Studies in Scripture

VOLUME FIVE The Gospels

Studies in Scripture

VOLUME FIVE The Gospels

Edited by Kent P. Jackson and Robert L. Millet

Deseret Book Company
Salt Lake City, Utah

Studies in Scripture Series:

Volume 1: The Doctrine and Covenants (Randall Book Co., 1974)

Volume 2: The Pearl of Great Price (Randall Book Co., 1985)

Volume 3: The Old Testament—Genesis to 2 Samuel (Randall Book Co., 1985)

Volume 4: The Old Testament—1 Kings to Malachi (future volume, 1989, Deseret Book Co.)

Volume 5: The Gospels (Deseret Book Co., 1986)

Volume 6: Acts to Revelation (Deseret Book Co., Summer 1987)

©1986 Kent P. Jackson and Robert L. Millet

All rights reserved

Printed in the United States of America

No part of this book may be reproduced in any form or by any means without permission in writing from the publisher, Deseret Book Company, P.O. Box 30178, Salt Lake City, Utah 84130. Deseret Book is a registered trademark of Deseret Book Company, Inc.

First printing November 1986

Second printing January 1987

Library of Congress Cataloging-in-Publication Data

The Gospels.

(Studies in Scripture; v. 5)
Includes index.
1. Jesus Christ—Biography. 2. Christian biography—Palestine. 3. Jesus Christ—Mormon interpretations.
I. Jackson, Kent P. II. Millet, Robert L. III. Series:
Studies in Scripture (Salt Lake City, Utah); v. 5.
BT301.2.G57 1986 226'.06 86-23981
ISBN 0-87579-064-X

CONTENTS

Preface vii

1 Jesus and the Gospels, *Kent P. Jackson* 1

2 The Setting of the Gospels, *Stephen E. Robinson* 10

3 The Testimony of Matthew, *Robert L. Millet* 38

4 The Testimony of Mark, *S. Kent Brown* 61

5 The Testimony of Luke, *Richard Lloyd Anderson* 88

6 The Testimony of John, *C. Wilfred Griggs* 109

7 The Prologue of John, *J. Philip Schaelling* 127

8 The Birth and Childhood of the Messiah, *Robert L. Millet* . 140

9 A Voice in the Wilderness: An Interview with John
   the Baptist, *Robert J. Matthews* 160

10 The Baptism and Temptations of Jesus, *S. Brent Farley* . . 175

11 The Early Judean Ministry, *Kay Edwards* 188

12 "No Prophet Is Accepted in His Own Country,"
   Stephen D. Ricks 201

13 The Miracles of Jesus, *Rex C. Reeve, Jr.* 213

14 The Calling and Mission of the Twelve, *H. Dean Garrett* . 227

15 The Sermon on the Mount: The Sacrifice of
   the Human Heart, *Catherine Thomas* 236

Contents

16 He That Is Not With Me Is Against Me, *Monte S. Nyman* . 251

17 The Parables of Jesus, *Richard D. Draper* 262

18 The Divine Sonship and the Law of Witnesses,
    Joseph F. McConkie 279

19 The Bread of Life, *Kent P. Jackson* 288

20 Tradition, Testimony, Transfiguration, and Keys,
    Robert J. Matthews 296

21 The Calling of the Seventy and the Parable of the
    Good Samaritan, *S. Brent Farley* 312

22 Jesus Is the Christ, *LaMar E. Garrard* 321

23 The Worth of a Soul, *Keith H. Meservy* 345

24 Fit for the Kingdom, *Larry E. Dahl* 357

25 Triumphal Entry and a Day of Debate, *Joseph F. McConkie* . 373

26 The Olivet Discourse, *David R. Seely* 391

27 The Farewell of Jesus, *Rodney Turner* 405

28 Treading the Winepress Alone, *Robert L. Millet* 430

29 The Arrest, Trial, and Crucifixion, *Andrew C. Skinner* . . 440

30 The Witnesses of the Resurrection, *Monte S. Nyman* . . 453

31 The Resurrected Lord and His Apostles,
    Thomas W. Mackay 461

    Scripture Index 471

    Subject Index 486

PREFACE

The following words of the Master, uttered in the meridian of time, are poignant and penetrating in regard to his mission among the sons and daughters of earth: "I am come that they might have life, and that they might have it more abundantly." (John 10:10.) This expression conveys in one sentence the essence of the Lord's mortal ministry: he came to teach and serve and save. He lived the abundant life and has extended the blessings of the same to all who will accept him and the principles of his gospel. Surely no life is more worthy of study and emulation than that of Jesus of Nazareth, known also as the Christ.

Studies in Scripture, Volume 5: The Gospels is another book in a series intended to enhance and supplement one's personal study of the revelations and truths found in the standard works of The Church of Jesus Christ of Latter-day Saints. Recognizing that there is no substitute for a sincere and serious study of the scriptures themselves, this series, *Studies in Scripture,* is presented as a resource, an aid in pointing members of the Church toward the profound realities to be discovered in the books that comprise our scriptural canon.

Sincere appreciation is expressed to many people, without whose active involvement and enthusiastic support this undertaking would not have been possible. The contributors have willingly shared their talents and their research and have been extremely cooperative during the months involved in writing, editing, and final preparation of the manuscripts for publication. A word of thanks goes to Morgan Tanner, a conscientious and capable research assistant, for many hours spent in readying the materials for the publisher. Gratitude is also extended to Ronald A. Millet, Eleanor Knowles, and the staff at Deseret

Book Company for their interest and editorial and production expertise in this project. And, as always, the editors owe a special debt of gratitude to their wives and children, who have been generous with their husbands' and fathers' time.

This volume consists of essays written to give deeper insight into the historical backgrounds and doctrinal significance of the messages contained in the four Gospels—Matthew, Mark, Luke, and John. These essays have been written by Latter-day Saints who have a commitment to the Lord Jesus Christ and a loyalty to his anointed servants in the Restored Church. We make no apology for the fact that this book is compiled with a bias of belief; it is an expression of testimony, a statement of faith.

Each of the contributors is responsible for his or her own conclusions, and this collection is a private endeavor and not a production of either Brigham Young University or The Church of Jesus Christ of Latter-day Saints. Although the writers and editors have sought to be in harmony with the teachings of the scriptures and the leaders of the Church, the reader should not regard this work as primary source for gospel understanding but should turn instead to the scriptures and the words of modern prophets for authoritative doctrinal statements.

We sincerely hope that this book will make a meaningful contribution in bringing Latter-day Saints to a greater understanding of and appreciation for our Savior, and that those who read it will be further motivated to be true to his teachings and actively involved in his church. This has proven to be an enjoyable and instructive experience for the editors, who hope that the reader will find similar inspiration and enjoyment.

KENT P. JACKSON
ROBERT L. MILLET

1

JESUS AND THE GOSPELS

KENT P. JACKSON

As Jesus spoke to the Father in his great intercessory prayer, he uttered these words: "And now, O Father, glorify thou me with thine own self with the glory which I had with thee before the world was." (John 17:5.) What was the glory that Jesus had with the Father "before the world was"? Abraham, beholding that time in vision, reported that Jesus was "like unto God." (Abr. 3:22, 24.) Into the hands of him who later was to become his Only Begotten in the flesh, the Father had given all power and all authority in the universe. Jesus was "the brightness of [the Father's] glory, and the express image of his person," who upholds "all things by the word of his power." (Heb. 1:3.) Such divine acts as the creation of worlds without number, the governing of the earth and millions of others like it, the revelation to the prophets, and the atonement for all of God's children were entrusted into the hands of Jesus Christ, Jehovah, the Lord God of the universe, the Father of heaven and earth. Jesus was, as Paul taught, "in the form of God" and "thought it not robbery to be equal with God." (Philip. 2:6.) How mighty this man was as a spirit son of God in premortality that the Father would endow him with all of the attributes of deity save only those that pertain to the possession of a physical body. How we, his spirit siblings but spiritual underlings, must have

---

Kent P. Jackson is associate professor of ancient scripture and Old Testament area coordinator at Brigham Young University.

stood in awe of him as we followed him in the course that the Father laid out for his children. How we must have admired the indescribable wisdom with which, even then, he administered the Father's plan. How we must have marveled at the unutterable courage with which he stepped forward to accept the burden of the holy atonement. If the present sensitivities that we feel for him, his sacred eternal work, and his gospel plan are any indication of the admiration that we had at that time in his presence, then heaven is a glorious place indeed. And if it is glorious because of the presence of the Son there, how glorious it must be because of the presence of the Father, the source of all glory in eternity.

From Glory to Glory

Jesus' mission was not limited to his acts of creation, his governing of the worlds, or his communication with prophets. As the Word of God, as the living embodiment of the Father and the Father's divine will in all things, his mission also included treading the paths of mortality, coming to earth to descend below all things —to be tested in all things to an even greater degree than we are, yet without committing sin. His coming to earth in the humblest of circumstances disguised his identity and the mission for which he was sent. Yet it was his coming under those very circumstances that made his work effective and his mission complete. As the children's hymn so sublimely testifies,

> He came down to earth from heaven,
> Who is God and Lord of all,
> And His shelter was a stable,
> And his cradle was a stall;
> With the poor, and mean, and lowly,
> Lived on earth our Saviour holy.[1]

As Paul wrote, Jesus "made himself of no reputation, and took upon him the form of a servant, and was made in the likeness of men: and being found in fashion as a man, he humbled himself." (Philip. 2:7-8.) The letter to the Hebrews teaches: "Wherefore in all things it behooved him to be made like unto his brethren, that he might be a merciful and faithful high priest in things pertaining to God, to make reconciliation for the sins of the people. For in that he himself hath suffered being tempted, he is able to succour them that are tempted. . . . For we have not an high priest which cannot be touched with the feelings of our infirmities; but was in all points tempted like as we are, yet without sin." (Heb. 2:17-18; 4:15.)

Indeed, one of the reasons for his descending from his divine throne to become as we are was to establish the pattern for all men and women to follow. Christ became one of us so he could demonstrate that commandments can be kept and that a righteous walk through life can be accomplished. To the millions who have experienced sorrow in their mortal existence, it is of great worth to know that there is One who has sorrowed more. And those who have suffered trials and temptations can know that there is One who not only has overcome such adversity but who also empathizes with those who are still learning how.

> For he is our childhood's pattern,
>   Day by day like us He grew:
> He was little, weak, and helpless,
>   Tears and smiles like us He knew;
> And He feeleth for our sadness,
>   And He shareth in our gladness.[2]

But Christ's mortality was much more than this. It included his atoning suffering—suffering that is beyond the comprehension of men. He descended below *all* things, suffered more than we can suffer, and sorrowed more than we can sorrow. And all this was done for others, an expression of his incredible grace, the greatest of his many divine attributes. Paul bore witness: "He humbled himself, and became obedient unto death, even the death of the cross." (Philip. 2:8.) As we ponder Paul's testimony, let us not forget of whom he spoke. This was Jehovah, Almighty God himself, who descended, humbled himself, suffered, and died—for us.

Jesus' atonement, the ultimate act of sacrifice and servitude, was also his greatest triumph. In carrying out this labor of supreme love, he demonstrated for all people in all places in all eternity what greatness really consists of. His atonement shows us how petty are our own vain delusions of grandeur and our obsession with rank and status and their symbols in whatever form they may be found. All definitions of worth must be measured against the example of Christ. Our man-made scales do not measure real value; they pervert it instead. When James and John and their mother came to the Master with requests for status and position in the hereafter, he gently taught them that real greatness comes not in rank but in service and commitment: "Ye know that the princes of the Gentiles exercise dominion over them, and they that are great exercise authority upon them. But it shall not be so among you: but whosoever will be great among you, let him be your minister; and whosoever will be chief among you, let him be your servant: even as the Son of man came not to be ministered unto, but to minister, and to give his life a ransom for many." (Matt. 20:25-28.) Jesus knew this better than anyone else, for he who was greatest of all had descended to the lowest, so that when he returned to his rightful place of glory, he could take others—some of *us*—with him.

And Jesus did return to his place of glory. Paul taught: "Wherefore God also hath highly exalted him, and given him a name which is above every name: that at the name of Jesus every knee should bow, . . . and that every tongue should confess that Jesus Christ is Lord, to the glory of God the Father." (Philip. 2:9-11.) He who was called the sacrificial Lamb of God in mortality is now "KING OF KINGS, AND LORD OF LORDS." (Rev. 19:16.) But even with that, his work is not yet accomplished, for his eternal mission, like that of his Father, is to "bring to pass the immortality and eternal life" of all who will receive it. (Moses 1:39.)

> And our eyes at last shall see Him,
>   Through His own redeeming love;
> For that Child so dear and gentle
>   Is the Lord in heaven above;
> And He leads His children on
>   To the place where He is gone.
>
> Not to that poor lowly stable,
>   With the oxen standing by,

We shall see Him, but in heaven,
Set at God's right hand on high;
When like stars His children crowned,
All in white shall wait around.[3]

The Vocabulary of Messiahship

The words used in sacred literature to describe Jesus proclaim his divinity and the nature of his mission. Let us examine a few of these.

1. *Savior,* "One who saves." Jesus is our Savior because he saves us.

First, he has saved us—all who ever have or ever will be born into mortality—from the bonds of physical death, the separation of body and spirit. All will be resurrected from the dead: those who have lived righteously to a resurrection of glory, and those who have lived unrighteously to a resurrection of damnation. That this is a marvelous gift of grace from the Lord is attested in the scriptures (see especially 2 Ne. 9:7-10).

Second, he has saved us from spiritual death, which means alienation from God, death as to the things of righteousness. We attain this condition when we sin in any degree. In doing so, we cut ourselves off from God and make it impossible for us to return to his presence, for "no unclean thing can inherit the kingdom of heaven" (Alma 11:37), and God "shall not save his people in their sins" (Alma 11:36). When we sin, we become unclean and therefore unworthy to enter his presence. Christ saved us from the eternal consequences of this situation. Yet the salvation that he brought about from spiritual death is not dispensed to the unworthy; it is conditioned on our faithfulness. We are indeed saved by grace, the unearned and eternally unmerited grace of Christ. Yet Christ has decreed that only those who live faithfully, in accordance with gospel standards and covenants, will be the recipients of his saving work. While we can never "earn" salvation from the bonds of spiritual death, it is only on condition of faithfulness to the laws and ordinances of the gospel that Christ will grant that saving blessing to us. In the Garden of Gethsemane and on the cross, he paid the price in full and did all of the work that brings

5

salvation. It was "an infinite and eternal sacrifice." (Alma 34:10.) Yet out of his incomprehensible love, he will grant his saving grace to us, his unworthy servants, if we will only do his will. We will be in his debt throughout all eternity.

In all things the atonement is the focus. Repentance is not a self-existing principle; it is possible only because Christ has already paid the penalty for our sins and thus can remove them from us if we repent of them. Our repentance, our resurrection, our redemption, and our ultimate exaltation are all products of Jesus Christ and his atoning work.

2. *Deliverer,* "One who delivers." This term is used in the scriptures in the same way that *Savior* is used; the terms are essentially synonymous.

3. *Redeemer,* "One who redeems." In most cases *Redeemer* is used the same way as *Savior* and *Deliverer.* But the focus of this word is on the fact that Christ paid for us. "To redeem" means "to pay for, to acquire something in exchange for proper payment." Thus Christ is our Redeemer because he paid for our sins; he purchased us and our future well-being at the price of his precious blood. He bought the burden of our souls in exchange for his suffering.

4. *Jesus.* This was a fairly common personal name in the days of the Savior. In the Aramaic original, Jesus was *Yeshu'a,* the equivalent of the Hebrew *Yoshu'a* (biblical Joshua), which means "The Lord is Salvation." Joseph and Mary gave that name to the Christ child at the command of a messenger from God, "for he shall save his people from their sins." (Matt. 1:21.) How appropriate it was that he should bear a name that teaches such a profound lesson, and that he himself should be the fulfillment of the message it bears.

5. *Messiah,* "Anointed One." This comes from the Hebrew word *mashiah* . In the Old Testament, the king was the "anointed one"; thus the term was primarily a royal title. But in later Old Testament times, and especially during the period between the Old and New Testaments, Jews anticipated the coming of *the* Anointed One, the One who would be sent from God to be their deliverer

from all foes. One Jerusalemite prophet, Lehi, spoke plainly to his people "of the coming of a Messiah, and also the redemption of the world," (1 Ne. 1:19.) And when Andrew heard the Savior speak, he exclaimed to his brother Simon, "We have found the Messias" (John 1:41), a Greek form of the word *Messiah*.

6. *Christ,* "Anointed One." This term, from the Greek word *christos,* is the Greek translation of *Messiah.* The two terms are synonymous.

The Testimonies of the New Covenant

The word *testament* means "covenant." It is used in this sense in both the Old and the New Testaments, and both volumes of scripture derive their name from this source. The New Testament refers to the new testament of Christianity, which is found within its pages. In the Old Testament, Jeremiah quotes the Lord concerning a new covenant that God would establish with his people—not the old covenant that was written on tablets of stone, but a new covenant to be written in the hearts of faithful Saints. (Jer. 31:31-33.) The epistle to the Hebrews uses similar terminology. (Heb. 8:8-13.) At the Last Supper, Jesus introduced the sacrament as a "new testament." (For example, Matt. 26:28; Mark 14:24; Luke 22:20; 1 Cor. 11:25.)

Testament also means "testimony." The New Testament is not only the record of God's new gospel covenant; it is also a testimony to its divinity. The Gospels are testimonies of Christ. They do not fit into the traditional categories of biography or history, but they fulfill well their role as witnesses to the divine mission of him whose life and works they record. In the titles of Matthew, Mark, Luke, and John in the Joseph Smith Translation, the words "The Gospel According to . . ." have been changed to read "The Testimony of. . . ." The modern scriptures—the Book of Mormon: Another Testament of Jesus Christ, and the Doctrine and Covenants and Pearl of Great Price, which are also latter-day testaments of Christ's eternal work—stand alongside the testaments of ancient Israel and the early church of Christ.

Reading and Understanding the Gospels

Perhaps nothing we do can have a more profound effect on our lives than to study the life of Christ. What we spend our time doing inevitably influences our personalities and the way we look at the world. If we immerse ourselves in the mission of the Savior and learn from his example and his words, we cannot help but feel the purifying influence of his character. Reading scripture is a life-changing exercise, and reading the Gospels will draw us nearer to Christ.

For various reasons, some find the scriptures, particularly the Bible, difficult to read. The New Testament comes from a culture that in many ways is quite different from our own, with a historical setting that may be strange to modern readers. Different customs are found throughout its pages, and words are expressed in ways unfamiliar to us in the twentieth century. Things that were common and quite simple in their original ancient setting have been obscured by the passage of time, requiring that the reader have other skills or resources from which to draw. No modern readers are native speakers of the ancient Greek language in which the New Testament was written, and translation very often fails to convey the intentions of the original author. Even in translation, readers of the King James Version must deal with an English text that is over 350 years old and in a dialect that few modern readers can understand without considerable effort. Yet Bible readers who pay the price of serious and prayerful study and thought will find great satisfaction in their reading.

I suggest the following four keys to gaining the most from reading the Gospels:

1. *Study the Gospels in light of gospel truth that has been revealed in modern times.* Modern scriptural sources that contribute to an understanding of the New Testament are the Book of Mormon, the Doctrine and Covenants, the Pearl of Great Price, and Joseph Smith's revision of the Bible (the Joseph Smith translation). Through the light of modern revelation, we have a better view, and with the perspective of the entire gospel plan, we can understand God's dealings with men and women of the past in a way not possible otherwise. (See D&C 20:11; 1 Ne. 13:39-40.) The

value of using modern revelation to illuminate the New Testament cannot be overstated. For example, the New Testament describes the historical event of the atonement, but it is only in the Book of Mormon and the Doctrine and Covenants that we learn the full significance of the Lord's sacrifice. Many other examples can be cited. Another modern source of revelation is found in the teachings and sermons of the Prophet Joseph Smith, through whose inspired witness the fullness of the gospel has been revealed in modern times.

2. *Rely upon the Holy Ghost.* The companionship of the Spirit is indispensable for scripture study. (See 2 Ne. 25:4.) Prayerful study of sacred literature draws readers close to the ultimate source of all knowledge. Righteous living makes a person worthy, and consistent prayer opens the channels of the heavens.

3. *Learn how the ancient writers expressed themselves.* This includes becoming familiar with their language, idioms, teaching methods, poetic styles, literary techniques, and general style of discourse. A consistent reading of the Gospels can help us become familiar with the expressions and styles of the New Testament. (See 2 Ne. 25:1.)

4. *Understand the Gospels within their own context.* Knowledge of the historical, cultural, and theological circumstances within which the mortal mission of Christ occurred is clearly of value. Our understanding is enhanced if we understand the nature of society in Jesus' day and the contemporary concerns of his disciples and detractors. Knowing the doctrinal and moral issues of the day helps us understand Jesus' message and its timely and timeless significance.

NOTES

1. Cecil Frances Alexander, "Once in Royal David's City," verse 2, from *A Treasury of Christmas Songs and Carols,* 2nd ed., ed. Henry W. Simon (Boston: Houghton Mifflin Co., 1955), pp. 186-87; also *Hymns of The Church of Jesus Christ of Latter-day Saints,* 1985, no. 205.

2. Alexander, verse 4.

3. Alexander, verses 5 and 6.

2

THE SETTING OF THE GOSPELS

STEPHEN E. ROBINSON

The Monarchy

In the years after the death of Saul, the first king of Israel, his successor, King David, was able to unite the various tribes into one nation under a strong central government and then to build Israel into something of a Near Eastern superpower. Under King David, the nation enjoyed growth and prosperity. There was a king, a high priest, a prophet. Israel's army was victorious, and its commercial and political interests outside of Israel were expanding. Under the son of David, Solomon, the temple that had been planned by David was finally built so that the rites of the temple could be properly observed and the Ark of the Covenant could be properly housed. Israel was never again to have such prosperity coupled with such complete enjoyment of its traditional institutions. In later years, Jews would remember the golden age of David and Solomon and would long for another "son of David" who could restore the glory of those days to the kingdom of Israel.[1]

After the reign of Solomon, a civil war divided the twelve tribes and the nation they had formed. The kingdom of David and Solomon was divided into the northern ten tribes, who continued to call themselves Israel but who followed the rebel Jeroboam, and the two southern tribes of Judah and Benjamin, who served

---

Stephen E. Robinson is associate professor of ancient scripture at Brigham Young University.

Rehoboam, the son of Solomon, and called themselves the kingdom of Judah. The modern terms *Jew* and *Judea* are derived from the name Judah. These divided kingdoms, Israel in the north and Judah in the south, were weaker than the original kingdom of David had been, and in 721 B.C. an Assyrian army defeated Israel and deported 27,290 of the aristocracy, the educated—anyone who might give the people leadership—to Assyrian territory.[2] Most of these people never returned to Israel and are still referred to as "the Lost Ten Tribes of Israel." But Assyrian colonists did come and settle in the land of Israel in their place. The descendants of these colonists who intermarried with the remaining Israelites ultimately were known as Samaritans, and the territory that had been called Israel was then called Samaria. The southern kingdom of Judah did not fall to the Assyrians, although Judah was forced to pay tribute to Assyrian kings.

Exile and Return

Eventually the Assyrians themselves were conquered by a new superpower in Mesopotamia, the Babylonians, and in 587 B.C. the Babylonians conquered Judah and destroyed both the city and the temple of Jerusalem.[3] Like the Assyrians before them, the Babylonians had a policy of deporting conquered peoples, and now, like Israel before them, it was Judah's turn to go away into exile. These mass deportations made it easy to integrate conquered territory and conquered peoples into the Babylonian Empire. The land, emptied of its original owners, could be parceled out to Babylonians and others whose loyalty was assured. At the same time, the conquered people, spread out in a foreign land, were too busy learning to cope with a new language and a new culture to worry about any further resistance. It was intended that such exiles would simply be absorbed into Babylonian society, but for generations the Jews in Babylon preserved their religion, their culture, and their sense of national identity by excluding Babylonian influence wherever possible. The tremendous commitment felt by many of the exiles is reflected in Psalm 137: "If I forget thee, O Jerusalem, let my right hand forget her cunning. If I do not remember thee, let my tongue cleave to the roof of my mouth; if I prefer not Jerusalem above my chief joy.'' (Psalm 137:5-6.)

With this kind of commitment, the Jews in exile were able to retain their identity and remain loyal to the institutions of their fathers and grandfathers. Unfortunately, one negative result of such single-minded devotion to the institutions and traditions of Judaism was a certain amount of Gentile phobia. The effort necessary for the preservation of Judaism in exile also resulted in an exclusivism that often reappeared in later times.[4]

In 539 B.C., the Babylonian Empire was conquered by Cyrus, king of Persia. Cyrus allowed the descendants of those nations that had been deported by the Babylonians to return to their ancestral homes. This policy was very successful in winning him the loyalty of those peoples. When Cyrus allowed the Jews to return to the land of their forefathers, the Jews repaid him and the Persians with loyalty and support as long as the Persian Empire lasted. Even afterward, in the time of Jesus, most Jews looked eastward to Parthia[5] rather than westward to Greece or Rome for a friendly ally.

After the fall of Babylon, the Jews returned to Judea in several stages over many years. In one stage of the return, associated with the governor Zerubbabel and with the prophets Zechariah and Haggai, the Jerusalem Temple was rebuilt (ca. 515 B.C.). At a later time, Nehemiah rebuilt the city walls of Jerusalem and thus secured its political future (ca. 444 B.C.). Later still, Ezra the scribe edited and published a new edition of the Hebrew scriptures and led the people in renewing their covenant with Jehovah (ca. 400 B.C.).

But the Jews who returned from exile were not the same Jews who were deported. By and large, the returnees were the children and grandchildren of the original exiles, returning to a land they had never seen. Also, the majority of Babylonian Jews chose not to leave Babylon, the land of their birth, and for centuries Babylon remained a center of Jewish population and intellectual life.[6] Despite all their efforts, Jews were influenced in many ways by Babylonian and Persian culture. For example, during the captivity, Aramaic replaced Hebrew as the common Jewish language, and the Jews also adopted the Babylonian alphabet and calendar.

The Greek Period

In 334 B.C., the young king of Macedon in Greece, Alexander, invaded the Persian Empire. By 331 Alexander had conquered Asia Minor, Syria, Palestine, and Egypt, and by the following year he was the master of Persia. By his thirty-third birthday, Alexander the Great had conquered most of the known world and ruled an empire that extended from Greece to India. When Alexander died in 323 B.C., his empire was divided among his four generals. Ptolemy, the ancestor of Cleopatra, got Egypt and Palestine. But some years later, Palestine was taken from the Ptolemies by descendants of Seleucus, another of Alexander's generals, who ruled in Syria and Babylon. It should be noted that from the time of Alexander the Great, most of the rulers and ruling families in the known world were Greeks, and as they ruled they imposed the Greek language and culture on the conquered peoples. The conquest of the world by Alexander created a great melting pot in which the native cultures were melted down and recast in Greek terms. In time and through a process of endless compromise, the effect was the creation of a universal language, Koine Greek, and a universal culture called Hellenism, a blending of Greek and native cultures with the Greek predominating.[7] This was the culture of the world in the days of Jesus.

In many ways the hellenistic world was much like our own. Very few people found much spiritual satisfaction in mainstream Greek religion anymore, except as a purveyor of a kind of bland ethical morality. Certainly very few Greeks could find meaningful answers to life's great questions in the worship of the Olympian gods, and many people in the hellenistic world were looking for answers in new religions.[8]

Greek intellectual life was not what it had been in an earlier period. For example, the classical philosophy of Socrates, Plato, and Aristotle had largely been succeeded by the rhetoric of the Sophists. Rhetoric is a discipline in which more value is placed on how one says a thing than on what one says, and the Sophists were professional intellectuals who placed a higher value on skillful arguing than on reaching correct conclusions; for them, therefore, everything was negotiable. Packaging became everything, content

13

nothing. Those disciplines that dealt with human questions and problems seemed to have lost their way, or, to use Professor Murray's famous phrase, experienced a "failure of nerve." Many of the arts as well had lost their originality and creativity.[9] Even so, the hellenistic age, like our own, was a technological age, and scientific knowledge made great advances. It seems that having despaired of finding the answers to life's great questions, hellenistic culture focused on finding answers to little questions instead. Many philosophers of this period had given up the search for objective truth entirely and had adopted a view of truth in which accommodation, flexibility, and compromise were the highest values. Thus, it was a thoroughly ecumenical age, since ecumenism is always easiest when people are least certain of their beliefs.

For a hundred and fifty years or so, the Greeks ruled Judea, and every effort was made to hellenize the Jews, that is, to make them adopt the values and culture of the rest of the world. In many ways, these attempts were successful. For example, Jews did adopt hellenistic dress and social customs.[10] Many of the institutions and practices known to us from the New Testament are hellenistic. Tenant farmers, tax collectors, moneylenders, customs officials, and landowners who hired day laborers—all of these come from hellenism and its institutions. During this period it became common for Jews to have Greek names like Nicodemus, Philip, or Stephen. Many Jews even left Judea and settled in Greek cities, such as Alexandria in Egypt (which was named after Alexander the Great). These Jews living in Greek lands were called collectively the *Diaspora* (a Greek word meaning dispersion). Perhaps the most famous of the Diaspora Jews was Saul of Tarsus, otherwise known as the Apostle Paul. Coins that circulated in Judea bore the "image and superscription" of hellenistic rulers, even though the law of Moses, as interpreted by the Jews, forbade such "graven images."[11] Even the governing council of the Jewish people, the Sanhedrin, had acquired a Greek name (*sunhedrios*). In fact, hellenism as a popular culture had such tremendous appeal and influence, and yet was so contrary to the values of traditional Jewish religion, that by 175 B.C., after 150 years of hellenistic Greek rule, Judaism was in real danger of being completely compromised. Even the high priests of the Jewish religion had become hellenized and cooperated slavishly with the Greek rulers in their attempts to make the Jews more like everyone else.

Finally, in 167 B.C., apparently with the full support of the reigning high priest, the Greek king of Syria-Palestine, Antiochus IV Epiphanes, outlawed the practice of circumcision and made it illegal to possess the Jewish scriptures. The temple at Jerusalem was converted to allow the worship of Zeus, and pigs were offered upon the altar in sacrifice to the pagan god.[12] Greek soldiers were sent to the towns and villages of Judea to enforce the ban on traditional Judaism and to encourage the people to offer sacrifice to Zeus. The Greek king was extremely anxious that his Jewish subjects finally comply with hellenistic religious ideas and the hellenistic spirit of compromise.

The Maccabean Period

In the village of Modin, north of Jerusalem, a local priest named Mattathias killed the Greek officer sent there to institute pagan worship, and with his five sons he went into the hills to wage a guerrilla war against the Greeks. Mattathias challenged all of Judea, saying, "Let everyone who is zealous of the law and supports the covenant come out with me!"[13] When Mattathias died, his eldest son, Judah, became the military leader of the Jewish rebels. The family name was Hasmon, and they are therefore referred to as the Hasmonean family, but because of Judah's prowess and success against the Greeks, he was also called the Maccabee, a word that means something like "the hammer." After Judah, the family is often referred to as the Maccabees as well as the Hasmoneans, and the Jewish revolt of 167 B.C. is called the Maccabean revolt. Time and again, Judah and his followers were able to defeat the Greek generals and their armies even though they were greatly outnumbered. In the fall of 165 B.C., Judah retook Jerusalem, and by December the Maccabees had torn down the altar of the temple, which had been desecrated by the sacrifice of swine, and had rebuilt it. They also replaced the Jerusalem priesthood, which had been disloyal, with "blameless priests who were devoted to the Law." The Jerusalem Temple was thoroughly cleansed and was rededicated to the worship of Jehovah on the twenty-fifth of the Jewish month of Kislev (December) amid great rejoicing, an event that is still commemorated every year in the Jewish festival of Hannukah.

The Maccabean revolt, which had begun as a fight for religious freedom, became a struggle for political freedom as well. Nevertheless, the Greeks were not completely driven out of Judea until 143 B.C. In the meantime (161 B.C.), Judah the Maccabee was killed in a battle in which he had been outnumbered twenty-five to one.

In 140 B.C., Simon, the last of the five Hasmonean brothers, was established as both high priest and political ruler (ethnarch) of the Jews. Moreover, these titles were declared to be hereditary, and thus the Hasmonean dynasty was founded. This was a momentous occasion, for although members of the Hasmonean family were priests, until the outbreak of the Maccabean revolt the high priesthood had been in the hands of one family, the Zadokite Oniads. Now the high priesthood had passed into the family of the Hasmoneans. While most Jews supported the Hasmoneans in their assumption of both political and religious power, there were those who believed that the high priesthood could not legitimately be taken away from the Oniad family. It was in this period that the Essenes withdrew to live in their desert communities, probably feeling that the Hasmoneans had usurped religious power. On the other hand, other Jews believed that the Maccabees had brought about the Messianic kingdom, or even that they were themselves Messiahs.

After 129 B.C. the Greek Seleucid kingdom was too troubled by internal problems to challenge Jewish independence. The Hasmonean rulers of Judea were able to extend their territory, defeat old enemies, and settle old scores. In 129-128 B.C., John Hyrcanus attacked the Samaritans around ancient Shechem and destroyed the Samaritan temple on Mount Gerizim.[14] He also conquered the Idumean towns of Adora and Marisa and forced the Idumeans (the Edomites of the Old Testament) to convert to Judaism.[15]

Decline of the Hasmoneans

Despite all the military successes, the decline of the Hasmonean family was rapid. Within a generation or two, the descendants of the Maccabees had become as weak and corrupt as the rulers and priests their fathers had replaced a century earlier. John Hyrcanus broke with the Pharisees and reinstated as religious authorities the Sadducees, who had direct ties to the corrupt establishment overthrown by Mattathias and his five sons. The son of John Hyrcanus, Alexander Jannaeus, used foreign troops to put down a rebellion against his corrupt rule, a rebellion in which fifty thousand Jews died. On one occasion, Jannaeus crucified eight hundred Pharisees in Jerusalem and then had their wives and children killed before them as they hung on the crosses.

Between 67 and 63 B.C., the two sons of Jannaeus, Hyrcanus II and Aristobulus II, fought over the succession to the throne and high priesthood. Hyrcanus was the rightful heir, but he was weak and incompetent. His chief supporter and adviser was the Idumean leader Antipater, the father of the future King Herod. Antipater knew Hyrcanus was weak, but he realized that his own fortunes would be better under a weak king than a strong one.

The rising power in the ancient world at that time was Rome; Roman legions had been in Syria since 65 B.C. Both Hyrcanus and Aristobulus had been trying to win Roman support for themselves but had succeeded only in drawing Roman attention to their vulnerability. When the Roman general Pompey decided in 63 B.C. to enter Jerusalem with his army, the supporters of Hyrcanus opened the gates to him, but the followers of Aristobulus and whoever else opposed Roman intervention barricaded themselves on the Temple Mount. When Pompey stormed the temple, twelve thousand Jews died, including the priests who were sacrificing at the altar and would not be distracted from their duties. When the fighting was over, Pompey himself entered the Holy of Holies, but he did no physical damage to the Temple. He installed Hyrcanus as high priest and nominal ruler of Judea, but Jewish independence had been lost; from that time forward Judea was in bondage to Rome.

The Roman Period

In the years following Pompey's incursion into Judea and the establishment of Hyrcanus upon the throne as a Roman puppet, the Idumean Antipater sat like a spider on Hyrcanus's shoulder, always looking for and taking advantage of ways to better the position of himself and his family. He was the true power behind the ineffectual Hyrcanus, and the Romans soon realized this. Antipater took pains to be of service to Rome, cheerfully supplying both troops and money as they were needed and often before they were requested. After the death of Antipater, his son Herod inherited the position and continued the tactics of his father.

In 40 B.C., the Parthians invaded all of the Roman Near East, including Palestine. The Parthians were a dynasty of the Persian Empire (the Arsacids) who fought with Rome for control of the Near East for three centuries. The Jews of Palestine looked upon the invasion of the Parthians as a liberation from the despised Romans. Jews had been on good terms with the Persians ever since Cyrus the Persian let them return home and rebuild after the Babylonian exile. Also, hundreds of thousands of Jews were still living in Babylon who fared better under Parthian rule than the Jews of Palestine were treated by the Romans. The invading Parthians deposed the Roman puppet Hyrcanus and placed his nephew Antigonus on the throne. Herod fled to Rome, where the senate decided to reward his constant service and loyalty to the empire and to do away with the figurehead Hasmonean kings altogether. Recognizing him as the real power behind the Jewish throne, the Roman senate appointed Herod, son of Antipater and the grandson of an Idumean forced to convert to Judaism, as king of the Jews.

Herod the Great

It took Herod three years of Roman support to reconquer Judea. He began by marrying Mariamne, the granddaughter of Hyrcanus. This gave him a connection to the royal Hasmonean family and strengthened his claim to the throne. However, it also caused him considerable trouble in that it made Herod's sons more acceptable to the people than Herod himself, since they were Hasmoneans by blood and he was not. In the end, Herod executed several of his sons and other relatives for real and imagined offenses.[16] Even his wife, whom he appears to have genuinely loved, was put to death. Herod was totally ruthless whenever his own interests were involved. He was a master politician and was able to stay on good terms with the Romans, even when Cleopatra, queen of Egypt, plotted against him.

In many ways Herod was an admirable ruler. He built or rebuilt public edifices on a magnificent scale, not only in Palestine but also throughout the eastern Mediterranean. He turned the rather modest temple in Jerusalem into one of the seven wonders of the ancient world. Personally, he was strong and athletic, and his skills as a warrior were extraordinary. He was disciplined, patient, and intelligent. He was also a monster. Nothing, no person, no matter how beloved or how innocent, no principle, could stand in the way of his ambition. Herod was larger than life, a truly great man, yet one who with all his extraordinary powers worshiped only himself. Josephus tells us that as Herod lay dying, in 4 B.C., the people found out and rejoiced. When Herod learned of this, he ordered the eldest sons from six hundred leading Jewish families to be arrested and held at the racetrack in Jericho. He wanted them all put to death when he died to ensure that the Jews would mourn the day of his passing.[17] His own son Antipater was executed just five days before his death.

When Herod died, his kingdom was divided among his three remaining sons, Archelaus, Antipas, and Philip, with Archelaus getting Judea. Archelaus had most of his father's vices and ambitions but few of his talents, and after nine years the Romans deposed him (A.D. 6). Antipas received Galilee and Perea (Trans-Jordan). He was the Herod who, according to the New Testament and Josephus,[18] beheaded John the Baptist. He was deposed and sent into exile by the emperor Caius (Caligula) in A.D. 39. Philip's territory was north and east of Galilee. When Archelaus was deposed in A.D. 6, the kingship was abolished and a Roman governor was appointed. From that time forward, Judea (but not Galilee or Perea, which until A.D. 39 were still ruled by Antipas) would be controlled directly by a Roman administration rather than through puppet kings.

In A.D. 26, Pontius Pilate was appointed governor of Judea. Pilate was described by contemporaries as vindictive, cruel, greedy, and stubborn.[19] Pilate resented the concessions that had been made to Jews by previous governors because of their religion, and he attempted on several occasions to ignore or revoke them. He also enjoyed teaching the crowds a lesson by unnecessarily setting his armed soldiers loose on them. Finally, in A.D. 36, he was removed from office by Vitellius, the Roman legate of Syria, and was sent back to Rome.[20]

In A.D. 38, two years after the departure of Pilate, the Roman emperor Caius (Caligula) ordered that his statue be placed in the Jerusalem Temple. Roman emperors since Augustus had been declared divine, but Caligula took his divinity seriously, and it irritated him that the Jews would neither believe in nor worship him. Moreover, Caius ordered the governor of Syria, Publius Petronius, to take half the legions in Syria with him and enforce the order. To the Jews, it seemed like a return to the decrees of Antiochus IV which precipitated the Maccabean revolt. Petronius, however, was a reasonable man. He knew the order was insane and that to obey it he would have to slaughter most of the Jewish nation. First he stalled, insisting that Caius should wait until after the harvest season, but finally he simply asked Caius to revoke the order. Enraged, Caius ordered Petronius to commit suicide, but since Caius himself was assassinated shortly afterward, neither the order for the statue nor the order for the suicide was ever obeyed.[21]

During this same time, between A.D. 37 and 41, a grandson of Herod the Great, Herod Agrippa, received first from Caius and then from Claudius (both of whom he had grown up with in Rome) all the lands that had been ruled by his grandfather. Agrippa was popular with the Jewish people for his piety according to the law of Moses and also for his persecution of the young Christian community (Acts 12). When he died after a very short reign, in A.D. 44, Palestine was again administered by Roman governors.

The First Revolt Against Rome

After the brief reign of Herod Agrippa, Roman policy in Judea grew increasingly oppressive. The later governors showed little of the intelligence and abilities displayed by their earlier counterparts. They robbed private citizens, despoiled the temple, and so ignored the administration of civil affairs that anarchy soon reigned. Finally, in A.D. 66, after several bloody confrontations with the governor, the Jews had had enough. First the temple sacrifices for the emperor were stopped; then the Roman garrison in Jerusalem was attacked. Although the Romans surrendered in exchange for a safe-conduct, they were all killed. Cestius Gallus, the military governor of Syria, came with his troops to Judea and barely escaped with his life. This would be a serious war.

At first, the regular Jewish authorities remained in charge—the chief priests and scribes. Later, as the Romans under Vespasian and his son Titus made advances and as conditions in the city of Jerusalem got worse and people grew more fanatical, the Zealots gained control. The moderate Jewish leaders who had begun the revolt were then put to death on the absurd charges of being too soft or too pro-Roman. Worse than that, the Zealots themselves split into factions and fought one another instead of the common enemy. While the besieging Romans patiently waited outside the city, the Zealot factions on the inside fought each other and mindlessly burned each other's food supplies.

In August of A.D. 70, Jerusalem fell. Thousands of its inhabitants were slaughtered and thousands more were sold as slaves or sent to the arenas as victims for Roman entertainment. The great Jerusalem Temple, the center of the Jewish religion and one of the seven wonders of the ancient world, was burned to the ground. About nine hundred rebels held out until A.D. 74 at the fortress of Masada on the shore of the Dead Sea, but when they chose mass suicide rather than be captured, the First Jewish Revolt was over.[22]

The Second (Bar Kokhba) Revolt

In A.D. 132, there was a second Jewish revolt against Rome. A certain Simon bar Kosiba (sometimes called Bar Kokhba, "son of the star") claimed to be the Promised Messiah. Rabbi Akiba, one of the most influential rabbis of the day, accepted and supported his claim; consequently, enough people followed him to bring the whole country into rebellion. The revolt lasted about three and a half years, and hundreds of thousands of Jews lost their lives or their freedom. When it was over, Jerusalem was so thoroughly destroyed that the site could be plowed. The emperor Hadrian built there an entirely new, pagan city named Aelia Capitolina. Jews were forbidden to enter on pain of death. Not until our own time would a Jewish Jerusalem be reestablished.

Religious Diversity

Just as the modern world we know has its religious denominations, so also were there denominations of Jews in the culture that Jesus knew. These sects had begun to develop in the period between the Babylonian exile and the revolt of the Maccabees.[23]

The Pharisees

In the first century, the most prominent of the Jewish sects was the Pharisees. The precise origin of the term *Pharisee* is unclear, but it seems most likely that it is derived from the Hebrew word *parash* and should be interpreted to mean something like "separatist." Certainly the Pharisees prided themselves on being "set apart" or "separated" from the rest of the Jews by their strict observance of the minutest requirements of the law of Moses. According to Josephus, there were approximately six thousand Pharisees in the first century.[24] They were the party that was most popular with the masses, and their interpretation of the scriptures was the one most readily accepted, even by those who were not themselves Pharisees. They were the popular party, the religion of the great mass of Jews—even though their actual membership was small.

Much of the Pharisees' influence was due to their control of what is called the "oral law." The Pharisees claimed that Moses had received the law on Mount Sinai in two parts—one written and one oral. The *written* part of the law made up the five books of Moses, which were accepted by all Jews: Genesis, Exodus, Leviticus, Numbers, and Deuteronomy. But according to the Pharisees, another part of the law had also been given to Moses *orally* and had been handed down and preserved by the Pharisees and their predecessors. This oral law, as interpreted and expanded by the Pharisees, was sometimes called "the tradition of the Fathers." Wherever the written scripture failed to give clear instructions, the Pharisees appealed to the oral law (which they alone controlled) for answers. For example, even though the written law directs that all debts are to be canceled in the seventh year, in the first century B.C. the Pharisaic rabbi Hillel was able to introduce an innovation called the *prosbul*, which allowed lenders to avoid cancellation of debt in the seventh year. He did this by insisting that the principle of the *prosbul* had actually been contained in the oral law since Sinai. In actuality, the antiquity of the oral law was largely a fiction, but it allowed the Pharisees to adapt the written law to new situations without admitting that any change had been made or that anything new had been added.[25] This tactic was necessary because the Pharisees denied that God could ever change or add anything to the revelation given once and for all on Mount Sinai. They insisted that any doctrine God was ever going to give, or ever could give, was already contained in "the one whole Torah [both the oral and written law] of Moses our rabbi." There could never be additional revelation. Nothing could be added—ever.[26] Jesus rejected the "tradition of the Fathers"[27] and insisted that the law of Moses was not immutable and ought in fact to be changed as he directed.[28]

Besides accepting both the written and the oral laws, the Pharisees believed in the existence of angels and demons. In this they differed from the Sadducees, who did not believe in the existence of these beings. The Pharisees also steered a middle course on the issue of free agency, believing that God predestined some things but that human beings could still be held accountable for their actions.

The Pharisees' strength was in the local synagogues, which they controlled; and their religious leaders were called rabbis (meaning teachers or masters). In matters pertaining to national government or to the administration of the temple and its rituals, they recognized the authority of the Sadducean priesthood, for the Pharisees were generally scholars and preachers rather than priests. From extant records, it appears that Jesus had more in common with the Pharisees than with the other Jewish sects known to us, and he was himself called "rabbi" on many occasions (as in John 1:49; 3:2).

Politically, the Pharisees were mildly anti-Roman. They believed that the Roman control of Judea was illegitimate, and they passively resisted Roman rule but stopped short of armed rebellion. After the Jewish revolt against Rome in A.D. 66-73, the Pharisees were the only Jewish sect to survive; consequently all later forms of mainstream Judaism are descended from the Pharisees. Modern-day Judaism is the offspring of the Judaism of the Pharisees.

The Sadducees

The Sadducees were a small party of very wealthy and influential aristocrats. Most Sadducees were priests, and the high priestly families (those families from whom the high priests traditionally came) controlled the sect and its membership. The term *Sadducee* comes from the name of Zadok, who had been high priest at the time of King Solomon, and whose descendants had served in the office ever since, except for the time of the early Maccabean period. The name thus underscores the nature of the Sadducees as an exclusive circle of wealthy and influential high priestly families and their followers.

The Sadducees controlled the Jerusalem Temple and derived their wealth, power, and influence from it. The temple generated tremendous revenues from the sacrifices and concessions,[29] and these riches were controlled by the Sadducees. The Sadducean high priest was also the head of the Sanhedrin (the governing council of the Jews), and therefore Sadducees were also very prominent in government. In any society, it is the aristocracy that resists changes in the status quo, since they benefit from things as they are.[30] Thus, politically the Sadducees cooperated with the Romans in return for the continued exercise of their many privileges. But it also followed that the Sadducees exerted almost no moral influence on the common people, who resented them for their aristocratic attitudes and for their cooperation with Rome.

Like Jesus, the Sadducees did not accept the Pharisaic oral law, the "traditions of the elders," and insisted that only the written Torah was valid. They did not believe in the existence of angels and demons, and they did not believe in the resurrection of the dead or in the continued existence of the spirit after death.[31] However, they did believe in free agency. The First Jewish Revolt in A.D. 66 spelled the doom of the Sadducees, for those who were not killed as traitors by their fellow Jews lost their base of power, their wealth, and their function in Jewish society when the temple was destroyed.

The Essenes

According to Josephus, the third major Jewish sect was the Essenes. It appears that there may have been more than one type of Essene, but those that are best known to us lived in a desert community on the shores of the Dead Sea. During the first Jewish revolt, when the Roman tenth legion scoured the Jordan River valley, the Essenes of this community, now called Qumran, buried their religious books in nearby caves. In 1947, the caves were discovered, and many of the books have come to light as the Dead Sea Scrolls. Through these scrolls, we know a great deal about the Essenes of Qumran, although how they differed from other Essenes is still unclear.

Basically, Essenes believed that the Sadducean Jerusalem priesthood was illegitimate and that all who associated with Sadducean priests were apostate.[32] The Essenes withdrew into their own wilderness community to wait for the end of the world and their own vindication. They believed that they were living in the last days, that the end of the world was near at hand, and that the Messiah would soon come to establish his kingdom and restore legitimate priests (Essenes, of course) to serve in a renewed temple. In the meantime, they withdrew as much as possible from what they perceived to be an apostate Jewish society.

Essenes were more strict and rigorous than even the Pharisees, whom they called "seekers after smooth things," that is, those who look for the easy way. Yet in their beliefs they were very close to the Pharisees, and it appears that the Essenes and Pharisees were two branches of a single movement that had its beginnings in Maccabean times. Like the Pharisees, the Essenes believed in the validity of some kind of oral law.[33] They believed in the existence of angels and demons, in the continued existence of the spirit after death, and in the resurrection of the body. Like the Pharisees, the Essenes were anti-Roman, and in the first Jewish revolt, Essenes were active in the fighting.

The Dead Sea Scrolls reveal that Essenes had many doctrines and practices in common with early Christianity. They practiced a ritual by immersion and believed in the necessity of receiving the Holy Ghost. They had a ritual meal of bread and wine (or perhaps grape juice) in which they anticipated the coming of the Messiah. Their leadership structure employed a group of three associated with a group of twelve. Individual communities were governed by an overseer who looked after the temporal welfare, controlled admission to the community, and acted as a common judge. They practiced communal living and "had all things in common." Nevertheless, the Essenes were not Christians, and many of the above beliefs and practices can also be found in other Jewish sects of the time. Moreover, Essenes believed many things that were contradicted in the teachings of Jesus and the early church.[34]

The Zealots

Strictly speaking, the Zealots should probably be considered as a branch of Pharisaism, because their theology was basically that of the Pharisees. However, the Zealots were rabid nationalists who actively resisted Roman rule of the Jews even to the point of armed insurrection. In the Old Testament, zeal for the law was always a positive thing. Out of zeal for the law, Phineas slew the Israelite man and the Midianite woman (Num. 25:1-8), and Mattathias slew the Greek officer (1 Macc. 2:15-28). Even Jesus was moved to violence when he drove the money changers out of the temple; John reports that the disciples remembered, "The zeal of thine house hath eaten me up." (John 2:17.) So there was ample precedent for Jews to resort to instant violence out of religious zeal.

Zealots believed that if Jews would only rise up and fight, God would send them victory as he had in the days of Judah the Maccabee. The Zealots, as an article of faith, would recognize no authority in Palestine but that of God and his appointed servants, and they rejected any kind of compromise or accommodation with Rome. Josephus and the New Testament call them "robbers" or "thieves."[35] Toward the end of the first century A.D., the Zealot movement grew stronger as the excesses of the Roman governors grew increasingly intolerable. The militant wing of the Zealot movement, called the *Sicarii* (Latin for "the Daggers"), practiced political assassination and other acts of terrorism directed both at the Roman occupation government and at those Jews, primarily the chief priests and scribes, who collaborated with Rome. Finally, in A.D. 66, the Zealots were able to precipitate what they had long sought, a general revolt against Rome. The war lasted for seven years, and when it was over Jerusalem had been conquered, the temple had been destroyed, and thousands upon thousands of Jews had lost their lives. Thousands of the survivors were sold into slavery and dispersed throughout the Roman world. Zealots, Essenes, and Sadducees were all gone forever; only the Pharisees remained to rebuild Judaism in their own image and create rabbinic or "orthodox" Judaism, the Talmudic or classical Judaism of a later time.

The Samaritans

According to 2 Kings, chapter 17, when the Assyrians conquered the northern kingdom of Israel, they took "all of Israel" out of the land and brought Assyrian colonists to replace them in the cities of Israel. When God sent ferocious lions among the colonists in their new home, they sent back to Assyria for an Israelite priest who could show them how to worship and appease the God of the land of Israel. However, they continued also to worship their foreign gods and thus polluted the religion of Israel. In the first century A.D., most Jews considered Samaritans to be only slightly less unclean than Gentiles, and certainly not bona fide members of the house of Israel.

Samaritan and Assyrian records show, however, that some of

the account in 2 Kings may be exaggerated. It does not appear that the Assyrians deported *all* the Israelites, but only 27,290 of them. This would be only a fraction of the whole population.[36] Moreover, Samaritan religion shows no influence from Assyrian ideas during this time, and the Samaritan version of the Pentateuch is very close to the Hebrew and implies a religion almost identical to Judaism, at least as far as the law of Moses is concerned, though naturally the Samaritans, like the Sadducees and Christians, rejected the oral law of the Pharisees and popular Judaism. Samaritans worshiped the God of Israel in a temple on Mount Gerizim, with rites similar to those of Judaism. So while it is certain that Israel lost its leadership along with large portions of its population in the deportation of 721 B.C., and that the Samaritans were a mixture of the Israelites who remained behind (predominately) and the Gentile colonists who moved in (partially), by and large the Samaritans were still descended from Israel and practiced a corrupted version of the religion of Israel. This explains why Jesus proselytized among the Samaritans,[37] though he intentionally avoided contact with Gentiles.

When the Jews returned from their Babylonian exile, the Samaritans attempted to establish cordial relations with them but were rebuffed, and an adversary relationship soon developed that was largely a continuation of the ancient hatred between Israel and Judah. (See Ezra 4:1-4.) The antagonism reached its peak, however, during the Maccabean period, for the Samaritans did not join the Jews in revolt against the Greeks, nor did they support the Jews who did. It was in retaliation for this policy, which the Jews viewed as treachery, that John Hyrcanus destroyed the Samaritan Temple in 128 B.C. After that event, there could be no friendly relations between Samaria and Judah. Such was the bitter state of affairs in the New Testament period that Jewish pilgrims from Galilee were often molested as they passed through Samaria, and Josephus wrote of Samaritans defiling the Jerusalem Temple at Passover by strewing human bones in the courts and sanctuary.[38] After about A.D. 300, the Jews treated Samaritans in all respects as Gentiles, except that they were not allowed even to become converts.

The 'Am Ha-'aretz

The vast majority of the population in Jewish Palestine did not go to church, that is, they did not have an active affiliation with any of the Jewish sects. Most people accepted the views of the Pharisees on the interpretation of the law, but few actually became Pharisees. These nonaffiliated Jews were called the *'am ha-'aretz*, the "people of the land," and they made up probably 90 percent of the crowds and multitudes to which John the Baptist and Jesus preached.

Scribes and Publicans

The terms *scribe* and *publican* do not refer to religious affiliation at all, but rather to occupation. Scribes or publicans could be Pharisees or Sadducees. They should not be conceived of as secretaries or clerks. The scribes were the lawyer class of Jewish life, the "doctors of the law." They were college-educated intellectuals, trained in the practical or civil aspects of the law of Moses, in applying and interpreting the law in everyday life to all denominations of Jews alike. Therefore the scribes represented, along with the Pharisees and the priests, a very influential class in Jewish society. Many scribes sat in the Sanhedrin, the ruling council of the Jewish people, just as many prominent lawyers become active in politics today.

The publicans were tax collectors. In Roman times, the right to collect transport tolls and other minor taxes in a given area was farmed out to private companies or individuals who bid for the privilege. Whatever they could collect above their bid was their profit. It was a system that invited and rewarded incredible dishonesty. Those who participated in such a business were considered by the Jews to be totally without moral scruples. Publicans were believed to be so certainly dishonest that they could not legally give testimony in a Jewish court. The owners of these tax franchises were usually Romans, but they often hired Jews (like Matthew/Levi) to do the actual tax collecting. These Jewish publicans were despised even more than the Romans. Not only did they rob and cheat their brethren, but they also served the enemies of their people. Thus they were viewed as both robbers and traitors.

Jewish Institutions

The Sanhedrin

The Greek term *sanhedrin* is a generic term for a council, and so there were many sanhedrins in different areas of Jewish life. However, when the term is used without explanation, usually the Great Jerusalem Sanhedrin, the ruling council of the Jewish nation, is meant. It was a body of seventy-two[39] influential men, appointed for life, which combined in one the legislative, executive, and judicial functions. The Sanhedrin interpreted the laws, enforced the laws, and judged those who broke the laws. Since the law of the land was the law of Moses, most of the members were scribes (doctors of the law), but the Sanhedrin was presided over by the Jewish high priest, and there were many of the "chief priests" (most of whom were Sadducees) in their number.

The Sanhedrin established the correct interpretation of the law when Pharisees and Sadducees (or others) disagreed, usually deciding in favor of the Pharisees. They declared war, supervised the activities of the priesthood, directed public works, adjusted the calendar, engaged in diplomacy with foreign governments, pronounced excommunications, and heard criminal cases. Local courts were also scattered about that were sometimes called sanhedrins, and they also heard criminal cases. The Jerusalem Sanhedrin sometimes decided points of law for cases before the local courts or occasionally took over a case that could not be decided by the local court, but the Jerusalem Sanhedrin was not an appeals court in the usual sense of the term.

The Romans did not interfere with the normal functions of the Sanhedrin or of the other Jewish courts. Rather, they set up parallel legal and governmental systems for non-Jews. As long as Jewish courts confined themselves to Jewish matters, the Romans let them alone. Where Roman and Jewish interests intersected, the Roman system had the last word.

Christian interest in the Sanhedrin has usually focused on its role in the trial and death of Jesus. It has often been claimed that the procedures by which Jesus were tried were grossly illegal under Jewish law. However, all such claims are based upon the Jewish laws as they are found in the Mishnah, which was not written down until the third century A.D., and which may not reflect the actual legal conditions at the time of Jesus. To criticize the trial of Jesus using the Mishnaic legislation would perhaps be like declaring illegal all the courts in colonial America for not abiding by the state codes of the 1980s.[40] Little is known about exact Jewish court procedures in Jesus' time.

The Synagogue

The Greek word *synagogue* means a place of gathering together. The synagogue in first-century Judaism was not primarily a place of worship, but a place of study. Worship in the strict sense was reserved for the temple in Jerusalem, which was the only "house of God" in Judaism. The local meetings in the synagogue were merely supplements to the actual worship that took place in the temple. Moreover, in the temple the worshiper was under the direction of the (Sadducean) priests, while in the synagogue the student was usually under the direction of the (Pharisaic) teacher or rabbi.

Synagogues seem to have developed during the Babylonian exile and were designed as places to pray and to educate the people in the religion of their fathers in the absence of the lost temple of Solomon. Especially after the destruction of Herod's Temple in A.D. 70, the synagogues began to take on even more elements of the lost temple, for example, being built on elevated points, facing east, and the torah scroll being kept in an ark behind a curtain in a holy of holies supported by two pillars.

In the first century, the local synagogue served as a sort of community center. The leader of the synagogue was a public official who administered floggings prescribed by the courts (as in Matt. 10:17). Charity drives and town meetings were held in the synagogues, and during the week they were used as schools. However, no eating, drinking, or sleeping was allowed; hence they could not be used for Christian worship where the sacrament of the Lord's Supper was administered. Synagogues could not be used as shelters or as places to conduct business.

Normally, in a synagogue service there was a series of recited prayers (the Eighteen Benedictions) and then the Shema'. (Deut. 6:4-7.) This was followed by a reading from the Hebrew Bible, which was delivered standing. Then the scripture was explained or commented upon by some qualified person. The explanation was delivered sitting down. (See Luke 4:16-21.) Gentiles were allowed to attend the synagogues but generally sat in the back or were somehow separated from the Jewish members. Women were not allowed to read or expound the scriptures in the synagogues.[41]

The Temple

The great Jerusalem Temple was the spiritual center of first-century Judaism. At one time there had been several different temples in Palestine, but after the Babylonian exile the priests and scribes insisted, more for political reasons than for religious ones, that there could be only one, and that one was in Jerusalem.[42] However, there was a Samaritan temple on Mount Gerizim near Shechem until 128 B.C., and there was also a full-scale Jewish temple at Leontopolis in Egypt (operated by priests descended from the Oniad family) until the second century A.D.

The temple built by Solomon in Jerusalem, which was destroyed by the Babylonians in 587 B.C., is usually called the First Temple. The temple built by Zerubbabel after the Babylonian exile is usually called the Second Temple. This was the temple, greatly remodeled by Herod, that stood in the days of Jesus.

As it stood in Jesus' day, the temple consisted of a huge area called the Temple Mount, surrounded by a wall. It was equivalent to our own Temple Square. Unclean persons and Gentiles could come up onto the Temple Mount. This was sometimes called the "Court of the Gentiles." This was where the Sanhedrin met and where there was a synagogue and also the concessions that made Jesus angry—the money changers and those who sold sacrifices to the pilgrims.[43] Inside the Court of the Gentiles, and placed a few steps higher, was an enclosure marked off by a low stone wall. Gentiles could not pass inside this wall. Within the enclosure was the Court of Women, also separated by a wall, and connected to the Court of Women and accessible from it was the Court of the Israelites. Here women could not come. A low barrier separated the Court of Israel from the Court of the Priests, where the actual sacrifices took place and where nonpriests could not enter. In the center of the Court of Priests stood the temple building itself. There was an outer porch, an inner room called the Holy Place, and, accessible only from the Holy Place, the innermost chamber, called the Holy of Holies. This was separated from the Holy Place by the veil of the temple. Only the high priest was allowed to enter the Holy of Holies, and that occurred only once a year on the Day of Atonement (Yom Kippur).

Individuals might attend the temple as they chose, but there were also temple assignments made up from twenty-four temple districts. The obligation to participate in these deputations fell on priests, Levites, and Israelites alike. However, those who were known to break the commandments or who were excommunicated were excluded from the temple. Temple worship in Jesus' time consisted mainly of the sacrifices, both personal and public, that were offered to God in the temple. An individual might bring his own personal offerings, but the assigned individuals were there to stand by the public offerings.

Those entering the temple first put aside their personal possessions and took off their shoes. They then performed a ritual washing and put on white clothes. Prayers, hymns, blessings, and the reading and expounding of the Torah were also part of the temple services in the first century.[44]

NOTES

1. Hence the question of the apostles to the risen Christ in Acts 1:6: "Lord, wilt thou at this time restore again the kingdom to Israel?"

2. The numbers come from the records of the Assyrian king Sargon, *Annals* 11-17. (See James B. Pritchard, ed., *Ancient Near Eastern Texts* [Princeton, N.J.: Princeton University Press, 1950], p. 284.) They indicate that the deportation was not total—in fact, that only a minority of the population was actually taken from Israel.

3. It was shortly before this catastrophe, in about 600 B.C., that the Lord warned the prophet Lehi and his family to leave Jerusalem.

4. Some have suggested that one purpose of the book of Jonah, which may have been written during this period or shortly after, is to combat the kind of narrow exclusivism that had crept into some of contemporary Judaism and to remind the chosen people that their religion must also deal with the Gentiles in a positive way.

5. Parthia included most of ancient Babylon and Persia.

6. In fact, it was this Babylonian Judaism that between A.D. 400 and 900 would produce the Babylonian Talmud.

7. Latin became a common language only in Europe and parts of North Africa, and only at a much later period. In classical antiquity, Greek was the true universal language, which is one reason why the New Testament documents all come to us in Greek.

8. A few years later, this fact would help explain the rapid expansion of Christianity in the hellenistic world: it answered life's questions when the traditional religions did not. See Gilbert Murray, *The Five Stages of Greek Religion* (Oxford: Clarendon Press, 1925), pp. 119-26.

9. For example, in the theater, hellenism had produced what was called new comedy—the ancient equivalent of television sitcoms. The arts of this period still displayed incredible technical skill and sophistication, but the old creativity was gone.

10. For example, the coat and cloak of Matthew 5:40 are the Greek *chiton* and *himation.*

11. This made money *changing*, that is, from hellenistic coins with images to temple coins without them, a necessity for those who wished to pay their tithes and offerings into the temple. For everyday purposes, most Jews compromised and used the image-bearing coins (as in Luke 20:24).

12. An account of these events and of the Jewish reaction can be found in the apocryphal books of 1 and 2 Maccabees. 1 Maccabees is a reliable historical narrative, while 2 Maccabees is more in the order of historical fiction—a dramatization of the same events. Additional information on this period can be found in Josephus, *Antiquities,* books 12 and 13.

13. 1 Macc. 2:15-27.

14. Relations between Jews and Samaritans never did improve after this campaign.

15. The future King Herod the Great was an Idumean whose family had been forced to convert to Judaism by the Hasmonean rulers.

16. This fact prompted Caesar Augustus to observe that it was better

to be Herod's pig than Herod's son (since the Jews don't eat pork, the pig is safe).

17. Josephus, *Antiquities* 17.6.5. The young men were not executed, since Herod, who was gone, was the only one who wanted them dead.

18. Josephus, *Antiquities* 18.5.2. See Matt. 14:1-10.

19. The description is that of King Agrippa I. It is quoted from Philo of Alexandria, *Legation to Caius,* 38.

20. Almost all of our information about Pilate comes from the New Testament; Philo's *Legation to Caius,* 38; and Josephus, *Antiquities* 18.3-4. As later Christianity grew increasingly hostile to Jews, Pilate was seen in a more positive light. He is a saint in the Coptic Christian Church.

21. The story is found in Josephus, *Antiquities* 18.8. The letter ordering suicide was delayed by bad weather and reached Petronius almost a month after he learned of Caius's death.

22. The best source for information about the first revolt is Josephus, *The Jewish War* (Grand Rapids, Mich.: Zondervan, 1982). A good shorter treatment can be found in David M. Rhoads, *Israel in Revolution, 6-74 C.E.* (Philadelphia: Fortress Press, 1976).

23. Convenient treatments of the Jewish sects can be found in Emil Schürer, *The History of the Jewish People in the Age of Jesus Christ,* 2 vols. (Edinburgh: T. & T. Clark, 1979), revised by Geza Vermes, Fergus Millar, and Matthew Black, 2:381-414, 555-606; and in Marcel Simon, *Jewish Sects at the Time of Jesus* (Philadelphia: Fortress Press, 1967).

24. Josephus, *Antiquities* 17.42.

25. It was to this practice that Jesus objected when he said, "Full well ye reject the commandment of God, that ye may keep your own tradition . . . making the word of God of none effect through your own tradition." (Mark 7:9, 13.)

26. This attitude, that once God has spoken he can never speak again, or that God's word once written can never be added upon, is a common error encountered in our own time as well. It is the inevitable result of the loss of continuing revelation, for when revelation to living prophets ceases, one must either admit the loss of it or deny the necessity of it.

27. See Mark 7:1-13; Matt. 15:1-9. The principle of *corban* mentioned here held that once assets had been designated as consecrated to the temple, they could not then be used for any other purpose, not even for the support of needy parents. (However, the third-century Mishnah says that support of parents has priority.) Like the *prosbul, corban* was an innovation of the oral law.

28. As, for example, in Matt. 19:7-9, or in the Sermon on the Mount at Matt. 5:21-22, 27-28, 31-34, 38-39.

29. Sacrifices, money changers, sale of wood and incense, and so on.

30. Thus the chief priests lamented concerning Jesus, "If we let him thus alone, all men will believe on him: and the Romans shall come and take away both our place and nation." (John 11:48.)

31. The Apostle Paul was able to capitalize on this in Acts 23:6-10. He got his opponents, Pharisees and Sadducees, quarreling with each other over the doctrine of the resurrection. Some of the Pharisees even turned to his defense.

32. It should be noted that unlike the Essenes, Jesus and the early Christians did not dispute the legitimacy of the Jerusalem priesthood—only their righteousness.

33. As might be expected, however, sometimes their version of the oral law differed from that of the Pharisees. For example, among the Essenes the obligation to support one's parents and family took precedence over the practice of *corban*. (Damascus Document 16:14-15.)

34. There is no substance to the popular speculation that Jesus and John the Baptist were influenced by the Essenes.

35. As with the thief Barabbas or the two thieves on the crosses. These men were being executed because they were rebels who had killed people in their insurrection. In today's terms, one side might have called them "freedom fighters" or "the underground," the other side "terrorists."

36. T. H. Gaster, "Samaritans," *The Interpreter's Dictionary of the Bible*, 4 vols., ed. G. A. Buttrick (New York: Abingdon Press, 1962), 4:190-97.

37. See John 4:4-42, although Jesus still insisted that the Samaritan version of the religion of Israel was incorrect and that the Jewish version was correct.

38. Josephus, *Antiquities* 18.2.2.

39. The exact number is disputed, but the best possibilities are that there were seventy (or seventy-one) council members and two (or one) presidents.

40. For information on the trial of Jesus, see Ernest Bammel, ed., *The Trial of Jesus* (Naperville, Ill.: A. R. Allenson, 1970). On the Sanhedrin, see S. Safrai and M. Stern, *The Jewish People in the First Century,* 2 vols. (Assen, Amsterdam: Van Gorcum, 1976), 1:379-400, and Schürer, *The History of the Jewish People* 2:199-226.

41. For information on the synagogues in general, see Safrai and Stern, *The Jewish People in the First Century* 2:908-44.

42. In Old Testament times, the prophet Samuel served at a sanctuary at Shiloh. There were others at Bethel (which means "house of God"), Nob, Gibeah, Arad (maybe), and elsewhere.

43. These concessions began as a service to pilgrims who otherwise would have had to go into town to change their foreign money into temple coin (which had no images on it and which alone could be used for the payment of religious obligations) and to find unblemished sacrifices. But what began on the pretext of being a service soon became a major source of revenue to the high-priestly families who controlled the concessions and who were taking unfair advantage of the tourists. There were also concessions that sold the wood and incense for the sacrifices.

44. Two good sources for understanding the temple and its worship are Menahem Haran, *Temples and Temple Service in Ancient Israel* (Oxford: Clarendon Press, 1978), and Safrai and Stern, *The Jewish People in the First Century* 2:865-907.

3

THE TESTIMONY OF MATTHEW

Robert L. Millet

The gospel is "the glad tidings . . . that he came into the world, even Jesus, to be crucified for the world, and to bear the sins of the world, and to sanctify the world, and to cleanse it from all unrighteousness; that through him all might be saved whom the Father had put into his power and made by him." (D&C 76:40-42.) Before ascending into heaven, the Master delivered a charge to his apostles to preach that gospel to all the world.

Oral and Written Testimonies

Acceptance of Christ and his gospel was accomplished first through the power of verbal human testimony: faith came by hearing the word of God, as taught by legal administrators whose oral witness was attended by the spirit of prophecy and revelation.[1] Much of the earliest scripture—that delivered by the power of the Holy Ghost (D&C 68:3-4)—in the meridian dispensation (as perhaps in all dispensations) existed in an oral and un-recorded form.[2] The *kerygma* or proclamation of the gospel, the *logia* (sayings of Christ), and the *agrapha* (unwritten things) circulated among the Saints as the witness of the apostles spread from Jerusalem to the ends of the known world. The gospel was preached then, as now, by word and by power, whether by mouth or by pen. In our own day, genuine faith-promoting stories circu-

Robert L. Millet is assistant professor of ancient scripture and New Testament area coordinator at Brigham Young University.

late throughout the Church orally at the same time that written accounts of the events are readily available. It does not require too much stretch of the imagination to suppose that in the first-century church, written documents recounting many of the events of the life of Jesus were contemporaneous with the members' reminiscences and personal oral testimonies of the same. The manner in which oral traditions were valued in early Christianity is highlighted by the following statement from Papias, bishop of Hierapolis in Asia Minor (ca. A.D. 130-140): "I will not hesitate to set down for you alongside my interpretations all that I ever learned well from the elders and remembered well, guaranteeing their truth. . . . Also, if ever a person came my way who had been a companion of the elders, I would inquire about the sayings of the elders—what was said by Andrew, or by Peter, or by Philip, or by Thomas or James, or by John or Matthew or any other of the Lord's disciples? . . . For *I did not suppose that what I could get from books was of such great value to me as the utterances of a living and abiding voice.*"[3]

The Challenge of the Gospel Writer

How does one write the story of a God, sketch the outlines or prepare the epoch of an Infinite One? "No man," observed Elder Bruce R. McConkie, "can write a *Life of Christ* in the true sense of the word, for two very good and sufficient reasons:

> 1. The data to do so do not exist. The material is simply not available. We do not know how he spent his youth, who his friends were, what part he played in church and civic affairs, how he conducted himself within the framework of the Jewish family system, and hosts of other things. Though we know a great deal about the historical and social circumstances of his day, very little authentic information is available of his actual life from either secular or spiritual sources. What Matthew, Mark, Luke, and John put in their Gospel accounts was written as their testimony of a small part of his divine doings. Personal items are scarcely mentioned. The Gospels contain only . . . those glimpses of selected acts and deeds, which the Spirit knew

beforehand should be preserved for presentation to the unbelieving and skeptical masses of men into whose hands the New Testament would come. Even God will not pour more knowledge and light and intelligence and understanding into human souls than they are prepared to accept. Such would be and is contrary to his whole plan for the advancement and growth and ultimate perfection of his children.

2. No mortal man, no matter how gifted he may be in literary craftsmanship, and no matter how highly endowed he may be with that spiritual insight which puts the words and acts of men into a true eternal perspective—no mortal, I say, can write the biography of a God. A biography is but the projection through the eyes of a penman of what the writer *believes* were the acts and what he *feels* were the thoughts and emotions of another man who had like feelings with his own. How, then, can any mortal plumb the depths of the feelings or understand in full the doings, of an Eternal Being?[4]

It would seem, therefore, that an initial obstacle facing the inspired author/editor is one of being able to discern the words and ideas that most closely approximate the ineffable. Indeed, some matters are such that "no tongue can speak [of them], neither can [they] be written by any man, neither can the hearts of men conceive so great and marvelous things." (3 Nephi 17:17; cf. D&C 76:115-16.) In the face of such overwhelming literary obstacles, however, it *was* given to certain chosen representatives to construct a limited but living and descriptive testimony of the Messiah—a carefully constrained chronicle of the life of the Son of God.

A second potential barrier encountered by the Gospel writers was the passage of time, the interval between the actual events and the accounts of those events. Most serious students of the New Testament feel that much of the material in our present canonical Gospels did not take final form until a number of years after the death and resurrection of Christ. In fact, the passing of years does occasionally lead to a loss of detail. The Lord Jesus did promise to his disciples, however, that "the Comforter, which is the Holy

Ghost, whom the Father will send in my name, . . . shall teach you all things, and bring all things to your remembrance, whatsoever I have said unto you." (John 14:26.) No doubt this was the case with Matthew and John, members of the original Twelve, who prepared Gospel accounts based upon their personal experiences with the Master. In regard to Mark and Luke—devoted disciples who may never have known the Savior intimately during his mortal ministry —we feel confident that the spirit of inspiration guided their minds and their pens and directed them to interview and inquire of persons whose firsthand dealings with Jesus needed to be preserved.

From another point of view, the passage of time also leads to a perspective and a breadth of clarity and context. Nephi began his small plates approximately thirty years after leaving Jerusalem (2 Ne. 5:28-32), but we as readers are so much the richer as a result of this period of rare and valuable spiritual gestation. With his eyes open to the works and wonders of the Lord during the previous three decades, Nephi the prophet/writer set forth in remarkable fashion his intriguing account of how the "tender mercies of the Lord are over all those whom he hath chosen." (1 Ne. 1:20.) Joseph Smith's 1838 account of the First Vision (the one contained in our Pearl of Great Price) was dictated some eighteen years after the dispensation-opening experience in the Sacred Grove. During that interval, Joseph the Prophet grew in spiritual graces and gained a mature frame of reference that sharply defined the significance of the appearance of the Father and the Son. In similar fashion, the Gospel writers, moved upon by the Holy Ghost, reflected upon personal or reported experiences with the Master, and then with mature minds and a grander vision set out to construct an extended written testimony of Jesus the Christ. Time frequently yields a peak in overall perception.

"Of all the disciples," wrote Eusebius, the fourth-century church historian, "Matthew and John are the only ones that have left us recorded comments [concerning the ministry of Christ], and even *they*, tradition says, *undertook it from necessity.*"[5] What was the necessity for written Gospels? Why was it essential that *the* gospel be formed into *a* Gospel, that the oral become textual? First of all, it is important to note that the power and the impact of oral traditions are bounded by the limitations and inabilities of human transmitters. George Reynolds and Janne Sjodahl have suggested that the written Gospels took shape to insure continuity and orthodoxy of doctrine:

> It may be supposed that those Disciples of Christ . . . like Matthew and John, would keep journals while they followed their Master, witnessing His works and listening to His teachings. These journals would, after the Crucifixion and Ascension, naturally be read in private and in public. They would be copied and distributed in the various branches of the Church and form texts for sermons and otherwise discourses, and thus be augmented with such incidents or sayings which were still retained in the memories of those who had been eyewitnesses. In this way several versions of the doings and sayings of our Lord began to circulate, some no doubt contradicting others, until the necessity became universally felt to have some authentic record showing exactly what was reliable of the many circulating reports, and what was not reliable. And the result is the four Gospels according to Matthew, Mark, Luke, and John.[6]

A "standard work" was needed in the first century as much as it is needed in the twentieth century in order that the Saints of the former day might "speak the same thing" and thus be "perfectly joined together in the same mind and in the same judgment." (1 Cor. 1:10.) The authorized Gospels helped to establish precise doctrinal and historical lines between orthodoxy and heresy, between the accepted and the aberrant. W. D. Davies has described the process as follows: "In the Graeco-Roman world, the Palestinian Gospel came into contact with all sorts of religious and philosophic movements. Men challenged it and could have perverted it by turning it into a metaphysical system or a mystery or Gnostic cult, without connection with that historic figure who gave it birth; that is, they could have cut it from its root. To prevent this, the Gospels came into being; they kept the Church attached to its base."[7] Two other biblical scholars have explained:

The infant Christian community demanded that oral tradition be rightly evaluated to avoid misunderstanding, in the knowledge that the original disciples would soon be dead and the community faced with the need to have more or less fixed patterns for recalling God's redemptive act in Jesus. There were other factors at work, too. We know from the evidence of both archaeology and secular writers that conditions in Palestine after A.D. 60 were fraught with uncertainty and pending civil strife, and that in these years (even before the fall of Jerusalem in A.D. 70) thousands of people left the country. In such a situation, it is understandable that only Christians would feel the need to record and preserve the earliest oral memories of the ministry of Jesus and its culmination.

Because of the nature of the Gospel proclamation, the original oral repetition of the story of Jesus and his teachings did not satisfy the early Christians for long. It was of the essence of the Gospel—supremely exemplified in Matthew and in Paul's teaching—that all Israel's experience had been gathered up, fulfilled in Jesus. But how, and in what manner, had it all been fulfilled? If the earliest Christians had the Old Testament as scripture, and presumably followed the old synagogue pattern of reading and prayers, then it is obvious that the Gospel had to be put into a form in which it could be similarly used. We know from Paul's letters (cf. Col iv 16) that he was able to order his letters to be read aloud in his convert-congregations, and we may infer from this that during worship there was teaching by the apostles and elders. It is only logical to assume, therefore, that there was pressure to have on record an authentic account of what Jesus had said and done, the better to show Christianity's roots in Israel.[8]

At the same time, the Gospels were written to secure and maintain the precious witness of those who had originally walked and talked with the Savior. "When these witnesses began to pass away," Davies has written, "their testimony had to be preserved. This is one of the fundamental reasons for the emergence of the Gospels—in part, at least, they were designed to supply the witness of those witnesses who were no longer alive."[9]

The Formation of the Gospels

Irenaus (ca. A.D. 180), in speaking out against doctrinal heresies of the second century, taught that "it is not possible that the gospels can be either more or fewer in number than they are." He further compared the four Gospels to the "four zones of the world in which we live," as well as the "four pillars" of the church. Jesus Christ, he added, "has given us the Gospel under four aspects, but bound together by one spirit."[10] Irenaus's statement was obviously intended to discourage and discount any and all apocryphal Gospels. At the same time, it is wise for us to recognize the hand of Providence in the formation, inspiration, and preservation of the four Gospels. Surely Matthew, Mark, Luke, and John were foreordained in premortality and raised up in mortality to make their particular contributions. Joseph Smith taught, "Every man who has a calling to minister to the inhabitants of the world was ordained to that very purpose in the Grand Council of heaven before the world was."[11] The impact of the ministries of our Gospel writers did not end with their own deaths; their compositions continue to turn men's minds toward their Redeemer twenty centuries later.

As noted earlier, there should be no doubt among Latter-day Saints that the canonical Gospels were compiled, composed, organized, and written by the spirit of revelation. At the same time, we in no way detract from the spiritual significance of the writers to suggest that Matthew, Mark, Luke, and John were also divinely directed editors as well as creative authors. Moses was a choice seer and a man familiar with and open to the revelations of the Lord. He was also a gifted compiler and editor of earlier records. "The only biblical account of the creation," writes Elder Bruce R. McConkie, "was revealed directly to Moses, but *we are left to suppose that he copied or condensed the historical portions of Genesis from the writings of Noah, Melchizedek, Abraham, and the patriarchs.* The fourteenth and fiftieth chapters of Genesis, both as restored by Joseph Smith, must have been written respectively by Melchizedek and Joseph (the son of Jacob) in the first instance."[12] Likewise, Mormon was an inspired author/editor whose timely commentary and whose "and thus we see" passages in the Nephite record help wondrously to demonstrate the wisdom of the ways of God. The Gospel writers undertook the task of producing authorized and written testimony-narratives, based upon accurate and authentic accounts and directed by that Spirit which Jesus had promised to send.

All four of the Gospel writers were prophets, men endowed with the testimony of Jesus, which is the spirit of prophecy. (Rev. 19:10.)[13] They all loved and served the same Lord. And yet their written testimonies of the Lord Jesus were expressed in varying ways and in a manner peculiar to each author. For example, Elder McConkie wrote: "It appears that Matthew was directing his gospel to the Jews. He presents Christ as the promised Messiah and Christianity as the fulfillment of Judaism. Mark apparently wrote with the aim of appealing to the Roman or Gentile mind. Luke's gospel presents the Master to the Greeks, to those of culture and refinement. And the gospel of John is the account for the saints; it is preeminently the gospel for the Church, for those who understand the scriptures and their symbolisms and who are concerned with spiritual and eternal things."[14] Each writer "had especial and intimate knowledge of certain circumstances not so well known to others," and thus each "felt impressed to emphasize different matters because of the particular people to whom he was addressing his personal gospel testimony."[15]

Also worthy of consideration is the possibility that the four Gospels may not always have existed in their present state or condition. First of all, we need to recognize the appropriateness for a writer—even an inspired writer—to add to or take away from his work as he matures or gains new or added perspective. In our Book of Mormon story, Moroni returned to his record after a period of fearful anticipation and (since he was still alive—see, for example, Moroni 1:1) provided additional doctrinal and historical insights to that which had previously been written. In the preparation of the first edition of the Doctrine and Covenants (1835), Joseph Smith made prophetic editorial changes in certain revelations that he had previously received and recorded in the Book of Commandments (1833).[16] The same is true of Joseph Smith's inspired translation of the King James Bible: whereas the

Prophet and his scribe had formally completed the work of translation by July 1833, Joseph continued to labor with the manuscripts, making changes where he felt the need to do so, until the time of his death.[17] Future discoveries may well reveal, therefore, that different editions of the Gospels existed through the years. In this connection it is worthwhile to consider an excerpt from a somewhat controversial document known as the "Secret Gospel of Mark." This document was discovered in 1958 by Morton Smith in the Mar Saba monastery, some twelve miles southeast of Jerusalem.

> Now of the things they keep saying about the divinely inspired Gospel according to Mark, some are altogether falsifications, and others, even if they do contain some true elements, nevertheless are not reported truly. For the true things being mixed with inventions, are falsified, so that, as the saying goes, even the salt loses its savor.
>
> As for Mark, then, during Peter's stay in Rome he wrote an account of the Lord's doings, not, however, declaring all of them, nor yet hinting at the secret ones, but selecting what he thought most useful for increasing the faith of those who were being instructed. But when Peter died a martyr, Mark came over to Alexandria, bringing both his own notes and those of Peter, from which he transferred to his former book the things suitable to whatever makes for progress toward knowledge. Thus *he composed a more spiritual Gospel* for the use of those who were being perfected. Nevertheless, he yet did not divulge the things not to be uttered.[18]

It may be that the Gospels as we now have them represent a truncated version of the Gospels as first written by Matthew, Mark, Luke, and John. Nephi saw in vision the day when the Old and New Testaments would suffer a willful interference by a church whose dominions were great and whose desires and actions were abominable. "Plain and precious things [would be] taken away from the book, which is the book of the Lamb of God" (1 Ne. 13:28); that is to say, "many important points touching the salvation of men, [would be] taken from the Bible, or lost before it was compiled."[19] We need, therefore, to be extremely grateful that the

Lord has seen fit to preserve those portions of the Gospels that have been secured for us.

In forming the message of *the* gospel into what we have come to call *a* Gospel, the writers became the initiators of a remarkably important literary genre. The Gospels are not, as we have seen, purely biographical, in the modern sense of revealing or developing the thoughts or personalities of the main characters; possibly not more than thirty days of the life of Christ receive treatment through all four Gospel accounts. On the other hand, the Gospels represent laudatory biographies written to elicit faith and emulation.[20]

The four Gospels "do not claim to be exhaustive accounts of all that Jesus said or did." Rather, "each gospel was selective according to the purpose of the author, and is complete in the sense that it carries out his intent."[21] The Gospels were "standard works" in the sense that they were given to guide the Saints in emulating the Sinless One as well as to transmit the witness that Jesus died, was buried, rose again the third day, and ascended into heaven. (See 1 Cor. 15:3-4.)[22] The Gospels were written to convey the "portion of the word" (to use Alma's words—Alma 12:9-11) that is appropriate for persons who are gaining or strengthening a conviction of Jesus as the Messiah. They were not written to convey the esoteric teachings of the Lord, those sacred truths preserved for those persons able to bear the added enlightenment. In a sense, the Gospels are public documents, created for display purposes. Surely there are "many other things which Jesus did, the which, if they should be written every one, I suppose that even the world itself could not contain the books that should be written." (John 21:25.)[23]

Matthew as a Gospel Writer

Matthew (Levi) was a member of the original Quorum of the Twelve Apostles, a publican or tax gatherer before his call. Edgar Goodspeed has suggested the following regarding the author of the first Gospel: "Matthew was probably a man of somewhat more education, as we would call it, than some of his fellow disciples. He must have been able to read and write, and to use the elements at least of arithmetic, in his work as a tax collector. . . . Matthew is more likely to have known Greek than any of the rest, for he was a tax collector. He is likelier to have been readier with the pen than most, perhaps than any, of the group, and he may even have jotted down for his own use not a few of Jesus' striking sayings, especially after the missionary travels of the Twelve about the Jewish towns."[24]

In the preparation of his Gospel, Matthew would no doubt have drawn upon his own reminiscences and notes, as well as other extant oral or written sources. After providing the genealogy of Jesus Christ, Matthew records (1:18): "Now the birth of Jesus Christ was on this wise . . ." The Matthean infancy narrative follows. Joseph Smith's translation of the same verse (JST, Matt. 2:1) reads: "Now, *as it is written*, the birth of Jesus Christ was on this wise . . ." This prophetic alteration of the King James text seems to point toward the possibility of a written source available to the apostle that predates his own Gospel.[25]

Christian tradition holds that Matthew collected the *logia* (sayings) of Jesus in Hebrew (presumably meaning Aramaic) and later translated the same into Greek. From Papias we have the following fragment: "Matthew put together the oracles [of the Lord] in the Hebrew language, and each one interpreted them the best he could."[26] Likewise, according to Irenaus, Matthew "produced his gospel written among the Hebrews in their own dialect."[27] Indeed, "if Matthew had made notes from time to time of things of especial interest and importance that Jesus had said, he would naturally have done so in Aramaic, the language Jesus spoke and they all used." Further, "in Antioch [the traditional source of Matthew's Gospel], of course, his public was largely Greek, and he naturally translated the sayings into that language as he had occasion to use them, or unwritten things that he simply remembered. This is doubtless the background of Papias's remarks."[28]

The "Synoptic Problem"

A close comparative study of Matthew, Mark, and Luke shows that they have much in common. Thus they are called "synoptic," meaning that they take a "similar look" at Christ. We find, for example, that the substance of 606 of the 661 verses of Mark appears in Matthew and that 380 of Mark's verses reappear with only slight alteration in Luke. From another perspective, of the 1,068 verses of Matthew, about 500 contain material also found in Mark; of the 1,149 verses in Luke, about 380 are paralleled in Mark. There are only 31 verses in Mark not found in Matthew or Luke.[29] To look at this another way, consider the following chart, which illustrates the material common and exclusive to each of the Gospels:

Gospel	Exclusive	Common
Mark	7%	93%
Matthew	42%	58%
Luke	59%	41%
John	92%	8%

In other words, 93 percent of the material in Mark is included in the other Gospels, while only 8 percent of the information in John is included in the other Gospels, and so on.

What is one to make of such statistics? What is the chronological and literary relationship between the Synoptic Gospels? The issues underlying these relationships constitute what biblical critics have come to denote the "synoptic problem." Since the nineteenth century many scholars have concluded that the resolution of the problem was to be found in stressing the priority and primacy of Mark, the shortest of the Gospels. The general consensus has been that Mark's was the first Gospel written and that Matthew and Luke drew upon Mark in preparing their own Gospels. This approach, known as the "Markan Hypothesis" or the "Two-Document Hypothesis," contends that Matthew relied upon Mark, upon a "sayings source" or collection of sayings of Jesus (known as the "Q Document," from the German word *Quelle,* "source"), and added his own peculiar style, perspective, and experiences (called "M") in preparing the Gospel we know as Matthew. Supposedly Luke did the same. In short, the Two-Document Hypothesis for the composition of Matthew and Luke is: Matthew = Mark + Q + M. Luke = Mark + Q + L.[30]

For Latter-day Saints, it is not difficult to believe that God could reveal the very same words to Matthew and Luke that he inspired Mark to record. In short, one resolution of the problem might well be the matter of revelation: all of the Gospel writers were inspired by the very same source. At the same time, it would not be out of harmony with principles of truth for one Gospel writer to utilize the writings of another. "Our understanding of the prophetic word," taught Elder Bruce R. McConkie, "will be greatly expanded if we know how one prophet quotes another, usually without acknowledging his source." Then, after giving illustrations of this principle (Micah and Isaiah; Zenos, Nephi, and Malachi; Paul and Mormon; John the Baptist and John the Beloved), Elder McConkie observed: "Once the Lord has revealed his doctrine in precise language to a chosen prophet, there is no reason why he should inspire another prophet to choose the same words in presenting the same doctrine on a subsequent occasion. It is much easier and simpler to quote that which has already been given." He concluded, "We are all commanded—including the prophets among us—to search the scriptures and thereby learn what other prophets have presented."[31]

Until further light and knowledge of the doings of the first century are available, we are left to our own reasoning as to the exact manner and time in which the Gospels were formed and prepared.

Prominent Themes in Matthew

Some of the most prominent themes in the Gospel of Matthew are (1) the importance of the Church and kingdom of God; (2) Jesus' condemnation of first-century Judaism and its traditions; and (3) Jesus Christ as the fulfillment of prophecy.

1. *The Importance of the Church and Kingdom of God.* Matthew's work is appropriately known as the "Gospel of the Church." It is, indeed, the only canonical Gospel to use the term *church* (Greek *ekklesia*) in referring to the Christian community. Peter's confession at Caesarea Philippi ("Thou art the Christ, the Son of the living God") was acknowledged and commended by the

Savior as of divine origin. The Lord continued: "And I say also unto thee, That thou art Peter, and upon this rock *I will build my church*; and the gates of hell shall not prevail against it. And I will give unto thee the keys of the kingdom of heaven." (Matt. 16:13-19, emphasis added.) The significant contribution of Matthew's Gospel in this regard (the matter of the church) is grasped by simply comparing the Synoptics in parallel. Mark's account (8:29-30) contains 23 words, Luke's account (9:20-21) contains 22 words, while Matthew's description of the occasion consists of 128 words.

Instructions on regulating the church are given in Matthew 18. Among the subjects discussed, the following are paramount: the need for conversion (vv. 1-5); removing harmful elements from the members' lives and thus from the church (vv. 12-14); resolving differences between individual Saints (vv. 15-17); and the need in the church for genuine forgiveness (vv. 21-35). The instructions regarding the resolution of differences between members (compare the similar counsel in D&C 42:84-92) conclude with the following: "And if he [the accused] shall neglect to hear them [witnesses], *tell it unto the church*: but if he neglect to hear the church, let him be unto thee as a heathen man and a publican." (Matt. 18:17, emphasis added.) The Joseph Smith Translation of Matthew is an even stronger witness than the King James Version that one of Matthew's areas of stress is the place of the church in administering the gospel to the Saints. The Joseph Smith Translation places a stronger emphasis upon the place of commandments (for example, JST, Matt. 5:50; 6:29-30; 9:35-36; 16:25-29) and ordinances (for example, JST, Matt. 5:1-4; 18:10-11).[32]

In a related manner, Matthew placed great stress upon the King and his kingdom. *Messiah* is a royal title, and Jesus' royal/messianic status was critically important to Matthew. The genealogy of Jesus given in Matthew (1:1-17) is the Lord's royal line. Matthew laid out the genealogy in such a manner as to divide the forty-two generations into three sections of fourteen (from Abraham to David, from David to Babylonian captivity, and from exile to Jesus). For Matthew, the very number *fourteen* has royal significance. How so?

51

The name *David* in Hebrew consists of three Hebrew consonants, each having numerical equivalents. Thus: Dahlet (d = 4) + Vav (v = 6) + Dahlet (d = 4) = 14.

Aspects of the Savior's life that highlight his royal status in Matthew include such things as the wise men searching for the King (messiah) of the Jews (2:1-12); Herod's alarm over the birth of a potential rival king (2:7-16); parables of the kingdom (13:1-52); the triumphal entry (21:1-11); Christ's mention of his eventual position at the throne of glory (25:31); and the inscription prepared by Pilate and placed above Jesus' head on the cross— "This is Jesus, the King of the Jews" (27:37). In the words of one New Testament scholar, "Matthew is the Jewish Gospel, dealing with the King and the Kingdom. In Greek, the term 'kingdom of heaven' occurs thirty-three times, and the term 'kingdom of God' four times."[33] Indeed, the ever-present plea of the disciple to the Father in the Gospel of Matthew is "Thy kingdom come. Thy will be done in earth, as it is in heaven" (6:10).

2. *Jesus' Condemnation of First-Century Judaism and Its Traditions.* Jesus chided the Jews of his day for becoming enamored with externals, with means rather than ends. He attacked their empty formalism and hypocrisy. This theme is far more prominent in Matthew than in any of the other Gospels.[34]

In the purest sense, Jesus was an observant Jew. He loved and honored the law of Moses and sought to keep the statutes and ordinances associated with it. "Christ Himself," said the Prophet Joseph Smith, "fulfilled all righteousness in becoming obedient to the law which he had given to Moses on the mount, and thereby magnified it and made it honorable, instead of destroying it."[35] The Master thus taught that until the infinite atonement was accomplished, the law was to be kept and observed. "Heaven and earth must pass away," he taught, "but one jot or one tittle shall in no wise pass from the law, until all be fulfilled. Whosoever, therefore, shall break one of these least commandments, and shall teach men so to do, he shall in no wise be saved in the kingdom of heaven; but whosoever shall do and teach these commandments of the law until it be fulfilled, the same shall be called great, and shall be saved in the kingdom of heaven." (JST, Matt. 5:20-21.) Had the Pharisees been more intense in their study of the pure law, rather than the traditions of the elders, the commentary upon the law, and more eager to apply its teachings, rather than seeking for further things they could not understand (see Jacob 4:14), they might have distilled the central message of the Torah and thereby recognized Jesus of Nazareth as the giver of the law and the promised Messiah. Such was not, however, the case. One of the most interesting contributions of the Joseph Smith Translation may be found in chapter 9 of Matthew's Gospel. Note the relationship between rejecting (or ignoring) the law and rejecting the Christ:

KJV, Matthew 9:15-16

And Jesus said unto them, Can the children of the bridechamber mourn, as long as the bridegroom is with them? but the days will come when the bridegroom shall be taken from them, and then shall they fast.

JST, Matthew 9:16-22

And Jesus said unto them, Can the children of the bridechamber mourn, as long as the bridegroom is with them?

But the days will come, when the bridegroom shall be taken from them, and then shall they fast.

Then said the Pharisees unto him, why will ye not receive us with our baptism, seeing we keep the whole law?

But Jesus said unto them, Ye keep not the law. If ye had kept the law, ye would have received me, for I am he who gave the law.

I receive not you with your baptism, because it profiteth you nothing.

For when that which is new is come, the old is ready to be put away.

No man putteth a piece of new cloth unto an old garment, for that which is put in to fill it up taketh from the garment, and the rent is made worse.	*For* no man putteth a piece of new cloth *on* an old garment; for that which is put in to fill it up, taketh from the garment, and the rent is made worse. (Emphasis added.)

Not only does this addition in the Joseph Smith Translation provide a marvelous topical transition and establish the social and doctrinal setting for the discussion of new cloth and new bottles (Jesus has rejected the baptism of the Pharisees—compare D&C 22), but it also underscores the fact that those who accept and follow divine direction come to recognize and accept the Divine Director, while those who set the law at naught and seek to become a law unto themselves are condemned by the law and rejected by the Lawgiver.

In the Sermon on the Mount, the Lord instructed the Twelve: "Beholdest thou the scribes, and the Pharisees, and the priests, and the Levites? They teach in their synagogues, but do not observe the law, nor the commandments; and all have gone out of the way, and are under sin. Go thou and say unto them, Why teach ye men the law and the commandments, when ye yourselves are the children of corruption?" (JST, Matt. 7:6-7; compare JST, Matt. 23:21.) In that same sermon, the Joseph Smith Translation uncovers an agnostic or atheistic attitude present among some of the Jews of the first century. The Twelve have voiced a concern about their missionary approach to the leaders of the Jews, anticipating the manner in which they would be spurned and rejected: "Then said his disciples unto him, they will say unto us, We ourselves are righteous, and need not that any man should teach us. *God, we know, heard Moses and some of the prophets; but us he will not hear.*" (JST, Matt. 7:14, emphasis added; compare JST, Luke 16:19-21.) Perhaps more than any other place in the Gospels, this passage demonstrates the static and inert condition of the days of Jesus. It appears that the spirit of true inquiry was all but gone. Absent was the awareness of the need for the spirit of prophecy and revelation.

3. *Jesus Christ as the Fulfillment of Prophecy.* Matthew presents Jesus, appropriately, as the fulfillment of God's promise to Israel. The Gospel of Matthew was written by one intent on building a bridge between the old covenant and the new, or between what we have come to call the two testaments. His was the witness, like Jacob's in the Book of Mormon, that "none of the prophets have written, nor prophesied, save they have spoken concerning this Christ." (Jacob 7:11.)

Jesus spoke clearly and directly to Simon and Andrew at the beginning of his ministry when he called them to their discipleship: "And he said unto them, *I am he of whom it is written by the prophets*; follow me, and I will make you fishers of men." (JST, Matt. 4:18, emphasis added.) At the Sermon on the Mount, the Savior repeatedly called the disciples to a higher righteousness. He who had delivered the law to Moses anciently on a holy mount (3 Ne. 15:5) now spoke again from a mount. "Think not that I am come to destroy the law, or the prophets," he said. "I am not come to destroy, but to fulfil." (Matt. 5:17.) Of this statement Elder Bruce R. McConkie wrote: "Jesus came to restore that gospel fulness which men had enjoyed before the day of Moses, before the time of the lesser order. Obviously he did not come to destroy what he himself had revealed to Moses any more than a college professor destroys arithmetic by revealing the principles of integral calculus to his students. Jesus came to build on the foundation Moses laid."[36] Jesus' repeated declarations of "Ye have heard that it was said by them of old time . . . but I say unto you . . ." (Matt. 5:21, 27, 31, 33, 38, 43) bear fervent testimony of him as the Lord of the law and the one qualified to amend and build upon the principles of the law. The Mediator of a new and everlasting covenant, the Mediator of Life was now on earth; one greater than Moses was in their midst. (See JST, Gal. 3:19-20.)

Perhaps the most important Matthean peculiarity is Matthew's desire to represent Jesus of Nazareth as the literal fulfillment of the law and the prophets, the realization of the hopes and prayers of the faithful for centuries. Matthew utilized what scholars have come to know as a "formula citation" method of tying the life and doings of Jesus Christ with the Old Testament prophecies of the

same. Matthew used this approach as many as fourteen times in his
Gospel, and of these, eight seem to come directly from the prophet
Isaiah. The formula citation method appears to be a Matthean
peculiarity, for although there was a constant reference during the
years of early Christianity to Jesus as the fulfillment of the prophecies, yet the other three Gospel writers do not apply this literary
technique in just the same way Matthew does. John uses nine
formula citations, but on five of those occasions John speaks in
very broad terms concerning the "fulfillment of scripture" rather
than a specific prophet.

Matthew's citations take the familiar form of "Now all this was
done, that it might be fulfilled which was spoken of the Lord by
the prophet, saying . . ." (Matt. 1:22), or "for thus it is written by
the prophet . . ." (Matt. 2:5), or "then was fulfilled that which was
spoken by . . . the prophet" (Matt. 2:17). The following is a list of
the formula citations in Matthew[37]:

Matthew	Citing
1:22-23	Isaiah 7:14
2:5b-6 (cf. JST)	Micah 5:1 and 2 Samuel 5:2
2:15b	Hosea 11:1
2:17-18	Jeremiah 31:15
2:23b	perhaps Isaiah 4:3 and Judges 16:17
3:3	Isaiah 40:3
4:14-16	Isaiah 8:23-9:1
8:17	Isaiah 53:4
12:17-21	Isaiah 42:1-4
13:14-15	Isaiah 6:9-10
13:35	Psalm 78:2 (though Matthew mentions Isaiah)
21:4-5	Isaiah 62:11 and Zechariah 9:9
26:56	a formula (cf. Mark 14:49) without citation
27:9-10	Zechariah 11:12-13 (see also Jeremiah 18:2-3; 32:6-15)

There can be little doubt that Matthew used his citations to
attract the attention of uninterested (and possibly even hostile)
Jews who still awaited a Messiah. Matthew's purpose was to

declare with boldness that the Messiah had come and that they should "believe the gospel, and look not for a Messiah to come who has already come." (D&C 19:27.) At the same time, a major function of the formula citations may have been didactic as well as apologetic. "The formula citations," writes Raymond Brown, "had a didactic purpose, informing the Christian readers and giving support to their faith. Some of the citations are attached to the minutiae of Jesus' career, as if to emphasize that the whole of Jesus' life, down to the least detail, lay within God's foreordained plan."[38]

During the last week of his life, the Lord delivered a scathing denunciation of the pretense and perverted priorities of the Jewish leaders. Matthew 23 is a stinging rebuke of those who should have known and acted better than they did. Note the following statement at the close of that sermon: "Behold, your house is left unto you desolate! For I say unto you, that ye shall not see me henceforth, *and know that I am he of whom it is written by the prophets,* until ye shall say, Blessed is he who cometh in the name of the Lord, *in the clouds of heaven, and all the holy angels with him. Then understood his disciples that he should come again on the earth, after that he was glorified and crowned on the right hand of God.''* (JST, Matt. 23:38-41, emphasis added.)

NOTES

1. *Teachings of the Prophet Joseph Smith,* p. 148; cf. Rom. 10:17.

2. See Bruce R. McConkie, *Docrinal New Testament Commentary*, 3 vols. (Salt Lake City: Bookcraft, 1965-73), 1:55-56.

3. In *The Ante-Nicene Fathers,* 10 vols., ed. Alexander Roberts and James Donaldson (Grand Rapids, Mich.: Eerdmans, 1981), 1:153.

4. *The Mortal Messiah—From Bethlehem to Calvary*, 4 vols. (Salt Lake City: Deseret Book, 1979-81), 1:xv-xvi.

5. Eusebius, *Ecclesiastical History*, 10 vols., trans. C. F. Cruse (Grand Rapids, Mich.: Baker Book House, 1977), 3.24.

6. *Commentary on the Pearl of Great Price* (Salt Lake City: Deseret Book, 1965), pp. 21-22.

7. *Invitation to the New Testament* (New York: Doubleday, 1969), p. 83.

8. W. F. Albright and C. S. Mann, *Matthew*, volume 26 in the Anchor Bible Series (New York: Doubleday, 1971), p. xxii.

9. *Invitation to the New Testament*, p. 81.

10. Irenaus, *Against Heresies*, 3.8, in *Ante-Nicene Fathers*, 1:428.

11. *Teachings*, p. 365.

12. *A New Witness for the Articles of Faith* (Salt Lake City: Deseret Book, 1985), p. 402, emphasis added. Note also the following from President Spencer W. Kimball: "How else do you think Moses, many hundreds of years later, got the information he compiled in the book of Genesis? These records had been kept, and he referred to them and got the history of the world, which wasn't in any library other than that." (*President Kimball Speaks Out* [Salt Lake City: Deseret Book, 1981], pp. 55-56.)

13. See *Teachings,* pp. 119, 160.

14. *Doctrinal New Testament Commentary* 1:65.

15. Ibid., p. 69.

16. See Melvin J. Petersen, "A Study of the Nature and Significance of the Changes in the Revelations as Found in a Comparison of the Book of Commandments and Subsequent Editions of the Doctrine and Covenants," Master's thesis, Brigham Young University, 1955; Robert J. Woodford, "The Historical Development of the Doctrine and Covenants," Ph.D. diss., Brigham Young University, 1974.

17. The definitive work on this subject is Robert J. Matthews, *A Plainer Translation: Joseph Smith's Translation of the Bible—A History and Commentary* (Provo, Utah: Brigham Young University Press, 1975). For a brief treatment of the process of translation, see Robert L. Millet, "Joseph Smith's Translation of the Bible: A Historical Overview," in *The Joseph Smith Translation: The Restoration of Plain and Precious Things,* ed. Monte S. Nyman and Robert L. Millet (Provo, Utah: Religious Studies Center, Brigham Young University, 1985), pp. 23-49.

18. From *The Other Gospels*, ed. Ron Cameron (Philadelphia: Westminster Press, 1982), pp. 69-70, emphasis added. See also Morton Smith, *The Secret Gospel* (New York: Harper & Row, 1973), p. 15.

19. *Teachings*, pp. 9-10.

20. See Charles H. Talbert, *What Is a Gospel? The Genre of the Canonical Gospels* (Philadelphia: Fortress Press, 1977); Philip L. Shuler, *A Genre for the Gospels: The Biographical Character of Matthew* (Philadelphia: Fortress Press, 1982).

21. Merrill C. Tenney, *New Testament Survey* (Grand Rapids, Mich.: Eerdmans, 1961), p. 133.

22. These matters are, in the words of Joseph Smith, those things which constitute the "fundamental principles of our religion." All other things that pertain to our religion, he noted, are only appendages to them. (*Teachings,* p. 121.)

23. "We understand," stated President Brigham Young, "from the writings of one of the Apostles, that if all the sayings and doings of the Savior had been written, the world could not contain them. *I will say that the world could not understand them.* They do not understand what we have on record, nor the character of the Savior, as delineated in the Scriptures; and yet it is one of the simplest things in the world, and the Bible, when it is understood, is one of the simplest books in the world, for, as far as it is translated correctly, it is nothing but truth, and in truth there is no mystery save to the ignorant." (*Journal of Discourses* 14:135-36, emphasis added.)

24. *The Twelve: The Story of Christ's Apostles* (New York: Holt, Rinehart, and Winston, 1957), pp. 27, 42-43. See also Edgar J. Goodspeed, *Matthew: Apostle and Evangelist* (Philadelphia: John C. Winston Company, 1959), pp. 13, 16-17.

25. Some might contend that the written source referred to here would be something from the Old Testament record concerning the birth of Jesus Christ. If such be the case, then the ancient source must certainly be more complete and detailed than anything we now have in the Old Testament. Others may feel that such is a reference to the Gospel of Mark, which most scholars believe to have preceded Matthew. (See S. Kent Brown, "The Testimony of Mark," chapter 4 of this volume.) This seems unlikely, inasmuch as Mark simply omits a discussion of the Annunciation and the Lord's early years.

26. "Fragments of Papias," in *Ante-Nicene Fathers* 1:155.

27. In Eusebius, *Ecclesiastical History* 5.8.

28. Goodspeed, *Matthew: Apostle and Evangelist*, pp. 101, 103. The following statement from Eusebius regarding the spread of the gospel to all parts of the earth is most interesting. Regarding one Pantaenus of Alexandria (ca. A.D. 180), Eusebius has written: "Pantaenus also was one of them and [is] said to have gone to India, where the story [goes] that he found the gospel according to Matthew, [which] had preceded his arrival, among certain people there who had learned of Christ; that Bartholomew, one of the Apostles, had preached to them; and that *he had left the writing of Matthew in Hebrew letters*, which also was preserved to the

time indicated." (*Ecclesiastical History*, V. 10, emphasis added.) For a detailed study of this tradition in Matthew's Gospel, see Matthew Black, *An Aramaic Approach to the Gospels and Acts,* 3rd ed. (London: Oxford University Press, 1967).

29. See F. F. Bruce,*The New Testament Documents: Are They Reliable?* (Grand Rapids, Mich.: Eerdmans, 1974), p. 31.

30. Though it is a common presupposition of some biblical critics to prefer the shortest document as the oldest (thus assuming that the longer ones evidence embellishments and additions), Latter-day Saints should take seriously Nephi's vision of the corruption of the earliest biblical texts (1 Ne. 13). Is it not just as reasonable to suppose that Mark, having before him the longer Matthew or the longer Luke, chose to prepare an abbreviated Gospel, placing less stress upon sermons and parables and more stress upon the movements and actions of our Lord? William R. Farmer has argued for the primacy of Matthew. See his discussion in *Jesus and the Gospel* (Philadelphia: Fortress Press, 1982), pp. 3-7. Further, Albright and Mann feel it is unnecessary to suppose that Matthew and Luke drew upon a single source of sayings: "All that an examination of the 'Q' material in Matthew and Luke seems likely at this stage to produce is evidence that more than one source was employed by all three evangelists." (*Matthew*, p. liii.)

31. "The Doctrinal Restoration," in Nyman and Millet, eds., *The Joseph Smith Translation,* pp. 17-18. See also *Doctrinal New Testament Commentary* 1:69-71.

32. A detailed treatment of the impact of the JST on Matthean themes is Robert L. Millet, "Joseph Smith and the Gospel of Matthew," *Brigham Young University Studies,* vol. 25, no. 1 (Winter 1985), pp. 65-80; see also "The JST and the Synoptic Gospels: Literary Style," in *The Joseph Smith Translation,* pp. 147-61.

33. H. C. Thiessen, *Introduction to the New Testament*, p. 138.

34. See Millet, "Looking Beyond the Mark: Insights from the JST into First-Century Judaism," in *The Joseph Smith Translation,* pp. 201-14.

35. *Teachings*, p. 276.

36. *Doctrinal New Testament Commentary* 1:219-20.

37. Adapted from Raymond E. Brown, *The Birth of the Messiah* (New York: Doubleday, 1977), p. 98. Citations in Mark include 15:28, citing Isa. 53:12. Citations in Luke include 18:31, a formula without any citation; 22:37, citing Isa. 53:12; and 24:44, a formula without citation.

38. *The Birth of the Messiah*, pp. 98-99.

4

THE TESTIMONY OF MARK

S. KENT BROWN

Few any longer doubt the pivotal place of the Gospel of Mark not only in inspiring the coming forth of the other records of Jesus' ministry but also in transmitting the essential message of Jesus' messiahship. Since the rise of the critical study of the Gospels, Mark's work has been singled out most frequently as the one record closest to the ministry of Jesus, both in time and in tone. And when we understand the reasons for this lofty assessment, we also quickly perceive the centrality of Mark for any serious study of the other three records that set out to encapsulate the Savior's earthly work.

Mark in the View of the Earliest Church

Any evaluation of the second Gospel must begin with the earliest assessment of Mark's record, which appeared in a work compiled by the second-century churchman Papias and is now pre-served only in later quotations. The passage appeared in Eusebius's *Ecclesiastical History:*

> This also the elder used to say. Mark, indeed, having been the interpreter of Peter, wrote accurately, howbeit not in order, all that he recalled of what was either said or done by the Lord. For he heard nothing of the Lord, nor was he a follower of his, but, at a later date (as I said) of Peter; who

S. Kent Brown is professor of ancient scripture and director of publications for the Religious Studies Center at Brigham Young University.

61

> used to adapt his instructions to the needs [of the hearers],
> but not with a view to putting together the teachings of the
> Lord in orderly fashion: so that Mark did no wrong in thus
> writing some things as he recalled them. For he kept a single
> aim in view: not to omit anything of what he heard, nor to
> state anything therein falsely. [1]

While the majority of modern commentators discredit the
historical reliability of Papias's notice, the reasons advanced to
disregard it appear seriously flawed upon close inspection. Papias,
writing probably between A.D. 120 and 140, exhibits every evidence of having been a reliable recorder who drew on knowledge
of Mark's activities, which reached back at least two generations
before himself, that is, well into the first century, thus underscoring the tradition's age and reliability.[2] As he wrote it, his
source for evaluating Mark was "the Elder" or "the Presbyter,"
usually thought to be a man named John from Asia Minor.[3] While
Papias does not accept the Elder's story uncritically (since he
makes it clear that he is relying on the Elder's accounting and not
on his own judgment), we do learn how Mark's work was viewed
in early Christian circles.

1. Mark was an interpreter of Peter. This should not surprise
us, since Peter, who was a moving force in the mission to Gentiles
as well as to Jews, would not have spoken Greek with fluency,
coming as he did from the fishing colony along the shores of the
Sea of Galilee. That Mark served as a companion to Peter is also
attested by 1 Peter 5:13.

2. Mark "wrote accurately, although not in order, all that he
recalled" of the Lord's words and deeds. Mark has frequently been
characterized as a writer who imposed his own order on the events
that he narrated.[4] Whatever discrepancies may have existed in the
memories of early Christians regarding the order and completeness
of Mark's account, the order of his narration must have derived
ultimately from Peter, who, in his preaching, "used to adapt his
instructions to the needs" of the moment.

3. Mark himself was not one of Jesus' disciples, an observation
that makes perfect sense because it is certain that he was the John
Mark whose mother's home in Jerusalem served as a meeting place

for early disciples (Acts 12:12-17) and who later accompanied Paul and Barnabas on their missionary journey to Cyprus and Perga in Pamphylia (Acts 12:25-13:13). Thus, Mark grew up in Jerusalem, was doubtless young when Jesus came there before his crucifixion, and was therefore probably not among Jesus' Galilean disciples.

Irenaeus, Bishop of Lyons in the late second century, had this to say about Mark and the other Gospel records: "Matthew composed his Gospel among the Hebrews in their own language, while Peter and Paul proclaimed the Gospel in Rome and founded the community. After their death Mark, the disciple and interpreter of Peter, transmitted his preaching to us in written form. And Luke, who was Paul's follower, set down in a book the gospel which he preached. Then John, the Lord's disciple who had reclined on his breast, himself produced the Gospel when he was staying at Ephesus, in the province of Asia."[5]

Two items become clear immediately. First, Irenaeus was aware of Mark's relationship to Peter, which consisted in Mark's service as an interpreter and his dependence on Peter's preaching for the material in the text of his Gospel. Second, Irenaeus stated that Mark wrote his account after Peter's death, an idea not explicitly found in Papias's fragmentary narration. Since Irenaeus doubtless drew his information from Papias, the former correctly surmised that Mark wrote after Peter's death; otherwise, Irenaeus —and we—would have expected a notation about Peter's approval.[6] As a matter of fact, the internal evidence in the second Gospel points to a date of composition after Peter's death in Rome (about A.D. 64).

Interestingly, evidence suggests that in the early church there was a second tradition concerning the timing of Mark's composition: that he wrote it before the death of Peter, who then had opportunity to read it. In its earliest form, it appeared in book six of the *Hypotyposes* of Clement of Alexandria, who was active at the end of the second century and the beginning of the third. Incidental passages of this work are preserved only in quoted form in later works, and the relevant account is found in Eusebius. Clement of Alexandria wrote: "The Gospel according to Mark came into being in this manner: when Peter had publicly preached the word at Rome, and by the Spirit had proclaimed the Gospel, that those present, who were many, exhorted Mark as one who had followed him for a long time and remembered what he had spoken, to make a record of what was said; and that he did this, and distributed the 'Gospel' among those that asked him. And that when the matter came to Peter's knowledge he neither strongly forbade it nor urged it forward.''[7]

This information agrees with the notices of both Papias and Irenaeus concerning Mark's dependence on Peter's recollections of Jesus. Where it differs, of course, is in its insistence both that Mark wrote before Peter's death and that Peter had opportunity to review the entire work and did not object to its content. A question naturally arises concerning the validity of this tradition. Because it was repeated by Clement at least a century after Papias wrote, it should thus be viewed as secondary.[8] Further, later traditions that locate the origin of Mark's Gospel in Alexandria need not be taken seriously.[9]

Evidence for Dating

While the evidence from early Christian sources points plainly both to Peter as the inspiration behind the second Gospel and to a date for its composition soon after A.D. 64, the likely date of Peter's death, we cannot fix the date more precisely without a careful review of the clues that lie within the Gospel itself, whereby, incidentally, we can buttress the case for rich ties to Peter.

Since it is extremely rare that a document written either in antiquity or in modern times does not leave any clues concerning the historical context in which it was composed or compiled, we are therefore justified in looking carefully at a text such as Mark's for indications that will tell us something of its date of composition.[10]

In his extremely important work on Mark's Gospel, Martin Hengel has argued persuasively for a date of A.D. 69.[11] The linchpin of his view consists of chapter 13 of Mark. But before examining this segment, let us review other features to which Hengel points in his study.

Relation to Matthew and Luke: Most students of the New Testament are aware of the so-called "Synoptic Problem," which concerns the chronological and literary relationships between the first three Gospels. Because Irenaeus supposed that Matthew's Gospel had appeared before the others, the view generally held since antiquity saw Mark as the abridger of Matthew's longer work. But the nineteenth century saw the rise of a type of detailed investigation whose results called into question the chronological priority of the first Gospel. While the primacy of Matthew's work has continued to find modern proponents,[12] it has become increasingly plain to many scholars that the least complex and most convincing solution to the Synoptic Problem holds that Mark was not only the earliest Gospel written but also served as one of the sources for both Matthew and Luke.[13] In this light, we would have to conclude that Mark was written before the Gospels of Matthew and Luke, that is, long before the end of the first century.

Mark 9:1: Jesus is quoted as saying, "Truly, I say to you, there are some standing here who will not taste death before they see that the Kingdom of God has come with power." (RSV.) It is not without basis to urge that Mark was writing in a day when some—that is, some of Jesus' original followers—were still alive. Mark must have known such persons; otherwise, the words of Jesus quoted here would make little sense either for himself or for his first readers. In this connection, we are justified in looking at Paul's statement made in A.D. 53 or 54 in which he affirmed that of the more than five hundred men who had seen the risen Jesus on one occasion, most were "still alive, though some have fallen asleep." (RSV, 1 Cor. 15:6.) In the middle 50s, then, the majority of the first generation of disciples remained alive, but by Mark's day, only some remained, pointing out that Mark wrote his Gospel well after Paul penned his first letter to the Corinthians but certainly within the lifetime of some first-generation Christians.[14]

Mark 15:21: It is important to notice that Simon of Cyrene is identified by the names of his sons, not by his father as is customary. Why? One probable answer is that Simon's sons, Alexander and Rufus, were still known to Mark's readers. In this connection, Mark identified other prominent persons who interacted with

Jesus in such a way that one must suppose Mark's audience was well acquainted with them and their roles. For instance, Mark calls Pilate simply by his name (15:1), without any note that his full name was Pontius Pilate or that he was the governor, appellations that Matthew and Luke apparently felt the need to add when introducing him to their readers. (Compare Luke 3:1; Matt. 27:2.) In a similar vein, Mark spoke simply of the high priest or chief priests without identifying anyone by name, a further indication that Mark's readers knew who they were.[15]

Portrait of Judaism: "No New Testament author portrays the different groups in Jewish Palestine at the time of Jesus as accurately and as true to their time as Mark." So wrote Martin Hengel. I would have to agree. His portrayals of the scribes as a distinctive group, the scribes of the Pharisees as the leading intellectuals of the Pharisaic party, the Pharisees as a unit, the Sadducees who were absent from Galilee, the Herodians in the territory of Antipas, and the disciples of John the Baptist all reflect accurately the religious and political situation in Palestine before the Jewish War (A.D. 66-70). In a sketch of Jesus' ministry in Jerusalem, Mark identified the real opponents of the Savior as the chief priests, the elders, and the scribes, all prominent members of the Sanhedrin.[16] When we combine this observation with that of Mark's carefully consistent and detailed portrait of Jesus' disciples, we can only conclude that Mark wrote both before the drastic changes effected in Palestinian Judaism with the fall of the Jerusalem Temple in August A.D. 70 and in a manner that points to the early, solid character of his account.[17]

Latinisms: While this issue is related to larger linguistic questions,[18] this unusual feature of Mark's record points to a place of origin in the western Roman Empire, doubtless at Rome, the location uniformly attested by the earliest accounts. Mark shows a penchant for employing not Greek, but Latin terms that were at home in Roman military, legal, and commercial enterprises.[19] What is more, Mark explained common Greek expressions twice by Latin terms: "two copper coins [*lepta*], which make a penny [*quadrans*]" (RSV 12:42), and "the hall, called Praetorium" (15:16). Related to this phenomenon is Mark's use of the Roman method of measuring time. For instance, he records four watches of the night and not the three that were customary among Jews (6:48; compare 13:35).

Mark, Chapter 13

Thus far, we have seen that both early Christian tradition and internal features of Mark's record point to an origin of his Gospel in Rome after Peter's death (A.D. 64) and before the final fall of the Jerusalem Temple (A.D. 70). Can the date of composition be delimited more precisely, and can the apparent place of composition (Rome) be buttressed more strongly? Hengel believes that a careful examination of chapter 13 will allow this. His observations are so compelling that a brief review is called for.

For most commentators, the events foretold in Mark 13:2-37 are to be understood not as prophesied occurrences but as events mentioned in retrospect. But Hengel speaks strongly against this common view. For him, the words "attributed" to Jesus must authentically go back to Jesus. For instance, Jesus' command to flee Judea when the "abomination of desolation" is seen (vv. 14-19) cannot have been invented by Mark or someone else after the destruction of Jerusalem, because it does not reflect the kind of detail expected when one looks back on that event. In the case of the siege of Jerusalem by the Romans, the land had been subdued by Titus's legions for miles around the city during the months before the first wall was breached and the assault on the temple courtyard was begun. By that point, there was no longer reason to flee. Thus, Jesus' warning here does not reflect in detail the situation in and around Jerusalem during the long, horrible months before the Roman army seized the temple and its grounds. Consequently, we can be assured that these words go back to Jesus and that Mark was unacquainted with the precise nature and order of events just before the city's fall and was thus writing both before the completion of the siege as well as at a distance from the scene. In a related vein, as soon as the Romans began to press toward Jerusalem from their long but victorious struggle in the Galilee area, the Christians living in and near Jerusalem fled to Pella, located across the Jordan and north of the city.[20] Why did Christians flee at the approach of the Romans? Why did they not flee into Jerusalem as others did? The most probable answer is that they had been warned to flee, and that warning went back to Jesus on the occasion described in Mark 13.

These observations lead necessarily to others. For Hengel, verse 14 is crucial to understand the meaning of chapter 13. First, the "abomination of desolation" is to be understood as coming *suddenly* to Jerusalem, a feature to which Jesus' warnings in the following verses point. In contrast, the three Roman legions first carefully constructed a circling wall around the city and then subdued the territory for miles around in order to rid the area of irregulars who might be tempted to launch occasional attacks at the Romans' backs. Following these actions, only then—and with difficulty—did Titus's armies fight their way into the city, through its several defenses, and finally to the temple's sanctuary after capturing its courtyard, a process of many months. There was nothing swift or sudden in the Roman action against Jerusalem. Second, the Greek participle that is translated by the English word *standing* in verse 14 is masculine in gender and also gives the clear sense of something or someone established permanently. By Mark's recounting, therefore, Jesus had prophesied that a *person* was to establish himself more or less permanently in the city. Of the possibilities, the most natural referent is the antichrist. One quickly thinks of Paul's words in 2 Thessalonians 2:1-4, written about A.D. 50, in which he maintained that the "man of sin . . . the son of perdition" was to appear "in the temple of god," that is, in Jerusalem,[21] before the Second Coming of Jesus occurred. Significantly, this theme of Jesus' delay is also present in Mark 13. For even after hearing of "wars and rumours of wars" and of serious natural disasters, Jesus' disciples were to know that the end was "not yet" (v. 7): "these are [only] the beginnings of sorrows" (v. 8). Much remained to happen.[22]

It seems significant that Jesus is quoted three times within the first half of chapter 13 as giving the warning "Take heed" (vv. 5, 9, 23). The first instance is followed initially by a warning against false Christs who were to come to deceive (v. 6) and then by a notation of a dramatic intensifying of human and natural disasters.

The second occurrence is followed by the prophecy that Christians were to be persecuted officially by both pagans and Jews (v. 9), to be betrayed by those closest to them (v. 12), and to be hated merely because they were his followers (v. 13). Jesus' last admonition was preceded by a second warning against false Christs, this time in company with false prophets (vv. 21-22). Significantly, in the middle of this section (vv. 5-23) stands Jesus' promise that "he that shall endure unto the end, the same shall be saved" (v. 13). The question arises whether we should make anything of this. In my view, the answer is yes. Hengel persuasively argues that Mark wrote his Gospel in part to try to address a distressing situation among his fellow Christians. Other commentators have regularly noted the very high profile that Mark has granted to the theme of persecution and enduring it.[23] But if Hengel is right, the elements of this motif in Mark 13 may allow us to determine rather accurately when and where he wrote his Gospel.

The Emperor Nero committed suicide on June 9, A.D. 68. Until shortly before that moment, events had remained rather calm in the empire for several decades[24] except for three disruptions that affected either Nero or Christians or both: (1) The first systematic persecution broke out in A.D. 64 when Nero pointed an accusing finger at Christians for starting the fire that had burned for weeks in Rome, the result of which was to bring a storm of almost universal hatred against Christians[25] who stood largely leaderless after the loss of the Lord's brother James and of Paul in A.D. 62 and Peter in 64. (2) In the autumn of A.D. 66, the Jewish revolt began in Judea, with the surprising defeat of the sixth legion under Cestius Gallus by Jewish insurrectionists. (3) In March A.D. 68, Julius Vindex rose against Nero; this uprising was soon followed by Galba's revolt in Spain and Clodius's rebellion in Africa, which cut the supply of grain to Rome. While events brewing in and near Judea may not have sent serious ripples throughout the empire, certainly Christians, including Mark, hearing reports from the east, must have sensed a drama slowly enclosing Jerusalem that would fulfill Jesus' prophetic words. For the rest, Nero's death set off a civil war that cost the lives of three emperors in A.D. 69, Galba, Otho, and Vitellius. In addition, a serious famine in Italy was one of the first consequences of the civil war. If we add to that the three recorded earthquakes in Italy during A.D. 68,[26] we sense the almost final force in Mark 13:8: "For nation shall rise against nation, and kingdom against kingdom: and there shall be earthquakes in diverse places, and there shall be famines and troubles." Yet, we are reminded, "these are [only] the beginnings of sorrows."

What are we to make of these events, compacted within a period of less than five years, that correspond so strikingly to Jesus' warnings? Most students would have us believe that Mark either reshaped the tradition that came to him in order to fit it to the events of the age or that he simply invented the whole in order to reinforce among Christians the impression of Jesus' prophetic insight. But because it can be shown that Mark was remarkably faithful in recording what came to him from Peter,[27] and because Mark must have completed his work before the fall of Jerusalem in August of A.D. 70, as we have already seen, no impelling reason exists to see this chapter as anything other than a faithful recording of the words that go back to Jesus himself through Peter. In fact, it was because of the serious consequences of events that swept through Italy and Rome, and therefore affected Christians who lived there, that Mark took pen in hand to record the words and deeds of Jesus that would illustrate to beleaguered Christians that (1) Jesus knew beforehand what was to transpire ("behold, I have foretold you all things" [13:23]), and (2) they must be willing to suffer consequences—as Jesus had—made inevitable by spiteful, hateful fellowmen ("he that shall endure unto the end, the same shall be saved" [13:13]). In one sense, then, Mark's work can be characterized as an effort to comfort Christians, who were victims of events more powerful than themselves but not more powerful than their Lord and Savior, who had fed five thousand and four thousand people on separate occasions and had also stilled the raging storm on the Sea of Galilee.[28]

In summary, therefore, both tradition and the internal evidence of the second Gospel demonstrate that: (1) It was in Rome that Mark wrote his Gospel. (2) The Gospel depended heavily on the preaching of the recently departed Peter, certainly for its content if not for its form[29] and order. (3) The Gospel was written either shortly after or during the last stages of the civil turmoil that gripped the empire in A.D. 68-69 and before the fall of the temple in Jerusalem in August 70. (4) Mark's work, viewed from one angle, was designed to comfort fellow Christians—especially in Italy—who had suffered both a major loss of leadership and repeated blows of official and unofficial persecution.

Modern Study of Mark

As noted above, it was the rise of the critical study of the Gospels that has led to the general view of the chronological and literary priority of Mark among the Synoptics. The history of this process has been rehearsed often. I simply want to focus on two of its phases, form criticism and redaction criticism.

Just before World War II, three scholars, Karl Ludwig Schmidt, Martin Dibelius, and Rudolph Bultmann, published works in German that formed the foundation for the form-critical approach to the study of the Gospels. The avowed purpose of this avenue was to discover "what the original units of the Synoptics were, both sayings and stories, [and] to try to establish what the historical setting was."[30] Bultmann's study became the most influential of the three, even though they all reached similar results whose effect was to leave the Gospels in small pieces, being viewed as a series of separate incidents without proper order except for the literary glue with which Mark originally stuck the individual stories or *pericopae* together. In this view, Mark has been portrayed simply as a collector of the individual units of tradition that had been augmented and embellished while the stories were being handed on orally within the early church. The form critics sought to understand the two levels of the tradition as they saw it: first to learn what the situation in life (*Sitz im Leben*)—that is, the use to which the piece had been put in the Church's preaching—was before it was taken into the Gospels in written form, and then to determine, when possible, what the original sociological and religious setting had been for the incident during Jesus' earthly ministry. The Prophet Joseph Smith seemed to have been pursuing a similar goal when, in the Gospels of the Joseph Smith Translation, he added notations that served to clarify the occasions on which Jesus delivered a certain sermon, responded to a particular situation, or acted in a particular way. In light of this, I have found no personal objection to the aims of this enterprise, that is, to identify the original words and deeds of Jesus as they in fact occurred. However, we must appreciate the difference between the prophetic, revelatory approach taken by the Prophet and an attempt to determine the "sociological setting" of Jesus' sayings and actions by starting with the texts themselves and proceeding by comparing the Synoptics to each other.

A particular problem with the form-critical approach derives from the set of assumptions from which it starts. They are at once theological—based upon early twentieth-century Protestantism—and literary, presuming that a literature always comes together in the same way, especially the kind of literature represented in the Gospels. I should note here that Bultmann was deeply influenced by an essay written by Axel Olrik in 1909.[31] Olrik argued that folk stories or oral materials always developed in a certain way. Bultmann accepted the entire argument of this rather obscure essay, applied it unrelentingly to the Gospel materials, and, in my view, simply left the Synoptic Gospels in tatters. For me, it is important to ask: Can it all have arisen from such a mound of bits and fragments?

To my mind, the related question of oral traditions lying behind the Gospel accounts must remain an open issue. The existence of *agrapha*, sayings of Jesus that do not appear in the Gospels but are quoted in later Christian sources, points to a rather rich, ongoing oral recitation of the words and deeds of Jesus. And this should not surprise us, since we are informed by John that he was forced to select among those that he knew when he drew up his own narrative. (John 21:25.) But modern students must surely question the assumption that any accounts from oral sources must be viewed as both late and unreliable because of the certain presence of embellishments added during transmission. As we have seen, the evidence clearly points to a long and deep association between Mark and Peter. One of the consequences for this observation is that any oral tradition embedded within Mark's narrative comes largely from Peter's recollections, a source as reliable as we could hope to find.[32]

Following the Second World War, a different approach to the Synoptic Gospels was advocated, also by European scholars.[33] Termed "redaction criticism" and built upon the form-critical results that seemed firm, this avenue looked at each of the Gospels as a whole and tried to understand them not as bits and pieces of tradition but as texts with their own integrity, an important recognition. In the view of redaction critics, the Gospel writers wrote for particular audiences who found themselves in particular circumstances. This led to choices on the part of the authors concerning the materials to be included and the emphases to be made in the story of the Savior. Because these choices were made largely for theological reasons, the Gospel writers were conceived to be theologians and therefore shapers of the accounts about Jesus rather than collectors who more or less stitched the individual stories together somewhat randomly, as the form critics had concluded. As a result, Mark and the other writers were understood to be composers or authors instead of mere collectors.

Thus far, this view possesses merit, for it is hard to deny that an author brings a point of view to the production of a literary work.[34] However, the radical view that Mark, having been the first to write, invented the literary form of his Gospel—often called a passion narrative with a biographical introduction—and that he was responsible for its order of events, its theological and ecclesiastical concerns, and its specific portrayal of Jesus places too much on his shoulders. It has recently been convincingly argued that Mark was repeating the story of Jesus just as it had been told from the earliest days following the Savior's death, certainly by Peter if not by others of the original disciples. Moreover, even though we might argue convincingly that Mark, as well as the other two synoptists, brought a point of view to his task, such an observation takes nothing away from the fidelity of the story repeated in the second Gospel. On the contrary, Mark is to be understood as a faithful recorder.[35]

Geography in Mark's Gospel

One important question to settle is that of Mark's knowledge of the contemporary Holy Land, since this issue has precipitated wide debate with ramifications for both the identity and competence of the Gospel writer. The observations of critics have run as follows: (1) The geography of events narrated in and around Jerusalem is consistent with what is known about first-century Judea, a fact that must be attributed not to Mark but to the earlier tradition of Jesus' passion, doubtless the first segment of the story of his ministry to coalesce, since it formed its most important part. (2) In Mark, the geography of Jesus' Galilean ministry betrays the hand of one who does not know the regions of Palestine outside of Judea. Interestingly, the coupling of these two observations has led some students to suggest that the author of the second Gospel had never even visited ancient Palestine and, therefore, could not have been the John Mark mentioned in Acts 12:12 – 13:13 and known to have grown up in Jerusalem. The further implication is that the geographical notes supplied by the Gospel writer, excluding those that were already part of the stories that came into his possession, whether oral or written, show him to have invented the geography of Jesus' Galilean activities, apparently relying on a vague set of ideas about Palestine and its environs. He therefore could not have been a Palestinian Jew.[36]

But having already affirmed the identity of the author to be John Mark, and having already seen that the Gospel was most probably authored in Rome, how shall we reply to these points? Do these geographical issues undercut seriously what we have so far concluded about Mark and his work? In my view, not at all. For one thing, the fact that the geography of Judea and Jerusalem, with one exception,[37] is faithfully represented by Mark fits with what we have concluded thus far. Whether the geographical elements were already embedded in the passion story before Mark wrote it down is quite beside the issue. It is just as plausible to argue that Mark, having lived in Jerusalem, would naturally have been able to write of such details with a confidence arising from first-hand knowledge and would have also been in a position to tidy up any inaccuracies in the information that came to him. In addition, when we consider that a typical person of antiquity, who was not able to travel much[38] and had no map, would probably have known almost nothing of areas more than fifty or so miles away, it is rather plain that Mark could write knowingly about Jerusalem but without much knowledge concerning Galilee, Samaria, and the Decapolis. As a matter of fact, the one road that Mark certainly traveled outside of Jerusalem in Palestine did not go north to Galilee but west to the Mediterranean Sea.[39] Thus, there exists no impelling evidence that Mark did not come from Jerusalem even though he apparently knew little of Galilee.[40]

The Character of the Second Gospel

We should observe that Joseph Smith knew the Gospels as "testimonies." In their titles in the JST, all four are entitled "testimonies," clearly implying that such records constituted rather personal views of Jesus, just as our own testimonies are personal. Such an observation explains in part the differences in tone and detail that we see among the Synoptic Gospels. (See D&C 88:141.) But much more can be said, particularly concerning Mark's work, which has been called by others a "witness document," whose purpose is to bear witness of Jesus' divinity and atonement, much in the spirit of John 20:31: "These are written, that ye might believe that Jesus is the Christ, the Son of God: and that believing ye might have life through his name." Following are some significant points.

Mark 1:1, the opening: The tone for the entire text is set by its first line: "The beginning of the gospel of Jesus Christ, the Son of God." Mark comes directly to the point and, by doing so, brings his readers immediately to the dramatic thrust of his work: The gospel or good news has its origin with Jesus, the anointed Son of God. In what follows, the reader will be introduced to that significant moment when Jesus appeared unexpectedly, and thus almost mysteriously, in fulfillment of prophecy.

The major question concerning this passage has focused on the authenticity of the phrase "the Son of God," since some early manuscripts of the New Testament omit it. But the apparent difficulty can be handled directly. While the solution to this problem is of small consequence because it is apparent throughout Mark's work that he was demonstrating his conviction that Jesus is indeed the Son of God,[41] the issue retains its importance simply because of the forceful character of the Gospel's initial line, its *incipit* title, as it were.

In terms of evidence from manuscripts and early quotations of this passage, the vast majority of texts and citations include the disputed phrase, with two important exceptions, Codex Sinaiticus (fourth century) and the church father Origen (about 185-254). But these notable omissions should be seen as unintentional. This title appears six other times in the second Gospel, including at obviously key points in the text, namely in Peter's confession of Jesus' messiahship (8:29) and, complementing this, in the Gentile centurion's acknowledgment of Jesus' sonship (15:39). Consequently, "Son of God," as a title that points forward from the opening of the text to the recorded events of the Savior's ministry through which this central testimony is revealed, must be considered an integral part of the text of Mark 1:1. From the side of the early witnesses to the reading of this text, in the two principle sources for omitting the phrase, Origen and Codex Sinaiticus, we are probably dealing with one rather than two omissions, since the text of Codex Sinaiticus was probably based upon papyri that Origen took with him from Egypt to Palestine. Thus the case for an unintentional omission is strengthened when we reduce to a common source the two most important witnesses for that omission. For the rest, the texts are late or derivative.[42]

Mark 1:1-13, the prologue: If the opening line has set the general tone for the story, the next twelve verses carry it through by introducing matters that further delineate what Jesus is and what stamp his ministry will bear.[43] First, verse 2 ties Jesus' actions directly to prophecy: "As it is written in the prophets . . ." For Mark and for Christians in general, Jesus' life had been lived in conformity to the voice of prophecy, be it written or be it currently alive, as in John's prediction about the one who was to come baptizing with the Holy Ghost (vv. 7-8). Further, the prophetic quotation called for events surrounding the Messiah to be played out in the wilderness. Interestingly, in the first few verses Mark employed the word *wilderness* three times, in quoting from Isaiah 40:3, in locating John the Baptist's ministry (v. 4), and in noting the place of Jesus' severe trial with Satan (v. 12). Thus, the first public acts of Jesus, the unveiling of the Messiah, so to speak, occurred in the desert. As a result, the symbolism of the Exodus is not to be missed in these events, especially because the passage quoted from Isaiah 40:3 was understood as the prophecy of the new Exodus. It was thus by the rich application of this single term, *wilderness*, that Mark established the initial revelation of Jesus as the Son of God to have occurred in the desert, much like Moses' call.[44] And as Moses emerged from the wilderness on the Lord's errand, so Jesus came out thence into Galilee bearing the divine mantle (v. 14).

The imagery of the Exodus is also present in the second unifying term, the Spirit, a word that occurs three times in the opening thirteen verses. First, John mentioned the one coming who was to be baptized with the Holy Ghost or Holy Spirit (v. 8). Next we read of the Spirit's descent upon Jesus after his baptism (v. 10). Finally, Jesus was led by the Spirit into the wilderness, there to suffer temptations for forty days, this last a numerical recollection of Israel's forty years in the desert. Consequently, Mark made it clear that the unveiling and first messianic actions of the Son of God were directed by the Spirit of God, the only proper beginning to the work of the "beloved Son" (v. 11).

Underscored in this initial section, of course, is the notion of Jesus' divine sonship. Both Mark (v. 1) and the divine voice from heaven (v. 11) solemnly affirmed this important fact. What is more, John's reference to the "one mightier" than himself fits intrinsically with this theme. It was that special quality of Jesus that brought him into direct conflict with the unseen world of Satan (v. 13), initiating a combat that would continue throughout the Savior's earthly mission. Naturally, this initial set of conflicts experienced by Jesus would eventually harden into systematic persecutions that would hound first him and then his followers (13:9-12).

The messianic secret: In 1901, Wilhelm Wrede published his influential study, which highlighted the aspect of secrecy in Jesus' messiahship as related in the second Gospel. Since that time, students of the New Testament have consistently followed Wrede's insight, even when critical of certain of its points, and have usually urged that this feature was largely due to Mark's personal view of Jesus. According to this outlook, Mark has imparted to his work a fundamental unity by employing the literary technique of carefully affirming that during Jesus' ministry, the essence of his messianic authority and mission remained hidden from the disciples, and this by Jesus' conscious actions. The foundation of Wrede's views rested upon his observation that the Savior consistently sought to hide his messiahship from others. This was accomplished in various ways: (1) he silenced demons who knew who he was, not allowing them to reveal his divine identity (1:25, 34; 3:12); (2) he charged benefactors of his healing powers not to speak of what he had done (1:44; 5:43; 7:36; 8:26); (3) even the disciples remained afraid to ask him about his marvelous and mysterious teachings and deeds (4:41; 9:32; 10:33; compare 6:51); (4) he frequently allowed the disciples to remain without enlightenment (8:17-21; 9:32); (5) he even scolded the disciples for their lack of understanding, rather than revealing the source and nature of his marvelous powers (8:17-21); and (6) after the disciples finally comprehended who he was, to a degree, he did not allow them to discuss this insight with others outside their number (8:30). To be sure, because of his miracles, notice of Jesus' remarkable powers spread far and wide, even though he sought to hide such (1:28, 45; 7:36).

This portrayal of Jesus, however, is not as one-sided as Wrede and others would have us believe. For instance, Jesus took occasion to enlighten his disciples by conscientiously teaching them (4:10-20, 34). Moreover, when he healed the man possessed of the demonic legion, he did not silence the demons (5:7-10). Furthermore, Jesus performed many miracles in public, some of which Mark described in detail, in which he did not charge the benefactor or the crowd to remain quiet about the matter (see 2:11-12; 3:1-5; 5:19).

Such complications have led recent researchers to raise questions concerning the unity, extent, and significance of the so-called messianic secret. As a matter of fact, according to Hengel, this feature applies strictly to only two passages, the first consisting of Jesus' charge to his disciples after Peter's confession (8:30) and the second being his instruction to the three disciples after the Transfiguration (9:9). In these two instances, Jesus' charges clearly grew out of the concern to keep his divine mission hidden until after his death and resurrection. But his motives in all other cases were based on different considerations, whether to slow the growing popular fervor over his miraculous powers or to teach the disciples in stages by employing a technique of obliging them to figure out some things for themselves. And in the cases in which Jesus obliged his followers to keep quiet about what they knew (8:30; 9:9), his concern arose from "the tremendous fact that the Messiah and Son of God" was not to "reveal himself immediately in 'the glory of his Father with the Holy angels' (8:38)," but was to walk obediently along the path toward the cross and toward his redeeming death and resurrection. Moreover, if we agree with Wrede that Mark intended to portray the messianic secret with consistency, we would be hard pressed to explain why this motif disappears after the Transfiguration (9:2-13). In fact, it was the disciples who tried to silence the blind Bartimaeus during Jesus' trip through Jericho, whereas Jesus accepted the appellation "Son of David" as a true title of honor (10:46-52). And precisely because of these ambiguities in the text, we can only conclude that Mark was not trying to portray Jesus in a consistent, unifyingly literary way. Rather, the portrait must go back to Jesus' actions and words, which arose from different motives dictated by the varying circumstances of his ministry.[45]

Theology versus biography: In recent decades, it has become fashionable to deny that any of the Gospel writers had any real interest in writing a biographical account of Jesus' life. In such a view, the main interests of the Gospel writers were theological, that is, they were centered on portraying Jesus in a particular manner that also conveyed certain messages about him to their readers. It was not history that Mark and the others sought to write, but theology. To a point, one must agree that the Gospel writers structured their accounts to bring about certain effects. We have already seen, for example, that Mark highlighted certain themes at his story's beginning in order to focus readers' attention on important elements in the message of his writing. But such a concept does not imply that his picture of Jesus was distorted so that it became nonbiographical, unhistorical. On the contrary, when we observe a life such as Jesus'—full of dramatic healings, conflicts with a growing number of opponents, and teaching that deeply impressed those who heard—we must admit that the course of his experiences lent itself to dramatic representation. As Martin Hengel has written: "One may say that Mark constructed his work as a dramatic narrative in several 'acts,' which might almost be said to correspond to the laws of ancient tragedy as worked out by Aristotle in his *poetics.*"[46] This lofty evaluation is a far cry from Bultmann's view that the Gospel materials grew out of simple folk stories. Nevertheless, Hengel goes on, "the fatal error in the interpretation of the gospels in general and of Mark in particular has been that scholars have thought that they had to decide between preaching and historical narration, that here there could only be an either-or. In reality, the 'theological' contribution of the evangelist lies in the fact that he combines both these things inseparably: he preaches by narrating; he writes history and in so doing proclaims."[47] Such was Mark's achievement: while bearing witness to Jesus as Messiah and Son of God, he wrote an account faithful to the events and course of Jesus' earthly ministry. Strengthening this view is the observation made earlier that Mark's Gospel was closely tied to the recollections of Peter.

The Purpose of Mark

Much has already been said about the purpose of Mark in writing his Gospel. In summary, his purpose was to strengthen faith in Jesus as the Son of God, particularly in light of the persecution and attendant difficulties that had come upon Christians in and near Rome. And, as I have argued elsewhere, the second Gospel, as well as the others, is a "brink document" written both on the eve of the expected apostasy and in an effort to set the record straight before the falling away predicted by Paul and others.[48] Even so, Mark's primary intent was to portray Jesus as the Son of

God. For him, like anyone else, the concern was how to succeed in sketching this portrait. In this connection, let us look at a few features of Mark's picture of Jesus that aided his purpose.

Abruptness of Mark's opening: Unlike the other three Gospels, which employ a good deal of introductory material before narrating Jesus' ministry, Mark comes directly to this later stage of the Savior's life. For him, it must have been central to focus attention on this period of time. The effect of this sudden, almost breathtaking introduction is to create a sense of awe, since the person introduced here is no less than the Son of God. Without explaining why John the Baptist was in the wilderness or why Jesus came to him, Mark let the two prophecies—the one an amalgam of Malachi 3:1 and Isaiah 40:3 (vv. 2-3) and the other from John himself (vv. 7-8)—set the stage for the activities of these two persons, whose contact at the Jordan River initiated the mission of God's Son.[49]

Jesus as a person of dynamic action: Mark employed the Greek term for "immediately" forty times.[50] By comparison, Matthew used it in fifteen passages and Luke in eight. The impact was to portray Jesus as a person of strong action, always exhibiting a remarkable power that moved persons or events. For Mark, there was never any indecision on Jesus' part. This is not to say, however, that Mark glossed over events in an unnatural way, making the occurrences of Jesus' life subservient to a personal impression or conception. On the contrary, Mark was faithful to what he had learned. For example, he related the healing of a blind man in Bethsaida (8:22-26), according to whose account Jesus was required to bless the man twice before he regained his full sight, a feature Mark would hardly have preserved if he were streamlining this story to fit his own preconceptions.

Sense of wonder among Jesus' followers: In discussing the so-called messianic secret earlier, I made the point that Wrede and his followers have put their fingers on an important concept, although it does not work out as neatly as they have maintained. Their insight is that in Mark's Gospel, Jesus was regarded with wonder and awe, even mystery, by his closest associates. The confessions of the demons heightened this sense of unseen glory and splendor, characteristics made visible in Jesus' words and deeds but only occasionally explained by him.[51] The point is that we readers are brought to observe very clearly throughout the pages of Mark's Gospel the majesty of the One who moved, taught, healed, had compassion.[52]

Suffering Son of Man: It becomes obvious early in Mark's text that Jesus is to be understood as the Son of Man of Jewish apocalyptic expectation who was to come on the clouds of heaven in order to deliver his people from their enemies and to usher in a reign of peace. But there was to be a twist. Instead of coming as the triumphal Son of Man, Jesus was to come as the suffering servant in fulfillment of Isaiah's prophecy (52:13 – 53:12). It was this concept that offended the disciples when he first expressed it on the way to Caesarea Philippi (8:31-33). And this idea of the suffering Son of Man must go back to Jesus himself, since the concept is so deeply embedded in the fabric of the early tradition, appearing as it does three times on occasions when Jesus taught his disciples concerning discipleship.[53]

Conclusions

Although our review has been brief, I am satisfied that we have established several characteristics concerning Mark's narrative. First, the book of Mark was probably the first Gospel written and was employed as a source by Matthew and Luke, undoubtedly because of its known association with Peter's teachings. Second, Mark served as Peter's interpreter, and, after Peter died, he set down an accurate record of what he had learned from the senior apostle. Third, Mark wrote his account in about A.D. 69, at the end of the furious persecution of Christians in Italy and Rome and before the fall of Jerusalem and its temple. Fourth, Mark is the John Mark of Acts 12:12 – 13:13 who grew up in Jerusalem but had little personal knowledge of Galilee, where the first part of Jesus' ministry was located. Fifth, Mark's major goal was to picture Jesus as the expected Messiah, the Son of God, who atoned for the sins of us all.[54]

NOTES

1. Eusebius, *Ecclesiastical History* 3.39.15. The translation of this passage appears in Martin Hengel, *Studies in the Gospel of Mark* (Philadelphia: Fortress Press, 1985), p. 47.

2. Hengel, pp. 47-50, and William L. Lane, *The Gospel According to Mark* (Grand Rapids, Mich.: Eerdmans, 1974), pp. 7-9, both accept the authenticity of Papias's notice. For an opposite view, see Dennis E. Nineham, *The Gospel of St. Mark* (Baltimore: Pelican Books, 1963), pp. 26-27, and Werner Georg Kümmel, *Introduction to the New Testament* (Nashville: Abingdon, 1966), pp. 43-44. These authors both find reason to mistrust Papias, but Hengel advances the more compelling arguments.

3. Hengel, p. 150, note 55. See also Hugh J. Lawlor and John E. L. Oulton, trans., *Eusebius, Bishop of Caesarea: The Ecclesiastical History and the Martyrs of Palestine* (London: SPCK, 1954), 2:114-15.

4. Nineham, pp. 36-38; Kummel, pp. 63-64.

5. *Against Heresies* 3.1.1. Translation is that of Hengel, p. 2.

6. A point made by Hengel, p. 2; also p. 119, note 14.

7. *Ecclesiastical History* 6.14.6-7. Translation is that of Lawlor and Oulton, vol. 1, p. 189.

8. As Hengel has noted (p. 4), Clement's view buttressed his own high opinion of John's Gospel as compared to that of Mark.

9. See Hengel, pp. 120-21, notes 24 and 27; p. 137, note 160.

10. One must realize that a work is not written in a vacuum. It is a fact that even forgeries betray the circumstances under which they were created.

11. Hengel, pp. 7-28.

12. The latest and most serious was that of William R. Farmer, *The Synoptic Problem* (New York: Mercer University Press, 1964). See also *Jesus and the Gospel* (Philadelphia: Fortress Press, 1982).

13. See the summary of the evidence in Kümmel, pp. 35-60. To say that Luke and Matthew employed the Gospel of Mark as a source for their own works should not disturb us. If it was Peter's recollections that stand at the foundation of Mark's work, as I have already tried to show, this fact would have been known to Mark's readers. Such would have been reason enough to recommend Mark's Gospel to Matthew and Luke.

14. Hengel, p. 8.

15. Hengel, pp. 9 and 123, note 53.

16. Hengel, pp. 9-10.

17. This has been noted by many; see Hengel's summary, pp. 10-11.

18. Such would include the question of an Aramaic source behind Mark's account as well as possible borrowings from collections of Jesus' sayings, as, say, those in the Gospel of Thomas and in the hypothetical "Q" source believed to have been used by Matthew and Luke.

19. Lane, pp. 24-25; Hengel, p. 29; Kümmel, p. 70.

20. Eusebius, *Ecclesiastical History* 3.5.3. Against those who discount the authenticity of this information, see the arguments of Hengel, pp. 130-31, note 111.

21. An expectation grew up that Nero would appear alive again, coming from the East: "Nero redivivus," see Hengel, pp. 25-28. Lane takes a completely different tack, avoiding the difficulty posed by the masculine participle (pp. 465-69).

22. Hengel, pp. 18-20.

23. Lane, pp. 12-17; Nineham, p. 42; Hengel, pp. 21-25.

24. For a review of this situation and the lament of Tacitus the historian about having little to report, see Hengel, pp. 22 and 132, note 125.

25. Compare Mark 13:13. The damage caused by the fire is summarized by Lane, pp. 13-14; for the hatred directed against Christians, see Hengel, p. 133, note 133.

26. For these events, see Hengel, pp. 22-23.

27. Consult Hengel's long discussion on pp. 31-58, especially pp. 50-56.

28. Mark 6:33-44, feeding the five thousand; 8:1-9, feeding the four thousand; 4:37-39, stilling the storm (compare 6:51).

29. See Hengel's very intriguing remarks on the possibility that the distinctive literary form of the Gospel went ultimately back to Peter (pp. 54-56). Most have postulated that it was Mark who was to be credited with initially composing the type of literature that came to be known as Gospels; compare Nineham, pp. 28-29, and Kümmel, pp. 31-33.

30. Rudolph Bultmann, *The History of the Synoptic Tradition,* 2nd ed. (New York: Harper & Row, 1968), the quote coming from pp. 2-3. The other studies were Karl Ludwig Schmidt, *Der Rahmen der Geschichte Jesu* (Berlin: Trowitzsch & Son, 1919), and Martin Dibelius, *From Tradition to Gospel* (London: Ivor Nicholson and Watson, 1934).

31. Axel Olrik, "Epische Gesetze der Volksdichtung," *Zeitschrift für deutsches Altertum und deutsche Literatur* 51 (1909): 1-12.

32. An entire school has grown up at Uppsala University in Sweden which studies the methods and achievements of oral transmission among

ancient societies, generally concluding that the oral recitation of stories, poems, and sagas is more reliable than the written mode. As an example, see Birger Gerhardsson, *Memory and Manuscript,* 2nd ed. (Lund, Sweden: C. W. K. Gleerup, 1964). Concerning the rapidity with which legendary elements can replace sober, historical accounts, see Hengel's remarks on the rapid growth of fanciful stories about Alexander the Great (pp. 11 and 124-25, note 70).

33. The three major studies, now in English translation, focused on the Synoptic Gospels: Gunther Bornkamm et al., *Tradition and Interpretation in Matthew* (Philadelphia: Westminster, 1963); Willi Marxsen, *Mark the Evangelist. Studies on the Redaction History of the Gospel* (Nashville: Abingdon Press, 1969); Hans Conzelmann, *The Theology of St. Luke* (New York: Harper & Row, 1961).

34. Consult the balanced and balancing view of Hengel, pp. 31-38.

35. For the variety of views current more than thirty years ago, see the essay by Joachim Jeremias, "The Present Position in the Controversy Concerning the Problem of the Historical Jesus," *Expository Times* 69 (1954): 333-39. I personally follow Hengel's results (pp. 53-56).

36. Proponents of this view include Kümmel, pp. 64-65, and Nineham, pp. 40-41, who calls the Gospel writer "a Gentile author . . . without the formal education to express himself in better Greek."

37. The issue concerns the sequence of "Bethphage and Bethany" as Jesus approached Jerusalem from Jericho (11:1). See Hengel's explanation on p. 148, note 51. For an opposite though less compelling view, see Nineham, pp. 294-95.

38. Without maps, one would have necessarily relied on the descriptions of those who had visited distant places. One can also note the interesting fact that peasants in Ptolemaic Egypt were forbidden by law to travel from their villages of residence; see William W. Tarn, *Hellenistic Civilization*, 3rd ed. (New York: Meridian Books, 1961), p. 187, and Michael Grant, *From Alexander to Cleopatra* (New York: Charles Scribner's Sons, 1982) pp. 41, 43.

39. Before Mark accompanied Paul on his first missionary journey from Antioch, they must have approached Antioch by sea, descending from Jerusalem to Caesarea or to Joppa, where they would have boarded a ship traveling north (Acts 11:27-30; 12:25), the land route being hazardous and slow. Moreover, when Mark returned to Jerusalem from Perga in Pamphylia, he most assuredly traveled by boat to a coastal port in Palestine, whence he went east up to Jerusalem (13:13).

40. Hengel, pp. 48 and 145-46.

41. See Nineham, p. 60; Lane, p. 40.

42. Consult the summary of textual evidence in Lane, p. 41, note 7.

43. Lane provides an insightful summary (pp. 39-41); also Nineham, pp. 55-64.

44. Concerning the connections to Moses made in Mark's work, see Hengel, pp. 56-58.

45. The theme of the messianic secret has been widely reviewed. See Kümmel, pp. 66-67; Hengel, pp. 41-45.

46. Consult Hengel's enlightening remarks on pp. 34-36; the quotation is to be found on p. 34. See also Kümmel, pp. 61-62.

47. Hengel, p. 41; his fuller discussion which exhibits a high esteem of Mark's achievement appears on pp. 34-41.

48. See my essay "The Four Gospels as Testimonies," *The Eleventh Annual Sidney B. Sperry Symposium Papers* (Provo, Utah: Brigham Young University Press, 1983), pp. 43-56. For a summary of the New Testament prophecies concerning the coming apostasy, consult Kent P. Jackson, "Early Signs of the Apostasy," *Ensign,* December 1984, pp. 8-16. The theme of the coming apostasy carries over into other early Christian documents; for a review of this feature in the Nag Hammadi materials, see my "The Nag Hammadi Library: A Mormon Perspective" in *Apocryphal Writings and the Latter-day Saints,* ed. C. Wilfred Griggs (Provo, Utah: Religious Studies Center, Brigham Young University, 1986), pp. 255-83, especially 263-64.

49. See Lane, p. 40.

50. Besides "immediately," the term is also translated in the King James Version by "straightway" and "forthwith." In one passage (1:30), it is rendered "anon."

51. Naturally, one can ask how many times Jesus needed to spell out to his disciples the significance of what he was doing. Presumably not many.

52. The feature of wonder or awe naturally leads to the question of the ending of Mark's Gospel. Most commentators hold the view that the text originally ended with 16:8, the variant endings that on the one hand add one verse and on the other add twelve being considered later additions; so Lane, p. 583, note 6; Hengel, pp. 71-72 and 167-68, note 47; and Nineham, 449-52. Internally, the consistency of the message of the Gospel text is not seriously violated if one opts for the shorter ending. The awe inspired in others by the majestic Son of God is deeply underscored thereby and the abruptness of the opening is matched by the same sort of ending. Theologically, however, verses 9 to 20 do not

seriously disrupt the Marcan flow as most have maintained. Textually, the longer ending appears principally in later texts and does not seem to be known by commentators until at least the end of the second century. But the textual evidence is not decisively clear either.

53. The teachings of Jesus concerning discipleship appear in 8:34-38; 9:31-50; 10:33-45.

54. Serious questions exist concerning both Pauline influences on Mark and whether or not Mark spelled out a clear doctrine of atonement. On these issues, see Hengel, pp. 37-38, 39-40, 45-46, 54.

5

THE TESTIMONY OF LUKE

RICHARD LLOYD ANDERSON

In 1961 the oldest copy of Luke (P^{75}) was published, in which the scribe added his note at the bottom of the last chapter: "The Gospel According to Luke." This was about A.D. 200. Then he moved down a few lines and started the next book with the similar title, "The Gospel According to John."[1] An independent copy of John of the same age exists, with the same title at the head.[2] Thus the authorship headings were part of the Gospels as early as records now exist. Evidence of four Gospels reaches back to mid-second century, and plural Gospels are indicated intermittently back to New Testament times. Anyone starting a new record of Jesus, as the opening of Luke describes, would of necessity distinguish his from records that had gone before. "According to" is a Christian formula with only minor variation in the handscripts; such essential unanimity suggests that "according to Luke" was on the earliest copies of that Gospel.

Some very significant things can be said about Luke, but the most prominent fact about him is that he was not prominent. With normal early Christian modesty, he does not directly name himself in his writings, nor is he mentioned except incidentally in the New Testament. So a relatively obscure person consistently appears as the author of Luke and Acts, the largest and most impressive block of writing in the New Testament from a literary and historical

Richard Lloyd Anderson is professor of ancient scripture and director of Bible research in the Religious Studies Center at Brigham Young University.

point of view. Contrary to the patristic debate that arose from the lack of "Paul" within the book of Hebrews, alternative authors are not suggested for the Gospel of Luke in the probings of the Ante-Nicene Fathers. For instance, several decades before the P^{75} scribe made his oldest known copy, Irenaeus, Bishop of Lyons, repeatedly named Luke and quoted from his Gospel in order to expose the inconsistencies of heretics.[3] History regularly speculates on what is probable, but it is most responsible when dealing more realistically with what is known. On the level of likelihood, a number of careful scholars ask about the authorship of Luke: "If people were guessing, would they not be much more likely to come up with an apostle?"[4] And on the restricted question of fact, Luke is the only author mentioned by the prominent church fathers and important hand-written copies of the Gospel in the early Christian centuries.

Paul profiles Luke. Besides giving Luke's general greetings in two letters (Col. 4:14; 2 Tim. 4:11), the apostle was specific at the end of Colossians, describing him as "the beloved physician" (Col. 4:14). While Christian leaders regularly addressed their converts by "beloved," this term of endearment applied to a fellow laborer amounts to a designation of intense trust. Paul was most sensitive about who instructed the volatile branches, so here he really designated Luke as an apostolic associate whose spiritual—and historical—knowledge could be trusted. This relationship gives important color to Luke's preface; he could record what apostles knew because he was their intimate companion. Luke was also called "physician," a term used only here outside the Gospels and clearly in a literal sense. If we did not have a hundred pages of Luke's prose, what kind of physician he was might be in doubt. But he reveals himself as a well-informed and careful thinker, qualities that evidently characterized his training and profession. Ancient medicine was obviously in its infancy by today's standards, but the best practitioners used pragmatic science within the limits of their technology. When such a man turned his whole attention to the Christian movement, he was in a unique position to investigate the healings, including the greatest healing—Christ's resurrection.

Paul adds a third insight to Luke that is clear but not as obvious.

Before noting the "beloved physician" in his letter from Rome to Colossae, the apostle mentioned three companions "of the circumcision" and immediately added the Greek phrase that they were his "only fellow workers" in the work of the kingdom of God. (Col. 4:10.) There certainly were such Jewish companions at other times and places, but Paul's concern to point out faithful Jewish companions makes an important point about Luke. For he is listed afterward with the Gentile missionaries laboring with the apostle. Paul's full characterization of this associate is importantly reflected in Luke's Gospel, but nothing is so evident as Luke's attraction to Jesus' concern with all classes and all nationalities. This emphasis in the selection of his materials reflects both Luke's non-Jewish origins and his experiences with Paul in the Gentile missions.

The other reliable insights to Luke's life come from his writings, since Christian traditions about him are late and carry no discernible link to the first century. But looking at Luke through his Gospel is only half the story, for he contributed two major books to the New Testament. Since he wrote the Gospel, he also wrote the Acts of the Apostles, for its preface tells Theophilus that the "former treatise" recorded Jesus' life to the resurrection and ascension. (Acts 1:1-2.) Theophilus appears twice in the New Testament, on both occasions in the prefaces tying Luke to Acts. Since this name basically signifies "friend of God," this could be Luke's literary device for writing to those who "feared God," the Gentile seekers who infiltrated the Jewish synagogues in Acts and Josephus; "Theophilus" could also be a well-educated Christian convert who merited "most excellent," a title of social or administrative status. (Luke 1:3.) In either event, Acts clearly continues the Gospel and adds significant insight into Luke and his purposes. The two books are also welded together by a distinctive prose that favors classical style and formal grammar not characteristic of other New Testament writers.

While Acts says nothing of Luke directly, there are autobiographical glimpses. The most subtle is worth passing mention. Ante-Nicene fathers sometimes gave Luke's home as Antioch, though it is hard to be sure whether this is valid tradition or an inference from Acts. If only the latter, it is still worth considering, for Luke's vivid detail about Paul begins about the time that Luke became a companion of the apostle. Paul had labored in Jewish areas and branches for about a decade until his official call to the Gentile work, when Barnabas came from the Twelve and brought Paul from Tarsus to Antioch. (Acts 11:19-26.) Before that event, Luke's record of that apostle is spotty, but full detail on his missionary work begins immediately after Paul comes to Antioch. Luke features only the Gentile missions from this time, either because of the subject, his own call, or first knowing Paul in the vicinity of Antioch, the base of operations for Paul's international labors. These interrelated possibilities justify an educated guess that Luke first knew Paul soon after the converted Jew from Tarsus was called to labor with Gentile converts in Antioch, some fifteen years after the crucifixion.

The more definite data from Acts concerns Luke's "we" passages. Roman historians of Luke's time typically begin their histories with no identification and minimal personal comment, but occasionally inject first-person observations into the body of their works later. Acts is normally written with the descriptive pronouns of the third person: *he, she,* and *they.* But in several significant sections Luke drops into *we,* identifying himself as one of the party in Paul's travels.[5] Thus Acts fits the three Roman epistles that name Luke as Paul's companion, and it adds further times when "the beloved physician" was with Paul. These "we" passages bring Luke from Asia Minor to northern Greece after Paul left Antioch with the apostolic revelation on duties of Gentile converts (Acts 16:10-13); they resume as Luke left northern Greece and traveled with Paul's party to Jerusalem with the Gentile welfare contributions. (Acts 19:5-15; 21:1-18.) They then dot the narrative after Paul spent two years in Palestine waiting for release. After the appeal to Rome, Luke boarded ship in Caesarea with Paul and his military escort (Acts 27:2), and references to "we" and "us" continue through the various stages of the trip until arrival at Rome (Acts 28:16).

Sources and Time of Writing

Did Luke remain in the Christian homeland while Paul stayed there in prison (about A.D. 59-61)? He virtually said that his mission was to attend Paul until freed. Right after the appeal to Rome, "it was determined that we should sail into Italy." (Acts 27:1.) Since he took for granted that he was a necessary member of Paul's party, the implication is that he was attending Paul prior to that. Indeed, Luke emphasized how Paul's associates were free to visit him throughout the Palestinian arrest. (Acts 24:23.) Luke was evidently saying that he was one of these attendants during the imprisonment, since he was one both at the beginning and the end. On any analysis Luke had substantial opportunities to locate those still on the scene who could speak firsthand on the Lord.

By the time Luke wrote about his trip to Judea with Paul, he had already penned his "former treatise," the Gospel of Luke (Acts 1:1), with its preface insisting that Christian beliefs stood solidly on the experience of those "which from the beginning were eyewitnesses" (Acts 1:2). The key term of time in that preface is repeated in the intensely personal account of his arriving at Jerusalem with Paul. This visit was highly significant for the historian, for as soon as the apostle's party arrived in Palestine, the style suddenly switched from generalizing to naming individuals. The trusted associate wrote moving accounts of Paul's forebodings and farewells to the Asian-Syrian churches, but adult saints and their hosts are nameless "disciples." Yet on landing at the Roman capital of Palestine, the personal pronouns intensify in ten verses that name the Christian pioneers that Luke met, all of which could give history of Jesus or of the early days of his Church.

Luke wrote about first arriving in Israel: "We entered into the house of Philip, the evangelist, which was one of the seven." (Acts 21:8.) Such a reference is more than accidental in a work marked by literary foreshadowing, retrospective emphasis, and specific illustrations of characteristic Christian events.[6] Personal contact with his source is the obvious point of Luke's labels of Philip, for when he wrote them, the historian had already written up the episode of choosing of the seven welfare assistants (Acts 6:1-6) and also the long stories of Philip's preaching to Samaria and to the

Ethiopian eunuch (Acts 8:5-40). And the same direct contact is apparent as Luke next mentioned Agabas coming to meet Paul's party staying in Caesarea "as we tarried there many days." (Acts 21:10.) Not long before writing these words, Luke had explained how this prophet came to Antioch prophesying of famine in Jerusalem, where he resided. (Acts 11:27-30.)

So Luke worked with the double level of history and implied historical accuracy as he next crafted his report of entering the city of Christ's preaching and passion. The early Christians just named at Caesarea were obviously sources for Acts. And Luke next named an earlier Christian that he met in Jerusalem, one apparently given as an example of contemporaries of Christ behind Luke's Gospel. The individual was the otherwise obscure "Mnason . . . an old disciple, with whom we should lodge." (Acts 21:16.) Here the Greek mirrors the preface of the Gospel, where Luke insisted that personal observers "from the beginning" had furnished facts for faith. The noun there is *arché*, which is the variant form of the adjective applied to *Mnason, archaios*, meaning in this context that he was a "disciple from the beginning." The latter term is emphatic because it is never used elsewhere by this writer in a Christian context. So Luke's dramatic mention of an original follower of Christ on coming to Jerusalem is personal foreshadowing like the earlier introduction of "a young man" named Saul, who guarded the clothes of those who stoned Stephen. (Acts 7:58.) Luke had introduced Paul in dramatic forecasting of the main theme of his subsequent story of how the Gospel went to the Gentiles. Likewise, "the disciple from the first" bridges the knowledge gap between Paul and Jesus, Luke's main theme prefacing his first work. Since this "we" passage puts the earliest disciple in the emphatic position as the first one met in Jerusalem, Luke essentially made a parenthetical comment on the authenticity of his writings before carrying on the main story of giving the welfare supplies to James, the brother of the Lord, the resident apostle.

Most scholars comment on the literary relationships of Luke and Acts, but the point here is the relevance of the people in Acts for Luke as a biographer of Jesus. The morning after arrival, "Paul went in with us unto James; and all the elders were present." (Acts

21:18.) Was meeting James the beginning of the historian's inquiries about Mary's experiences in the miraculous events of Jesus' birth? Luke's is the only Gospel that mentions them. One good result from Paul's subsequent arrest was that Luke spent substantial time, if not all of his time, in the land of the Lord with access to many individuals who had personal experiences with him. After naming the above four people first met in Palestine, Luke dropped himself out of the record in favor of the notable imprisonment of the apostle about the years A.D. 59 to 61. But the aware physician did not drop out of life. Whom he talked to in Judea in this period is not known, but one would lack a healthy curiosity not to ask. James was articulate and literate, and might well have furnished family records. He was just past thirty during Jesus' ministry, and highly competent to remember early events when Luke saw him at about sixty. There were other men in the same category, especially in the villages, not to speak of women, a larger group because of their longer life span. Females between twenty and forty during Jesus' ministry were still available for Luke's inquiries three decades later when he waited for Paul. In fact, five years before this arrest, Paul had insisted that the majority of the 500 who saw Jesus in the resurrection were still alive. (1 Cor. 15:6.)

Luke's contacts with Jesus' generation about A.D. 60 perhaps completed a process of gathering information during the previous decade, when Luke is known to have been a companion of Paul. The date when the physician wrote his two volumes on Christian beginnings is not known. There are educated guesses, and this paper will argue briefly for the earliest choice. However, the authenticity of Luke's two records should not depend on whether they were written about A.D. 63, soon after A.D. 70, or a decade beyond that. These later dates are claimed by a majority of commentators but on highly debatable arguments of when early Christian theology had evolved to Luke's point of view, or of how some details of Jesus' prophecy against Jerusalem (Luke 21) must have been written after the seige in A.D. 70. The latter reasoning fails to impress one who accepts the possibility that prophecy can really predict. About the only objective data is the sudden ending of Acts, since its preface defines it as Luke's second work. Toward the end,

Luke built suspense through Paul's appeal to Caesar to avoid risking assassination in Palestine. Then the exciting close of Acts brings the apostle to Rome, but only to wait two years for trial, where the final verse leaves the apostle in loose custody, waiting and preaching. Here is a strange anticlimax from a literary artist, which convinces me that the story stopped then because at the time of writing Paul had not yet appeared before the imperial court. On this ground Acts was composed about A.D. 63, and the Gospel would have been written earlier. This reasoning envisions Luke finishing the fact-gathering process in Palestine before Paul came to Rome about A.D. 61 and afterward compiling the Gospel and Acts while he waited for Paul's trial, the period when Paul's letters from the capital include Luke's greetings.

Luke's Historical Reliability

To repeat, Luke's date of composition should not affect the great historical value of that Gospel. His preface gives the reason for this view, backed up by insights in Acts and New Testament letters of the Christian historical process at work. A modern translation better communicates Luke's introductory thoughts, and the New International Version answers that purpose here: "Many have undertaken to draw up an account of the things that have been fulfilled among us, just as they were handed down to us by those who from the first were eyewitnesses and ministers of the word. Therefore, since I myself have carefully investigated everything from the beginning, it seemed good also to me to write an orderly account for you, most excellent Theophilus, so that you may know the certainty of the things you have been taught (Luke 1:1-4)."[7]

Luke's goal was verification. Records of Jesus already existed, one of which was surely Mark. Other possibilities are the Gospel of Matthew and/or its predecessors that officially collected the main teachings of Jesus, a subject beyond our scope here. Buy why would Luke write another account after admitting that several already existed? He obviously thought he could add something, and the stated purpose of his account is to doublecheck earliest Christian events. Here is a man of education insisting that the Christian story could stand up under his own standards. "Investigated" is a preferred translation now, but on any analysis Luke took pains to be independently informed about the founding story and certified that it was correct.[8]

This process puts Luke at the second stage of information, which came from "eyewitnesses and ministers of the word." "Minister" (*hupéretés*) was used in that period in the sense of an assistant or helper, regularly applied to administrators of some status. So the strong implication is that eyewitnesses are the apostles who in every Gospel have the commission to carry the word or message to the world. Some scholars have sought to put Luke at the third stage after eyewitnesses, getting his information from anonymous Christian preachers who taught traditional stories to a later generation. However, we have seen Luke picturing himself through the "we" passages as in contact with the generation that knew Jesus. Thus, as many scholars insist, the "eyewitnesses and ministers of the word" are to be taken together.[9] They were really those who knew Jesus personally and who were also commissioned to preach the gospel. Luke opened Acts with just such an example. Matthias was chosen as an apostle from the body of those who walked with Jesus. (Acts 1:22-23.) Then he was given the second status of an eyewitness invested with the preaching authority of the Twelve. (Acts 1:25-26.) This eyewitness-apostle combination throws light on Luke's own definition of those who had already written accounts of Christ's work. He later recorded the same double description of Paul, qualified through his call and vision to be "a minister and a witness." (Acts 26:16.) In the light of these dual descriptions of the apostles Matthias and Paul, "eyewitnesses and ministers of the word" in Luke's preface should be seen as a combination term referring to the Galilean Twelve with personal knowledge of Christ and delegated authority to testify of him. Thus Luke gives two main ideas in his preface: that he was one step away from original information from the first leaders, and that he could go back to those who could verify written records.

Yet critical New Testament scholarship is generally not satisfied with Luke's straightforward testimony. Form criticism is heavily stressed by analysts representing the academic establishment, though there are protests. In this theory, authors of the

Gospels merely gathered up circulating stories that were remembered for their religious message but had changed in the retelling. This skeptical approach attempts to go behind the New Testament record by speculating about earlier forms of the main stories about Jesus. But by distrusting the objectivity of the Gospels, scholars have created a crisis of subjectivity. One expert on Luke reacts to this intellectual maze: "It is notorious that today questions regarding the ministry and teaching of the historical Jesus have become immensely complex and difficult, so much so that some scholars (wrongly, in our opinion) have despaired of ever answering them."[10]

For this reason the New Testament student will find many current books on the Gospels to be shortsighted. Rather than read heavily in secondary literature, serious students should define people and places with the aid of an up-to-date Bible dictionary and mainly search the Gospels themselves, perhaps with the aid of a harmony printed in parallel columns. Most commentaries and some Bible dictionaries state theoretical positions as though they were proved. With the New Testament as the base, one should develop insights and explanations that are justified by the New Testament, for Luke had access to those who knew and to the earliest records, each of which told a consistent story of the miraculous powers of the Lord. One clear New Testament example of what was available to Luke is 1 Corinthians. About A.D. 56 Paul wrote that letter, predating Luke's Gospel and probably Mark's. The apostle opened his testimony of the resurrection (1 Cor. 15) with language close to Luke's preface about what was received from eyewitnesses before him. Paul listed resurrection appearances (1 Cor. 15:3-7) and also summarized the Last Supper (1 Cor. 11:23-25). Both of these short histories harmonize with the Gospels that appeared later. So evidence supports Luke's model of a settled historical record rather than today's fashionable hypothesis of evolving oral stories.

This is not to say that Luke even attempted verbal photography or mechanical sequence. His writing structure suggests that the "order" of his preface means effective presentation, and his prose suggests that he valued artful expression. But for the best ancient historians, such views did not place rhetoric above accuracy: they sought excellence of form *and* content. This means that Luke may have paraphrased, since he tended to avoid Jewish titles and phrases that would not be understood by non-Jewish readers. But he clearly stayed close to his sources, since he retold incidents from Mark with a tendency to summarize but with care, and he quoted his Matthew source verbatim in long sentences of agreement between those two Gospels. In fact, Luke's goal of a new presentation was clearly limited by the historical framework already established in writing a gospel. Since his events generally harmonize with Matthew and Mark, the three are called "synoptic," taking a "common view" of their material. Such correlated history sharply distinguishes the canonical Gospels from second- and third-century compilations that plagiarized and imitated them to serve the ends of Christian Gnosticism or exaggerated piety. Luke's preface is backed up by a gospel that says by its content that prior writings on Jesus told the truth but did not contain a complete record of Jesus. Moreover, John wrote late in the first century with Luke's same goals, to verify and supplement.

Scholars study interrelationships of Matthew, Mark, and Luke under the label of the "synoptic problem." Its solutions amount to seemingly endless searching for their order of composition and ultimate sources. The majority vote goes today for the two-document hypothesis, claiming that Mark came first and was used by Matthew and Luke independently, together with mutual use of a common collection of Jesus' sayings. But continuing books of dissent prove that Mark before Matthew is not proved, though the existence of an early-sayings source is suggested by historical and literary investigation. That fits Luke's preface describing existing written sources plus additional personal investigation. The latter produced his unique addition of two long chapters of family history on the birth and youth of John the Baptist and Jesus, and also about ten middle chapters that have a missionary theme in reporting Jesus' work in Gentile areas bordering Israel.

Obviously Paul's missionary companion to the Gentiles was interested in similar work in the Savior's life. Each Gospel reflects not only Jesus but also special interest in Jesus in the mind of each author. The pendulum swings high in this area of study today, labeled by the question-begging term *redaction criticism.* Since *redaction* is simply another word for *editorial revision,* the concept is that the writers of Gospels took stories in general circulation and refashioned them to support the evolved theological needs of a later church. Thus the Gospels are supposedly compilations of religious folklore. They are "a mixture of historical reminiscence, interpreted tradition, and the free creativity of prophets and the evangelist."[11] Thus it is now commonly said that the Gospels tell us little about Jesus but much about the author of each Gospel. As with many exaggerations, there is truth in the position, provided the historical concern of the writer is balanced against the obvious fact that every historian reveals himself in writing about others. But to deny Luke a passion for accuracy is to contradict his prefaces and his Christian commitment to truth. The extreme forms of redaction criticism write about Luke the theologian instead of Luke the historian. This is a crude either-or fallacy, for he was both.

There are three accounts of Jesus healing the woman with chronic bleeding. Here the synoptic authors reveal different points of view, but they also verify Christian history by agreeing on a dozen main details of the miracle. With the distantness of an official record, Matthew objectively stated that the woman had been afflicted twelve years; with blunt personal details fitting Peter as the source behind Mark, Mark's Gospel says that the woman had endured physicians, "and had spent all that she had, and . . . rather grew worse" (Mark 5:25-26); but Luke empathizes with both the woman and the physicians: she "had spent all her living upon physicians, neither could be healed of any" (Luke 8:43). Here there is definite but limited injection of personality by each evangelist. Yet editing here is not modifying details, but selective omission and selective comment. Different personalities thus strengthened the historical record of Jesus, for Luke and John added many tested incidents to the first writings. In doing so they served their personal interests but also the cause of history.

The Contributions of Luke

Distinctive features of Luke include: the detailed birth account, which correlates with Luke's contact with Jesus' family; Luke's unique parables on love, which correlate with his lack of sexual or racial bias, as well as Paul's characterization of him as "beloved"; his insightful summary of the Last Supper, which correlates with his probable contact with John, who was there, and his close association with Paul, who gave us our earliest known record of blessing the bread and wine (1 Cor. 11:23-25); the summary record of Jesus' trial, which correlates with Luke's travels in the Empire and his sense of the legal and political realities behind Pilate's moves; and finally, the most detailed account of Christ's resurrection by the most informed early Christian on psychology and physiology, the areas that Luke had practical experience with as a physician. All of these contributions reflect the keen interest of an individual inquiring at a time when first-generation memories were broader than written records. The breadth of Luke's Gospel matches the unusual journeys, probably visiting with traveling apostles and perhaps even going to villages where miracles took place, such as Nain, where he gave the touching sketch of Jesus' healing of the widow's son. Of course, it is not known where Luke learned of the events that he alone reports, but it is known that he insisted that information come to him accurately, whether from apostles with Jesus or from participants in their homes.

This essay makes no attempt to summarize Luke's Gospel. No explanation of it can take the place of experiencing its impact through consecutive reading. Luke blended documents and oral history into a powerful statement of the divinity of Christ. In the words of Thucydides, the Greek pioneer of careful history, Luke produced "a possession for all time." He insisted that he did not alter but organized his stories after establishing them as true by personal inquiries. The reader of this introduction to his introduction should have a feeling for the man behind the third Gospel, and his commitment both to truth and to Christ, who came to bring gospel truth. Luke's interests were broad, his spirit tolerant, his mind inquisitive, his experiences international. He brought a strength to the Christian witness as a convert with special qualifications to examine who Jesus was and what he did.

After John later finished his Gospel, there were three apostolic testaments of Christ: from Matthew, whose Gospel preserves the great discourses of the Master and no doubt reflects Matthew's record-keeping abilities as a tax collector; from Mark, whose detail of events consistently reflects personal knowledge, which, according to traceable Christian tradition, came directly from Peter;[12] from John, who could say of himself and his fellow apostles, "We beheld his glory" (John 1:14), and give the intimate details of divine love and power displayed by the Lord. These three Gospels incorporate information and insights on Jesus stemming from the inner circle. The problem with such incredible events is that they reach so far beyond comfortable normality. But incredible breakthroughs in medical or scientific research are finally believed because additional investigators can duplicate laboratory conditions and validate the discoveries.

The historical process has analogies here, as Luke reverified by going back to observers. He was in the position of an accountant charged with making an independent audit. The three other evangelists were Jewish, Palestinian, not highly educated, and had direct contact with the Lord. Luke was a polished outsider who had become a convert. Yet true education produces multiple loyalties, and Luke was deeply educated or he would not have written the polished preface that shows knowledge of the histories of his period, nor would he have used the most extensive vocabulary of the New Testament and the most literary style of any evangelist. The point is that Luke had seen the world, had glimpsed much truth outside of a Christian context, and would not narrowly commit himself to something questionable. That he saw the need of verification in his preface shows that. So the strength of Luke's testament is the support of the insider's story by an informed outsider. He was virtually the journalist assigned to get at the bottom of an incredible event, the one whose writings featured participants telling the world what it was and how it was.

Luke's introduction shows that other accounts of Jesus were written before he organized his own. And writing is a firm act of preservation that guards against change. Since Luke's gathering process preceded his writing, the autobiographical glimpses in Acts show that by A.D. 60 he was probing, comparing, and finding the consistency that he described in the prologue of his Gospel. Paul's similar testimony was given at A.D. 56 in 1 Corinthians 15, insisting that all the apostles told the same story of Christ's resurrection, the summit event in Luke's biography of Christ. Thus basic records of the resurrection are clear by mid-century, a mere two decades after it took place. At this time literacy and Christian conviction were at work to publish private records and recollections, and Luke's Gospel was a part of that process.

Those who write family history rescue detail from oblivion. And Luke saved specifics on the most significant individual of all history. Because of his concern and discipline in writing, there is a clearer understanding of Jesus' private meditations, personal compassion, and timeless challenges to all to believe, to live with strict integrity and generous empathy, and to enter and sacrifice for God's kingdom. Luke's ultimate authentication is his fuller record of the first day of the resurrection. Reality is constructed from ingredients and particulars, and Luke satisfied himself that Jesus returned that day not in the minds, but in the sustained physical experiences of the apostles. The short eight verses that establish this obviously came after many questions directed to at least some of the ten who first stood together in Jesus' presence. Luke recorded their conversation just before Jesus appeared, their total shock at seeing him, his firm assurance of comfort and identity, and his invitation to examine his "flesh and bones," which they accepted. Only Luke added the truth that Jesus ate before these overwhelmed associates in a final assurance of materiality that they could not doubt. It is tempting to see the physician's preoccupation with anatomy at a time when much about the body was known. Luke's resurrection account reveals the same inquiring mind glimpsed in the opening verses of his Gospel. Such a man probed Jesus' private life, public works, teachings, miracles, and the ultimate miracle of conquering death. On all of these he left his stamp of verification.

Postscript: Some Textual Issues in Luke

The Gospels are mutually illuminating, and studying them brings far more benefits than studying any number of commentaries on them. Yet accurate understanding of wording is a barrier in the King James Version, which uses a number of archaic meanings not apparent in casual reading. The "GR" footnotes of the recent Latter-day Saint edition of the Bible help; so do modern translations, which also raise textual problems. Most modern versions choose the shorter Greek readings on the general theory that pious scribes were prone to additions. On the other hand, careless scribes tend to delete, a statistically more likely case for the average manuscript difference, though each problem needs to be settled on a case by case basis. The reader without Greek has a fuller statement of these variant readings and a longer text in the New King James Version. Yet most variants are doctrinally and historically insignificant, though three main textual questions emerge in the sections of Luke most commonly studied by Latter-day Saints. The King James Version rarely indicates alternative readings because its translators used a traditional text without notes on differences between manuscripts, many of which were more recently discovered.

The first variant in sequence is the vivid description of Gethsemane, with the bloody sweat and the comforting angel. (Luke 22:43-44.) Such a verse obviously caused problems with Christian Gnostics and orthodox theologians, who were uncomfortable with Jesus' physical nature and human passions. Thus a knowledgeable patristic scholar considers deletion in many manuscripts on both grounds: "perhaps omitted by Marcion for docetic reasons, and by Alexandrians as doctrinally difficult."[13] Such double jeopardy for this verse has specific grounds because the heretic Marcion manufactured a shortened version of Luke, and earliest-known New Testament manuscripts stem from Egypt, the center of Christian revisionism on the nature of God. Although the A.D. 200 Lucan copy deletes the verse, some thirty years before that Irenaeus insisted on the physical passion by reciting that Christ

103

"sweated great drops of blood."[14] And a decade before that, Justin Martyr specifically quoted the "memoirs . . . drawn up by his apostles and those who followed them," where it was written that Christ's "sweat fell down like drops of blood while he was praying."[15] Thus there are two witnesses to the bloody sweat prior to the oldest copy of Luke, one of them naming the Gospels.

The next relevant textual problem concerns Jesus' prayer for his enemies on the cross: "Father, forgive them, for they know not what they do." (Luke 23:34.) At first glance one remembers that Luke is the Gospel stressing both prayer and forgiveness, for that evangelist added special parables and examples of Christ's compassion, as well as produced the only note of Jesus' prayers at the special occasions of his life—his baptism, temptation, choosing the Twelve, and transfiguration. The earliest extra-biblical evidence for the incident is Irenaeus, who about A.D. 180 quoted Christ's words of forgiveness that he "exclaimed upon the cross."[16] So even though these words do not appear in the A.D. 200 copy of Luke, they were already attributed to Jesus by a bishop who insisted that knowledge of Jesus came only through the four Gospels. Some scholars think the prayer was deleted because forgiveness seemed to go against Jesus' recent prophecy of the destruction of Jerusalem, reiterated in warning to the women who wept as he carried the cross to Calvary. But there is a more likely contradiction to cause the deletion, for Peter expressly told the Jews that national forgiveness would not come until the latter days (Acts 3:19); the other side of that coin was Luke's report of Jesus saying that Jerusalem would be in bondage until the age of Gentile dominance was over (Luke 21:24). Joseph Smith, who preached on the delayed forgiveness of corporate Israel, noted in his translation that the forgiving words from the cross applied to the Roman soldiers. But an early copyist, feeling that Jesus' prayer was not restricted and therefore would be interpreted as a contradiction, perhaps acted to save Luke from ridicule at an early point when anti-Christian polemics were harsh and increased the danger of persecution for the faithful. The hard fact remains that the words are quoted from Jesus before the earliest manuscripts and by a traditionalist who insisted that authentic teachings of Jesus came from the four Gospels.[17]

The final textual problem has a lesson attached to it. Luke obviously thought deeply and apparently inquired carefully about the Lord's appearance to ten apostles on the first day of the resurrection. Luke's account uses a progressive heightening as Jesus led the disciples from one level of stunned realization to the next. After the opening shock and assurances, Jesus extended his hands in invitation to touch, followed by the natural crescendo of Luke's narrative: "And when he had thus spoken, he shewed them his hands and his feet." (Luke 24:40.) However, a fifth-century Greek manuscript, labeled D, omitted this verse and a number of others in the resurrection account of Luke 24. Since D contains intriguing additions to Acts, Westcott and Hort developed a theory that the omissions of this manuscript reflected an earlier shorter text. Conservative scholars protested, but from about 1900 to 1960 this position carried the day, resulting in the omission of Jesus showing his hands and feet in both the Revised Standard Version and the New English Bible. In both cases a footnote printed the verses as added by other manuscripts, a type of notation that was misleading because only one known Greek manuscript deleted the verse out of hundreds of significant ones that included it. Yet a majority of textual scholars clearly supported the reasoning behind these deletions.

The industrious LDS New Testament student, President J. Reuben Clark, Jr., protested such treatment in a compilation of conservative quotations and also in a concise pamphlet.[18] Calling the proponents of deletion "extreme textualists," he lamented the doubt that had been projected to "become the ruling text."[19] His dissent was vindicated when the A.D. 200 copy of Luke was published in 1961, containing the verse wherein Jesus showed the apostles his hands and feet, as well as the other segments of Luke 24 deleted in the atypical fifth-century manuscript. Scholarly opinion has since reversed itself to the point that mainstream Joseph Fitzmeyer labels the former Luke 24 deletions a fad.[20] Thus the later committee translations have included the verse where

Jesus shows his hands and feet.[21] The whole episode sustains Luke's testimony of the physical resurrection and serves as a warning that agreement of Bible scholars on any theory is no substitute for evidence.

NOTES

1. Victor Martin and Rodolphe Kasser, *Papyrus Bodmer XIV* (Geneva: Bibliotheca Bodmeriana, 1961), p. 150 of the transcription, p. 61 of the photo supplement.

2. Victor Martin and J. W. B. Barns, *Papyrus Bodmer II, Supplement* (Geneva: Bibliotheca Bodmeriana, 1962), p. 1 of the photo supplement.

3. Irenaeus, *Against Heresies* 3.1 and 3.10.1-4. Quotations from church fathers in this article may be found in Alexander Roberts and James Donaldson, *The Ante-Nicene Fathers* (Grand Rapids, Mich.: Eerdmans Publishing Co., 1956). For a survey of early patristic comments on Luke, see Daniel J. Theron, *Evidence of Tradition* (Grand Rapids, Mich.: Baker Book House, 1958), pp. 41-65, 69-71.

4. Leon Morris, *The Gospel According to St. Luke* (London: Inter-Varsity Press, 1974), p. 15.

5. The argument that Luke incorporated another's diary is not convincing because of "the overwhelming linguistic evidence that the author of the book was also the author of the diary." (G. B. Caird, *Saint Luke* [New York: Penguin Books, 1963], p. 16.) Furthermore, interjecting personal comments in a third-person narrative was a recognized pattern in ancient literature, and Luke's preface shows that he followed the polished practices of his day in presentation of his material.

6. For Luke's practice of giving typical cases instead of exhaustive detail, see Richard Lloyd Anderson, *Understanding Paul* (Salt Lake City: Deseret Book, 1983), pp. 45-46, 48, 57, 61.

7. I have changed "servant" to "minister" in this translation for reasons explained in the following discussion.

8. Luke's verb means literally that he "followed along" or "followed up," and the two connotations here roughly reflect the modern debate that contained some hair splitting. The preface represents Luke as coming after the eyewitnesses to certify to Theophilus that information from them is correct. Since "follow" fits into an investigation context,

recent translations have Luke "go over," "trace," or "investigate" the founding events. For current comments, see E. Earle Ellis, *The Gospel of Luke* (Grand Rapids, Mich.: Eerdmans Publishing Co., 1975), p. 66; Joseph A. Fitzmeyer, *The Gospel According to Luke (I-IX)* (Doubleday, 1981), pp. 296-97.

9. For a strong opinion on this pairing, see I. Howard Marshall, *The Gospel of Luke* (Grand Rapids, Mich.: Eerdmans Publishing Co., 1978), p. 42: "The syntax demands that the eyewitnesses and servants are one group of people." My argument is that Luke's vocabulary and thought on succeeding apostles show an intent to combine the "eyewitnesses and ministers of the word" of the preface. Rengstorf correctly sees Luke's purpose in making the two groups the same, since the resulting expression "establishes continuity between the preaching of Jesus and the history of Jesus." (Gerhard Friedrich et al., *Theological Dictionary of the New Testament,* trans. Geoffrey W. Bromiley [Grand Rapids, Mich.: Eerdmans Publishing Co., 1972] 8:543.)

10. I. Howard Marshall, *Luke: Historian and Theologian* (Grand Rapids, Mich.: Zondervan, 1970), p. 217.

11. Norman Perrin, *What Is Redaction Criticism?* (Philadelphia: Fortress Press, 1969), p. 75.

12. For a convenient reprinting of the Peter-Mark information gathered by early second-century bishop Papias, see Theron, p. 67 (quoting Eusebius), and also p. 45 for the "tradition of the early elders" from Clement of Alexandria. See also S. Kent Brown, "The Testimony of Mark," chapter 3 in this volume.

13. G. W. H. Lampe, commenting on Luke in Matthew Black and H. H. Rowley, eds., *Peake's Commentary on the Bible* (London: Thomas Nelson & Sons, 1962), p. 841.

14. *Against Heresies* 3.22.2.

15. *Dialogue with Trypho* 103.

16. *Against Heresies* 3.18.5.

17. Irenaeus is characterized by a number of apparently naive arguments that there can be only four Gospels, but they are really analogies because of his insistence that the imitation gospels of his century contradict "the Gospels of the Apostles" (*Against Heresies* 3.11.9). Luke is expressly included in this terminology (ibid., 3.1), an accurate statement in the sense that Luke's data came from apostles.

18. The detailed treatment is *Why the King James Version?* (Salt Lake City: Deseret Book, 1956).

19. "Our Bible," reprint of the 1954 pamphlet by J. Reuben Clark, Jr., in David H. Yarn, Jr., ed., *J. Reuben Clark: Selected Papers* (Provo, Utah: Brigham Young University Press, 1984), p. 89.

20. Fitzmeyer, pp. 130-31.

21. The following committee translations include the verse: The Jerusalem Bible (1966), The New American Bible (1970), The New International Version (1978), The New King James Version (1982). Editors made no qualifying comment in these versions except for the last: "Some printed New Testaments omit this verse. It is found in nearly all Greek manuscripts." Compare the comment of Bruce M. Metzger on the application of redaction criticism to ancient editorial decisions in copying the D-type text of the Gospels: "Scholars have begun to give renewed attention to the possibility that special theological interests on the part of scribes may account for the deletion of certain passages in Western witnesses." (*A Textual Commentary on the Greek New Testament* [New York: United Bible Societies, 1975], pp. 192-93.)

6

THE TESTIMONY OF JOHN

C. Wilfred Griggs

A brief article on the Gospel of John cannot pretend to be a commentary, for any brief part of the text can command a response as lengthy as (or more so than) this brief essay. During a long discussion on John, I once asked a very learned friend why he had not written a commentary on that Gospel. The response seemed frivolous at first, but it was seen to be insightfully accurate with the passage of time: "I would have to write some eight hundred pages—and then I could move on to verse two." This essay, then, will simply reflect some of the impressions I had during one reading of the text. Each reading has brought different insights and new ideas. The purpose of this chapter is to suggest a few themes and ideas that will enhance understanding of and appreciation for John's testimony of the Word of God, whom John served as an apostle for much of the Christian church's first century.

Authorship and Date

No Gospel author identifies himself by name in his work, but the uniqueness of each writer's style serves as an identification for his writings. It is generally agreed, for example, that the same person is responsible for both Luke and Acts. Likewise, even a

C. Wilfred Griggs is professor of ancient scripture and director of ancient studies research in the Religious Studies Center at Brigham Young University.

casual reading of John, 1 John, and Revelation would show sufficient similarities in vocabulary and style to argue for common
authorship. Although they are brief, 2 John and 3 John also display
characteristics that would argue for Johannine authorship. While
modern scholars commonly deny authorship of the Gospels to
those whose names are associated with them, or argue for multiple
redactions, the practice is more illustrative of theories of literary
analysis than of dependence upon firm historical evidence. The
earliest available evidence unquestionably attributes the Gospels to
their respective authors, and the lack of historical evidence in the
early decades of the early church relating to alternative authorship
possibilities further supports the traditional assignations. One need
not feel intellectually shy about an assertion that John the Beloved
Apostle is the author of the fourth Gospel.

The date of the writing of the Gospel is not easily determined,
and many of the reasons usually given for assigning it to the end of
the first century are not so compelling as they seemed to be in
recent decades. Some have argued that the highly stylized vocabulary of opposites, such as light and dark, spirit and flesh, or truth
and falseness, was a response to an incipient gnosticism at the end
of the first century. But discoveries of ancient documents, like the
Community Rule and War Scroll of the Dead Sea Scrolls, demonstrate that precisely the same vocabulary was used in Jewish circles
before the time of Jesus and the apostles. Others have contended
that the uniqueness of John (compared with the three Synoptic
Gospels) occurred partly because the author was filling in gaps of
information or otherwise responding to them in some particular
way. Such a theory is based on the untenable assumption that there
was one developed Gospel format from which any other must be
considered a later deviation or derivation.

Arguments for a later first- or second-century completion of the
fourth Gospel based on perceived redactional or editorial layers, or
on imaginative developments between Jews and Gentiles in early
Christian communities, must likewise be accepted only as hypothetical. The reader should understand that the genius of the
proponents of such theories is their greatest support, for we
cannot identify such communities by name or documented

history, nor can we identify the editors, either by name or by extant texts of the earlier forms of the Gospel. Textual variants do occur in the manuscripts of John, but not to the extent expected in a much-edited work; and much can be known about early Christian communities, but not enough to say which ones might be Johannine in origin or development.

In sum, attractive arguments can be put forth for a late dating of John, but they are not sufficiently strong or decisive to rule out the possibility of an early date, perhaps even as early as A.D. 35 to 45. It is less important to choose a date than to realize the tenuousness with which we must do so. It is natural that proposing reasons for writing the Gospel and assigning a date for its composition will be closely related to each other, but no one should become so attached to either the purpose of writing or the date as to preclude a reevaluation of one in the face of new or conflicting evidence relating to the other.

An excellent case can be made for each of the synoptic Gospels (Matthew, Mark, and Luke) being a missionary tract to a particular audience. I believe that John, however, is written to those who were already disciples of Jesus and who were to be guided into a more profound understanding of and appreciation for the redeeming mission of Jesus. Events and discourses illustrate and illuminate rituals and doctrines that were part of the liturgy of the apostolic church and some that were practiced and accepted even before Jesus' atonement. The Gospel of John presents these materials in such detail that instruction appears to be the primary goal of the author.

All spiritual teaching can lead to conversion, and John's testimony has doubtless brought many to discipleship. But the contents of the Gospel of John are not likely to be comprehended well until a person has embraced the practices and beliefs they elucidate. The Gospel of John was written to the Saints to teach them about the Savior and his mission. The miracle of the wine at the wedding in Cana, the miracle of the loaves and fishes in feeding the five thousand men (plus women and children), and the Sermon on the Bread of Life enhance understanding of the sacred sacramental meal rather than argue for acceptance of it. The act of washing and anointing to give light and knowledge to a man blind from birth likewise is not so much to use in preaching to investigators of Christianity as to enlighten disciples in the meaning of sacred rituals. Even the conflict between Jesus and those who opposed him can be seen in the context of a great conflict in a ritual drama that culminated during the Last Supper with the dismissal of Judas. After explaining some matters relating to the great drama of his mission, Jesus concluded the discourse of the Last Supper with the statement, "But take heart, I have conquered the world." (John 16:33.)

Old Testament Allusions

Each of the Gospel authors begins his account with reference to the Old Testament, either by quotation or by allusion. John takes the reader to the introduction of the Old Testament with his opening phrase, "In the beginning . . ." Apart from observing that numerous (and often better) translations could be given for the early verses in the Gospel, John brings all of the essential elements of the Creation account into focus. God is the major reference in verses 1 and 2, and all things were brought into their present state by His Word (who also is a God). Life, light and darkness, and the coming forth of a man from the presence of God are mentioned by John, but not in the same way as in Genesis. The light and darkness of the Gospel do not simply designate day and night, for the light is the life of God in everyone who comes into the world, and the darkness was unable to capture or resist the light shining in it. John wrote of a man sent from God, John the Baptist, whose purpose was to bear witness of the light and life of the world. In verses 10 and 11, the reader notes that the world did not know its Creator and, more specifically, that his own people rejected him when he was in the world. This rejection is especially poignant, for whereas God's presence and glory were veiled in the tabernacle or temple of the Old Testament when Israel usually rejected God, in John's day "the Word also became flesh and was tabernacled in our midst, and we saw and observed his glory, glory as of an only-begotten from the Father, full of grace and truth." (John 1:14, translation mine.) People now rejected God even though they could see and associate with him.

In this spiritual account of the Creation and the mortal tabernacling of God on the earth, men become begotten children of God as they receive him and receive authority to be born through him. Thus the relationship between Genesis and John's opening verses can be summarized: Although the world was created by God and the law for men was given through Moses, the fullness of life and light within the Creation can be achieved only through Jesus Christ, who was tabernacled in flesh so that men might see his glory, accept him, and come to God through him.

Among the few incidents from Jesus' life that John selected to relate, the making of wine at a wedding in Cana (John 2:1-11) has special Old Testament connections. There is no way of knowing from the text whose wedding was being celebrated (there are numerous reasons why it could not have been Jesus' own wedding, as some have suggested), but it was apparently a grand affair lasting for many days. Extending proper hospitality to the guests was a serious obligation for a host, and to run short of wine before the end of the feast could even result in a lawsuit.[1] Knowledge of this requirement and concern for the hosts may have motivated Jesus' mother to approach him when the wine supply ran out. His response (better translated, "Of what concern is that to you and me, mother? My hour has not yet arrived," for the word translated *mother* is technically *woman,* but is more polite than the English word suggests) shows the reader that he is already thinking of a different wine that he will produce when his hour arrives.

Just as the Creation account in Genesis provided John an opportunity to teach the role of Jesus in the spiritual creation and birth of each person, so also the miracle at Cana gives a setting in which one can learn of the wine of life. Wine was a symbol of life and fertility throughout the ancient world, and its association with a wedding feast in this episode reinforces that meaning. The six stone vessels that were to contain water for purification rituals or washings are also significant in this context. A Jew was not to pray, worship, or eat, even at a public wedding banquet, without first washing off the filth and corruption of the world around him, and thus arose the necessity for having a number of large vessels available for the guests invited to this feast (stone vessels are better than ceramic ones in that they did not have to be destroyed if inadvertently touched by unclean hands). At an earthly feast for a bride and bridegroom, then, the Heavenly Bridegroom provided the necessary and desired wine from jars in which water was placed for the cleansing and purification of the mortal body. When his hour came, however, this Bridegroom would provide through the shedding of his blood the wine of eternal life and the means for cleansing the spiritual being. The number seven signifies perfection and completeness in John's writings (and elsewhere, to be sure), and some suggest that only Jesus can compensate for the incompleteness or imperfection of the *six* water vessels. (See the number *six* associated with the beast in Revelation 13:18, for example.)

Even if the reader does not wish to attribute special significance to the number of vessels, the amount of wine Jesus miraculously produced deserves attention. Each vessel had a capacity of twenty to thirty gallons, making the total in excess of 120 gallons. In the revelation of Enoch, held to be scriptural and authoritative by Christians and many Jews in Jesus' day, both before and after the distinction was made between Jew and Christian, many prophecies are found relating to the Messianic age, to the end of the world, and to the eternal destinies of men. In one of the Messianic passages, Enoch foretold of the abundant life the coming Messiah would provide in the last days: "And then shall the whole earth be tilled in righteousness, and shall all be planted with trees and be full of blessing. And all desirable trees shall be planted on it, and they shall plant vines on it: and the vine which they plant thereon shall yield wine in abundance, and as for all the seed which is sown thereon each measure (of it) shall bear a thousand, and each measure of olives shall yield ten presses of oil. And cleanse thou the earth from all oppression, and from all unrighteousness, and from all sin, and from all godlessness: and all the uncleanness that is wrought upon the earth destroy from off the earth. And all the children of men shall become righteous, and all nations shall offer adoration and shall praise Me, and all shall worship Me." (1 Enoch 10:18-21.)[2]

Even more specific in its reference to the abundant production of wine in the Messianic era is the Apocalyptic work entitled 2 Baruch. The prophet states that when the "Messiah shall begin to be revealed, the earth also shall yield its fruit ten thousandfold and on each vine there shall be a thousand branches, and each branch shall produce a thousand clusters, and each cluster produce a thousand grapes, and each grape produce a cor of wine." (2 Baruch 29:5.)[3]

The great miracle of producing a vintage wine miraculously at a wedding feast is thus a fulfillment of a Messianic prophecy, in addition to which Jesus satisfied a very real social need and presaged the greater miracle of the eternal "wine" that his own suffering would produce.

One of the best-known allusions to Old Testament history in the Gospel of John occurs immediately after Jesus miraculously fed five thousand men (plus women and children) from five barley loaves and two small fish. (John 6:1-15.) To ensure that the reader not overlook or underestimate the greatness of this accomplishment, John observed that the disciples picked up twelve baskets of leftovers from the five loaves (the number five is repeated for emphasis of the small beginning amount of food in 6:13). His is the true leaven or yeast that can make much from little, as opposed to the leaven of the Scribes and Pharisees, which could not give any increase. It is within this context that the sermon often entitled "The Bread of Life," was given.

During the night following the miraculous feeding of the thousands, Jesus walked across the Sea of Galilee to the boat in which his disciples were struggling against a strong wind. In this episode, the disciples took him into the boat, and they immediately arrived at the shore of the lake. The crowds sought Jesus the next day, and, taking boats to Capernaum, they found him in the synagogue. To their query concerning his means of travel to Capernaum (and therefore emphasizing for the reader his miraculous crossing), Jesus responded that they should not work for perishable food, but for eternal nourishment that the Son of Man alone can give. (See John 6.) Just as with the making of wine at Cana, where Jesus had performed a miracle that resulted in satisfying physical needs and at the same time conveyed a spiritual lesson, so the reader here also should expect a spiritual lesson to be taught through the recent miracle of the feast. The crowd challenged Jesus anew to perform a miracle so that they might have confidence in him, and specifically referred to the heavenly gift of manna to their fathers as the kind of miracle they expected. (From this John infers that most of the crowd in Capernaum did not really comprehend the heavenly source of the previous day's feast.) Jesus first applied a corrective to his audience, declaring that it was his Father, not Moses, who gave the heavenly bread. He then explained that he, Jesus, is the Bread of Life who had been sent from heaven as the true manna for mankind. His assertion that he had been sent from heaven by his Father caused an argument to erupt in the synagogue (6:41), not over the doctrine of the Bread of Life but concerning his supposed parentage and birthplace. He then repeated that he is the Bread of Life, adding that their fathers had eaten manna and still died (6:49). Only by partaking of his flesh could they have eternal life. The crowd became violent in response to a doctrine they considered blasphemous and cannibalistic (6:52). The sermon concluded in that hostile atmosphere with him telling them that they not only must eat his flesh but also drink his blood in order to have eternal life. Far from building upon the foundation of the Old Testament stories to learn spiritual lessons as Jesus invited them to do, the majority of his disciples—to say nothing of those not yet in that circle—henceforth refused to associate with him (6:66).

Jesus had earlier taught that Jewish unwillingness to accept the Old Testament, and specifically the writings of Moses, as a witness of his Messianic role would be a source of condemnation to them (5:45). He even went so far as to say that rejecting him meant that they were also rejecting Moses: "For if you had faith in Moses, you would also have faith in me, for he wrote concerning me. For if you do not believe in his writings, how will you believe in my words?" (5:46-47; translation mine.) It is clear that believing in the lore of the ancients involved more than simply being steeped in their traditions, but few in Jesus' day were willing to add commitment to knowledge. The indictment was given in John 1:11-12: "He came into his own creation and his own people did not accept him. But to as many as did accept him, to those who have confidence in his name, he gave authority to become children of God." (Translation mine.) The Old Testament provided analogues from which spiritual lessons could be taught, but most were unwilling to follow Jesus in his interpretation of the scriptures and to gain confidence in him.

The synagogue audience to whom Jesus spoke concerning the Bread of Life either could not or would not understand the doctrine being taught. Although a reader might suspect the latter in the way John narrated the incident, the ideas Jesus presented may simply have been too strange for their orthodox minds to grasp or accept. In John 1:11-12, the word translated *received* also included the sense of *accept, employ,* or *ascertain.* The inability of the Jews to accept Jesus, whether because of sins (3:19) or traditions (5:39-40), is restated in the Bread of Life sermon, for he declared: "No one is able to come to me unless my Father who sent me shall draw him to me" (6:44, translation mine; compare with verse 65, where the wording is "except it were given unto him of my Father"). Elsewhere in the Gospel, it is clear that rejection of God is the real reason for rejecting the One whom God had sent (5:37-38, for example).

Lack of acceptance was not always accompanied by lack of understanding, however, for the actions of Jesus' hearers often demonstrated that they knew well what he meant, even if they did not agree with him. In John 8:39-59, a group of Jews declared themselves to be children of Abraham, to which Jesus responded that if they were really children of Abraham, they would do as Abraham did, rather than try to kill him. The Jews then declared God to be their father, but Jesus countered by saying that he came from God, and that they should love him if they were of God. He further charged that they were acting as if the devil were their father, and they rejoined by name calling, saying that Jesus was a Samaritan (a strong ethnic slur) with an evil spirit. This war of words concluded with Jesus stating that Abraham had seen his day and rejoiced, and that he was ("I am") before Abraham was born. This assertion is a clear reference to the name given to Moses in the Old Testament ("I Am that I Am"—Exodus 3:14). For their conclusion to the discussion, the Jews picked up stones to kill him for blasphemy, bearing witness by such action that they had at least understood what he had said and meant.

Similarly, a group of Pharisees heard Jesus discourse about sheepfolds and shepherds after the healing of the man born blind, which will be considered below (John 9, with the discourse in John 10). The antagonism of the Pharisees toward Jesus was established in the narrative of the trial of the man whom the Savior had given sight. They not only prejudged Jesus to be a sinner, but they also excommunicated the healed man from fellowship in Judaism because he would not likewise condemn his benefactor. Despite their antipathy toward Jesus, these men listened to him as he spoke using the imagery of the pastoral world so commonly found in the Old Testament. The portrayal of the sheepfold, or a shepherd protecting the sheep from harm in a sheepfold, and the love of the real shepherd for his sheep would have brought the great shepherd king David to the minds of Jesus' Jewish audience, and the statement "I am the good shepherd" would have been a clear reference to Psalm 23 and other Old Testament passages. His clear reference to this psalm constituted a claim to his divinity ("The Lord is my shepherd"), and this identification with Deity was not missed by the Pharisees. Some argued that he was a demoniac, while others asked if a demoniac could heal a blind person. As the division grew more heated in succeeding days, some of the Jews again displayed their understanding of the matter, though not their acceptance of his claim, by taking up stones to stone him. The reason was clear, for Jesus asked them the charge behind their action. They declared it to be blasphemy, saying, "Although you are a man, you make yourself a god." (See 10:33.)

Style and Historicity

The Old Testament provides the scriptural foundation upon which the New Testament is built, and the Gospel of John does not depart from the pattern of using Old Testament prophecies and stories to establish continuity and fulfillment. When John did allude to the Old Testament, he did so primarily to illustrate spiritual analogues for prophetic words and deeds. Furthermore, incidents were not simply recorded for narrative value in the fourth Gospel as they often are elsewhere in the New Testament, for the author selected a few miracles and teachings that best illustrated the spiritual themes he wanted his readers to consider and understand. His narrative style is both more probing and more analytic than is common elsewhere in the New Testament, and there is purposeful ambiguity in his choice of words that allows a reader to find many meanings and levels of understanding in the text. This highly selective and didactic technique was not new with John; one of its best practitioners in ancient times was the Greek historian Thucydides, long recognized as the best historian of Classical Antiquity. The artist and historian combine to give form and meaning to real events beyond the skills of a less skilled writer or editor. Prejudice and ignorance have combined to prevent modern scholars from giving John similarly high marks for the historicity of his Gospel, but such judgments should not overly concern us. Negative assessments of such historians as Herodotus and Caesar have seen reversals in recent years as scholars reevaluate the canons and criteria for writing historically accurate accounts. John's work should not suffer in future reexaminations of the historicity of his Gospel, for there is growing scholarly opinion that literary artistry and symbolism are not incompatible with historical accuracy.

Light and Darkness

One of the literary characteristics of John most often observed by commentators is his use of opposites to emphasize key doctrines. Not all can be considered here, but a brief demonstration of some occurrences will illustrate the author's methods.

The first juxtaposition of opposites occurs in 1:4-5: "That which has come to be through him is life, and his life is the light of man; and his light shines in the darkness, and the darkness did not overtake it." (Translation mine.) The light is equated with the life that came into the creation through the Word, and that (see verse 9) illuminates everyone who comes into the world. The Word is a God, and the light and life he bestows in the creation are to be considered of God. The darkness therefore represents the opposites of God and life, such as death, ignorance, selfishness, and all else associated with a devilish realm. The verse quoted above states that darkness did not overtake the light, and much of John's Gospel is an exposition of that assertion. The light and darkness are in constant conflict, and the darkness is always trying to overcome the light, but Jesus, the Light of the world, clearly triumphs at the end. One episode that illustrates well the conflict between light and darkness is the healing of the blind man in John 9. When Jesus and his disciples happened upon the man who had been blind from birth, the disciples asked if sin had caused the problem, sin either by the man's parents or by himself in some premortal setting. Jesus' answer was that the man's blindness was not a result of sin (there is no indication here that sin and physical ills are never related), but that his blindness occurred so that God might work through him. Jesus continued: "It is necessary for us to accomplish the works of the One who sent us while I am in the world. I am the light of the world" (9:4-5; translation mine). Jesus then granted sight—light—to the man, first by anointing his eyes and then by sending him to wash in the pool of Siloam. (Siloam means *sent,* corresponding with John the Baptist, who was *sent* from God, Jesus who was *sent* from God, and so forth. All who are sent from God are to give sight and light to the blind, to those who are in darkness.) As soon as the man received his sight, the darkness tried to overtake him in the form of a Jewish council of Pharisees. These representatives of darkness tried to catch the man in his words, threatened him, berated him, and even called in his parents to bring pressure against him. When all failed and the man who could now perceive light held firmly to his joyful testimony of gaining sight and overcoming blindness, the council reacted by excommunicating him from their association. There was to be no light shining in *their* darkness!

Jesus heard of the man's ordeal and its result and sought him out to give even more light and truth to the one not overtaken by darkness. "Do you have faith in the Son of Man?" he asked. The man answered, "And who is he, sir, that I might have faith in him?" Jesus said to him, "You have now seen him, and he is the one who is speaking with you." The individual's final recorded response was, "I do have faith, sir," and he then fell down and worshipped him. (See 9:35-38.) By Light, light. Jesus stated that his purpose was to bring sight—light—to those who do not see, but that those who claim to see would become blind in their darkness. Some of the Pharisees heard Jesus and asked if he really thought they were blind. He answered, "If you were blind, you would have no sin, but because you claim to see, your sin remains." (See 9:41.) Now the reader understands better the opening remarks by the disciples concerning the man's blindness and sin. Because his blindness was not caused by sin, he could receive light and sight, but those who were blind because of their sins must remain in their darkness. Stated yet another way, the darkness in its sin, especially pride and greed, is not able to overcome the light in its righteousness.

Another example of light–darkness contrast is found within the context of Jesus' meeting with Nicodemus. That experience is also set in a larger contrast with another meeting, that between Jesus and the woman of Samaria. The light–darkness theme will be treated in greater detail here, and the other meeting will be given only brief attention in this essay.[4]

Jesus had been performing numerous miracles in Jerusalem (the use of imperfect indicative form of the verb in 2:23 denotes repeated activity), and many were gaining testimonies of his divinity based upon the signs they saw. One of them, a Pharisaic ruler named Nicodemus (his name means "prevail over the people," a fitting definition in view of his position in society and his role in this episode), came to him professing his knowledge that Jesus was a teacher from God, since nobody could do such marvelous deeds unless God be with him. Nicodemus actually used the editorial "we," as if he were including others in his declaration of knowledge, but he may also have been trying to impart a greater sense of personal authority by implying that he represented a group rather than only himself. John mentions that Nicodemus came to Jesus "at night," and many have assumed that he did so out of fear that his peers would see him, or for some other similar reason. That may be so, but reason will be given later to show an alternative way of understanding that phrase.

Because miracles and signs are not a proper base upon which testimonies are founded, Jesus invited Nicodemus to be born "from above" and become able to really *see* the kingdom of God (the reader should perceive a foreshadowing of the experience with the blind man in John 9, which has been treated already). Nicodemus turned Jesus' spiritual invitation back to an earthly interpretation, asking how a man can enter into the womb a second time to be reborn. Jesus patiently explained that one must be born of water and spirit in order to enter the kingdom of God. He further challenged Nicodemus to begin thinking in spiritual rather than physical terms, repeating his statement that a man must be born from above. The ambiguity of verse 8 can be seen only in the Greek, but the word translated *wind* can also be *spirit.* Nicodemus had a choice of hearing Jesus say that the wind blows where it wishes, and one may not know the origin or destiny of the wind, just that he is blown by it; or, the Spirit breathes wherever it desires, and a man may not know whence the Spirit comes nor where it will lead him, just that he hears the voice of the Spirit. Thus, said Jesus, is everyone who is blown by the wind or begotten of the Spirit. Nicodemus was unable to pursue the matter or unwilling to make such an obvious choice, so he begged out of the conversation by declaring, "I don't understand these things at all." (See 3:9.) It should not be surprising, in view of Nicodemus's earlier declaration that Jesus was a teacher from God and his subsequent inability or unwillingness to grasp even the rudiments of spiritual rebirth, that Jesus should give him a stinging rebuke: "Are you the teacher of Israel, and yet you do not understand these things." (See 3:10.) One does not know precisely what Nicodemus's position was, but Jesus called him *the* teacher, not *a* teacher, of Israel. The chastisement continued: "Verily I say to you that what we know we speak and what we have seen we bear witness, but you [plural] do not receive our testimony." (See 3:11.) Nicodemus had begun the conversation with a declaration of knowledge based on what he had seen, but his knowledge was not from God, as he had inferred, nor was it spiritual knowledge about Jesus, even though Jesus was the declared object of his knowledge. Jesus continued explaining to Nicodemus that he spoke of heavenly, not earthly, knowledge, and that he was qualified to speak of such knowledge because he had descended from heaven and would be raised up again. He likewise sought to raise man to eternal life through spiritual knowledge, but although "the light had come into the world, men loved the darkness rather than the light, for their deeds were evil." (See 3:19.)

The meeting with Nicodemus was finally placed within the context of light and darkness: being reborn through water and the Spirit brings one to the light. It is surely obvious now that Nicodemus had come to Jesus not only "at night" but also "in the dark." Unfortunately, he preferred to remain in the darkness of spiritual ignorance rather than come to the light of spiritual insight through being born from above. Even more tragic than his darkened condition was the claim he brought of being able to see—of being in the light. As Jesus would later tell the Pharisees after healing the blind man, "Although you claim to see, your sin (and your blindness) remains." (See 9:41.)

Nicodemus came declaring knowledge of Jesus as a teacher from God, and from all prospective indications he was a candidate for Christian baptism. We might compare him to those who seek out Latter-day Saint missionaries, declaring that they know Joseph Smith to be a prophet, for nobody could translate the Book of Mormon or establish such a religious community without God's help. However laudable such assertions, they are not sufficient for conversion without spiritual confirmation, and no number of external proofs or social benefits will compensate for the heavenly revelation. Nicodemus would not make the transition from physical to spiritual in his approach to Jesus, although he at first seemed a likely candidate to do so.

Jesus' next encounter in John's Gospel was with a person who seemed to be almost an exact opposite of Nicodemus in spiritual background and capacity. Because this person was a woman, traditional avenues of educational and religious training were not open to her; because she was a Samaritan, her social status was that of an outcast in Jewish society; and because she had lived with five men before her present male companion, her moral standing was considered the worst imaginable. We cannot easily think of a less likely candidate for spiritual conversion under normal circumstances than such a person, and her meeting with Jesus did not begin on an auspicious note.

At midday, as Jesus and his disciples were passing through Samaria to Galilee (itself an unusual route for Jews, who usually went around Samaria rather than through it), Jesus sat on the edge of Jacob's well while the disciples went to the nearby village to purchase food. The woman came to the well with her bucket attached to a rope in order to draw water from the deep well. She was shocked at Jesus' request for a drink, surmising either from his clothes or his accent that he was a Jew, and knowing that Jews did not associate with Samaritans. He responded to her surprise with the observation that if she knew who he was, she would ask *him* for living water. The reader already knows that Jesus was not referring to well water, but to spiritual refreshment. The woman, however, who had no pretensions to such matters as Nicodemus had, countered by noting that Jesus had no bucket or rope, and, in case he hadn't noticed, the well was deep. She taunted him, asking if he was greater than Jacob, who gave the well from which men and animals had drunk water for centuries. Jesus answered that the water he promised would quench thirst forever, and it would, in fact, be a free-flowing spring and not simply a well. The woman still could not grasp the spiritual level of his comments, but she did ask for the water so that she would not have to return often to the well with her bucket. Having finally captured her interest in his offer of spiritual water, Jesus told her to go home and bring back her husband, but she demurred, stating that she was not married. Then the revelation from Jesus of her immorality followed, after which the woman expressed a surprising interest in matters relating to worship. At the conclusion of that portion of the dialogue, she even expressed the hope that when the Messiah did appear, he would teach everything to the people. Jesus then identified himself to her as the Messiah, following which she departed for the village to announce him as the Messiah, since he had made known her deeds (4:28-29).

The terms *light* and *darkness* are not used in this pericope, but there can be no doubt that the woman came to the light out of darkness in a way that Nicodemus had refused to do. Both Nicodemus and the Samaritan brought a bias toward physical rather than spiritual interpretations of their conversations with Jesus, and both had misconceptions about what was important in religious understanding (he regarding miracles, and she concerning the place of worship). The fact that Nicodemus came to Jesus and initiated a religious conversation, coupled with his extensive training and prominent position as the religious teacher of Jews, should have made him susceptible to Jesus' invitation to think spiritually. Likewise, the deficiencies in the very same areas would seem to rule out the Samaritan woman's susceptibility toward spiritual matters, but receptivity to spiritual light is not determined by worldly criteria such as status or education.

The light–darkness contrast in John occurs elsewhere, but enough has been presented to show how it is woven like a literary thread through the tapestry of the fourth Gospel. Other threads are likewise found in John's testimony of Jesus Christ, but consideration of them must be deferred to another time and place.

Conclusion

This brief essay has dealt with two significant aspects of John's Gospel, the Old Testament foundation on which it is based and the use of opposites to emphasize particular doctrines. Both could have been treated in greater length, and numerous other themes deserve consideration as well. Another major focus in John is on the sacred ordinances of Christianity, which are emphasized greatly in the later chapters of John. Much of this will be discussed in subsequent chapters of this book. The ancient world was suffused with ritual activities, all growing out of and centering on a cosmic drama of creation and renewal. Scholarly awareness of the importance of early Christian ritual has increased in recent decades, and John's Gospel should be read and evaluated from that perspective as well.

The richness of John's Gospel in its multiple levels of meaning should explain in part why this work has been the most popular in the New Testament for commentators of a wide range of religious and theological persuasions. It was the first Gospel to attract a commentator (one of the so-called Gnostics), and it has enjoyed the uninterrupted attention of writers ever since. Such attention, even if occasionally misguided and faulty in scope, is deserving of the testimony of this ancient apostle. In any study of John, however, the reader must be aware of the ancient author's own stated purpose in selecting and including particular sayings and events of Jesus in his account:

> There are many other signs (wonders) which Jesus did before His disciples, which have not been written in this book; but these things have been written in order that you might have faith that Jesus is the Christ, the Son of God, and that because you believe you might have life through His name. (John 20:30-31, translation mine.)
>
> Now there are also many other things which Jesus did, which, if each one should be written, I do not believe the world itself could contain the books that would be written. (John 21:25, translation mine.)

NOTES

1. Leon Morris, *Reflections on the Gospel of John: The Word Was Made Flesh, John 1-5* (Grand Rapids, Mich.: Baker Book House, 1986), p. 72.

2. R. H. Charles, *The Apocrypha and Pseudepigrapha of the Old Testament* (Oxford: Oxford University Press, 1913), 2:195.

3. The translator states that a *cor* is about 120 gallons. Ibid., pp. 497-98.

4. See Stephen D. Ricks, "No Prophet Is Accepted in His Own Country," chapter 12, in this volume.

7

THE PROLOGUE OF JOHN
(John 1:1-18)

J. Philip Schaelling

The Prologue of John (John 1:1-18) has long been favored as a jewel in the crown of biblical scholarship. One author has written: "If John has been described as the pearl of great price among the NT writings, then one may say that the Prologue is the pearl within this Gospel. In her comparison of Augustine's and Chrysostom's exegesis of the prologue, M. A. Aucoin points out that both held that it is beyond the power of man to speak as John does in the Prologue. . . . All these attestations of sublimity, however, do not remove the fact that the eighteen verses of the Prologue contain for the exegete a number of bewildering textual, critical, and interpretative problems."[1]

Modern revelation can help us with some of these problems, but the Prologue of John is still one of the most intriguing, exciting, challenging, and absolutely transcendent passages ever written. Let no one feel that these eighteen verses carry no depth. They not only have depth—they transcend both time and space to reveal to us the purpose of Christ's ministry. These verses crystallize, in the testimony of one who knew, not only our heritage but also our eternal destiny as children of the living God.

John is a witness. His stress is on those things he had seen and experienced himself: "That which was from the beginning, which we have heard, which we have seen with our eyes, which we have

J. Philip Schaelling is an instructor at the LDS Institute of Religion in McAllen, Texas.

looked at and our hands have touched—this we proclaim concerning the Word of life.'' (1 John 1:1, NIV.) The first eighteen verses of his Gospel serve as a prologue. Before John started his actual story, he wanted to give a preview to define the parameters of his account. His purpose was not to catalog all of the deeds and works of the Savior during His mortal life: "If they should be written every one, I suppose that even the world itself could not contain the books that should be written." (John 21:25.) The Gospel of John is not a hodgepodge of randomly remembered recollections, but a carefully constructed historical account with design and purpose. "That which we have seen and heard declare we unto you, that ye also may have fellowship with us: and truly our fellowship is with the Father, and with his Son Jesus Christ." (1 John 1:3.) A fundamental purpose of John's Gospel is to show us how we can have fellowship with the Father and the Son. The purposes of the Prologue are to summarize that process of achieving fellowship so that we will not miss it as we proceed through the account of the Savior's ministry, and to set the stage for this story of eternal sweep by introducing us to the Savior in his eternal context.

Setting the Stage

"In the beginning" (1:1). This phrase is identical in the Greek of the Gospel of John with the beginning of the book of Genesis in the Septuagint. There are many "beginnings" in our span of forever. Though we have always existed, there was a "beginning" when we became children of our Heavenly Father; there was a "beginning" when the great premortal council was held and plans for this earth were laid; there was a "beginning" as the creation of this earth was initiated.

"Was the Word" (1:1). The word *was* does not do justice to the Greek verb tense. In Greek, the author could have chosen from either the *aorist* or the *imperfect* verb tense. While the aorist refers to a single, completed occurrence, the imperfect defines an ongoing, continuous state. The use of the imperfect tense here defines that which lies beyond time. "In the beginning, place it where you may, the Word already existed. In other words, the

Logos is before time, eternal."[2] John is telling us that when time began, the Word not only already existed, but the Word already existed in a timeless state, and existed as the "Word."

Next we must deal with "Word." In verse 14, the "Word" is identified as the Savior. Would it not have been easier to have said, "In the beginning was Jesus Christ"? Why use the personification? What was John trying to tell us by identifying the Savior as the "Word"? In the English translation, "Word" is probably the best translation of *logos,* but it is also a very limited translation. *Logos* is a word replete with nuances and great depth. It can refer to a single word, a phrase, a discussion, or even a whole book. Hugh Nibley uses it in this broad sense when he translates John 1:1 as, "In the beginning was the *Logos* [counsel, discussion], and the *Logos* was in the presence of God, and all things were done according to it."[3] Many useful articles and books are available that discuss *logos.* For our purposes, and for the sake of brevity, let us simply note a few aspects of this intriguing word.

1. *Logos* "is never the mere word as an assemblage of sounds, but the word as determined by a meaning and conveying a meaning."[4] In other words, it is the outward form that expresses the inner thought.

2. While *logos* does not represent the mere "assemblage of sounds," neither does it represent the thought itself. *Logos* is tangible, whether it represents "a phrase or sentence, or a prolonged discourse, or even a book."[5]

3. *Logos* from God is always dynamic. It does not just exist as a static lump. "The Word is seen to be a heavenly force which creatively accomplishes its work on earth."[6] Isaiah referred to the word of God in this same way when he said: "For as the rain cometh down, and the snow from heaven, and returneth not thither, but watereth the earth, and maketh it bring forth and bud, that it may give seed to the sower, and bread to the eater: so shall my word be that goeth forth out of my mouth: it shall not return unto me void, but it shall accomplish that which I please, and it shall prosper in the thing whereto I sent it." (Isa. 55:10-11.) *Logos* from God always has purpose and always has power.

"In the beginning, the *logos* already existed." *The reason for the personification is to help us understand that Christ was to be the outward expression of the Father's inner nature, having the same purpose and the same power.* This principle helps us to better comprehend the Savior's statement to Philip, "He that hath seen me hath seen the Father" (John 14:9) and gives new depth to the following passage: "Believest thou not that I am in the Father, and the Father in me? the words that I speak unto you I speak not of myself: but the Father that dwelleth in me, he doeth the works. Believe me that I am in the Father, and the Father in me." (John 14:10-11.)

John's introduction helps us understand that Jesus, in fulfilling his destiny in the eternal plan of salvation, was the *dynamic* expression of the Father's inner being. He was and is, since before the beginning, the actor and doer of the Father's will, filled with his purpose and power. While on earth, he was the *visible* expression of his Father's inner nature. If we wish to learn more about the Father, we merely need to learn more about his Son. Through Joseph Smith much of this concept was revealed in modern times: "He was the Word, even the messenger of salvation." (D&C 93:8.) The Plan of Salvation is eternal, and for us, the embodiment of that plan is Jesus Christ.

"And the Word was with God" (1:1). "The word *with* (in the Greek), while emphasizing the communion of the Logos with God, yet safeguards the idea of his individual personality: it expresses *nearness* combined with the sense of *movement towards* God, and so indicates an active relationship. The Logos and God do not simply exist side by side, but are on terms of living intercourse, and such fellowship implies separate personality."[7]

"And the Word was God" (1:1). In the Greek, the word *God* comes first in this phrase, which gives it special emphasis. Though it comes first, it is predicative and without an article. This means that John wanted us to know that in the beginning, the *logos* had already achieved Godhood: He had developed within himself the divine nature. By this we do not merely mean that he developed *a* divine nature. The absence of the article implies that he has acquired *the very same* character and divine attributes as *The God* with whom he associated in the previous phrase. The emphatic arrangement of this word gives special stature to the *logos*. Not only was Jesus to be the one who would actively implement the plan of our Father, not only did he have a close and personal fellowship with the Father, but "in the beginning" the Savior had already developed the very same attributes and character of the Father, thus attaining Godhood.

"The same was in the beginning with [the] God" (1:2). I have placed a bracketed *the* here simply to mirror John's emphasis; the word *the* exists in the Greek text. John has wanted to communicate clearly that while the *logos* has developed the qualities of the Father, he is also a distinct and separate individual. The repetition and structure of this phrase is so emphatic that it may imply an attempt by John to address any misunderstanding or confusion on the doctrine of the trinity within the early church. This is a very difficult thing to translate because the absence or presence of articles (that is, *the*) in English does not communicate the same thing as it does in Greek.

Thus we can see that there are three things that John wanted to establish in these first two verses:

1. Jesus Christ was to be the outward and dynamic expression of both his Father's essence and his Father's will.

2. Jesus was eminently suited to this task, for he had developed the very same character and attributes as His Father.

3. We should not confuse the issue and think that they are the same individual. They are clearly separate.

Achieving Fellowship

After John established the majesty of the *logos* in its premortal eternal state, he gave us a brief outline of how the *logos* fits into the plan of salvation. This is divided into three stages:

1. John 1:3-9: The existence of light as a fundamental part of the *logos,* which he shares freely with all who come into the world.

2. John 1:10-13: Our free agency to accept him or reject him, and the right and power given to those who accept him to become children of God.

3. John 1:14-17: The actual achievement of that relationship, together with an emphasis on the Savior as role model and the very embodiment of those principles which develop our capacity to be sons and daughters.

The Light

"And the light shineth in darkness; and the darkness comprehended it not" (1:5). As soon as John identified *light* with *logos,* he informed us that a great rivalry exists in the universe between the *logos* and "the Prince of Darkness." *Light* and *darkness* are active elements and are personified, as was *logos.* John did this to help us identify certain basic principles that pertain to the individuals thus personified. In this very powerful verse, he encapsulated one of the fundamental dramas of his entire narrative, the struggle that inherently exists between good and evil.

In King James's time, the word *comprehend* could mean either "to seize, grasp, lay hold of, catch," or "to grasp, take in, or apprehend with the senses."[8] The Greek word from which it is translated has the basic meaning of seizing with hostile intent, or overtaking. In one verb voice, not used here, it can also be used to express an ability to understand or perceive. Certainly it is imperative that we develop the capacity to perceive the light. But in the only other place where John used this word, it was again in relationship to darkness, and assumes the active role of "to seize with hostile intent, to overtake": "Walk while ye have the light, lest darkness come upon you." (John 12:35.) "In these cases the sense cannot be doubtful. The darkness comes down upon, enwraps men. As applied to light, this sense includes the further notion of overwhelming, eclipsing. The relation of darkness to light is one of essential antagonism."[9] Another interesting contrast is offered in this verse. The verb *shineth* is given in the timeless present tense, while the verb *comprehended* is in a tense that is used for a given point in time. The effect of this contrast is to say that this dispelling of darkness is an inherent and enduring quality of light and of the One who is personified as light. On the other hand, there was a time when the darkness, or the one of whom it is a personification, attempted to seize and overcome the light. It refers to a specific attempt, a single occurrence, not an ongoing, timeless quality. *John was foreshadowing a main theme of his Gospel: a record of the specific time when, as the light shone in the darkness that had come upon this world, the Prince of Darkness attempted and failed to overcome and extinguish that light.* A major effort of his Gospel is to mirror and witness the dynamic conflict between light and dark which was to culminate in the Savior's dynamic victory.

"That was the true Light, which lighteth every man that cometh into the world" (1:9). It is as though we are all in a huge arena, in total darkness, searching for a way out. Some panic, some give up, many search aimlessly, all are lost. Suddenly someone opens a door and the light shines in. *He* is the light that shines in the darkness! Now we can find our way out! Now we can go back home! He shows us the way and helps us be sensitive to the light. He also places within each of us our own little light, so that we can always see in the darkness. But it works only if we follow that light: "And he that repents not, from him shall be taken even the light which he has received." (D&C 1:33.) *The possession of light gives us the ability to see our way out of the darkness of this world and find our way back to our Father in heaven.* This understanding of light harbors intriguing implications in the definition of *intelligence* as found in D&C 93:36-39.

Becoming Children of God

"And the world knew him not" (1:10). The word translated *knew* can mean either *perceive, realize* or *acknowledge, recognize.*[10]

"And his own received him not" (1:11). The word translated *received,* in this context, means *to accept.*[11]

"To them gave he power" (1:12). The word translated *power* "does not describe mere ability, but legitimate, rightful authority, derived from a competent source which includes the idea of power."[12]

"To become the sons of God, even to them that believe" (1:12). The word *tekna,* here translated as *sons,* is a neuter form and simply means *children,* without reference to gender.[13] A contrast is here drawn between the first phrase and the last by the use of different verb tenses. The phrase "to become" is in the aorist tense, meaning that it is a specific event. The phrase "to them that believe" is in the present tense, implying an ongoing condition. The thrust of the passage is that becoming a child of God occurs only to those for whom belief has become an ongoing part of their very nature.

A word or two about the word *believe* is also appropriate. In the New Testament, the words *belief* and *faith* are used as translations for a single Greek word, *pistis. Pistis* in this sense is a "faith in the Divinity that lays special emphasis on trust in his power and his nearness to help, in addition to being convinced that he exists and that his revelations or disclosures are true."[14] This describes what happens when we trust him to such an extent that we simply do whatever he tells us and refuse to do that which he tells us not to do. It is to such people that he gives both the right and the power to become "children of God."

"Which were born . . . of God" (1:13). Verse 13 amplifies the principle of belief or faith and causes the term to apply only to those who so thoroughly reconstruct their lives that they are no longer children of this world, but children of God. Elder Bruce R. McConkie described it as follows: "Those who are sons of God (meaning the Father) are persons who, first, receive the gospel, join the true Church, obtain the priesthood, marry for eternity, and walk in obedience to the whole gospel law. They are then adopted into the family of Jesus Christ, become joint-heirs with him, and consequently receive, inherit, and possess equally with him in glorious exaltation in the kingdom of his Father."[15]

"And the Word was made flesh" (1:14). As a mortal man, the Lord Jesus was subject to all of the trials, tribulations, temptations, and vicissitudes of mortality.[16]

"And we beheld his glory" (1:14). The word translated *beheld* means more than merely to see. It means that one has carefully observed. For this reason, one translator, attempting to bring out the full meaning, has rendered it: "And we gazed with attentive and careful regard and spiritual perception."[17]

"The glory as of the only begotten of the Father" (1:14). *Glory* is being used here to describe the relationship that John had observed to exist between the Father and the Son. The Greek word used here, *doxa,* has as one of its base meanings *opinion.* When applied to another, it means "the opinion which others have of one, estimation, repute." [18] In the New Testament it is also used to represent radiance or splendor, but its use here refers to the esteem that the Father holds for His Son. John wrote that during the mortal life of Christ, he (John), along with others, was able to observe the special relationship that existed between the Father and the Son, along with the esteem and honor given to Jesus by the Father. This is reinforced often in his account: "For the Father judgeth no man, but hath committed all judgment unto the Son: that all men should honour the Son, even as they honour the Father" (5:22-23). "As the Father hath life in himself; so hath he given to the Son to have life in himself; and hath given him authority to execute judgment also, because he is the Son of man" (5:26-27). "The Father hath not left me alone; for I do always those things that please him" (8:29). "I and my Father are one" (10:30). "Father, I will that they also, whom thou hast given me, be with me where I am; that they may behold my glory, which thou hast given me: for thou lovedst me before the foundation of the world" (17:24).

In the first verse of his Gospel, John tells us about the strong and special relationship between the Father and the Son. In this phrase he desires us to know that he personally witnessed this special relationship.

"Full of grace and truth" (1:14). When John observed that the Savior is *full* of grace and truth, it of course means that nothing exists in him that is not composed of these elements. There is no untruth in him, and there is nothing that does not partake of grace. The Greek word translated as *grace* is a challenging word to grasp, with many meanings and nuances. In the secular usage of this period, this word *charis* was employed as "a fixed term for demonstrations of a ruler's favour." [19] In earlier antiquity it represented "the 'favour' of the gods." [20] Some help in understanding this verse is given in verse 17 as John contrasted the law of Moses with the grace and truth that comes by Jesus Christ. The law of Moses was strict justice. Through Christ we receive the benefit of his love for us as a free gift. Though we must qualify for that gift, we in no way earn it; this gift is so glorious that it is far beyond our capacity to earn. In describing the Savior as being "full of grace," John wanted us to know that there exists in him nothing but pure, selfless love for us, which he gives freely and with joy whenever he can. Being "in His grace" also implies that we have special access to him and that he is readily available to listen to our needs.

"And of his fulness have all we received, and grace for grace" (1:16). This phrase described the process by which we acquire the same qualities and character as the Savior. It can be translated to mean that we can receive either "grace upon grace" or "grace in exchange for grace." In the Doctrine and Covenants we find this same phrase applied to Jesus and including both meanings. "And I, John, saw that he received not of the fulness at the first, but received *grace for grace;* And he received not of the fulness at first, but continued from *grace to grace,* until he received a fulness." (D&C 93:12-13, emphasis added.)

In the phrase "grace for grace," we understand that as we reach out with love and joy to bless freely those around us, we are blessed freely and with joy from above. As we give grace, we receive grace.

In addition, we *move* from "grace to grace." The Lord does not wait until we have developed the quality of grace fully before bestowing blessings upon us, but lets us move from level to level. We are always in his favor, but as we develop we are blessed accordingly. When no feeling exists within us except the desire to bless and bring joy, then he can reach out and bestow upon us that fellowship which brings a fullness of joy. "Neither pray I for these alone, but for them also which shall believe on me through their word; that they all may be one; as thou, Father, art in me, and I in thee, that they also may be one in us." (John 17:20-21.)

As we have seen, verses 3 to 17 of chapter 1 take us through our eternal development in three stages:

1. Our relationship with the Light,

2. The rebirth and our use of agency, and

3. The process of "grace for grace" as we partake of his fullness.

The same sequence is mirrored in the actual record of John's Gospel. It begins with the witness to the Light (John the Baptist) that is so strongly stressed in verses 6 to 9 of the Prologue, then continues with the great rebirth discourse given to Nicodemus. John expands this with illustrations of how some reject the light and others accept it with faith. This section makes up a large portion of his record and includes stories of great faith as well as some of the great discourses and discussions with the Pharisees and Sadducees. John vividly portrays the love and compassion of the Savior and his greatness as a teacher, as he records the Savior's discourses on the choices that exist for all of us in this world. This section is followed by the only detailed account of the proceedings of the Last Supper, in which the Savior revealed to his disciples the great law of love: the foundation of grace. The structural organization of the Prologue mirrors the structural organization of John's Gospel.

Knowing the Father Through Christ

"No man hath seen God at any time" (1:18). Joseph Smith added, "except he hath borne record of the Son" (JST, 1:19). President Spencer W. Kimball noted: "It is noteworthy that the Father, God, Elohim came to the earth upon each necessary occasion to introduce the Son to a new dispensation, to a new people; then Jesus Christ, the Son, carried forward his work. This has happened again in our own dispensation when both separate beings, the Father and the Son, came again to the earth in person and appeared unto man. This holy occurrence was described by the devout and prepared young man who was the principal recipient of the vision."[21] This highlights the point brought out in verse 1, that we are to learn of the Father through the Son.

"The only begotten Son" (1:18). The oldest and best ancient manuscript read, "the only begotten God."[22]

"Which is in the bosom of the Father" (1:18). "The image is

used of the closest and tenderest of human relationships, of mother and child (Num. xi. 12), and of husband and wife (Deut. xiii. 6), and also of friends reclining side by side at a feast (comp. xiii. 23), and so describes the ultimate fellowship of love. The exact form of the words is remarkable. The phrase is not strictly 'in the bosom,' but 'into the bosom.' Thus there is the combination (as it were) of rest and motion, of a continuous relation, with a realization of it."[23]

"He hath declared him" (1:18). The Greek word translated *declared* means to "explain, interpret, tell, report, describe."[24] John completed the Prologue with a restatement of the thought with which he began it. The purpose of Christ's ministry was to reveal to us the essential character of the Father and to dynamically bring about his plan. Through Jesus, we can learn about the Father's plan, discover his design for our personal destiny, see his power, and feel his love for us. Jesus is the visible personification of the Father. *Jesus is the Word.*[25]

NOTES

1. Raymond E. Brown, *The Gospel According to John, I-XII,* Anchor Bible 29 (Garden City, N.Y.: Doubleday & Co., 1966), p. 18.

2. M. Dods, "The Gospel of St. John," *The Expositor's Greek Testament,* W. Robertson Nicoll, ed. (Grand Rapids, Mich.: Eerdmans, 1974), 1:683.

3. Hugh Nibley, *Nibley on the Timely and the Timeless* (Provo, Utah: Religious Studies Center, Brigham Young University, 1978), p. 282.

4. C. H. Dodd, *The Interpretation of the Fourth Gospel* (Cambridge: Cambridge University Press, 1965), p. 263.

5. Ibid.

6. O. Procksch, "Lego," in *Theological Dictionary of the New Testament,* G. Kittel, ed., 10 vols. (Grand Rapids, Mich.: Eerdmans, 1967), 4:98.

7. G. H. C. Macgregor, "The Gospel of John" in *The Moffatt New Testament Commentary,* James Moffatt, ed. (London: Hodder and Stoughton, 1949), 4:4.

8. *The Oxford English Dictionary* (Oxford: Clarendon Press, 1933), 2:741.

9. Brooke Foss Westcott, *The Gospel According to St. John* (London: John Murray, 1908), 1:9.

10. Walter Bauer, *A Greek-English Lexicon of the New Testament,* trans. W. F. Arndt and F. W. Gingrich, 2nd ed. (Chicago: University of Chicago Press, 1979), p. 161.

11. Ibid., p. 619.

12. Westcott, p. 16.

13. Bauer, p. 808.

14. Ibid., p. 665.

15. Bruce R. McConkie, *Doctrinal New Testament Commentary,* 3 vols. (Salt Lake City: Bookcraft, 1965-73), 1:74.

16. Ibid., p. 75.

17. Kenneth S. Wuest, *The New Testament: An Expanded Translation* (Grand Rapids, Mich.: Eerdmans, 1961), p. 209.

18. Henry George Liddell and Robert Scott, *A Greek-English Lexicon* (Oxford: Clarendon Press, 1925), p. 444.

19. Gerhard Friedrich, "Charis," *Theological Dictionary of the New Testament* (Grand Rapids, Mich.: Eerdmans, 1974), 9:375.

20. Ibid., 9:374.

21. Spencer W. Kimball, *Conference Report,* October 1977, p. 112.

22. Dods, p. 691.

23. Westcott, p. 28.

24. Bauer, p. 275.

25. For a discussion of the mission of John the Baptist, see Robert J. Matthews, "A Voice in the Wilderness: An Interview with John the Baptist," chapter 9 in this volume.

8

THE BIRTH AND CHILDHOOD
OF THE MESSIAH
(Matthew 1-2; Luke 1-2)

ROBERT L. MILLET

Inasmuch as the four Gospels are testimonies of the Lord Jesus Christ, it is appropriate that Matthew and Luke should begin their faithful narratives with a brief discussion of the events associated with the miraculous birth and early childhood of our Savior. These earliest scenes are integral parts of the written testimonies of Matthew and Luke; they bear vital testimony of the hand of the Almighty in setting the stage for the greatest mortal life and ministry in all eternity. Elder Bruce R. McConkie has written: "A God [was] coming to earth and everything connected with his birth and life and ministry and resurrection and ascension to eternal glory—everything!—must be perfect. It must conform to what the prophets have foreseen, foreknown, and foretold. . . . Truly Omnipotent Wisdom had left nothing to chance. A God was coming into the world, and the world must be ready for his Advent."[1]

Whose Son Is He?

To the casual reader of the Bible, few things are more meaningless than the "begat" sections. In fact, many of us are prone to skip lightly through (or perhaps skip entirely) those chapters or portions of chapters that trace genealogical lines. To do so, however,

---

Robert L. Millet is assistant professor of ancient scripture and New Testament area coordinator at Brigham Young University.

is to miss an important message of the writer. Matthew, for example, was a student of Jewish history and culture and was careful to discuss the ancestry of Jesus, since he was addressing his Gospel to a people who needed to understand the position of Jesus of Nazareth as a son of David, a son of Abraham, and the rightful king of Israel. Comparisons are frequently made between the genealogies of Matthew (1:1-17) and Luke (3:23-38). Elder James E. Talmage has given us to understand that "Matthew's account is that of the royal lineage, establishing the order of sequence among the legal successors to the throne of David, while the account given by Luke is a personal pedigree, demonstrating descent from David without adherence to the line of legal succession to the throne through primogeniture or nearness of kin."[2]

Genealogies help to establish one's place within the house of Israel, to establish tribal identity. "Another aspect of genealogies," writes one scholar of the New Testament, "may be related to the biblical concept of collective personality: if something of the ancestor is thought to reappear in the descendant, then one's genealogy may reflect on one's character, personality, or traits. Related to this is the tendency to narrate stories about famous ancestors or descendants within the framework of a genealogy, so that history becomes an expansion of a genealogy."[3] Finally, we might with appropriateness state that the genealogy of Jesus is far more than a record of man's biological productivity: it is evidence and demonstration of God's providence, a reflection of the Almighty working out his great and wondrous plan of salvation through history.

The Announcement of the Forerunner

As indicated earlier, all things must be in readiness for the coming of the Mortal Messiah. All things must bear record of his divine Sonship. Even the circumstances surrounding the birth of Christ's chief witness and forerunner were miraculous and wondrous. Luke chronicles (1:5-25) the inspiring story of the angelic appearance to the aged Zacharias and the miraculous birth of John to the faithful Elisabeth, a noble woman who was childless and "well stricken in years." The name of John, *Yohanan* in Hebrew, was especially appropriate: it meant literally "Jehovah is gracious." The details of the announcement of John's birth and the events surrounding his naming, circumcision, and setting apart will be treated in a subsequent chapter.[4]

The Annunciation

A wealth of information is contained in the four short verses in Matthew (1:18-21) dealing with the preparation of Mary and Joseph for the conception and birth of Jesus. We simply cannot praise too highly the one chosen to bear the Son of God. "There was only one Christ," Elder Bruce R. McConkie has written, "and there is only one Mary. Each was noble and great in preexistence, and each was foreordained to the ministry he or she performed. We cannot but think that the Father would choose the greatest female spirit to be the mother of his Son, even as he chose the male spirit like unto him to be the Savior."[5] Luke preserved the details concerning the visit of Gabriel to Mary and the subsequent Annunciation (*the* announcement), but Matthew wrote simply that Mary, engaged to Joseph, was "found with child of the Holy Ghost" (1:18). It was Nephi who was instructed by the Spirit of the Lord concerning the condescension of God the Father—that the Almighty Elohim would step down from his divine throne, join with one who was finite and mortal, and beget a son, an Only Begotten Son in the flesh. (1 Ne. 11:16-25.) In the words of Alma, Jesus Christ "shall be born of Mary, at Jerusalem, . . . she being a virgin, a precious and chosen vessel, who shall be overshadowed and conceive by the power of the Holy Ghost, and bring forth a son, yea, even the Son of God." (Alma 7:10.)

One can only imagine the agony and torment of uncertainty and doubt that must have filled the soul of Joseph the carpenter. Matthew teaches us that Joseph was a *just man* and hence was "not willing to make her [Mary] a publick example," choosing rather to "put her away privily." (Matt. 1:19.) Why was Joseph called a just man? First, he was just and upright in that he showed kindness and mercy toward Mary between the time that Mary was "found with child of the Holy Ghost" and the time that he learned in a vision[6] that Mary was involved in a marvelous part of the divine drama whereby the Son of God would soon take upon himself a "tabernacle of clay." The unwritten part of this story is simply that Joseph showed mercy toward his beloved Mary, who was now, it seemed (what else was there to believe?), expecting someone else's child. Joseph chose not to accuse Mary publicly of immorality and thus not to subject her to trial.

Joseph's status as a just man is seen in his awe and respect for the plan of salvation, which he recognized in unfolding fashion in the conception of the Promised Messiah within his espoused wife. Thus the message of the angel in the vision—"Fear not to take unto thee Mary thy wife: for that which is conceived in her is of the Holy Ghost" (Matt. 1:20)—was intended to assure the carpenter that a part of God's plan did include Joseph's marriage to Mary, and that he too had a significant role in the long-awaited Messianic era that was about to be ushered in.

Finally, some students of the Gospels have proposed that Joseph was a just man in that he was obedient to the law. Raymond Brown has written concerning this possibility: "The particular law that would have concerned Joseph was Deut. 22:20-21, which deals with the case of a young woman who is brought to her husband's home and found not to be a virgin. Deuteronomy required the stoning of the adultress; but in a less severe legal system the command to 'purge the evil from the midst of you' could have been met by divorcing her. In this interpretation, while Joseph's sense of obedience to the Law forced him in conscience to divorce Mary, his unwillingness to expose her to public disgrace led him to proceed without accusation of serious crime. He was upright *but* also merciful."[7]

In summary, we conclude that of the three explanations considered, the first two understand the expression in verse 19 to mean "a just man and *therefore* not willing to make her a public example," while the latter means "a just man, *but* unwilling to make her a public example." Also worthy of note is the simple but important fact that within two short chapters we find Joseph receiving four separate visions in which he was given instructions regarding the birth and protection of Jesus and Mary. Obviously his soul was in tune with the Infinite. This is as it must be, for the step-father of our Lord had to be capable and ready to receive divine direction.

The Christmas Story

In what has become the traditional "Christmas Story," Luke records (2:1-20) the significant scenes surrounding the birth of Jesus. The drama begins with Joseph and his wife Mary, who was now in the advanced stage of her pregnancy, leaving their home in Nazareth. They traveled a distance of from eighty to ninety miles to Bethlehem, "to enroll their names as members of the house of David in a census which had been ordered by the Emperor Augustus. In the political condition of the Roman Empire, of which Judea then formed a part," Frederic Farrar has noted, "a single whisper of the Emperor was sufficiently powerful to secure the execution of his mandates in the remotest corners of the civilized world." Further, Farrar added, "in deference to Jewish prejudices, any infringement of which was the certain signal for violent tumults and insurrection, it was not carried out in the ordinary Roman manner, at each person's place of residence, but according to Jewish custom, at the town to which their family originally belonged."[8]

When they had arrived in Bethlehem, the city of David, a city whose name means literally "house of bread" (appropriately, the place from which will go forth the true Bread of Life), they sought earnestly a comfortable setting for the birth of their baby. Because of the crowded conditions in Bethlehem and perhaps the insensitivity that too often exists in and among masses of people, "there was none to give room for them in the inns." (JST, Luke 2:7.) *Inns* presumably refers to places of lodging that are sometimes called *khans,* or caravanseries. They were locations where caravans or companies of people settled down for the night. Such places may have consisted of no more than crudely constructed roofs over open courts. Farrar offered his own perspective (from the nineteenth century) of these locations. They were "perfectly public; everything that takes place in them is visible to every person in the khan. They are also totally devoid of even the most ordinary furniture."9 In the words of Elder Bruce R. McConkie: "In the area of Bethlehem, sometimes the whole khan, sometimes only the portion where the animals were kept, was located within a large cave, of which there are many in the area. But unless or until some of the saints—and such a thing is by no means improbable or beyond the realm of expectancy—see in a dream or a vision the inn where Joseph and Mary and Jesus spent that awesome night, we can only speculate as to the details."10 Thus here in the humblest of circumstances we become witnesses of the condescension of God the Son, the Holy One of Israel, leaving the courts of glory, coming down to earth, taking a tabernacle of clay, and becoming the most helpless of all forms of life—a human infant.

On the plains of Bethlehem, shepherds were "abiding in the field, keeping watch over their flock by night." (Luke 2:8.) "These were not ordinary shepherds nor ordinary flocks," wrote Elder McConkie. "The sheep there being herded—nay, not herded, but watched over, cared for with love and devotion—were destined for sacrifice on the great altar in the Lord's House, in similitude of the eternal sacrifice of Him who that wondrous night lay in a stable, perhaps among sheep of lesser destiny. And the shepherds —for whom the veil was then rent: surely they were in spiritual stature like Simeon and Anna and Zacharias and Elisabeth and Joseph and the growing group of believing souls who were coming to know, by revelation, that the Lord's Christ was now on earth. As there were many widows in Israel, and only to the one in Zarephath was Elijah sent, so there were many shepherds in Palestine, but only to those who watched over the temple flocks did the herald angel come; only they heard the heavenly choir."11

An angel appeared and spoke with authority the long-awaited "good tidings of great joy," the singular message that the Lord of Life had been born, that the age of the Anointed One had now burst upon all creation. An angel had appeared to King Benjamin in the Americas over a century earlier and said: "I am come to declare unto you the *glad tidings of great joy*." (Mosiah 3:3, emphasis added.) What were those glad tidings? Simply that "the time cometh, and is not far distant, that with power, the Lord Omnipotent who reigneth, who was, and is from all eternity to all eternity, shall come down from heaven among the children of men, and shall dwell in a tabernacle of clay, and shall go forth amongst men, working mighty miracles." More specifically: "And he shall be called Jesus Christ, the Son of God, the Father of heaven and earth, the Creator of all things from the beginning; and his mother shall be called Mary." (Mosiah 3:5, 8.) Likewise Samuel the Lamanite taught that Jesus Christ "surely shall come into the world, and shall suffer many things and shall be slain for his people. And behold, an angel of the Lord hath declared it unto me, and he did bring *glad tidings* to my soul." (Hel. 13:6-7, emphasis added.)

"And this is the way you shall find the babe," the angel continued to the attentive shepherds: "He is wrapped in swaddling clothes, and is lying in a manger." (JST, Luke 2:12.) After the preceding directions were given regarding our Lord's place of birth, the heavens resounded with anthems of praise: "Glory to God in the highest heaven! Peace upon earth among men of good will!" (Phillips Translation, Luke 2:14.) Or, as translated in a slightly different manner: "Glory to God in the highest heaven, and peace to men who enjoy his favor." (Jerusalem Bible.) Having found the humble dwellings of the holy family, and then no doubt having visited at length with Joseph and Mary and sensed the sacredness of the occasion, the shepherds were among the first mortals to bear Messianic witness, to testify of those "things which they had heard and seen, as they were manifested unto them." (JST, Luke 2:20.) Many heard the inspired words of the shepherds and marveled at the implications of what had come to pass. "But Mary kept all these things, and pondered them in her heart" (Luke 2:19), "awaiting the day when she too will bear witness of all that she feels and believes and knows concerning the Son of David, who was born in the city of David, and who came to reign on the throne of David forever."[12]

Messianic Testimonies on the Eighth Day

It had become customary among the Jews to name their children on the eighth day after birth, the same day on which males were to be circumcised. The act of circumcision was originally given to Abraham as a token, a reminder of the covenant God had made with his people. Jehovah had said to him: "I will establish a covenant of circumcision with thee, and it shall be my covenant between me and thee, and thy seed after thee, in their generations; that thou mayest know forever that *children are not accountable before me until they are eight years old.*" (JST, Gen. 17:11, emphasis added.) For almost two thousand years male infants were circumcised at *eight days* of age as a reminder to parents to teach and prepare their children for the time of moral accountability, the age of *eight years.*

At eight days the infant son of Mary was circumcised and given the name Jesus, or, more directly, *Yeshua,* literally "Jehovah is salvation," a name foreknown centuries before this occasion (Moses 6:52; 7:50; 8:24; 2 Ne. 25:19; Mosiah 3:8; Alma 7:10), and the name that had been given to Joseph and Mary by the angel Gabriel (Matt. 1:21; Luke 1:31). Mary, in obedience to the law of Moses, underwent a forty-day period of purification following the birth of her child (an eighty-day period was required for a female child). At the end of that period, she and Joseph, with Jesus, returned to Jerusalem to perform two ceremonial acts: to present the Christ child—Mary's firstborn—unto God, to "redeem him" from a life of priestly service through the payment of five shekels at the sanctuary (Ex. 13:1-2); and to present a sin offering at the temple, which offering would serve as a pronouncement of ritual cleanliness for the mother (see Lev. 12:1-8). "On this occasion Mary entered the Court of the Women; dropped the price of her sacrifice into one of the thirteen trumpet-shaped chests; heard the sound of the organ, announcing that incense was about to be kindled on the Golden Altar; made her way, as one for whom a special sacrifice was being offered, to a place near the Sanctuary; and there, while the ordinance was performed, offered up the unspoken prayers of praise and thanksgiving of a grateful heart. Thus she became Levitically clean."[13]

While in the courts of the temple, on temple square as it were, the young Nazarean family encountered one Simeon, a man who was "just and devout, waiting for the consolation of Israel: and the Holy Ghost was upon him. And it was revealed unto him by the

Holy Ghost, that he should not see death, before he had seen the Lord's Christ." (Luke 2:25-26.) As Mary and Joseph underwent their solemn duties within the temple precincts, Simeon (whose name appropriately means one "that hears,") took the child into his arms and said: "Lord, now lettest thou thy servant depart in peace, according to thy word: for mine eyes have seen thy salvation, which thou hast prepared before the face of all people." (Luke 2:28-31.) Simeon then broke forth into psalmic prophecy, speaking of the Savior's mission to Jew and Gentile and of his ministry as the Light of the world. And then in a poignant moment Simeon spoke prophetically to Mary of a painful but inevitable time yet future: "Yea, a spear shall pierce through him to the wounding of thine own soul also." (JST, Luke 2:35; cf. John 19:25.)

Also in attendance at this early testimony meeting was a woman named Anna, a prophetess of the tribe of Asher. "She was of great age, and had lived with a husband only seven years, whom she married in her youth, and she lived a widow about fourscore and four years, who departed not from the temple, but served God with fastings and prayers, night and day." Aged Anna, now over a century in age, was undimmed in her spiritual capacities, undaunted in her hunger and thirst for the things of the Spirit. Like Simeon, she rejoiced in the God of her salvation and bore witness of the newly come Christ "to all those who looked for redemption in Jerusalem." (JST, Luke 2:36-38.)

The Visit of the Magi

Some time after the presentation of Jesus in the temple (a period that may have been as much as two years—see Matt. 2:7, 16), certain "wise men from the east" were led by a new star to Jerusalem. (Matt. 2:1).[14] Christian tradition is replete with suggestions as to their native countries, their names, and their numbers. Were the eastern visitors from Babylon, Persia, or Arabia? Were they two in number, or perhaps three, as millions have supposed? We simply do not know, for our primary source, the Gospel of Matthew, is silent beyond the twelve verses contained in the second chapter.

About five years before the birth of Christ, Samuel the Lamanite prophesied of "a new star" that would serve as one of the signs of the Savior's birth. (Hel. 14:5.) Elder McConkie wrote: "As to the star, there is nothing mysterious about it. The Magi, if so they are to be designated, were not reading portents in the skies nor divining the destinies of men by the movement of celestial bodies in the sidereal heavens. The new star was simply a new star of the sort we are familiar with. No doubt it exhibited an unusual brilliance, so as to attract special attention and so as to give guidance to those who walked in its light, but it was, nonetheless, a star."[15]

There seems to have been in Jewish prophecy or legend the knowledge that the Messiah's coming would be heralded by a special appearance of a star. Alfred Edersheim wrote: "There is . . . testimony which seems to us not only reliable, but embodies most ancient Jewish tradition. It is contained in one of the smaller *Midrashim*. . . . The so-called Messiah-Haggadah *(Aggadoth Mashiach)* opens as follows: 'A star shall come out of Jacob. There is a Boraita in the name of the Rabbis: The heptad in which the Son of David cometh—in the first year, there will not be sufficient nourishment; in the second year the arrows of famine are launched; in the third, a great famine; in the fourth, neither famine nor plenty; in the fifth, great abundance and *the Star shall shine forth from the East, and this is the Star of the Messiah.*' "[16]

It is generally supposed that the wise men were Gentiles from foreign soil who had come to behold the babe in Bethlehem. This supposition seems at variance with the fact that these are men guided in personal religious quests for the Anointed One of Israel: "Where is the child that is born, *the Messiah of the Jews?* for we have seen his star in the east, and have come to worship him." (JST, Matt. 3:2, emphasis added.)[17] Elder McConkie concluded: "As to the men themselves, one thing is clear. They had prophetic insight. It was with them as it had been with saintly Simeon. . . . The probability is *they were themselves Jews* who lived, as millions of Jews then did, in one of the nations to the East."[18]

Word of the inquiries by the wise men and the subsequent stir among the people reached Herod the Great. Herod "gathered all the chief priests, and scribes of the people together, [and] demanded of them, saying, Where is the place that is written of by the prophets, in which Christ [i.e., the Messiah] should be born? For he greatly feared, yet he believed not the prophets. And they said unto him, It is written by the prophets, that he should be born in Bethlehem of Judea, for thus have they said, The word of the Lord came unto us, saying, And thou Bethlehem, which lieth in the land of Judea, in thee shall be born a prince, which art not the least among all the princes of Judea; for out of thee shall come the Messiah, who shall save my people Israel." (JST, Matt. 3:4-6.)

Herod learned from the wise men when they had first encountered the new star, and he asked them to bring word back to him once they had found the Christ, so that, in his own lying and deceitful words, "I may come and worship him also." (Matt. 2:8.) Having found the house to which the holy family had relocated, the wise men worshiped the Lord and presented him with gifts of gold, frankincense, and myrrh. That these souls were spiritually sensitive is attested by the fact that they were warned in an inspired dream not to return to Jerusalem to discuss the matter with Herod further. Consequently, "they departed into their own country another way." (Matt. 2:12.)

The Death of the Innocents

Perhaps nowhere do we gain greater insight into the depraved disposition of Herod the Great (of whom it was wisely observed by the Emperor Augustus that it was safer to be Herod's pig than his son!) than in the brief episode described by Matthew in which he, in demonic and paranoid frenzy, ordered the death of innocent children. After inquiring of the magi as to the time of the rising of the new star and subsequently finding that the visitors from the East had left the area (that he had been "mocked of the wise men"), this spineless creature ordered the death of all *boys* (not children, but boys—the plural of *pais* in Greek) in Bethlehem two years of age or younger. Considering that Bethlehem was a small town with a population of approximately one thousand to two thousand, as well as that there was a high infant mortality rate, with an annual birthrate of about thirty, then the number of boys killed probably did not exceed twenty.[19] "But," wrote Edersheim, "the deed was none the less atrocious; and these infants may justly be regarded as the 'protomartyrs,' the first witnesses of Christ." Continuing, Edersheim remarked: "The slaughter was entirely in accordance with the character and former measure of Herod. Nor do we wonder, that it remained unrecorded by Josephus, since on other occasions also he has omitted events which to us seem important. The murder of a few infants in an insignificant village might appear scarcely worth notice in a reign stained by so much bloodshed."[20]

Jesus was delivered from Herod's murderous decree through revelatory instruction to Joseph prior to the carrying out of Herod's order. An angel came to him in a vision, saying: "Arise and take the young child and his mother, and flee into Egypt, and tarry thou there until I bring thee word; for Herod will seek the young child to destroy him." (JST, Matt. 3:13.) The family remained in Egypt until word reached them of the death of Herod. One apocryphal source suggests how it was that John the Baptist was also spared.

> But Elizabeth, when she heard that John was sought for, took him and went up into the hill-country. . . .
>
> Now Herod was searching for John, and sent officers to Zacharias at the altar to ask him: "Where have you hidden your son?" And he answered and said to them: "I am a minister of God and attend continually upon his temple. How should I know where my son is?" And the officers departed and told all this to Herod. Then Herod was angry and said: "Is his son to be king over Israel?" And he sent the officers to him again with the command: "Tell the truth. Where is your son? You know that your blood is under my hand." And the officers departed and told him all this. And Zacharias said: "I am a martyr of God. Take my blood! But my spirit the Lord will receive, for you shed innocent blood in the forecourt of the temple of the Lord." And about the dawning of the day Zacharias was slain. And the children of Israel did not know that he had been slain.[21]

Concerning the hideous manner in which the sadistic ruler met his death, Josephus wrote:

> But now Herod's distemper greatly increased upon him after a severe manner, and this by God's judgment upon him for his sins: for a fire glowed in him slowly, which did not so much appear to the touch outwardly, as it augmented his pains inwardly; for it brought upon him a vehement appetite to eating, which he could not avoid to supply with one sort of food or other. His entrails were also exulcerated, and the chief violence of his pain lay on his colon. . . . And when he sat upright he had a difficulty of breathing, which was very loathsome, on account of the stench of his breath and the quickness of its returns; he had also convulsions in all parts of his body.[22]

Fearing that his passing would not be accompanied by what he felt to be the appropriate level of remorse among his subjects, Herod ordered the mass death in the Hippodrome of "all the principal men of the entire Jewish nation," thus assuring himself of the "honour of a memorable mourning at his funeral."[23] According to historians, Herod the Great died in March of 4 B.C. Just prior to his death, Herod made arrangements for the settlement and governance of his territories by his sons.

> Herod's youngest son, Antipas, was now named heir to the throne. Antipas was Herod's son by a secondary wife, a Samaritan woman named Malthake. Herod had an elder son by Malthake, Archelaus by name, but he passed him over at this stage because his mind had been poisoned against him by Antipater [his son by his first wife, Doris]. . . . Four or five days before his death he ordered the execution of Antipater, and changed his mind once more about the succession, for in his last will and testament his kingdom was divided among three of his sons. Antipas was to rule Galilee and Peraea as tetrarch, his full brother Archelaus was to receive Judaea (including Samaria and Idumaea) with the royal title, while Philip, Herod's son by yet another wife (Cleopatra of Jerusalem), was nominated tetrarch of the territory which Herod had received from Augustus east and north-east of the Lake of Galilee.[24]

Joseph feared to return to Israel when he heard that Archelaus had received the title from his father, but after receiving comfort and instruction in a vision, he settled his young family in Nazareth, a city in the province of Galilee. (JST, Matt. 3:21-22.) Matthew explained that this settlement of the holy family was in fulfillment of a now unknown prophecy about the Messiah that "he shall be called a Nazarene." (Matt. 2:23).[25]

Boyhood and the "Missing Years"

As to the preparation and training—the education—of a Jewish male child in the first century, Alfred Edersheim wrote:

> . . . while the earliest religious teaching would, of necessity, come from the lips of the mother, it was the father who was "bound to teach his son." To impart to the child knowledge of the Torah conferred as great spiritual distinction, as if a man had received the Law itself on Mount Horeb. . . . Directly the child learned to speak, his religious instruction was to begin—no doubt, with such verses of Holy Scripture as composed that part of the Jewish liturgy, which answers to our Creed [the Shema—Deut. 6:4-6]. Then would follow other passages from the Bible, short prayers, and select sayings of the sages. Special attention was given to the culture of the *memory,* since forgetfulness might prove as fatal in its consequences as ignorance or neglect of the Law. . . . The earliest hymns taught would be the Psalms for the days of the week, or festive Psalms, such as the *Hallel* [Psalms of praise such as Ps. 113-18, 120-26, 135-36], or those connected with the festive pilgrimages to Zion.
>
> The regular instruction commenced with the fifth or sixth year (according to strength), when every child was sent to school. There can be no reasonable doubt that at that time [the first century] such schools existed throughout the land. . . . From the teaching of the alphabet or of writing, onwards to the farthest limit of instruction in the most advanced Academies of the Rabbis, all is marked by extreme care, wisdom, accuracy, and a moral and religious purpose as the ultimate object. For a long time it was not uncommon

to teach in the open air; but this must have been chiefly in connection with theological discussions, and the instruction of youths. But the children were gathered in the Synagogues, or in the School-houses, where at first they either stood, teacher and pupils alike, or else sat on the ground in a semicircle, facing the teacher. . . .

Roughly classifying the subjects of study, it was held, that, up to ten years of age, the Bible exclusively should be the textbook; from ten to fifteen, the . . . traditional law; after that age, the student should enter on those theological discussions which occupied time and attention in the higher Academies of the Rabbis. . . . The study of the Bible commenced with that of the Book of Leviticus. Thence it passed to the other parts of the Pentateuch; then to the Prophets; and, finally, to the Hagiographa [Writings].

Finally, in speaking of the atmosphere and training in the home of Joseph and Mary, Edersheim has suggested: "That [Jesus'] was preeminently a pious home in the highest sense, it seems almost irreverent to say. . . . We know that from earliest childhood [the scriptures] must have formed the meat and drink of the God-Man."[26]

The scriptures are silent regarding particular incidents in the life of Christ between the ages of twelve and thirty. Luke records that at the age of twelve, Jesus, perhaps what would now be called a *bar mitzvah,* a "son of the commandment" and a man in his own right, accompanied his parents into the holy city for the Feast of the Passover. It was expected that those men who resided within a reasonable distance of Jerusalem would go to the city to celebrate three sacred occasions: the feasts of Passover ("feast of unleavened bread," in the spring of the year), Pentecost (the feast of "first fruits," fifty days after Passover), and Tabernacles (the "feast of booths," held during the fall of the year). Frequently large caravans of Israelites would travel together to enjoy the social benefits occasioned by the pilgrimages, as well as to protect themselves from marauding bands of robbers. It was at the end of a week of feasting and celebration following Passover that Mary and Joseph discovered, after a full day's journey from Jerusalem, that their twelve-year-old was missing. "And it came to pass, after three days they found him in the temple, sitting in the midst of the doctors [the scribes, the experts on the law], and *they were hearing him, and asking him questions.* And all who heard him were astonished at his understanding, and answers." (JST, Luke 2:46-47, emphasis added.) Already we see in the mind and soul of the young Messiah the spiritual depth and infinite wisdom that would characterize his ministry. Even as a boy he demonstrated the originality and freshness and animation that comes only through one who is imbued with the powers of his Eternal Father. Indeed, Jesus "taught them as one having authority from God, and not as having authority from the scribes." (JST, Matt. 7:37.)

Mary questioned his wisdom and seemed to stress the inconsiderateness of causing such anxiety to his parents: "Son," she asked, "why hast thou thus dealt with us? Behold, thy father and I have sought thee sorrowing." Jesus responded with mature confidence, his words evidencing both his growing knowledge of his singular ministry and a firm assurance as to his Divine Sonship and relationship to his true Father: "Why is it that ye sought me? *Knew ye not that I must be about my Father's business?*" The account continues: "And [Jesus] went down with them, and came to Nazareth, and was subject unto them. And his mother kept all these sayings in her heart." (JST, Luke 2:48-49, 51, emphasis added.) "What marvelous and sacred secrets were treasured in that mother's heart," writes Elder Talmage. "And what new surprises and grave problems were added day after day in the manifestations of unfolding wisdom displayed by her more than mortal Son! . . . At every new evidence of His uniqueness she marveled and pondered anew. He was hers, and yet in a very real sense not wholly hers."[27]

Luke's statement that "Jesus increased in wisdom and stature, and in favour with God and man" (Luke 2:52) speaks volumes. He developed in understanding and intellectual powers. He developed physically, such that his body would prove a benefit and blessing to his work. He developed in his relationship with God, line upon line, precept upon precept. Jesus did not receive the fullness of light and power and glory at the first of his life but received "grace for grace"; that is, our Lord was blessed by his Father as he continually gave of himself to others in service. He thereby progressed "from grace to grace," from one level to a higher, from a lesser spiritual endowment to a greater. (See D&C 93:12-20.) Finally, Jesus of Nazareth developed socially, "in favor with man." Jesus loved people, for people were his reason for being: his work and glory were to "bring to pass the immortality and eternal life of man." (Moses 1:39.)

The Gospels of Matthew and Luke are accurate and appropriate in what they present in regard to our Lord's beginnings. During the time of the apostasy, men and women sought to fill in the gaps, to provide details as to the "missing years" of his life where details were not intended, to supplement the record. Many of the particulars of these accounts are readily discerned as spurious by those who are sensitive to the Spirit of the Lord; they stand in stark contrast to the sacred silence of the Gospels of Matthew and Luke. As I have written elsewhere: "The presence of sensational and titilating elements often evident in the apocryphal gospels are absent in the canonical Gospels. Absent also are attempts to explain the unexplained or to reconcile the seemingly estranged or disparate. There are no attempts to 'lie for God,' to appease the questioning mind, to conciliate by appending the authoritative. The canonical Gospels combine simplicity with the power of their message, and present a dignified and appropriate glimpse into the life and words of the Savior."[28]

One final contribution from the Joseph Smith Translation of Matthew provides us with a temporal link to the formal ministry of our Lord: "And it came to pass that Jesus grew up with his brethren, and waxed strong, and waited upon the Lord for the time of his ministry to come. And he served under his father, and he spake not as other men, neither could he be taught; for he needed not that any man should teach him. And after many years, the hour of his ministry drew nigh." (JST, Matt. 3:24-26.) What a remarkable manner in which to describe the divine process by which the Son of Man of Holiness made his transition from infancy through boyhood into manhood! Building upon a solid foundation, the time of his ministry was now at hand.

NOTES

1. Bruce R. McConkie, *The Mortal Messiah: From Bethlehem to Calvary,* 4 vols. (Salt Lake City: Deseret Book, 1979-81), 1:284-85.

2. James E. Talmage, *Jesus the Christ* (Salt Lake City: Deseret Book, 1972), p. 86.

3. Raymond E. Brown, *The Birth of the Messiah* (New York: Doubleday & Co., 1977), p. 65.

4. See Robert J. Matthews, "A Voice in the Wilderness: An Interview with John the Baptist," chapter 9 of this volume.

5. *The Mortal Messiah* 1:326-27, note 4.

6. Note in all four cases where the King James Version speaks of Joseph receiving instructions through *dreams* (Matt. 1:20, 24; 2:13, 19, 33) that the Joseph Smith Translation refers to these experiences as *visions.*

7. *The Birth of the Messiah,* p. 127.

8. Frederic Farrar, *The Life of Christ* (Portland, Ore.: Fountain Publications, 1964), pp. 35-36.

9. Ibid., p. 33.

10. *The Mortal Messiah* 1:344.

11. Ibid., 1:347.

12. Ibid., 1:349.

13. Ibid., 1:353.

14. The Greek word used by Matthew (translated as "wise men" in the KJV) is *magoi,* rendered in English as *magi.* What does Matthew mean by *magoi?* A typical scholarly opinion is as follows: "Long before, Herodotus (*Histories* 1) had intrigued his Greek readers with a description of a priestly caste of magi among the sixth-century Medes, a caste that has special power to interpret dreams. The magi survived both the transfer of power from the Medes to the Persians (ca. 550 B.C.) and the emerging religious dominance of Zoroastrianism, so that by Herodotus' time (ca. 450) the magi were Zoroastrian priests. In the subsequent centuries there was a diversification in the functions of magi as the title was loosely applied to men adept in various forms of secret lore and magic. . . . Thus, the term 'magi' refers to those engaged in occult arts and covers a wide range of astronomers, fortune tellers, priestly augurers, and magicians of varying plausibility." (Brown, *The Birth of the Messiah,* p. 167.) This approach to the identity of the magi has been popularly received over the centuries, since it points to the role of Jesus Christ as Savior and King to all the world. Though this has some attraction, I agree

with Elder McConkie's assessment (hereafter) that the magi were Jews of the dispersion.

15. *The Mortal Messiah* 1:359.

16. Alfred Edersheim, *The Life and Times of Jesus the Messiah* (Grand Rapids, Mich.: Eerdmans, 1971), 1:211-12, emphasis added.

17. The reader should note the differences in the numbering of chapters and verses in early Matthew in the KJV and the JST. Joseph Smith began chapter 2 in his inspired version after the genealogy of Jesus (after KJV, 1:17). By Matthew 4 the KJV and the JST chapters are the same again.

18. *The Mortal Messiah* 1:358, emphasis added.

19. See McConkie, *The Mortal Messiah* 1:363; Farrar, *The Life of Christ,* p. 62; Edersheim, *The Life and Times of Jesus the Messiah* 1:214; Brown, *The Birth of the Messiah,* p. 204.

20. *The Life and Times of Jesus the Messiah* 1:214-15.

21. From "The Protevangelium of James," trans. A. J. B. Higgins, in Edgar Hennecke, *New Testament Apocrypha,* 2 vols., ed. Wilhelm Schneemelcher (Philadelphia: Westminster Press, 1963), 1:387. It is worthy of note that a very similar account of the death of Zacharias is found in an editorial in the September 15, 1842, issue of *Times and Seasons* (also found in *Teachings of the Prophet Joseph Smith,* p. 261). There is some question as to whether the editorial was indeed prepared by Joseph Smith, who was probably out of town at the time.

22. Flavius Josephus, "Antiquities of the Jews," XVII. 6.5, in *Josephus: Complete Works,* trans. William Whiston (Grand Rapids, Mich.: Kregal Publications, 1974), p. 365.

23. Ibid.

24. F. F. Bruce, *New Testament History* (New York: Doubleday & Co., 1972), pp. 23-24.

25. Three main points of view have surfaced in regard to the meaning of this prophecy: (1) Jesus as one who lived in Nazareth, as noted, the specific prophecy of which is unknown; (2) Jesus as a *nazir,* a Nazarite, one consecrated and made holy to God by a vow (see Num. 6:1-21); and (3) Jesus as *neser,* a branch, in fulfillment of the passage in Isaiah 11:1. For a detailed discussion of these matters, see Brown, *The Birth of the Messiah,* pp. 209-12.

26. *The Life and Times of Jesus the Messiah* 1:230-34, emphasis in the original.

27. *Jesus the Christ,* pp. 115-16.

28. " 'As Delivered from the Beginning': The Formation of the

Canonical Gospels," in *Apocryphal Writings and the Latter-day Saints,* ed. C. Wilfred Griggs (Provo, Utah: Religious Studies Center, Brigham Young University, 1986), p. 211. See also Richard Lloyd Anderson, "Imitation Gospels and Christ's Book of Mormon Ministry," ibid., pp. 53-107.

9

A VOICE IN THE WILDERNESS:
AN INTERVIEW WITH JOHN THE BAPTIST

ROBERT J. MATTHEWS

Most of us know two things about John the Baptist: he baptized Jesus, and he ordained Joseph Smith and Oliver Cowdery to the Aaronic Priesthood. These may be the two most important things about John, but they are not enough knowledge about him to satisfy us. As members of the Church, we will want to know a good deal more of this man about whom Jesus said, "Among those that are born of women there is not a greater prophet than John the Baptist." (Luke 7:28.)

A biographical entry in an encyclopedia might read as follows:

> John. Also known as the Baptist. Born: Judea, October, about six months before Jesus Christ. Parents: Zacharias and Elisabeth, tribe of Levi, family of Aaron. Blessed by his father at the age of eight days. Blessed also by an angel on the same day. Taken into the hill country by his mother to escape Herod's order that babies be slain. Grew to maturity in the desert. Food: locusts and wild honey. Clothing: the rough garb of the desert—leather girdle and raiment of camel's hair. Was baptized during childhood. At about thirty years of age received divine call to begin ministry to prepare a people to receive the Son of God. Went among the people of Judea and proclaimed that the Messiah would shortly appear. Baptized many people in Jordan River. His counsel was sought by common people, publicans, soldiers,

Robert J. Matthews is professor of ancient scripture and dean of Religious Education at Brigham Young University.

and even Jewish religious leaders. Among his notable baptisms was that of Jesus, the Messiah. Gathered many disciples and at the height of his popularity was mistakenly thought by some to be the Messiah. This identification he vigorously denied. His popularity was felt throughout Israel, even in areas he had not visited personally. One of his admirers was Herod Antipas, a Roman appointee as tetrarch of Galilee and Perea. Herod later imprisoned him for several months (he was kept in chains and tortured) and then ordered his execution. Place of imprisonment: probably Machereus, on the northeast side of the Dead Sea. Buried by some of his disciples; place unknown. His total public ministry was about a year and one-half. He died in his thirty-second year. Nothing is known concerning wife or children, although it is almost certain that he had both. Resurrection: a short time after death. Ordained Joseph Smith and Oliver Cowdery to the Aaronic Priesthood, near Harmony, Pennsylvania, on May 15, 1829.

Having thus reviewed the basic facts of John's life and actions, we shall interview some of those who knew him personally. Among them are his father, Zacharias; his mother, Elisabeth; the angel Gabriel, who announced his birth; a disciple who was converted by him; a publican who was impressed by him; a Roman soldier who believed him; a lawyer who interrogated him; John the Beloved and Andrew, who followed him; Herod Antipas, who respected and feared him; two of his disciples who visited him; and Joseph Smith, who was ordained by him. The interviews are, of course, imaginary, but they are based on the knowledge we have of John and his contemporaries given to us in the holy scriptures and in the teachings of the Prophet Joseph Smith. The inquirer is any man or woman. Let us talk to Zacharias first.

INQUIRER. Brother Zacharias, when did you first learn that you would have a son who would be a prophet and the forerunner of the Lord?

ZACHARIAS. It was when I was attending to my duties in the temple in Jerusalem. As I went to burn incense, the angel Gabriel stood before me and said that the Lord had heard our prayers, and my wife Elisabeth would bear a son, notwithstanding our old age.

161

He told me to name him John, that he would be great in the sight of the Lord, that he would drink no wine or strong drink, and that he would be filled with the Holy Ghost from his mother's womb. He specifically said that my son would turn many to righteousness and would make ready a people for the Lord. [See Luke 1:7-17.]

INQUIRER. How did this information strike you?

ZACHARIAS. It overwhelmed me. I could hardly believe it; therefore, the angel told me that I would be struck dumb until the baby was born and named. That meant I'd be unable to speak for nearly a year.

INQUIRER. Why do you think you and Elisabeth were selected to be the parents of John?

ZACHARIAS. We don't know why it was us, but one thing we do know. The office of the forerunner was a preparatory role and therefore came under the jurisdiction of the Aaronic Priesthood. In order for John to be a legal heir and hold the keys to that priesthood, he had to be a firstborn son of the family of Aaron. As you know, I am a priest, which means I am of that lineage. Elisabeth also was a direct descendant of Aaron. Our son John was the firstborn of just the right lineage in order to be fully representative of the Aaronic Priesthood and the law of Moses. [See Luke 1:5-7; Ex. 30:30-31; 40:15.]

INQUIRER. Thank you, Zacharias. Your explanation is informative. I think our listeners would also enjoy hearing from John's mother. Elisabeth, would you tell us your feelings when you learned of the forthcoming birth of your son, John?

ELISABETH. It made me very happy, and yet I was awed by the responsibility. It was wonderful to know that the Lord had heard our prayers after all these years, and we would have a son. Then when Mary came to visit me and stayed for three months until the baby was born, we had many pleasant and inspiring times together. It was a great blessing to us to contemplate that Mary's son would be the Messiah and that my son would prepare the way before him. When Mary entered into my home, the Holy Ghost came upon me, and I knew that she had been selected to be the mother of our Lord. At the same time the Holy Ghost came also upon John, and he leaped for joy in my womb, even though he would not be born for three months yet. Thus, according to the prophecies in the scriptures, John had the Holy Ghost even from the time of the womb. [See Luke 1:15, 36-57; D&C 84:27.] I did not see the angel, but I believed the things the angel told my husband. I thanked the Lord in my prayers many times for his kindness and tender mercies to me.

When the baby was born, the neighbors and relatives wanted to name him Zacharias. I insisted that he must be called John because that is what the angel had said. But not until they inquired of my husband were they convinced. We had never had anyone in the family named John, and, as you know, it is customary among us to name children after near relatives. Zacharias couldn't speak, but he wrote the name for them to see. [See Luke 1:56-61.]

INQUIRER. Thank you, Elisabeth. Zacharias, do you want to say anything about the naming of the child?

ZACHARIAS. Yes, I do. It was one of the busiest days in John's early life. He was eight days old. On that day he was circumcised. I had not been able to talk for nearly a year. The relatives and neighbors knew that, so they handed me a tablet on which I wrote, "His name is John." Suddenly I could speak again. Everyone was awestruck. The Holy Ghost came upon me, and I gave my son a father's blessing. I first praised the God of Israel that he would send his Son into the world to redeem us. Then I blessed John and spoke of his mission to teach and baptize the children of Israel and to prepare the way before the face of the Lord. The blessing is now called "the Benedictus." The people saw and heard these things, and it was noised abroad, and they wondered what manner of child this would be. [See Luke 1:67-79.]

But what also made that day memorable is that an angel also came and blessed John and set him apart for his mission to wrest the kingdom from the apostate Jews, make straight the way of the Lord, and prepare a people to receive the true Savior, Jesus Christ. [See D&C 84:28-29.] This was to be a mighty task for one man—a mere mortal, my son. But he had been called of God in the premortal life. Born through the prescribed lineage and proclaimed by the angel Gabriel, he was a child of promise.

INQUIRER. We've mentioned the angel Gabriel several times.

Let's see if we can talk to him. Gabriel, we understand that you are also Noah, the ancient patriarch and builder of the ark.[1] You have certainly fulfilled some important assignments. Would you tell us about your announcement of the coming of John and Jesus?

GABRIEL. The Lord has given me the keys of the restoration of all things. [See D&C 27:6.] And it was a great honor bestowed upon me to make an announcement to Zacharias of the coming of John and then to tell Mary of the approaching birth of the Son of God. These were momentous events, and I was greatly honored that the Lord would choose me to make the announcements. As you know, John was selected in the grand councils of heaven before the world was formed to be the great forerunner of the Lord Jesus Christ. He was chosen by the Lord and sustained by those present. It was a most important mission. He was not only to baptize many of the people but was to baptize the Lord himself. And what a preacher he had to be! It was a time of great turmoil and wickedness among the Jews. He had to prepare a people to receive the Lord Jesus Christ. Several of the future apostles of the Church of Jesus Christ in New Testament times would be tutored by John. When the Lord chose a man in the premortal councils to fulfill this mission, he selected a man who could do the job—a man who could teach, explain, bear testimony, persuade, and perform—and do it magnificently. A man of intellect, courage, and stamina was needed. And he had to be of the lineage that would make him a legal heir to the keys of the Aaronic Priesthood, which is the preparatory priesthood. John was that man in every way. He was in person what the law of Moses was on the tablets, and that was a schoolmaster to bring men and women to Christ.

INQUIRER. Thank you for that insight into the premortal calling and the personality of John. But we need to go back to Zacharias. Brother Zacharias, how long did you live after the birth of John? Were you able to be father to him during his formative and teenage years?

ZACHARIAS. That was one of the saddest times of my long life. When Herod the Great ordered the death of the babies in order to slay Jesus, my own son came under that edict. John's birth was well known throughout Judea, and everyone knew of the miracles involved, such as the angel's coming to me in the temple and my being struck dumb and regaining my speech when the child was named. And so the soldiers came to find him. I had previously sent Elisabeth and John into the hill country to hide. When I refused to tell them the hiding place, they killed me instead. Elisabeth was left a widow to rear him. I would have liked to be with them longer, but it was more important to save him alive.[2]

INQUIRER. That is a very touching story. Thank you for sharing it with us. We will now inquire of one of the citizens of Judea who heard John preach and was baptized by him. We don't know his name, so we'll call him Disciple. Brother Disciple, what did you feel when you heard John preach?

DISCIPLE. I had never felt anything like it before. He was very open and to the point. First I heard him preach that Jesus would come and later that Jesus had come; and he told us, his disciples, to leave him and follow Jesus. I heard him bear testimony that when he baptized Jesus, he saw the sign of the dove. He also heard the voice of the Father declaring Jesus to be the Son of God. I heard John teach by the Spirit and give counsel to all who came to him. Multitudes from Jerusalem and Judea came to the Jordan to be baptized. For a year I heard him teach. He was fearless. How he could handle those Pharisees and Sadducees! He called them a generation of vipers and told them to bring forth fruits worthy of repentance. To retaliate, they said he had a devil. [See Luke 7:33.] He was so filled with the Spirit that most of us wondered if he were the Messiah. [See Luke 3:15.] But he would have no nonsense about that. He plainly told us that he was not the Christ but was sent to testify of him. We never ceased to marvel at his loyalty and devotion to his Master. He had an eye single to the glory of God. He told us that he must decrease, but that Jesus would increase. He told us that Jesus was the Lamb of God who would take away the sins of the world. [See John 3:22-36; 1:29.]

I heard him teach faith, repentance, confession of sins, baptism, and the necessity of receiving the Holy Ghost. He taught honesty, brotherly kindness, charity, fasting, prayer, moral cleanliness, Gentile adoption into the house of Israel, the resurrection, the Second Coming of Jesus, the burning of the earth, the judgment, and ever so many principles of the gospel. He didn't perform any miracles, but everything he told us about Jesus was true. I tell you, he was magnificent! He had a special dignity. Even the publicans, the soldiers, and Herod Antipas were impressed. He roused the people to action. [See Matt. 3:1-17; JST, Luke 3:1-25; John 1:18-40; 3:25-36; 10:41.]

INQUIRER. We're glad we talked to you. We can feel your enthusiasm. Let's visit with one of those soldiers over there. Soldier, is it true that you and the others were on hand and that you believed the preaching of John the Baptist?

SOLDIER. Yes, that is true. We used to accompany the tax collectors ("publicans" to you) on their calls. When we'd press a customer, it was easy to collect a little extra for the collector and ourselves. But when we heard John preach about the coming judgment, we felt guilty, and so we asked him what we should do. He told us to do violence to no man, to be content with our wages, not to rob the people, and not to accuse anyone falsely. [See Luke 3:9, 14.] Here is one of the publicans. Ask him. He can tell you how it was.

INQUIRER. Incredible! We have heard it ourselves from a Roman soldier! Mr. Publican, sir, did John the Baptist really make that big an impression among the Jews and the Roman soldiers?

PUBLICAN. Yes, he was immensely popular. We had never seen or heard anything like him: dressed in rough clothing, claiming divine authority, testifying of what he had seen and heard. He told us that the Messiah was already born and was among us and would soon be made manifest. John was great, but he told us that the Messiah was much greater than he. We heard his testimony of Jesus Christ and his warning of a day of judgment. We were touched in our hearts; we wanted to confess our sins and be baptized. We asked him what we should do. He counseled us to exact no more taxes than that which was appointed to us. Many of us believed him and were baptized. [See Luke 3:9-13; 7:29.]

INQUIRER. Thank you. All of these people we have interviewed have spoken highly of John. We wonder if he had any enemies. A man is judged by who his enemies are as well as by who his friends are. What about those Pharisees and lawyers whom he called vipers? Let's find one of them and hear what he ways. Ah, here's one now. You can tell he's an important man; see how richly he's dressed—and such a pious look. Let's ask him. Mr. Pharisee, or Mr. Sadducee, or whoever you are, can you tell us anything about John the Baptist? We've heard of him from others, but we would like to hear from you.

PHARISEE. I'm a Pharisee! a lawyer! I work for the Sanhedrin. Yes, I heard John on several occasions. I even met him personally once. I, along with several others, was sent as an official delegate from the council in Jerusalem to the river Jordan to examine John and, if possible, to refute him. He was stealing our flock—baptizing them and telling them of an approaching Messiah. He called us vipers—snakes—yet he attracted thousands of the common people. He was so convincing and so successful that the council became worried and sent us to listen to his preaching and to cross-examine him. He was not hard to find, since multitudes were attending his meetings. But he was hard for us to talk to, since he knew the scriptures better than we did and insisted also on telling us of the revelations that he had received in addition to the written word. We asked John a number of questions. He always had answers.

INQUIRER. What did you ask him?

PHARISEE. We asked him if he were the Christ. He said he was not. There were some prophecies among us about the coming of a Messiah and of an Elias. The scribes often talked about them. So we asked if he were Elias. He did not deny being an Elias to prepare, but said he was not the Elias to restore. He made a distinction we had not understood before. We knew of a series of prophecies that when the Messiah came, he would baptize with water and also with the Holy Ghost. We also knew that an Elias would come. But when we asked John if he were the Messiah, he said he was not. [See JST, John 1:20-25.] So we asked him why he baptized, if he was neither the Messiah nor the Elias to restore. He said he had been divinely commissioned to teach and baptize and that we ought to be able to figure out for ourselves that he was not the Messiah, since he, John, baptized with water only, whereas the prophecies showed that the Messiah would baptize with water and with the Holy Ghost. John made it clear to us. He was the Elias to prepare, whereas Jesus was the Elias to restore, and Jesus came with both kinds of baptism, representing both the Aaronic and Melchizedek priesthoods, whereas John exercised the Aaronic Priesthood only. We didn't understand those prophecies until we heard the explanations from John. [See JST, John 1:26-33.]

We were impressed with John, as were the people, but he told us he wasn't anything compared to the Messiah. He said he wasn't even worthy to untie the Messiah's sandals. The day after we questioned John, he showed us Jesus of Nazareth walking along the way. He said he knew for certain that this Jesus was the Lamb of God, because he had seen the sign at the time he had baptized him. For a while we were willing to rejoice in John's testimony. But before long we realized that if we believed what John said, we'd have to accept Jesus as the Messiah and give up our profession. So we rejected John and his testimony and helped Herod imprison him.

Later, on another official assignment from the Sanhedrin, we interrogated Jesus. He told us that John was a burning and a shining light, a righteous man, and he said that the preaching of John the Baptist would condemn us on the day of judgment. [See John 1:29-34; 5:32-35; JST, Matt. 21:33-34.] We did not thank him for that. There was no mistake that John was loyal to Jesus and carefully proclaimed who Jesus was. And Jesus didn't leave John to struggle alone. He defended him publicly and testified of his greatness on many occasions. [See Luke 7:24-35; John 5:32-36; Matt. 21:23-32.] He told the people in our hearing that there never was a greater prophet born of woman than John the Baptist. [See Luke 7:24-30.] Our delegation didn't accept John or Jesus, but we knew absolutely who and what they claimed to be.

INQUIRER. Both friends and enemies say that John was loyal to Jesus, but I recall hearing that when John was in prison, he seemed to waver and to doubt that Jesus was the Christ, and so he sent two of his disciples to ask Jesus for reassurance. Is that not a weakness in John's testimony? Can anyone come forth and explain that for us? Through the crowd I see two young men approaching. Who are you, and why do you think you can reply to the question?

TWO DISCIPLES. We are the two men whom John sent to see Jesus. We were disciples of John. He often told us to leave him and follow Jesus, but we didn't do it. Finally, toward the end of John's life when he was in prison, we stayed with him, still hoping that maybe he was the Messiah. One day he told us that we should go ask Jesus himself. So we left John in the prison and searched until we found Jesus over a hundred miles away in Galilee. He had recently raised a man from the dead and was surrounded by a multitude. We told him who we were and that John had sent us to ask if he were the one to look for as the Savior. Jesus often would not give direct answers, for that would substitute for an inquirer's own responsibility to think and to have faith and gain his own testimony. So he told us of his works and of his words and told us to return to John. We didn't realize it at first, but Jesus was directing us to get a testimony for ourselves. It was not John who was wavering in his faith or devotion—it was us! Jesus also said that John was no "reed shaken with the wind." [Luke 7:24.]

INQUIRER. I see your point. It was necessary that you should experience a conversion for yourselves. Such conversions are born of faith, prayer, obedience, and a seeking for the witness of the Spirit.

Well, let's go on with more interviews. We mentioned earlier that many of the early leaders of the New Testament church received their first lessons in the gospel from John the Baptist. Two of these are identified as John the Beloved and Andrew, who later became members of the Quorum of the Twelve. Since they are so well known and can tell us so much from firsthand experience of both Jesus and John the Baptist, let's visit with them. Andrew and John, would you tell us of your experiences and your feelings about John the Baptist?

ANDREW AND JOHN. Yes, we will. We received our introduction to Jesus from John the Baptist. We heard him preach and became his disciples. We were taught the basic principles of the gospel by him, and one day he showed us Jesus in person. He called him the Lamb of God, emphasizing his mission to redeem the world with his blood. We thereafter became disciples of Jesus, although that did not mean we had to renounce John. There was complete compatibility between them. Since it was part of John's mission to prepare people to receive the Lord, it was natural that those who were to be future leaders in the Church should be attracted to John. Jesus didn't pick the Twelve off the street. We had first been tutored and spiritually awakened and baptized by John. Although it may seem in some instances that Jesus abruptly called men from the fishing nets into the Quorum of the Twelve, the record clearly shows that we were trained first by John, then were called by the Lord into his vineyard, and we later became apostles. Jesus loved John and often told us about his goodness. Our brother Matthew has written that when John was in prison, he was chained and tortured. [See Matt. 14:3; 17:12-13; Mark 6:17. Some modern translations read *chained* in preference to the King James Version *bound*.] Also, Jesus sent angels to minister to him there. [JST, Matt. 4:11.]

INQUIRER. Thank you, John and Andrew. Your insight is helpful in giving us an impression of John the Baptist.

Let's see if we can find Herod Antipas, who imprisoned John and finally ordered his execution. He's probably quite a long distance from here, but maybe we can find him. Ah, there he is now. Herod, some say that you were a friend of John. Is that true, and if so, why did you imprison and finally slay him?

HEROD ANTIPAS. Yes, it is almost true. I don't know that I could be called John's friend, but I was impressed with him. He had the kind of moral courage I admired but couldn't quite find within myself. I knew he was a holy man, but I didn't want to live by his standards. I did many things for him and obeyed his counsel for a time [JST, Mark 6:21], but when he told me I had committed a grave sin by leaving my wife and enticing Herodias, my brother's wife, that was too much! I felt that prophets should stay in their own realm and leave the business of the kingdom to the kings. My new wife, Herodias, who was also my niece, was more angry than I. She hated him. She would like to have killed him. Finally she tricked me with a birthday party, too much wine, and Salome, her dancing-girl daughter. My unrepented habits caught up with me, and I succumbed to the lust of the flesh. I let the girl get a promise from me of anything she wanted, up to half of my kingdom. Being instructed by her scheming mother, who was now almost delirious

170

with the success of her plot, she asked for the head of John the Baptist to be delivered immediately to us on a platter. I was sorry, for I knew John was a prophet and popular with the people; but to save face in the presence of my friends and the nobles of the kingdom, I gave in to the pressure and ordered the death of John. Within a few minutes the executioner returned with the blood dripping from the plate.

Later, Jesus came through my area preaching the gospel and performing miracles. I heard of his great works, and fear struck deep in my breast. I really thought that John had come back from the dead to torment me. The description, the popularity, and the doctrine sounded like John, and I was fearful. My advisers told me it was not John, but my conscience would not allow me to believe them. [Matt. 14:1-12; Mark 6:14-29.]

INQUIRER. Thank you, Herod. We appreciate your views about your contact with John in life and in death. Thus ended the mortal life of John the Baptist, one of God's noble men. A short time later he rose in the resurrection, after Jesus, and he is still engaged in the ministry of his Lord. He is a man of three dispensations. He was the last prophet under the law of Moses and the first prophet of the New Testament, and he restored the Aaronic Priesthood to Joseph Smith and Oliver Cowdery in the fullness of times. He was and is a burning light, a fire that cannot be quenched. He is the greatest Aaronic Priesthood hero that we have—an example for every teenage boy and girl as well as every adult man and woman.

We have the extreme good fortune now to meet with the Prophet Joseph Smith. Could you give our listeners your impressions of John the Baptist?

JOSEPH SMITH. Oliver Cowdery and I really did feel the hands of John on our heads when he ordained us to the Aaronic Priesthood. We knew him personally. We saw him, felt him, and heard his voice. He was true and faithful to the end of his life. He helped to bring to pass the restoration of all things spoken by all the holy prophets since the world began. He was a martyr for the gospel. He appeared to us as a resurrected being and said he was working under the direction of Peter, James, and John, who would soon bring us the Melchizedek Priesthood. [JS-H 1:68-74.]

INQUIRER. President Smith, one time Jesus referred to John, saying there had risen no greater prophet born of woman than John the Baptist. He also said that he that was least in the kingdom of heaven was greater than John. Could you enlighten us on the meaning of that statement?

JOSEPH SMITH. John's greatness lay in his privileges and opportunities and his loyalty. He alone was chosen to prepare the way for Jesus and even to baptize Jesus.[3] He saw the sign of the dove. He was faithful and diligent and successful in all that he was entrusted to do. These favored opportunities of baptizing Jesus and preparing a path for him constituted John's greatness. No other prophet had the honor of doing those things. He that is "least in the kingdom of heaven" was Jesus himself. It was an irony for the unbelieving Jews. At that time the Jews felt that Jesus had the least claim on heaven of any man. Jesus was saying that great as John is, he is actually less than "I myself."[4]

INQUIRER. Thank you, President Smith. Through the Doctrine and Covenants, the Pearl of Great Price, the Joseph Smith Translation, and your other writings, our knowledge and appreciation of John the Baptist have greatly increased. We are grateful for the wisdom God has given to you.

We will now interview John himself. We are happy that he has agreed to respond to our questions. First, are the things written about you in the New Testament really true?

JOHN. Yes, all those things are true. However, some have misunderstood through the years and have thought that I got my teachings from the Essenes and other desert religious groups. But this is not so. I gained a testimony of the Messiah from reading the Old Testament and learned what I was to say and do from the revelations of the Holy Ghost to me. I was also visited by angels.

INQUIRER. Why did you wear such rough clothing and eat such bizarre food? A shirt of itchy camels' hair, a leather girdle, and locust and honey! [Matt. 3:4.]

JOHN. That was the food and dress of the poorer people of the desert. When I began my ministry, I kept the same appearance so as to be as unlike the Pharisee and Sadducee as I could. I was a plain-spoken man, with a straightforward mission and announcement. My food, my clothing, and my speech were all plain truth. [Luke 7:24-25.] I did not want anything about my manner to detract from the work I was sent to do.

INQUIRER. Your ministry has spanned twenty centuries. Tell us how you feel about your calling.

JOHN. My privileges have been great. Truly the Lord has used the so-called "weak and simple things" to break down the strongholds of worldly power, false pride, and wickedness. The Messiah, in referring to me, said there was no greater prophet. [Luke 7:28.] He had reference not to any personal greatness about me but to my privileges as the one to prepare the way and to announce the Messiah's presence in the flesh, to baptize him in Jordan, to see the Holy Ghost descend upon him and hear the voice of the Father say that this was the Son of God.[5] My mission included pointing out to thousands the actual person of the Messiah and giving several of the future members of the Twelve their first lessons in the gospel. I held the keys of the Aaronic Priesthood and taught the preparatory gospel. [D&C 84:26-28.]

INQUIRER. Would you tell us about the Messiah?

JOHN. He was superb in every way. A master in debate against the perfidy and pride of so many of the religious and political leaders. He was patient and kind to all who were open and honest in their lives, but he was an enemy of hypocrisy and deception. He knew the hearts of people. There was no other like him. You remember I said that I was not even worthy to untie his shoelaces. [John 1:27.] That means I would be entirely unable to fill his shoes or take his place. [JST, John 1:28.] I knew that he must increase, but I must decrease. He was divine, I was but a mortal. [John 3:30-31.] Though I was imprisoned, tortured, and slain because of my testimony, I was resurrected and received this very body as you now see me. [D&C 133:55.] My resurrection and everlasting salvation I owe to the Messiah.

INQUIRER. You have been involved in three dispensations. Isn't that a bit unusual?

JOHN. Yes, in some ways unusual. I was the last prophet under the law of Moses and essentially the first prophet in the New Testament dispensation. Also, I helped in the restoration of all things in the fullness of times by bringing the Aaronic Priesthood to Joseph Smith and Oliver Cowdery. Others have also functioned in three dispensations; for example, Moses and Elijah, first in mortality, and then at the Transfiguration, and also in the Kirtland Temple in Ohio.

INQUIRER. Your ministry has placed you in association with some of the greatest men of all time—the Messiah, Elijah, Moses, and the Prophet Joseph Smith. It is unfortunate there is not more written *about* you and even something *by* you.

JOHN. There is a record made by me, but only part of it is available today in the world. [John 1:19.] Someday, when the Lord sees fit, the entire record will be available among the believers.[6]

INQUIRER. Thank you, John. We wish we had more time to learn from you. We will await the coming of your record.

Our interviews have been designed not to give a theological pronouncement or a historical treatise but to create an appreciation for John the Baptist.[7]

NOTES

1. *Teachings of the Prophet Joseph Smith,* p. 157.
2. Ibid., p. 261.
3. See S. Brent Farley, "The Baptism and Temptations of Jesus," chapter 10 of this volume.
4. *Teachings,* pp. 275-76.
5. Ibid.
6. D&C 93:6-18. See Robert J. Matthews, *A Burning Light: The Life and Ministry of John the Baptist* (Provo, Utah: Brigham Young University Press, 1972), pp. 81-82, for statements by Elders Orson Pratt, John Taylor, and Bruce R. McConkie affirming the existence of such a record.
7. An extensive study is presented in the author's *A Burning Light.*

10

THE BAPTISM AND TEMPTATIONS OF JESUS
(Matthew 3:1-17; 4:1-11)

S. BRENT FARLEY

The Baptism of Jesus

Jesus taught his disciples: "I am the way, the truth, and the life." "If any man serve me, let him follow me." "I am the good shepherd." "My sheep hear my voice, and I know them, and they follow me." (John 14:6; 12:26; 10:14, 27.) To Nicodemus, the investigator, Jesus taught, "Except a man be born of water and of the Spirit, he cannot enter into the kingdom of God." (John 3:5.)

In a profound example of obedience, Jesus, the shepherd of the faithful, led the way by walking into the waters of baptism and submitting to that heavenly ordinance performed upon earth. "Even the King of the kingdom could not return to his high state of pre-existent exaltation without complying with his own eternal law for admission to that kingdom."[1]

The scriptural setting for the Lord's compliance with baptism shows John "preaching in the wilderness of Judea, and saying, Repent ye: for the kingdom of heaven is at hand." (Matt. 3:1-2.) Matthew testified that John was fulfilling a prophecy from the lips of the prophet Isaiah that there would be one to prepare the way for the Son of God, and that John was that individual: "This is he that was spoken of by the prophet Esaias, saying, The voice of one crying in the wilderness, Prepare ye the way of the Lord." (Matt. 3:3.)

S. Brent Farley is an instructor at the LDS Institute of Religion at Utah State University.

To prepare such a way, the people were to "bring forth . . . fruits meet for [appropriate to, or worthy of] repentance" (Matt. 3:8), and to "make his paths straight" (Matt. 3:3). The Greek word *euthus,* represented by the English *straight,* also denoted *upright* and right.[2] Jesus the Christ was soon to walk visibly among the crowds of Jews; they would listen to him, question him, and dine with him, but to receive him in the fullest sense went beyond public or private hospitality. It meant that they would straighten their lives by repentance and conformity to that which Jesus would personify: uprightness and correctness.

To those stirred by the Spirit of Truth, John promised: "I indeed baptize you with water, upon your repentance." (JST, Matt. 3:38.) Those who received worthily of the Lord's commissioned prophet would later receive from the Lord, who, John said, "is mightier than I, whose shoes I am not worthy to bear, (or whose place I am not able to fill)." (JST, Matt. 3:38.) John's admission referred both to a humble contrast of himself with the Son of God and to a lack of ability to do what the Lord himself would do. Years later another John, on the Isle of Patmos, added light that helped in the understanding of John the Baptist's statement. John the Apostle saw in vision a book representing the events of our earth, and there were seals on the book. "And I saw a strong angel, and heard him proclaiming with a loud voice, Who is worthy to open the book, and to loose the seals thereof?" (JST, Rev. 5:2.) The seals, among other things, must have represented the effects of mortality, for "no man in heaven, nor in earth, neither under the earth, was able to open the book, neither to look thereon. And I wept much, because no man was found worthy to open and to read the book, neither to look thereon." (Rev. 5:3-4.) Perhaps the anxious expectation of premortal spirits for mortal experience was also accompanied by the anxiety of how to return from a fallen world to an exalted sphere with God. No one was worthy to unseal the book.

But there was another who was worthy: he was to be the literal Son of God both in the spirit and in the flesh. He, the "Lion of the tribe of Juda, the Root of David," the "Lamb as it had been slain," upheld the plan of the Father and "came and took the book out of the right hand of him that sat upon the throne." (Rev. 5:5-7.) Then a song rang out in the heavens: "Thou art worthy to take the book, and to open the seals thereof: for thou wast slain, and hast redeemed us to God by thy blood." (Rev. 5:9.) These very events, hailed from the realms of premortality, were about to be fulfilled on the stage of mortal life, and John the Baptist was preaching of the very one, the only one, who could redeem mankind by his atoning sacrifice. He, the forerunner, left no misunderstanding of the exacting and noble role of Jesus, who was soon to follow.

"I indeed baptize you before he cometh, that when he cometh he may baptize you with the Holy Ghost and fire." (JST, Matt. 3:38.) John's commission was of an Aaronic order, not holding the authority of the conferral of the Holy Ghost. (See D&C 107:20; 53:3.)[3] Jesus, the great high priest (see Heb. 4:14), would make possible the conferral of the Holy Ghost, which would cleanse and purify those baptized worthily unto repentance (see D&C 55:1). He who was deserving of the witness of the Spirit of Truth would extend that right and gift himself, which was more than John was authorized to do.

The day that Jesus approached John for baptism is worthy of inclusion among historical events deserving of reverential awe. From the scriptural accounts we have, it appears that Jesus and John had been separated from the moment they left the premortal realm until now, some thirty years later. Jesus knew who John was and sought him out; John's recognition of Jesus probably did not come because of any physical characteristics. But just as when, some thirty years before, "the babe leaped in [Elisabeth's] womb; and Elisabeth was filled with the Holy Ghost" (Luke 1:41) when Mary, the expectant mother of the Son of God, approached the mother-to-be of John, so John the Baptist, now a man, must have felt the electricity of the Spirit when that Holy Being of whom he was the forerunner approached. "Then cometh Jesus from Galilee to Jordan unto John, to be baptized of him." (Matt. 3:13.)[4]

The event was foreseen and prophesied by Lehi over six hundred years before its occurrence, and the river Jordan was named as the place where John "should baptize the Messiah with water." (1 Ne. 10:9.) It was over three thousand years ago that all the Israelites miraculously crossed the Jordan waters "until all the people were passed clean over." (Josh. 3:17.) Two great prophets, Elijah and Elisha, had both miraculously parted the waters of the Jordan and crossed over. (2 Kgs. 2:6-8, 14.) But the greatest parting of these waters would occur when John immersed the Son of God and brought him out again. And though the Son of God was pure and had no need of remission of sins, yet his act stood for obedience to God's commandments necessary for entrance into his kingdom. Every other person who has parted the waters of baptism in any other age in any other place in the world would need immersion for the remission of sins. And, as the leper Naaman was cleansed of his physical disease by washing in the Jordan's waters (2 Kgs. 5:10-14), so could all be cleansed of their spiritual maladies by worthily submitting to the ordinance now to be graced by the cleanser himself, Jesus, the Son of God. And Jesus, the sinless one, would teach by his baptism that perfection includes not only being free from sin, but also freely complying with the ordinances of God. (2 Ne. 31:5-7.)

John, again sensing the disparity between himself and a perfect being, stated: "I have need to be baptized of thee, and comest thou to me?" (Matt. 3:14.) But his humble restraint was superseded by the Master when he said, "Suffer [permit] me to be baptized of thee, for thus it becometh us to fulfill all righteousness." (JST, Matt. 3:43.)

Given the revealed pattern for the manner of baptism today (see D&C 20:73-74), it would be a justifiable assumption that John raised his right hand to the square and pronounced an authoritative and inspired prayer, perhaps embellished with words appropriate for the special nature of that particular occasion. He then completely immersed the Savior in the waters of the Jordan, following which Jesus "went up straightway [immediately] out of the water." (Matt. 3:16.)

Lehi's 600 B.C. prophecy stated that after the Son of God was baptized by John, "he should behold and bear record that he had baptized the Lamb of God, who should take away the sins of the world." (1 Ne. 10:10.) The Matthew account confirms that prophecy by recording that following the baptism of Jesus by John, "the heavens were opened unto him, and he saw the Spirit of God descending like a dove, and lighting upon him." (Matt. 3:16.) Elder Bruce R. McConkie explained: "John sees the heavens open and the Holy Ghost descend in bodily form, in serenity and peace, like a dove."[5]

Since the Holy Ghost is a *personage* of Spirit (see D&C 130:22), the only bodily form he could come in is that of his own self. But as a dove would descend in its heavenly flight, so the Holy Ghost descended to the earth from its heavenly sphere. And as the dove is a symbol of peace, so the Holy Ghost as a witness of God speaks that peaceful yet powerful witness to the souls of the faithful. Joseph Smith explained:

> [John] had the privilege of beholding the Holy Ghost descend in the form of a dove, or rather in the *sign* of the dove, in witness of that administration[.] The sign of the dove was instituted before the creation of the world, a witness for the Holy Ghost, and the devil cannot come in the sign of a dove. The Holy Ghost is a personage, and is in the form of a personage. It does not confine itself to the *form* of the dove, but in *sign* of the dove. The Holy Ghost cannot be transformed into a dove; but the sign of a dove was given to John to signify the truth of the deed, as the dove is an emblem or token of truth and innocence.[6]

We have little else to help in further understanding the sign of the dove, but we do know that there, at that place and that moment in mortal time, was a grand gathering of the Godhead, for as the Savior went up out of the water and the Holy Ghost appeared to give his witness for Christ, the voice of the Father issued from the heavens in supreme testimony: "This is my beloved Son, in whom I am well pleased." (Matt. 3:17.) Thus John beheld, and he bore witness. (See also D&C 93:15-17.)

Wherein did Jesus fulfill all righteousness in being baptized? An aspect that is often overlooked is the verification of the validity of prophecy. If inspired prophets recorded the future baptism of Jesus by John, then that word could not have been fulfilled had the events occurred other than foreseen. But the word of God is truth, and the representatives of God who prophesied of these very events had their heavenly edicts verified by their fulfillment.

With analytical insight, Nephi highlighted the following ways in which Jesus fulfilled all righteousness by being baptized:

1. "He showeth unto the children of men that, according to the flesh he humbleth himself before the Father." (2 Ne. 31:7.) Here was Jehovah, creator of worlds without number (see Moses 7:30); the very God who appeared amid fire and smoke on quaking Mount Sinai. (Ex. 19:18.) And yet, in the flesh as a mortal he set the pattern for all who would strive to become more like him: he humbled himself before his Father in heaven. With such an example, no earthly inhabitant, great or small, rich or poor, should dare to presume the stature of that pride and power which shuts out the quality of humility exemplified by Jesus the Christ.

2. He "witnesseth unto the Father that he would be obedient unto him in keeping his commandments." (2 Ne. 31:7.) Obedience is a many-faceted diamond. Humility is included; so also are love, self-mastery, ability to put in proper priority one's life and devotions, ability to subdue earthly passions and desires, the freedom of correct service. All of these and many more are reflected. But important above all was the focus of these qualities: it was obedience, not to the powers and doctrines of men or nations, but to God in heaven. They were *his* commandments that beautified the setting of obedience that the Savior manifested.

Nephi then emphasized that after Jesus was baptized, "the Holy Ghost descended upon him." (2 Ne. 31:8.) This was the pattern with Adam, the first man (see Moses 6:64-65); it was the pattern restored through Joseph Smith, prophet of the latter-day restoration, who stated it in simplicity in the fourth Article of Faith.

It was not that Jesus needed to qualify for the gift of the Holy Ghost any more than he needed to seek repentance, for as Elder McConkie suggested, "This was a formality only in his case, for he being holy and without sin, the Spirit was his companion always. At baptism he simply went through the form that is required for all men, and that he should have done so is manifest by the fact that 'the Holy Ghost descended upon him in the form of a dove.' "[7]

After describing the Savior's baptism, Nephi concluded that "it

180

showeth unto the children of men the straitness of the path, and the narrowness of the gate, by which they should enter, he having set the example before them." (2 Ne. 31:9.) Thus, in the example of baptism of water and of the Spirit (as well as all other conditions for exaltation), Jesus fulfilled all righteousness in that he accomplished "all that was required of him according to the terms and conditions of his Father's plan."[8] And, in so doing, he added a living letter of credence for the importance and authority of a legal administrator in God's kingdom when he sought out John for baptism.

The Temptations of Jesus

Paul wrote: "For we have not an high priest [Christ] which cannot be touched with the feeling of our infirmities; but was in all points tempted like as we are, yet without sin." (Heb. 4:15.) "Wherefore in all things it behoved him to be made like unto his brethren, that he might be a merciful and faithful high priest in things pertaining to God, to make reconciliation for the sins of the people. For in that he himself hath suffered being tempted, he is able to succour them that are tempted." (Heb. 2:17-18.)

The temptations following his baptism were not the first Jesus confronted, for the Lord said, "Power is not given unto Satan to tempt little children, until they begin to become accountable before me." (D&C 29:47.) Jesus was now a mature man and surely had been tempted before. Neither would these be the last temptations he would endure. But these were exemplified by the Gospel writers for a teaching purpose, probably that of example. And they most probably were unique.

"Then was Jesus led up of the Spirit, into the wilderness, to be with God." (JST, Matt. 4:1.) What communion took place between Jesus and his Father is not now in written form for us to examine. But after he had undergone forty days and nights of fasting and communion, it is recorded that Jesus was hungry. At this seemingly opportune moment, Satan entered the stage with a proposition and a challenge: "If thou be the Son of God, command that these stones be made bread." (Matt. 4:3.) Had not Esau, in a moment of hunger, traded his birthright to satisfy his physical appetite? Perhaps the power of appetite would again prevail.

This confrontation between Jesus and Lucifer was no mythological or hypothetical setting. Elder McConkie wrote: "We must assert that this was a personal appearance, one in which the spirit Lucifer, who was cast out of heaven for rebellion, came in person and spoke to Jesus face to face. It was no mere placing of thoughts in his mind, but an open and spoken conversation."[9]

Jesus would later work miracles that would provide food for the hungry (e.g., Matt. 14:16-21). Previously, manna had been provided miraculously to preserve the Children of Israel from starvation, being in fact a type of Jesus himself, who was the "bread from heaven." (See John 6:28-35, 47-51.)[10] Jesus, now hungry, could indeed satisfy his physical appetite with bread. He had the power to perform such a miracle. But to do so would have been to obey a command of Satan (cf. Moses 5:18), who seeks the "misery of all mankind." (2 Ne. 2:18.) It would also be an abuse of his divine powers for convenience' sake.

Jesus answered, "It is written, Man shall not live by bread alone, but by every word that proceedeth out of the mouth of God." (Matt. 4:4.) He lived the lesson he would teach in John 6—in sustaining and nourishing spiritual life, to eat and drink of the divine nature is to live by God's words. (John 6:56-57, 63.) The "Bread of Life" himself had no intention of following the words of Satan: it was his Father's words that brought eternal life; his priorities were ordered correctly. The hunger of his body was overridden by the strength of his spirit.[11] Spiritual sustenance took precedence over physical satisfaction, and the temptation was overcome.

When Jesus stated, "It is written . . ." (Matt. 4:4), he emphasized the recognition of scriptural authority and reaffirmed its importance. He also highlighted the need to apply the written word to daily life. (See 1 Ne. 19:23.) Note that Jesus emphasized living by *every* word of God.[12] There would be no picking and choosing, but rather a total commitment. His example in overcoming this temptation provides some valuable insights and encouragement for all. Satan often makes his approach when the desire and need are both prominent.[13] It will thus be difficult to resist unless there is a higher, spiritual morality dominating our lives. We must know as a point of fact and experiential logic that when temptation is resisted and we look back upon the victory, the sweetness of accomplishment will always far outweigh the depression of sin inherent in succumbing to the will of the evil one. Jesus did satisfy his physical hunger in an appropriate way and time, unrecorded as far as we know. But Satan's hunger for dominance left a gnawing pain, and he was soon to return.

"Then Jesus was taken up into the holy city, and the Spirit setteth him on the pinnacle of the temple." (JST, Matt. 4:5.) The holy city was Jerusalem. The pinnacle of the temple, apostate though its officiators were, symbolized the house of God. Jesus would later cleanse it of the moneychangers and command, "Make not my Father's house an house of merchandise." (John 2:16.) He was appropriately placed on a high point of what should have been the holy house in the holy city. In addition to spiritual purposes that we can only wonder at, it was perhaps a symbolic act confirming the freely chosen and yet-to-be earned destiny of returning to his Father's celestial home at the conclusion of his mortal ministry.

Physically, the Savior was raised to the top of the temple. His mission in life could be lost now by a plunge from the pinnacle to the ground. Satan taunted: "If thou be the Son of God, cast thyself down: for it is written, He shall give his angels charge concerning thee: and in their hands they shall bear thee up, lest at any time thou dash thy foot against a stone." (Matt. 4:6.) Perhaps the tempter thought that the mingling of scripture with his satanic philosophy would add convincing weight to his enticement, as it likely had among many mortal prospects at other times and in other places. Whether or not Jesus would have survived the fall physically is not the most critical point; but it is critical that his status of perfection would have died in the plunge, for it was not the Father who beckoned, but the rebellious brother of premortal war who sought again to exalt himself by debasing another.

There was no question of the validity of the prophecy to protect the Son of God. Later he would pass unharmed through an angry crowd whose motive was to cast him to his death from the brow of a hill. (Luke 4:28-30.) When Peter drew his sword to protect Jesus from those who would lead him to the trial of death, the Master testified, "Thinkest thou that I cannot now pray to my Father, and he shall presently give me more than twelve legions of angels?" (Matt. 26:53.) The protection of Jesus was a given; perhaps the barb was the word *if:* "If thou be the Son of God . . ." (Matt. 4:6.) If Satan could establish even a wedge of doubt, perhaps he could split in two the mission of the Son of God. But such was not to be allowed by Jesus. His power was not for show to a wicked and rebellious brother whose intent was neither the manifestation of the Savior's power nor the establishment of the validity of prophecy, for Jesus knew that Satan "was a liar from the beginning." (D&C 93:25.)

In addition, that prompted plunge to the earth was but a pattern in disguise of Lucifer's trend from the premortal realms, from which he had been cast, to his final demise at the end of time. By the inspiration of Jehovah (whom Lucifer now faced), Isaiah revealed: "How art thou fallen from heaven, O Lucifer, son of the morning! how art thou cut down to the ground, which didst weaken the nations! For thou has said in thine heart, I will ascend into heaven, I will exalt my throne above the stars of God. . . . I will ascend above the heights of the clouds; I will be like the most High." (Isa. 14:12-14.) If Jesus would cast himself from his own Father's house, what a delight and a victory that would be for Satan! Isaiah continued concerning Satan: "Yet thou shalt be brought down to hell, to the sides of the pit." (Isa. 14:15.) Lucifer's pattern was one of downward progression. That thought alone should serve as a solemn warning to those who would contemplate following him in any degree.

In contrast, the Savior's pattern was upward. He had condescended to be born on earth with the sacred purpose of leading the way back up to his Father in heaven. The downward pattern was foreign to his commitment and desires; he would not move in the direction of his obstinate spirit brother. Again, unruffled, he resisted and overcame temptation. Satan would sink to the depths, but the Savior would not follow. By his own free agency, he chose to look to the heights of his Father and of his own chosen mission.

And he stayed atop the pinnacle of his Father's house, saying, "It is written again, Thou shalt not tempt the Lord thy God." (Matt. 4:7.) It is a common understanding among Latter-day Saints that Satan tempts men and women to do evil. But in what way would one tempt God? The Hebrew meaning of *tempt* is *to try, test.* The promise of protection for Jesus was scriptural fact. But it was not for the Savior to test the Father's promise just for the sake of a display of power. It was to be accomplished as willed by the Father. There are many promises extended to man from God. It is for men to seek to do the will of God, not to tempt or try to force or prove God's power by the will of men.

"And again, Jesus was in the Spirit, and it taketh him up into an exceeding high mountain, and showeth him all the kingdoms of the world, and the glory of them." (JST, Matt. 4:8.) Again, we have no record of the purpose or the events that were spiritual in this experience. In the pattern of many prophets who went up to commune with God, up into the top of a mountain, Jesus too had a vantage point from a height that revealed in a spiritually understood panorama all the kingdoms of this world. Included was their glory, presumably the power and status recognized by the worldly. All the mortal greatness was there in a composite vista. It must have been impressive to Satan, for at the conclusion of Jesus' spiritual experience, Satan came again and said, "All these things will I give thee, if thou wilt fall down and worship me." (Matt. 4:9.) This was the most blatant manifestation of the purpose in all of his temptations, the ultimate motive of his persistence: to gain worshipers, to counterfeit the throne of godhood that he had lost forever. "Fall down" indeed—another plunge toward his decayed realm. Men would bow the knee to their Maker, but it would be in properly placed reverential awe, motivated by love. Satan would rule the nations in anger for a season (see Isa. 14:6); the Lord would offer love to the point of divine sacrifice. The children of God would bow down in the thankful humility of free choice; the choice to fall down before Satan carried the force and deathly weight of sin.

Holy writ (to which Jesus turned in adding emphasis to his resistance of temptation) already had recorded: "The nation and kingdom that will not serve thee shall perish; yea, those nations shall be utterly wasted." (Isa. 60:12.) John would record, "The kingdoms of this world are become the kingdoms of our Lord and of his Christ; and he shall reign for ever and ever." (Rev. 11:15.) To Satan it must have been an attractive offer; to Christ it was but a synthetic jewel, and a poor one at that. All Satan could possibly offer was the transitory, unfulfilling, worldly power that would be terminated when (perhaps in Satan's hope, "if") Christ reigned anyway. What Satan had sold his soul to possess was worth nothing to the God he openly confronted. Again the Master's voice resounded in triumph: "Get thee hence, Satan: for it is written, Thou shalt worship the Lord thy God, and him only shalt thou serve." (Matt. 4:10.)

"Then the devil leaveth him." (Matt. 4:11.) Luke noted, appropriately: "And when the devil had ended all the temptation, he departed from him *for a season.*" (Luke 4:13, emphasis added.) None of his weapons had even scratched the surface, let alone destroyed the mission of the Savior. Jesus had left a perfect pattern for resistance. In turn, Satan had left a pattern for his attack upon mankind, the perception of which could be very helpful in overcoming his enticements. President David O. McKay taught: "Now, nearly every temptation that comes to you and me comes in one of those forms. Classify them, and you will find that under one of those three nearly every given temptation that makes you and me spotted, ever so little maybe, comes to us as (1) *a temptation of the appetite;* (2) *a yielding to the pride and fashion and vanity of those alienated from the things of God;* or (3) *a gratifying of the passions,* or a desire for the riches of the world, or power among men."[14]

Jesus, the Light that would be held up for all the world to see (3 Ne. 18:24), had conformed to the words of God while resisting the enticements of Satan. His example of humble obedience to the will and ordinances of his Father had clearly marked the path by which others could attain similar blessings. The detractor from the path, Satan, had thrown his poisonous darts without effect. The Savior's love for his fellow beings led him on to the infinite atonement whereby all who desired to follow him could gain power to do so.

NOTES

1. Bruce R. McConkie, *Mormon Doctrine,* 2nd ed. (Salt Lake City: Bookcraft, 1966), p. 71.

2. W. Bauer, W. F. Arndt, and F. W. Gingrich, *A Greek-English Lexicon of the New Testament* (Chicago: University of Chicago, 1957), p. 321.

3. Elder Bruce R. McConkie stated: "Without the Melchizedek Priesthood salvation in the kingdom of God would not be available for men on earth, for the ordinances of salvation—the laying on of hands for the gift of the Holy Ghost, for instance—could not be authoritatively performed." (*Mormon Doctrine,* p. 479.) "John the Baptist 'was a descendant of Aaron' and held the keys of the Aaronic Priesthood. . . . Faith, repentance, and baptism—comprising as they do the preparatory gospel—fall within its province, though the laying on of hands for the gift of the Holy Ghost is not a prerogative that attends it." (Ibid., pp. 10-11.) See also Robert J. Matthews, "A Voice in the Wilderness: An Interview with John the Baptist," chapter 9 in this volume.

4. For a beautiful description of circumstances that might have attended the baptism of Jesus, see Bruce R. McConkie, *The Mortal Messiah: From Bethlehem to Calvary,* 4 vols. (Salt Lake City: Deseret Book, 1979-81), 1:399-401.

5. McConkie, *The Mortal Messiah* 1:401.

6. *Teachings of the Prophet Joseph Smith,* pp. 275-76, emphasis added.

7. *The Mortal Messiah* 1:402.

8. Ibid., p. 401.

9. Ibid., p. 411.

10. See also Kent P. Jackson, "The Bread of Life," chapter 19 in this volume.

11. This is one of the purposes of the fast, that those who properly fast gain spiritual strength and discipline their bodily appetites by the strength of their spirits. (See Isa. 58.)

12. "And I give unto you a commandment, that ye shall forsake all evil and cleave unto all good, that ye shall live by every word which proceedeth forth out of the mouth of God." (D&C 98:11.)

13. The need may be real or perceived. Some individuals' needs are really wants, but Satan will take their perceived "need" and build upon it.

14. David O. McKay in *Conference Report,* October 1911, p. 59.

11

THE EARLY JUDEAN MINISTRY
(John 2 and 3)

KAY EDWARDS

The second and third chapters of John detail a series of events at the beginning of the Savior's public ministry from which some powerful lessons can be drawn. It seems safe to conclude, at the very least, that these events were viewed as significant moments in the Savior's life, since they were considered worthy of recording and preservation. The Savior's public ministry was brief and the surviving record circumscribed. It is logical to assume that each event in the limited record preserved down through the ages is a precious pearl from which wisdom and guidance can be derived.

From the beginning, Jesus's ministry to his people on the earth took the very steps we must take when we accept his gospel and begin our own ministry as his disciples. An understanding of and compliance with these steps ensures that our feet will be set firmly on the "strait and narrow path." (1 Ne. 8:20.) The following discussion will review each major event and seminal principle taught, as it is recorded in John 2 and 3.

The Miracle at Cana

The miracle at Cana was the first of the recorded miracles of Jesus. (See John 2:1-11.) While attending a wedding feast, in which his mother and his disciples also were present, Jesus turned water into wine, bringing honor to the bridegroom and to him who presided at the feast. (See John 2:9-10.) John did not tell us much

Kay Edwards is professor of family sciences at Brigham Young University.

about the event except to say that it "manifested forth his glory" and increased his disciples' faith in him. (John 2:11.) Worthy of note is Jesus' comment to his mother in verse 4, which he uttered after she told him that the wine had run out: "Woman, what have I to do with thee? mine hour is not yet come." Various ideas have been proposed concerning the nature of the Lord's seemingly harsh rebuke of his mother. Perhaps it can be viewed as a public declaration of commitment. With these words, Jesus aligned himself specifically with his Father's work. Although he continued to be solicitous of his mother's welfare and concerned for her care, a transition seems to have been taking place between the "Jesus of Nazareth" and "Jesus the Christ," who was finally embarking on his long anticipated service in behalf of his Father's children. He had put his hand to the plow and could not now pause or turn back (see Luke 9:62), but had to move on with the inexorable series of events leading to his destiny in Gethsemane and upon Golgotha.

The Joseph Smith Translation makes a significant change in this verse that removes the issue of the Lord's seemingly sharp tone in addressing his mother: "Woman, what wilt thou have me to do for thee? that will I do; for mine hour is not yet come." (JST, John 2:4.)

Just as Jesus did, we too find ourselves required to make a public declaration of our commitment to a new life, with new responsibilities and new purposes. As each individual accepts the gospel covenant, he or she faces the challenge of communicating to family, friends, colleagues, and others that their former associate is no more, and that new allegiances exist and new concerns must be addressed.

A Visit to Capernaum

John 2:12 mentions briefly a short trip that Jesus took to Capernaum before leaving Galilee for the beginning of his ministry in Jerusalem. Although this episode may seem out of place or disruptive to the writer's narrative of these early days in the Savior's ministry, or at least unimportant, one author has characterized it as a watershed in Christ's life:

As long ago as Aristotle's day it was a recognized literary canon that a skilled dramatist does not allow episodes and characters with no significance for the unraveling of the plot to obtrude into his play. And this evangelist is much too expert a writer to crowd his meager space with pointless irrelevancies that mean nothing and lead nowhere. If he sets down this sojourn in Capernaum, it is because something momentous must have happened there. But what? Every life has its watersheds, where things begin to run in a new direction. A youth from some remote glen sets out for a new life in a city; and when the road reaches its highest point before it dips down on the farther side, instinctively he pauses to look back at the familiar scenes that he is leaving, soaking every item of it all into his memory, and then turns and faces out into the new and unknown bigger world into which he is venturing. These few days at Capernaum were such a watershed for Jesus Christ. There the old definitely was finished. There the new just as definitely was begun.[1]

Apparently in this brief visit to Capernaum with family and disciples, the Savior bade farewell to the former and solidified his relationship to the latter. His public ministry in Judea was soon to commence, and his life would never be the same.

Cleansing the Temple

After leaving Capernaum, Jesus traveled to Jerusalem to celebrate the Passover, present himself to his Father, and pay homage in his holy temple. Upon his arrival in Jerusalem, he apparently hurried directly to the temple to present himself and observe the religious customs of his people. Elder James E. Talmage pointed out that Jesus probably had attended other Passovers during the interval between his recorded visit to the temple at the age of twelve (Luke 2:42-50) and this visit. However, "he, not being thirty years old, could not have assumed the right or privilege of a teacher without contravening established customs." Elder Talmage explained further that to teach in the synagogue, a man had to be thirty years old.[2]

What Jesus found at the temple was noise and dirt and

confusion, a cacophony of sounds from birds, animals, people of diverse languages, merchants of sacrificial emblems, and money-changers—all polluting the sanctity of this great edifice. That place, which should have been the scene of utmost reverence and spiritual uplift where he could refresh himself spiritually for the demanding days ahead, was instead a scene of chaos and confusion.

In righteous indignation, Jesus set about the task of driving out wickedness and restoring his Father's house to the religious purpose, order, and faith that should reign there. (See D&C 88:119.) What is most surprising, perhaps, about this event is that there appeared to be little, if any, protest made or resistance raised against his actions. Even when he had finished, there was no condemnation of what had transpired, only a query as to the authority he claimed that justified his having acted in such a way: "What sign shewest thou unto us, seeing that thou doest these things?" (John 2:18.) Why this seeming acquiescence, by those most directly affected, to violent action on the part of this young stranger from Galilee? Frederic Farrar has offered this explanation: "Because Vice cannot stand for one moment before Virtue's uplifted arm. Base and grovelling as they were, these money-mongering Jews felt, in all the remnant of their souls which was not yet eaten away by infidelity and avarice, that the Son of Man was *right*."[3]

Christ responded to the Jewish leaders' request for a sign of his authority to carry out a task that was their responsibility and in which they knew they had failed to do their duty. He declared himself: "Destroy this temple, and in three days I will raise it up." (John 2:19.) From the way he phrased his response to their queries, it appears that they had become somewhat threatening in their questioning. However, it was at this moment, in this place, to these people, that he revealed his calling and earthly mission and foretold the events that would culminate in the freedom of all mankind from death and sin. The most momentous message in all time had been delivered, and it fell on deaf ears; blinded eyes looked upon its speaker—not a prophetic messenger this time, but even Jesus Christ, the Son of the Living God.

For those of us who heed his words, the example is set: "No

man, having put his hand to the plough, and looking back, is fit for the kingdom of God." (Luke 9:62.) The call had come, the commitment was made; he must be about his Father's business. So, too, must we get on with this new life we have chosen. "Our assignment is affirmative: . . . to carry the gospel to our enemies, that they might no longer be our enemies," President Spencer Kimball has said.[4] Reluctance and hesitation in moving forward with our Father's work is unseemly. A clear declaration of allegiance and purpose is required.

The Conversation with Nicodemus

As Christ continued his ministry in Jerusalem, a ruler of the Jews, one Nicodemus, came to him, as the scripture says, "by night." (John 3:1-2.) A number of authors have written about this encounter between Jesus and Nicodemus. President Kimball used the incident to illustrate the difficulties some encounter in receiving the witness and accepting the fullness of the gospel of Jesus Christ.[5] Elder Bruce R. McConkie interpreted Nicodemus's choice of time to visit the Savior as an attempt to protect his worldly position while investigating the gospel preached by this new Rabbi.[6] Arthur John Gossip suggests that Nicodemus came at night because he was a cautious man, sensitive to his responsibility as "a religious leader to whom others looked for guidance, and whom they were likely to follow. It was not fair to the people, or to God, that he should plunge enthusiastically after every seeming prophet. He must find means to see for himself, to question, to meet Christ face to face, to base his decision not on carried stories, but on firsthand experience and evidence. And he did it."[7] Elder Talmage felt that Nicodemus's belief failed to develop into a condition of true faith, but that he did more than most of his associates.[8]

Whatever Nicodemus's motivation may have been, his questions elicited specific instruction as to the next step he must take: "Verily, verily, I say unto thee, Except a man be born again, he cannot see the kingdom of God" (John 3:3), followed by a powerful statement of the Savior's calling and mission.

Nicodemus appears to have been a very literal man in his thinking. He had great difficulty comprehending the words of the Savior and did not easily grasp the analogy being used. This concept of being "born again" continues to be a stumbling block in the understanding of the people of the world as they struggle to find the "strait and narrow path." Why does it matter so much that we understand? Because this new birth is the *gateway* to that path that leads to eternal life. God explained to Adam:

> That by reason of transgression cometh the fall, which fall bringeth death, and inasmuch as ye were born into the world by water, and blood, and the spirit, which I have made, and so became of dust a living soul, even so ye must be born again into the kingdom of heaven, of water, and of the Spirit, and be cleansed by blood, even the blood of mine Only Begotten; that ye might be sanctified from all sin, and enjoy the words of eternal life in this world, and eternal life in the world to come, even immortal glory;
>
> For by the water ye keep the commandment; by the Spirit ye are justified, and by the blood ye are sanctified;
>
> Therefore it is given to abide in you; the record of heaven; the Comforter; the peaceable things of immortal glory; the truth of all things; that which quickeneth all things, which maketh alive all things; that which knoweth all things, and hath all power according to wisdom, mercy, truth, justice, and judgment. (Moses 6:59-61.)

It is a mistake to assume that baptism, even when performed by proper authority, is all that is involved in being "born again." It is only one step in a process of change whereby we "have put off the old man with his deeds; and have put on the new man, which is renewed in knowledge after the image of him that created him." (Col. 3:9-10.) The entire process is "a gradual thing," Elder McConkie explained. "We are born again by degrees, and we are born again to added light and added knowledge and added desires for righteousness as we keep the commandments."[9]

Why is it so important that we be "born again"? The Prophet Joseph Smith taught:

> Except a man be born again, he cannot see the kingdom of God. . . . A man may be saved, after the judgment, in the

terrestrial kingdom, or in the telestial kingdom. But he can never see the celestial kingdom of God, without being born of water *and* the Spirit . . . he can never come unto Mount Zion, and unto the city of the living God, the heavenly Jerusalem, and to an innumerable company of angels; to the general assembly and Church of the Firstborn, . . . and to God the judge of all, and to the spirits of just men made perfect, and to Jesus the Mediator of the new covenant, unless he becomes as a little child, and is taught by the Spirit of God.[10]

What does it mean to be "born of water and of the spirit"? It means to be born of God, so that we are changed from a "carnal and fallen state, to a state of righteousness" (Mosiah 27:25), thereby becoming new creatures of the Holy Ghost. Peter said that we must become newborn babes in Christ. (1 Pet. 2:2.) King Benjamin taught that conversion results in being "spiritually begotten" of God, being born of Christ, and thus becoming his sons and daughters. (Mosiah 5:7.)

Elder McConkie explained the process further:

The first birth takes place when spirits pass from their pre-existent first estate into mortality; the second birth or birth "into the kingdom of heaven" takes place when mortal men are born again and become alive to things of the Spirit and of righteousness. . . . The second birth begins when men are baptized in water by a legal administrator; it is completed when they actually receive the companionship of the Holy Ghost, becoming new creatures by the cleansing power of that member of the Godhead. Mere compliance with the formality of the ordinance of baptism does not mean that a person has been born again. No one can be born again without baptism, but the immersion in water and the laying on of hands to confer the Holy Ghost do not of themselves guarantee that a person has been or will be born again. The new birth takes place only for those who actually enjoy the gift or companionship of the Holy Ghost, only for those who are fully converted, who have given themselves without restraint to the Lord.[11]

The importance of this full conversion was stressed by Alma in his address to his "brethren of the church." He pointedly asked them if they had "spiritually been born of God," received the Lord's image in their countenances, and had the "mighty change" in their hearts that always attends the birth of the Spirit. (Alma 5:14.) If they had not, he warned them, "Ye cannot suppose that such can have place in the kingdom of heaven; but they shall be cast out for they are the children of the kingdom of the devil." (Alma 5:25.)

Being born again puts us on the strait and narrow path, but it takes constant devotion to the Savior and diligence in keeping his commandments to remain there. We are cautioned that once the process is complete and the state of spiritual rebirth again is achieved, we can lose it. Alma asked his brethren, "If ye have experienced a change of heart, and if ye have felt to sing the song of redeeming love, . . . can ye feel so now?" (Alma 5:26.) He had referred to their fathers, saying that "a mighty change was also wrought in their [the fathers'] hearts, and they humbled them-selves and put their trust in the true and living God. And behold, *they were faithful until the end; therefore they were saved.*" (Alma 5:13, emphasis added.)

The Son of Man Which Is in Heaven

During the recorded interview between Jesus and Nicodemus, Jesus foretold his ascension into heaven, reaffirming his relation-ship to his Father. (John 3:13.) In his discussion of this verse, Elder Talmage proposed the following: "There is . . . a profound signif-icance attaching to the Lord's use of the title 'The Son of Man', and this lies in the fact that He knew His Father to be the one and only supremely exalted Man, whose Son Jesus was both in spirit and in body—the Firstborn among all the spirit-children of the Father, the Only Begotten in the flesh—and therefore, in a sense applicable to Himself alone, He was and is the Son of the 'Man of Holiness,' Elohim, the Eternal Father."[12]

It was revealed to Enoch that "in the language of Adam, Man of Holiness is his name, and the name of his Only Begotten is the Son of Man, even Jesus Christ." (Moses 6:57.) The Father later proclaimed himself to Enoch: "Behold, I am God; Man of Holiness is my name; Man of Counsel is my name; and Endless and Eternal is my name, also." (Moses 7:35.) In this short verse, Jesus revealed to Nicodemus, and to those of us who read his scriptures, the nature of God the Eternal Father.

A Type of Christ

When Jesus referred to his ascension into heaven, he likened his crucifixion to the serpent staff raised by Moses in the wilderness. (John 3:14; see Num. 21:8-9.) If a man had been bitten by a poison serpent and he looked upon the bronze serpent set upon a pole, he lived. Jesus promised that those who believe in him—his mission and its purpose—also will not perish, but shall be blessed with eternal life. One Latter-day Saint commentator has written the following concerning this event:

> The brazen serpent, like so many incidents in Israel's wanderings and religious life, was a type, an actual historical reality which pointed beyond itself to a greater and more powerful reality. What is remarkable is that these things were known long before Calvary. Nephi the son of Helaman, approximately twenty years before the coming of Christ to earth, spoke of the testimony of Moses regarding the Redeemer. "Yea, did he [Moses] not bear record that the Son of God should come? And as he lifted up the brazen serpent in the wilderness, even so shall he be lifted up who should come." Nephi continued: "And as many as should look upon that serpent should live, even so as many as should look upon the Son of God with faith, having a contrite spirit, might live, even unto that life which is eternal." (Hel. 8:14-15.)[13]

God Loved Us So He Sent His Son

Probably the most powerful testimony of the love of our Father in heaven for us, collectively and individually, was then borne by Jesus: "For God so loved the world, that he gave his only begotten Son, that whosoever believeth in him should not perish, but have everlasting life." (John 3:16.) In an effort to help us to understand the enormity of the gift of God and the depth of the love revealed in this verse of scripture, Gossip has written:

> In the day of the world's desperation [referring to World War II] people gave their means, their time, their strength, even their boy on whom their homes were centered, making no effort to hold him back, prepared to run even that risk; feeling that for the emancipation of the multitudes enslaved or threatened, and for the upholding of our tottering human liberties, even that price was not too vast. All that they paid down, unflinchingly, and having paid it, sit now in an emptied home. That, says this scripture, is the nearest human analogy to what God did to save the world. Always the New Testament asserts that that is the background of the gospel and the origin from which it flows. He who out of the hugeness of his liberality has devised for us so many and such gracious benefits, has added this last crowning act of generosity, than which even God can do no more: has given us his only Son.[14]

When all else is done—the gospel has been accepted, we have turned our back on the old life and on old companions who continue in that way, repentance and the cleansing of our bodily temples have occurred, we have been spiritually born again and have received his image in our countenance—we are left with this one last step, without which all else is vain. We must accept the gift of God's Only Begotten Son and believe in him. In essence, "this is the condemnation, that light is come into the world, and men loved darkness rather than light." (John 3:19.)

Humility and Self-abnegation

In the third chapter of John we find one final lesson of what it means to be spiritually reborn as a son or daughter of Jesus Christ. A few short verses highlight the relationship between Jesus and John the Baptist that had begun when they were yet in the womb.

Jesus and his disciples had left Jerusalem and journeyed into Judea, where they began baptizing not far from the area where John still labored in his ministry. Those who had been taught by

John and who loved him were apparently confused as to the implications of Jesus' new activities as they pertained to the work John had been doing, including even the baptizing of Jesus himself. (See John 3:26.) John's response of self-abnegation and declaration is poetical in its imagery and the example *par excellence* of humility and submission to God: "Ye yourselves bear me witness, that I said, I am not the Christ, but that I am sent before him. He that hath the bride is the bridegroom: but the friend of the bridegroom, which standeth and heareth him, rejoiceth greatly because of the bridegroom's voice: this my joy therefore is fulfilled. He must increase, but I must decrease." (John 3:28-30.)

Concerning this Elder Talmage wrote: "In such a reply, under the existent condition, is to be found the spirit of true greatness, and of a humility that could rest only on a conviction of divine assurance to the Baptist as to himself and the Christ. In more than one sense was John great among all who are born of women. He had entered upon his work when sent of God so to do; he realized that his work had been in a measure superseded, and he patiently awaited his release, in the meantime continuing in the ministry, directing souls to his Master."[15]

Humility is a precondition of progress in spiritual things. It is required, along with repentance, to qualify for baptism. (D&C 20:37.) Without it, one cannot see God and gain entrance to the kingdom of God hereafter. (D&C 67:10; 2 Ne. 9:41-42.) In the interval between these two events, humility is required of all those who embark in the service of God (D&C 4:6; 12:8) and is a prerequisite to gaining wisdom (D&C 136:32-33).

Without humility, self-abnegation is impossible. Pride, conceit, haughtiness, and vainglory are of the world. To keep the commandments of God requires a denial of the desires of our own heart and a renunciation of self in favor of God. John's example of both these virtues is striking. As he exemplified, so, too, should we be: humble before God, denying our own desires, patiently awaiting our release from this carnal existence, serving diligently where and how we are called, and declaring in word and deed that Jesus is the Christ, the Son of the Living God, the Savior of all mankind. Only in this way can we assure that our feet are still on the strait and narrow path, that our lives are worthy of acceptance, and that we will hear him say, "Well done, thou good and faithful servant" (Matt. 25:21) as he welcomes us into his kingdom.

NOTES

1. Arthur John Gossip, "The Gospel According to St. John: Exposition," in *The Interpreter's Bible* (New York: Abingdon Press, 1952), 12:495.

2. James E. Talmage, *Jesus the Christ* (Salt Lake City: Deseret Book, 1979), p. 166. Here he quotes Clarke, *Bible Commentary:* " '[Thirty] was the age required by the law to which the priests must arrive before they could be installed in their office.' Jesus may possibly have had regard for what had become a custom of the time, in waiting until He had attained that age before entering publicly on the labors of a Teacher among the people. . . . To have taught in public at an earlier age would have been to arouse criticism, and objection, which might have resulted in serious handicap or hindrance at the outset."

3. Frederic W. Farrar, *The Life of Christ* (New York: John B. Alden), p. 102; emphasis added.

4. Spencer W. Kimball, "The False Gods We Worship," *Ensign,* June 1976, p. 6.

5. Spencer W. Kimball, *Faith Precedes the Miracle* (Salt Lake City: Deseret Book, 1972), pp. 14-20.

6. Bruce R. McConkie, *The Mortal Messiah: From Bethlehem to Calvary,* 4 vols. (Salt Lake City: Deseret Book Co., 1979-82), 1:470.

7. Gossip, p. 504.

8. Talmage, p. 170.

9. Bruce R. McConkie, "Jesus Christ and Him Crucified," in *1976 BYU Devotional Speeches of the Year* (Provo: Brigham Young University Press, 1976), p. 399.

10. *Teachings of the Prophet Joseph Smith,* p. 12; emphasis added.

11. Bruce R. McConkie, *Mormon Doctrine,* 2nd ed. (Salt Lake City: Bookcraft, 1966), p. 101.

12. Talmage, p. 143.

13. Robert L. Millet, "Lessons in the Wilderness," *Studies in Scripture, vol. 3: The Old Testament—Genesis to 2 Samuel* (Sandy, Utah: Randall Book, 1985), pp. 197-98.

14. Gossip, p. 511.

15. Talmage, pp. 164-65.

12

"NO PROPHET IS ACCEPTED IN HIS OWN COUNTRY"
(Luke 4; John 4)

STEPHEN D. RICKS

As the congregation in Nazareth turned angrily on Jesus for announcing the fulfillment of the Servant prophecies in Isaiah 61, he responded, "No prophet is accepted in his own country." (Luke 4:16-24.)[1] Conversely, Jesus was received as prophet and Messiah by the Samaritans of Sychar, where, at the well of the city, he had plainly told the woman that he was the expected Messiah. (John 4:25-26.) While an underlying theme of both of these accounts is the rejection/acceptance of Jesus as the Son of Man, each presupposes a religious, cultural, and political situation—in Luke 4, synagogues and synagogue worship, and in John 4, the relations between the Jews and the Samaritans, as well as Samaritan beliefs—that were an inherent and self-evident part of the life of first century A.D. Palestine, but are in many respects foreign to us. Only with some understanding about these cultural facts can these passages be fully understood.

Synagogue Worship in the Time of Christ

Jewish worship in the time of Jesus was centered in the temple and the synagogue. From its beginning, the synagogue served a function different from that of the temple. The temple was primarily a site of priestly sacrifice and the destination of national pilgrimage at the three great pilgrim feasts: Passover, Tabernacles,

Stephen D. Ricks is associate professor of Hebrew and Semitic languages at Brigham Young University.

and Weeks.[2] The synagogue, on the other hand, was the place of regular communal worship as well as a significant locus of religious education.[3]

The origins of the synagogue remain somewhat obscure, although most scholars are agreed that it was already a well-established institution in the early pre-Christian centuries.[4] Unlike the temple, which was located at a single site in Palestine at this time, synagogues were found in individual communities throughout the land of Israel.

The synagogue at the time of Christ was generally oriented to the east or toward Jerusalem,[5] and was rectangular in shape, with a single nave and a raised platform in the front third of the building from which readings from selected texts of the scriptures were given during services. In many ancient synagogues of Palestine, seating was built into the walls adjacent to the speaker's platform; additional seats may also have been set up in the interior of the synagogue in the rear two-thirds of the building.[6] Seating was arranged in a particular order, with the younger members of the synagogue seated behind the older and more distinguished members.[7] Although it is a matter of dispute, women in the congregation seem to have been separated from the men.[8]

The order of service was already well developed at the time of Christ. From sources that are nearly contemporary with the New Testament, synagogue services at this period included the following elements: (1) private prayer upon entrance to the synagogue; (2) the recitation of the *Shema'*, a canonical confession of faith in one God; (3) communal prayers; (4) reading from a part of the Torah (the first five books of the Old Testament); (5) reading from the prophets; and (6) following a prayer, a sermon from one of the members of the congregation.[9]

The *Shema'*, named from the opening words of Deuteronomy 6:4, consists of Deuteronomy 6:4-9 and 11:13-21, and Numbers 15:37-41, preceded and followed by one or two benedictions. These passages were recited as the great confessions of faith among the Jews: "Hear, O Israel: The Lord our God is one Lord: and thou shalt love the Lord thy God with all thine heart, and with all thy soul, and with all thy might. And these words, which I command thee this day, shall be in thine heart: and thou shalt teach them diligently unto thy children, and shalt talk of them when thou sittest in thine house, and when thou walkest by the way, and when thou liest down, and when thou risest up." (Deut. 6:4-7.)

Prayers were offered standing[10] facing the Holy of Holies in Jerusalem, a practice mentioned several times in the Old Testament; for example, Daniel 6:10, where Daniel "went into his house; and his windows being open in his chamber toward Jerusalem, he kneeled upon his knees three times a day, and prayed, and gave thanks before his God, as he did aforetime."[11] The communal prayers were not offered by the whole congregation but by a person designated to do so. The congregation made only certain verbal responses, such as the *Amen*.[12]

The synagogue service in New Testament times also included readings from both the Pentateuch (the first five books of the Old Testament) and the prophets.[13] Readings from the Pentateuch were based on a lectionary cycle of three or three-and-a-half years, that is, during this period of time all of the chapters of the first five books of the Old Testament were read in the course of the synagogue service. The readings from the prophets at this period may also have been based on such a three- or three-and-a-half-year cycle, but the evidence is less clear on that point.[14]

A major element of each synagogue service was the sermon given by one of the members of the congregation, who might be chosen by the synagogue leader before the service or might be called from among the congregants. (See Acts 13:15.) Whereas the readings in the scriptures were given standing up, the sermon was given seated. (See Luke 4:20.)

"As his custom was," Jesus, like many observant Jews of his day, went to synagogue services on the Sabbath. (Luke 4:16.) We need not suppose that all of the elements of the synagogue service are outlined in Luke 4:16-30, since it was not the intention of the writer to provide a detailed description of the order of service. Jesus read from Isaiah 61:1-2 one of the great messages of hope: "The Spirit of the Lord is upon me, because he hath anointed me to preach the gospel to the poor; he hath sent me to heal the brokenhearted, to preach deliverance to the captives, and recovering of sight to the blind, to set at liberty them that are bruised, to preach the acceptable year of the Lord." (Luke 4:18-19.) Whether Jesus himself selected the passage in Isaiah that he read to the congregation or had it selected for him is unclear from the text in Luke, though it seems, based on the later Jewish practice, that the latter is more likely. Thereafter, he was given the opportunity to deliver the sermon to the congregation. The thrust of Jesus' sermon was unmistakable: in him the great message of hope had found its fulfillment. So great was the anger of certain members of the congregation at what they thought was the unwarranted arrogance of "Joseph's son" that they "thrust him out of the city, and led him unto the brow of the hill whereon their city was built, that they might cast him down headlong" (Luke 4:29), but Jesus was able to pass through the crowd, perhaps through miraculous means, and make his way to Capernaum (see also John 7:30; 8:59; 10:39).

Jesus and the Samaritan Woman at the Well

There was probably no group with which the Jews had lived in longer tension than the Samaritans. Thus, it is not surprising that the Jewish and Samaritan views of Samaritan origins show considerable divergency. According to the Jewish view, the Samaritans were descendants of the intermixture of the few Israelites of the Northern Kingdom who were left at the time of the destruction of that kingdom by the Assyrians and the various peoples whom the Assyrians brought in. (See 2 Kgs. 17:24; Ezra 4:2, 10.) Whereas, according to the Jewish view, the Samaritans claimed nominal allegiance to the Mosaic faith—much of which had been taught to the Samaritans by an errant Jewish priest (the same mentioned in Neh. 13:28)—this Hebrew overlay barely concealed the deep heathen roots of their religion (2 Kgs. 17:24-41). According to the Samaritan version, on the other hand, the Israelite inhabitants of the Northern Kingdom had indeed been deported but never in large numbers. After fifty-five years of exile, even many of them were allowed to return to their homes.[15] Thus, according to the Samaritan view, the religion of the Samaritans had always remained predominantly Mosaic, with no heathen substrate. Further, the proximate cause of the breach between the two groups pre-dated the fall of the Northern Kingdom and resulted from the illegitimate transference of the sanctuary from its original location on Mount Gerizim, the "holy mountain" that faced the city of Shechem, to Shiloh in the time of Eli.[16] In the light of the actual features of Samaritan belief (which will be discussed below), which betray no more clear indications of influence from contiguous Ancient Near Eastern religions than do the beliefs and practices of Judaism of the same period, it seems likely that the Jewish claims of heathen influence are more the result of the historical tensions between the two groups than from any deeply rooted impulse in Samaritanism that lies outside of the Israelite tradition.

The tensions between the Jews and Samaritans were height-ened by the Jews' sense that they had been betrayed by the Samar-itans during the period of the Babylonian exile and immediately after. According to the account of the exile and return of the Jews in Ezra and Nehemiah, the Samaritans conspired with the foreign overlords of Palestine in order to prevent the Jews from rebuilding the walls of Jerusalem and reconstructing the city. (Ezra 4; Neh. 2:19-20; 4.) The result of these years of rancor and suspicion was a sharp division between members of the two groups that was tanta-mount to mutual ostracism.

The major beliefs in the Samaritan faith included: (1) belief in one God; (2) acknowledgment of Moses as the greatest and final, or "seal" of the prophets; (3) the acceptance of the first five books of the Old Testament as the word of God, and rejection of all else as scripture; (4) belief that Mount Gerizim is the chosen place of God, and acceptance of the temple that stood there as God's chosen sanctuary, with the concomitant rejection of all other sites (such as the temple in Jerusalem); (5) the appearance at the end of time of a *Taheb (Ta'eb)* or "Restorer," who would appear to usher in a new dispensation, teach the law, and restore the proper modes of worship; and (6) expectation of a final day of rewards for the righ-teous and punishment for the wicked.[17] Of these beliefs, the ones of particular importance for understanding the actions in John 4 are points 3, 4, and 5.

As mentioned above, Mount Gerizim was, in the Samaritan

view, the true holy mountain of God, not Mount Zion or any other mountain in the land of Israel. The Samaritan text of Deuteronomy 12:5 indicates that God "has chosen" Gerizim as his sacred mountain, not, as in the canonical version, that he "shall choose" it. Further, after each version of the Ten Commandments (Ex. 20:17; Deut. 5:21), the Samaritan text contains a passage commanding sacrifice on that mountain. In Samaritan tradition, the holiness of Mount Gerizim has all of the elements of sacredness that later rabbinic tradition accords to Mount Zion (that is, the Temple Mount): It existed before creation, was the first land to appear out of the watery deep, was the only elevation to escape the effects of the Flood, was the site of the true temple, and will be the only place to survive destruction at the time of the eschatological travails, and it is further identified with numerous places that are mentioned in the Pentateuch.[18]

Although it was often longer and inconvenient to do so, Jews traveling from Galilee to Jerusalem would often skirt the areas around Shechem (Sychar in the New Testament) in order to avoid the Samaritan population centers. In John 4, however, the initial motivation for going into Samaritan country appears to be a wish to escape as quickly as possible the dangers that Jesus confronted in Judea: "When therefore the Lord knew how the Pharisees had heard that Jesus made and baptized more disciples than John, . . . he left Judaea, and departed again into Galilee. And he must needs go through Samaria." (John 4:1, 3-4.) Implied in this was the "divine hand" working to create a teaching opportunity for Jesus.[19]

The Samaritan expresses surprise that Jesus would ask for a drink from her, since, John parenthetically explains, "the Jews have no dealings with the Samaritans." (John 4:9; Raymond Brown renders this passage, "Jews, remember, use nothing in common with Samaritans."[20]) The reason for this lack of contact between the two people results from the Jewish view that Samaritans were ritually impure: Samaritan women were, according to one passage in the Mishnah, menstruants from the cradle.[21] The Jewish attitude toward the Samaritans may also be reflected in a regulation enacted in A.D. 65 that declared all Samaritan women unclean and, consequently, any food or drink likewise ritually impure.

When the woman asks Jesus, "Art thou greater than our father Jacob, which gave us the well?" (John 4:12), she is reflecting the deep commitment felt by the Samaritans toward the patriarchal and Exodus figures in Israelite history. Conversely, all of the writings from the period after the entrance of Joshua and Israel into Canaan that were accepted by the Jews as canonical (with their accompanying theology) were viewed by the Samaritans as unauthorized accretions. There is, of course, an unconscious irony in the woman's statement, since she herself will shortly recognize Jesus as the Messiah and one greater than Jacob.

After recognizing Jesus as a prophet who had correctly detailed to her her sad and sordid domestic history, the Samaritan woman further says to him: "Our fathers worshipped in this mountain; and ye say, that in Jerusalem is the place where men ought to worship." (John 4:20.) The mountain where her ancestors worshiped was, of course, Gerizim. Her statement implies a prime source of contention between the Samaritans and the Jews: the proper site of worship. Jesus' response does not immediately affirm the correctness of the one location as a site of worship and deny the legitimacy of the other. Rather, his answer serves to affirm that worship is potentially universal: "Woman, believe me, the hour cometh, when ye shall neither in this mountain, nor yet at Jerusalem, worship the Father. . . . But the hour cometh, and now is, when true worshippers shall worship the Father in spirit and in truth." (John 4:21, 23.) There is something importantly prophetic in this as well: just as the temple of the Samaritans had already been destroyed (in ca. 128 B.C.),[22] Jesus' statement portends the end of the temple in Jerusalem as well. Christ's utterance should not, however, be construed as a temple-denying statement. Rather, it affirms that the proper site of worship need not be restricted solely to the location of an epiphany.

The woman's further statement, "I know that Messias cometh, which is called Christ: when he is come, he will tell us all things" (John 4:25), seems to be an allusion to the Samaritan belief in the *Taheb* or restorer. The *Taheb* is not a messiah in the Jewish sense of a deliverer or an anointed prince. Rather, he is like the prophet foretold in Deuteronomy 18:18, where God says: "I will raise them up a Prophet from among their brethren, like unto thee, and will put my words in his mouth; and he shall speak unto them all that I shall command him." He will appear to usher in a new dispensation, instruct the people in the law, restore the temple on Gerizim, reinstitute the sacrificial cult, and obtain the recognition of the heathen.[23] Indeed, much of John 4:19-25 suggests this Samaritan view of the *Taheb,* one who will teach and restore "all things" to their proper and rightful place.

In terms of dramatic sense and literary artistry, John 4:4-42 is one of the most skillfully crafted pieces in the Gospels. Irony (John 4:12), words spoken and understood at different levels of meaning (John 4:10-11), along with the skillful use of the Samaritan townspeople in the manner of a Greek chorus (John 4:39-42),[24] all combine to create a powerful episode in which the Samaritan woman is led, step by step, along a path of recognition of Jesus, first as man, then as Jew, a prophet, and, finally, the Messiah. What began as a simple request for water resulted in the conversion of many Samaritans to Jesus.

Conclusion

Paradox and foreshadowing characterize both Luke 4 and John 4. Jesus, who had himself asserted that he had been sent only to the lost sheep of the house of Israel, was rejected by fellow Israelites but accepted by the despised Samaritans as Lord. Conversely, the disciples, whose great commission would be to go into all the world (see Matt. 28:19-20), can scarcely understand, but dare not question, Jesus' speaking to the Samaritan woman. The rejection of Jesus by his own townspeople in Luke 4 may serve as a veiled foreboding of his later rejection, and crucifixion, by the Jews.[25] On the other hand, Christ's success among the Samaritans foreshadows the situation of the early church, where the message of Jesus' Messiahship was spread among all the nations. Christ's famous paradox, "the last shall be first, and the first last" (Matt. 20:16), finds vivid illustration in these chapters.

NOTES

1. The British evangelical biblical scholars I. Howard Marshall and F. F. Bruce see Isaiah 61 as a Servant prophecy. (See I. Howard Marshall, *The Gospel of Luke* [Exeter: The Paternoster Press, 1978], p. 183. See also headnote to Isaiah 61 of the 1981 LDS edition of the Bible, where these verses are understood as referring to the Messiah.) But as Marshall also points out, Jesus appears in this passage in Luke 4 "as the eschatological prophet—a figure who is to be identified with the Messiah and the Servant of Yahweh." (Ibid., p. 178.)

2. The sacrificial cult associated with the temple is treated in greatest detail in the canonical text of the Bible in Leviticus, while the three pilgrim festivals—passover, Weeks, and Tabernacles—are mentioned several times in the Pentateuch (e.g., Ex. 23:14-17; Lev. 23:4-8, 15-21, 33-44).

3. The functional distinction between the worship of the synagogue (communal worship) and the rites of the temple (private devotion and ritual renewal) are paralleled by similar distinctions between the functions of temple and house in numerous other cultures. (See Harold W. Turner, *From Temple to Meeting House: The Phenomenology and Theology of Places of Worship* (The Hague: Mouton Publishers, 1979.) Certain of the differences between the two types—the temple admitting only those who belong to the community (and, in some instances, only those who are worthy to enter—cf. Moshe Weinfeld, "Instructions for Temple Visitors in the Bible and in Ancient Egypt," *Scripta Hierosolymitana* 28 [1984]), the synagogue admitting all who are desirous of participating, Jew and Gentile alike—are paralleled by the functional distinction between the chapel and temple among the Mormons; thus Turner (ibid., p. 46) notes that Mormon temples "became distinguished from Mormon chapels and tabernacles by being confined to those deemed ready to receive the mysteries of advanced religion. In no sense is it a Mormon congregational meeting place. It is reserved for special functions which all seem to have some cosmic reference. . . . Mormon temples . . . reveal some of the marks of the temple type and make the term entirely appropriate."

4. For a recent discussion (with some bibliography) on the antiquity and origins of the synagogue, see Joseph Gutmann, *Ancient Synagogues: The State of the Research* (Brown Judaic Studies Series 22) (Chico, Calif.: Scholars Press, 1981), pp. 1-6. Gutmann himself favors an origin in second century B.C. Palestine, but notes the wide variety of scholarly

opinion, the current balance weighing in favor of sixth-century B.C. Babylonia. Synagogues are mentioned in the Book of Mormon (2 Ne. 26:26; Alma 21:4; 26:29; 31:12; Hel. 3:9; 3 Ne. 18:32; Moro. 7:1), but this need not be taken as *prima facie* evidence for the existence of synagogues in the preexilic period, that is, during the time before the departure of Lehi's family from Jerusalem, since the forces that led to the creation of the synagogue were probably already operative during that period of time, even if the synagogue itself was not realized as an institution until a later period.

5. Geza Vermes, F. Millar, and Matthew Black, eds., *The History of the Jewish People in the Age of Jesus Christ (175 B.C.-A.D. 135),* 2 vols. (Edinburgh: T. & T. Clark, 1983), 2:442, n. 67.

6. Paul Billerbeck, "Ein Synagogengottesdienst in Jesu Tagen," *Zeitschrift für die neutestamentliche Wissenschaft* 55 (1965): 143-44.

7. Philo, *Quod Omnis Probus* 12; cf. 1QS 6:8-9.

8. The segregation of the sexes is not explicitly mentioned in the ancient literature. Philo's statement concerning the Therapeutae in *De Vita Contemplativa* 9 is not relevant, according to Vermes et al., eds. (*History of the Jewish People* 2:448, f. 98). There is no special mention of the separation of the sexes in the Talmud. Still, Vermes et al. assert that "the segregation of the sexes must be taken for granted." Galleries that may have been intended for women (as they are sometimes used in modern orthodox synagogues) have been found in several ancient synagogues in the Galilee. (See E. Goodenough, *Jewish Symbols in the Graeco-Roman World,* 13 vols. [New York: Pantheon Books, 1953], 1:182, 193.)

9. Marshall, *The Gospel of Luke,* p. 181; Vermes et al., *History of the Jewish People* 2:447-63. However, as Jacob Neusner has pointed out in numerous articles and books, great caution must be exercised to avoid retrojecting into an earlier period practices that were observed in later eras.

10. Matt. 6:5; Mark 11:25; Luke 18:11; Mishnah Berakhot 5:1; Mishnah Ta'anit 2:2.

11. Cf. 1 Kgs. 8:48; Ezek. 8:16; Mishnah Berakhot 4:5-6; Tosefta Berakhot 3:16; Jerome, *Commentarius in Ezechielem* 8:16. Franz Landsberger ("The Sacred Direction in Synagogue and Church," *Hebrew Union College Annual* 28 [1957]: 181 [= Joseph Gutmann, ed., *The Synagogue: Studies in Origins, Archaeology and Architecture* (New York: KTAV, 1975), 239]) wishes to avoid the word *orientation* in speaking of direction of prayer since it "signifies a turning toward the

east, while we are concerned not only with the east but also with the west, the north, and the south," i.e., whatever direction it was necessary to turn in order to face toward the Holy of Holies of the temple in Jerusalem. See also Erik Peterson, "Die geschichtlich Bedeutung der judischen Gebetsrichtung," *Theologische Zeitschrift* 3:1 (1947): 1-15 (= Erik Peterson, *Fruhkirche, Judentum un Gnosis* [Rome: Herder, 1959], pp. 1-14; E. Peterson, "La croce et la preghiera verso oriente," *Epheme-rides Liturgicae* 58 [1945]: 52-68 (= "Das Kreuz und das Gebet nach Osten," in Peterson, *Fruhkirche,* pp. 15-35).

12. Vermes et al., *History of the Jewish People* 2:449-50.

13. Besides the evidence for liturgical readings from the prophets in Luke 4:17, there is a similar account in Acts 13:14-15: "When they departed from Perga, they came to Antioch in Pisidia, and went into the synagogue on the sabbath day, and sat down. And after the reading of the law and the prophets the rulers of the synagogue sent unto them, saying, Ye men and brethren, if ye have any word of exhortation for the people, say on." Compare Mishnah Megillah 4:1-5.

14. Marshall, *Luke,* p. 181; L. C. Crockett, "Luke iv. 16-30 and the Jewish Lectionary Cycle: A Word of Caution," *Journal of Jewish Studies* 17 (1966): 13-46; J. Heinemann, "The Triennial Lectionary Cycle," *Journal of Jewish Studies* 19 (1968): 41-48; Charles Perrot, "Luc 4, 16-30 et la lecture biblique de l'ancienne synagogue," *Revue des Sciences Religieuses* 47 (1973): 324-40 (= Jacques-E. Menard, ed., *Exegese biblique et judaisme* [Strasbourg: Faculté de théologie catholique]), 170-83.

15. For a convenient summary of Samaritan history during the ancient and early medieval periods, from both the Jewish and Samaritan points of view, see J. Macdonald, "Samaritans," in *Encyclopedia Judaica,* 16 vols. (Jerusalem: Keter Publishing, 1975), 14:727-31; Theodor H. Gaster, "Samaritans," in G. A. Buttrick, ed., *The Interpreter's Dictionary of the Bible,* 4 vols. (Nashville: Abingdon Press, 1962), 4:191-92.

16. Shechem is mentioned numerous times in the Pentateuch; for example, Gen. 12:6; 33:18; 35:4; 37:14. Shechem was the site of the covenant renewal ceremony mentioned in Joshua 24 and was the place where the bones of Joseph were interred. (Josh. 24:32.) Mount Gerizim is also mentioned in the Pentateuch, as in Deuteronomy 11:29, where the blessing is "put" on Gerizim, the curse on Ebal, a mountain due north of Gerizim and also facing Shechem. In Deuteronomy 27:11-13, Moses commanded representatives of certain of the tribes to stand on Gerizim to bless the people, while representatives of other tribes would stand on

Ebal to curse the people in the event that they failed to observe God's laws.

17. Gaster, "Samaritans," pp. 193-94.

18. Gaster, "Samaritans," p. 194; Jonathan Z. Smith, "Earth and Gods," in *Map Is Not Territory* (Leiden: Brill, 1978), pp. 112-15. Similar beliefs developed in Christian tradition surrounding the sanctity of Golgotha; see J. Jeremias, "Golgotha und der heilige Felsen," *Angelos: Archiv für neutestamentliche Zeitgeschichte und Kulturkunde* 2 (1926). There are similar accounts in Muslim tradition outlining the primeval and eschatological significance of the Ka'ba in Mecca.

19. Ernst Haenchen, *John I,* Robert W. Funk, trans. (Philadelphia: Fortress Press, 1984), p. 218; Raymond E. Brown, *The Gospel According to John I-XII* (Garden City, New York: Doubleday & Co., 1981), p. 169.

20. Ibid., p. 170.

21. See David Daube, "Jesus and the Samaritan Woman: The Meaning of *sunchraomai,*" *Journal of Biblical Literature* 69 (1950): 137-47. Daube himself translates this passage, "The Jews do not use vessels together with Samaritans," ibid., p. 139.

22. According to Josephus, *Antiquities of the Jews* 13.9.1, the Jewish ruler John Hyrcanus had destroyed the Samaritan temple in 128 B.C.

23. John Bowman, "Early Samaritan Eschatology," *Journal of Jewish Studies* 5 (1955): 163-72; John Bowman, "Samaritan Studies," *Bulletin of the John Rylands Library* 40 (1957-58): 299.

24. Brown, *John,* p. 176.

25. Joseph Fitzmeyer, *The Gospel According to Luke I-IX* (Garden City, New York: Doubleday & Co., 1981), p. 529.

13

THE MIRACLES OF JESUS

REX C. REEVE, JR.

From the days of Adam down to the present time, people have sought to know and understand the true God. For the most part this search has been in vain and has produced only confusion and a proliferation of false ideas. The true God and his gospel can only be known as they are revealed from God by his own voice, the voice of angels, and by the Holy Ghost. (See Moses 5:6-9, 14-15.) From time to time he has revealed himself to certain individuals and made available a full understanding of his gospel to those who would see, hear, and follow.

The brief earthly ministry of Jesus Christ was a testimony that he was the true God sent from the Father to complete the Atonement and bring all men unto him through the principles of his gospel. His personal testimony was openly rejected by all except a few humble followers, even when accompanied by powerful teachings and great miracles. After his death and resurrection, his faithful disciples raised their voices in testimony of his divine Messiahship. To generations past and future, they testified that Jesus Christ was the Son of God and that all persons must come unto him to receive eternal life.

We believe in the literal reality of the miracles of Jesus. We believe that he actually healed the sick, fed the multitudes, calmed the sea, and raised the dead. The miracles of his earthly ministry,

---

Rex C. Reeve, Jr. is assistant professor of ancient scripture at Brigham Young University.

213

however, were not his first nor his greatest miracles. His power was made manifest prior to his mortal birth when he created the heavens and the earth, gave order to the universe, and placed Adam and Eve in the Garden of Eden. After the Fall, Jesus Christ was known as Jehovah, the God of the Old Testament, and by his power he performed the mighty miracles of ancient Israel. The miracle of his divine birth and his resurrection from the dead stand for all time as God's greatest miracles.

Miracles Show Christ's Divinity

The miracles Jesus performed during his earthly ministry were intended, among other things, to be proof to the Jews and to all people that he was the Messiah, the Son of God, and to reveal his character and power. When John the Baptist was in prison, he sent two of his disciples to Jesus to persuade his (John's) disciples to forsake him and follow Jesus. John's disciples asked: "Art thou he that should come, or do we look for another? Jesus answered and said unto them, Go and shew John again those things which ye do hear and see: The blind receive their sight, and the lame walk, the lepers are cleansed, and the deaf hear, the dead are raised up, and the poor have the gospel preached to them." (Matt. 11:3-5.) Jesus used his miracles to verify that he was the Messiah, the one to come, and not an imposter. After the man born blind was healed, the man said, "If this man were not of God, he could do nothing." (John 9:33.) When the Jews at the Feast of Dedication asked Jesus to tell them plainly if he were the Christ, he answered, "I told you, and ye believed not: the works that I do in my Father's name, they bear witness of me." (John 10:25.) On the day of Pentecost, Peter called Jesus "a man approved of God among you by miracles and wonders and signs, which God did by him in the midst of you, as ye yourselves also know." (Acts 2:22.)

One writer has stated that "the miracles were Jesus' credentials, presented to the people in general and the leaders in particular as signs of his divinity. . . . In this context some miracles were directed specifically to the people, some to the leaders of the Jews, some to the Law, and some to the Apostles. All this that they might prove, attest, and verify that Jesus was the Christ, the expected Messiah."[1]

A latter-day apostle explained how the miracles establish Christ's divinity. He declared: "Jesus performed miracles by the power of God, which he could not have done unless God was with him and approved of his ministry (John 9:30-33). His crowning teaching was: 'I am the Son of God' (John 10:36). Therefore, his miracles proved his divine Sonship, for God would not have endowed him with healing power if he were a false teacher."[2]

Finally, the apostle John, near the end of his Gospel, declared his reason for including a record of the signs Jesus performed during his ministry: "Many other signs truly did Jesus in the presence of his disciples, which are not written in this book: But these are written, that ye might believe that Jesus is the Christ, the Son of God; and that believing ye might have life through his name." (John 20:30-31.)

Why Did Christ Perform Miracles?

In addition to their central purpose, that of testifying that Jesus is the Christ, the variety of miracles and the various circumstances under which they were performed provide for additional purposes and meaning. In addition to witnessing Christ's divinity, each miracle with its own unique details may well have been performed for one or more of the following reasons:

1. To witness that Christ had power over all things by showing his power over disease, physical imperfections, nature, evil spirits, and death.

2. To reveal the character of Jesus and demonstrate his love and compassion for all mankind by showing love and compassion for individuals faced with the daily challenges of life.

3. To motivate men to recognize and cast off their spiritual infirmities in the same manner that physical infirmities were eliminated.

4. To create teaching opportunities to present sacred gospel truths. Through miracles Christ taught proper judgment, correct use of his power, testimony of the Father, and more.[3]

5. To give evidence, confirmation, and example to his teachings.

6. To prevent men in their ignorance or wickedness from frustrating the purposes of God. (See examples in Luke 4:28-30; John 8:59.) This may be consistent with Jesus' frequent comment that his "time had not come."[4]

7. To reward and strengthen the faith of individuals who believed in him and followed his teachings.

8. To set an example for his apostles and followers, as he would then command them to perform similar miracles.

9. To open the hearts of nonbelievers to receive further instructions, with the possibility of true conversion.

10. To stand as a witness against nonbelievers in the day of judgment.

The Miracles As Signs of Christ's Power

The Gospel writers, while able to record only a small portion of the teachings and doings of Jesus, devoted an average of about 14 percent of their text to reporting the miracles (Matthew, 12 percent; Mark, 25 percent; Luke, 13 percent; and John, 9 percent). With limited space, it is significant that each of the writers committed such a large portion of his record to the miracles as a testimony of Christ. The Gospels testify that the kingdom of God has been set up, and they outline the teachings and requirements of that kingdom. The writers' select accounts of specific miracles testify that as Messiah and King, Christ had power over all things, including power to provide redemption and salvation. He gave the power to perform miracles to the Twelve and sent them forth to heal the sick and to cast out devils.

Power over Sickness

When he was come down from the mountain, great multitudes followed him. And, behold, there came a leper and worshipped him, saying, Lord, if thou wilt, thou canst make me clean. And Jesus put forth his hand, and touched

216

him, saying, I will; be thou clean. And immediately his leprosy was cleansed. And Jesus saith unto him, See thou tell no man; but go thy way, shew thyself to the priest, and offer the gift that Moses commanded, for a testimony unto them. (Matt. 8:1-4; see also Mark 1:40-45; Luke 5:12-14.)

Leprosy, as we know it today, was a familiar disease in Mesopotamia and the Orient as far back as the third millennium B.C. In the Bible the term *leprosy* was quite probably used in a more general way to include several other diseases as well as true leprosy. The law of Moses gave the priest the responsibility to diagnose an individual afflicted with a skin disease and, according to carefully spelled out symptoms, pronounce him either clean or unclean. The law also contained instructions concerning rites and sacrifices for the ritual cleansing of lepers, their garments, and leprous houses.

Through the compassionate act of healing the leper, Jesus demonstrated his power over the vilest of physical ailments as well as over sin and even death. To the Jews, the power to cure leprosy should have been a special testimony that Jesus was their Messiah.

Luke alone recorded the account of the healing of ten lepers who asked for mercy from Jesus as he went to Jerusalem. (Luke 17:11-19.) In addition to Jesus' power over leprosy, the four Gospel writers provide ample testimony of his power over all manner of sickness, disease, and physical deformity. For example, a man infirm thirty-eight years was healed (John 5:1-15); a man with a withered hand was healed (Matt. 12:10-13; Mark 3:1-5; Luke 6:6-10); a deaf man with an impediment in speech was healed (Mark 7:32-37); a blind man was healed (Mark 8:22-26); a man born blind was healed (John 9:1-7); a man with dropsy was healed on the Sabbath (Luke 14:1-6); sight was restored to Bartimaeus and another blind beggar (Matt. 20:30-34; Mark 10:46-52; Luke 18:35-43); the ear of Malchus, the high priest's servant, was healed (Luke 22:50-51; John 18:10); and on other occasions multitudes were healed (Matt. 8:16-17; Mark 1:32-34; Luke 4:40-41). The testimony of the Gospel writers is that Jesus did have power over all manner of sickness and disease.

Power for All Nations

> When Jesus was entered into Capernaum, there came unto him a centurion, beseeching him, and saying, Lord, my servant lieth at home sick of the palsy, grievously tormented. And Jesus saith unto him, I will come and heal him. The centurion answered and said, Lord, I am not worthy that thou shouldst come under my roof: but speak the word only, and my servant shall be healed. . . . Jesus said unto the centurion, Go thy way; and as thou hast believed, so be it done unto thee. And his servant was healed in the selfsame hour. (Matt. 8:5-13; see also Luke 7:2-10.)[5]

The centurion was a commander of up to one hundred men in the Roman army; he was of non-Jewish lineage and would have been considered by most Jews unfit for the kingdom. This particular centurion, however, showed humility and great faith, and, according to Luke, he had gained the love and respect of some of the Jewish leaders. (Luke 7:3-5.) Jesus chose this ideal occasion to show that his kingdom was not confined to any one race, but his power unto salvation was for the righteous and faithful of all nations. He demonstrated that his power extended to the Gentiles, and he warned that without faith and righteousness, even the Jews would lose their blessings: "Many shall come from the east and west, and shall sit down with Abraham, and Isaac, and Jacob, in the kingdom of heaven. But the children of the kingdom shall be cast out into outer darkness: there shall be weeping and gnashing of teeth." (Matt. 8:11-12.)

Another example of the power of Jesus extending beyond the Jews to the Gentiles was recorded by Matthew and Mark, as Jesus healed the daughter of a Phoenician woman who showed great faith. (Matt. 15:22-28; Mark 7:25-30.)

Power for Both Men and Women

> When Jesus was come into Peter's house, he saw his wife's mother laid, and sick of a fever. And he touched her hand, and the fever left her: and she arose, and ministered unto them. (Matt. 8:14-15; see also Mark 1:29-31; Luke 4:38-39.)

Jesus rewarded righteous faith by responding to the request to heal Peter's mother-in-law. With a touch of his hand, she was immediately healed and able to extend hospitality to family and guests. Additional examples of Christ healing women include the woman with the issue of blood (Matt. 9:20-22; Mark 5:25-34; Luke 8:43-48) and the woman healed on the Sabbath (Luke 13:11-17).

By selecting the miracles of Jesus healing the leper, the centurion's servant, and Peter's mother-in-law, the Gospel writers have testified that the power and the kingdom of Jesus extend to include faithful persons of all nations, both Jew and Gentile.

Power over Nature

> When he was entered into a ship, his disciples followed him. And, behold, there arose a great tempest in the sea, insomuch that the ship was covered with the waves: but he was asleep. And his disciples came to him, and awoke him, saying, Lord, save us: we perish. And he saith unto them, Why are ye fearful, O ye of little faith? Then he arose, and rebuked the winds and the sea; and there was a great calm. But the men marvelled, saying, What manner of man is this, that even the winds and the sea obey him! (Matt. 8:23-27; see also Mark 4:35-41; Luke 8:22-25.)

By including an account of calming the winds and the sea, the Gospel writers testified that the power of Jesus included power over nature. Jesus is the Lord of nature; he created the heavens and the earth and has control over his creations.

The Gospels also record the miracle of Jesus walking on the sea, the wind ceasing, and the boat being immediately at land. (Matt. 14:24-33; Mark 6:47-51; John 6:16-21.) John recorded the first miracle performed by Jesus, that of changing water into wine (John 2:1-11), and Luke recorded the miracle of the draught of fishes (Luke 5:4-9). All four writers testified of the power of Jesus as expressed in the feeding of the five thousand (Matt. 14:15-21; Mark 6:33-34; Luke 9:11-17; John 6:5-14),[6] and Matthew and Mark recorded the feeding of the four thousand (Matt. 15:30-38; Mark 8:1-9). Matthew recorded the tribute money being found in the fish's mouth (Matt. 17:24-27), and John recorded the great haul of fishes (John 21:6-14). Ample testimony is given that Jesus is the Lord of nature with power over all of the elements.

At the time of the calming of the sea, Jesus rebuked the disciples for their fear and their lack of faith in his power over nature. (Matt. 8:26.) Elder Bruce R. McConkie wrote: "Implicit in Jesus' reproof of the weak faith of the disciples is the assurance that by faith they also could have commanded the elements and had them obey. By faith all things are possible, and when the Lord's servants rise in the full majesty of their callings, they have 'power to command the waters' (D&C 61:27)."[7]

Power over Devils

When he was come to the other side into the country of the Gergesenes, there met him two possessed with devils, coming out of the tombs, exceeding fierce, so that no man might pass by the way. And, behold, they cried out, saying, What have we to do with thee, Jesus, thou Son of God? art thou come hither to torment us before the time? And there was a good way off from them an herd of many swine feeding. So the devils besought him, saying, If thou cast us out, suffer us to go away into the herd of swine. And he said unto them, Go. And when they were come out, they went into the herd of swine: and, behold, the whole herd of swine ran violently down a steep place into the sea, and perished in the waters. (Matt. 8:28-32; see also Mark 5:1-20; Luke 8:26-39.)

Other miracles that show Christ's power over evil spirits were recorded, such as an unclean spirit cast out (Mark 1:23-27; Luke 4:33-36), a dumb demoniac healed (Matt. 9:32-34), a demoniac boy healed by Jesus after the failure of the disciples to do so (Matt. 17:14-21; Mark 9:14-29; Luke 9:37-42), and a dumb devil cast out (Luke 11:14-26).

In addition to teaching the reality of evil spirits, their power to possess the bodies of people, and their recognition of Jesus as the Son of God, the Gospel writers testified that Jesus had power over devils and unclean spirits. The kingdom of Jesus is not just of this earth; his power and authority, which began prior to the foundation of the earth, now extend to include complete power over evil spirits and will result in his ultimate triumph over Satan and all evil.

Power over Sins

> They brought to him a man sick of the palsy, lying on a bed: and Jesus seeing their faith said unto the sick of the palsy; Son, be of good cheer; thy sins be forgiven thee. And, behold, certain of the scribes said within themselves, This man blasphemeth. And Jesus knowing their thoughts said, Wherefore think ye evil in your hearts? For whether is easier, to say, Thy sins be forgiven thee; or to say, Arise, and walk? But that ye may know that the Son of man hath power on earth to forgive sins, (then saith he to the sick of the palsy,) Arise, take up thy bed, and go unto thine house. (Matt. 9:2-6; see also Mark 2:1-12; Luke 5:17-26.)

The Synoptic authors used this miracle and the words of Jesus to extend his power to include the power to forgive sin and cleanse the repentant sinner. Luke recorded that on another occasion a sinful woman washed the feet of the Savior. He said to her, "Thy sins are forgiven. . . . Thy faith hath saved thee; go in peace." (Luke 7:48-50.)

Much of the law of Moses dealt with sacrifice and offerings to cleanse individuals from sin. The law also anticipated the future day when Christ would come with power to cleanse repentant individuals from all sin and make possible a reuniting with God. By including this miracle, Matthew, Mark, and Luke testified that Jesus was the anticipated Messiah with all earthly power, and that through him sins could be forgiven and individuals brought to stand clean and pure before God.

Power over Death

> While he spake these things unto them, behold, there came a certain ruler [Jairus], and worshipped him, saying, My daughter is even now dead: but come and lay thy hand upon her, and she shall live. . . . And when Jesus came into the ruler's house, and saw the minstrels and the people

> making a noise, he said unto them, Give place: for the maid
> is not dead, but sleepeth. And they laughed him to scorn.
> But when the people were put forth, he went in, and took
> her by the hand, and the maid arose. (Matt. 9:18, 23-25; see
> also Mark 5:22-24, 35-43; Luke 8:41-42, 49-56.)

In addition to these reports of the raising of Jairus's daughter
from the dead, Luke recorded the miracle of Jesus raising the son of
the widow of Nain (Luke 7:11-16), and John recorded the raising
of Lazarus after his body had lain four days in the grave (John
11:17-46). For persons in all ages, death has been the ultimate and
sure enemy; no one can escape its reality. As a witness that Jesus
had the power to perform the promised resurrection, the Gospel
writers gave their testimonies that he raised three individuals from
the dead.

Power Shared with Others

After testifying that Jesus had power over all enemies by including accounts of his miracles, Matthew recorded that Jesus called
the twelve apostles and "gave them power against unclean spirits,
to cast them out, and to heal all manner of sickness and all manner
of disease." (Matt. 10:1.) The Savior instructed them and sent them
forth, saying, "As ye go, preach, saying, The kingdom of heaven is
at hand. Heal the sick, cleanse the lepers, raise the dead, cast out
devils: freely ye have received, freely give." (Matt. 10:7-8.)
Matthew identified the pattern that Jesus followed in his kingdom,
that of demonstrating the power of his miracles and then sending
others forth to use his power in the same manner and for the same
purposes. As an additional witness of this principle, Mark closed
his record with the testimony that other followers of Jesus could
also perform miracles: "These signs shall follow them that believe;
in my name shall they cast out devils; they shall speak with new
tongues; . . . they shall lay hands on the sick, and they shall
recover." (Mark 16:17-18.) The reality that the followers of Christ
can use his power to perform miracles in his name is an identifying
sign of the true Church of Christ.

Conclusion

The miracles performed by Jesus were an important part of his earthly ministry. He used miracles to show compassion, to teach, to inspire, to motivate, and to testify that he was the true Messiah. After his death and resurrection, his disciples continued to perform miracles and to testify that he was the Messiah, the Son of God who had come in power and authority. The Gospel writers used his miracles to testify that he had power over all enemies. The healing of the leper, the centurion's servant, and Peter's mother-in-law testified that his power extends to persons of all nations, both Jew and Gentile. The calming of the sea extended his power to include power over nature and the elements. Casting out the unclean spirits testified of his power over devils and all evil. Healing the man with palsy demonstrated his power to forgive sin and to cleanse men before God. And, finally, the raising of individuals from the dead showed his power to include power over death and the grave. For individuals in all generations, accounts of the miracles reveal the power of Jesus over all enemies and testify that he was the Son of God and that he had sufficient power to perform the Atonement and bring immortality and the possibility of eternal life to all men.

A Catalog of Jesus' Miracles[8]

Miracle	Where Recorded
First miracle, water converted into wine	John 2:1-11
Healing the nobleman's son	John 4:46-54
Jesus passes unseen through the crowd	Luke 4:28-30 John 8:59
Draught of fishes	Luke 5:4-11
Unclean spirit cast out	Mark 1:21-28 Luke 4:31-37
Peter's wife's mother healed	Matt. 8:14-15 Mark 1:29-31 Luke 4:38-39

Multitude healed	Matt. 8:16-17 Mark 1:32-34 Luke 4:40-41
Leper healed	Matt. 8:1-4 Mark 1:40-45 Luke 5:12-15
One sick with palsy healed	Matt. 9:1-8 Mark 2:1-12 Luke 5:17-26
Man with an infirmity of thirty-eight years healed	John 5:2-16
Man with a withered hand healed	Matt. 12:10-13 Mark 3:1-5 Luke 6:6-10
Centurion's servant healed of palsy	Matt. 8:5-13 Luke 7:1-10
Son of a widow of Nain raised	Luke 7:11-17
Blind and dumb demoniac healed	Matt. 12:22
Storm stilled	Matt. 8:23-27 Mark 4:35-41 Luke 8:22-25
Two Gadarene demoniacs healed (including swine that rushed down into the sea and perished)	Matt. 8:28-34 Mark 5:1-20 Luke 8:26-39
Daughter of Jairus raised	Matt. 9:18-19, 23-26 Mark 5:21-22, 35-43 Luke 8:41-42, 49-56
Woman with issue of blood healed	Matt. 9:20-22 Mark 5:25-34 Luke 8:43-48
Two blind men healed	Matt. 9:27-31
Dumb demoniac healed	Matt. 9:32-34

Five thousand fed	Matt. 14:16-21 Mark 6:33-34 Luke 9:11-17 John 6:5-14
Jesus walks on the sea (including rescue of Peter and ceasing of wind)	Matt. 14:22-33 Mark 6:45-52 John 6:15-21
People healed by touch of Jesus' garment	Matt. 14:34-36 Mark 6:53-56
Daughter of the Phoenician woman healed	Matt. 15:21-28 Mark 7:24-30
Deaf man with impediment in speech healed	Mark 7:31-37
Four thousand fed	Matt. 15:32-38 Mark 8:1-9
Blind man healed by stages	Mark 8:22-26
Demoniac boy healed after failure of disciples	Matt. 17:14-21 Mark 9:14-29 Luke 9:37-43
Tribute money in the fish	Matt. 17:24-27
Jesus casts out a dumb devil	Luke 11:14-15
Jesus heals a man born blind	John 9:1-7
Woman healed on Sabbath	Luke 13:11-17
Man with dropsy healed on Sabbath	Luke 14:1-6
Raising of Lazarus from the dead	John 11:17-46
Ten lepers healed	Luke 17:11-19
Sight restored to Bartimaeus and another blind beggar	Matt. 20:29-34 Mark 10:46-52 Luke 18:35-43
Barren fig tree cursed	Matt. 21:18-22 Mark 11:12-14, 20-26

Those sent to take Jesus fall to the ground	John 18:3-6
Ear of Malchus, high priest's servant, healed	Luke 22:50-51
Great haul of fishes	John 21:1-14

NOTES

1. E. Keith Howick, *The Miracles of Jesus the Messiah* (Salt Lake City: Bookcraft, 1985), p. 10.

2. Bruce R. McConkie, *Doctrinal New Testament Commentary,* 3 vols. (Salt Lake City: Bookcraft, 1965-73), 2:38.

3. Howick, p. 11.

4. Robert J. Matthews, *The Miracles of Jesus* (Provo, Utah: Brigham Young University Press, 1968), p. 15.

5. In the Greek, this use of the word *servant* may also connote *child* or *son*. See John 4:43-54.

6. See Kent P. Jackson, "The Bread of Life," chapter 19 in this volume.

7. McConkie, 1:307.

8. This list is adapted from J. Reuben Clark, Jr., *Our Lord of the Gospels* (Salt Lake City: Deseret Book, 1954), pp. 535-37.

14

THE CALLING AND MISSION OF THE TWELVE
(Matthew 10)

H. DEAN GARRETT

An apostle is "one sent forth."[1] The calling of the Apostles was to be "special witnesses of the name of Christ in all the world." (D&C 107:23.) The ministry of the Savior had developed a need for "twelve men who [would] be his witnesses; who [would] bear, with him, the burdens of the kingdom; who [would] accept martyrdom and defy the rulers of the world."[2] This type of witness would require preparation and training.

The Early Disciples

The preparation began early with the ministry of John the Baptist, whose life intertwined with that of Jesus on several occasions, in ways that had eternal effect. Perhaps the greatest effect on the development of the kingdom was the introduction of some of the future apostles to the Christ.

One day beyond Jordan in Bethabara, John saw Jesus coming toward him. John bore record of him to the people, saying, "This is he of whom I said; After me cometh a man who is preferred before me; for he was before me, and I knew him, and that he should be made manifest to Israel; therefore am I come baptizing." (JST, John 1:30.) The next day John and two disciples, John and Andrew, Simon's brother, went to see the Christ. Two future apostles heard John testify that Christ was "the Lamb of God." (John 1:36.) Their focus was now on

---

H. Dean Garrett is assistant professor of Church history and doctrine at Brigham Young University.

Christ. They heard him teach, went with him to his home, and "abode with him that day." (John 1:39.)

With the excitement of a convert, Andrew went to find his brother Simon, saying, "We have found the Messias." (John 1:41.) He wanted Simon to see the Christ, although Simon probably was not prepared for the greeting that he received from Jesus. When Jesus saw him, he exclaimed: "Thou art Simon the son of Jona: thou shalt be called Cephas." (John 1:42.) They had never met, yet he had called Simon "Cephas, which is, by interpretation, a seer, or a stone." (JST, John 1:42.) This prophetic utterance impressed Simon Peter and his brother Andrew, "and they straightway left all, and followed Jesus." (JST, John 1:42.)

John, the son of Zebedee, apparently went to his home in Galilee after hearing Jesus. He perhaps discussed with his family the experience. He was convincing enough that when the Savior passed by sometime later and called to them while they were mending their nets, not only John but also his brother James responded to the call: "They immediately left the ship and their father, and followed him." (Matt. 4:22.)

These disciples joined Christ in his travels: They heard him teach in the synagogues; they watched him heal the sick and cast out devils; they saw future companion apostles respond to the messages of the Christ and join them in their discipleship. They were with him as he searched out another future apostle, Philip. Philip lived in Bethsaida, the home town of Peter and Andrew. Little is known of his life before his encounter with the Savior. The record simply states that the Savior commanded him to follow him. (John 1:43.)

Philip was excited. He found his friend Nathanael (Bartholomew)[3] and exclaimed: "We have found him, of whom Moses in the law, and the prophets, did write, Jesus of Nazareth, the son of Joseph." Nathanael was not convinced; it would take more than just the excited declaration of a friend. He apparently was influenced by local attitudes—"Can there any good thing come out of Nazareth?"—whereupon Philip invited him to "come and see" for himself. Nathanael was about to receive a witness far exceeding that of his friend, for when Jesus saw Nathanael coming, he announced to those around him that here came one without guile. Nathanael was surprised and wanted to know how Christ knew him. The answer was rather startling: "Before that Philip called thee, when thou wast under the fig tree, I saw thee." Nathanael proclaimed, "Thou art the Son of God." The promise was then made to him that he would "see heaven open, and the angels of God ascending and descending upon the Son of man." (John 1:45-51.)

Thus soon after the beginning of his ministry, Christ developed discipleship with six members of the future Quorum of Twelve. Others would soon hear the Master and leave whatever they were doing to follow him. They were still disciples but not yet called to the apostleship. This was a period of training and preparation. They spent a year with the Savior, hearing him testify of his divine mission. They watched him heal the sick and cast out devils; they watched the multitudes gather. Yet this year was not spent constantly with him. On one occasion as the multitudes praised him, he asked Peter, who was working on the fishing nets in his boat, to row him a small distance out from shore. Simon Peter had been fishing all night without success. When the Savior suggested they drop their nets over the sides, Peter protested that it would do no good. But it did. So many fish were caught that the nets broke. Peter fell to the Master's feet and proclaimed his unworthiness. The Savior taught Peter and others with him that they would soon "catch men." (Luke 5:1-11.) They began to understand: he was the Messiah!

The Calling of the Apostles

Perhaps a year passed after some of the future apostles gathered themselves to the Savior. During that time they learned much concerning his mission. They heard him proclaim his own divine sonship as the Lord of the Sabbath. (See Matt. 12:1-8.)

In preparation for the calling of the Twelve, the Savior went to a mountain to pray. After a night of communion with his Father, he called to him his disciples. Then he chose twelve of them and named them apostles. (Luke 6:12-13.) The listing of the apostles as a group appears four times in the New Testament: once each in Matthew, Mark, Luke, and Acts. No two lists are alike. "No two of these listings give the same order of seniority," Elder Bruce R. McConkie wrote, "and in some instances the name applied to the same person varies. All of the lists place Peter first, and the three that mention Judas place him last."[4] The account in Acts does not mention Judas Iscariot, as he had already died. (Matt. 27:3-5; Acts 1:15-19.) The following chart gives a comparison of each list of the Twelve:[5]

Matthew 10:2-4	Luke 6:14-16	Mark 3:16-19	Acts 1:13
Simon Peter	Simon Peter	Simon Peter	Peter
Andrew	Andrew	James	James
James	James	John	John
John	John	Andrew	Andrew
Philip	Philip	Philip	Philip
Bartholomew	Bartholomew	Bartholomew	Thomas
Thomas	Thomas	Matthew	Bartholomew
Matthew	Matthew	Thomas	Matthew
James, son of Alphaeus	James, son of Alphaeus	James, son of Alphaeus	James, son of Alphaeus
Lebbaeus Thaddaeus	Simon Zelotes	Thaddaeus	Simon Zelotes
Simon the Canaanite	Judas, brother of James	Simon the Canaanite	Judas, brother of James
Judas Iscariot	Judas Iscariot	Judas Iscariot	

The only difference in sequence is with the order of Andrew, Bartholomew, Thomas and Matthew, which appears to have had no impact on the leadership of the Quorum. The listing of Peter, James, and John at the head of the lists and in order is significant. "From other sources we know that Peter, James, and John were the preeminent three," Elder McConkie wrote, "and were in fact the First Presidency of the Church in that day, although we have no way of knowing whether they served as a separate quorum apart from the others of the Twelve."[6]

The Savior ordained the Twelve and gave them "power to heal sicknesses, and to cast out devils." (Mark 3:15.) In due time he granted to them the keys of the kingdom, giving them power, saying: "Whatsoever ye shall bind on earth shall be bound in heaven: and whatsoever ye shall loose on earth shall be loosed in heaven." (Matt. 18:18.) He desired that they might "be with him, and that he might send them forth to preach." (Mark 3:14.)

Preparation for Mission

Soon after the calling of the Twelve, the Savior saw the large multitudes and "went up into a mountain; and when he was set down" (JST, Matt. 5:1), the disciples came to him and were taught by him. One of the greatest sermons of all time was delivered to the multitude. Insights received from a careful study of the Joseph Smith Translation account and the pattern given in 3 Nephi give evidence that the bulk of the Sermon on the Mount was directed to the Twelve, to aid them in understanding their mission and purpose in the kingdom. As Jesus said to his Nephite disciples, "Remember the words which I have spoken. For behold, ye are they whom I have chosen to minister unto this people." (3 Ne. 13:25.) The Twelve were to take "no thought for the morrow" (3 Ne. 13:34), nor to concern themselves with earthly things that the Lord would provide (Matt. 6:25-34). They were to be concerned about spiritual things and about building the kingdom of God on this earth: "Go ye into the world, and care not for the world; for the world will hate you, and will persecute you, and will turn you out of their synagogues. Nevertheless, ye shall go forth from house to house, teaching the people; and I will go before you. And your heavenly Father will provide for you, whatsoever things ye need for food, what ye shall eat; and for raiment, what ye shall wear or put on." (JST, Matt. 6:25-27.)

The apostles were instructed as to the nature of their mission, as the Lord taught them what "they should say unto the people." (JST, Matt. 7:1.) This included instruction on righteous judgment, how to respond to the scribes and the Pharisees, and counsel to be wise in what mysteries of the kingdom they gave the world: "The world cannot receive that which ye, yourselves, are not able to bear," he said; "wherefore ye shall not give your pearls unto them, lest they turn again and rend you." (JST, Matt. 7:11.) Thus the Sermon on the Mount was to the apostles a collection of instructions. They now had both the experience of watching the Savior and the basic knowledge to serve in their apostolic callings.

The Mission of the Twelve

The time had come for the apostles to go forth and preach the gospel. It had been between one and two years since the first of them had become disciples. Before their departure, the Savior called the Twelve to him and instructed them on their behavior and expectations. (See Matt. 10.) He commanded them to preach only to "the lost sheep of the house of Israel." (Matt. 10:6.) The time of the Gentiles was not yet at hand; their ministry was to Israel. The time would come when they would stand alongside the Savior "at the day of [his] coming . . . to judge the whole house of Israel, even as many as have loved [him] and kept [his] commandments, and none else." (D&C 29:12.)

The message to be preached to the house of Israel was that "the kingdom of heaven is at hand." (Matt. 10:7.) In other words, "the Church of Jesus Christ is here; it has been organized and established; it is the kingdom of God on earth; enter into it through the waters of baptism, and be ye saved."[7]

The apostles were not to spend time with those who were not worthy. (Matt. 10:11-15.) Elder McConkie explained: "Jesus is not sending his disciples out to find harlots and whoremongers and thieves and robbers—although any of these may repent and be saved—but he is sending them to find the honest in heart, the upright among men, those whose prior living has made them worthy to hear an apostolic voice. Such are the ones in whose homes the Twelve shall abide and where they shall leave their blessings."[8] If the people refused to hear their message, the apostles were to leave that home or city and shake off the dust of their feet. This dusting of feet would be "against them as a testimony." (D&C 24:15.) The servants of the Lord would have power "to seal both on earth and in heaven, the unbelieving and rebellious; yea, verily to seal them up unto the day when the wrath of God shall be poured out upon the wicked without measure." (D&C 1:8-9.) They would know "that in the day of judgment [they] shall be judges of that house, and condemn them." (D&C 75:21.) As Elder McConkie observed: "It is as though those who reject the message are not worthy to receive even the dust that cleaves to an apostolic sandal."[9]

As a result of rejection and hatred, the mission of the apostles would not be easy. The Savior warned: "I send you forth as sheep in the midst of wolves: be ye therefore wise as serpents [be ye therefore wise servants—JST, Matt. 10:14], and harmless as doves." (Matt.

10:16.) Although their message was one of peace, yet they would generate by that very message hatred and suffering. Their message would generate an atmosphere of trial. Jesus said: "They will deliver you up to the councils, and they will scourge you in their synagogues; and ye shall be brought before governors and kings for my sake, for a testimony against them and the Gentiles." (Matt. 10:17-18.) Yet the apostles should not fear or be hesitant in proclaiming the message. Even under those conditions, the Lord told them, "Take no thought how or what ye shall speak: for it shall be given you in that same hour what ye shall speak." (Matt. 10:19.) It was necessary, however, for them to understand the effects that their preaching would have on others. They would "be hated of all men" (Matt. 10:22), but they must endure. They should not seek confrontation or persecution, but should flee from it: "When they persecute you in this city, flee ye into another." (Matt. 10:23.) Later he taught, "Then shall they deliver you up to be afflicted, and shall kill you: and ye shall be hated of all nations for my name's sake." (Matt. 24:9.) Yet the Master gave them the reassuring knowledge that their Father in heaven was even aware of sparrows that were sold in the market. God had "the very hairs" of their head all numbered. (Matt. 10:30.)

The result of their preaching would be one of division. The Savior warned them: "I am come to set a man at variance against his father, and the daughter against her mother, and the daughter in law against her mother in law. And a man's foes shall be they of his own household." (Matt. 10:35-36.) If circumstances so demanded, it would be necessary that a person choose Christ over family: "He that loveth father or mother more than me is not worthy of me: and he that loveth son or daughter more than me is not worthy of me. And he that taketh not his cross, and followeth after me, is not worthy of me." (Matt. 10:37-38.)

Elder James E. Talmage observed: "The significance of this figure [of the cross] must have been solemnly impressive, and actually terrifying; for the cross was a symbol of ignominy, extreme suffering, and death. However, should they lose their lives for His sake, they would find life eternal; while he who was not willing to die in the Lord's service should lose his life in a sense at once literal and awful. They were never to forget in whose name they were sent; and were comforted with the assurance that whoever received them would be rewarded as one who had received the Christ and His Father; and that though the gift were only that of a cup of cold water, the giver should in no wise lose his reward."[11] With that charge, the apostles went on their missions. Luke stated simply that "they departed, and went through the towns, preaching the gospel, and healing every where." (Luke 9:6.)

For the rest of that dispensation, the apostles of the Lord Jesus Christ proclaimed the gospel, functioning under the leadership of Peter, James, and John. They indeed faced the struggles and trials of which the Lord warned them. Judas Iscariot, the betrayer of Christ, was the first apostle to die. (See Matt. 27:5.) James, the son of Zebedee, was ordered killed by the sword by King Herod Agrippa. (See Acts 12:2.) Peter, Elder Talmage wrote, died a difficult death of crucifixion during "the reign of Nero, probably between A.D. 64 and 68. Origen states that the apostle was crucified with his head downward."[12] John the Beloved was exiled many years later to the island of Patmos, where he wrote the book of Revelation (he also wrote the Gospel of John and the epistle of John). In the age of apostasy, he was taken from the earth, and the ministry of the apostleship ceased in the church. It was these three—Peter, James, and John—who appeared to Joseph Smith in the late spring of 1829 and conferred upon him and Oliver Cowdery the keys that were given them by the Savior.[13]

The fate of the other original apostles is not known.[14] Little is written about them or their activities except as they interacted with the Savior in his mortal ministry. But this we do know: "They went forth, and preached every where, the Lord working with them, and confirming the word with signs following." (Mark 16:20.)

NOTES

1. Karl Heinrich Rengstorf, "Apostéllō," "Apóstolos," *The Theological Dictionary of the New Testament,* ed. Gehard Kittel, 10 vols. (Grand Rapids, Mich.: Eerdmans, 1964-76), 1:398, 407-45.

2. Bruce R. McConkie, *The Mortal Messiah: From Bethlehem to Calvary,* 4 vols. (Salt Lake City: Deseret Book, 1979-81), 2:99.

3. Ibid., p. 109.

4. Ibid., p. 104.

5. See Richard O. Cowan: "The Twelve Then and Now," *A Symposium on the New Testament* (Salt Lake City: Church Educational System, The Church of Jesus Christ of Latter-day Saints, 1984), p. 93.

6. McConkie, 2:104-5.

7. McConkie, *Doctrinal New Testament Commentary,* 3 vols. (Salt Lake City: Bookcraft, 1966-73), 1:325.

8. McConkie, *The Mortal Messiah* 2:311.

9. Ibid., p. 313.

10. James E. Talmage, *Jesus the Christ* (Salt Lake City: Deseret Book, 1958), pp. 330-31.

11. Ibid., p. 219.

12. See Kent P. Jackson, "Early Signs of the Apostasy," *Ensign,* December 1984, pp. 15-16.

13. Larry C. Porter, "The Priesthood Restored," in *Studies in Scripture, Vol. 2: Pearl of Great Price,* ed. Robert L. Millet and Kent P. Jackson (Sandy, Utah: Randall Book, 1985), pp. 389-409; see also *History of the Church* 1:139-41.

14. Legends concerning their deaths are found in *Foxe's Book of Martyrs* (Chicago: John C. Winston).

15

THE SERMON ON THE MOUNT:
THE SACRIFICE OF THE HUMAN HEART
(Matthew 5-7; Luke 6:17-49)

CATHERINE THOMAS

The Greek text of Matthew describes Jesus ascending *the mountain,* where he delivered the Sermon on the Mount. This mountain evokes another ancient mountain from the Old Testament: Mount Sinai, where Jehovah delivered the great law to Moses. The allusion is no accident. Jehovah had again ascended a mount from which he would deliver another law. Allusions from the Old Testament permeate his address and illuminate his message. Especially important to a grasp of this discourse is an understanding of the relationship of the law of Moses to the law of the gospel, which Jehovah had come to earth to institute. The major themes of the address, then, are Jesus' authority to deliver the new law and the means by which one may come to the Savior through that law.

The Beatitudes, or the "Blesseds," form the introduction to the sermon and foreshadow its major themes. One definition of the word *blessed* (makarios in Greek) means "privileged to receive divine favor."[1] It could be retranslated as "Oh, the happiness of."[2] The word signifies a state of true well-being. As the first word in the address, it signals a theme and a promise. Mary used a form of this word when she exclaimed, "All generations shall call me blessed." (Luke 1:48.) *Blessed* occurs several times in the Old Testament, especially in Psalms, where again it is the first word. Thus the word was not new to Jesus' Jewish audience and indeed bore with it an intensified meaning because of its Old Testament use.

Catherine Thomas is a doctrinal candidate in ancient history and an instructor in ancient scripture at Brigham Young University.

236

Jesus' Audience

Undoubtedly many curiosity seekers had come to the mountain; others hovered on the edge of commitment to the gospel, while several had committed themselves and become disciples through baptism. Evidences from the parallel sermon to the Nephites suggest that the teachings of the sermon had meaning primarily for Jesus' disciples, those who had entered into the covenant of baptism or were preparing to do so. Each blessing was offered to those who came to Christ through baptism. (3 Ne. 12:2.) Thus the address has meaning primarily for those who have entered into or are about to enter into the covenant of baptism and who thereby have a special claim on divine help. The teachings are particularly suited to those who have just become new members of the kingdom, because they illustrate the disciple's new way of life. The Joseph Smith Translation of Matthew 7:1 indicates that Jesus directed his remarks to his disciples and told them to teach them to others. In 3 Nephi 12, the remarks were delivered directly to the people whom we may also term new disciples. Since *disciple* in the New Testament denotes both a member of the Twelve and the larger group of the Savior's followers, it is not always obvious to which group the word refers. The sermon, then, was for the benefit of the newly ordained Twelve, being a type of missionary preparation, as well as for that larger group of disciples also present. No teaching in the sermon need be seen as specific to the Twelve only. The Lord invited each disciple in the kingdom to embrace the freedom in these teachings.

The Beatitudes

The words used in the individual beatitudes evoke significant Old Testament meanings. Jesus called the "poor in spirit," the "meek," and those who "mourn" to come to him and obtain the kingdom of heaven. Compare Isaiah 61:1-2: "The Spirit of the Lord God is upon me; because the Lord hath anointed me to preach good tidings unto the *meek;* he hath sent me to bind up the *brokenhearted,* to proclaim liberty to the captives, and the opening of the prison to them that are bound; to proclaim the acceptable year of the Lord, and the day of vengeance of our God; to comfort all that *mourn."* (Emphasis added.) By his allusion to this Messianic text, a passage well known from frequent reading in the synagogue (the Lord himself read it there, as described in Luke 4:16-20), Jesus proclaimed that he had the power and authority to bring the blessed state of the kingdom to everyone who was prepared to receive it. Jesus is Jehovah.

"Blessed are the poor in spirit. . . . Blessed are they that mourn. . . . Blessed are the meek. . . . Blessed are they which do hunger and thirst after righteousness: for they shall be filled." (Matt. 5:3-6.) The would-be disciple of Jesus Christ, sensing his estrangement, comes in his emptiness, hungering and thirsting for the Holy Ghost. (See 3 Ne. 12:6.) The Lord promised satisfaction. Compare this passage from the Psalms where the context is redemption: "They wandered in the wilderness in a solitary way; they found no city to dwell in. *Hungry* and *thirsty,* their soul fainted in them. Then they cried unto the Lord in their trouble, and he delivered them out of their distresses. And he led them forth by the right way, that they might go to a city of habitation. . . . For he *satisfieth* the longing soul, and *filleth* the hungry soul with goodness." (Ps. 107:4-7, 9; emphasis added.)

"Blessed are the merciful. . . . Blessed are the pure in heart. . . . Blessed are the peacemakers. . . . Blessed are they which are persecuted." (Matt. 5:7-10.) At this point the Lord made a transition. In the foregoing we have the debits; here follow the credits. Instead of the spiritual bankruptcy of verses 3-5, now mercy, purity of heart, and peacemaking fill the soul; there is love for those who lack peace—the troublemakers and persecuters. The transition point, verse 6, is the longing for the Holy Ghost. The longing evokes the gift.

The giving and receiving of mercy evoke a passage on the principle of restoration from Alma: "Therefore, my son, see that you are merciful unto your brethren; deal justly, judge righteously, and do good continually; and if ye do all these things then shall ye receive your reward; yea, ye shall have mercy restored unto you again; ye shall have justice restored unto you again; ye shall have a righteous judgment restored unto you again; and ye shall have good rewarded unto you again. For that which ye do send out shall return unto you again, and be restored." (Alma 41:14-15.) As in the other beatitudes, the principle of restoration applies here as well as hereafter. The good that one does to another is restored through the creation of peace and confidence inside himself; the evil that he does to another creates fear in himself.

The blessing on the pure in heart alludes to another passage in the Psalms: "Who shall ascend into the hill of the Lord? or who shall stand in his holy place? He that hath clean hands, and a pure heart; who hath not lifted up his soul unto vanity, nor sworn deceitfully. He shall receive the blessing from the Lord, and righteousness from the God of his salvation. This is the generation of them that seek him, that seek thy face." (Ps. 24:3-6.) Purity fills the disciple with spiritual confidence, drawing the kingdom of heaven to him and making possible his entrance into the Lord's presence. (See D&C 121:45.)

Persecution is the last of the states of blessedness mentioned. Its position in the Savior's catalog enhances its significance. This state is shared by the prophets and other holy ones. One reason that it is described as *blessed* is that it provides the greatest opportunity to triumph over hate and fear and to love one's enemies; love of one's enemies is also the last point the Lord made before the injunction to be perfect. Perhaps it is the final spiritual frontier.

The Beatitudes introduce the major themes of the Savior's sermon, and we may continually observe that the Lord expanded each beatitude in the text of his sermon. In addition, the first and last beatitudes enclose the others with the promise of the kingdom of heaven. The promise is essentially the same for each beatitude and is twofold: (1) triumph over alienation from God and spiritual death by reception of God's spiritual presence through the Holy Ghost here; and (2) God's physical presence in the next life. It is interesting to note the paradox underlying the beatitudes: one's suffering is the field in which the blessing is planted and nourished.

"Ye are the salt of the earth." (Matt. 5:13.) Mark 9:49-50 contributes meaning to this verse: "For every one shall be salted with fire, and every sacrifice shall be salted with salt. Salt is good: but if the salt have lost his saltness, wherewith will ye season it? Have salt in yourselves, and have peace one with another." Both salt and fire were used in the offering of sacrifices in the temple. Salt, a preservative, represented the covenant between God and Israel. (Lev. 2:13; Num. 18:19.) The priest kept the fire burning on the altar in the temple, symbolizing the perpetual "covenant which made the ordinance of sacrifice efficacious."[3] Salt, like fire, is also a purifier. With the illustrations of salt and light (below), ideas that may at first seem random, the Lord turned to the theme of men making *themselves* sacrifices to God. He linked personal sacrifice and purification with peace: when one purifies himself, he has peace with others. Sustained peace is never an accident, but always a triumph of spiritual principle.

"Ye are the light of the world." (Matt. 5:14.) Personal sanctification cannot exist in a vacuum: it includes extending the kingdom to others. The Savior spoke to potential and actual missionaries. To the Nephites, he identified the light of Matthew 5:14 as himself. (3 Ne. 18:24.) When an individual ignites this light within himself or herself it cannot be hidden, just as a lighted city set on a hill cannot be hidden. The light draws others to the Savior. However, the disciple without salt is savorless or, retranslating the Greek word *moranthe,* is *empty, insipid* (our word *moron* comes from this Greek word). In speaking of covenant people, a modern revelation explained: "They were set to be a light unto the world, and to be the saviors of men; and inasmuch as they are not the saviors of men, they are as salt that has lost its savor, and is thenceforth good for nothing but to be cast out." (D&C 103:9-10.) The true disciple draws others consciously, while unconsciously giving off light. The Lord referred to the link between self-purification and its effect on others in John 17:19: "For their sakes I sanctify myself, that they also might be sanctified through the truth."

Sacrifice and the Law of Moses

The sacrifices included in the law of Moses were given expressly to point individuals to Jesus Christ. (See Gal. 3:24.) Abinadi taught: "Therefore there was a law given them, yea, a law of performances and of ordinances, a law which they were to observe strictly from day to day, to keep them in remembrance of God and their duty towards him. . . . All these things were types of things to come." (Mosiah 13:30-31.) Mormon wrote: "Now they did not suppose that salvation came by the law of Moses; but the law of Moses did serve to strengthen their faith in Christ; and thus they did retain a hope through faith, unto eternal salvation, relying upon the spirit of prophecy, which spake of those things to come." (Alma 25:16.) The components of the law of sacrifice were "types of things to come" in that every element in the offering of sacrifices reflected the eternal ministry of Jesus Christ.

The Mosaic ordinance of sacrifice consisted of two main types of offerings: the voluntary (burnt offering, peace offering, and meat or cereal offering) and obligatory (sin offering and trespass offering). Though each was performed differently, they shared the same elements: an offering, an offerer, a place of offering, a laying on of hands, a priest, salt, fire, and blood. Layers of meaning rested on each element; the *offering* symbolized not only the Savior (unblemished and so on), but also the offerer. (See Rom. 6:6.) The *priest* acted as mediator between humans and God. The *altar* was the place where Jehovah promised to meet with his people and reconcile them to him. (See Ex. 29:42.) *Fire* symbolized the eternal covenant, as mentioned above; it also represented the purifying action of the Holy Ghost. With respect to the obligatory offering, the *laying on of hands* accompanied confession of sins, making the animal a substitute for the person who vicariously suffered the consequences of sin. *Salt* has been mentioned above as symbolizing a preservative of the covenant. *Blood* symbolized both life and death, since the shedding of the Savior's blood affected the giving of life.[4] When the three offerings—sin, burnt, and peace—were offered together, they symbolized respectively the progression from *atonement* through *sanctification* to *fellowship* with the Lord.[5] Thus the law of sacrifice was instituted to point men to Christ and finally to sanctify them. The word *sacrifice* comes from the latin word meaning to make sacred. We encounter the recurring theme of the sacrificer making himself a sanctified offering.

The law of sacrifice is eternal, but the Lord changed the form: "Think not that I am come to destroy the law, or the prophets: I am not come to destroy, but to fulfil." (Matt. 5:17.) These were provocative words to Jewish ears. For them, the law had ceased to be a means to an end and had become the end itself. They viewed the law as the source of salvation. Jesus' message here was that he, not the law, is the source of salvation.[6] With the old law fulfilled in Christ's coming, a new covenant with Israel became necessary. The Sermon on the Mount is a statement of that new covenant.[7] In Matthew 5:21-48, the Lord compared the requirements of the law of Moses with those of the new law of the gospel. The major difference lies between the outward act and the inward state of the heart.

The Holy Ghost is essential to the process of being born again through the new law. In ancient times the Lord removed the Melchizedek Priesthood from Israel's midst (D&C 84:25), which loss deprived them of certain blessings pertaining to godhood, for example, the gift of the Holy Ghost. The Lord said, "This greater priesthood administereth the gospel and holdeth the key of the mysteries of the kingdom, even the key of the knowledge of God. Therefore, in the ordinances thereof, the power of godliness is manifest. And without the ordinances thereof, and the authority of the priesthood, the power of godliness is not manifest unto men in the flesh; for without this no man can see the face of God, even the Father, and live." (D&C 84:19-22.) The gift of the Holy Ghost, bestowed only by the Melchizedek Priesthood, was not generally received as an individual gift from the time of Moses to the time of Jesus Christ, or, in particular, until the day of Pentecost after his ascension. (See Acts 2:1-4.) But the Savior taught the Holy Ghost in anticipation of the day when individual disciples would receive the gift.

The Old and the New Laws Compared

How then was the new law to be lived? As terrified Nephites cowered in darkness, the voice of Christ penetrated their hearts: "I am the light and life of the world. I am Alpha and Omega, the beginning and the end. And ye shall offer up unto me no more the shedding of blood; yea, your sacrifices and your burnt offerings shall be done away, for I will accept none of your sacrifices and your burnt offerings. And ye shall offer for a sacrifice unto me a broken heart and a contrite spirit. And whoso cometh unto me with a broken heart and a contrite spirit, him will I baptize with fire and with the Holy Ghost." (3 Ne. 9:18-20.)

When the light returned in the New World following the storms and earthquakes that signaled the Savior's crucifixion, the Nephites saw an earth they did not recognize. Its face was transformed. The ruptured land graphically demonstrated just how complete the new change would be. The Latin word behind *contrite* means "to grind down to powder." A *broken-up* and *ground-down* heart was required of the new disciples. The first three beatitudes—poor, mournful, meek—describe the state precedent to the broken heart and contrite spirit.

Jesus compared the old with the new. Where the outward act of murder was earlier forbidden, now the inner state of anger, of contempt, of condemnation, of mocking one's brother was proscribed for the one who wishes to come to the Lord's altar. Anger and contempt, even for one's enemy, must be sacrificed. (See Matt. 5:21-26.) Verses 25 and 26 suggest that where physical death was the penalty for murder (Ex. 21:12: "He that smiteth a man, so that he die, shall be surely put to death"), now spiritual death with its accompanying suffering is the penalty for anger and failure to forgive. In addition, true disciples must sacrifice lust and observe the sanctity of marriage. (See vv. 27-32.) They must sacrifice oath making for the ungarnished truth. (See vv. 33-37.) They must sacrifice retaliation and vengeance, doing good to those who seem least to deserve it, sharing with all who need what they have. (See vv. 38-47.) These last triumphs over fear and hate prepare them for perfection.

"Be ye therefore perfect, even as your Father which is in heaven is perfect." (Matt. 5:48.) Lest we dismiss as divine hyperbole this injunction to be perfect, we may observe that many people have been described as perfect in the scriptures: Seth was a perfect man, like his father Adam, in all things (D&C 107:43); Noah was a just man and perfect in his generation (Gen. 6:9); to Abraham the Lord said, "Walk before me, and be thou perfect" (Gen. 17:1); Job is described as a perfect and upright man (Job 1:1); Moroni was "a man of perfect understanding" (Alma 48:11); and Nephihah "filled the judgment-seat with perfect uprightness" (Alma 50:37).

But something enigmatic attends their perfection, especially if we define a perfect person as one who does not make mistakes, since the scriptures record mistakes that many of these men made. In D&C 132:49-50, the Lord says to Joseph Smith, "I seal upon you your exaltation" and then adds, "and will forgive all your sins." Apparently these great men were imperfect in some ways and partook of the same fallen nature that all of us do, yet they were able to please God and walk guiltless before him. How then shall we understand *perfect?*

To focus on the Greek and Hebrew words behind the English *per-*

fect helps clarify understanding of what the Lord is asking. These words may also be translated as *whole, complete, the end product of a process.* An individual's opportunity as an imperfect, unfinished being is to become *whole* through the power of Jesus Christ. During the Savior's mortal ministry, he likened the healing of physical infirmities to the forgiveness of sins. (See Luke 5:23-24.) Infirmities of the spirit reflected a state of unwholeness, as did infirmities of the body. The Savior has the power to make people completely whole (*teleos* in Greek, the word translated in Matthew 5:48 as *perfect*) in body and spirit and offers that wholeness to all who want it.

To understand what kind of perfection the Lord is inviting us to, it is helpful to see mankind's mistakes as divided into two kinds: errors of judgment and errors of intent. Individuals are held accountable for *intent* to do wrong, of course, though they may repent and be completely forgiven. People make many errors in *judgment,* but, where intent is pure, they need not pronounce harsh judgments on themselves, for, in fact, they may have done their best and should continue in faith.[8] The Savior summarized his plan in 3 Nephi 27:16: "Whoso repenteth and is baptized in my name shall be filled [with the Holy Ghost]; and if he endureth to the end, behold, him will I hold guiltless before my Father." This passage conveys profound insight: if we repent, are baptized, receive the Holy Ghost, and endure with the Holy Ghost to the end, we will be found not perfect yet, but *guiltless* before the Father. A study of the scriptural contexts in which *perfect* is used reveals that the Lord often used the word in the sense of *guiltless,* of being in a state of repentance and pure intent.

Studying the Sermon on the Mount closely, we discover that the Savior spoke specifically of the condition of the human heart, of *our* hearts. To the Nephites he explicitly taught that no anger, no condemnation, no grudges, no lust need enter our hearts: "I give unto you a commandment, that ye suffer none of these things to enter into your heart; for it is better that ye should deny yourselves of these things, wherein ye will take up your cross, than that ye should be cast into hell." (3 Ne. 12:29-30.) The cross is, of course, the cross of self-denial, or sacrifice to the cause of righteousness, which is the cross he took up. He invites each of his disciples—each of *us*—to bless those that curse them, do good to them that hate them, and make other such heart-expanding efforts. Love must overcome fear at the Lord's altar. It is in this context that he issued the injunction to be perfect. He could not command us to be perfect in his judgment, but he could invite us to be perfect in the intents of our hearts, which perfection we have power over through agency and through Christ's freely offered power; such perfection puts us on the road to that final perfection. However, the Lord kindly observed: "Ye are not able to abide the presence of God now, neither the ministering of angels; wherefore, continue in patience until ye are perfected." (D&C 67:13.)

Acceptable Sacrifice

Matthew 6 treats the state of heart that is single to God. No deed is acceptable on the Lord's altar except that which is motivated by love. The spiritual deed—fasting, prayer, loving acts—that is motivated by desire for the good opinion of others, or by the expectation of some other personal gain, will not make us whole and therefore is unacceptable to the Lord. James labeled that act "double minded" and added that "a double minded man is unstable in all his ways." (James1:8.) "No man can serve two masters." (Matt. 6:24.) Darkness and confusion, even fear, cloud the perception of such a person: "If therefore thine eye be single, thy whole body shall be full of light. But if thine eye be evil, thy whole body shall be full of darkness." (Matt. 6:22-23.) Self-magnification is unacceptable, but the pure act performed before the Lord enlarges and clarifies the soul. The Lord increases the power for good of those who make themselves independent of the praise (or scorn) of others: "Thy Father, which seeth in secret, shall reward thee openly." (Matt. 6:18.)

An intriguing promise emerges from verses 25 to 34 and is linked to all the sacrifices that precede them. In these verses the Lord used the phrase "take no thought for," a bland translation of the Greek word *merimnesete,* which means to be very anxious about something. He used the word six times in this passage. In effect he invited us to *sacrifice our anxiety* over the many elements of our lives that are beyond our control (such as adding a cubit to our stature—v. 27), but that we think affect our well-being. However, he implied that this sacrifice of fear is possible only if we first give up anger, lust, vengeance, and glory seeking, which in themselves produce fear. He pointed out that if we make the single aim of our lives the will of God and the promotion of the cause of Zion, those uncontrollable elements of life will, one day at a time, take care of themselves, and we can live knowing that the forces of the universe are working to our benefit. Matthew 6:34 translates the Greek word *kakia* as *evil*. The verse could be accurately translated, "Do not be unduly anxious about the morrow, for the morrow will take thought for the things of itself; sufficient to the day are the *problems* (or *troubles*) thereof."

"Judge not, that ye be not judged." (Matt. 7:1.) Here Jesus treats another sin that interferes with true perception. The Joseph Smith Translation adds, "Judge not *unrighteously,* that ye be not judged: *but judge righteous judgment.*" What is righteous judgement? The *unrighteous* judgment we make of another leads to condemnation of that person, resulting in a sense of self-superiority, in anger, or in some retributive action. If we had in the beginning given the person the benefit of the doubt, realizing that we could never know the motives or the conditioning of another, we would have avoided falling into a sin at least as great as the one that provoked our judgment, that is, condemnation. Had we not first judged and condemned another for what that person did, there would be no reason for us to forgive. If we do judge—no matter how great the injury or how deliberate—*we* are at fault. How helpful it is to turn our focus inward instead and concentrate on clarifying our own souls.

Righteous judgment may often not belong to us at all, but to a priesthood leader, such as a bishop. But where we must judge, we should try to see through the lens of love rather than the dark glass of demeaning or retaliation. The Savior's mote-beam discussion illustrates that true perception of another is obscured by our own sins. If we react against what turns out to be a fabrication of our own imaginations, namely our negative interpretation of another person, we choose sorrow and cannot blame the other person for our spiritual predicament. For our own sakes, we must accept others as they are. We recall the law of restoration in Alma 41:14: what we do to another, even in our hearts, has great power over our own happiness and well-being. The Golden Rule takes on new meaning: "Therefore all things whatsoever ye would that men should do to you, do ye even so to them" (Matt. 7:12), because truly we do them to ourselves.

"Ask, and it shall be given you; seek, and ye shall find; knock, and it shall be opened unto you: for every one that asketh receiveth; and he that seeketh findeth; and to him that knocketh it shall be opened." (Matt. 7:7-8.) We restrain the Lord's gifts to us until we have identified the things we need most and then ask him for those gifts. Repeatedly throughout the scriptures the Lord invites, indeed commands, us to come to him with our real needs: strength in temptation, forgiveness, love, insight, knowledge of his will, a blessing on another, a change of heart. It is in the asking, seeking, and knocking process that we come to understand intimately the Lord's accessibility and his ongoing function as Savior.

"Enter ye in at the strait gate." (Matt. 7:13.) "Not every one that saith unto me, Lord, Lord, shall enter into the kingdom of heaven; but he that doeth the will of my Father which is in heaven." (Matt. 7:21.) Total submission to God's will eludes us as we keep trying to take the reins back, to do things our way. Elder Neal A. Maxwell has said, "We need to break free of our old selves—the provincial, constraining, and complaining selves—and become susceptible to the shaping of the Lord. But the old self goes neither gladly nor quickly. Even so, this subjection to God is really emancipation."[9]

By refusing to place God's will first, we deprive ourselves of his help and even of an understanding of how ever-present his help is. The words "Of myself I am nothing, the Father doeth the works" carry bright insight and promise. Then what prevents us from yielding our hearts to God? A deeper self-analysis may reveal that fear lurks at the base of many personality defects: fear that we will lose something we already have, or fear that we will not get something we think we must have. People thus afflicted do not believe that the Father really is a giver of good gifts. (See Matt. 7:11.) Sacrifice and submission build love and confidence and dissolve such fear. As that exchange takes place in our hearts, a wonderful sense of security, of stillness, undergirds our existence at its deepest levels. We cannot know God through the veil of our own will. Only as we deliberately become conscious of him, submitting to his plan for us, do we see him moving in his tender and gracious majesty through the moments of our lives.

The Power of Sacrifice

One of the great foundation insights from this sermon is the extent to which we can come to the Savior and the extent to which he will come to us. To give up finally all that stands between us and him seems at first a heavy task as we see how all-encompassing the requirements are. Nevertheless, the reward is incomparable. The old concept of God as primarily an emergency source evaporates, as does the idea that we might still live our own lives, God helping a little now and then. "I am the vine, ye are the branches: he that abideth in me, and I in him, the same bringeth forth much fruit: for without me ye can do nothing." (John 15:5.) Perhaps we think that God speaks in hyperbole—that we cannot take him literally when he invites total dependence. Perhaps we are afraid to interpret him literally because the full truth seems to require so much of us. Or perhaps it seems too wonderful to be true.

At first we perceive the law of sacrifice as an external observance. We do the outward things: pay tithing, contribute to the ward budget, do our visiting teaching, and so on. Through time and experience we come to feel that we could give all that we own for the Lord's work. After more time, the revelation of the meaning of sacrifice penetrates to the yet deeper level, and our opportunities to sacrifice come more often as we try to merge our will with the Lord's. All opportunities to serve the cause of righteousness require something of us, and that something often feels like sacrifice—it requires an exertion, an extension of ourselves that is often not convenient or comfortable or even safe. We have fences of limitation around us that extend grudgingly. Exertion and even pain accompany us beyond where we have gone before. To keep extending the boundaries is the process of becoming like God. The process by which we extend those boundaries is obedience to the law of sacrifice.

We have seen that this sermon represents a covenant: sacrifice of sin elicits power from God to have the kingdom here and to enter the kingdom in the world to come. Joseph Smith observed:

A religion that does not require the sacrifice of all things never has power sufficient to produce the faith necessary unto life and salvation; for, from the first existence of man, the faith necessary unto the enjoyment of life and salvation never could be obtained without the sacrifice of all earthly things. . . . God has ordained that men should enjoy eternal life; and it is through the medium of the sacrifice of all earthly things that men do actually know that they are doing the things that are well pleasing in the sight of God. When a man has offered in sacrifice all that he has for the truth's sake, not even withholding his life, and believing before God that he has been called to make this sacrifice because he seeks to do his will, he does know, most assuredly, that God does and will accept his sacrifice and offering, and that he has not, nor will not seek his face in vain. Under these circumstances, then, he can obtain the faith necessary for him to lay hold on eternal life.[10]

The covenant of sacrifice actually distinguishes the Saints: "In the last days, before the Lord comes, he is to gather together his saints who have made a covenant with him by sacrifice."[11]

The practice of sacrifice fortifies the Saints against the power of evil. The Prophet explained: "[Those who made sacrifice] were enabled, through faith, to combat the powers of darkness, contend against the wiles of the adversary, overcome the world, and obtain . . . even the salvation of their souls. . . . [Those who do not make sacrifice] will not be able to contend against all the opposition, tribulations, and afflictions which they will have to encounter in order to be heirs of God, and joint heirs with Christ Jesus; and they will grow weary in their minds, and the adversary will have power over them and destroy them."[12]

Amaleki offered a fitting summary: "My beloved brethren, I would that ye should come unto Christ, who is the Holy One of Israel, and partake of his salvation, and the power of his redemption. Yea, come unto him, and *offer your whole souls as an offering unto him,* and continue in fasting and praying, and endure to the end; and as the Lord liveth ye will be saved." (Omni 1:26, emphasis added.)

"When Jesus had ended these sayings, the people were astonished at his doctrine: for he taught them as one having authority, and not as the scribes." (Matt. 7:28-29.) The scribes were the experts on the law of Moses. They were the ones to whom the people turned for an explication of it. Yet here was a man who was no scribe, who even denounced the scribes for their distortion of the law and attempted to change the law. Nevertheless, despite their resistance to the fulfillment of the law of Moses, they had to acknowledge that he had the authority of the Lawgiver himself.

NOTES

1. Walter Bauer, W. F. Arndt, and F. W. Gingrich, *A Greek-English Lexicon of the New Testament,* 2nd ed. (Chicago: University of Chicago Press, 1979), p. 486.

2. James H. Moulton and George Milligan, *The Vocabulary of the Greek Testament* (Grand Rapids, Mich.: Eerdmans, 1952), p. 386.

3. Richard Draper, "Sacrifices and Offerings: Foreshadowings of Christ," *Ensign,* September 1980, p. 24.

4. See Kent P. Jackson, "The Law of Moses and the Atonement of Christ," *Studies in Scripture, Volume 3: The Old Testament,* pp. 159-72.

5. Draper, pp. 24-25.

6. As suggested in the Bible Dictionary in the LDS edition of the King James Bible, p. 767.

7. The King James Version translates *diatheke* as *testament,* but it also means *covenant* or *contract,* which definition gives added insight to the term *new testament.* See Matt. 26:28, "my blood of the new testament." See also Kent P. Jackson, "God's Testament to Ancient Israel," *Studies in Scripture, Volume 3: The Old Testament,* p. 3.

8. See Howard W. Hunter, "Parents' Concern for Children," *Ensign,* November 1983, p. 65.

9. Neal A. Maxwell, "Willing to Submit," *Ensign,* May 1985, p. 71.

10. *Lectures on Faith* (Salt Lake City: Deseret Book, 1985), 6:7.

11. Ibid., 6:9.

12. Ibid., 6:11-12.

16

HE THAT IS NOT WITH ME
IS AGAINST ME
(Matthew 12:14-50; Mark 3:22-35; Luke 8:1-3, 19-21)

MONTE S. NYMAN

The setting for the events of these chapters is Capernaum and the cities in its vicinity. (Luke 7:1; 8:1.) The time is during the second year of the Savior's ministry. Accompanying the Savior on a tour of the cities, a part of the great Galilean ministry, were "the twelve who were ordained of him." (JST, Luke 8:1.) This was a training mission for the recently called Twelve.

The Casting Out of Devils

Among the miracles Jesus performed on this Galilean tour was the casting out of a devil from a man who was blind and dumb. He also healed the man of his blindness and his inability to speak. (Matt. 12:22.) This great miracle amazed the people of the area and convinced them of Jesus' Messiahship. When word reached Jerusalem, however, the Pharisees came from Jerusalem[1] to explain away the miracle. "Unless this and like miracles are explained away," Elder Bruce R. McConkie wrote, "the priestcrafts of the priests will be replaced by a new order; the scribes and Pharisees must disabuse the public mind or lose their positions of power and influence over the people."[2]

The miracle had been observed; it was an established incident. The Pharisees could not deny the miracle; therefore they had to find

Monte S. Nyman is professor of ancient scripture, associate dean of Religious Education, and director of Book of Mormon research in the Religious Studies Center at Brigham Young University.

another explanation. They chose to attribute it to Satan. Little did they realize that this choice would draw from the Savior the great doctrine of the condemnation that comes upon those who choose to follow Satan, the one whom they were following in making such an accusation. Before presenting this doctrine, Jesus pointed out the absurdity of their accusation.

A Kingdom Divided Against Itself

The Messiahship of Jesus was again illustrated as he encountered the Pharisees. Before they spoke to him, he perceived their thoughts.[3] He declared to them the obvious fallacy of their claims before asking the incriminating questions. A kingdom, a city, or even a house that is divided will not endure but will fail in its goals. Therefore, if their accusations were correct, Satan "is divided against himself" (Matt. 12:26), and "he cannot stand, but hath an end" (Mark 3:26).

The Joseph Smith Translation account of Mark adds the concept that Satan would "speedily" come to an end if divided against himself. (JST, Mark 3:19.) The kingdom of Satan was destined to come to an end, but not speedily. Satan would be allowed to remain upon the earth until the millennial reign of Christ. Satan and his followers knew this, as shown by the reaction of the devils when they were cast out of two men in the country of the Gergesenes. (See Matt. 8:28-29.) To have Satan's kingdom divided at this point would prevent their seeking "the misery of all mankind." (2 Ne. 2:18.) The logic of the Pharisees was thus soundly refuted.

Jesus was not content with refuting the Pharisees' logic; he had a more important goal to accomplish. His mission included testifying of the kingdom of God that had been established. His next question would confirm this establishment. He asked how others among the Pharisees, their "children," were casting out devils; was it by the same power that they claimed Christ was using? (See Matt. 12:27.) Their "children" were other people who were performing similar miraculous healings of people possessed by evil spirits. These persons had power not possessed by the accusers, and they were therefore more powerful than the Pharisaic rulers. The logic was that if these healings were done by the power of Satan, then Satan had more power than the

Pharisees and they would become subject to him. Again they were caught in their faulty reasoning.

On the other hand, if Jesus had "cast out devils by the Spirit of God, then the kingdom of God" had come unto the Pharisees (Matt, 12:28), and they were rejecting or fighting against it. Jesus then declared by what power these others were performing miracles (a truth restored in the Joseph Smith Translation): "They also cast out devils by the Spirit of God, for unto them is given power over devils, that they may cast them out." (JST, Matt. 12:23; cf. Matt. 12:28.) These others, members of the Church of Jesus Christ who held priesthood power, were not using the power of Satan but were using the power of God delegated to them as members of the kingdom of God. The kingdom was restored and the Pharisees were fighting against it.

As a further attestation to his own and his associates' power, Jesus declared that a strong man must first be bound before someone can spoil or take the desired contents of his house. (Matt. 12:29.) In casting out devils, he and his followers were binding the power of Satan over the precious souls of men and were spoiling Satan's house or freeing souls from captivity by taking them out of Satan's grasp.

As a final declaration of the Pharisees' present position, Jesus declared: "He that is not with me is against me; and he that gathereth not with me scattereth abroad." (Matt. 12:30.) That the kingdom of God was established had been proven. The conclusion was, therefore, that since these Pharisees were not with him, they were against him and were opposing the movement of the kingdom of God. Furthermore, since they were not a part of the gathering to this kingdom, they were a part of the scattering. Those who reject the opportunity of the gospel and the kingdom will not only lose the blessings of that kingdom but will also be left desolate and will remain so until Christ comes again. (See Matt. 23:37-39.) There were and are only two kingdoms or two churches—the kingdom of God and the kingdom of Satan; the church of the Lamb and the church of the devil—and "whoso belongeth not to the church of the Lamb of God belongeth to that great church, which is the mother of abominations; and she is the whore of all the earth." (1 Ne. 14:10.) This stern teaching from the Book of Mormon is not unique to that book but was taught by the Savior on this occasion.

The Sin Against the Holy Ghost

Having refuted the Pharisees in their logic and undoubtedly in their egos, the Savior capitalized upon the opportunity to teach the seriousness of their sins. From Mark's account in the Joseph Smith Translation, we learn that at this point others joined the group Jesus was teaching. These were not of the Pharisees, but they were critical of his association with the Pharisees, whom they considered to be sinners. These were apparently self-righteous individuals who abhorred the Pharisees. Jesus' answer to these accusers shows that he was offering the Pharisees an opportunity to repent, but he was also giving them a warning against further serious sin. It may also illustrate that the accusers were really not for Jesus but were against him. Because of the Joseph Smith Translation additions in both Matthew and Mark, and to illustrate the effects of a harmony of the two accounts, the JST verses are compared below:

JST, Matthew

Wherefore I say unto you, All manner of sin and blasphemy shall be forgiven unto men *who receive me and repent;* but the blasphemy against the Holy Ghost, *it* shall not be forgiven unto men.

And whosoever speaketh a word against the Son of *Man,* it shall be forgiven him; but whosoever speaketh against the Holy Ghost, it shall not be forgiven him; neither in this world; neither in the world to come.

Either make the tree good and his fruit good; or else make the tree corrupt, and his fruit corrupt; for

JST, Mark

And then came certain men unto him, accusing him, saying, Why do ye receive sinners, seeing thou makest thyself the Son of God.

But he answered them and said, Verily I say unto you, All sins *which men have committed, when they repent,* shall be forgiven *them; for I came to preach repentance unto the sons of men.*

And blasphemies, wheresoever they shall blaspheme, *shall be forgiven them that come unto me, and do the works which they see me do.*

But there is a sin which shall not be forgiven. He that shall blaspheme against the Holy Ghost, hath never forgiveness; but is in danger of *being cut down out of*

the tree is known by *the* fruit. (JST, Matt. 12:26-28; cf. Matt. 12:31-33. Italics designate changes and additions of the JST.)

the world. And they shall inherit eternal damnation.

And *this he said unto them* because they said, He hath an unclean spirit. (JST, Mark 3:21-25; cf. Mark 3:28-29. Italics designate changes and additions of the JST.)

In commenting on these words of Jesus, Joseph Smith declared:

> I have a declaration to make as to the provisions which God hath made to suit the conditions of man—made from before the foundation of the world. What has Jesus said? All sin, and all blasphemies, and every transgression, except one, that man can be guilty of, may be forgiven; and there is a salvation for all men, either in this world or the world to come, who have not committed the unpardonable sin, there being a provision either in this world or the world of spirits. Hence God hath made a provision that every spirit in the eternal world can be ferreted out and saved unless he has committed that unpardonable sin which cannot be remitted to him either in this world or the world of spirits. God has wrought out a salvation for all men, unless they have committed a certain sin; and every man who has a friend in the eternal world can save him, unless he has committed the unpardonable sin. And so you can see how far you can be a savior.[4]

The Pharisees had not committed the unpardonable sin. They had sinned against Jesus, but he was still their friend in offering salvation to them. However, this was their opportunity to be ferreted out. "This life is the time for men to prepare to meet God." (Alma 34:32.) Joseph Smith further declared:

> A man cannot commit the unpardonable sin after the dissolution of the body, and there is a way possible for escape. Knowledge saves a man; and in the world of spirits no man can be exalted but by knowledge. So long as a man will not give heed to the commandments, he must abide without salvation. If a man has knowledge, he can be saved; although, if he has been guilty of great sins, he will be punished for them. But when he consents to obey the Gospel, whether here or in the world of spirits, he is saved. . . .

255

> I know the Scriptures and understand them. I said, no man can commit the unpardonable sin after the dissolution of the body, nor in this life, until he receives the Holy Ghost; but they must do it in this world. Hence the salvation of Jesus Christ was wrought out for all men, in order to triumph over the devil; for if it did not catch him in one place, it would in another; for he stood up as a Savior. All will suffer until they obey Christ himself.[5]

Jesus was attempting to prevent the Pharisees and others from committing this serious sin and to allow them to escape the punishment for serious sins by obeying him. He had given them knowledge, and the way of escape was open to them. He had shown that his power was greater than the devil's. They had not sinned against the Holy Ghost, for the Holy Ghost had not yet been given. (See John 7:39.) What, then, is the sin against the Holy Ghost? Joseph Smith explained:

> All sins shall be forgiven, except the sin against the Holy Ghost; for Jesus will save all except the sons of perdition. What must a man do to commit the unpardonable sin? He must receive the Holy Ghost, have the heavens opened unto him, and know God, and then sin against Him. After a man has sinned against the Holy Ghost, there is no repentance for him. He has got to say that the sun does not shine while he sees it; he has got to deny Jesus Christ when the heavens have been opened unto him, and to deny the plan of salvation with his eyes open to the truth of it; and from that time he begins to be an enemy. This is the case with many apostates of the Church of Jesus Christ of Latter-day Saints.[6]

Although the Pharisees had spoken against the Son of Man, he was willing to forgive them. They had not had the sure witness of the Holy Ghost, but he warned them that when it came, if they denied it they could not be forgiven. This is possibly in conjunction with the law of witnesses: in the mouth of two or more witnesses is the Lord's word established. (Deut. 19:15; Matt. 18:16.) The Savior was the first witness. When the Holy Ghost was poured out upon the world through him (3 Ne. 20:27), they would have two witnesses and would therefore be condemned.

As a further warning, those who accused Jesus of having an unclean spirit were victims of that very spirit, and if they did not cease to be an enemy to his work, they might be guilty of that unpardonable sin. Joseph Smith used his own life and the life of the Savior to illustrate this: "When a man begins to be an enemy to this work, he hunts me, he seeks to kill me, and never ceases to thirst for my blood. He gets the spirit of the devil—the same spirit that they had who crucified the Lord of Life—the same spirit that sins against the Holy Ghost. You cannot save such persons; you cannot bring them to repentance; they make open war, like the devil, and awful is the consequence."[7]

As a conclusion to this terse and stern doctrine, Jesus again warned of the polarity of the situation. They should either become a good tree, a part of the kingdom, and produce fruit, or they would become more corrupt, with corrupt fruit. Again, he taught that there would eventually be two churches only.

By Thy Words

In an apparent broadening of the audience to include his latest self-righteous accusers, Jesus warned of venom or poison coming from their mouths. Calling them vipers or snakes that produce the poisonous venom, he declared that the mouth speaks those things which are in the heart. (Matt. 12:34.) If their hearts are good, they will speak good things. If their hearts are evil, they will speak evil things. (Matt. 12:35.) He concluded with this warning: "Every idle word that men shall speak, they shall give account thereof in the day of judgment. For by thy words thou shalt be justified, and by thy words thou shalt be condemned." (Matt. 12:36-37.)

Although the audience was broadened, Jesus did not intend that this warning be isolated from the unpardonable sin, the sin of denying the Holy Ghost. A thought precedes words; a word precedes actions. As one thinks and as one says, so one will do. In a further comment upon the sin against the Holy Ghost, Joseph Smith makes this tie and gives this warning to our day:

> I advise all of you to be careful what you do, or you may
> by-and-by find out that you have been deceived. Stay your-
> selves; do not give way; don't make any hasty moves, you may
> be saved. If a spirit of bitterness is in you, don't be in haste. You

may say, that man is a sinner. Well, if he repents, he shall be forgiven. Be cautious: await. When you find a spirit that wants
bloodshed—murder, the same is not of God, but is of the devil.
Out of the abundance of the heart of man the mouth speaketh.[8]

For a second witness to this great principle, we turn to the Book of
Mormon. Alma testified that "our words will condemn us, yea, all our
works will condemn us; we shall not be found spotless; and our
thoughts will also condemn us." (Alma 12:14.)

Sign Seekers

Jesus' conversation next turned back to the scribes and Pharisees,
who displayed their spiritual nature by asking Jesus for a sign. (Matt.
12:38.) His rebuking answer that "an evil and adulterous generation
seeketh after a sign" (Matt. 12:39) was later repeated in another setting—see Matthew 16:4—but could be repeated many times more in
every age and generation. Sign seeking and adulterous relations are as
compatible as are the two participants in the illicit relationship. The
reason for this is explained by Elder Bruce R. McConkie: "Adultery so
dulls the spiritual sensations of men that it becomes exceedingly hard
for them to believe the truth when they have it. In their hardened
state they seek for a sign."[9] Again we turn to the Prophet Joseph Smith
to verify this teaching of our Savior:

> When I was preaching in Philadelphia, a Quaker called out
> for a sign. I told him to be still. After the sermon, he again asked
> for a sign. I told the congregation the man was an adulterer;
> that a wicked and adulterous generation seeketh after a sign;
> and that the Lord had said to me in a revelation, that any man
> who wanted a sign was an adulterous person. "It is true," cried
> one, "for I caught him in the very act," which the man after-
> wards confessed when he was baptized.[10]

The Pharisees had had many signs. They had come seeking Jesus
because of the reported miracles he had done. They also had the scriptures as signs. The prophet Jonas (Jonah) had experienced a miraculous physical salvation from the belly of a whale in similitude of the
Savior's burial in the earth and coming forth after three days in the resurrection. (Matt. 12:39-40.) The Savior's statement about Jonah was

used here to show that since the Pharisees had been given these and other scriptural witnesses of the past, as well as the miraculous witnesses of the present, they would be given no other signs until the Savior's resurrection gave irrefutable evidence that Jesus was the Christ. They had had signs enough. Unless they repented of their immoral practices, discontinued their venomous speaking, and became good trees producing good fruit, their only sign would be "not unto salvation" but to their condemnation. (D&C 63:7-11.)

Furthermore, they who were the royal lineage would be condemned by those Gentiles who would accept the witnesses voluntarily given, as did Gentiles in the days of Jonah and Solomon. (Matt. 12:41-42.) Jesus was not on trial—this generation had greater evidence than either Ninevah or the Queen of the South; rather, the world was on trial. In our day, the Book of Mormon is not on trial. The Lord has provided the witnesses, and they will condemn us or bring us to salvation. (See D&C 20:13-15.)

A Worse End

The Pharisees did not give up easily. They sent their scribes to try one more argument to justify their sinful actions, accusing Jesus of giving instructions contrary to the written scriptures:

> *Then came some of the scribes and said unto him, Master, it is written that, Every sin shall be forgiven; but ye say, Whosoever speaketh against the Holy Ghost shall not be forgiven. And they asked him, saying, How can these things be?*
>
> *And he said unto them,* When the unclean spirit is gone out of a man, he walketh through dry places, seeking rest and findeth none; *but when a man speaketh against the Holy Ghost,* then he saith, I will return into my house from whence I came out; and when he is come, he findeth *him* empty, swept and garnished; *for the good spirit leaveth him unto himself.*
>
> Then goeth *the evil spirit,* and taketh with himself seven other spirits more wicked than himself; and they enter in and dwell there; and the last *end* of that man is worse than the first. Even so shall it be also unto this wicked generation. (JST, Matt. 12:37-39; cf. Matt. 12:43-45. Italics designate changes and additions in the JST.)

In their apostate condition, did they not know that they were dealing with the giver of the scriptures? (See 3 Ne. 15:5.) Undoubtedly not. Again, Jesus more than answered their question. He taught them that not only must they rid themselves of the spirit of the devil, but they must also replace that evil spirit with the spirit of God and retain it; for if the person who had rid himself or herself of the devil speaks against the Holy Ghost, then the Spirit of God will withdraw. The evil spirit will return, bringing with him seven other evil spirits worse than himself, and the person will be worse off than before.

The body is the tabernacle of God. The devil also desires a body. The spirit of God will not dwell in an unclean tabernacle, but the devil will. Apparently many evil spirits can occupy one body. (See Luke 8:2.) Therefore, it will be much more difficult to rid oneself of these multiple evil spirits than it was before to get rid of the devil. In a prophetic statement, Jesus declared that this would be the state of "this wicked generation." (Matt. 12:45.) Those who rejected the Spirit of God would become so obsessed with the devil that they would actually crucify their Savior, the only one who could save them.

Jesus' Brothers and Sisters

Jesus' conversation had by now drawn a crowd. The crowd was so large that his mother and his brethren, who had come seeking him, could not get to him, so a message that they were there was relayed to him. (Matt. 12:46-47.) Jesus capitalized on this occasion to summarize his teachings. While his comments verify that Mary was the mother of other children (Matt. 12:48-49; cf. Matt. 13:55-56), the spiritual connotation of his response was that all who would accept him as their Messiah and follow his instructions would be his brothers and sisters (Matt. 12:50). He was literally the Son of God in the flesh, but he was here to make it possible for all to be his brothers and sisters—joint heirs to all that the Father has—in eternity. Although they (and all of us) are all the spirit offspring of God, only those who do the will of the Father of their spirits, as manifest through Jesus on earth, will attain that blessing.

NOTES

1. Mark records that the scribes came down from Jerusalem. (Mark 3:22.) Matthew merely states that the Pharisees heard it. (Matt. 12:24.) Scribes were persons responsible for the detail of the law and its application to the time. They were usually, but not always, Pharisees. Since Jesus was a threat to the "traditions of the elders," which was the scribes' responsibility to maintain, it is probable that they were sent by the Pharisees to monitor this situation.

2. Bruce R. McConkie, *The Mortal Messiah,* 4 vols. (Salt Lake City: Deseret Book, 1979-81), 2:209-10.

3. Only Matthew's account records that Jesus knew their thoughts, but the Joseph Smith Translation adds this detail to Mark's account.

4. *Teachings of the Prophet Joseph Smith,* pp. 356-57.

5. Ibid., p. 357.

6. Ibid., p. 358.

7. Ibid.

8. Ibid.

9. McConkie, *The Mortal Messiah* 2:225.

10. *Teachings of the Prophet Joseph Smith,* p. 278.

17

THE PARABLES OF JESUS
(Matthew 13)

RICHARD D. DRAPER

The disciples of the Lord stood puzzled, perhaps even perplexed. For over a year they had followed their Master—hearing him, learning from him, drinking deep from the clear water of life that he offered. His doctrine was declared in unveiled plainness. This is not to say that he did not rely on the power of imagery. Indeed, his sayings were full of it: "Ye are the salt of the earth: but if the salt have lost his savour, wherewith shall it be salted? it is thenceforth good for nothing, but to be cast out." (Matt. 5:13.) And again, "Every tree is known by his own fruit. For of thorns men do not gather figs, nor of a bramble bush gather they grapes." (Luke 6:44.) These word pictures enhanced his message and gave it beauty.

But on this day his method of teaching changed. One after another, nothing but stories—parables—flowed from his mouth. What did they mean? Why did he suddenly change his approach? How were these parables to be understood? These and other questions puzzled the disciples.

Literary Devices in Scripture

From ancient times, symbolism has been one of the important means by which people have communicated ideas. Such figurative speech can range from single words to extended stories. Names have been given to these kinds of utterances. Among them are the following:

Richard D. Draper is an instructor at the LDS Institute of Religion at Utah Technical College in Orem, Utah.

Metaphor

A metaphor is a word or group of words denoting one object or idea used in place of another to suggest a likeness between them. Some examples are: "I am the bread of life" (John 6:35), and "Judah is a lion's whelp" (Gen. 49:9). In these cases, it is not implied that the person so described is actually the object used as identification; rather some characteristic of that object is attributed to the person, suggesting a likeness between the two. Metaphors cover a broad range of subjects and can include animals, plants, actions, ideas, topographical features, or inanimate objects. An example of the latter is "The prophet is a pillar."

Simile

A simile is the same as a metaphor, but with the use of such words as "like" or "as." Thus, "The kingdom of heaven is like unto treasure hid in a field" (Matt. 13:44), or "the prophet stands like a pillar at the head of the Church."

Allegory

An allegory is a metaphor in story form. There is usually a plot (in most cases quite simple), and the event is often metaphorical, as are the characters also. Generally speaking, Jesus' parables in the New Testament fall into this category.

Hyperbole

Hyperbole is the use of extreme exaggeration to emphasize a point. In the scriptures, hyperbole is used not to mislead but to emphasize. A good New Testament example is in Jesus' mention of the mustard tree, which grows from the smallest of seeds into the greatest of trees. (Matt. 13:32.) This is not technically accurate, but the exaggeration emphasizes the lesson that he taught.

Parable

The word *parable* (Greek *parabole*) stems from the ancient Greek word *ballō* (to throw or set) with the prefix *para* (alongside or near). Though most of the New Testament parables are allegories, since most are metaphorical stories, the Gospels use the word *parable* to designate all types of figurative language, including simile and metaphor.

The Appeal of Parables

Because of its symbolic nature, the real point of any kind of parable can remain hidden from the hearer. Even so, there is a twofold advantage to teaching by this method. First, it makes the assimilation of truth easier. As one old Jewish proverb states: "Truth embodied in a tale shall enter in at lowly doors," meaning that even the most simple person can understand truth given by this means.[1] Second, truth taught in this way is more likely to be remembered, especially when hearers make their own deductions about its significance. In this way the hearers, in effect, teach themselves. The reason the Lord chose this form of teaching is not expressly stated in the scriptures but its use was deliberate.[2] To Ezekiel he commanded, "Son of man, put forth a riddle, and speak a parable unto the house of Israel." (Ezek. 17:2.) The parable was the riddle. Only the wise could deduce or the prophet supply the answer.

That the message in a parable was hidden suggests a reason for its use. The dissonance caused by curiosity led the people either to the Lord or to his prophet. This allowed a second revelation to be given for the purpose of satisfying their curiosity,[3] and placed the people in a position of double responsibility: first, they had asked for the revelation, and second, the revelation was repeated in plainness such that they could not misunderstand. In this way the Lord stood justified, whether or not the people obeyed. In addition, to those who were spiritually prepared, the parable brought understanding that could lead to life and salvation. In this light, Elder McConkie wrote:

> Parables are a call to investigate the truth; to learn more; to inquire into the spiritual realities, which, through them, are but dimly viewed. Parables start truth seekers out in the direction of further light and knowledge and understanding; they invite men to ponder such truths as they are able to bear in the hope of learning more. Parables are a call to come unto Christ, to believe his doctrines, to live his laws, and to be saved in his

kingdom. They teach arithmetic to those who have the capacity to learn calculus in due course. They are the mild milk of the word that prepares our spiritual digestive processes to feast upon the doctrinal meat of the kingdom.[4]

Parables in the Gospels

In the New Testament we find all variations of metaphorical speech. In the King James Translation, the word *parable* is used to identify all these forms. Thus, the definition includes simple metaphor, simile, and hyperbole—as when the Lord called Herod "that fox" (Luke 13:32); when he told the Pharisees that they were "blind guides, which strain at a gnat, and swallow a camel" (Matt. 23:24); or, more elaborate, when he taught them, "Give, and it shall be given unto you; good measure, pressed down, and shaken together, and running over, shall men give unto your bosom" (Luke 6:38). It also includes fully developed stories, allegories, such as the parables of the prodigal son (Luke 15:11-32) and the ten virgins (Matt. 25:1-13).

In some ways, Jesus' parables resembles those of the Pharisaic rabbis, who wrote in the centuries following the time of Christ but whose teachings may have their roots in Jesus' day. Both the rabbis and Jesus used parables to clarify and illustrate some of the main themes of their religious and ethical teachings. But it can hardly be assumed that Jesus borrowed from them or they from him. Both took their parables from the same relationships and customs, and these are reflected in their works. B. T. D. Smith notes the following about the use of parables by the rabbis and the Savior:

> In Talmud and Midrash we find parables of sowing and harvesting, sheep-farming and house-building, of stewards and farmlands, landlords and tenants, as well as many others drawn from a different environment and unrepresented in the Gospels. There is a Rabbinic story of hid treasure, of a Pharisee and a Publican, of a prodigal son, of a feast meant for others but given to the poor, of guests rejected because unsuitably dressed, of laborers who grumble at the wage paid to others. But it is only very rarely that the resemblance between these and the Gospel parables is so close as to suggest any direct re-

lationship, and it is probable that the parallelism is in all cases to be accounted for by the fact that behind both lies a common background of popular tales and illustrations and Scripture exposition.[5]

Both the rabbis and the Lord used parables for their own purposes, and it is here that one of the most striking differences can be found. For the rabbinic schools, the main concern was the exposition of the Torah or law of Moses. For the Lord, it was the kingdom of God and especially its eschatological significance for the chosen people living in his day.[6] This manifested itself primarily in three aspects. First, the time of decision was at hand and the people needed to decide, because the spiritual kingdom was actually being set up among them. The decision that all had to make was to accept the Lord for what he was and join his church or suffer the consequences. Second, while not minimizing the awful fate of those who willfully rejected him, Jesus emphasized the joy that would be found in the coming kingdom for the weak, oppressed, and distressed. (See Luke 15:4-10.) And third, Jesus set forth the standards by which men must prepare for entrance into his kingdom. Thus, some of his parables stressed singleness of devotion toward God. This, he showed, could be expressed only in actual deeds of faith, repentance, and love toward both God and men.[7] In other parables he stressed the value of obtaining entrance into the kingdom but also warned of its cost. Still others stressed the need to prepare for the full manifestation of his glory when the kingdom of God would be permanently established on the earth.

Another striking difference between the parables of the Redeemer and those of the rabbis is the Lord's superior development of the form, "whether in the wealth of imagination, the power of short and realistic depiction, or the spiritual force of the ideas presented."[8] Stressing this idea, one scholar has written:

> There were many parables before the day of Jesus. They can be found in the Old Testament, in the extra-canonical writings of the Jews and in the literature of other ancient peoples. . . . Jesus did not invent the form of story, but under His transforming touch its water became wine. . . .
>
> Jesus would have failed to make contact with His hearers

had He been unwilling to speak to them in their own tongue and to some extent, within the range of prevalent ideas. . . . Nor need we shrink, as some have felt they must, from the admission that Jesus sometimes adopted a well-known parable, and retold it in His own way for his own purpose. . . . The difference between the rabbinical parables and those of Jesus is precisely the difference between their mind and His. Their parables are mostly arid and artificial, . . . beyond the limits of ordinary human interest.[9]

It is interesting that the Lord turned to teaching in parables at the very moment open opposition began to mount against him and his message. How did the use of parables assist him in his ministry? The answer lies in the power of parables to do a number of things at the same time. Some of these have been mentioned already. Here I shall focus on two that seem to best illustrate how the Lord used them.

When his perplexed disciples came to him asking why he had turned to the use of parables, he explained: "Because it is given unto you to know the mysteries of the kingdom of heaven, but to them it is not given. For whosoever hath, to him shall be given, and he shall have more abundance: but whosoever hath not, from him shall be taken away even that he hath. Therefore speak I to them in parables: because they seeing see not; and hearing they hear not, neither do they understand." (Matt. 13:11-13.) The Lord's answer to the Twelve revealed his reasons for using parables: both to reveal and to conceal his doctrine. We shall look at the latter first.

The Power of Parables to Conceal

In speaking in parables, the Savior followed his own instructions to the Twelve. They were told to preach the gospel and teach repentance. The deeper mysteries, however, they were to keep within themselves: "Give not that which is holy unto the dogs, neither cast ye your pearls before swine, lest they trample them under their feet, and turn again and rend you." (Matt. 7:6.) The Lord knew that "such unbelieving and rebellious people would first reject the message, and then use the very truths they had heard to rend and destroy and wreak havoc among those whose faith was weak."[10]

Through parables, the Lord protected sacred truths from being used to thwart his work. But there was another reason why he used them. Elder Bruce R. McConkie wrote: "Had Jesus taught all of his doctrine in plainness, such would have added to the condemnation of his hearers (D&C 82:2-4). His use of parables to hide the full and deep import of portions of his message was an act of mercy on his part."[11] He observed: "Parables are for nonmembers of the Church, for those outside the kingdom, or, at best, . . . for those who are weak in the faith; who are not prepared to receive the truth involved in plain words; from whom the full truth must, as yet, remain hidden."[12] At the same time, Jesus used parables to enlighten those who were faithful.

The Power of Parables to Reveal

Elder McConkie continued:

> With it all, parables are majestic teaching devices, and they do reveal truth, and they do add light and understanding to those who already have the gift of understanding, as well as to those who are sincerely seeking truth. . . .
>
> Parables, planted in the minds of truth seekers, help them remember the issues involved until such time as the full and plain knowledge parts the parabolic veil and stands revealed for all to see. And parables form a reservoir of knowledge about which even the saints can ponder and inquire as they seek to perfect and expand their limited views of gospel themes.[13]

It was also because of the ability of parables to reveal things in a graphic way that the Lord was able to use them against his enemies. This idea is seen in his instructions to the Twelve: "Unto you it is given to know the mystery of the kingdom of God: but unto them that are without, all these things are done in parables: that seeing they may see, and not perceive; and hearing they may hear, and not understand; lest at any time they should be converted, and their sins should be forgiven them." (Mark 4:11-12.) This explanation should not be taken to suggest that the Lord used parables to deny light to the unenlightened or to harden the unbeliever in his unbelief. It is true that many may have become hardened toward the Lord, but that was not his purpose. His statement is really not a clause of purpose but of consequence. As one scholar has explained:

The truth is that the parables of Jesus are unique. The parables of other teachers and moralists can to some extent be separated from the teachers themselves. But Jesus and His parables are inseparable. To fail to understand *Him* is to fail to understand His parables. Consequently, to those who remain unaware of who He really is, or ignorant of the nature of the gift that He came to bring mankind, the mysteries of the kingdom of God, however many parables they may hear about it, must remain mysteries.[14]

It is important to remember that Jesus said that it was not those who had accepted him but those who were "without" for whom he spoke in parables. Acts and deeds, not simply instruction and doctrine, were parables to those who stood deliberately apart from the disciples. This suggests that it was the whole of his ministry—not just his parables or his unveiled teachings, or even his miracles, but the whole of his deeds—that could not be understood by those who refused to accept him for what he really was. To such, even his miracles remained (and still do remain) only stories and portents devoid of real meaning. As he said, quoting Isaiah, it was because "they seeing see not; and hearing they hear not, neither do they understand," that all remained a mystery to them. (Matt. 13:13; see also Isa. 6:9-10; 2 Ne. 16:9-10.)[15]

This was the same indictment leveled by Isaiah against the corrupt Israelites of his day. It revealed that deliberate kind of spiritual blindness through which they brought upon themselves temporal and everlasting destruction. The beloved John quoted this very passage to explain why the Jewish leaders refused to accept the Savior, "though he had done so many miracles before them." (John 12:37, 39-40.) The Lord's parables, as well as his acts and other teachings, expressed his disturbing new thinking, as compared with Judaism. His entire ministry was a message both clear and succinct. Thus we find some of his more detailed parables directed not to his disciples but to his antagonists, and not to obscure his message but to force it. (For example, see Matt. 21:23–22:14.) Those who refused to believe did so not because they did not understand, but because they understood very well. Having spiritually blinded themselves, they could not see the Light and Life of the world, and they were thus left to walk the dark path of the second death.

Interpreting and Applying Parables

Because the parables had power to reveal the mysteries of the kingdom, their message is timeless. Modern disciples, like the ancient, can learn much by understanding their deep truths. In order to do so, it is important to interpret them properly. A few keys are important.

Each parable had a definite message when it was spoken by the Lord, and a proper understanding of each can come only as we understand the original meaning. But how do we find out that original meaning? The best source is generally the New Testament itself. The Lord gave explanation of many of his parables. For those in which he did not, the Prophet Joseph Smith gave a key: "I enquire, what was the question which drew out the answer, or caused Jesus to utter the parable? . . . To ascertain its meaning, we must dig up the root and ascertain what it was that drew the saying out of Jesus."[16] Reading the parable in context, then, often provides either the question or the Lord's own interpretation. Understanding these provides the best tools for the proper interpretation of the message. There are, however, additional helps. These are found in the latter-day scriptures and the inspired writings of modern prophets. In the Doctrine and Covenants, the Lord both uses and explains a number of parables; and in the writings and discourses of Joseph Smith, important interpretations are given.[17]

The Message of the Lord's
First Recorded Parables

Matthew, Mark, and Luke all described the setting in which the Lord delivered his first recorded parables. He had risen early and walked down to the Sea of Galilee, where people gathered to him until there was a great multitude. Many of those who came to hear and see him did so not out of desire to follow him, but out of curiosity and a hope to see the sensational. So great was the multitude that he moved into a fishing boat and, while sitting there, taught the people.

Seven parables are recorded that were given at this time. These are usually designated as "The Sower," "The Seed Growing by Itself," "The Wheat and the Tares," "The Mustard Seed," "The Treasure Hid in a Field," "The Pearl of Great Price," and "The Fish Net." Some were given to the multitude, while others may have been shared only with the disciples. The text is clear that the two longer parables—"The Sower" and "The Wheat and the Tares"—were given as public discourses, but the setting of the shorter ones is not clear. What is important is that the disciples were present when all the parables were given. Since the message was often especially for them, the importance of the utterance does not depend on whether it was public or private. The record is clear that the interpretation of the parables was private. Thus their fullest meaning was for those of the kingdom who would benefit by the word.

Joseph Smith taught that the first parables spoken by the Lord all form a part of one prophetic whole that the Savior wanted his disciples to understand. These parables focus on various aspects of the gathering of the house of Israel, both in the meridian of time and in the dispensation of the fullness of times.[18]

The first recorded parable of the Lord is "The Sower," or, more appropriately, "The Soils." (Matt. 13:3-8, 18-23; Mark 4:3-8, 14-20; Luke 8:5-8, 11-15.) The grain that the sower sowed fell on different kinds of ground. Some grains were immediately parched and dried; others took root but soon died due to the action of sun, weed, or fowl; and others grew to maturity and produced different amounts of grain. The Savior told his disciples that the parable represented the various ways people receive the gospel and why some abandon it while others thrive in it.

Joseph Smith taught that this parable had an "allusion directly, to the commencement, or the setting up of the Kingdom in that age."[19] The Savior set in motion at that time the forces to gather Israel. One of the major purposes was to set up temples and begin the work for the dead.[20]

Closely connected with this parable was that which is called "The Wheat and the Tares." (Matt. 13:24-30.) In this parable the Lord told of a villain who sowed seeds of weeds among the newly planted grain and how, though distressed, the husbandman decided to leave the two growing together until the time of harvest, when each would be gathered—one for saving, one for burning. The Savior explained that this parable was meant to teach that though the tares would be allowed to do their work for a time, they would eventually be destroyed. (Matt. 13:36-43.)

According to the Prophet Joseph Smith this parable referred to conditions from Jesus' day to the Second Coming. During this period the truth would be opposed and falsehood would flourish, due to false doctrines and corrupt creeds. These would bind many down so that they would not receive the truth. As the work of gathering commenced at the time of the coming of the Lord, the good would respond to this word and be prepared, while the wicked would be left to burn.[21]

The Lord spoke yet another parable describing conditions between the time of his mortal preaching and his second coming. (Mark 4:26-29.) This also concerned grain but focused on its power to grow by itself while the husbandman slept or worked at other things. Only when the harvest had fully come did his attention have to return to the grain. In applying this parable to the last days, Joseph Smith suggested that the word operated even during the long night of apostasy until, at the time of the restoration, there were many who were prepared to receive it. At that time, when harvest time had fully come, the Lord noted that it would be necessary for the husbandmen, his servants, to work with all their might.

Five parables dealt with conditions near the time of the Second Coming. Two of these, "The Treasure Hid in a Field" and "The Pearl of Great Price," focused on the cost of discipleship at that time. (Matt. 13:44-46.) Together they show that whether the gospel is accidentally discovered or deliberately sought, the price of acquisition is everything one has. But the Savior also taught that the reward transcends any cost. Joseph Smith applied the meaning of the parables directly to the requirements of the gathering and the establishment of Zion and her stakes.[22]

A third parable focused on how a little leaven enriches a whole loaf and makes it light and delicious. (Matt. 13:33.) This referred to the effectiveness of the spread of the kingdom. The Prophet Joseph Smith likened the leaven to the testimony of the Three Witnesses, who testified to the truthfulness of the Book of Mormon. This testimony grew in the hearts of many, he explained, and the Church was growing mightily because of it.[23]

In the parable of the mustard seed, the focus of the Savior was on the ability of the tiny seed to grow into a mighty plant. So great was it that in its limbs birds could find roost. (Matt. 13:31-32; Mark 4:30-32.) Again the Prophet, through application, showed that the parable relates also to the Church in the last days. He compared the seed to the Book of Mormon, which was hidden in a field. Once found, it caused the establishment of a mighty kingdom upon the earth to which "God [was] sending down His powers, gifts and angels, to lodge in the branches thereof."[24]

The final parable focused attention on the fishing net, which draws all types of fish indiscriminately into it, such that sorting is always found necessary. (Matt. 13:47-50.) Joseph Smith tied this directly to the judgment that will take place when the Lord comes. The judgment will be necessary because of the diversity of faithfulness and unfaithfulness in the Church at that time. The sorting will be done by the angels, who the Prophet said, will "sever the wicked from among the just, and cast them into the furnace of fire: and there shall be wailing and gnashing of teeth."[25]

In these parables we see the Savior working to strengthen the faith of those who had accepted him. These parables reveal that the work started by the former-day saints would expand and continue, in spite of the opposition leading to the great apostasy, and that judgment would eventually come. In the end the righteous would be fully rewarded and the wicked would be punished. In these simple comparisons, a wealth of prophetic detail is revealed to those who have ears to hear.

Conclusion

The parable has a special place in the work of the Lord. Even today he speaks in parables to reveal and conceal his will. This is seen not only in the ordinances of his church but in the deeds of the kingdom as it spreads into ever more lands. Many cannot see the kingdom for what it is and explain it away just as they did the ministry of the Lord, but for those who have ears to hear and eyes to see, the fullness of the gospel is revealed and they will be fully prepared for the coming of the Lord.

A Catalog of Jesus' Parables[26]

Parable	Where Recorded
Temple, if destroyed, to be raised in three days	John 2:19-22
Candle under bushel	Matt. 5:14-16
House on rock and on sand	Matt. 7:24-27
Children of the bridechamber	Matt. 9:14-15 Mark 2:18-20 Luke 5:33-35
Piece of new cloth in an old garment	Matt. 9:16 Mark 2:21 Luke 5:36
New wine in old bottles	Matt. 9:17 Mark 2:22 Luke 5:37-38
New wine as against old wine	Luke 5:39
Blind leading the blind	Matt. 15:14 Luke 6:39
The beam and the mote	Luke 6:41-42
The two debtors	Luke 7:36-50
The sower	Matt. 13:3-23 Mark 4:3-25 Luke 8:5-18

Parable	Where Recorded
The seed growing by itself	Mark 4:26-29
The tares	Matt. 13:24-30
The mustard seed	Matt. 13:31-32 Luke 13:18-19 Mark 4:30-32
The leaven	Matt. 13:33 Luke 13:20-21
Parable of the tares explained	Matt. 13:36-43
Treasure hid in a field	Matt. 13:44
Pearl of great price	Matt. 13:45-46
The dragnet	Matt.13:47-50
What defiles a man	Matt. 15:11, 15-20
The lost sheep, and the ninety and nine	Matt. 18:12-14 Luke 15:3-7
The harsh servant and the debt	Matt. 18:23-35
The good Samaritan	Luke 10:25-37
The friend at midnight	Luke 11:5-13
The unclean spirit	Luke 11:24-26
The foolish rich man	Luke 12:13-21
The watchful servants	Luke 12:36-40

Parable	Where Recorded
The faithful and wise steward	Luke 12:41-48
The unfruitful fig tree	Luke 13:6-9
The good shepherd	John 10:1-6
The shut door	Luke 13:23-30
The wedding feast	Luke 14:7-14
The great supper	Luke 14:15-24
The building of the tower	Luke 14:25-30
The king going to make war	Luke 14:31-33
The ten pieces of silver	Luke 15:8-10
The return of the prodigal son	Luke 15:11-32
The unjust steward	Luke 16:1-13
The rich man and Lazarus	Luke 16:19-31
Servant and master supping	Luke 17:7-10
The importunate widow	Luke 18:1-8
The Pharisee and the publican	Luke 18:9-14
The labourers in the vineyard	Matt. 20:1-16
The two sons	Matt. 21:28-32
The wicked husbandman	Matt. 21:33-34 Mark 12:1-12 Luke 20:9-18

Parable	Where Recorded
The king's son	Matt. 22:1-14
The fig tree leaves	Matt. 24:32-33 Mark 13:28-29 Luke 21:29-31
The man taking a long journey	Mark 13:34-37
The faithful and the evil servant	Matt. 24:42-51
The ten virgins	Matt.25:1-13
The talents or the ten pounds	Matt. 25:14-30 Luke 19:11-27
The sheep and the goats	Matt. 25:31-46

NOTES

1. As quoted in J. D. Douglas, ed., *New Bible Dictionary* (Grand Rapids, Mich.: Eerdmans, 1962), p. 932.

2. Ezekiel was commanded to deliver some of his prophecies in the form of parables. For examples, see Ezek. 17:2-10; 24:3-8.

3. This process can be seen in Ezekiel as the people came to the prophet to inquire as to the meaning of his sayings and doings. For example, see Ezek. 24:19.

4. Bruce R. McConkie, *The Mortal Messiah,* 4 vols. (Salt Lake City: Deseret Book, 1979-81), 2:245.

5. B. T. D. Smith, *The Parables of the Synoptic Gospels* (Cambridge: The University Press, 1937), p. 70.

6. For examples, see Mark 1:15; Matt. 6:10; 21:42-44; Luke 14:7-11, 16-24; 16:19-31.

7. L. Mowry, "Parable," in *The Interpreter's Dictionary of the Bible,* 5 vols., ed. G. A. Buttrick (Nashville: Abingdon, 1962-1976), 3:653-54.

8. F. Huack, *"Parabole,"* in *Theological Dictionary of the New Testament,* 10 vols., ed. G. Friedrich and G. W. Bromiley (Grand Rapids, Mich.: Eerdmans, 1967), 5:754.

9. From George A. Buttrick, *The Parables of Jesus,* as cited in Robert J. Matthews, *The Parables of Jesus* (Provo: Brigham Young University Press, 1969), p. 3.

10. McConkie, *The Mortal Messiah* 2:238.

11. Bruce R. McConkie, *Doctrinal New Testament Commentary,* 3 vols. (Salt Lake City: Bookcraft, 1966-73), 1:284.

12. *The Mortal Messiah* 2:239.

13. Ibid., 2:239-40.

14. Douglas, *New Bible Dictionary,* p. 934.

15. Joseph Smith taught that the reason the Jews would not receive the Lord as the Messiah was that they "would not understand; and seeing, they did not perceive." The reason for their misunderstanding "was because they were not willing to see with their eyes, and hear with their ears; not because they could not, and were not privileged to see and hear, but because their hearts were full of iniquity and abominations." (*Teachings,* pp. 95-96.)

16. Ibid., pp. 276-77.

17. D&C 35:15-16 gives insight into the parable of the fig tree; while D&C 86:1-7 is important for understanding the parable of the wheat and the tares. D&C 101:43-65 is a unique parable, but bears some points of resemblance with the parable of the wicked husbandman. For some of Joseph Smith's insights, see *Teachings,* pp. 63-64 on the parable of the talents, pp. 94-102 on the parables of the kingdom of God, and pp. 276-77 for the prodigal son.

18. Ibid., p. 94.

19. Ibid., p. 97.

20. Ibid., pp. 183, 222.

21. Ibid., p. 101.

22. Ibid., pp. 101-2.

23. Ibid., p. 100.

24. Ibid., p. 98.

25. Ibid., p. 102. See also Matt. 13:49-50.

26. Adapted from J. Reuben Clark, Jr., *Our Lord of the Gospels* (Salt Lake City: Deseret Book, 1954), pp. 538-40.

18

THE DIVINE SONSHIP AND THE LAW OF WITNESSES
(John 5)

JOSEPH F. MCCONKIE

How are we to know with perfect assurance that Jesus of Nazareth is indeed the Son of God, the fulfillment of the prophets? What obligation rested upon the Nazarene to establish for his own and all future generations his claim to divine Sonship? By what standards are we to assess such assertions? We accept or reject the Christ at the peril of our eternal lives. What evidence are the heavens required to produce to establish the truth of such a claim? And by what standards are we to assess this and like declarations? Such are the matters with which the Gospel, or Testimony, of John deals. No chapter in that Gospel does so more directly than the fifth chapter.

Two major themes dominate this chapter of John: Christ's repeated affirmation that he had been sent of the Father, that he could do nothing of himself, that he received no honor from men, that he came in his Father's name to do his Father's will; and the evidences or testimonies of his divine Sonship. Every word and event in the chapter is directed to the accomplishment of that dual purpose. The events of this day center in his healing a lame man at the pool of Bethesda and subsequently giving a great discourse on the grounds of the temple in which he testified in perfect plainness that he was God's Son. He further challenged his detractors to return to the scriptures for collaboration of his testimony, with the warning that to reject him in the

Joseph F. McConkie is associate professor of ancient scripture at Brigham Young University.

name of Moses would but cause Moses to be their accuser on the day of judgment. We have read the story often; let us now ponder its implications.

Jesus as Lord of the Sabbath

The setting of our story finds us in Jerusalem at feast time, either Passover or Purim (on which, scholars are divided). Of a certainty it was the Sabbath, that holy day upon which servile work was to cease and the children of the Lord of the Sabbath were to identify themselves by keeping the day holy. Yet the long years that separated this people from the announcement of Sinai and the covenants associated therewith had witnessed a perversion of those covenants in general and of this day in particular, a perversion that astounds the modern mind. The refreshing waters of the Sabbath had become as the Dead Sea, a place in which there was no life, while the fertile lands of faith had been so heavily salted with traditions and ritual that no living thing could survive in their parched soil. The rabbis had determined thirty-nine chief or principal types of work that were forbidden. In application, this came to mean that "scattering two seeds was sowing; sweeping away or breaking a single clod was ploughing; plucking one blade of grass was sin; watering fruit or removing a withered leaf was forbidden; picking fruit, or even lifting it from the ground, was reaping; cutting a mushroom was a double sin, one both of harvesting and of sowing, for a new one would grow in place of the old; fishing, or anything that put an end to life, ranked with harvesting; rubbing ears of corn together, or anything else connected with food, was classed as binding of sheaves."[1] One could spit upon a rock but not upon the ground, for by scratching the earth you were guilty of cultivating. You could eat an egg laid by a fryer on the Sabbath but not an egg laid by a laying hen, because it was not the work of a fryer to produce eggs. Such distinctions, which went on endlessly, included prohibition against administering to the sick or afflicted. A broken bone could not be set or a dislocated joint put back, for if this were done, the body would start to heal itself, thus causing it to work. However, it was ruled that labor could be performed to save life. Thus, if someone were buried under ruins on the Sabbath, they might be dug and taken out if they were found alive, but if dead, they were to be left until the Sabbath was over.

Christ, who kept with exactness and honor the law as given on Sinai, had no reverence for these trappings with which men had embellished that law. It is not for mortals to tamper with the commandments of God, either adding to or taking therefrom; those doing so build upon a sandy foundation, and the gates of hell open to receive them. (See 3 Ne. 11:39-40.) Thus with deliberation and intent Christ sought for one in need of his healing powers that holy day, one upon whom a miracle could properly be performed. How more perfectly to dramatize the issue—was the love of his fellow Jews centered in the God who made them or in traditions of their own making? Would they rejoice in the healing of their brother or would they offend the very spirit of the Sabbath with anger that some inconsequential taboo of their concocting had been violated?

Among those with whom Christ chose to honor his Father in worship that day were the afflicted souls who stood vigil over the waters of the pool of Bethesda. It was their tradition, of what origin we know not, that the first of their number to enter the waters when they were disturbed, supposedly by an angel, would be healed. The pool was evidently a mineral spring whose waters bubbled intermittently as escaping gases broke the surface. Among those gathered that morning was a man who had been crippled for thirty-eight years. Jesus addressed him, asking, "Wilt thou be made whole?" The man responded that because of his infirmity he was unable to reach the troubled waters first, and that he could do so only with the help of another. Jesus then told him, "Rise, take up thy bed, and walk." Without hesitation, the man—impotent in body but not in faith—responded to God's Son and took up his bed and walked. (See John 5:6-9.)

The scripture records no rejoicing at the man's good fortune, nor does it contain any hint that his nation saw reason to praise God for the miracle they had witnessed. We read no commendation of Jesus, no suggestion that he might be their long-promised Messiah, but rather condemnation of a man who carried his bed on the Sabbath day and efforts to kill the person who directed him to do so. It was the tradition that was loved and honored, not the living Christ.

Jesus Proclaims His Divine Sonship

The scene of our story now shifts to the temple ground, where Christ had gone to teach. It was there that he was identified as the one who had defiled holy traditions by healing a man. The bitter opposition of the people had the desired effect of attracting a sizeable multitude; among their number were those, howbeit few in number, who would hear with listening ears. Jesus was readily condemned for his violation of the Sabbath, yet we are left to wonder at the nature of his offense. He of himself had lifted no burden, he had administered no medicine, he had walked no more than the requisite number of steps the rabbis had decreed appropriate, he had done no work save that of the Spirit, he had done nothing save utter the healing words. No charges, according to their system of legalism, were brought against him, yet he had shown his disdain for that system in his direction to another to defy it. If there be sin in what had transpired, it rested with God, for it was his power that worked that day to perform the miracle of healing.

The matter of healing and the petty Sabbath observances were of little interest to Christ. It is not of such things that he chose to speak. The occasion could not pass save he used it to declare his own divine Sonship. Thus he responded to their charges, saying, "My Father worketh hitherto, and I work." (John 5:17.) The implication of the statement was lost on none. If God, who is his Father, chose to do works of righteousness on the Sabbath, can he as his Son choose to do less?

We need no other evidence as to how completely and perfectly Christ's testimony of his divine Sonship was understood than the subsequent efforts to kill him. Now he had added the charge of blasphemy to that of breaking the Sabbath. Again his testimony was distorted—his announcement that he was God's Son was perverted to be an announcement that he was equal with God. Christ said no such thing. He did say he was God's Son, that as God's Son he could do "nothing of himself, but what he seeth the Father do," and that he had been sent of the Father. He testified of the power that was in God and announced that to reject him was to reject the Father, and conversely to accept his word and believe in him was to believe in the Father and accept him. To those who did so, he promised eternal life, while those who rejected his testimony were assured condemnation. (John 5:19-24.)

Jesus Announces Himself as God
of the Living and the Dead

Having announced his divine Sonship and having made the acceptance or rejection of his claim the hinge upon which the door of salvation swings, Christ then responded to the question that must be the natural sequel to such an announcement. If, indeed, he was the Messiah, and if the acceptance of him was the central point of salvation, what becomes of the innumerable host who had died without a knowledge of him? 'My Father has "committed all judgment" to me,' he had declared. (John 5:22.) No plainer statement professing Messiahship could be given. If he was to render justice to all, and surely God could do no less, how were those who died without the knowledge of him to be judged? Such was the matter to which Christ then responded: "The hour is coming, and now is, when the dead shall hear the voice of the Son of God: and they that hear shall live. For as the Father hath life in himself; so hath he given to the Son to have life in himself; and hath given him authority to execute judgment also, because he is the Son of man. Marvel not at this: for the hour is coming, in the which all that are in the graves shall hear his voice, and shall come forth; they that have done good, unto the resurrection of life; and they that have done evil, unto the resurrection of damnation." (John 5:25-29.)

We could paraphrase Christ's words thus: In very fact you live in the age and generation in which this same gospel will be taught to those who are dead, that they might be judged according to men in the flesh. They too must accept or reject my claim to divine Sonship, and they too must do so at the peril of their eternal lives. Indeed, all must have the opportunity to hear. This I do because I have inherited from our Father that power of life which is in him. From my mortal mother, Mary, I inherited the gift of death. From God, who fathered this earthly tabernacle, I have life within myself. The power to break the bands of death is mine, and through me all will come forth in the resurrection—the good to everlasting life, the evil to everlasting damnation.[2]

Of John's statement that there are but two resurrections—that of the just and that of the unjust—Elder Bruce R. McConkie observed: "With the exception of the statement in James (Jas. 1:5) which led to the appearance of the Father and the Son to the Prophet, thus ushering in the dispensation of the fullness of times, this one verse has probably done more to open the door to the mysteries of salvation than any other single verse of scripture. It is the verse that paid off a thousand fold for all the struggle that ever went in to the preparation of the Inspired Version of the Bible, for it was meditation upon this verse that caused the Prophet to receive the vision of the degrees of glory."[3]

"While we were doing the work of translation, which the Lord had appointed unto us," Joseph Smith wrote, "[this verse] was given unto us as follows—speaking of the resurrection of the dead, concerning those who shall hear the voice of the Son of Man: and shall come forth; they who have done good, in the resurrection of the just; and they who have done evil, in the resurrection of the unjust. Now this caused us to marvel, for it was given unto us of the Spirit. And while we meditated upon these things, the Lord touched the eyes of our understandings and they were opened, and the glory of the Lord shone round about. And we beheld. . . . " (D&C 76:15-20.) Then follows the vision of the degrees of glory, one of the most marvelous visions ever penned by a prophet.

Jesus Obeys the Law of Witnesses

If there be justice in the heavens, the matter of accepting or rejecting Jesus as our Savior cannot be a matter of good fortune contrasted with another's misjudgment. There must be a divinely ordained system whereby all might know with perfect surety those truths upon which salvation rests, and so there is. The laws that govern heaven assure that all, be it in this life or the next, will be granted full and complete opportunity to hear the gospel message. As a birthright, all are bequeathed the light of Christ, and all may lay claim to the companionship of the Holy Ghost through purity and obedience. Further, we have been assured that all saving truths will have both manifestation and confirmation. The divine law states it thus: "In the mouth of two or three witnesses shall every word be established." (2 Cor. 13:1.) No testimony is to stand alone. There are no exceptions: the message of all who would claim themselves prophets must comply with this heaven-given standard. It is for this very reason that the Godhead consists of three separate and distinct personages—two Gods to bear witness of the third. Thus Christ explained: "I bear record of the Father, and the Father beareth record of me, and the Holy Ghost beareth record of the Father and me." (3 Ne. 11:32.)

It was absolutely essential that Christ comply with this principle in his mortal ministry. Had he failed to do so, none would be obligated to accept his claim to Messiahship. Knowing this, the Pharisees came to him, saying, "Thou bearest record of thyself; thy record is not true." (John 8:13.) Responding to their challenge, Jesus replied: "I am not alone, but I and the Father that sent me. It is also written in your law, that the testimony of two men is true. I am one that bear witness of myself, and the Father that sent me beareth witness of me." (John 8:16-18.)

In the text before us, Christ is recorded as saying, "If I bear witness of myself, my witness is not true." (John 5:31.) In his inspired translation, Joseph Smith rendered the verse, "I bear witness of myself, yet my witness is true." (JST, John 5:32.) In either case the sense is the same—his testimony cannot stand alone. In this instance Christ appealed to the witness of John the Baptist, who came as "a burning and shining light" to prepare the hearts of mortals to accept Jesus as the Christ. John came declaring the gospel of repentance, so that we might see with pure eyes; he came baptizing, so that the cataracts of sin might not impede our vision; he came announcing Jesus of Nazareth as the Lamb of God. (See John 5:32-35; 1:36.)

In addition, Christ cited *the works* he had done as evidence of his divine nature. (John 5:36.) Every miracle he performed, every word he preached, every prophecy he uttered, had one common element: to testify of him as the great Redeemer. To this he added the witness of his Father, who had rent the heavens—and would do so again—and who in audible voice proclaimed Jesus of Nazareth as his Son. (John 5:37-38.) Jesus then cited yet another evidence that he was what he professed to be—the testimony of the scriptures. To those who used the scriptures to war against him, he said, "Search the scriptures; for in them ye think ye have eternal life: and they are they which testify of me." (John 5:39.)

Oh, how foolish is mind of anyone to suppose that eternal life is to be found within a book rather than in the living witness of the Spirit. No people have professed a greater love for the scriptures than those who have used them as the pretext to reject the Lord's anointed, and as they rejected those who came in his name, so they rejected him. To those of his day, those who rejected him in the name of loyalty to the law of Moses, Christ said, "Do not think that I will accuse you to the Father: there is one that accuseth you, even Moses, in whom ye trust." (John 5:45.) Moses, who under divine direction established a law every jot and tittle of which was intended to testify of Christ and prepare a people to accept him, will, of all men, be most offended by that which has been done inappropriately in his name.

There is a marvelous constancy in the spirit of disbelief; to find it in one dispensation is to know it in others. In our day some claim allegiance to Peter, while rejecting his testimony that in the last days there would be a restoration of all things (see Acts 3:19-21); others pay homage to Paul, while ignoring his injunction that we must "work out [our] own salvation with fear and trembling" (Philip. 2:12). It is not without significance that in our day those who are the most vociferous in their defense of the Bible are also the most selective in what they choose to see within its covers. Like the Pharisees, their ancient counterparts, they read with blind eyes—one blinded by their traditions, the other with their excessive zeal. In the meridian of time, the scriptures were used to reject Christ and his servants. Their ancient craft has been bequeathed to modern successors, who in like manner use the Bible to sustain their position of spiritual supremacy and salvation while rejecting the living Christ and his servants who have been commissioned to proclaim the message of the restoration. The story of John 5 is as much the story of our day as it is the story of ancient days.

NOTES

1. Bruce R. McConkie, *The Mortal Messiah,* 4 vols. (Salt Lake City: Deseret Book, 1979-81), 1:207.

2. The Gospels, and that of John in particular, are full of such statements. We are left to wonder about the rather astonishing ignorance manifest in discussions and writings that question whether Christ ever announced himself as divine.

3. Bruce R. McConkie, *Doctrinal New Testament Commentary,* 3 vols. (Salt Lake City: Bookcraft, 1965-73), 1:195.

19

THE BREAD OF LIFE
(Matthew 14:13-36; Mark 6:30-56; Luke 9:10-17; John 6)

KENT P. JACKSON

The feeding of the five thousand was one of the most stunning of the miracles of Jesus, so impressive, in fact, that it is one of the rare events of which all four Gospel writers gave accounts.[1] That fact in itself attests to the magnificence of the occurrence and its importance in the minds of the early Saints. As has already been shown, it is characteristic of the Gospel of John to complement and supplement the events described in the synoptic Gospels.[2] The record of the feeding of the multitude is no exception. Of the Gospel writers, John alone completed the account by recording the fascinating discussion that followed soon after the miraculous feeding. That discussion, the discourse on the Bread of Life, is one of the most profound utterances of all time, and it stands as a witness to the divinity of him from whose lips it came.

The Feeding of the Five Thousand

During Jesus' great ministry in Galilee, it was not uncommon for him to preach to extremely large groups of intrested listeners. Among those who heard him were some who had already committed themselves to following him—the Twelve and other disciples—as well as a multitude of other individuals who were attracted to him because of what they had heard concerning his doctrine and his power to perform miracles. The miraculous feeding of five thousand and the events

---

Kent P. Jackson is associate professor of ancient scripture and Old Testament area coordinator at Brigham Young University.

288

that followed it demonstrate that witnessing a miracle does not necessarily lead to the kind of faith that brings salvation. Perhaps John's emphasis on the aftermath of the feeding was included to teach that very point.

On the occasion of the feeding of the multitude, which followed soon after Jesus received word of the death of John the Baptist (Matt. 14:12-13) and soon after the apostles returned from missions (Mark 6:30-31; Luke 9:10), Jesus went to an isolated location. When the people of Galilee heard of his whereabouts, they "ran afoot thither out of all cities, . . . and came together unto him." (Mark 6:33.) Although it appears that the Twelve, and perhaps Jesus also, were seeking rest from their labors and refuge from the crowds (see Matt. 14:13; Mark 6:31), when the people arrived the Lord welcomed[3] them, and he attended to their physical and spiritual needs. Matthew and Mark both wrote that he "was moved with compassion toward them" (Matt. 14:14; Mark 6:34), yet, interestingly, each recorded in the same verse a different response of Jesus to his feelings for the people. Matthew reported that Jesus "healed their sick," while Mark's account emphasizes another healing: he "was moved with compassion toward them, because they were as sheep not having a shepherd: and he began to teach them many things." Luke recorded that Jesus "spake unto them of the kingdom of God, and healed them that had need of healing."

When it became late and the apostles anticipated the hunger of the multitude, they suggested to the Master that he send the people away so they could find food. The Savior's response, found in all three of the synoptic Gospels, was: "Give ye them to eat." (Matt. 14:16; Mark 6:37; Luke 9:13.) John added another passage, which reveals the Lord's intent: "He saith unto Philip, Whence shall we buy bread, that these may eat? And this he said to prove him: for he himself knew what he would do." (John 6:5-6.) When a search produced five loaves of barley bread and two fish, Jesus took them, "and looking up to heaven, he blessed them, and brake, and gave to the disciples to set before the multitude. And they did eat, and were all filled." (Luke 9:16-17.) Not only did five thousand individuals eat their fill on five loaves of bread and two fish,[4] but the remainder that was not eaten filled twelve baskets, which certainly amounted to much more than the original quantity from which the miracle was generated!

In addition to showing his miraculous power over the elements,[5] Jesus also demonstrated an important gospel principle on this occasion. When he gave food to his apostles and then commanded them to give it to others, he was teaching the order of priesthood government. (See Matt. 14:19.) The Lord's pattern is to call and instruct individuals to whom he gives responsibility and through whom he then works for the benefit of all. So it is with priesthood, with temple ordinances, with church administration, and with parenthood. Jesus blessed and divided the food, but perhaps the miraculous proliferation of it took place while it was in the hands of the apostles. Their distributing of the food, blessed and prepared as it was by divine power, typified their service in the church in other ways, as the Master gave into the hands of these mortals a portion of his mission and a portion of his authority, and sanctified their labors of righteousness.

Walking on Water

Following the feeding of the five thousand, Jesus dismissed first the Twelve, who set off across the Sea of Galilee in a boat, and then the multitude, who presumably went back to their homes. He then went by himself to a mountain to pray. In the middle of the night the disciples were still out on the lake, unable to reach the shore because of a storm. While they were "toiling in rowing; for the wind was contrary unto them" (Mark 6:48), Jesus walked out to meet them. The disciples were frightened, supposing that they saw a ghost. Only Matthew recorded that when Jesus identified himself, Peter desired to walk on the water to meet him. In response to Peter's request, Jesus said simply: "Come."

Matthew continues the narration: "And when Peter was come down out of the ship, he walked on the water, to go to Jesus. But when he saw the wind boisterous, he was afraid; and beginning to sink, he cried, saying, Lord, save me. And immediately Jesus stretched forth his hand, and caught him, and said unto him, O thou of little faith, wherefore didst thou doubt?" (Matt. 14:29-31.) The record adds that as soon as Jesus entered the boat, the storm stopped. (Matt. 14:32; Mark 6:51.) The disciples "were sore amazed in themselves beyond measure, and wondered. For they considered not the miracle of the loaves: for their heart was hardened." (Mark 6:51-52.) Then they testified: "Of a truth thou art the Son of God." (Matt. 14:33.)

The account of the walking on the water is remarkable for several reasons: It demonstrates again the power of the Lord over the elements and the forces of nature, not only in his walking on water, but in his stilling of the storm as well.[6] More remarkably, perhaps, it attests to the powerful faith of Peter, to whom would soon be entrusted the keys of the kingdom and the leadership of the Lord's work on earth. This was no ordinary man who sought to have enough faith to defy the power of gravity. Aside from the case of the Lord himself, scripture records no other example of a person walking on water. Although Peter's faith did not allow him to walk as far as he might have desired, those who would make light of it should duplicate his accomplishment before they chide him. Only Jesus—who constantly challenges us to progress beyond the artificial limits of our faith—could say, "O thou of little faith, wherefore didst thou doubt?"

After the boat carrying Jesus and his disciples landed on the shore of the Sea of Galilee, crowds soon gathered, bringing with them those who were in need of Jesus' healing powers. (Matt. 14:34-36; Mark 6:53-55.)

"I Am the Bread of Life"

Only the Gospel of John records Jesus' teaching of the next day, preserving for us his Bread of Life discussion, which he gave while in the synagogue at Capernaum. (See John 6:12-59.) True to the style of his teaching in John, the Bread of Life discourse was actually much more of a conversation than a sermon, with Jesus teaching aspects of the gospel to dumbfounded and baffled listeners. Also typical of his teaching method, as recorded by John, were his powerful and provocative assertions about who he was and what the Father had sent him to accomplish. Further, his use of vivid, descriptive metaphor,[7] especially with reference to himself and his mission, is typical of his teaching style in John.[8] Metaphor is used in the Bread of Life discussion in a powerful manner that is never excelled elsewhere in Jesus' teachings.

When the feeding of the five thousand took place, some witnesses testified that Jesus was the great prophet of whom Moses had foretold. (See Deut. 18:15, 18-19; John 6:14.) He had left after the miraculous meal because he "perceived that they would come and take him by force, to make him a king." (John 6:15.) Now, on the following day, people still sought him. Jesus was aware of their interest in him: "Ye seek me, not because ye desire to keep my sayings, neither because ye saw the miracles, but because ye did eat of the loaves and were filled." (JST, John 6:26.) They sought him not out of desire to be his disciples, nor out of wonderment because of his divine power, but because he had filled their stomachs! He took this as an opportunity to teach them about spiritual food: "Do not labor for the food[9] which perishes, but for the food which endures to eternal life, which the Son of man will give to you." (RSV, John 6:27.)

When Jesus implied that he was the one sent by the Father in whom his listeners should believe, they asked, "What sign shewest thou then, that we may see, and believe thee? what dost thou work?" (John 6:30.) That they would ask such a question the day after the miraculous feeding of thousands suggests that they still had much to learn. Yet perhaps the multiplying of earthly food was not a sufficient demonstration of divine power. "Our fathers did eat manna in the desert," they said, as though to challenge Jesus with a miracle of greater magnitude than his. (John 6:31.) He accepted the challenge and taught them of the greatest miracle of all history—himself: "My Father giveth you the true bread from heaven. For the bread of God is he which cometh down from heaven, and giveth life unto the world." (John 6:32-33.)

Jesus' brief statement must have stirred feelings in the hearts of his listeners. Although they clearly did not understand the implications of what he said, their longing was evident in their words: "Lord, evermore give us this bread." (John 6:34.) Then the Lord taught them: "I am the bread of life: he that cometh to me shall never hunger; and he that believeth on me shall never thirst. . . .

"I am that bread of life. Your fathers did eat manna in the wilderness, and are dead. This is the bread which cometh down from heaven, that a man may eat thereof, and not die.

"I am the living bread which came down from heaven: if any man eat of this bread, he shall live for ever: and the bread that I will give is my flesh, which I will give for the life of the world. . . .

"This is that bread which came down from heaven: not as your fathers did eat manna, and are dead: he that eateth of this bread shall live for ever." (John 6:35, 48-51, 58.)

The bread metaphor was most appropriate on this occasion because the topic of food had been raised in conjunction with the events of the previous day. Jesus used the metaphor brilliantly to teach the people who he was and what a person's relationship to him must be in order to obtain eternal life. While it is clear that many of his ancient listeners either missed the point or refused to open their minds to his message (see John 6:41, 52, 60, 66), Latter-day Saints have no excuse to not understand and live according to his words.

Hunger and thirst (John 6:35): Jesus was not speaking here of physical hunger and thirst, but of that which is spiritual. Since physical hunger and thirst are instincts with which every mortal is familiar, they serve as ideal metaphors to teach about hunger and thirst after higher things. Yet Jesus was not speaking simply of satisfying a temporary spiritual need. He was speaking of eternal life and everlasting satisfaction in the kingdom of heaven.

Life (John 6:48, 51, 53-54, 58): Jesus taught about eternal life in the presence of the Father, which means exaltation, a glorious eternal reward in the celestial kingdom of God, with family and loved ones. It means obtaining an inheritance of all that the Father has.

Death (John 6:50): Physical death is a reality that all shall face, even those who are worthy to live in the presence of God. Jesus spoke here about *spiritual* death, which is alienation from the Father, banishment from his presence, and death as to things of righteousness. Those who partake to the fullest of Christ's atoning grace will not taste of that death but will enjoy eternal life. John wrote elsewhere, "He that overcometh shall not be hurt of the second death." (Rev. 2:11.)

Bread of Life (John 6:35, 48-51, 53-54, 58): Jesus Christ is the Bread of Life. Eternal life and all other good things in the universe, present and future, are made possible to mankind through him. In mortal life food sustains existence—but only temporarily. Even though they were fed divinely provided manna, the forefathers of

Jesus' hearers had suffered physical death. Yet the bread that Jesus offered would provide life everlasting. Jesus told the Jews, "Except ye eat the flesh of the Son of man, and drink his blood, ye have no life in you. Whoso eateth my flesh, and drinketh my blood, hath eternal life." (John 6:53-54.)

Jesus invited not only those who heard him, but all others as well, to partake of his atonement. Through the fatal piercing of his flesh and shedding of his blood, he overcame death and made possible eternal life. The invitation to partake of his flesh and blood is an invitation to take part in the atonement that he worked out in our behalf. His redeeming grace, the true power by which we can be saved, is made available to all who desire to take part in it and demonstrate this by their devotion to his gospel plan. The ordinance of the sacrament, in which we consume the symbolic emblems of his redemptive act, signifies profoundly our consuming of his atoning grace and of his plan that makes it effective in our lives.

Many of Jesus' listeners found his words too provocative or too difficult to comprehend. They said, "This is an hard saying; who can hear it?" "Doth this offend you?" he responded. "The words that I speak unto you, they are spirit, and they are life." (John 6:60-61, 63.) Clearly his words were to be understood on a higher, more spiritual, plane than many of his hearers could comprehend. And truly they were words of everlasting life.

John recorded the results of the Savior's discussion with those who heard him and who had followed him in search of physical and spiritual nourishment: "From that time many of his disciples went back, and walked no more with him." Then Jesus asked the Twelve, "Will ye also go away?" (John 6:66-67.)

The challenge of discipleship was great, and many chose not to continue with it. It should not be surprising that those who left Jesus then were not offended by his miracles, his popularity, his healings, or his feeding of those who were hungry. Rather, they were offended by his doctrine. Even today, it is the doctrine that sets the Church apart. Neither the programs nor the life-styles of the members make the Church true or provide the measuring rod by which it and those who are in it will be judged. Rather, the truth of the doctrine and the authority to administer that doctrine make it indeed the Church of Jesus

Christ. Latter-day Saints who live the gospel and understand the role that Jesus Christ plays in their lives can respond to his question and can, with Peter, bear testimony: "Lord, to whom shall we go? thou hast the words of eternal life. And we believe and are sure that thou art that Christ, the Son of the living God." (John 6:68-69.)

NOTES

1. The only other events described in all four Gospels are the following: the triumphal entry (Matt. 21:1-11; Mark 11:1-11; Luke 19:29-44; John 12:12-19); the Last Supper and parts of the subsequent discourse (Matt. 26:20-35; Mark 14:17-31; Luke 22:14-34; John 13); the events at Gethsemane (Matt. 26:36-56; Mark 14:32-52; Luke 22:39-53; John 18:1-12); the trials of Jesus (Matt. 26:57-27:31; Mark 14:53-15:20; Luke 22:54-23:25; John 18:12-19:16); the crucifixion and burial (Matt. 27:32-66; Mark 15:21-47; Luke 23:26-56; John 19:16-42); and the resurrection morning (Matt. 28:1-10; Mark 16:1-11; Luke 23:56-24:12; John 20:1-18).

2. See C. Wilfred Griggs, "The Testimony of John," chapter 6 in this volume.

3. The Greek word, translated *received* in Luke 9:11, means *welcomed.*

4. Mark 6:44, Luke 9:14, and John 6:10 give the total number of participants at "five thousand men." Matthew 14:21 gives the number as "five thousand men, beside women and children."

5. For other examples, see Rex C. Reeve, Jr., "The Miracles of Jesus," chapter 13 of this volume.

6. See Reeve, "The Miracles of Jesus."

7. Metaphor is a literary device in which one word, or a series of words, is used to represent something else, to suggest a likeness between the two. A typical example would be, "Jesus is the Good Shepherd," referring to Jesus' compassionate leadership of those who follow him.

8. See Griggs, "The Testimony of John." For an introduction to the use of metaphor in the teachings of Jesus, see Richard D. Draper, "The Parables of Jesus," chapter 17 in this volume.

9. The word translated in the King James Version as *meat* means *food.*

20

TRADITION, TESTIMONY, TRANSFIGURATION, AND KEYS
(Matthew 15-17; Mark 7-9; Luke 9)

ROBERT J. MATTHEWS

The period of which we write is the autumn, about six months previous to the Crucifixion. The Twelve had been called and ordained for more than a year and had recently returned from their missions throughout the cities and villages of Galilee. John the Baptist, after a vigorous and highly successful ministry of nearly a year, had languished in the dreadful dungeon at Herod's palace for more than another year and then had recently suffered a martyr's death when he was beheaded by Herod's executioner.

Jesus was in northern Galilee and had just healed many people of their sicknesses. He was immensely popular with the multitudes, but there was rising opposition from the Jewish rulers. A delegation of scribes and Pharisees came from Jerusalem. Finding Jesus with his disciples, the delegation registered a complaint about the disciples' behavior—for they had eaten without first washing their hands.

The Tradition and the Law

Before investigating the Pharisees' complaint, it will be helpful to discuss some of the reasons why there was frequently a difference in the views of the Savior and the Jewish rulers.

The Jews' religion at the time of Jesus included many traditions that influenced their thinking and behavior. They judged illness and calamity to be the immediate result and also evidence of sin (John 9:2,

Robert J. Matthews is professor of ancient scripture and dean of Religious Education at Brigham Young University.

34; Luke 13:1-5), and they practiced extravagant ceremonial cleansings and washings. Eating habits and Sabbath day observances were very rigid. They called their performances the law of Moses, but they had gone far beyond the actual provisions of the law. Jesus did not subscribe to their extreme position (although he kept every valid commandment of the law) and spoke harshly against their traditions, which had led them away from the commandments of God.

The Lord had given Moses the Melchizedek Priesthood and the principles and ordinances of the gospel of Jesus Christ. Moses sought diligently to confer these on the children of Israel, but they were unable, or at least unwilling, to live by the standard of the high priesthood and the gospel, so the Lord gave them a lesser law, governed by a lesser priesthood. This lower law, which was known as the law of Moses, functioned under the Aaronic order of priesthood. It contained a law of carnal commandments, putting forth many "performances and ordinances" that the people were "to observe strictly from day to day, to keep them in remembrance of God and their duty towards him." However, because of the hardness of their hearts, "they did not all understand the law" (D&C 84:23-27; Mosiah 13:29-32) and did not realize it was intended to lead them to Christ.

The law of Moses was a good law and was adapted to the capacities of people who were not living as high a standard as required in the gospel. The gospel is the law of Christ.

Through the centuries after Moses, well-meaning but uninspired Jewish religious philosophers—reacting to the inroads made upon the law by foreign cultures and especially the Babylonian captivity—put "a hedge around the law" (as they called it). In so doing they invented many burdens and excessive legal requirements as safeguards to preserve the law. These inventions were the "traditions of the elders," or the "oral law."

By the time of Jesus, the spirit of the law had been smothered in interpretations and definitions. Intricate definitions were given concerning Sabbath day activities, ceremonial cleansing and purification, eating habits, washing of pots and pans, washing of hands, tying of knots, Sabbath-day travel, and so forth. The scribes felt obliged and pleased to give instructions on many things.

When Jesus and his disciples refused to heed the many traditions developed by the scribes and rabbis, they came under criticism of the rulers. Jesus obeyed every provision of the law of Moses; in fact, it was he who gave the law (3 Ne. 15:5), but he was not under any obligation to obey the traditions that the Jews themselves had added. His controversies with the Jews were often occasioned by the difference in the law as it was first given and the profuse interpretations of the law by the scribes and rabbis. He informed them that they were neglecting "the weightier matters of the law" while observing the lesser (Matt. 23:23), and that their traditions were preventing them from keeping the commandments of God.

In Joseph Smith's translation of Mark 7 we find the following (italics show variants from the King James Version):

> When they [scribes and Pharisees from Jerusalem] saw some of his disciples eat bread with defiled (that is to say with unwashen) hands, they found fault.
>
> For the Pharisees, and all the Jews, except they wash *hands* oft, eat not; holding the tradition of the elders.
>
> And when they come from the market, except they wash *their bodies,* they eat not.
>
> And many other things there be, which they have received to hold, as the washing of cups, and pots, brazen vessels, and of tables.
>
> *And* the Pharisees and scribes asked him, Why walk not thy disciples according to the *traditions* of the elders, but eat bread with unwashen hands? (JST, Mark 7:2-6.)

Jesus called the complainers hypocrites, citing the words of Isaiah as evidence: "This people honoureth me with their lips, but their heart is far from me. Howbeit, in vain do they worship me, teaching *the* doctrines *and* commandments of men." (JST, Mark 7:7; cf. Isa. 29:13.)

He then applied Isaiah's words to those who were finding fault:

> For laying aside the commandment of God, ye hold the tradition of men; the washing of pots and of cups: and many other such like things ye do.
>
> And he said unto them, *yea, altogether* ye reject the commandment of God, that ye may keep your own tradition.
>
> *Full well is it written of you, by the prophets whom ye have rejected.*

*They testified these things of a truth, and their blood shall
be upon you.* (JST, Mark 7:8-11.)

However, these people had developed another tradition more
spiritually destructive than the washing of pots and the excessive
washing of hands. This was the willful neglect of parents under the
guise of religious duty and holy consecration. Jesus continued:

Ye have kept not the ordinances of God; for Moses said,
Honor thy father and thy mother; and whoso curseth father or
mother, let him die the death *of the transgressor, as it is written in your law; but ye keep not the law.*

Ye say, if a man shall say to his father or mother, *Corban,*
that is to say, a gift, by whatsoever thou mightest be profited by
me, he *is of age.* And ye suffer him no more to do aught for his
father or his mother; making the word of God of none effect
through your tradition, which ye have delivered; and many
such like things do ye. (JST, Mark 7:12-13.)

The practice referred to as "corban" is that a son, if he were of independent age, could pledge his property to God, and thus it would
not be available to be used to support needy parents, although the son
could continue to use it for himself as long as he lived. Such a vow
(which was permitted by the religious leaders) became more binding
than the command of God, and hence the law of God was made "of
none effect" by the tradition.

Having thus shown the delegation that they themselves were
guilty of gross negligence and corruption far greater than eating with
unwashed hands, Jesus then proceeded to explain that defilement that
comes from within the heart is worse than defilement from the soil on
one's outer body:

And when he had called all the people, he said unto them,
Hearken unto me every one, and understand;

There is nothing from without, that entering into a man,
can defile him, *which is food;* but the things which come out of
him; those are they that defile the man, *that proceedeth forth
out of the heart.*

If any man have ears to hear, let him hear.

And when he was entered into the house from among the

people, his disciples [Matt. 15:15 says it was Peter] asked him concerning the parable.

And he said unto them, Are ye without understanding also? Do ye not perceive, that whatsoever thing from without entereth into the man, cannot defile him; because it entereth not into his heart, but into the belly, and goeth out into the draught, purging all meats?

And he said, That which cometh out of a man, defileth the man.

For from within, out of the hearts of men, proceed evil thoughts, adulteries, fornications, murders, thefts, covetousness, wickedness, deceit, lasciviousness, an evil eye, blasphemy, pride, foolishness;

All these evil things come from within, and defile the man. (JST, Mark 7:14-21.)

Matthew 15 gives a close parallel to Mark's account but adds an interesting exchange between Jesus and his disciples about the plain talk of Jesus to the delegation:

Then came his disciples, and said unto him, Knowest thou that the Pharisees were offended, after they heard this saying?

But he answered and said, Every plant, which my heavenly Father hath not planted, shall be rooted up.

Let them alone: they be blind leaders of the blind. And if the blind lead the blind, both shall fall into the ditch. (Matt. 15:12-14.)

Seeking Signs Instead of Faith

A short time later, Jesus again emphasized to his disciples his dislike and disapproval of the doctrine of the Pharisees and the Sadducees and their desire to seek a sign from heaven:

The Pharisees also with the Sadducees came, and tempting desired him that he would shew them a sign from heaven.

He answered and said unto them, . . .

A wicked and adulterous generation seeketh after a sign; and there shall no sign be given unto it, but the sign of the prophet Jonas. And he left them, and departed. (Matt. 16:1-2, 4.)

Mark added the informative comment that when Jesus was approached by these critics, "He sighed deeply in his spirit, and saith, Why doth this generation seek after a sign?" (Mark 8:12.)

Jesus then entered a ship with the disciples and crossed the Sea of Galilee. He told them to "beware of the leaven of the Pharisees and of the Sadducees." (Matt. 16:6. Mark 8:15 adds "beware . . . of the leaven of Herod.") The Savior's reference to leaven puzzled them:

> And they reasoned among themselves, saying, It is because we have taken no bread.
>
> Which when Jesus perceived, he said unto them, O ye of little faith, why reason ye among yourselves, because ye have brought no bread? . . .
>
> How is it that ye do not understand that I spake it not to you concerning bread, that ye should beware of the leaven of the Pharisees and of the Sadducees?
>
> Then understood they how that he bade them not beware of the leaven of bread, but of the doctrine of the Pharisees and of the Sadducees. (Matt. 16:7-8, 11-12.)

Jesus was wearied with even the disciples' lack of understanding and said, "Perceive ye not yet, neither understand? have ye your heart yet hardened? . . . How is it that ye do not understand?" (Mark 8:17, 21.)

The particularly unholy character of the Pharisees is exposed in another passage, which contains a scathing denunciation of the Pharisees because of their marital infidelity, showing that they were in fact an adulterous generation. The Joseph Smith Translation alone offers these words:

> [Then said Jesus unto the Pharisees,] Why teach ye the law, and deny that which is written; and condemn him whom the Father hath sent to fulfil the law, that ye might all be redeemed?
>
> O fools! for you have said in your hearts, There is no God. And you pervert the right way; and the kingdom of heaven suffereth violence of you; and you persecute the meek; and in your violence you seek to destroy the kingdom; and ye take the children of the kingdom by force. Woe unto you, ye adulterers!
>
> And they reviled him again, being angry for the saying, that they were adulterers. (JST, Luke 16:20-22.)

It is not difficult to see that the Savior had very strong feelings against the false doctrine and the life-style of the Pharisees and other Jewish leaders and that he was also concerned when even the believers were sometimes slow to sense the important difference between true doctrine and false doctrine. The differences between the Savior's doctrine and the Jewish leaders' traditions and practices were deep-rooted and fundamental. Only by repentance and reformation could those leaders come into harmony with their Lord.

Mark tells of Jesus entering "into an house, and would have no man know it: but he could not be hid." (Mark 7:24.) However, a woman with an ailing daughter found him. The Joseph Smith Translation adds an important dimension totally missing in other Bibles, which shows that Jesus, in spite of his apparent physical weariness, allowed himself to be approached, listening and responding favorably to the woman's plea. As rendered in the Joseph Smith Translation account of Mark 7:22-23, we can see the true situation: Jesus "entered into a house, and would that no man *should come unto him. But he could not deny them; for he had compassion upon all men.*" (See also Mark 6:34.)

We see in this passage an instance of the dual nature of the Savior: a weary body, craving rest, as contrasted to the compassionate love of one who came to save and help mankind. And compassion prevailed. The Joseph Smith Translation thus presents an important aspect of his divine nature that is lost in this passage in other translations.

The Testimony of Christ

Shortly thereafter, Jesus with the Twelve came into the region of Caesarea Philippi, north of the Sea of Galilee near the source of the Jordan River. He questioned them as to who others said he was. They replied that some thought he was John the Baptist (risen from the dead), some that he was Elijah, or Jeremiah, or one of the prophets of olden times.

Jesus then asked the Twelve, "But whom say ye that I am?" He was teaching by contrast. He wanted no mistake or blurred vision in the thinking of the chosen Twelve as to who he really was. To be thought of and even mistaken for a prophet would ordinarily be an honor, and

Jesus *was* a prophet, but he was much more than that. *Ye* is a plural designation, and he was asking the question of all the Twelve (their calling is to be special witnesses of him): But whom say *ye?* Peter, as the chief and senior member of the quorum, spoke for his fellows, with great assurance, in the plainest of terms: "Thou art the Christ, the Son of the living God." (Matt. 16:15-16.)

Peter's utterance was borne of knowledge, not of opinion or guesswork. Jesus said that Peter's testimony was not revealed by flesh and blood (mortality) but that it was revealed from the Father himself. This revealed knowledge—which is called *testimony*—is the basis of all saving knowledge and is the rock foundation upon which the gospel of Jesus Christ is promulgated among mortals.

Revelation is the only true source of testimony about Jesus Christ, and it comes through the Holy Ghost. As recorded in the King James Version, Paul wrote to the Corinthians that "no man can say Jesus is the Lord, but by the Holy Ghost." (1 Cor. 12:3.) The Prophet Joseph Smith explained that the true meaning of this concept is that "no man can *know* that Jesus is the Lord, but by the Holy Ghost."[1] A testimony of Jesus Christ, borne of the Holy Spirit, is the greatest knowledge a mortal can obtain and is the beginning of true wisdom. No one can be saved in ignorance of that testimony. No man was ever a true prophet who did not possess that knowledge (Rev. 19:10; Jacob 7:11; Hel. 8:13-20), and no revelation of the saving principles was ever given nor will be given that does not make known the role of Jesus Christ (JST, John 1:19; JST, 1 Jn. 4:12). No one can ever be saved by any other name, as is repeatedly affirmed in scripture. (2 Ne. 25:20; Mosiah 3:17; Hel. 5:9; Acts 4:12; D&C 18:23; Moses 6:52.)

It is possible for the natural senses to be deceived, but a testimony of Christ through the Holy Ghost is pure knowledge without deception. It exceeds in value and clarity anything that could be gained by the eyes or the ears or by physical touch, because it is God's Spirit speaking to man's spirit. Since the knowledge of Christ, as revealed through the Holy Ghost, is the greatest of all truths, the sin against that knowledge is the greatest of all sins. Revelation through the Holy Ghost has always been the way of salvation and always will be.

There is a difference between the *power* and the *gift* of the Holy Ghost.[2] The testimony of Peter was given to him by the power of the

Holy Ghost. This power must always be operative whenever the gospel is taught. Both the teacher and the hearer must be influenced by it. (See 2 Ne. 33:1.) This power bears convincing witness to the hearts of honest men and women. If they hearken to that testimony, they will then be baptized and receive the greater *gift* of the Holy Ghost by the laying on of hands of those who have authority to confer it. The *power* brings divine knowledge. The *gift* makes it possible for one to become sanctified and to be baptized with fire—totally cleansed. Some have thought that the Holy Ghost in any form was not operative in the days of Jesus' mortal ministry, or before the day of Pentecost, but this is a mistaken notion based on a lack of understanding of John 7:39, which specifies that "the Holy Ghost was not yet given," and John 16:7, which states that unless Jesus goes away, the Holy Ghost (Comforter) cannot come. However, the Holy Ghost *was* active both during Jesus' time and before, as is seen in various passages. (See Luke 1:41, 67; 4:1; 2 Pet. 1:21; 1 Ne. 10:17; D&C 20:26-27.) The truth of the matter is that no one could be converted by the preaching of John, or of Jesus, or of the Twelve, if the power of the Holy Ghost had not borne witness to the hearers. It was the *gift* of the Holy Ghost that was not operative until the day of Pentecost in Acts 2, and to which John 7:39 also refers.

At this time, Peter was promised the keys of the kingdom, with which he could bind or loose on earth and it would be valid in heaven. (Matt. 16:19.) More will be said later of the function of these keys. Jesus then charged the Twelve that they should tell no man that he was the Christ.

The directive to refrain from identifying Jesus as the Christ was a temporary restraining order, probably given for at least two reasons. One, a straightforward proclamation at that time would probably have angered the Jews and brought increased persecution upon Jesus and the Twelve. The time was near but not yet for his death. Second, the Twelve apparently were not yet prepared for the opposition that would arise, so it was expedient that they be restrained for a few more months from proclaiming who Jesus really was. This was a local restraint, for their time and place and for those persons only. By contrast, *our* responsibility is to declare openly, with meekness but with clarity, that Jesus Christ is the Son of the living God, that he alone is the Savior of the world, and that he has established his church—a church that bears his name—on this earth and in our generation through the Prophet Joseph Smith.

Transfiguration and Keys

According to the biblical account, about one week after Peter's great declaration and the Savior's promise that the keys of the kingdom would be given, Jesus took Peter, James, and John on a high mountain and there he was transfigured before them. Matthew's account says that Jesus' clothing became "white as the light" and "his face did shine as the sun." (Matt. 17:2.) Mark wrote that the clothing "became shining, exceeding white as snow." (Mark 9:3.) Luke said the clothing "was white and glistering." (Luke 9:29.) *Glistering* is not only bright but also means shiny and even sparkling. Moses and Elijah (KJV, "Elias") appeared and spoke to Jesus about his forthcoming death and atonement, which he would accomplish in Jerusalem. The Father spoke out of a cloud, testifying to the three apostles that Jesus is the Son of God. All these things are recorded in Matthew 17, Mark 9, and Luke 9, and Peter made reference to the event in 2 Peter 1:16-18. Even with these details, it is evident that the biblical record is not complete regarding what really took place on the mount.

The Prophet Joseph Smith explained that priesthood keys were given on the mount: "The Savior, Moses, and Elias, gave the keys of the priesthood to Peter, James and John, on the mount, when they were transfigured before him."[3] The bestowal of these keys is possibly the most important thing that transpired on the mount. The promise of the keys, given a week earlier, was now fulfilled. The three apostles, with Peter at the head, now held the keys of the holy priesthood, the same keys that Moses and Elijah held, keys that had the power to bind and to loose both on earth and in heaven.

The Twelve had been given the Melchizedek Priesthood a year earlier, when they were ordained apostles and sent on missions (Matt. 10), but the keys were not at that time transferred to them for the fullness of the blessings and the organization of the church upon the earth. The keys are the directing power in the priesthood. Without them, a person might hold the priesthood, but he could not use it in performing ordinances or directing the affairs of the church. So far as the establishment of the kingdom is concerned, the bestowal of keys upon the Twelve appears to be the single most important event in the ministry of the Savior between his baptism and the Garden of Gethsemane.

There are numerous similarities between the establishment of the church with the accompanying restoration of the priesthood keys and powers in our own time and that which is recorded in the New Testament. Since we have more precise information about the present dispensation, it can serve as a guide toward understanding the development and sequence of events in the meridian of time. Please note the following parallels:

Meridian of Time	Fullness of Times
Jesus himself held the Melchizedek Priesthood (Heb. 6:20)	Melchizedek Priesthood restored [May or June 1829]
Twelve Apostles called, ordained, and sent on missions. The Seventy also called (Luke 6:13-16 and 10:1-20; Matt. 10) [A.D. 31]	Twelve Apostles and the Seventy called and ordained (D&C 107) [1835]
Keys of the priesthood given to Peter, James, and John (Mount of Transfiguration) by Moses and Elijah (Matt. 17:1-9; Mark 9:2-9; Luke 9:28-36) [A.D. 32]	Keys of priesthood given to Joseph Smith and Oliver Cowdery by Moses, Elijah, and others in the Kirtland Temple (D&C 110) [1836]

The similarity of the events on the Mount of Transfiguration with those of the Kirtland Temple seems to certify that the main accomplishment of the visitation of the holy beings on the mount was the bestowal of priesthood keys, in order to establish the dispensation of the meridian of time on a solid and complete foundation, with power to preach the gospel, to seal up the faithful to eternal life, and to communicate all of the gifts, powers, and graces of the gospel of Jesus Christ. This important and significant event is all but lost in the biblical account. Without latter-day revelation, we would know nothing about the significance of this event and why the occurrences on the Mount of Transfiguration were so necessary.

The Prophet Joseph Smith explained the postmortal mission of

Elijah in these words: "Elijah was the last Prophet that held the keys of the Priesthood, and who will, before the last dispensation, restore the authority and deliver the keys of the Priesthood, in order that all the ordinances may be attended to in righteousness. . . . Why send Elijah? Because he holds the keys of the authority to administer in all the ordinances of the Priesthood; and without the authority is given, the ordinances could not be administered in righteousness."[4]

Elijah, as a mortal, had lived approximately 800 B.C. in and around the country of Samaria and was a prophet to the northern kingdom of Israel in the days of King Ahab and Jezebel. The account of his translation is given in 2 Kings 2:9-12.

Although it is recorded in Deuteronomy that Moses died and supposedly was buried by the hand of the Lord (Deut. 34:1-8), it is certain that he did not die but was translated. If this were not so, he could not have appeared on the Mount of Transfiguration to lay on hands and bestow keys of the holy priesthood. Since this event took place before the resurrection of Jesus (or of anyone else), and since Moses had lived as a mortal thirteen or fourteen centuries earlier, it follows that Moses was a translated being, even as Elijah. Perhaps this is why "no man knoweth of his sepulchre" and why it was assumed that he was "buried by the hand of the Lord" in Moab. (Alma 45:19.)

There is no doubt that Jesus could have given the keys of the priesthood himself to Peter, James, and John. However, there is an added message with Moses and Elijah being present. The lesson would be unmistakable that Jesus is the Savior of men in every age of the world when the three mortal brethren saw the earlier prophets ministering to him and sharing with him in the activities. Furthermore, for Peter, James, and John to see these prophets in their glorified condition, hear their voices, and feel their hands on their heads would convey clear and lasting impressions.

In addition to the foregoing events, it is learned from latter-day revelation that Peter, James, and John, while on the Mount, saw a vision of the earth as it will appear in its glorified state: "He that endureth in faith and doeth my will, the same shall overcome, and shall receive an inheritance upon the earth when the day of transfiguration shall come; when the earth shall be transfigured, even according to the pattern which was shown unto mine apostles upon the mount; of which account the fulness ye have not yet received." (D&C 63:20-21.) The same subject is also referred to by the Prophet Joseph: "They saw the glory of the Lord when he showed the transfiguration of the earth on the mount."[5] We are persuaded, therefore, that the happenings on the Mount of Transfiguration are among the most important in the New Testament.

The precise mount of the Transfiguration is not specified in the scriptures, but it is evident that it was in Galilee, probably not far from Caesarea Philipi. (Matt. 16:13; 17:1.) The probable location is either Mount Hermon or Mount Tabor.

The Joseph Smith Translation of Mark 9:1-4 suggests that John the Baptist was also present on the Mount of Transfiguration. John would be a spirit only, since he had been slain some months before and the resurrection had not yet taken place. Just what his mission would be at this event is not clear, but perhaps there were many holy and angelic beings present for a number of reasons. Elder Bruce R. McConkie expressed his understanding of the event as follows: "For some reason that remains unknown because of the partial record of the proceedings—John played some other part in the glorious manifestation—perhaps he was there, as the last legal administrator under the Old Covenant, to symbolize that the law was fulfilled."[6]

The Role of Two Eliases

As Jesus and the three disciples descended the mountain, they asked him why the scribes had taught "that Elias must first come." (Matt. 17:10.) The emphasis in the question has to be on the word *first*—that is, they were asking "Why is it that you, the Messiah, have been with us for thirty-two years, and now Elias has finally appeared on this mount, whereas the teaching of the scribes has been that Elias would come first or before the Messiah?"

The King James account of Jesus' reply seems to contain only fragments of the conversation, and as a result identifies John the Baptist as the one to restore all things. This account misses the point that there are two Eliases, each having different missions. The matter is clarified in the Joseph Smith Translation, which clearly speaks of one Elias to prepare the way and another to restore all things: *"I say unto you,*

Who is Elias? Behold, this is Elias, whom I send to prepare the way before me. Then the disciples understood that he spoke unto them of John the Baptist, *and also of another who should come and restore all things, as it is written by the prophets."* (JST, Matt. 17:13-14.)

This clarification of the two Eliases and their separate missions harmonizes perfectly with the Joseph Smith Translation rendition of Matthew 11:15, which identifies John as an Elias to "prepare all things," and also with John 1:21-28 in the Joseph Smith Translation, wherein John distinctly affirms that he (John) had a preliminary work and came before the Messiah, but that Jesus himself is the Elias to restore all things.

In the dispensation of the meridian of time, John prepared the way with the Aaronic Priesthood, and Jesus subsequently restored all things through the Melchizedek Priesthood. As a type of parallel, in the fullness of times, John again prepared the way with the Aaronic Priesthood, and the Prophet Joseph Smith is the prophet to whom the Lord granted the privilege of restoring all things through the Melchizedek Priesthood. Joseph Smith is thus the Elias to restore all things in the last days.

It is evident that the scribes had access to a prophecy or prophecies by which they knew more about Elias than our present Bibles contain, except the Joseph Smith Translation.

A Priesthood Endowment

The Lord placed the three disciples under a strict requirement to tell no one about the events on the mount until after the resurrection of the Savior from the dead. Since the keys of the priesthood are inseparably connected with the holy endowment of the temple, it could well be that Peter, James, and John received their endowments on the mount. This could account for the imposed silence.

On this matter, Elder Bruce R. McConkie wrote: "It appears that Peter, James and John received their own endowments while on the mountain. . . . Peter says that while there, they 'received from God the Father honour and glory,' seemingly bearing out this conclusion. It also appears that it was while on the mount that they received the more sure word of prophecy, it then being revealed to them that they were sealed up unto eternal life (2 Peter 1:16-19; D&C 131:5)."[7] President Joseph Fielding Smith explained: "These keys were given to Peter, James, and John on the mount when they received this power from Elias and Moses. . . . Christ told these three men, who I believe received their endowments on the mount, that they were not to mention this vision and what had taken place until after he was resurrected."[8]

Summary

The Lord has often appeared to his servants on a high mountain, away from the multitude and ways of the world. In the absence of a dedicated, unpolluted temple building, a mountaintop seems to be an acceptable place for divine communication. This appears to be the case with the Mount of Transfiguration.

The topics covered in this chapter identify three major areas of Jesus' mortal life: (1) The terrible opposition he encountered from institutionalized, organized priestcraft, supported by spiritual wickedness and cultural tradition, the opposition that eventually led men to crucify him; (2) the absolute necessity of obtaining a testimony of Jesus Christ through the Holy Spirit if one wishes to obtain salvation; (3) the remarkable spiritual manifestations and priesthood endowment necessary for the development of the kingdom of God on earth. These three subjects, found in Matthew 15-17, Mark 7-9, and Luke 9, absolutely basic to an understanding of the mission of Jesus Christ on this earth.

NOTES

1. *Teachings of the Prophet Joseph Smith,* pp. 223, 243; emphasis added.
2. Ibid., p. 199.
3. Ibid., p. 158.
4. Ibid., p. 172.
5. Ibid., p. 13.

6. Bruce R. McConkie, *Doctrinal New Testament Commentary,* 3 vols. (Salt Lake City: Bookcraft, 1965-73), 1:404.

7. Ibid., p. 400.

8. Joseph Fielding Smith, *Doctrines of Salvation,* 3 vols. (Salt Lake City: Bookcraft, 1954-56), 2:165.

21

THE CALLING OF THE SEVENTY
AND THE
PARABLE OF THE GOOD SAMARITAN
(Luke 10:1-37)

S. Brent Farley

The Sending of the Seventy

It is the duty of the Seventy "to preach the gospel to every creature, to every tongue and people under the heavens, to whom they may be sent."[1] "It is expected of this body of men that they will have burning in their souls the testimony of Jesus Christ, which is the spirit of prophecy; that they will be full of light and of the knowledge of the truth; that they will be enthusiastic in their calling, and in the cause of Zion, and that they will be ready at any moment, when required, to go out into the world, or anywhere throughout the Church and bear testimony of the truth, preach the Gospel of Jesus Christ, and set examples before the world of purity, love, honesty, uprightness and integrity to the truth."[2]

It was of men of such qualities that the scriptures record, "The Lord appointed other seventy also, and sent them two and two before his face into every city and place, whither he himself would come." (Luke 10:1.) They were sent without purse, scrip, or shoes; that is, rather than relying upon their own financial store and personal provisions, they would walk in common sandals and modest clothing and would rely upon the hospitality of those among whom they were sent (as was the custom of the day). They would eat the same as did those to whom they preached—nothing greater, nothing less. Their power would not be symbolized by their dress or their food; it would come by their tesimony of the Lord and his kingdom. To those inclined toward peace, the heavenly provisions of the gospel were offered as hos-

---

S. Brent Farley is an instructor at the LDS Institute of Religion at Utah State University.

312

pitably as the mortal provisions of those families with whom the Seventy stayed. For those who were sick and deserving of a blessing, the Seventy would lay their hands upon them and heal them. (See Luke 10:4-9.)

What was the message of the Seventy? They were to declare in words of soberness, attended by the Spirit of Truth, "The kingdom of God is come nigh unto you." (Luke 10:9.) Jesus the Christ, Son of the Almighty Father, is near. His kingdom is being set up upon the earth, that those with receptive hearts might enter and receive the blessings of the gospel both in this world and in eternity.

Their message was of such significance that those who rejected them would also be rejected by God; that as dust is shaken from the feet, so would those who rejected them be shaken from the kingdom of God if they did not repent. (See Luke 10:10-16.) Those who rejected the Seventy rejected Jesus, for he stated: "He that heareth you heareth me; and he that despiseth you despiseth me." (Luke 10:16.)[3]

With their divine commission, the Seventy went forth in faith and power, as witnessed by their joyful return and report that "even the devils are subject unto us through thy name." (Luke 10:17.) They surely would have witnessed the power of the word among the faithful, but the implication in the text is that they were surprised that the disobedient spirits who followed Satan were subject to the power of the priesthood exercised in the name of the Lord. With an insight that stretched back beyond the normal veil of forgetfulness that we experience at birth, the Savior recalled: "As lightning falleth from heaven, I beheld Satan also falling." (JST, Luke 10:19.) This same message had been given to Moses, perhaps to enable the "soldiers of righteousness" to conceive of the beginnings of that commander of evil, Lucifer:

> I, the Lord God, spake unto Moses, saying: That Satan, whom thou hast commanded in the name of mine Only Begotten, is the same which was from the beginning, and he came before me, saying—Behold, here am I, send me, I will be thy son, and I will redeem all mankind, that one soul shall not be lost, and surely I will do it; wherefore give me thine honor. But, behold, my Beloved Son, which was my Beloved and Chosen from the beginning, said unto me—Father, thy will be done, and the glory be thine forever. Wherefore, because that Satan

rebelled against me, and sought to destroy the agency of man, which I, the Lord God, had given him, and also, that I should give unto him mine own power; by the power of mine Only Begotten, I caused that he should be cast down; and he became Satan, yea, even the devil, the father of all lies, to deceive and to blind men, and to lead them captive at his will, even as many as would not hearken unto my voice. (Moses 4:1-4.)

The possible symbolism of lightning falling from heaven as a parallel to Satan's course is interesting to contemplate. Lightning is a powerful force that strikes with a downward motion toward the earth. Joseph Smith learned that Lucifer was "an angel of God who was in authority in the presence of God and the Son." (D&C 76:25.)

Jesus knew that the war waged in heaven by Satan continued upon the earth, for because Lucifer "had fallen from heaven, and had become miserable forever, he sought also the misery of all mankind." (2 Ne. 2:18.) Adding comfort and strength to his wondering servants, Jesus said, "I will give unto you power over serpents and scorpions, and over all the power of the enemy; and nothing shall by any means hurt you." (JST, Luke 10:20.) Were it to be the Lord's will, even the poisonous strike of serpents and scorpions would not harm the disciples. However, there is a deeper, symbolic meaning to these words. Isaiah symbolized the works of wicked and deceitful men as follows: "They hatch cockatrice' eggs, and weave the spider's web: he that eateth of their eggs dieth, and that which is crushed breaketh out into a viper."[4] (Isa. 59:5.) The terrible poison of serpents that brings pain and physical death was used to connote the seriousness of the poison of wickedness, which itself would cause the pains of hell and the spiritual death suffered by the wicked. Thus, as Elder James E. Talmage wrote, "The promise that they should tread on serpents and scorpions included immunity from injury by venomous creatures if encountered in the path of duty and power to prevail over the wicked spirits that serve the devil, who is elsewhere expressly called the serpent."[5] They were not to rejoice, however, in their power, "but rather rejoice, because [their] names are written in heaven." (Luke 10:20.) This may have been a revelation, or a confirmation of prior revelations, that their callings and elections were made sure, or it may have been a goal for which they should seek, or it may have been either, depending upon the individual servant. Regarding this passage, Elder Bruce R. McConkie wrote: "The faithful saints who have gained the promise of eternal life have their names recorded in the Lamb's Book of Life."[6] Such was the goal of the gospel, whereas the spirits of the evil one would seek to counter the works of the Lord's ministers so that others might fall from the grace of God, as did their leader in the premortal existence.

Having reflected upon the self-assumed power of Satan and his evil horde, Jesus "rejoiced in spirit, and said, I thank thee, O Father, Lord of heaven and earth, that thou hast hid these things from them who think they are wise and prudent, and hast revealed them unto babes." (JST, Luke 10:22.) Perhaps he was thinking of the scribes and Pharisees of the day, counterparts of those individuals in the last days who Paul prophesied would be "ever learning, and never able to come to the knowledge of the truth." (2 Tim. 3:7.) Jesus loved teachable followers, for they could be made into saints. Like babes anxious to learn, they would absorb the knowledge of the Spirit. The Greek word translated *babe,* as used in this context, denotes one who was without speech.[7] It was the speech of the Spirit that the disciples were willing to learn (see 1 Cor. 2:9-16), whereas those schooled only in worldly traditions and who were unwilling to change blocked out the language of the Spirit of Truth. To them it was a foreign tongue. They were not pliable, not ready to be fashioned into something better by God. Isaiah proclaimed, "O Lord, thou art our father; we are the clay, and thou our potter; and we all are the work of thy hand." (Isa. 64:8.) Such was the nature of the Seventy whom Jesus had commissioned.

The Parable of the Good Samaritan

In the narrative of Luke 10, it is recorded that a lawyer stood up and asked the Master a question. The lawyer may have personified the rigidity of knowledge that stemmed more from men than from God, a man who thought he was wise and prudent. In the New Testament, a lawyer was equivalent to a scribe, a person who was a professional teacher of the law, including the written law of the Pentateuch and the oral traditions of the Jews. His motivation was to "tempt," meaning "to try, or test."[8] The lawyer's question, according to Elder Talmage, was likely a conscious attempt "to annoy and if possible disconcert Jesus on questions of law and doctrine, and to provoke Him to some overt utterance or deed."[9] The lawyer lacked the childlike qualities of babes (to which Jesus had just referred in verse 21), such as humility, trust, faith, and willingness to learn. Rather, as has been suggested by Elder McConkie, the lawyer was "one of those intellectual religionists who thrive on contention and delight in dissension."[10]

"What shall I do to inherit eternal life?" the man asked. (Luke 10:25.) The question was simple to ask, but it could have opened an endless debate in the courts of worldly wisdom. However, the Savior in divine perception turned the question back to the man schooled in the law and asked simply, "What is written in the law? how readest thou?" (Luke 10:26.) With precision, the lawyer quickly drew from holy writ the great commandments: "Thou shalt love the Lord thy God with all thy heart, and with all thy soul, and with all thy strength, and with all thy mind; and thy neighbour as thyself." (Luke 10:27; see also Lev. 19:18 and Deut. 6:5.) He had exhibited his knowledge with quick perfection. Jesus said, "Thou hast answered right." (Luke 10:28.)

Perhaps the lawyer's desire to be exalted in the eyes of the public had prompted him to such a quick response when his own question was returned. The commendation by Jesus, an individual who drew much public attention, probably added more light to the lamp of his own conceit. If it did, it was short-lived, for the completion of the sentence carried the challenge that "to know" and "to do" must be harmonized to be effective: "This do, and thou shalt live." (Luke 10:28.) He had expected a debate but had received a powerful sermon: live your life in harmony with these teachings. His conscience may have twinged a little at this time; in addition, he probably sensed that he was not doing well in a debate that he himself had begun, which debate now seemed to be aborted. Hoping to salvage such reputation as he could in a confrontation that had gone against him; desiring to justify his own hatred rather than love for many of his fellowmen, and knowing, by instinct or from some previous statement of Jesus, that the Lord and the other rabbis differed widely as to who fell in the category of a neighbor, the lawyer asked: "And who is my neighbour?" (Luke 10:29.)[11] This time the Savior answered with a parable, one so typical of the times that it may have been history as well as parable:

> A certain man went down from Jerusalem to Jericho, and fell among thieves, which stripped him of his raiment, and wounded him, and departed, leaving him half dead. And by chance there came down a certain priest that way, and when he saw him, he passed by on the other side. And likewise a Levite, when he was at the place, came and looked on him, and passed by on the other side. But a certain Samaritan, as he journeyed, came where he was: and when he saw him, he had compassion on him, and went to him, and bound up his wounds, pouring in oil and wine, and set him on his own beast, and brought him to an inn, and took care of him. And on the morrow when he departed, he took out two pence, and gave them to the host, and said unto him, take care of him: and whatsoever thou spendest more, when I come again, I will repay thee. (Luke 10:30-35.)

The answer to the lawyer's first question, regarding eternal life, was merely a matter of quoting the law. The answer to the second, regarding one's neighbor, involved something far more difficult: the application of the law in one's own life. "Which now of these three, thinkest thou, was a neighbour unto him that fell among the thieves?" (Luke 10:36.) As the parable had been structured, only one answer could be given, and it would have been perceived by the less-learned observers. The lawyer could only respond, "He that shewed mercy on him." Then followed the challenge to put life in his learning: "Go, and do thou likewise." (Luke 10:37.) Twice the lawyer had been told that his actions must follow correct teachings. One would hope that his encounter would have opened the door to a higher understanding of the truth; it is not recorded, however, what became of him thereafter.

A look at the characters in the parable adds interest to its interpretation and applications. The first to pass by the wounded man was a priest. It was his religious duty to act as a mediator between his people and God; he was, by virtue of his office, supposed to draw the people closer to God. One would think that a priest would be a logical individual to lead out in demonstrating the principle of neighborly love that would help lead to eternal life. But such was not the case; he went out of his way to avoid contact with the sufferer. Next came a Levite, an authority who was to assist the priests, one who was traditionally viewed as fulfilling a role of sanctuary service.[12] Should he not understand the significance of his commission in the Lord's kingdom? Should he not exemplify the love of neighbor that God would desire? Yet the Levite also passed by on the other side, as did the priest, "for they desired in their hearts that it might not be known that they had seen him." (JST, Luke 10:33.) It was a Samaritan, one hated of the Jews, one not considered as being worthy to be termed a neighbor; a Samaritan, one viewed by the Jews as not being of the chosen lineage, one in whose veins flowed blood tainted by Gentile mixture. He was viewed as least likely to act appropriately, even to be considered for eternal life.[13] Yet of the three, it was he who put the others to shame; he alone loved his neighbor enough to sacrifice in his behalf.

Was not this parable a declaration of the apostasy of the Jewish religious leaders from the pure religion lived by the Old Testament prophets? Was not Jesus illustrating to them the need for his own restoration of the true religion taught to Adam and the other patriarchs?

Many pages could be written to interpret and apply principles in this parable to the lives of others. But out of it all ought to come one lesson more grand than all others: it was a declaration of the Messiahship of Jesus, a truth veiled in parabolic form to be discovered by those who were willing to learn the language of the Spirit. The afflicted man was wounded by evil thieves; are not all of God's children also wounded, to one degree or another, by submission to sin? And is it not Satan who is the thief seeking to rob us of eternal life? And who loved his neighbor more than Jesus, who would fulfill in the sacrificial Garden of Gethsemane and upon the cross his own declaration that "greater love hath no man than this, that a man lay down his life for his friends"? (John 15:13.) As I have written elsewhere:

> I wonder if the disciples, sometime after the atoning sacrifice and resurrection of the Savior, reflected upon the parable of the good Samaritan and saw some distinct parallels portrayed in the life of Jesus. Just as the Samaritans were not regarded by the Jews as a chosen race, so have the Jews themselves been looked down upon by others who felt themselves superior. It was to the often unpopular race of Jews that Jesus was born. As in the parable, the Savior (as a "good Samaritan" to all men) stopped and stooped to help the wounded. If the wounded were likened to sinners, then the Savior did what

contemporary authorities (the priest and the Levite) not only did not do in the parable but could not do in life: he atoned for their sins. As the parabolic Samaritan offered unconditionally to pay the cost for his friend's recovery, so the Savior paid a price unlimited by time or amount when he atoned for his fellow beings in the Garden of Gethsemane.[14]

What the lawyer could have learned was that to love God with all his heart required his acceptance of the Son of God, Jesus the Christ, who would offer himself for the salvation of all. And to accept the Christ would in turn require his sacrifice for his neighbors, regardless of their learning, ancestry, or social status, for all were spirit children of God.

The Seventy, as babes, were progressing toward eternal life; the lawyer, as one wise in his own sight, was not.

NOTES

1. Joseph F. Smith, *Gospel Doctrine* (Salt Lake City: Deseret Book, 1975), p. 183.

2. Joseph F. Smith, *Conference Report,* October 1904, p. 3.

3. This constant principle was revealed to Joseph Smith as part of the Oath and Covenant of the Priesthood. (See D&C 84:33-39.)

4. A cockatrice was a very poisonous serpent.

5. James E. Talmage, *Jesus the Christ* (Salt Lake City: Deseret Book, 1961), pp. 427-28.

6. Bruce R. McConkie, *Doctrinal New Testament Commentary,* 3 vols. (Salt Lake City: Bookcraft, 1966-71), 1:465.

7. Robert Young, *Young's Analytical Concordance to the Bible* (Grand Rapids, Mich.: William B. Eerdmans, 1970), p. 66.

8. This meaning is listed in the same category as the passages stating, "Thou shalt not tempt the Lord thy God" (Matt. 4:7; Luke 4:12), and "Neither let us tempt Christ" (1 Cor. 10:9); Young, *Concordance,* p. 966.

9. Talmage, *Jesus the Christ,* p. 429.

10. McConkie, *The Mortal Messiah,* 4 vols. (Salt Lake City: Deseret Book, 1979-81), 3:176.

11. "To the Jews their neighbors were the members of the congregation

of Israel; the Gentiles and all who opposed the Jewish people not only failed to qualify as neighbors, but were, in fact, enemies." (McConkie, *The Mortal Messiah* 3:178.) Hence, Jesus taught in the Sermon on the Mount, "Ye have heard that it hath been said, Thou shalt love thy neighbour, and hate thine enemy. But I say unto you, Love your enemies." (Matt. 5:43-44.)

12. See Kent P. Jackson, "The Law of Moses and the Atonement of Christ," *Studies in Scripture, Vol. 3: The Old Testament,* 3:156-59.

13. McConkie, *The Mortal Messiah* 3:179.

14. S. Brent Farley, "The Parables: A Reflection of the Mission of Christ," *Religious Educators' Symposium on the New Testament* (Salt Lake City: The Church of Jesus Christ of Latter-day Saints, August 1980), p. 78.

22

JESUS IS THE CHRIST
(John 7-11)

LaMar E. Garrard

Chapters 7 through 11 in the Gospel of John cover that period in the life of Jesus when he was, for the most part, in Judea (Jerusalem or the near vicinity), testifying to the Jewish people and their religious leaders that he was their Christ or promised Messiah. Almost everything he said or did during this period is related to the fact that he is the Christ, the Lord God, the Savior or Redeemer of this world. The Jewish nation, as a whole, rejected his claim that he was the Christ, the promised Messiah. (John 1:11; 3 Ne. 9:16.) This was especially so in the vicinity of Jerusalem, where the temple and the hierarchy of the Jewish religion were located.[1] It was there that he encountered the most opposition, including threats on his life. In fact, orders had been given that he be taken prisoner, but he always managed to escape. Then, after he had finished his Judean ministry, he rode openly and triumphantly on a donkey at the head of a procession of followers into the city of Jerusalem, thus fulfilling a prophecy that he was their King and promised Messiah.[2] (Matt. 21:1-11.) He was crucified five days later.

Before his Judean ministry, Jesus spent most of his time in Galilee, preaching the gospel and healing the sick. During this Galilean ministry, he made several journeys to Jerusalem to attend the annual Passover feasts, staying only briefly each time. The last time he was in Jerusalem for the Passover feast, he healed a cripple on the Sabbath and was criticized for breaking the Sabbath. He answered his accusers,

LaMar E. Garrard is professor of Church history and doctrine at Brigham Young University.

"My Father worketh hitherto, and I work." (John 5:17.) This caused the Jewish leaders to seek to kill him because they felt "he not only had broken the sabbath, but said also that God was his Father, making himself equal with God." (John 5:18.) Thereafter, he stayed mostly in Galilee, "for he would not walk in Jewry, because the Jews sought to kill him." (John 7:1.)

The end of Jesus' Galilean ministry came when his half-brothers— who had not yet accepted his divine status—asked him to go to Jerusalem with them for the Feast of Tabernacles and perform great works there as he had done in Galilee. He knew that if he did as they requested, it would bring about his death prematurely, for he said: "I go not up yet unto this feast; for my time is not yet full come." (John 7:1-8.) However, he later went down privately with his apostles. The time had now come for him to leave his beloved Galilee forever (except when he would return as a resurrected being, Matt. 28:16-18) to go to Jerusalem and bear testimony of his divine status and mission.[3] He knew that as a result of the testimonies, he would eventually be crucified. (Matt. 16:21; 20:17-19.) Yet this was part of God's plan to leave a final witness with the Jews that Jesus was the Christ, the promised Messiah, and at the same time provide for his great atonement. Elder Bruce R. McConkie wrote:

> Nearly three years have passed since our Lord's baptism and the commencement of his formal ministry; in another six months he will eat his last Passover with his disciples, be crucified, and received up into eternal glory with his Father. The final hours of his ministry before his final ascension into heaven are at hand. . . .
>
> Jesus was leaving Galilee forever; his great Galilean ministry was ended. In Judea and Perea his voice would yet be heard, his mighty works seen. But the course of his life was toward the cross, and he was steadfast and immovable in his determination to follow this very course, one laid out for him by his Father. He had said of himself through the mouth of Isaiah, "I set my face like a flint, and I know that I shall not be ashamed." (Isa. 50:7.) Clearly, there was to be no turning back.[4]

The events in chapters 7 to 11 of John's Gospel, designated as the

Judean ministry, took place in either Jerusalem or Bethany except for the following: (1) John 7:1-9, when he was still in Galilee preparing to journey to Jerusalem; (2) John 10:40-11:16, when he left Jerusalem and went east across the Jordan River into Perea because the Jews "sought again to take him: but he escaped out of their hand" (John 10:39); (3) John 11:54, when, after returning from Perea, he left Jerusalem again, and "walked no more openly among the Jews; but went thence unto a country near to the wilderness, into a city called Ephraim, and there continued with his disciples." After a short stay in Ephraim, he returned to Jerusalem to begin the Passion Week just six days prior to the Passover and his death.

When Jesus arrived in Jerusalem from Galilee, he accused the Jews of seeking to kill him because of the incident involving the healing of the cripple on the Sabbath. The people were confused because they did not at first know who he was. (John 7:19-26.) Once they knew his identity, though, "they sought to take him." (John 7:30.) During this part of his ministry, there are three references where he either avoided going to Jerusalem or left the vicinity to avoid the Jews; at least five references where they sought to take him prisoner in Jerusalem (John 7:30, 32, 44-46; 10:39; 11:57); two references where they attempted to stone him (John 8:58-59; 10:30-33); and finally, after he healed Lazarus, a reference to a plot to kill him (John 11:47-53).

Views Concerning Christ

When Jesus arrived in Jerusalem, there was no small stir concerning who he really was. Many "marvelled, saying, How knoweth this man letters, having never learned?" (John 7:15.) Others "believed on him, and said, When Christ cometh, will he do more miracles than these which this man hath done?" (John 7:31.) On the other hand, some said he had a devil when he accused them of breaking the law of Moses by seeking to kill him. (John 7:20.)

Many rejected Jesus as the Messiah because, according to their traditions, the coming of the Messiah would be hidden in mystery so that no one would know where he came from (see John 7:27); since Jesus' home in Nazareth was known and also his parents were known, they surmised that he could not be the promised Messiah (see Matt. 13:55; John 6:42). Still others rejected him as the Messiah because, as the seed of David, he should have come from Bethlehem rather than Galilee. At the Feast of Tabernacles, Jesus quoted certain Messianic prophecies and implied that they referred to him: "Many of the people therefore, when they heard this saying, said, Of a truth this is the Prophet. Others said, This is the Christ. But some said, Shall Christ come out of Galilee? Hath not the scripture said, That Christ cometh of the seed of David, and out of the town of Bethlehem, where David was? So there was a division among the people because of him." (John 7:40-43.) Because of their apostate condition, a tradition had arisen among some of the Jews that the prophet spoken of by Moses (Deut. 18:15-19) was different from the promised Messiah. They believed that Jesus fulfilled the role of this prophet rather than that of the Messiah or Christ.

As we read these accounts, it becomes readily apparent that the Jews lacked spiritual insight into and understanding of the scriptures as a result of disobedience and apostasy. (See John 8:43-45.) Their leaders, who claimed to be able to see and understand the scriptures, were actually blind as to their true meaning. They had changed the meaning of the scriptures, relying more on traditions of uninspired predecessors.[5] By contrast, many of the common people, humble persons who were considered spiritually blind by their leaders, were in fact able to see and understand the scriptures and Christ's role, once it was explained to them by an inspired teacher. Jesus pointed this out when he healed the blind man (who typified the common people), who was not only able to see physically but also to see spiritually once Jesus had healed him and testified to him. The Pharisees, who cast the man out of their synagogue, claimed to *see spiritually* but were actually *spiritually blind*:

> Jesus heard that they had cast him out; and when he had found him, he said unto him, Dost thou belive on the Son of God?
>
> He answered and said, Who is he, Lord, that I might believe on him?
>
> And Jesus said unto him, Thou hast both seen him, and it is he that talketh with thee.

> And he said, Lord, I believe. And he worshipped him.
>
> And Jesus said, For judgment I am come into this world, that they which see not might see; and that they which see might be made blind.
>
> And some of the Pharisees which were with him heard these words, and said unto him, Are we blind also?
>
> Jesus said unto them, If ye were blind, ye should have no sin: but now ye say, We see; therefore your sin remaineth. (John 9:35-41.)

It is difficult to tell from the New Testament record exactly how much the common people understood concerning the role and mission of Christ or the Messiah. However, the fact remains that whenever they felt he was implying by his words or actions that he was divine, many became angry at him:

> Jesus walked in the temple in Solomon's porch.
>
> Then came the Jews round about him, and said unto him, How long dost thou make us to doubt? If thou be the Christ, tell us plainly.
>
> Jesus answered them, I told you, and ye believed not: the works that I do in my Father's name, they bear witness of me. But ye believe not. . . . I and my Father are one.
>
> Then the Jews took up stones again to stone him.
>
> Jesus answered them, Many good works have I shewed you from my Father; for which of those works do ye stone me?
>
> The Jews answered him, saying, For a good work we stone thee not; but for blasphemy; and because that thou, being a man, makest thyself God. (John 10:23-25, 30-33.)

The Roles of the Messiah

With only the New Testament record—which is often incomplete—it is sometimes difficult for us to understand just what Jesus was saying regarding his role as the Christ or Messiah. With the aid of modern scripture and prophets, however, we can gain a better understanding of the Messiah's role. (See 1 Ne. 13:34-41.) Modern scripture indicates that his role is twofold: he is the Lord God of this world, and he is the Savior and Redeemer of this world. He told John and Peter Whitmer that he was their Lord *and* their Redeemer. (See D&C 15:1;

16:1.) Sometimes he identified himself to Joseph Smith and others as their Lord or God (see D&C 5:2; 18:33), and at other times as their Savior or Redeemer (see D&C 29:1; 43:34). Furthermore, the role of the Christ seems to be divided into two parts: Alma emphasized that Christ must be a God of justice (the Lord God) as well as a God of mercy (Savior or Redeemer). In fact, Alma explained that the role of Christ as a God of mercy cannot be overemphasized to the point that it detracts from or nullifies his role as a God of justice; if mercy robs justice, he said, then the works of justice are destroyed and God would cease to be God. (Alma 42:15-25.)

It should be noted that Moses was a prototype of Christ because he fulfilled two roles that were quite similar to the roles fulfilled by Christ: both were to be rulers, lawgivers, and judges, and both were to be deliverers and saviors to Israel. Moses prophesied to Israel that God would raise up a prophet "like unto me; unto him ye shall hearken." (Deut. 18:15.)

Lehi emphasized this dual role associated with the Christ by telling us that "the law which the Holy One hath given" has a punishment affixed if we do not obey it. (2 Ne. 2:10.) He also stated that this same Holy One "offereth himself a sacrifice for sin, to answer the ends of the law, unto all those who have a broken heart and a contrite spirit." (2 Ne. 2:7.) In other words, Christ as our Deliverer, Savior, or Redeemer can save us from the very laws he gave to us as our ruler or Lord and God.

The words *Messiah* (from Hebrew) and *Christ* (from Greek) are synonymous.[6] In modern scriptures, *Messiah* often appears in the text where one would normally expect *Christ* to appear: John the Baptist bestowed the Aaronic Priesthood upon Joseph Smith and Oliver Cowdery in the name of the Messiah (D&C 13:1), Lehi referred to the fullness of the gospel of the Messiah (1 Ne. 15:13), and Joseph Smith prayed that scattered Israel would come to believe in the Messiah (D&C 109:67). Furthermore, in the Book of Mormon the title *Messiah* is used in conjunction with Christ's first role as the Lord God of the world,[7] as well as in conjunction with his second role as the Savior or Redeemer of the world.[8] The title *Messiah* appears over thirty times in the Book of Mormon in books written before Christ's birth but not once in any books written after his birth.[9] This would seem to indicate that the title was used primarily in reference to the future coming of Christ.[10] Furthermore, the Book of Mormon definitely identifies Jesus of Nazareth as this promised Messiah. (2 Ne. 25:19.)

In the original uncorrupted version of the Bible, the title *Messiah* appeared much more often than in our modern Bible, where it is found only four times. In the Book of Mormon the title was sometimes used to indicate the future coming of the Holy One who would save or deliver Israel from spiritual and temporal death (2 Ne. 3:5; 25:16, 18),[11] whereas among the apostate Jews the term had traditionally come to mean the advent of a great national Deliverer who would save Israel from their worldly enemies.[12]

Jesus as the Lord God

In order to better understand Christ's words and works in John 7 through 11, it will be helpful to review, through modern as well as ancient scriptures, the first role associated with Jesus as the Christ: as the Lord God of this world.

All of us were born in premortality as spirit children of God the Father (D&C 76:24; Heb. 12:9),[13] Christ being the firstborn of all these spirits (D&C 93:21; Col. 1:15). Each spirit was given the opportunity to obey or disobey the words of God the Father, which came in the form of light and truth.[14] (D&C 93:29-33.) As we obeyed, our spirits received more light and truth, and as we disobeyed, we damned ourselves by not receiving further light and truth and thereby came under condemnation.[15] (Alma 12:9-13.) After a period of time in this premortal state, some spirits excelled above their fellow spirits because they possessed more light and truth or glory as a result of their obedience.[16] (Abr. 3:22-23.) Because he was so obedient and gained so much light and truth (glory), Christ became more intelligent than all the rest of these spirits. (Abr. 3:19; John 17:5; Heb. 1:9.) He attained the status of a God and was made the ruler over all the other spirits.[17] Acting under the direction of his Father, he was given the authority and power to create this earth and all things therein. (D&C 38:1-3; Heb. 1:2.) He became a Divine Monarch, or the Lord God, over this earth[18] and all the spirits who were to come here.

Although they never attained the status that Christ attained, some of the spirits in premortality were obedient enough to be called great and noble and were chosen by Christ to be his rulers. (Abr. 3:22-23; Jer. 1:5.) Abraham was one of these great spirits. He understood Christ's eminence in premortality and the importance of his mission on earth, so he looked forward to the future coming of Christ upon the earth and rejoiced.[19] The Jewish leaders, however, rejected Christ's testimony that he was the God of this world. They accused him of blasphemy for making such a statement and attempted to kill him by stoning; but since it was not yet time to die, he escaped from their midst. (See John 8:52-59.)

The Light of the World

The purpose of mortality was to prove us to see if we would continue to obey God's words and therefore obtain additional light and truth. (Abr. 3:24-26.) Mortality provides the opposition necessary for further refinement, bringing us toward a future goal of attaining a fullness of light and truth with a resurrected body.[20] Lucifer and his followers in the premortal state did not have a love for truth as did most of the other spirits. "A liar from the beginning" (D&C 93:25), "a murderer from the beginning" (John 8:44), he rebelled against God and persuaded one-third of the spirits to follow after him. As a result, they became subject to spiritual death, were cast out of the presence of God down to the earth, and became the devil and his angels. (Moses 4:1-4; D&C 29:36-37.) Here they continue their war against God's plans and purposes and attempt to persuade mortals to disobey Christ. (D&C 29:28-32; Moro. 7:12.)

In the treasury of the temple, Jesus bore witness to the Jews of his divinely appointed status. However, the Jewish leaders rejected not only his words but also the confirming testimony sent to them by God the Father through the Spirit of God.

> Then spake Jesus again unto them, saying, I am the light of the world: he that followeth me shall not walk in darkness, but shall have the light of life.
>
> The Pharisees therefore said unto him, Thou bearest record of thyself; thy record is not true.
>
> Jesus answered and said unto them, Though I bear record of myself, yet my record is true: for I know whence I came, and

whither I go; but ye cannot tell whence I come, and whither I go; Ye judge after the flesh. . . .

I am one that bear witness of myself, and the Father that sent me beareth witness of me.

Then said they unto him, Where is thy Father? Jesus answered, Ye neither know me, nor my Father: if ye had known me, ye should have known my Father also.

These words spake Jesus in the treasury, as he taught in the temple: and no man laid hands on him; for his hour was not yet come. (John 8:12-15, 18-20.)

Elder McConkie pointed out: "It appears to have been our Lord's deliberate design to dramatize the great truths relative to himself by associating them with the religious and social practices then prevailing."[21] He therefore chose an appropriate time during the Feast of Tabernacles to emphasize that he was the light of the world. As Elder McConkie explained:

And so now, apparently while the great golden lamp-stands in the temple were blazing forth their light as part of the festivities of the Feast of the Tabernacles, he took occasion to associate himself with the Messianic prophecies by announcing, *"I am the light of the world."*

His hearers well knew that their Messiah should stand as a light to all men; that is, they knew that he as the very source of light and truth, would stand forth as a light, an example, a dispenser of truth; they knew that his would be the mission to mark the course and light the way which all men should travel. (3 Ne. 15:9; 18:16, 24.) Messianic prophecies given to their fathers promised that he would be "a light to the Gentiles" (Isa. 49:6), a light piercing the darkness of error and unbelief (Isa. 60:1-3). Jesus' application of these prophecies to his own person was a clear proclamation of his own Messiahship.[22]

The Good Shepherd

The scriptures indicate that the tendency to accept or reject Christ's voice in premortality carries over into this mortal life, for Christ has said that "whoso cometh not unto me is under the bondage of sin. And whoso receiveth not my voice is not acquainted with my voice, and is not of me." (D&C 84:51-52.) The only place we could have become acquainted with the voice of Christ, before we heard it in this mortal state, was in our premortal life. Referring to himself as the Good Shepherd, he said:

> He that entereth in by the door is the shepherd of the sheep. To him the porter openeth; and the sheep hear his voice: and he calleth his own sheep by name, and leadeth them out. And when he putteth forth his own sheep, he goeth before them, and the sheep follow him: for they know his voice. And a stranger will they not follow, but will flee from him: for they know not the voice of strangers. . . .
>
> I am the good shepherd, and know my sheep, and am known of mine. . . .
>
> But ye believed not, because ye are not of my sheep, as I said unto you. My sheep hear my voice, and I know them, and they follow me: And I give unto them eternal life; and they shall never perish, neither shall any man pluck them out of my hand. My Father, which gave them me, is greater than all; and no man is able to pluck them out of my Father's hand. (John 10:2-5, 14, 26-29.)

This metaphor carries an even greater impression to the mind if one is acquainted with the relationship that existed between the shepherd and his sheep in ancient biblical times. One observer has noted:

> By day and by night the shepherd is always with his sheep. . . . This was necessary on account of the exposed nature of the land, and the presence of danger from wild animals and robbers. One of the most familiar and beautiful sights of the East is that of the shepherd leading his sheep to the pasture. . . . He depends upon the sheep to follow, and they in turn expect him never to leave them. They run after him if he appears to be escaping from them, and are terrified when he is out of sight, or any stranger appears instead of him. He calls to them from time to time to let them know that he is at hand. The sheep listen and continue grazing, but if any one else tries to produce the same peculiar cries and gutteral sounds, they look around with a startled air and begin to scatter. . . .
>
> As he is always with them, and so deeply interested in them, the shepherd comes to know his sheep very intimately. Many of them have pet names suggested either by the appearance or character of the particular sheep, or by some incident

connected with it. . . . One day a missionary, meeting a shepherd on one of the wildest parts of the Lebanon, asked him various questions about his sheep, and among others if he counted them every night. On answering that he did not, he was asked how he knew if they were all there or not. His reply was, "Master, if you were to put a cloth over my eyes, and bring me any sheep and only let me put my hands on its face, I could tell in a moment if it was mine or not." Such is the fulness of meaning in the words of the good Shepherd, "I know mine own, and mine own know Me" (John 10:14).[23]

Living Water

Those who continue to accept the promptings of the Spirit of Christ to the point where they accept and live the gospel (D&C 84:43-48) will overcome spiritual death by receiving the gift of the Holy Ghost, which is an even greater source of light and truth (2 Ne. 31:18; 32:5).[24] Since they now receive light and truth through the power of the Holy Ghost, they are able to influence others, by their example and words, to accept and live the gospel and thereby also receive light and truth.[25]

"In the last day, that great day of the feast, Jesus stood and cried, saying, If any man thirst, let him come unto me, and drink. He that believeth on me, as the scripture hath said, out of his belly shall flow rivers of living water. (But this spake he of the Spirit, which they that believe on him should receive; for the Holy Ghost was promised unto them who believe, after that Jesus was glorified.)" (JST, John 7:37-39.) Again, we see Jesus portraying himself as the Messiah or God of this world by using dramatic moments in Jewish worship at one of the annual feasts. Elder McConkie wrote:

> In the majesty of his own eternal might, the Lord Jehovah had proclaimed to ancient Israel: "I will pour water upon him that is thirsty, and floods upon the dry ground: I will pour my spirit upon thy seed, and my blessing upon thine offspring." (Isa. 44:3.) "Ho, every one that thirsteth, come ye to the waters." (Isa. 55:1.)
>
> Now the same Eternal One, tabernacled in the flesh, ministering as the Lord Jesus unto the seed and offspring of them of old, proclaimed his willingness to give the Holy Ghost to men

so that floods of living water might be poured out upon them. His solemn invitation, "If any man thirst, let him come unto me, and drink," was a plain and open claim of Messiahship. In making it he identified himself as the very Jehovah who had promised drink to the thirsty through an outpouring of the Spirit. After such a pronouncement his hearers were faced with two choices: Either he was a blasphemer worthy of death, or he was in fact the God of Israel.

For the publicizing of such a sobering and transcendent doctrine Jesus chose one of the most solemn and dramatic moments of Jewish worship. On each of the eight days of the feast of Tabernacles, as most authorities agree, it was the custom, for the priest as part of the temple service, to take water in golden vessels from the stream of Siloam, which flowed under the temple-mountain, and pour it upon the altar. Then the words of Isaiah were sung: "With joy shall ye draw water out of the wells of salvation." (Isa. 12:3.) And it was at this very moment of religious climax that Jesus stepped forth and offered draughts of living refreshment which would satisfy the deepest spiritual cravings of the thirsty soul.[26]

The Healing of the Blind Man

In addition to his verbal testimonies and use of metaphors, Christ performed miracles to testify to the Jews that he was the God of this world. (John 10:24-25.) Two great miracles were performed by him at this time in the environs of Jerusalem: the giving of sight to the man who was blind from birth (John 9:1-38) and the bringing of Lazarus back from the dead (John 11:1-45). The motive he gave for performing the first was "that the works of God should be made manifest in him" (John 9:3), and for the latter, "for the glory of God, that the Son of God might be glorified thereby" (John 11:4). Although the blind man, Lazarus, and others present benefited personally from these miracles, perhaps the primary reason Christ performed these miracles was to give irrefutable evidence to the Jews that he had divine powers, that he had control and power over the elements of this earth, and that he was indeed Christ, the Lord God of this world.[27]

The man born blind did not ask to be healed. He received his sight only after he was noticed by Christ and then followed his instructions;

later he testified that it was through Christ's power that he was healed.

> As Jesus passed by, he saw a man which was blind from his birth. And his disciples asked him, saying, Master, who did sin, this man, or his parents, that he was born blind?
>
> Jesus answered, Neither hath this man sinned, nor his parents: but that the works of God should be made manifest in him. . . .
>
> When he had thus spoken, he spat on the ground, and made clay of the spittle, and he anointed the eyes of the blind man with the clay, and said unto him, Go, wash in the pool of Siloam. . . .
>
> He went his way therefore, and washed, and came seeing. (John 9:1-3, 6-7.)

The question the disciples asked obviously referred to a sin committed in premortality. Christ's reply confirms that both he and other Jews believed in a premortality where one could disobey God.[28] The reality of the miracle became public because those who had known the blind man could now see that he was no more blind. (John 9:8-12.) The news soon reached the Jewish leaders, especially since the miracle was performed on the Sabbath day. They failed in their attempt to discredit it (John 19:13-25), but they did not want to admit that Jesus had divine powers.[29] Hence, they tried to escape the obvious by the fallacy of *ad hominem:* they accused the healed man of being a sinner and cast him out of the synagogue:

> Then said they to him again, What did he to thee? how opened he thine eyes?
>
> He answered them, I have told you already, and ye did not hear: wherefore would ye hear it again? will ye also be his disciples?
>
> Then they reviled him, and said, Thou art his disciple; but we are Moses' disciples. We know that God spake unto Moses: as for this fellow, we know not from whence he is.
>
> The man answered and said unto them, Why herein is a marvellous thing, that ye know not from whence he is, and yet he hath opened mine eyes. Now we know that God heareth not sinners: but if any man be a worshipper of God, and doeth his will, him he heareth. Since the world began was it not heard

that any man opened the eyes of one that was born blind. If this man were not of God, he could do nothing.

They answered and said unto him, Thou wast altogether born in sins, and dost thou teach us? And they cast him out. (John 9:26-34.)

Since the man did not ask to be healed, and since Christ stated that the man was born blind so that "the works of God should be manifest in him," it is obvious that the miracle was performed primarily as a witness to the Jews that Jesus was the Christ, the Lord God of this world.

The Raising of Lazarus

The bringing of Lazarus back from the dead seems to be an even greater witness of Christ's divine power over the elements. The body of Lazarus had been in the grave for four days, with the decomposition process well under way. (John 11:17.) To bring him back from the dead required not only that his spirit be brought back from the spirit world to be united again with his body, but also that the physical elements of the body be changed from a decomposed or unorganized state to their former or more organized state, thus seemingly defying laws of nature.[30]

Jesus was in Perea when he learned that Lazarus was sick. Had he performed the miracle strictly out of compassion or love for Mary and Martha, he no doubt would have rushed to Bethany immediately. However, he apparently delayed his coming so that the incident would be more miraculous, thus demonstrating more vividly his divine powers:

Now a certain man was sick, named Lazarus, of Bethany, the town of Mary and her sister Martha. . . .

Therefore his sisters sent unto him, saying, Lord, behold, he whom thou lovest is sick.

When Jesus heard that, he said, This sickness is not unto death, but for the glory of God, that the Son of God might be glorified thereby.

Now Jesus loved Martha, and her sister, and Lazarus. When he had heard therefore that he was sick, he abode two days still in the same place where he was. Then after that saith he to his disciples, Let us go into Judaea again. (John 11:1, 3-7.)

Jesus used this incident to test Martha's faith. Because of her obedience to God, she was spiritually alive, having light and truth to be able to testify that Jesus was the Christ, Thus, she knew that he had the power to bring Lazarus back from the dead. She told him: "Lord, if thou hadst been here, my brother had not died. But I know, that even now, whatsoever thou wilt ask of God, God will give it thee. . . . Yea, Lord: I believe that thou art the Christ, the Son of God, which should come into the world." (John 11:21-22, 27.)

By the time Jesus arrived at Lazarus's tomb, a large crowd had gathered. Thus, when Lazarus came forth from the tomb, there were numerous witnesses to the great miracle, including many who had great faith; the raising of Lazarus confirmed their belief that Jesus was the Christ. (John 11:45.) However, when the news reached the ears of the chief priests and Pharisees, "they took counsel together for to put [Jesus] to death." (John 11:53.) The miracle performed two functions: it helped to confirm the faith of those who had already accepted the testimony of the Spirit of God and had believed, and it served as a further witness against those who fought against the testimony of the Spirit and hence disbelieved. (3 Ne. 29:5-7.)

In his role as the Lord God of this world, Christ is not only our law-giver but also our final judge as to how we have kept his law; in this respect he is a God of justice. He has stated that he "cannot look upon sin with the least degree of allowance" (D&C 1:31), and if we do not keep his laws, he must see to it that we are punished. His laws are given not only in the scriptures and through the prophets but also through the Holy Ghost. If we ask for revelation and he answers through one of these mediums, it becomes a law unto us. If we do not then obey that law, we "become transgressors; and justice and judgment are the penalty which is affixed unto [the] law." (D&C 82:4.) We will be punished by remaining spiritually dead, and eventually we will die in our sins. (2 Ne. 9:38; Moro. 10:26.)

Since the Jewish leaders were not seeking the truth, they did not accept Christ as their God or Lawgiver. As a result, they became and remained spiritually dead and would die in their sins:

> Then said Jesus again unto them, I go my way, and ye shall seek me, and shall die in your sins. . . . Ye are from beneath; I am from above: ye are of this world; I am not of this world. I

said therefore unto you, that ye shall die in your sins: for if ye believe not that I am he, ye shall die in your sins.

Then said they unto him, Who art thou? And Jesus saith unto them, Even the same that I said unto you from the beginning. (John 8:21, 23-25.)

Evidently these Jewish leaders loved their sins so much that they did not want to accept the truth and could not admit that they were wrong. (John 3:19-20.) They preferred to listen to the voice of the devil, who was a liar from the beginning (in premortality) and hates light and truth.

[Jesus said:] I know that ye are Abraham's seed; but ye seek to kill me, because my word hath no place in you. I speak that which I have seen with my Father: and ye do that which ye have seen with your father.

They answered and said unto him, Abraham is our father.

Jesus saith unto them, If ye were Abraham's children, ye would do the works of Abraham. But ye seek to kill me, a man that hath told you the truth.... Ye do the deeds of your father.... Why do ye not understand my speech? even because ye cannot hear my word. Ye are of your father the devil, and the lusts of your father ye will do. He was a murderer from the beginning, and abode not in the truth, because there is no truth in him. When he speaketh a lie, he speaketh of his own: for he is a liar, and the father of it. And because I tell you the truth, ye believe me not....

He that is of God heareth God's words: ye therefore hear them not, because ye are not of God. (John 8:37-41, 43-45, 47.)

Jesus knew that the Jewish leaders would not accept him in mortality but would crucify him. (Matt. 20:17-19.) Then, after he had risen from the grave and they had risen from the grave, they would have to face him at the judgment bar. At that time they would know who he really was and would have to confess that he was the Christ, the Lord God of this world, and that they had trampled and broken his laws:[31] "Then said Jesus unto them, When ye have lifted up the Son of man, then shall ye know that I am he, and that I do nothing of myself; but as my Father hath taught me, I speak these things." (John 8:28.)

Jesus as the Savior or Redeemer

The second role associated with the title *Christ* was that of a Savior or Redeemer. In this role, he was to redeem or save mankind from the consequences of the very laws he had given in his first role as the Lord God of this world. (2 Ne. 2:9-10.) As a result of Adam's and Eve's transgression of God's law in the Garden of Eden, they, as well as all their posterity, became subject to temporal and spiritual death. (Moses 6:48; D&C 29:41.) This meant that after temporal or mortal death, the bodies of all mankind would remain in the grave to rot and crumble, never to rise again. At the same time, all the spirits of mankind would be cast out of the presence of God, doomed to dwell forever with Satan and his angels. (2 Ne. 9:7-9.) Therefore, an atonement was needed to overcome the effects of these two everlasting deaths: to resurrect all mankind from the grave to an immortal state and to bring all back after the resurrection, into the presence of God to be judged. (2 Ne. 9:10-15.)

Not only was an atonement needed to overcome Adam's transgression, but it was also needed to overcome the spiritual death people bring upon themselves in this mortal life through disobedience to God's laws. Because of the power Satan gained over the physical world (including our physical bodies as well as our environment) through the Fall, it is very difficult for persons in this fallen condition to resist the temptation of Satan without the help of God.[32] Consequently, all persons, after they reach the age of accountability, disobey Christ's laws at one time or another (some more than others) and become subject to spiritual death. (Alma 42:11, 14.) Although they are deprived of the presence of the Father, the Son, and the Holy Ghost in this state of spiritual death, they can still receive the promptings of the Spirit of Christ directly or when they hear the prophets or read the scriptures here on earth. (Moro. 7:16-19; D&C 84:46.) Christ was the only person upon the earth who always obeyed his own laws as well as his Father's. Therefore, he was always spiritually alive.

Since it is impossible for people to relive their lives, Christ has provided a way, through the power of the Atonement, for us to become spiritually alive by going directly from spiritual death to spiritual life, providing we do the things he requires. (Alma 42:9-15.)

First, he requires us to have godly sorrow for our sins and to confess that we have broken his laws.[33] (D&C 58:43.) Once we have a sincere desire to change our lives to be more in conformity with God's laws, then the power of the Atonement can be used to help us resist Satan's power and overcome the tendency to disobey God.[34] Once this change is made, we are then in a position to make restitution for past sins.[35] After we show further obedience by being baptized, God can use the power of the Atonement to wash away our sins so that we are clean and ready to receive the Holy Ghost. (2 Ne. 31:5-17.) When we receive the Holy Ghost, we are back in the presence of God and have overcome spiritual death. As long as we continue to feast upon the words of Christ and obey him, we will never again taste of spiritual death.[36]

In a conversation with some of the Jews who had begun to believe on him as their Lord and God, Jesus said that if they would accept his word and obey it, then as their Savior or Redeemer he could free them from the bondage of sin and help them to overcome the tendency to sin so that they could overcome spiritual death. Furthermore, as long as they continued to obey, they would never again taste of spiritual death:

> Then said Jesus to those Jews which believed on him, If ye continue in my word, then are ye my disciples indeed; and ye shall know the truth, and the truth shall make you free.
>
> They answered him, We be Abraham's seed, and were never in bondage to any man: how sayest thou, Ye shall be made free?
>
> Jesus answered them, Verily, verily, I say unto you, Whosoever committeth sin is the servant of sin. . . . If the Son therefore shall make you free, ye shall be free indeed. . . . If a man keep my saying, he shall never see death.
>
> Then said the Jews unto him, Now we know that thou hast a devil. Abraham is dead, and the prophets; and thou sayest, If a man keep my saying, he shall never taste of death. Art thou greater than our father Abraham, which is dead? And the prophets are dead: whom makest thou thyself? (John 8:31-34, 36, 51-53.)

The obvious answer to their question was that Jesus *was* greater than Abraham or any of the other prophets. (John 8:58.) He was not just a teacher or preacher; his role as the Redeemer and Savior of the world far outshadowed his role as a teacher.[37] Many have preached and could preach the gospel, but one—and only one—person could be the Savior of the world. Only one person could free others from being servants of sin and release them from spiritual death. That person was the Christ, the Savior and Redeemer of the world.[38]

Just what did Jesus have to be and to do in order to accomplish the Atonement? The scriptures indicate that he had to be born the Son of God the Father; he had to live a sinless life; he not only had to shed his blood but also to suffer so tremendously that he sweat blood from every pore, and he had to voluntarily sacrifice his life. (D&C 45:3-4.) At the time he gave up his life on the cross he said, "It is finished" (John 19:30), indicating that the requirements of the Atonement had been met (Heb. 9:12, 25-28; 10:14). He not only had the power to lay down his life voluntarily, but now he also had the power to take it up again, thereby bringing to pass his resurrection as well as the resurrection of all mankind. (2 Ne. 2:8.)

In raising Lazarus from the dead, Jesus performed a miracle to help teach the Jews his role as the Great Redeemer or Savior. (See our discussion earlier in this chapter.) Even though Lazarus was not resurrected at this time but was brought back to life as a mortal, this miracle was a foreshadowing of the resurrection from the dead. Jesus tested Martha's faith in his future ability to raise all mortals from the dead in the resurrection; then he confirmed that faith by bringing Lazarus back from the dead. He also used this incident to teach Martha his ability to raise people from spiritual death to spiritual life and keep them there until they gain eternal life, if they are willing to accept him as both their Lord God and their Redeemer and to obey his will:

> Jesus saith unto her, Thy brother shall rise again.
> Martha saith unto him, I know that he shall rise again in the resurrection at the last day.
> Jesus said unto her, I am the resurrection, and the life: he that believeth in me, though he were dead, yet shall he live: and whosoever liveth and believeth in me shall never die. Believest thou this?
> She saith unto him, Yea, Lord: I believe that thou art the Christ, the Son of God, which should come into the world. (John 11:23-27.)

339

As odd as it may seem, God the Father even inspired Caiaphas, the high priest, to bear testimony that Jesus was the Great Redeemer who would die for his people, so that he could save them from spiritual and temporal death: "Caiaphas, being the high priest that same year, said unto them, Ye know nothing at all. Nor consider that it is expedient for us, that one man should die for the people, and that the whole nation perish not. And this spake he not of himself: but being high priest that year, he prophesied that Jesus should die for that nation; and not for that nation only, but that also he should gather together in one the children of God that were scattered abroad." (John 11:49-52.)

Summary

John 7 through 11 covers a very important part of the life of Jesus of Nazareth: He knew that he would be rejected and crucified by the Jewish nation, so he came to Jerusalem to bear a final witness that he was the promised Messiah. He bore that testimony in his conversations, through parables and metaphors, through performing miraculous healings, and by associating himself with various religious practices performed at the annual feasts. It is apparent that in these five chapters of John, Jesus emphasized both of his roles as the Christ: as the Lord God of this world and as the Savior or Redeemer of the world. To accept him as the Christ in either of these roles is necessary, but not sufficient to gain salvation. To accept him as the Christ in both of these roles is both necessary and sufficient for us to be saved from our sins and eventually gain eternal life.

NOTES

1. The city of Jerusalem and especially the temple typified the Jewish nation. When Jesus pronounced a judgment against Jerusalem (JST, Luke 13:34-36) and the temple (Mark 13:1-2), it was a pronouncement against both the people and their nation, for "with the passing of the temple the Jews, as a distinct nation, also ceased." See Bruce R. McConkie, *Doctrinal New Testament Commentary,* 3 vols. (Salt Lake City: Bookcraft, 1966-73), 1:636-37.

2. It was at this time that "Jesus, as though to place the capstone on all the testimony of Messiahship which he had previously borne, arranged to fulfil in detail one of the great Messianic prophecies." (McConkie, 1:577.)

3. Christ warned that those who would follow him and preach the same message would be persecuted and killed also. (Matt. 10:16-40.) Peter preached that Jesus was the Christ (Acts 2:22-36) as did Paul (Acts 26:1-24). Both men were persecuted and eventually killed for that testimony. The Book of Mormon and the Doctrine and Covenants bear testimony that Jesus is the Christ, and Joseph and Hyrum Smith were martyred as a result of that testimony. (D&C 136:36-39.) Modern-day elders are commanded to bear testimony of Christ (D&C 68:6) so that they will not be held accountable for the sins of their generation (D&C 88:81-88) and also so that the wicked—who do not accept that testimony—will be left without excuse when God visits them with his judgments (D&C 124:2-3, 7-10).

4. McConkie, 1:439.

5. Up until the days of John the Baptist, there had been no prophets among the Jews for approximately five hundred years. The last prophet, Malachi, had condemned the Jewish nation for tendencies toward apostasy. Uninspired scribes and Pharisees interpreted the scriptures to fit their own desires and needs, and from these false interpretations there arose false traditions that later Jewish leaders accepted as more binding than the scriptures. See James E. Talmage, *Jesus the Christ* (Salt Lake City: Deseret Book, 1949), pp. 63-68.

6. See Talmage, pp. 35-36. The premortal Christ was anointed the Lord God and the Savior over the human family. See Ps. 45:6-7.

7. Abinadi referred to the coming of the Messiah: "God himself shall come down among the children of men, and redeem his people." (Mosiah 15:1.) Lehi spoke of the Messiah as the Holy One who had given the law "unto the inflicting of the punishment which is affixed." (2 Ne. 2:10.) He also referred to the Messiah in this same role, saying that "if the day shall come that they will reject the Holy One of Israel, the true Messiah, their Redeemer and their God, behold, the judgments of him that is just shall rest upon them." (2 Ne. 1:10.)

8. Nephi spoke of the coming of the Messiah in terms of "the redemption of the world." (1 Ne. 1:19.) Lehi referred to him in one verse as a prophet who would be raised up among the Jews, "even a Messiah, or, in other words, a Savior of the world" and in the following verse as "this Messiah . . . or this Redeemer of the world." (1 Ne. 10:4-5.) Lehi also explained that "redemption cometh in and through the Holy Messiah. . . . He offereth himself a sacrifice for sin, to answer the ends of the law, unto all those who have a broken

heart and a contrite spirit." He elaborated: "No flesh . . . can dwell in the presence of God, save it be through the merits, and mercy, and grace, of the Holy Messiah, who layeth down his life according to the flesh." (2 Ne. 2:6-8.)

9. The last reference to the Messiah is in Helaman 8:13, which was written between 23 and 20 B.C.

10. 1 Nephi 1:19, 2 Nephi 25:19, Jarom 1:11, Mosiah 13:33, and Helaman 8:13 indicate how the title was used in an anticipatory sense.

11. The Book of Mormon also teaches that the Messiah will save Israel in the latter days from temporal or worldly enemies. (2 Ne. 6:13-14.)

12. Talmage, pp. 71-72.

13. See also *Teachings of the Prophet Joseph Smith,* pp. 48, 353. This premortal state is discussed in greater detail in the following articles: LaMar E. Garrard, "What Is Man?" in *Hearken, O Ye People* (Sandy, Utah: Randall Book Co., 1984), pp. 133-52, and LaMar E. Garrard, "The Origin and Destiny of Man" in *Studies in Scriptures, Vol. 1: The Doctrine and Covenants* (Sandy, Utah: Randall Book Co., 1984), pp. 365-78.

14. Evidently, the voice or word of God comes to our spirits in the form of light and truth and through the power of the Spirit of God. (D&C 84:43-47.) This is sometimes referred to as testimony or promptings of the Spirit of God. (See Alma 32:28-35.)

15. Individual spirits can accept or reject the promptings of the Spirit of God. When they reject the Spirit, either in premortality or mortality, it is because they love their sins and do not want to change their lives. The Spirit of God prompts them to believe in God and accept his laws and change their lives to be in accordance with these laws. (John 3:16-21.)

16. *Glory, light and truth,* and *intelligence* are synonymous terms in this context: "The glory of God is intelligence, or, in other words, light and truth." (D&C 93:36.) Those who are more obedient to God in this mortal life go into the next life with more intelligence. (D&C 130:18-19.) For God to be just, it seems that the same would apply to a spirit coming into this mortal life.

17. Evidently he was chosen and anointed to this position of authority in premortality. (Ps. 45:6, 7; Heb. 1:8-12; 5:5-6; *Teachings of the Prophet Joseph Smith,* pp. 181, 265.) Sometimes he is known as Jehovah. (Abr. 1:16; Ex. 6:3.)

18. Christ depicts himself as a Divine Monarch sitting upon his throne who rules over all things. (D&C 60:4; 88:12-13.)

19. *Teachings of the Prophet Joseph Smith,* p. 60; Hel. 8:17-18.

20. For more detailed information on the purpose of the Fall and the role of opposition in life, see LaMar E. Garrard, "The Fall of Man," *Principles of the Gospel in Practice* (Sandy, Utah: Randall Book Co., 1985), pp. 39-70.

21. McConkie, 1:452.

22. Ibid., 1:452-53.

23. George M. Mackie, *Bible Manners and Customs* (Beirut: Fleming H. Revell Co.), pp. 33-35.

24. When we receive the Holy Ghost, we come back into the presence of God and overcome spiritual death. (Mosiah 27:24-27; McConkie, 1:141-42, 357, 469, 532.) A more detailed discussion on spiritual death and spiritual life is given in the following articles: LaMar E. Garrard, "Spiritual Death, Temporal Death, and the Atonement of Christ," *The Eleventh Annual Sidney B. Sperry Symposium: The New Testament* (Provo, Utah: Religious Education, Brigham Young University, 1983), pp. 57-72, and Garrard, "The Fall of Man," pp. 43-58.

25. McConkie, 1:446.

26. Ibid., 1:445-46.

27. Ibid., 1:479, 531.

28. Ibid., 1:480.

29. Those who do not love the truth do not seek after truth because it would require them to change their lives to be in conformity with God's laws. Therefore, these Pharisees did not want to believe that Jesus was the God of this world, for that would require them to recognize that they were wrong, be sorry for their sins, confess them, and then forsake them. (D&C 56:14-15.)

30. Natural law is merely a description of the way the elements obey God's commands. Since Jesus was the Lord God of this world, he could revoke a former commandment for a new one (D&C 56:4), which appears to mortals as a miracle. Those who refuse to acknowledge that he has this power take a naturalistic view of the world that eliminates God or his power over the elements. When people take this position, they may also deny God's laws over themselves. Hence, if there is no God, or a God with no power to enact laws, there is no need to repent for breaking these laws. (Alma 42:17-21.) Such persons resist the Spirit of God, the words of the prophets, and the scriptures because they love their sins. They prefer to listen to Satan rather than God. (Alma 30:50-53.) For further discussion on this subject of natural law, see Garrard, "What Is Man?," pp. 134-39.

31. McConkie, 1:455. See also 2 Ne. 9:46.

32. For further information on this subject, see Garrard, "The Fall of Man," pp. 39-70. Because of the power Satan gained over us through the Fall, we are commanded to call upon God for help in overcoming Satan's temptations. (D&C 29:39-40; 10:5.)

33. There must be godly sorrow (a broken heart and contrite spirit),

which is sorrow that we have offended God by breaking his laws, not just sorrow that we have offended a neighbor or that we were caught. Paul said that "godly sorrow worketh repentance to salvation not to be repented of: but the sorrow of the world worketh death." (2 Cor. 7:10.)

34. If we have free agency, then it is our desires that ultimately determine the choices we make (Alma 29:4-5; 2 Ne. 2:27-29), and consequently our actions or works (Alma 41:3-7).

35. Once we desire to change our lives and humbly call upon God for help, as he has commanded us to do (Ether 3:2), then that help comes to us as the Holy Ghost fills our spirits (2 Ne. 12:6) and enlightens them (Alma 19:6; D&C 11:13). As we are born of God, we gain the power or strength (Philip. 4:13; Col. 1:9-11) to change our carnal natures and can eventually overcome the world (Mosiah 27:25; D&C 50:34-35). Restitution cannot be completed until we cease to do those things for which we are making restitution.

36. The Holy Ghost will continue to guide and direct us (2 Ne. 31:19–32:3) as long as we do not turn against God and disobey him (Heb. 6:4-6).

37. To characterize Jesus as just a great moral teacher of ethics would be to humanize him and destroy him in his role as the Redeemer and Savior. One of the requirements necessary to be Savior of this world was that he had to be the Son of God the Father.

38. As the Son of God, Christ is the only one who could "not be a human sacrifice" but "an infinite and eternal sacrifice." (Alma 34:10.)

23

THE WORTH OF A SOUL
(Luke 11-15)

Keith H. Meservy

The Prophet Joseph Smith taught: "Happiness is the object and design of our existence."[1] Lehi taught his sons, "Men are, that they might have joy." (2 Ne. 2:25.) Since Jesus came that we "might have life, and that [we] might have it more abundantly" (John 10:10), it seems apparent that happiness as implied by the abundant life is the goal of existence. Thus we would expect to find that every generation would determine how best to be happy and would eagerly pass that information on to the next generation. Each succeeding generation in turn would discover more of the means to a happy life and would be happier than the preceding one. Ours, then, being the latest in the series, should be happiest of all.

Ironically, this does not follow. Each generation regards itself as unique and its challenges as so novel that all past solutions are outmoded and old-fashioned. Thus, each generation, regarding anything from the past as unreliable, sets out anew to discover the secrets of the happy life.

In this *material world,* values tend to be material. Obtaining material possessions, gaining power and wealth, and earning the plaudits of the world all appear to provide the key to success and happiness. In the *physical world,* values tend to be physical. Each human body arrives on earth with highly developed sensory equipment that hates to be hurt and loves to feel good. Fully satisfying the pleasurable feelings of the body by eating, drinking, and making merry, while at the same

---

Keith H. Meservy is associate professor of ancient scripture at Brigham Young University.

345

time avoiding pain at any cost, would seem to epitomize happiness. Happiness, then, seems to depend upon satisfying the here-and-now needs of a physical, material person.

But this easy, rational conclusion is contradicted by Christ. He teaches us to trade the tangible but unreal world for the intangible but real one—the eternal world of the soul. If souls are meant to be happy, he says, caring for souls is of major importance. (D&C 18:10; Moses 1:39.) It takes good soul care, including a liberal investment of time and talent, to save souls. Without this, souls can be lost or exchanged for something of far less value.

At one point Jesus asked his disciples what a person in this material world might give in exchange for his soul. (Matt. 16:26.) Any self-respecting person might quake at the thought that anything could be more highly valued than his soul; no one would knowingly trade it. Unless one knowingly sacrifices or mistakes the shadow for the essence, nothing can be *more* important than what is *most* important— one's essence, one's being, one's soul. So any question about the rate of exchange for souls must be a contradiction. But a soul may get lost in the process of living. In living a life, choices are made that determine whether one's soul is won or lost. The value, then, of the things chosen establishes the exchange rate for a lost soul.

Obtaining the Goal Through Sacrifice

Luke 11 through 15 records several things that Jesus did and said that show how to care for souls so they are not exchanged. He was constantly valuing the nature of life and its experiences. He emphasized the need for us to receive guidance throughout life, to seek God's interests above all else, and to commit ourselves so intensely to the building up of God's kingdom that we would pay whatever costs were necessary, including making any sacrifice that had to be made, in order to inherit it. Those who value life will study and follow his teachings carefully.

Wisdom to make good choices is to be coveted, and Jesus at times contrasted the wise and the foolish souls who may or may not have planned ahead and counted the cost of saving their souls. "Which of you," said he, "intending to build a tower, sitteth not down first, and counteth the cost, whether he have sufficient to finish it? Lest haply, after he hath laid the foundation, and is not able to finish it, all that behold it begin to mock him, saying, this man began to build, and was not able to finish." (Luke 14:28-30.)

Since choices are based upon one's desires, then, by way of contrast, anything that stands between us and our soul's desire must be hated. On one occasion Jesus rebuked his friend Peter when Peter tried to convince him that his suffering need not be undertaken. (Matt. 16:22-23.) Said Jesus, "If any man come to me, and hate not his father, and mother, and wife, and children, and brethren, and sisters, yea, and his own life also, he cannot be my disciple. And whosoever doth not bear his cross, and come after me, cannot be my disciple." (Luke 14:26-27.) Nothing that life has to offer must deter a person from following Jesus, who declared: "Whosoever he be of you that forsaketh not all that he hath, he cannot be my disciple." (Luke 14:33.) All of this talk of sacrifice came in the context of counting the cost of building the tower.

One value of the scriptures is that they show the price others (for example, Abraham, Joseph, Saul, David, Solomon, Isaiah, Jeremiah, Jesus, Paul, Peter, Joseph Smith) were asked to pay for their souls and how their lives turned out, depending upon whether or not they were willing to pay it. As we read their stories, we are perhaps prone to ask, Am I willing to pay a similar cost? And since none of us knows the specific costs for building our own soul, each of us must walk humbly with God and keep training continually for the call to perform, hoping that our strength to execute our task will be adequate when the time for performance comes. Yea, "blessed is that servant, whom his lord when he cometh shall find so doing. Of a truth I say unto you, that he will make him ruler over all that he hath." (Luke 12:43-44.) But not so the person who is slothful.

Those who clearly see their desired goal will sacrifice whatever they must to reach it. How exciting it is during athletic events to look at the jubilant faces and see the tears of joy and relief on the faces of champions. How often young boys and girls who look at them hope someday to be the same, and listen intently to individual stories as they are told what is required to attain victory with its related honor. It means the sacrifice of a normal life, often including painful injury, long and grueling hours of practice when others are at play, frustration, heartache, and sometimes failure. These are some of the prices that winners are willing to pay because their hearts are set single-heartedly on reaching their goal.

Taking Jesus as our example, it is clear that from the earliest day, the vision he had of the meaning of his life and the intensity with which he kept that vision alive determined what he did. He remembered who he was and why he was here, and he constantly made his choices based on these considerations.

At Caesarea Philippi, Jesus began to "shew unto his disciples, how that he must go unto Jerusalem, and suffer many things, . . . and be killed, and be raised again the third day." He then used this example to teach his disciples: "If any man will come after me, let him deny himself, and take up his cross, and follow me. For whosoever will save his life shall lose it: and whosoever will lose his life for my sake shall find it." (Matt. 16:21, 24-25.) He emphasized how clear the vision must be of those who seek God. "The light of the body is the eye: therefore when thine eye is single [to God], thy whole body also is full of light; but when thine eye is evil, the body also is full of darkness. Take heed therefore that the light which is in thee be not darkness. If thy whole body therefore be full of light, having no part dark, the whole shall be full of light, as when the bright shining of a candle doth give thee light." (Luke 11:34-36; compare D&C 88:67-68.)

Those souls who love light inevitably turn toward the light and receive from God what they are and what they aspire to be, "for intelligence cleaveth unto intelligence; wisdom receiveth wisdom; truth embraceth truth; virtue loveth virtue; light cleaveth unto light; mercy hath compassion on mercy and claimeth her own; justice continueth its course and claimeth its own." (D&C 88:40.)

The Holy Ghost Comes Through Prayer

Those who want to know who they are and why they are on the earth must turn to God. But God does not force his way into the sovereign soul. He enters by invitation, and the invitation is sent by personal prayer and sometimes by fasting. (D&C 63:64; 42:14.)

The disciples had heard Jesus pray and had pled: "Lord, teach us to pray." (Luke 11:1.) He not only provided a model prayer for them but also emphasized in the parable following the prayer that those who desire God must seek him persistently and must not be put off in their quest any more than was the eager householder, whose guests dropped in on him at midnight when he had no means to satisfy their hunger. He asked his neighbor for help, but his neighbor was in bed and refused to answer the door even for friendship's sake. Persistent knocking, however, finally produced the necessary results. (Luke 11:5-8.)

All parables are analogies, and analogies have limitations.[2] In this light, God is not a sleepy neighbor who cannot go back to sleep until he answers the door. Neither does he respond, if the request is all wrong, simply because of persistent pressure. The point here as well as in the parable of the unjust judge (Luke 18:2-8) was "that men ought always to pray, and not to faint" (Luke 18:1). Without persistence the prayer would fail. The petitioner might be unready, his faith might be inadequate on a given day, it might not be the right time in God's economy.

All righteous prayers are answered, but in the due time of the Lord. There may be some delay until his time is due, as a man well-stricken in years learned when Gabriel appeared to him and said: "Fear not, Zacharias: for thy prayer is heard." (Luke 1:13.) Though the answer was much-delayed, the prayer was answered in God's time. This experience says much about God's need and his timing. To become as God, a person needs the power of the Holy Ghost. Through it, all other blessings are possible; whether the person needs intelligence, personal power, priesthood power, or testimony power, the Holy Ghost tailors the divine grace to each personal request and need.

Jesus completed this parable by showing how God, as a father, responds to his needy children. These children hunger for righteousness more fully than does a loving parent, who, despite imperfections, knows how to give good gifts to his or her children. "How much more," then, "shall your heavenly Father give the Holy Spirit to them that ask him?" (Luke 11:13.) "And ye receive the Spirit through prayer." (D&C 63:64.)

God blesses lives when his children hear his message. How earnestly this simple but profound point comes out. When someone exclaimed: "Blessed is the womb that bare thee, and the paps which thou hast sucked," Jesus responded, "Yea rather, blessed are they that hear the word of God, and keep it." (Luke 11:27-28.)

Seeking After Real Treasure

In discussing the value of life and things of worth, we must distinguish between apparent and real worth. No one who could have pearls wants baubles. And eyes and ears that see only the good things of this world can deceive a person into thinking that such things are the only good. It is precisely in these areas that Jesus provided heavenly counsel to earthbound fellow residents. He identified things that God esteems to be of great worth and that mankind tends to esteem lightly, as well as those things that God esteems lightly that mankind tends to esteem highly. By questioning the popular perceptions of reality, he questioned the nature of the world as it really is and as it will be. Those who are honest with themselves want to know the truth about themselves and the world in which they live.

Having made this world and all that is in it, Jesus was well qualified to give advice about its nature and what is of greatest importance. He knows who we are, why we are here, and where we are going, what is temporal and eternal, what is true and false. He knows what we can be. He is the truth, the way, and the life. Because those things most desirable in this world are often least desirable to God, we are required to sacrifice that which, in his eyes, is of little value in favor of that which is of true worth.

What are life's baubles and what are its pearls? What is real? When people die, they leave behind all of the material that they have striven so hard to acquire in this world. At that point, there must be not only a great sense of shock, but perhaps even bitterness, anger, and resentment, that things work this way. How can things that have dominated a lifetime be abandoned so casually? Why, in the divine accounting, is the inventory of life wiped out without any apparent qualms?

But, we might ask, how can anyone blame God when our own hearts are set on the wrong goal? Hasn't God always counseled through his prophets and his Son Jesus that mortality is ephemeral?

Doesn't common observation show us that we can't take it with us? Shouldn't that fact arouse us to ask for deeper meanings of life? Those who set out to acquire wealth as their supreme value set out to build their lives without finding out what the one who created them said about why life was given to them. Are they careless or merely arrogant? Why do they assume that they know better than God what will bring them joy? Ignorance of divine intent and of the nature of eternity is no excuse. Why don't they ask so they could receive? How important it is to see things as they are and not as we wish they were! How important it is to be honest with ourselves as well as with God! The penalty for ignorance applies forever. Now is the time to draw near to God and talk about it.

To help us keep our perspective, Luke relates an incident that occurred while the Savior was teaching the multitude. Two brothers contested with each other over who would inherit their fair share of their inheritance. When they asked Jesus to arbitrate their differences, he gently reminded them how costly it is to souls to set their hearts on the things of this world. He counseled them: "Take heed, and beware of covetousness: for a man's life consisteth not in the abundance of the things which he possesseth." (Luke 12:13-15.) He implied in this example that a person could lose his soul by being obsessed with possessing life's abundance.

Then he related the parable about the rich man who died and had to leave behind all of his hard-earned wealth. In conclusion, he said, God told the unwise man: "Thou fool, this night thy soul shall be required of thee: then whose shall those things be, which thou hast provided? So is he that layeth up treasure for himself, and is not rich toward God." (Luke 12:20-21.)

Treasures in heaven—the wealth of eternity—consist of such things as a strong testimony of the truth of the gospel, love for God and his children, a loving family, good relationships with neighbors, a life of service, and good character. These are things of the heart. We can carry them over into the next world because they are stored in our hearts. How foolish for individuals such as the foolish rich man to spend the only mortal life they will ever have chasing after the things of this world without any concern for what lies ahead! Why don't they know, as they climb the ladder of success, that it is leaning against the wrong wall? If they were to stop to pray about their goals, to seek counsel day by day in the living of their lives, and humble themselves to respond to the divine Spirit, they might succeed. But they seem never to find out what God's world is really like. They are living out a fantasy, creating an illusion, building on sand. They are never in the real world.

Things As They Really Are

Jesus' lessons seem hard but only because of our limited perspective. Any sacrifices God imposes are apparent and not real—a process merely of trading baubles for pearls, a nonsacrifice. On the other hand, when the soul is saved, then any material or earthly thing that interferes is not only of no value but is actually detrimental to growth of the soul. And in the process of acquiring it, if the soul has suffered irreparable damage, gaining it would be the real sacrifice. In this perspective, any impediments to acquiring one's soul becomes hateful and repulsive rather than highly desired.

To his disciples, Jesus emphasized: Life has too great a value to spend it for full barns, gourmet foods, or clothes with designer labels. God helps take care of the necessities. Have faith; God looks after ravens, lilies, and even the grass of the field. If God can "clothe the grass . . . how much more will he clothe you, O ye of little of faith?" Therefore, "seek not ye what ye shall eat, or what ye shall drink, neither be ye of doubtful mind. For all these things do the nations of the world seek after: and your Father knoweth that ye have need of these things. But rather seek ye the kingdom of God; and all these things shall be added unto you." (Luke 12:28-31; see also Isa. 55:1-2.)

"Fear not, little flock; for it is your Father's good pleasure to give you the kingdom. Sell that ye have, and give alms; provide yourselves bags which wax not old, a treasure in the heavens that faileth not, where no thief approacheth, neither moth corrupteth. For where your treasure is, there will your heart be also." (Luke 12:32-34.) This challenge was warmly extended to the rich young man whom Jesus loved: "If thou wilt be perfect, go and sell that thou hast, and give to the poor, and thou shalt have treasure in heaven: and come and follow me." (Matt. 19:21.) He went away sorrowing because he had great riches. It is hard for the rich to enter heaven—as hard even as for a camel to go literally through the eye of a needle. "It is impossible," said the Savior, "for them who trust in riches, to enter into the kingdom of God; but he who forsaketh the things which are of this world, it is possible with God, that he should enter in." (JST, Luke 18:27.)

In the world people may feel that true indication of their worth is reflected in how much others value their life or their influence. Jesus castigated those who sought for human recognition, the upper seats in the synagogue, and greetings in public. And the Pharisees, who set such a negative example, must not be allowed to spread their leavening hypocrisy into the lives of the disciples. (Luke 12:1.) There is no hope for hypocrites, rationalizers who lie to God, their neighbors, and themselves. They are the real losers. All hidden motives and agendas will ultimately be made known. Schemes made in darkness will all be brought to light, spoken from the housetops and proclaimed in all ears. (Luke 12:2-3.)

Jesus' compassion can be seen in his commitment to truth. Compassion might be defined as the right response to the real needs of others, whether it be for mercy, healing, chastisement, invitation, enlightenment, encouragement, rebuke, or a call to repentance. Each response is based on real needs, and needs are based on things the way they really are or the way they really will be. Jesus had the ability to look at all things, including eternity, as they are, not as one wants them to be or hopes they will be. Reality is always governed by law and order. To teach about reality is to teach the truth.

We might suggest that real blessedness, for Jesus, was to cope with or live in harmony with reality. Real misery, on the other hand, was trying to reject or fight it. He taught people how to see truth clearly, to overcome dishonesty, and to stop rationalizing. Wherever he could get people to be honest enough to acknowledge a problem and brokenhearted enough to accept a solution, he could teach them. He showed them that sin is contrary to divine nature; that being hateful, giving offense, being angry, being unjust, or lacking mercy goes against the nature of souls and breaks down the order of things. Those who engage in such acts to find happiness are inevitably frustrated in their attempt. Disharmony with reality brings pain rather than joy, restlessness rather than peace, and disharmony rather than unity.

The Value of Souls and of Repentance

Whoever fights reality ends up in a state of despair. Moroni said, "Despair cometh because of iniquity." (Moro. 10:22.) It is a predictable result. Seeking the right goal by the wrong means always is frustrating, and when frustration accumulates to a high degree, despair sets in. Despair comes from believing in the lies of him who is an enemy of the soul. Satan wants us to be as frustrated, despairing, and miserable as he is, so he teaches us to seek for happiness by the wrong means. He persuades us of the apparent advantage in living a lie. On the other hand, God teaches us the consequences of living in harmony with the truth and the disadvantages of living a lie. Jesus did not come to judge the world but to save it. Punishment inevitably comes from breaking the laws that govern the world the way it is—from fighting reality. The final punishing judgments come when the person who might have been meets the one who really is and discovers that he or she could have known the truth and faced up to reality but chose instead to hide in the dark and live by wishful thinking.

The Prodigal Son

The ultimate justification for Jesus' ministry and his willingness to give his life relates to his concern for those who fail to face reality. If he makes the sacrifice and such individuals offer no recognition, no confession of wrongdoing, and do not return to the Father, for them his sacrifice was in vain. Part of God's great joy comes whenever anyone who leaves him to walk in deviant paths decides to return and walk again with him. He does not give up on those who reject truth or refuse to face reality. He empathizes with their pain and despair and sets out to find them.

In reflecting on the importance of being faithful to God, we have not emphasized the needs of the unfaithful (which, to a certain extent, includes us all), and perhaps have raised the idea that if a person has gone very far away from God, he has gone too far and there may be no hope for him. But if Christ worked with the publicans and harlots precisely because they could be reclaimed, it is clear that a new life is possible. The alcoholic can regain his resistance and live soberly. The harlot can purify herself through repentance and faith in Christ and live a virtuous life. God challenges all of his children to live beyond themselves in Christ—to overcome sinful tendencies, to live in harmony with truth and reality, and to recognize the deeply ingrained needs each person has for integrity, truth, and genuine bonds of love. Thus, the greatest joy in heaven comes when a soul turns to God and faces life the way it really is—by accepting truth and living in harmony with it.

That this is possible is illustrated in the parable of the prodigal son. (Luke 15:11-32.) This is the account of a young man who took his inheritance and "wasted his substance with riotous living." When his degraded circumstances later brought him to an awareness of his sins, he determined to return to his father and accept whatever grace might be given him. The father greeted the son with open arms, demonstrating the love of our Father in heaven for the soul that repents and returns. The young man came back home, meaning that he turned away from his way of life and repented, and returned to his father. Perhaps there is no more powerful picture in all the scriptures than that of the father who runs to met his errant son and who, upon meeting him, embraces and kisses him. What a sign of the depth of the love our Father in heaven has for each of us and of his desire that we return to him!

The practice of the Church of Jesus Christ shows how we should interpret the scriptures concerning God's forgiveness. The Church welcomes back errant sons and daughters. And those who return to the folds of the Church—who repent of past sins, submit to any required Church discipline, dedicate their lives to the Lord, give of themselves in full service to the Lord, qualify themselves to go to the temple, and live up to their covenants—have hope for exaltation in the kingdom of our Father if they endure in faithfulness to the end and overcome all things.

The principle still applies that "whatever principle of intelligence we attain unto in this life, it will rise with us in the resurrection. And if a person gains more knowledge and intelligence in this life through his diligence and obedience than another, he will have so much the advantage in the world to come." (D&C 130:18-19.) The older, more faithful son will rise with all of the intelligence he gained by his diligence and obedience; his younger brother, all things being equal, will not have his advantage. On the other hand, if the older brother becomes careless and decides that he has lived faithfully enough that he can deviate somewhat, then his younger brother, by greater diligence, might pass by him.

Conclusion

We are basically spiritual, and if our spiritual needs are not met, then regardless of how many other physical and material satisfactions we may have, we are not happy. There are several things that Jesus did and said, as recorded in Luke 11 through 15, that illustrate his concern for the soul and how to make it happy. He takes all of our needs into consideration when he tells us about those things that are of most value. If we accept him, we will repudiate those material things that appear to us to be of value and will accept the intangibles that he tells us are really of greatest worth. Commitment to him is commitment to deny ourselves those things that the world views as important—physical pleasures and material acquisitions.

Sacrifice, by definition, is to deny oneself. And sacrificing for God brings forth the blessings of heaven, though it may lead to the ridicule of the world. Jesus sacrificed and was ridiculed, though he insisted that he was the one who was in touch with reality. His eye was single to the glory of the Father and he followed the Father implicitly, making the necessary sacrifices along the way.

Those who make God the center of their lives, who seek to know his will and follow it, and who are willing to sacrifice and accept any subsequent persecution (a type of sacrifice) are sustained with the conviction that they are doing the right thing. There is a whispering in their souls that tells them they are of God and that God is with them. They know that as long as they stay close to God, their souls are not for sale or trade under any circumstances.

NOTES

1. *Teachings of the Prophet Joseph Smith,* p. 255.
2. See Richard D. Draper, "The Parables of Jesus," chapter 17 in this volume.

24

FIT FOR THE KINGDOM
(Luke 16; Matthew 18-20)

LARRY E. DAHL

The Parable of the Rich Man and Lazarus

Luke is the only Gospel writer who records the parable of the rich man and the beggar named Lazarus. (Luke 16:19-31; JST, Luke 16:20-36.) Among the important messages of the parable are the following:

1. Life does not cease at the death of the mortal body.

2. All persons are accountable to God for what they choose to do with their earthly lives.

3. "That which is highly esteemed among men is abomination in the sight of God." (Luke 16:15.)

4. It is a serious matter in the eyes of God for those with means to ignore or disdain those in need.

5. At death all persons will reap rewards or punishments according to their works.

The Prophet Joseph Smith helped us understand what prompted the parable and also the unrighteousness of the Pharisees to whom it was given. Luke 16:20-23 in the Joseph Smith Translation adds the following information to the account in the King James Version:

> Why teach ye the law, and deny that which is written; and condemn him whom the Father hath sent to fulfil the law, that ye might all be redeemed? O fools! for you have said in your hearts, There is no God. And you pervert the right way; and the

Larry E. Dahl is associate professor of Church history and doctrine and director of Doctrine and Covenants research in the Religious Studies Center at Brigham Young University.

kingdom of heaven suffereth violence of you; and you persecute the meek; and in your violence you seek to destroy the
kingdom; and ye take the children of the kingdom by force.
Woe unto you, ye adulterers!

And they reviled him again, being angry for the saying, that
they were adulterers. But he continued, saying, Whosoever
putteth away his wife, and marrieth another, committeth adultery; and whosoever marrieth her who is put away from her
husband, committeth adultery. Verily I say unto you, I will
liken you unto the rich man.

It is clear from these verses that the Savior was scolding the
Pharisees for more than being selfish with material wealth. They were
also being selfish and hypocritical, even abusing spiritual opportunities to the detriment of both those who looked to them for
spiritual sustenance and those who were concerned about the kingdom of God. By their own admission, they had "the law, and the
prophets" (JST, Luke 16:16) and even taught it to others, but in their
hearts they said, "There is no God." It is also significant that in the parable, Lazarus, who represents those in need of and desiring nourishment, had to beg for whatever he got from those who "fared sump-
tuously." At death, both types reap the rewards of their earthly
behavior, being judged by a very different standard than is honored in
the world. The one reward is hell; the other is "Abraham's bosom."

Of these two rewards, Alma said:

> Now, concerning the state of the soul between death and
> the resurrection—Behold, it has been made known unto me
> by an angel, that the spirits of all men, as soon as they are de-
> parted from this mortal body, yea, the spirits of all men,
> whether they be good or evil, are taken home to that God who
> gave them life.
>
> And then shall it come to pass, that the spirits of those who
> are righteous are received into a state of happiness, which is
> called paradise, a state of rest, a state of peace, where they shall
> rest from all their troubles and from all care, and sorrow.
>
> And then shall it come to pass, that the spirits of the
> wicked, yea, who are evil—for behold, they have no part nor
> portion of the Spirit of the Lord; for behold, they chose evil
> works rather than good; therefore the spirit of the devil did

enter into them, and take possession of their house—and these shall be cast out into outer darkness; there shall be weeping, and wailing, and gnashing of teeth, and this because of their own iniquity, being led captive by the will of the devil.

Now this is the state of the souls of the wicked, yea, in darkness, and a state of awful, fearful looking for the fiery indignation of the wrath of God upon them; thus they remain in this state, as well as the righteous in paradise, until the time of their resurrection. (Alma 40:11-14.)

In describing hell, or the status of one who does not repent but dies an enemy to God, the prophet-king Benjamin taught: "The demands of divine justice do awaken his immortal soul to a lively sense of his own guilt, which doth cause him to shrink from the presence of the Lord, and doth fill his breast with guilt, and pain, and anguish, which is like an unquenchable fire, whose flame ascendeth up forever and ever." (Mosiah 2:38.) Joseph Smith added: "A man is his own tormenter and his own condemner. Hence the saying, They shall go into the lake that burns with fire and brimstone. The torment of disappointment in the mind of man is as exquisite as a lake burning with fire and brimstone. I say, so is the torment of man."[1]

Such was the state of the spirit of the rich man of the parable after he died and was buried. In contrast, Lazarus was carried by the angels into Abraham's bosom, or into a "state of rest, a state of peace, where [he could] rest from all [his] troubles, and from all care, and sorrow." (Alma 40:12.)

What was the gulf that separated Lazarus and the rich man and prevented Lazarus from helping? That they could see and converse with one another seems obvious. The Prophet Joseph taught that "the righteous and the wicked all go to the same world of spirits until the resurrection."[2] He also said, however, that within that spirit world there are "bounds, limits, and laws by which [wicked spirits] are governed or controlled."[3] In the same world of spirits, the state of righteous spirits is very different from the state of wicked.

President Joseph F. Smith was privileged to see the world of spirits in vision. (D&C 138.) He saw the Savior visit the spirit world between his crucifixion and resurrection, and organize the righteous spirits to preach the gospel of Jesus Christ there. He saw that the gospel was to be preached to "all the spirits of men" (v. 30), "all who would repent of their sins and receive the gospel" (v. 31), "those who had died in their sins without a knowledge of the truth, or in transgression, having rejected the prophets" (v. 32), "the unrighteous as well as the faithful" (v. 35), even to "all the dead, unto whom he could not go personally, because of their rebellion and transgression" (v. 37). "Where these [the wicked spirits] were, darkness reigned, but among the righteous there was peace." (V. 22.) That he met with the righteous but did not (the record even says "could not") go personally among the wicked, and the statement "where these were," both indicate that there is some physical separation of the righteous and the wicked in the world of spirits. However, it is not clear whether that separation is because of bounds, limits, and laws, or by choice. (See D&C 88:38.)

It seems certain that one aspect of the gulf was that the rich man did not at that time have the opportunity to sooth his torments with the fullness of the gospel of Jesus Christ. However, Christ's mission to the spirit world bridged that gulf, giving all the opportunity to hear the gospel and relieve their sufferings by conforming their minds, hearts, and actions to it—all this made possible by the power of the atonement. That the rich man and others like him can overcome their torments by hearing and accepting the gospel in the spirit world seems clear. Their ultimate destiny will depend upon what level of law they did and can abide. (See D&C 88:21-24.) Perhaps the gulf in the parable referred to the fact that at that time Lazarus was not permitted to help the rich man by taking him the gospel. It might also mean that the rich man was suffering the natural, inevitable, irrevokable consequences of wickedness—a gulf that neither Abraham nor Lazarus, even if they desperately wanted to, could bridge for the rich man. He had to work it out himself. (See 1 Ne. 15:28-29; 2 Ne. 1:13; Alma 26:20; Hel. 5:12.)

There is another intriguing principle in the parable of the rich man and Lazarus. Not wanting his brothers yet on earth to suffer as he was suffering, the rich man implored Abraham to send Lazarus to warn them. Abraham replied that the rich man's brethren had Moses and the prophets, to which the rich man responded, "Nay, father Abraham: but if one went unto them from the dead, they will repent." (Luke 16:30.) The parable then has Abraham speaking an eternal truth, which is difficult for many to accept: "If they hear not Moses and the prophets, neither will they be persuaded, though one rose from the dead." (Luke 16:31.) Contrary to popular notion, seeing is *not* necessarily believing. Knowledge, even testimony born of the Spirit, does not guarantee faith. James wrote that even the devils believe and tremble, but have not faith to keep the commandments of God. (James 2:19.) Laman and Lemuel experienced repeated demonstrations of the power of God, yet they did not believe or have faith sufficient to submit to his will. (See 1 Ne. 3:29-31; 7:16-20; 16:37-39; 17:45-55; 18:8-21; 2 Ne. 5:1-7.)

Faith comes as a gift from God to those who hear Moses and the prophets and who have enough real intent to honestly experiment with the principles of the gospel. (See Alma 32:26-43.) Learning without humility, or simply being shown all things—even someone returning from the dead will not bring faith.

The last few verses of the parable may have been intended to direct the Pharisees (and perhaps later readers of the parable) to a careful study of Moses and the prophets, an invitation to be among those who are blessed because they believe without seeing. (See John 20:24-29.)

Becoming Heirs of Eternal Life

The contents of Matthew 18–20 fit nicely under the theme: "Who is the greatest in the kingdom of heaven?" (Matt. 18:1), and "What good thing shall I do, that I may have eternal life?" (Matt. 19:16).

Anyone who is truly concerned about what is required to qualify for eternal life in the kingdom of heaven must confront the challenges of Jesus' teachings.

Become As a Little Child

References: Matthew 18:1-6; 19:13-15. See also Mark 9:33-37; Luke 9:46-48; JST, Matthew 18:1-5; JST, Mark 9:30-35; JST, Luke 9:46-48.

The apostles had been reasoning together about who would be greatest in the kingdom of heaven. (Luke 9:46.) Jesus, perceiving their thoughts, "called a little child unto him, and set him in the midst of them, and said, Verily I say unto you, Except ye be converted, and become as little children, ye shall not enter into the kingdom of heaven." (Matt. 18:2-3.)

What does it mean to be converted? And what does it mean to become as little children? To be converted means to be changed. Alma testified: "Marvel not that all mankind, yea, men and women, all nations, kindreds, tongues and people, must be born again; yea, born of God, changed from their carnal and fallen state, to a state of righteousness, being redeemed of God, becoming his sons and daughters; and thus they become new creatures; and unless they do this, they can in nowise inherit the kingdom of God." (Mosiah 27:25-26.) In being thus changed, or converted, we become "children of Christ, his sons, and his daughters; for behold, this day he hath spiritually begotten you; for ye say that your hearts are changed through faith on his name; therefore, ye are born of him and have become his sons and his daughters." (Mosiah 5:7.)

There is another sense in which those who gain eternal life must become as little children. "Little children are whole" (Moro. 8:8) and "innocent before God" because of the atonement (D&C 93:38). All who enter the kingdom of heaven must apply the atoning blood of Jesus Christ through repentance and obedience to become whole and innocent as are little children, "for no unclean thing can dwell there." (Moses 6:57.)

The Savior's statement that we must become as little children, then, was a call to become *his* children, whole and innocent before God, "submissive, meek, humble, patient, full of love, willing to submit to all things which the Lord seeth fit to inflict upon him, even as a child doth submit to his father." (Mosiah 3:19.)

Seek First the Kingdom of God

References: Matt. 18:7-14; Mark 9:43-50; JST, Matthew 18:6-14; JST, Mark 9:40-50.

"If thine eye offended thee, pluck it out, and cast it from thee." (Matt. 18:9.) "If thy hand or thy foot offend thee, cut them off, and cast them from thee." (Matt. 18:8.) Matthew 18:9 in Joseph Smith Translation explains that "a man's hand is his friend, and his foot, also; and a man's eye, are they of his own household." (JST, Matt. 18:9.)

What is the message? It seems clear the Lord is teaching that seeking the kingdom of God is the *first* priority, even if it must be that we choose it above friends, mentors, or family members. This is reminiscent of the Savior's earlier teaching that "he that loveth father or mother more than me is not worthy of me: and he that loveth son or daughter more than me is not worthy of me." (Matt. 10:37; see vv. 32-39.) The Prophet Joseph Smith taught that to ensure exaltation, we must be "thoroughly proved" and demonstrate that we are "determined to serve [God] at all hazards."[4] He also taught the apostles in Nauvoo that to be thoroughly proved may require the wrenching of the heartstrings. President John Taylor recalled: "I speak of these things to show how men are to be tried. I heard Joseph Smith say—and I presume Brother Snow heard him also—in preaching to the Twelve in Nauvoo, that the Lord would get hold of their heart strings and wrench them, and that they would have to be tried as Abraham was tried. Well, some of the Twelve could not stand it. They faltered and fell by the way. It was not everybody that could stand what Abraham stood. And Joseph said that if God had known any other way whereby he could have touched Abraham's feelings more acutely and more keenly he would have done so."[5]

What would wrench heartstrings more than to be torn between the kingdom of heaven and a dearly loved family member, friend, or leader? Yet the possibility exists, and if we are faced with such a difficult situation, the right choice is clearly given for us.

But the instruction does not end here. As if anticipating that some may use (or abuse) this principle as an excuse to ignore, reject, or give up on one who has "become a transgressor" (JST, Mark 9:46), or who has "gone astray," the Savior taught the parable of the lost sheep. (Matt. 18:12-14.) If we honor agency, it may be ultimately necessary for us to choose between the kingdom and a loved one. However, for now, until the ultimate choice must be made, we are to do all we possibly can to bring them to understand and live the saving principles of the gospel. As we contemplate priorities, it is important to remember the Savior's promise that if we seek the kingdom of God first, all other considerations will fall into place (see Matt. 6:33)—a comforting thought in connection with a rather difficult doctrine.

Forgive Others

References: Matthew 18:15-17, 21-35.

The necessity of forgiving others in order to be forgiven is a recurring theme in scripture. The Lord instructed that we pray, "forgive us our debts, as we forgive our debtors" (Matt. 6:12), and emphasized the point by adding, "For if ye forgive men their trespasses, your heavenly Father will also forgive you: but if ye forgive not men their trespasses, neither will your Father forgive your trespasses" (Matt. 6:14-15).

In our own dispensation it has again been made clear that we are to forgive others: "Wherefore, I say unto you, that ye ought to forgive one another; for he that forgiveth not his brother his trespasses standeth condemned before the Lord; for there remaineth in him the greater sin. I, the Lord, will forgive whom I will forgive, but of you it is required to forgive all men." (D&C 64:9-10.) It is also clear that we are to forgive again and again, even seventy times seven. Though numbers are used in the Lord's response to Peter's question of "how oft?" (Matt. 18:21), the underlying principle is the same as that taught in Doctrine and Covenants 98:39-48, Mosiah 26:29-30, and Moroni 6:8—we should forgive as often as people repent and seek forgiveness with real intent. Some special instructions are given in Doctrine and Covenants 98:41-48 concerning those who repeatedly sin against us and do not repent.

There is a point of special significance in the parable of Matthew 18:23-35, which a twentieth century reader who is not familiar with the value of a talent and a pence may miss. That point is that the debts we owe to each other are a mere pittance compared to the debt we all owe to the Savior and our Heavenly Father. The servant of the king owed the king ten thousand *talents,* while the fellowservant owed the king's servant one hundred *pence.* One pence equaled a denarius, which was the value of one day's pay. It took six thousand pence to equal one talent. Therefore, the debt of the king's servant to the king was sixty million pence, while the fellowservant's debt to the king's servant was a mere one hundred pence—a six hundred thousand to one comparison. After being freely forgiven for such an overwhelming debt, how utterly silly was the servant's refusal to forgive another such a comparatively tiny obligation.

As we are tempted to hold grudges toward or withhold forgiveness from each other, and at the same time appeal to the heavens for forgiveness of our sins, perhaps we should remember this powerful lesson about pence and talents.

"Cleave unto [Your Spouse] and None Else" (D&C 42:22)

References: Matthew 5:31-32; 19:1-12; Mark 10:1-12; JST, Matthew 5:35-36; JST, Mark 10:1-10.

"Is it lawful for a man to put away his wife for every cause?" (Matt. 19:3.) Also, is it lawful for a woman to put away her husband for every cause? The Lord's response was disturbing to those who listened then, and is also disturbing to many who read it now.

The Pharisees who asked the question were not honestly seeking to know gospel standard in reference to divorce. They were tempting the Savior—pitting his anticipated teachings (he had earlier spoken of divorce in the Sermon on the Mount—see Matt. 5:31-32) against the teachings of Moses, an acknowledged prophet. (Mark 10:2-4.) In essence, they were asking Jesus, "Why are you teaching a different standard than the prophet Moses taught?" A similar question might be asked today: "Why are church members now permitted to divorce, seemingly for every cause, and marry others in the holy temples without charges of adultery?"

Perhaps the answer to both questions lies in the words "hardness of your hearts" both in Moses' day and our own. Jesus explained, "Moses because of the hardness of your hearts suffered [allowed] you to put away your wives: but from the beginning it was not so." (Matt. 19:8.) The Savior then stated God's intention ("from the beginning") that marriages were not to be dissolved, "except it be for fornication" (the Greek word translated into English as *fornication* clearly means sexual immorality), indicating that those who divorce for lesser reasons and then marry another are guilty of adultery. That is hard doctrine in a world where divorce "for every cause" is becoming more and more common. The question still presses: Why are such things allowed in the Church of Jesus Christ? Are we not supposed to be in but not of the world? Elder Bruce R. McConkie taught:

> Divorce is not part of the gospel plan no matter what kind
> of marriage is involved. But because men in practice do not al-

ways live in harmony with gospel standards, the Lord permits divorce for one reason or another, depending upon the spiritual stability of the people involved. In ancient Israel men had power to divorce their wives for relatively insignificant reasons. (Deut. 24:1-4.) Under the most perfect conditions there would be no divorce permitted except where sex sin was involved. In this day divorces are permitted in accordance with civil statutes, and the divorced persons are permitted by the Church to marry again without the stain of immorality which under a higher system would attend such a course.[6]

It appears that when the people are unprepared or unwilling to live the higher law (the celestial law, the intended standard "from the beginning") the Lord allows them to have a lesser standard, a "schoolmaster law." (Gal. 3:24.) But even strict obedience to the schoolmaster law is not the goal, nor is it sufficient to exalt us. (See Mosiah 3:13-17; 12:31-37; 13:28-35.) The schoolmaster is to "bring us unto Christ." It is a temporary measure, a minimum standard, to keep us tethered to the kingdom of God and help prepare us to live willingly the fullness of the law of Christ. All who will be exalted must, through a process of repentance and obedience, become the kind of people who desire and obey "the law of the celestial kingdom." (D&C 88:22.) In President Ezra Taft Benson's words, "a better day . . . surely must come."[7]

But are there not divorces in which one of the partners is an innocent victim? If such an innocent victim remarries, is it considered adultery in the eyes of the Lord under the highest law (that is, "whoso marrieth her which is put away doth commit adultery"—Matt. 19:9)? One of the foundation principles of the gospel of Jesus Christ is that all persons "will be punished for their own sins, and not for Adam's transgression." (Article of Faith 2.) Some of the instruction given by the Savior about divorce and adultery was not given in an open forum, but "in the house" (Mark 10:10) after the public exchange. Do we have record of all that was discussed in this more private setting? What might he have said to those honestly seeking the truth about the question of innocent victims?

Mark's account is somewhat helpful. Notice that in Mark 10:11-12, the charge of adultery is assigned only to the marriage partner who put away his or her spouse. No charge of adultery is mentioned in reference to the one who was being put away: "Whosoever shall put away his wife, and marry another, committeth adultery against her. And if a woman shall put away her husband, and be married to another, she committeth adultery."

Is sexual immorality the only justifiable reason for divorce in the eyes of the Lord? Again, if this question had been put to the Savior "in the house" by those truly wanting to do what is right, how would he respond? Thankfully, God has provided means whereby we can seek and know the will of heaven. We have a living prophet and apostles who hold the keys of the kingdom. We have additional Church leaders, and we have personal prayer. Joseph Smith taught: "This is the principle on which the government of heaven is conducted—by revelation adapted to the circumstances in which the children of the kingdom are placed."[8] Through his appointed leaders, God will continually reveal his will and direct his people on how to apply gospel principles "to the circumstances in which the children of the kingdom are placed," generally and individually. And through personal revelation, the Lord will confirm the rightness of following those leaders. That is the appointed way to resolve searching questions about divorce, and other things not explicitly clarified in the scriptures. Of all of us it requires listening ears, honesty, humility, and obedience.

What Lack I Yet?

References: Matthew 19:16-30; Mark 10:17-31; Luke 18:18-30; JST, Matthew 19:26; JST, Mark 10:26; JST, Luke 18:27.

Although these verses deal with a rich young man and his particular spiritual nemesis, there is a broader principle inherent in this encounter. It is interesting to compare this incident with another recorded in Luke 10:25-37. Both incidents begin with the same basic question posed to the Savior: "What good thing shall I do, that I may have eternal life?" (Matt. 19:16) and "What shall I do to inherit eternal life?" (Luke 10:25). The answers, however, were customized. The rich young man needed instruction about not trusting so much in wealth; the lawyer evidently needed to be taught the importance of loving his neighbor. How sad that the young man, who had kept so many of the commandments from his youth up, would allow his love of riches to stand between him and eternal life. Elder McConkie taught:

> We might well ask, "Isn't it enough to keep the commandments? What more is expected of us than to be true and faithful to every trust? Is there more than the law of obedience?"
>
> In the case of our rich young friend there was more. He was expected to live the law of consecration, to sacrifice his earthly possessions, for the answer of Jesus was: "If thou wilt be perfect, go and sell that thou hast, and give to the poor, and thou shalt have treasure in heaven: and come and follow me."
>
> As you know, the young man went away sorrowful, "for he had great possessions." (Matt. 19:16-22.) And we are left to wonder what intimacies he might have shared with the Son of God, what fellowship he might have enjoyed with the apostles, what revelations and visions he might have received, if he had been *able* to live the law of a celestial kingdom. As it is he remains nameless; as it might have been, his name could have been had in honorable remembrance among the saints forever.[9]

Jesus taught: "It is easier for a camel to go through the eye of a needle, than for a rich man to enter into the kingdom of God." (Matt. 19:24.) Our perceptions and our experience tell us that camels cannot go through the eye of a needle. What hope is there then for rich men to enter the kingdom of God? In the Joseph Smith Translation, Matthew (19:26), Mark (10:26), and Luke (18:27) all clarify that the impossibility refers not to those who have riches, but to those who trust in riches. Mark's account reads: "With men that trust in riches, it is impossible; but not impossible with men who trust in God and leave all for my sake, for with such all these things are possible."

With the question of whether the rich can gain eternal life settled, Peter asked what blessings he and others who had "forsaken all" and followed Christ could expect. (Matt. 19:27.) The Savior's response was a reassurance that all righteousness and sacrifice will be amply rewarded both now and in the hereafter, but it was also a caution, even a warning, to Peter against focusing unduly on comparative rewards and status:

"There is no man that hath left house, or brethren, or sisters, or father, or mother, or wife, or children, or lands, for my sake and the gospel's, but he shall receive a hundredfold now in this time, houses, and brethren, and sisters, and mothers, and children, and lands, with persecutions; and in the world to come, eternal life. But there are many who make themselves first, that shall be last, and the last first. This he said, rebuking Peter." (JST, Mark 10:28-31.)

The issues and principles illuminated here are as alive and necessary today as they were in Jesus' day. Perhaps they have special meaning today, inasmuch as we have been repeatedly taught that affluence, luxury, and ease are a subtle and very difficult tests of faithfulness that currently face many saints. President Harold B. Lee explained: "We're tested and we're tried. Perhaps we don't realize the severity of the tests we're going through. In the early days of the Church, there were murders committed, there were mobbings. The Saints were driven out into the desert. They were starving, they were unclad, and they were cold. We're the inheritors of what they gave to us. But what are we doing with it? Today we're basking in the lap of luxury, the like of which we've never seen before in the history of the world. It would seem that probably this is the most severe test of any we've ever had in the history of this Church."[10]

President Ezra Taft Benson has added: "Ours then seems to be the toughest test of all for the evils are more subtle, more clever. It all seems less menacing and it is harder to detect. While every test of righteousness represents a struggle, this particular test seems like no test at all, no struggle and so could be the most deceiving of all tests. Do you know what peace and prosperity can do to a people—it can put them to sleep."[11]

If affluence is not the problem for an individual, perhaps he or she could ask, "What lack I yet?"

Not Where We Serve, but How

References: Matthew 20:1-34; JST, Matthew 20:1-34.

What lessons did the Savior want his disciples (then and now) to learn from the parable of the laborers in the vineyard, and from his response to the mother of James and John that they be granted special place in the kingdom of heaven? Considering the introduction to and the summary statement of the parable is helpful. Jesus introduced the parable with this statement: "But many that are first [or as it is expressed in JST, Mark 10:30: "many who make themselves first"] shall be last; and the last shall be first." (Matt. 19:30.) He concluded, "So the last shall be first, and the first last: for many are called, but few chosen." (Matt. 20:16.) It seems that the words *first* and *last* have double meanings as used here: (1) sequence—some were sent to labor first, and others last, and (2) position or greatness—some who have high position or opportunity or reputation in this life may not be looked upon with the same favor in the next life, and some who are considered lowly here may receive high station there.

To sit at Christ's right or left in the kingdom of heaven is not given as a favor to an influential mother, nor because of high earthly calling (James and John were apostles), nor on the basis of how long one serves (even though a person has "borne the burden and the heat of the day"—Matt. 20:12). That high place is given to those "for whom it is prepared of my Father." (Matt. 20:23.)

And for whom is it prepared? The parable teaches that it is prepared for those who willingly contract to labor in the vineyard, having faith that the Lord will reward them "whatsoever is right." (Matt. 20:4, 7.) It is interesting to note that except for the laborers hired first, the laborers went to work without negotiating wages. It is also interesting to consider the reason those hired in the eleventh hour were not laboring before: "Because no man has hired us." (Matt. 20:7.) They were willing, even anxious to work. They only lacked opportunity. The Lord of the vineyard is mindful of all the laborers and can see that each is sent appropriately to labor when and where and for how much. If he has a spot that he wants us to tend, he will see that we get there, either with the help of or, if need be, in spite of other laborers involved. "Therefore, let every man stand in his *own* office, and labor in his *own* calling; and let not the head say unto the feet it hath no need of the feet; for without the feet how shall the body be able to stand? Also the body hath need of every member, that all may be edified together, that the system may be kept perfect." (D&C 84: 109-110, emphasis added.) "Wherefore, now let every man learn *his* duty, and to act in the office *in which he is appointed,* in all diligence." (D&C 107:99; emphasis added.)

In addition to the parable, Jesus explained to the disciples that it is not position but disposition—the disposition to serve—that qualifies one to sit at his right or left in the kingdom of heaven: "Whosoever will be great among you, let him be your minister; and whosoever will be chief among you, let him be your servant: even as the Son of man came not to be ministered unto, but to minister, and to give his life a ransom for many." (Matt. 20:26-28.)

The spirit of this important principle was captured by President J. Reuben Clark: "In the service of the Lord, it is not where you serve but how. In the Church of Jesus Christ of Latter-day Saints, one takes the place to which one is duly called, which place one neither seeks nor declines."[12]

Conclusion

"What good thing shall I do, that I may have eternal life?"

There are many requirements to qualify for eternal life. Luke 16 and Matthew 18 through 20 address some important ones. As we begin to recognize those things we yet lack, we are compelled to cry with the two blind men, "Have mercy on us, O Lord, thou Son of David." (Matt. 20:30.) For we are all as dependent upon the Savior for eternal life as they were for their sight. In our strivings to serve and to better ourselves we would do well to remember King Benjamin's counsel: "See that all these things are done in wisdom and order; for it is not requisite that a man should run faster than he has strength. And again, it is expedient that he should be diligent, that thereby he might win the prize; therefore, all things must be done in order." (Mosiah 4:27.)

NOTES

1. *Teachings of the Prophet Joseph Smith,* p. 357.
2. Ibid., p. 310.
3. Ibid., p. 208.
4. Ibid., p. 150.

5. John Taylor, *Journal of Discourses* 24:264.

6. Bruce R. McConkie, *Doctrinal New Testament Commentary,* 3 vols. (Salt Lake City: Bookcraft, 1965-73), 1:547.

7. Ezra Taft Benson, *Speeches of the Year* (Provo, Utah: Brigham Young University, 1975), pp. 304-5.

8. *Teachings of the Prophet Joseph Smith,* p. 256.

9. Bruce R. McConkie, *Conference Report,* April 1975, pp. 75-76.

10. Harold B. Lee, address to Church employees, Salt Lake Tabernacle, December 13, 1973.

11. Ezra Taft Benson, address to Regional Representatives, September 30, 1977.

12. J. Reuben Clark, Jr., Conference Report, April 1951, pp. 153-54.

25

TRIUMPHAL ENTRY AND
A DAY OF DEBATE
(Matthew 21–23)

JOSEPH F. MCCONKIE

Though we treasure all the words and acts of Christ, none have made a deeper imprint upon the hearts and minds of his followers than those things he said and did immediately before his death. This chapter will consider the events of the first three days of the passion week.

Jesus Enters the Holy City as Its King

At the time of the Passover it had become the habit of Jesus to take refuge in the village of Bethany, which rested near the eastern crest of the Mount of Olives facing Jericho and the Dead Sea. In distance it was little more than a mile and one-half from Jerusalem and the temple. Here Christ was the honored guest of Lazarus, his sisters Mary and Martha, and Simon the leper, in whose home he would yet receive a holy anointing preparatory to his burial. That Sunday morning his disciples gathered so that they might walk together to the temple, where it was anticipated that Jesus would preach to the great throngs assembling from many nations for the commemoration of the Passover, setting in motion events by which he would be proclaimed the Messiah and fulfill ancient prophecy.

As the little band left Bethany for Jerusalem, they soon had a multitude following them. The raising of Lazarus from the dead after his body had begun to decay was a miracle of such magnitude that as

Joseph F. McConkie is associate professor of ancient scripture at Brigham Young University.

word of it spread, people were drawn to the vicinity to see for themselves this man who once was dead and to hear the words of this miracle-working prophet from Galilee. At Bethphage, Jesus told two of his disciples, presumably Peter and John, to go to a nearby village, where they would find an ass with a colt that had never before been ridden. They were to untie the colt and bring it to him. If they were asked what they were doing, they were instructed to say, "The Lord hath need of him," and without further question they would be allowed to take it.[1]

The disciples then went into the village as they had been instructed, found the colt as they had been told, were challenged as anticipated, responded according to their instructions, and were allowed to bring the young donkey to the Master. Then they set their coats on the colt, "and Jesus took the colt and sat thereon; and they followed him." (JST, Matt. 21:5.) The gathering multitude commenced to throw their own outer garments, along with palm branches, in the path of the colt with such cries as "Hosanna to the Son of David: Blessed is he that cometh in the name of the Lord; Hosanna in the highest." (Matt. 21:9.)

Like much that was to take place in that last week, this procession was richly symbolic and deeply rooted in scriptural tradition. One writer has said: "To ride upon *white asses* or *ass-colts* was the privilege of persons of high rank, *princes, judges,* and *prophets.*"[2] Christ's doing so attested that he entered the Holy City as its rightful king, as did the shouts of Hosanna—meaning "save now," "save we pray," or "save we beseech thee." The matter could not be stated more plainly; the people were announcing Jesus of Nazareth as their king and deliverer. The declarations that he was David's son—the promise of kingship having been given David's heirs (2 Sam. 7:12-16)—announced him as their king, as did the palm leaves and garments that were strewn before him. Nor was this all, for this very event had been detailed by the prophet Zechariah. "Rejoice greatly, O daughter of Zion," he had written. "Shout, O daughter of Jerusalem: behold, thy King cometh unto thee: he is just, and having salvation; lowly, and riding upon an ass, and upon a colt the foal of an ass."[3] (Zech. 9:9.)

The implication of this ritual entrance into Jerusalem was not lost on those who witnessed it, for some of the Pharisees among the multitude demanded that he rebuke his disciples and constrain their expressions. To this he responded, "I tell you that, if these should hold their peace, the stones would immediately cry out." (Luke 19:40.)

We must not suppose that the honor thus paid to Jesus in this moment of triumph was born of ignorance. The testimony of this multitude of believers would stand as a witness against the city of Jerusalem over which Christ now wept. Luke alone records the event: "When he was come near, he beheld the city, and wept over it, Saying, If thou hadst known, even thou, at least in this thy day, the things which belong unto thy peace! but now they are hid from thine eyes. For the days shall come upon thee, that thine enemies shall cast a trench about thee, and compass thee round, and keep thee in on every side, and shall lay thee even with the ground, and thy children within thee; and they shall not leave in thee one stone upon another; because thou knewest not the time of thy visitation."[4] (Luke 19:41-44.)

The nation of Judah, with Jerusalem as its chief city, was doomed for rejecting its Messiah, yet as Jesus walked the temple grounds that day before he returned to Bethany, he blessed his disciples. (JST, Mark 11:13.) They, by watchful obedience to his words, would be spared the calamity that was to befall the wicked. (Mark 13:14-16.)

Jesus—One Having Authority

The holy party returned to Bethany for refuge and rest that Sunday evening. How the night was spent we do not know; perhaps Christ continued his instruction to the Twelve, or perhaps the time was spent in meditation and prayer, or maybe they just rested quietly at the home of Simon the leper. In the scriptural account we are invited to join them again Monday morning as they were en route to the temple. As they walked and talked, Christ saw "afar off" a fig tree "having leaves," to which he went in the obvious expectation of obtaining fruit, so that he and the disciples might take refreshment. The tree, however, was barren. Mark tells us that "the time of figs was not yet," meaning that it was too early in the season for figs to have ripened. Christ, finding the tree to be without fruit, cursed it and then proceeded to the temple. The following morning, when he and the apostles passed that way again, Peter observed that the cursed tree had already "withered away." (Mark 11:12-14, 20-24.)

We have no indication that the Savior explained his action to his disciples, nor does the scriptural account offer explanation. Apparently it was left to them, as it has been for us, to discern the purpose of the Master Teacher in so doing. May I suggest that the event combined an ingenious teaching moment with the spirit of prophecy. As I have written elsewhere:

> All present knew that fig trees bring forth their fruit before their leaves. All were equally aware that it would be some weeks before fig trees normally gave fruit. Yet the profusion of leaves on this tree constituted an announcement that it was laden with fruit. Christ was thus attracted to it. The symbol was perfect—a tree professing fruits and having none standing in the very shadows of the temple where a corrupt priesthood professed righteousness and devotion to Israel's God as they plotted the death of his Son. How better could Christ have typified the rustling leaves of religious pretense that took refuge within the temple walls? And does not such hypocrisy, be it individual or national, merit the disdain and curse of that very authority it mocks?
>
> The stage was set, the lesson was most timely, and in the false pretense of the fig tree was to be found perfect typecasting. The moment now belonged to the Master Teacher, who used it to dramatize his power over nature and evidence once again his claim to Messiahship, while making the fig tree a prophetic type of what befalls those who profess his authority and fail to bring forth good fruits. Of such he has said that he will curse them "with the heaviest of all cursings." (D&C 41:1.)[5]

When Jesus entered the temple, his heart and soul filled with righteous indignation for the manner in which his Father's house, this sacred place of prayer and revelation, was being polluted with the hypocrisy of a corrupt priesthood and a nation that willingly partook of evil fruits offered them. Repeating an action that had introduced his ministry some three years previously (John 2:13-17), he cast out all those who made merchandise of his Father's house, overthrowing "the tables of the moneychangers, and the seats of them that sold doves," and telling them they had made "the house of prayer" into "a den of thieves." (Matt. 21:12-13.) "Then, having with physical force driven the wicked from the holy sanctuary, he remained to heal, teach, and receive again from believing disciples a renewal of the same acclaim, hosannas, and vocal acceptance of his divine Sonship, as he previously accepted while entering Jerusalem in triumph."[6]

That night as Jesus again sought refuge and rest in Bethany, the councils of Beelzebub met in Jerusalem, seeking his destruction. Tuesday morning, as he taught in the temple, the body of his listeners parted to admit a delegation consisting of the chief priests, elders of the Sanhedrin, and learned rabbis. They had devised a scheme to discredit him in the eyes of the people and to show him to be in violation of the Mosaic law. Their question was twofold: By what authority did he preach, and who had given him that authority?

This question is most interesting. First, when he had previously cleansed the temple, he was challenged to prove his authority by showing a sign. (John 2:18.) Signs were no longer sought; they had been given in all too great abundance. The previous day these same men had themselves witnessed "the wonderful things that he did." (Matt. 21:15.) The issue now was one of authority to teach the gospel. It was well understood that no one could take that honor unto himself. If Jesus could claim no authority, he would obviously be in conflict with the Mosaic law and would have no right to preach the gospel. On the other hand, should he claim such authority, but not having received it from his questioners or those they represented, he would be accused of blasphemy.

Christ responded to their question with a question, assuring them that if they would answer his question, he would most certainly answer theirs. He then asked them by what authority John the Baptist performed baptisms. Was it from heaven or of men? As they huddled together, they quickly realized that if they acknowledged that John's authority came from heaven, they would be condemned for not having recognized it and not having been baptized at his hands. On the other hand, if they said that the Baptist's authority was of men, they would offend the people, "for all [held] John as a prophet." (Matt. 21:26.) Thus they had ensnared themselves in the trap they had laid for the Master, and they were forced to admit that they could not answer. He responded, "Neither tell I you by what authority I do these things." (Matt. 21:27.) His answer was tantamount to saying: "You have your answer; John gave it to you at Bethabara, and my Father confirmed it by his own voice out of heaven when he said at my baptism: 'This is my Beloved Son, in whom I am well pleased. Hear ye him.'"[7]

Three Parables to the Jews

Without explanation of any sort, the scriptural text appears to leave the matter of authority (growing out of the questions put to Christ by the chief priests, scribes, and elders), and has Christ relate the "Parable of the Two Sons." (Matt. 21:28-32.) In fact, the parable skillfully answers the question about authority. It is a simple story about a man with two sons whom he asked to labor in his vineyard. The first son said he would not go but repented and went, while the second son said he would go but did not. The question was, which of the two did the will of their father?

The simplicity of the story compelled those to whom it was directed to respond that it was the first son who did his father's will, whereupon Jesus made this application: "Verily I say unto you, That the publicans and the harlots shall go into the kingdom of God before you. For John came unto you in the way of righteousness, and bore record of me, and ye believed him not; but the publicans and the harlots believed him; and ye, afterward, when ye had seen me, repented not, that ye might believe him. For he that believed not John concerning me, cannot believe me, except he first repent. And except ye repent, the preaching of John shall condemn you in the day of judgment." (JST, Matt. 21:31-34.)

To those spiritually in tune, the message was plain. The father is God; the first son represents the publicans and harlots who repented of their sins and became faithful followers of Christ; the second son represents the Jewish leaders who professed to be about their Father's business but were in fact cankering in wickedness, refusing the most overwhelming array of evidence ever vouchsafed to mortal men to testify that Jesus was the Christ. John had come to bear witness of

Christ; his message was one of righteousness and salvation. The publicans and harlots repented and thus were led by John to Christ. The lawyers and Jewish leaders rejected John and, having done so, could not accept Christ, for John and Christ were one. To accept John and his heaven-sent authority was to accept Christ and his authority; to reject John was to seal the heavens—to reject Christ, and to reject the message and authority of salvation.

In the hardness of their hearts and the bitterness of their souls, we witness the abomination that would precede the desolation of both the temple and the nation of the Jews. Here within the very walls of the temple, where every ritual movement had been designed in the councils of heaven to testify of Christ, and every officiator to personify his likeness, those so chosen stood in open rebellion to him. To them he spoke in parables, that their "unrighteousness might be rewarded" to them. (JST, Matt. 21:34.)

Christ then related the "Parable of the Wicked Husbandmen," by which those corrupt priests, scribes, Pharisees, and elders pronounced their own judgment. (Matt. 21:33-44.) The parable concerns a householder who planted a vineyard, hedged it, dug a winepress in it, built a tower to protect it, placed it in the trust of husbandmen, and then left for a distant country. At the time of harvest he sent servants to receive the fruits of his vineyard, only to have them beaten or killed in one manner or another. Finally he sent "his son, saying, They will reverence my son. But when the husbandmen saw the son, they said among themselves, This is the heir; come, let us kill him, and let us seize on his inheritance." (Matt. 21:37-38.) Thus they killed the son.

Christ asked of his antagonists, "When the lord therefore of the vineyard cometh, what will he do unto those husbandmen?" To that they responded, "He will miserably destroy those wicked men, and will let out his vineyard unto other husbandmen, which shall render him the fruits in their seasons." (Matt. 21:40-41.) By their own mouths, and that too while acting in their official capacity, those corrupt "husbandmen" of Israel had passed judgment upon themselves. According to their own word, they were "wicked men" who ought to be "miserably destroy[ed]" and their stewardship properly given to others. For the third time in a row this contingent of scribes, elders, Pharisees, and chief priests (who but represented their counterparts throughout the nation) had become entangled in their own web and found themselves admitting their own guilt. Let it not be lost upon the reader that in this parable the wicked husbandmen, who had now been identified as the leaders of the Jews, recognized the heir of the Father and knowingly killed him!

At this point Jesus asked them if they had not read in the scriptures how it was prophesied that the stone rejected by the builders of the temple would yet be discovered to be the chief cornerstone.[8] (Matt. 21:42; Ps. 118:22.) Again the meaning was clear: Jesus of Nazareth was announcing himself to be the Chief Cornerstone in his Father's house and was identifying the spiritually blind and hostile Jewish leaders as the builders who would reject him, along with their nation, until the time of his second coming.

Humiliated and angered, these devils cloaked in piety sought to lay hands on Christ but were prevented by his followers. (Matt. 21:46.) Away from their presence, Christ spoke plainly to his disciples, saying, "I am the stone, and those wicked ones reject me. I am the head of the corner. These Jews shall fall upon me, and shall be broken. And the kingdom of God shall be taken from them, and shall be given to a nation bringing forth the fruits thereof." (JST, Matt. 21:51-53.) Those upon whom the stone fell, he said, would be ground to powder. He extended his prophecy to the last days, when, he said, the vineyard of the Lord would be given to other husbandmen who would render its fruits to the Lord. (JST, Matt. 21:54-56.)

Jesus then related a third parable, one commonly known to us as the "Parable of the Royal Marriage Feast." (Matt. 22:1-14.) Jewish tradition had long held that the Messianic era would be ushered in by a great feast, one symbolic of the covenant that would exist between Israel and her Redeemer. In this parable Jesus likened that covenant meal to a royal wedding feast and prophetically announced who the children of the covenant would be.

The kingdom of heaven, he said, would be like a king who, having prepared a feast for his son's wedding, sent his servants to summon the guests he had invited, but they would not come. Other servants were sent to tell of all the good and rich things that had been prepared for those invited. Still those whom the king desired to honor would not come, being involved in their own affairs. Some of their number even attacked the king's messengers and killed them. In anger, the king sent an army to destroy the murderers and burn their city. With the wedding feast ready and the guests both unwilling and unworthy to come, the king sent his servants to the highways to invite to the feast all that would come. Many were gathered, "both bad and good: and the wedding was furnished with guests." (Matt. 22:10.) When the king made his appearance, he saw among his guests a man who was not clothed in a wedding garment. Asked why he was not properly dressed, the man was speechless. The king then directed his servants to "bind him hand and foot, and take him away," casting him into "outer darkness," the place of "weeping and gnashing of teeth." Concluding the parable, Jesus said, "Many are called, but few are chosen." (Matt. 22:13-14.)

"The interpretation of much of the parable is obvious. The king is God; the son is Christ; the place of the wedding feast is the kingdom of heaven; those bidden to the feast are those to whom the message of the gospel is taken; the servants are obviously the prophets who had been rejected and killed by those of their own nation; the army, it appears, was that of Rome; and the city, Jerusalem. After their rejection by Israel, the servants went to the gentile nations, preaching to all, the righteous and unrighteous alike."[9]

What is not evident to the modern reader is why a particular dress was required for the king's guests and why the penalty for improper dress was so severe. To those of the Savior's audience, it was well known that one had to be suitably dressed to appear before a king. The apparel of the guest was a reflection of respect for the host. It was also commonly understood that the appropriate dress for such an occasion would be white robes.[10] Apparently the people invited from the highways of the earth would have neither time nor means to procure the appropriate wedding clothing, so the king supplied his guests from his own wardrobe, a common practice. Thus all had been invited to clothe themselves in the garments of royalty. The man cast out had chosen to trust in his own dress rather than that provided by the king. "By interpretation, he had chosen to join the true worshippers, that is, the church or kingdom of God, yet he had not chosen to dress as the others had dressed. He was not one with them. He desired the full blessings of the kingdom, but on his own terms, not those of the king. He had spurned the ritual garment and the righteousness associated with it. This is emphasized in the JST, which adds to the statement that 'many are called, but few chosen' the explanation, that 'all do not have on the wedding garment' (JST, Matt. 22:14)."[11]

Thus Jesus reminded his listeners of truths long known to them—that the children of the covenant must be found wearing the garments of purity and holiness, garments made white through "the blood of the Lamb." (Rev. 7:14.) John the Revelator would yet write to explain that this "fine linen, clean and white" represented "the righteousness of the saints," and thus the clothing of those "called unto the marriage supper of the Lamb." (Rev. 19:8-9.)

In telling this parable, Jesus corrected the tradition of the Jews that they alone would be numbered among the covenant people, and he emphasized that the covenant could be entered into only in purity and righteousness. The Book of Mormon, our most perfect witness of Christ, teaches this doctrine thus: "As many of the Gentiles as will repent are the covenant people of the Lord; and as many of the Jews as will not repent shall be cast off; for the Lord covenanteth with none save it be with them that repent and believe in his Son, who is the Holy One of Israel." (2 Ne. 30:2.)

Render to God and Caesar Their Own

Hatred makes strange bedfellows. Next we read of the Pharisees striking hands with the Herodians in an attempt to entrap the Savior. Of this event Elder McConkie wrote: "If ever a plot was conceived in hell, born in hate, and acted out with satanic cunning, it was the jointly concocted stratagem of the Pharisees and Herodians on the matter of paying tribute to Caesar."[12] The Herodians were Jews who had sold their souls to Herod and, with him, were fawning sycophants of Rome. The Pharisees, on the other hand, were Jews fanatic in their profession of devotion to the law of Moses and the observance of traditions they extorted from it. Between Pharisee and Herodian there was no common ground, yet both were servants of the same master, at whose bidding they now united in the effort to betray the Son of God.

This delegation of devils came, as devils so often do, with pretended sincerity and words flowing like a river of praise. "Master," they said, "we know that thou art true, and teachest the way of God in truth, neither carest thou for any man: for thou regardest not the person of men. Tell us therefore, What thinkest thou? Is it lawful to give tribute unto Caesar, or not?" (Matt. 22:16-17.)

Their trap was most clever. Were Christ to say, "Yes, pay the hated tax to Rome, as the law requires," the Pharisees would inflame a beleaguered and oppressed people against him. Should he say, "No, God alone is our king, we ought to pay no tribute to a foreign power," the Herodians would have him arrested for sedition and rebellion against the government. "Why tempt me, ye hypocrites?" came the response, evidencing that he had not been beguiled by their flattery. "Shew me the tribute money," he said, and they produced a coin that bore the effigy and name of Tiberius Caesar, emperor of Rome. "Whose is this image and superscription?" Jesus asked. They answered, "Caesar's." Then he said to them, "Render therefore unto Caesar the things which are Caesar's; and unto God the things that are God's." (Matt. 22:18-21.)

With inspired insight Elder James E. Talmage observed:

> One may draw a lesson if he will, from the association of our Lord's words with the occurrence of Caesar's image on the coin. It was that effigy with its accompanying superscription that gave special point to His memorable instruction, "Render therefore unto Caesar the things which are Caesar's". This was followed by the further injunction: "and unto God the things that are God's". Every human soul is stamped with the image and superscription of God, however blurred and indistinct the lines may have become through the corrosion or attrition of sin; and as unto Caesar should be rendered the coins upon which his effigy appeared, so unto God should be given the souls that bear His image. Render unto the world the stamped pieces that are made legally current by the insignia of worldly powers, and give unto God and His service, yourselves—the divine mintage of His eternal realm.[13]

Resurrection and Marriage in Heaven

Perhaps it was by the invitation of Providence that the contending sects of Judaism, whether religious or political, confronted Jesus in the temple this day to challenge his Messiahship. All in turn manifested their murderous hatred, were confounded and silenced, and affirmed their zealous devotion to the Prince of Darkness. The last of their number to do so were the Sadducees, who came baiting Jesus with a question about the resurrection. The scriptural text is at pains to point out that the Sadducees did not believe in a resurrection, so there could be no doubt about the hypocritical nature of their question. Their purpose was to discredit the doctrine of the resurrection through ludicrous, exaggerated circumstance. "Master," their spokesman said, "Moses said, If a man die, having no children, his brother shall marry his wife, and raise up seed unto his brother." (Matt. 22:24.) Now the dilemma: one after another each of his brothers married his wife and died without issue. The question was, to whom would she be married in the resurrection?

Christ made two telling points in response. First, he told the Sadducees that the question they asked was the result of their lack of scriptural understanding. Of their number there would be none that would marry or be given in marriage in the resurrection. This is not to say that others cannot marry or be given in marriage in the resurrected state.[14] It is to say simply that those who have refused the proper authority by which such marriages are performed cannot lay claim to such blessings. (D&C 132:15-19.) Then Christ showed them the fallacy of their refusing to believe in a resurrection. The God of Moses, through whom they got the law they professed to believe, announced himself as "the God of Abraham, and the God of Isaac, and the God of Jacob." (Matt. 22:32.) Yet Abraham, Isaac, and Jacob were dead. How then could Deity be their God unless they continued to live and unless they would arise in the resurrection?

The First Great Commandment

The Savior's adversaries had been defeated in each of their encounters with him. Had they been wise, they would have acknowledged their defeat and troubled him no more. But the Pharisees, exulting in the immediate discomfiture of the Sadducees, sought to make yet another attempt to discredit him. Huddling in some corner of the temple ground, they continued to plot, this time choosing the most learned of their number, a lawyer (meaning scribe or doctor of the

Mosaic law), to approach Christ and submit what appeared to them a most vexing question. It was reckoned by the rabbis that the law contained 613 precepts—248 statements of duty and 365 prohibitions. As to the relative importance of each, they could argue endlessly. Thus the question, "Master, which is the great commandment in the law?" (Matt. 22:36.) In response, Jesus brushed aside the cobwebs of their debate and turned the attention of his hearers to the foundation upon which the law rested, saying: "Thou shalt love the Lord thy God with all thy heart, and with all thy soul, and with all thy mind. This is the first and great commandment. And the second is like unto it, Thou shalt love thy neighbour as thyself. On these two commandments hang all the law and the prophets." (Matt. 22:37-40.)

Again the Pharisees had erred, perhaps in this instance in the choice of a questioner, for he appears to have been a man of integrity. "Well, Master," he responded spontaneously, "thou hast said the truth: for there is one God; and there is none other but he: and to love him with all the heart, and with all the understanding, and with all the soul, and with all the strength, and to love his neighbour as himself, is more than all whole burnt offerings and sacrifices." To this Jesus responded, "Thou art not far from the kingdom of God." (Mark 12:32-34.)

Whose Son Is the Christ?

It was not enough that all quietly slip away impressed that Jesus of Nazareth was a prophet of great wisdom, for he was more than that: he was the Savior of all mankind, and such testimony needed now to be borne. To call attention to his Messiahship, he turned questioner and asked of the Pharisees, "What think ye of Christ? whose son is he?" (Matt. 22:42.) They responded that he would be the son of David and in so doing they illustrated that they sought a temporal deliverer who would wield David's sword, sit upon David's throne, and do the works of David. Jesus retorted by asking why David by the spirit of prophecy referred to the Messiah as Lord, saying, "The Lord said unto my Lord, Sit thou on my right hand, till I make thine enemies thy footstool? If David then call him Lord, how is he his son?" (Matt. 22:44-45; cf. Ps. 110:1.)

The issue was clearly set: The scribes said that the Messiah was to be David's son, but David by the power of the Holy Ghost called him Lord. Do we properly give such title to children of our own conception? Why did David do so if he were not testifying that the Son would be divine? Could they understand that through his mother Jesus would claim the throne of David, while through his Father he would claim a far greater throne and a far greater power? Such was his testimony of himself, and so great was the spirit of it and the power of his teachings that we read: "No man was able to answer him a word, neither durst any man from that day forth ask him any more questions." (Matt. 22:46.)

The Great Denunciation

Addressing himself to the multitude but more specifically to his disciples, Jesus then spoke with great plainness about the damning religious hypocrisy that had been so fully displayed that day. "The scribes and the Pharisees sit in Moses' seat," he said, and "whatsoever they bid you observe, that observe and do; but do not ye after their works: for they say, and do not." (Matt. 23:2-3.) Until the Paschal Lamb had been slain, until Jesus the Christ had offered himself as a sacrifice for all, they were to respect the authority that rested in those who controlled the temple and performed its sacred ordinances.

This is a lesson of the greatest magnitude, reminiscent of David's refusal to lift his hand against Saul who sought his life, for Saul was the Lord's anointed (1 Sam. 26:9); the Lord had called him and, notwithstanding his wickedness, it was for the Lord to release him. Yet, though the scribes and Pharisees respected the authority of those sitting in "Moses' seat," the people were not to follow their example, for, as Christ said, "they bind heavy burdens and grievous to be borne, and lay them on men's shoulders; but they themselves will not move them with one of their fingers." (Matt. 23:4.) They were masters of religious pomp, making great display of their supposed righteousness and glorying in the honors of their fellow worshipers. As one cannot be saved in falsehood, so one cannot be edified in following bad examples. All are agents unto themselves, and all will be judged for what they have done or failed to do; none will be excused in works of wickedness on the guise that they mistakenly followed the example of false prophets or the unworthy example of hypocritical religious leaders.

Christ further warned against those who exalt themselves, for such, he said, "shall be abased; and he that shall humble himself shall be exalted." (Matt. 23:12.) He then burst forth upon the scribes and Pharisees with eight denunciations, which aptly typify the world of religious hypocrisy. They are as follows:

First, he condemned those who "shut up the kingdom of heaven," not qualifying themselves and hindering any that would desire to do so. (Matt. 23:13.) Such are those who rejected Jesus as the Christ and the plan of salvation. Today they are found rejecting the testimony that Joseph Smith is a prophet and opposing the message of the restored gospel.

Second, he condemned those who hide their greed and meanness under the cloak of piety. Such, he said, "devour widows' houses, and for a pretence make long prayer." (Matt. 23:14.)

Third, he denounced missionaries of false faiths who travel over "land and sea to make one proselyte, and when he is made, [they] make him twofold more the child of hell than [themselves.]" (Matt. 23:15.) There is no salvation in false religion, notwithstanding the enthusiasm of its converts.

Fourth, he directed condemnation at those who perfect the art of breaking their bond while appearing sanctimonious. (Matt. 23:16-22.) The word or oath of such is nothing more than bait in games of trickery. They are indeed morally blind.

Fifth, he denounced the "blind guides" who subverted eternal truths in their excessive zeal for trifles. Exactness in the performance of outward ordinances supplanted for them even an interest in the inward or spiritual meanings intended behind their ritual. They jealously tended to the rituals that testified and taught of Christ at the same time that they rejected and killed him. (Matt. 23:23-24.) Their modern counterparts can be found praising the Bible while rejecting the spirit of revelation from which it sprang, and using it as the justification to reject the testimony of living prophets.

The sixth and seventh woes are essentially the same. Here Christ denounced that which is ceremonially clean, while being filthy within. He aptly used the figure of a whited sepulchre filled with decaying bodies to make his point. Commenting on this imagery Elder Talmage wrote:

It was an awful figure, that of likening them to whitewashed tombs, full of dead bones and rotting flesh. As the dogmas of the rabbis made even the slightest contact with a corpse or its cerements, or with the bier upon which it was borne, or the grave in which it had been lain, a cause of personal defilement, which only ceremonial washing and the offering of sacrifices could remove, care was taken to make tombs conspicuously white, so that no person need be defiled through ignorance or proximity to such unclean places; and, moreover, the periodical whitening of sepulchers was regarded as a memorial act of honor to the dead. But even as no amount of care or degree of diligence in keeping bright the outside of a tomb could stay the putrescence going on within, so no externals of pretended righteousness could mitigate the revolting corruption of a heart reeking with iniquity.[15]

The eighth or final woe, which is the crown to all the others, is that they reject the living prophets while they "garnish the sepulchres of the righteous." (Matt. 23:29.) Indeed, to reject the prophet of any age is to reject those of all ages, for all teach the same truths and bear the same witness.

Accountability for Their Ancestors' Sins

None can be saved alone and none come to this earth without responsibility to others. That responsibility spans generations; thus we are taught that "we without them [those of past dispensations] cannot be made perfect; neither can they without us be made perfect." (D&C 128:18.) Christ applied this principle to those of his day who would reject and kill the prophets. Upon them, he said, would come "all the righteous blood shed upon the earth, from the blood of righteous Abel unto the blood of Zacharias son of Barachias." (Matt. 23:35.)[16] Thus they would become "accountable for the sins of their fathers who through ignorance rejected the message of salvation.... All these could have been freed from their spirit prison by the men of Jesus' day, if those to whom Jesus then preached had believed his words."[17]

Jesus Laments over Doomed Jerusalem

Christ's teaching in the temple ended with his oft-quoted lament over Jerusalem, the city he loved: "O Jerusalem, Jerusalem, thou that killest the prophets, and stonest them which are sent unto thee, how often would I have gathered thy children together, even as a hen gathereth her chickens under her wings, and ye would not! Behold, your house is left unto you desolate." (Matt. 23:37-38.) "Truly Jerusalem's history is like that of no other place; and truly Jesus with cause, wept because of the rebellion of her children."[18]

NOTES

1. All four Gospel writers give an account of this event. (Matt. 21:1-11; Mark 11:1-11; Luke 19:29-40; John 12:12-19.) Matthew's account has the disciples bringing Christ both a colt and its mother. This is not in harmony with the other accounts and is corrected in the Joseph Smith Translation, Matthew 21:5.

2. Adam Clarke, *Clarke's Commentary,* 3 vols. (Nashville: Abingdon, 1977), 1:268. "The mule was the proper riding beast for the king and his sons (2 Samuel 13:29; 18:9)." George Arthur Buttrick, ed., *The Interpreter's Bible,* 12 vols. (Nashville: Abingdon Press, 1954), 3:26. See also Judges 5:10; 10:4.

3. Even this did not constitute the complete fulfillment of Zechariah's prophecy. His prophecy was one of a kingdom of peace, a day when Ephraim and Judah would again be one, a day when that peace (that is, the gospel message) would cover the earth "from sea even to sea, and from the river even to the ends of the earth." (Zech. 9:10.) We look to a future day when that part of the prophecy not fulfilled in Christ's first coming finds completion in the era of millennial rest.

4. Literal fulfillment of this prophecy would come in A.D. 70, when Titus and his Roman legion would lay siege to the city, destroy the temple so that not one stone would be left standing upon another, and take into slavery that remnant of his people who did not suffer death in its siege and destruction. Those of his captives who did not die in bondage would eventually be scattered to the ends of the earth.

5. Joseph Fielding McConkie, *Gospel Symbolism* (Salt Lake City: Bookcraft, 1985), pp. 10-11.

6. Bruce R. McConkie, *Doctrinal New Testament Commentary,* 3 vols. (Salt Lake City: Bookcraft, 1965-73), 1:585. See also JST, Matt. 21:13.

7. Bruce R. McConkie, *The Mortal Messiah,* 4 vols. (Salt Lake City: Deseret Book, 1979-81), 3:356.

8. These words were part of the *Hallel*, which all Jewry chanted in their ceremonies. As such, they were well known to those whom the Savior addressed. A tradition among the Jews held that in the building of the temple, one stone was originally rejected by the builders, who did not know for what purpose it had been quarried. Later it was discovered that it was indeed the chief cornerstone. See J. R. Dummelow, *A Commentary on the Holy Bible* (New York: Macmillan, 1973), p. 372.

9. Joseph Fielding McConkie, *Gospel Symbolism,* p. 132.

10. *Clarke's Commentary* 3:210.

11. *Gospel Symbolism,* pp. 132-33.

12. *The Mortal Messiah* 3:369-70.

13. *Jesus the Christ* (Salt Lake City: Deseret Book, 1957), pp. 546-47.

14. This issue has been confused among Latter-day Saints. Critics of Mormonism have frequently used this passage to discount the principle of eternal marriage. A typical response to this criticism has been to agree that there will be no marriage after the resurrection, for all such matters will be attended to prior to that time. Whether that will be the case or not, we have no way of knowing. We should remember, however, that the first resurrection precedes the millennial era, when it is supposed that such matters will be attended to. This passage does not say that there cannot be marriage in the Millennium or at some subsequent time. It simply states that unbelievers, "Sadducees," be they ancient or modern, cannot be sealed for time and eternity. See Robert L. Millet and Joseph Fielding McConkie, *The Life Beyond* (Salt Lake City: Bookcraft, 1986), pp. 98-100.

15. *Jesus the Christ,* p. 558.

16. Jesus here referred to "Zacharias son of Barachias, whom ye slew between the temple and the altar." This has been thought to be John the Baptist's father, but this tradition of his death comes from a late Christian apocryphal book. (See Robert L. Millet, "The Birth and Childhood of the Messiah," chapter 8 of this volume, note 20.) The idea also finds expression in *Teachings of the Prophet Joseph Smith,* p. 261, which may not have been written by the Prophet. The Zechariah familiar to Jesus' audience was the son of Jehoiada who rebuked Israel and was stoned "in the court of the house of the Lord." (2 Chr. 24:20-22.) The Hebrew Bible arranged Genesis first and Chronicles last, so Jesus probably gave the first and last martyrs in his testimony to the Jews.

17. *The Mortal Messiah* 3:405.

18. *Doctrinal New Testament Commentary* 1:626.

26

THE OLIVET DISCOURSE
(Matthew 24-25; Mark 13; Luke 21:5-36)

DAVID R. SEELY

"Behold, your house is left unto you desolate. For I say unto you, Ye shall not see me henceforth, till ye shall say, Blessed is he that cometh in the name of the Lord." (Matt. 23:38-39.) With these foreboding words from the Old Testament,[1] Jesus ended his discourse found in Matthew 23. In the discourse, he condemned the hypocrisy of the scribes and Pharisees, who fastidiously attended to the forms of the law but neglected its ethical substance, pronouncing woes upon them for their behavior and lamenting Jerusalem's long history of rejecting the Lord's prophets. He then made these veiled references to the impending destruction of Jerusalem and the temple and to his return in glory.

Not One Stone upon Another

As he left the temple, Jesus pointed to the magnificent buildings in the temple complex and said to his disciples: "See ye not all these things? Verily I say unto you, There shall not be left here one stone upon another, that shall not be thrown down." (Matt. 24:1-2.) This prophecy of the destruction of the temple set the stage for his Olivet Discourse, which is found in Matthew 24 and 25. Juxtaposed with the preceding discourse, it echoes the ancient words of Jeremiah's Temple Sermon, which had been uttered in a similar situation. (Jer. 7, 26.)

David R. Seely is a doctrinal candidate in Near Eastern Studies at the University of Michigan and an instructor in religion at Albion College in Albion, Michigan.

In the final days before the Babylonian destruction in 587 B.C., Jeremiah was disturbed that the people were confident of deliverance from their enemies and trusted in "lying words, saying, The temple of the Lord, The temple of the Lord, The temple of the Lord." (Jer. 7:4.) While they were guilty of adultery, murder, lying, and stealing, and of oppressing the poor, the stranger, the fatherless, and the widow (Jer. 7:6, 9), they came and stood before the Lord—before the house that bore his name—and declared, "We are delivered to do all these abominations." (Jer. 7:10.) Jeremiah reminded the people of the previous destruction of the temple at Shiloh and then prophesied, "This house shall be like Shiloh, and this city shall be desolate without an inhabitant." (Jer. 26:9.) And it was Jeremiah's words from the same sermon that Jesus earlier had used when he had cleansed the temple: "My house shall be called the house of prayer; but ye have made it a den of thieves." (Matt. 21:13; Jer. 7:11.) He alluded to Jeremiah to make the same point: just as the Lord did not deliver his people in their wickedness from the Philistines at Shiloh, or from the Babylonians in 587 B.C., neither would he deliver "whited sepulchres" from the Romans.

The burning of Herod's grandiose temple implied a national disaster that transcended the physical destruction of a building. The temple represented first and foremost the presence of the Lord in the midst of his people—the true King in the midst of his kingdom—the kingdom of God. It represented the covenant he had made with his people from the beginning that they would be his people and he would be their God. In Old Testament times, it came to represent the eternal covenant that had been made with the dynasty of David, from whose loins would come Jesus the Messiah, and was a symbol of a once great empire. In the New Testament period, it represented the proud national religion of a semi-autonomous state, which in the days of the Maccabees had cleansed the temple from the "abomination of desolation" decreed by Antiochus Epiphanes in 168 B.C.

Therefore, this prophecy must have been a shock to the disciples who had witnessed the coming of the "kingdom of heaven" and the presence of the King. How were they to understand the destruction of this great symbol and the devastation it would entail? And how was this event to be related to the return of the Savior in his glory, signaling the end of the world?

"When Shall These Things Be?"

As they sat on the Mount of Olives, with the temple and the Holy City spread out before them, the disciples voiced their perplexity: "Tell us, when shall these things be? and what shall be the sign of thy coming, and of the end of the world?" (Matt. 24:3.)[2] The key to understanding the Olivet Discourse is to find the answers to these two questions, both of which Jesus carefully addressed.[3] It is important also to note the purpose of apocalyptic or eschatological[4] prophecy. While it is apparent that one of the primary functions of such prophecies is to warn the wicked and righteous alike of impending destruction and judgment, it is also clear that such prophecies provide comfort and assurance to the righteous. For example, throughout Matthew 24 and 25 the Lord provided promises for those who are prepared to meet him: "He that shall endure unto the end, the same shall be saved" (Matt. 24:13); "Blessed is that servant, whom his lord when he cometh shall find so doing" (Matt. 24:46); "Then shall the King say unto them on his right hand, Come, ye blessed of my Father, inherit the kingdom prepared for you from the foundation of the world" (Matt. 25:34). These prophecies demonstrate that in spite of the future calamities, the Lord God knows and controls the course of history; eventually justice will prevail, and whoever "shall endure unto the end, the same shall be saved." (Matt. 24:13.)

Matthew 24 and Latter-day Revelation

The importance of the assurance provided by such warnings for the Latter-day Saints, as well as the ancient disciples, was reiterated in 1831, when the Lord revealed a much expanded version of this prophetic discourse to the restored church in section 45 of the Doctrine and Covenants. In fact, in the period of persecution and crisis in the early days of the Church, the Lord gave several important revelations on the subject of the last days in Doctrine and Covenants 29 (1830), 1, 43, 45, and 133 (1831), and 116 (1838), which helped the Saints to keep a proper perspective and to recognize that in spite of difficulties of mortality, the Lord had not forgotten them and would not forsake them. The prophecy was further clarified when Joseph Smith, in the process of his inspired translation of the New Testament, expanded and reordered the New Testament text in what is now contained in the Pearl of Great Price as Joseph Smith–Matthew. Serious study of Matthew 24 is greatly facilitated by a careful reading and comparison of these three accounts. While a comprehensive analysis of these versions of the text (as well as the parallel synoptic accounts found in Mark 13 and Luke 21) is beyond the scope of this study, several Latter-day Saint scholars have recently published excellent discussions of the contents of and relationships between the texts.[5]

Matthew 24, as it stands in the New Testament, addresses both the destruction of Jerusalem, which was to happen in A.D. 70, and the Second Coming of the Messiah, which is to occur in the future. Most agree that the two periods are described in Matthew in similar language, with no absolute distinction between which signs and events applied to each period.

On the other hand, section 45 contains a significantly different text and makes a clear division between those events that transpired in the days of the apostles and those that are still to take place in the future. Doctrine and Covenants 45:16-25 deals with events pertaining to the destruction of Jerusalem in A.D. 70 while verses 26-59 deal with events connected with the present and the future—from the "times of the Gentiles" (the restoration of the gospel) until the glorious return of the Son of God, when he will declare to all the world, "I am he who was lifted up. I am Jesus that was crucified." (D&C 45:52.)[6]

Richard Draper has recently described Joseph Smith's inspired translation of Matthew 24 as both a substantial expansion and a reordering of the text: "To the basic text the Prophet added nearly four hundred fifty new words, representing about a fifty percent increase in the text size. . . . Even so, there is only one verse (v. 55) to which there is not correlation in the King James Bible. Yet it is not only in adding material that the revealed version gives understanding but more especially in the *reordering* of the material."[7] Joseph Smith's reorganization (and repetition) of many of the verses in Matthew 24 has also resulted in a general division of the material between that which pertains to the Roman destruction of the temple and the fate of the apostles (JS–M 1:1-21a), and the portion that is relevant to the future return of the Savior (JS–M 1:21b-55). Perhaps this reorganization is best demonstrated by the following table.

Joseph Smith–Matthew	Matthew 24
1	23:39
2-6	1-5
7-11	9-13
12-18	15-21
19	8
20-21a	22
———————————division past/future———————————	
21b-22	23-24
23	6
24-27	25-28
28-29	6-7
30	12
31-32	14-15
33	29
34-35	34-35
36-39	30-33
40-54	36-51
55	

Note that Matthew 24:6, 7, and 14 have been relocated in Joseph Smith–Matthew to clearly refer to the future. Several verses in Matthew 24 are repeated in Joseph Smith–Matthew: 24:6 = JS–M 1:23 and 28; 24:12 = JS–M 1:10 and 30; and 24:15 = JS–M 1:12 and 32. In several cases this suggests that these verses are relevant to both time periods.

It is clear that the prophecies contained in Matthew 24 are very important for Latter-day Saints. The dramatic fulfillment of those prophecies that were given to the apostles of the early Church testify of the veracity of those prophecies that apply to the future. The Lord, through his servant Joseph Smith, has provided much modern revelation that illuminates the ancient biblical record and stands as a solemn witness of his love and concern for his children and as a warning that we should carefully heed.

The Signs of the Times

In Matthew 24:4-31, Jesus prophesied the many "signs of the times" that would accompany the destruction of Jerusalem and the eventual coming of the Son of Man. As indicated above, often in the biblical account there is little distinction between the two times of crisis. In this study we will follow the order of Matthew 24, noting significant relocations and important expansions provided by Joseph Smith–Matthew, and keeping in mind the two questions the disciples asked: "*When* shall these things happen?" and "*What* will be the signs?"

Verses 4-8 indicate that there will be false Christs, wars, famines, pestilences, and earthquakes, but that this will only be "the beginning of sorrows." At the same time Jesus told his disciples that they should not be troubled: "for all these things must come to pass, but the end is not yet." (Matt. 24:6.) History bears witness that all of these things occurred.

In verses 9 through 14, Jesus described what would happen to the disciples and the Church, indicating that they would be killed and that there would be confusion, betrayal, and deception in the Church. The prediction that "iniquity shall abound, the love of many shall wax cold" is repeated twice, in verses 10 and 30 of Joseph Smith–Matthew, and apparently applies to both time periods. Then Jesus added the assurance that those who endure to the end would be saved. The prophecy that "the gospel of the kingdom shall be preached in all the world for a witness unto all nations" (Matt. 24:14), even in its present position in the biblical text, makes good sense—that the "end" cannot come until the gospel is taken to all the nations. Nevertheless, it has been moved to verse 31 in Joseph Smith–Matthew, and thus it clearly refers to the period before the return of the Son of Man.

Verses 15-22 seem to relate specifically to the destruction of Jerusalem. The abomination of desolation, prophesied by Daniel (Dan. 11:31, 12:11), is cited as one of the telltale signs of the destruction. The prophecy about the abomination of desolation is clearly a symbol of desecration and/or destruction of the Temple of Jerusalem, a prophecy that clearly may have more than one fulfillment. In the apocryphal literature, it was applied to the desecration of the temple in 168 B.C. by Antiochus Epiphanes (1 Macc. 1:54; 2 Macc. 6:2), which precipitated the Maccabean Revolt and resulted in the eventual cleansing and rededication in 165 B.C. Jesus was most certainly referring to the desecration and destruction of the temple by the Romans under Titus in A.D. 70. Those who were in Judea were urged to "flee into the mountains" and to do so in haste. Many have seen this admonition as the motivating force behind the fact that many of the Jerusalem Christians apparently heeded the signs of the times and fled to safety in Pella just before Jerusalem fell in A.D. 70.[8]

Again there is a faint note of hope that "for the elect's sake those days shall be shortened." (Matt. 24:22.) Verse 20 of Joseph Smith–Matthew adds, "but for the elect's sake, *according to the covenant,*" which suggests the elect are members of the covenant community—the Church. Matthew 24:15, the prophecy about the abomination of desolation, appears twice in Joseph Smith–Matthew—in verses 12 and 32—and therefore appears to be both a prophecy of the destruction in A.D. 70 and a prophecy that will be fulfilled by an unspecified act or acts of unrighteousness, desecration, or blasphemy at some future date before the Second Coming. (See D&C 84:117; 88:84-85.)

The time of the end and the coming of the Son of Man are the focal points of verses 25-31. Again, warnings are made about not being deceived by the rise of false Christs, or those who would say that he has come in secret. Jesus declared that "as the lightning cometh out of the east, and shineth even unto the west; so shall also the coming of the Son of man be." (Matt. 24:27.) The image of the eagles gathered together over the carcass in verse 28 is interpreted in verse 27 of Joseph Smith–Matthew as a parable signifying the gathering of the elect from the four corners of the earth. The signs of the Son of Man will not be obscure and unnoticed, but will be of cosmic proportions involving the sun, the moon, and the stars; and all of the "tribes of the earth" shall see him as he comes in his glory. The expanded account in Doctrine and Covenants 45:40-59 recounts, along with many other terrible portents and wonders, that he will come to the Mount of Olives—the very site of the discourse—and split it asunder as a sign to the Jews of his return.

"Watch, Therefore: for Ye Know Not the Hour"

In his discourse, Jesus included four short examples that help to illustrate the points he was making. The parable of the fig tree (Matt. 24:32-35) teaches that the signs, while not specifying the exact time, will give a general indication as to the "season" of the coming of the Son of Man; Jesus assured his disciples that all of these prophecies would indeed come to pass. In its original context, the phrase in verse 34, "this generation shall not pass away," may have applied to the destruction in A.D. 70, which many at the time of Jesus would live to see. In Joseph Smith—Matthew 1:34 it is related to the return of the Son of Man.

Using the example of the destruction in the days of Noah, Jesus taught that while the signs of the times will indicate the season, no one knows the day and the hour of the end. (Matt. 24:36.) As in the days of Noah, so the Son of Man will come while many are carrying on their normal day-to-day activities, and "two women shall be grinding at the mill; the one shall be taken, and the other left." (Matt. 24:40-41.)

Furthermore, because no one will know the precise moment, many will be unprepared when the end comes. Jesus illustrated the day of the Lord coming as a thief in the night and warned the disciples that they should always be ready: "for in such an hour as ye think not the Son of man cometh." (Matt. 24:42-44.) This point is further emphasized by the parable of the wise and faithful servant (Matt. 24:45-51) who diligently fulfills his duties even when his master is away—in contrast to the evil servant who, because his master delays his coming, is caught unexpectedly abusing his stewardship when the master does arrive.

In short, the answer to the disciples' questions as to when these things will occur is that there will be many signs of the coming, and yet the end will come when many least expect it.

The Parable of the Ten Virgins

"Then shall the kingdom of heaven be likened unto ten virgins." (Matt. 25:1.) With this phrase, Jesus introduced two parables, the ten virgins and the talents, that illustrate the necessity of preparation for the Second Coming. In Matthew's account of the Lord's ministry, Jesus introduced many of his parables with the phrase "likened unto." He likened the kingdom of heaven to the sower in the parable of the tares (13:24); the mustard seed (13:31); leaven (13:33); the pearl of great price (13:45); the net (13:47); the king in the parable of the unmerciful servant (18:23); the laborers in the vineyard (20:1); and the marriage feast (22:2). All of these comparisons demonstrate that the kingdom of heaven in the context of the parables represents the members of the earthly kingdom or the Church.[9]

The parable of the virgins portrays the coming of the king of the kingdom of heaven as the coming of the Bridegroom. The relationship of the Lord with his people—that is, the covenant—is often symbolized in the Old and New Testaments by the imagery of marriage. It is perhaps one of the most poignant images in the Bible and eloquently describes the intimacy, mutual commitment, and eternal nature of the covenant.[10] The Lord often referred to Israel as his maiden bride whom he took by covenant at Sinai: "I remember thee, the kindness of thy youth, the love of thine espousals, when thou wentest after me in the wilderness, in a land that was not sown." (Jer. 2:2.) Marriage as a covenant captures the conditional nature of the Mosaic covenant as well, and Israel's idolatry and her going after strange gods is aptly portrayed throughout the Old Testament as adultery. (See especially Hosea 2.) The New Testament continues this imagery, and in Revelation 19:7-9, the righteous saints are portrayed as the bride awaiting the consummation of the marriage at the Second Coming of the Lamb.

In the parable of the virgins, the ten are apparently attendants of the Bridegroom.[11] Five of them are wise and carefully supply their lamps with oil; the other five are foolish and neglect to procure the necessary oil. When the bridegroom finally does come, only half of the virgins are properly prepared to meet him. There is only enough oil for those who brought it themselves, and they are allowed to enter into the marriage ceremony. Those without oil are unable to enter. The point of the parable in relationship to the questions initially posed by the disciples is that the bridegroom tarries longer than expected, and no one knows "the day nor the hour wherein the Son of man cometh." (Matt. 25:13.) It is necessary to be prepared always to meet him, and the preparation is not merely a community effort; rather, it is the responsibility of each individual involved.

The relevance of this parable for members of the Church in all ages is obvious. Besides illustrating the necessity to be prepared for the judgment that will accompany the Second Coming, the fragile nature of mortality itself—which can unexpectedly come to an end at any moment—necessitates the same constant preparation. In latter-day revelations contained in the Doctrine and Covenants, the Lord refers to this parable several times in instructions to individuals as well as to the Church in general as a warning to prepare for his coming. (See D&C 33:17-18; 45:56; 63:54; 65:3; 88:92; 133:10, 19.)

The Parable of the Talents

The parable of the talents is a continuation of the simile with the kingdom of heaven. While the phrase "the kingdom of heaven" does not appear in the Greek (as indicated by the italics in the King James Version), the Greek particles that do appear suggest that this phrase has been ellipsed, and, as with the first parable, that this one is to be compared with the kingdom of heaven.

The language of the parable is financial, perhaps because people have always been able to understand these terms. The meaning of the word *talent* as a "natural ability" is a secondary definition of a word that originally meant a Greek monetary weight or coin. The meaning of *ability* did not occur until the Middle Ages, perhaps due largely to its usage in this parable. While of course the meaning of *talent* as "natural ability" can well be one of the meanings of this parable, we should not be limited to this interpretation. The parable proceeds to show how the Lord has blessed *everyone* in the kingdom with varying abilities and opportunities to serve. Those who are willing to use these blessings are able to double their worth to the kingdom. The one who is unwilling to use his endowment from the Lord is cast out as an "unprofitable servant," and that which was given to him is lost. In fact, the nature of service in the kingdom may well be referred to in the section following the parable, Matthew 25:35-46, where the Lord defines what a "profitable" servant does in order to "inherit the kingdom prepared" for him in the hereafter. Again the parable relates to two basic issues: (1) "after a long time the lord of those servants cometh" (Matt. 25:19), which suggests that there will be delay in his coming; and (2) at his coming many will not be prepared.

"Inasmuch as Ye Have Done
It unto One of the Least"

The final section of the Olivet Discourse contains one of the most sublime principles taught by the Son of Man. The theme is judgment, and Jesus clearly taught his disciples the priorities of membership in the kingdom of heaven both on earth and in heaven. Matthew 25:31-34 describes how the Son of Man—the Messiah—will return, and explains that it is he who will be the judge of all of his creation. The judgment will consist of a basic separation of the two groups that were illustrated in the two preceding parables: those who are prepared and have magnified their opportunities as members of the kingdom and those who are unprepared and therefore are to be cast out.

The image of judgment is a pastoral one: the King will come to his kingdom as the Shepherd to separate the sheep from the goats. The King of heaven and earth, the Judge of all nations, the Son of Man, sat before his disciples and taught them the dignity and divinity of each of the sons and daughters of God. He illustrated the pivotal point of the judgment that determined each individual's eternal reward: "Then shall the King say unto them on this right hand, Come, ye blessed of my Father, inherit the kingdom prepared for you from the foundation of the world: for I was an hungred, and ye gave me meat: I was thirsty, and ye gave me drink: I was a stranger, and ye took me in: naked, and ye clothed me: I was sick, and ye visited me: I was in prison, and ye came unto me." (Matt. 25:34-36.) Not remembering any such occasions, the righteous will question, "Lord, when saw we thee an hungred, and fed thee? or thirsty, and gave thee drink? When saw we thee a stranger, and took thee in? or naked, and clothed thee? Or when saw we thee sick, or in prison, and came to thee? And the King shall answer and say unto them, Verily I say unto you, Inasmuch as ye have done it unto one of the least of these my brethren, ye have done it unto me." (Matt. 25:37-40.)

With these words Jesus summed up the substance of the Mosaic law that had been on the lips of all the prophets before him—echoing the words of Jeremiah in the shadow of the temple when he warned the people that their survival did not depend on ritual purity and sacrifical offerings, but that they "oppress not the stranger, the fatherless, and the widow." (Jer. 7:6.)

In the events of the ensuing days, Jesus would himself become as the "least" in kingdom, and he would descend below all things in order to raise man from death and sin. He, as the Suffering Servant, would take upon himself the sins of all mankind, and he would give his life that man might live. He would set the ultimate example for all who would take upon themselves his name and witness that "pure religion and undefiled before God and the Father is this, To visit the fatherless and the widows in their affliction, and to keep [oneself] unspotted from the world." (James 1:27.)

NOTES

1. "Behold, your house is left unto you desolate" is reminiscent of the prophecies that refer to the presence of the Lord departing from Jerusalem in Jeremiah 12:7; 22:5; and Ezekiel 10:18-19; and 11:22-23. "Blessed is he that cometh in the name of the Lord" is from Psalm 118:26. Joseph Smith's inspired translation of this verse, Joseph Smith–Matthew 1:1, adds, "Then understood his disciples that he should come again on the earth, after that he was glorified and crowned on the right hand of God," explicitly stating that the disciples clearly understood that he was referring to his return in glory.

2. Joseph Smith–Matthew 1:4 adds, "Tell us when shall these things be which thou hast said concerning the destruction of the temple, and the Jews; and what is the sign of thy coming, and of the end of the world, or the destruction of the wicked, which is the end of the world?" This further demonstrates that the disciples realized the import of what Jesus had prophesied and clarifies the meaning of the term "end of the world."

3. Joseph Smith identified this as a useful method of scripture study: "I have a key by which I understand the scriptures. I enquire, what was the question which drew out the answer, or caused Jesus to utter the parable." *(Teachings of the Prophet Joseph Smith,* pp. 276-77.)

4. *Eschatology* is a term derived from a Greek word that means *last things* and refers to teachings about the end-time (judgment, resurrection, Second Coming of Christ, and so forth). Matthew 24 and its synoptic parallels in Mark 13 and Luke 21 are also often referred to as "The Little Apocalypse," as compared with the larger New Testament apocalyptic book of Revelation. The term *apocalyptic* literally means *from hiding, disclosure,* or *revelation,* and refers to visionary writings that also deal with the end of the world. The two terms are often interchangeable.

5. For an excellent discussion of Doctrine and Covenants 45, along with the other latter-day revelations (sections 29, 43, 116, and 133) about the signs of the times, see Kent P. Jackson, "The Signs of the Times: Be Not Troubled," in *Studies in Scripture, Vol. 1: The Doctrine and Covenants,* ed.

Robert L. Millet and Kent P. Jackson (Sandy, Utah: Randall Book, 1984), pp. 186-200. Recent studies comparing Joseph Smith's inspired translation of Matthew 24 (found in Joseph Smith—Matthew in the Pearl of Great Price) are Richard L. Anderson, "Joseph Smith's Insights into the Olivet Prophecy: Joseph Smith 1 and Matthew 24," *Pearl of Great Price Symposium* (Provo, Utah: Brigham Young University, 1975), pp. 48-61, and Richard D. Draper, "Joseph Smith—Matthew and the Signs of the Times," *Studies in Scripture, Vol. 2: The Pearl of Great Price,* ed. Robert L. Millet and Kent P. Jackson (Sandy, Utah: Randall Book, 1985), pp. 287-302.

6. For a detailed discussion of the contents and structure of Doctrine and Covenants 45, see Jackson, pp. 188-92.

7. Draper, pp. 289-90. Draper discusses throughout the article the implications of this chronological reordering for an understanding of Joseph Smith—Matthew. (Note Draper's note 9, p. 300, which should read "verse 7 became *29* [instead of 23], v. 8 became *19* [instead of 29] and v. 9 became v. 7 [instead of 19]."

8. Eusebius records, "Furthermore, the members of the Jerusalem church, by means of an oracle given by revelation to acceptable persons there, were ordered to leave the City before the war began and settle in a town in Peraea called Pella. To Pella those who believed in Christ migrated from Jerusalem." *(Ecclesiastical History* 5:4, translation from G. A. Williamson's *Eusebius: The History of the Church from Christ to Constantine* [Minneapolis: Augsburg Publishing House, 1965], p. 111.) While it is not clear if the passage in Matthew 24 had anything to do with the preservation of the Jerusalem Christian community as Eusebius records, it certainly is not impossible that it was circulating at the time. In fact, some have interpreted the editorial remark in parentheses in verse 15 "(whoso readeth, let him understand)" as an addition to a document containing Jesus' Olivet Discourse that was circulated at this time to facilitate the Christian exodus from Jerusalem.

9. The kingdom of heaven in the scriptures often refers to the heavenly or celestial kingdom. (See, for example, D&C 6:37; 10:55; 58:2; Alma 11:37-40.) Even in Matthew, it sometimes refers to the heavenly kingdom. For example, see Matthew 7:21-23. It appears, however, that the specialized usage of the phrase in the parables almost always refers to the covenant community of the Church.

10. See Kent P. Jackson, "The Marriage of Hosea and Jehovah's Covenant with Israel," in *Isaiah and the Prophets,* ed. Monte S. Nyman (Provo, Utah: Religious Studies Center, Brigham Young University, 1983), pp. 57-73.

11. Some have observed that Near Eastern marriage customs generally attest to groups of virgins waiting on the bride rather than on the bride-

groom. Several Greek manuscripts include in Matthew 25:1 the phrase "the bridegroom and the bride," which would suggest that the virgins are part of the bride's party waiting for the couple, making it easier to see a one-to-one correspondence in the parable, with the virgins and the bride as the church and the bridegroom as the Son of Man.

27

THE FAREWELL OF JESUS
(Matthew 26:20-35; Mark 14:17-25; Luke 22:1-38; John 13–17)

RODNEY TURNER

The public ministry was over. For three years Jesus had walked among the people bearing witness in word and deed of his divine calling. Although rejected by most (but not all) local and national Jewish leaders (John 3:1-2; 12:42), he was esteemed by many of the common people as a miracle worker, a great teacher, a prophet, and even among some as the long-sought Messiah (John 1:41; 7:40-43; 10:19-25).

But it may well be that no one comprehended that he was the Lord God Jehovah come to earth as the literal Son of God.[1] Although the Holy Scriptures described God in anthropomorphic terms, Judaism did not define him as a material being. Then too, Judaism was, and is, totally monotheistic; there is only one God.[2] Belief in a Godhead comprised of three deities (tritheism) was quite unthinkable. Equally absurd to them would have been the notion that God could have a literal Son.[3] Thus, references to God as "Father," or to his children (as in Ps. 82:6), were employed only metaphorically.[4] Jesus' disciples were raised in this centuries-old tradition. Only with the passage of time were they enlightened as to Jesus' real identity and God's true nature.

The awesome truth that Jesus was more than a mortal man—however spiritually empowered—first began to dawn upon his grieving, bewildered disciples with his appearance to them the night following his resurrection.[5] That his resurrection was totally unexpected is evi-

---

Rodney Turner is professor of ancient scripture at Brigham Young University.

dent in the combined testimony of the Gospel writers. (Luke 24:6-12, 22-25; Matt. 28:17; Mark 16:9-11, 14; John 20:9-15, 24-29.) The claim of the women that Jesus had appeared to them was rejected by the apostles "as idle tales, and they believed them not." (Luke 24:11.) "For as yet they knew not the scripture, that he must rise again from the dead." (John 20:9.) No one was more surprised to see the risen Christ than those who were called to be his special witnesses. Indeed, the chief priests and Pharisees paid more heed to Jesus' statement, "After three days I will rise again" (Matt. 27:63), than did his own disciples— hence the guard at the tomb (Matt. 27:62-66).

The Last Supper and the Sacrament

It is against this background of apostolic uncertainty concerning who and what Jesus really was that the solemn events associated with his farewell to the Twelve took place. The patience, the love, and the gentle instruction he manifested on that occasion must be seen in the context of his own terrible loneliness—to be at heart unknown and a stranger to those nearest and most precious to him. His loneliness was intensified beyond human comprehension in the greatest ordeal ever imposed upon any soul in all eternity. That ordeal was but hours away, as he ministered to his uncomprehending apostles for the last time in mortality.

The Savior's thirty-third birthday occurred just four days before he sat with the Twelve for the last time.[6] According to John's account, the week-long feast of unleavened bread would begin with the Passover meal the following evening. However, Jesus would not live to partake of it; the Last Supper was to be his last Passover as well.[7]

The death of the Lamb of God at about the ninth hour (3 P.M.) the following afternoon officially ended the practice of animal sacrifice that had been instituted in the days of Adam.[8] It also rendered null and void the law of Moses, together with all of its ritual aspects. The death of Jesus was the legal death of the old covenant, even as his resurrection symbolized the rebirth of the new covenant—the law of Christ. (Jer. 31:31-34; Heb. 8:6-13.) Consequently, Jehovah, the God of Israel who gave the feast of the Passover (Ex. 12:1-11) was, with his apostles, the last to lawfully partake of that feast on this earth.

Washing of Feet

Only John recounts Jesus washing the feet of the Twelve. This lesson in humility was to be a graphic reminder to the apostles of the spirit that was to accompany all that they did as the Savior's special witnesses. No service was to be beneath them; no soul was unworthy of their ministrations.

In a way not now fully understood, the washing of feet also figured in Jewish ritual: "Now this was the custom of the Jews under their law; wherefore Jesus did this that the law might be fulfilled." (JST, John 13:10; see Ex. 30:19; 40:31.) That he did so demonstrates the exactness with which he observed every "jot and tittle" of the law that he himself had given ancient Israel. (See Matt. 5:18.)

Those who acted in the Savior's behalf were to be both physically and morally clean. "Be ye clean, that bear the vessels of the Lord." (Isa. 52:11.) In modern times, any brother participating in the "School of the prophets" in Kirtland, Ohio, in 1833 was to be "clean from the blood of this generation; and he shall be received by the ordinance of the washing of feet, for unto this end was the ordinance of the washing of feet instituted."[9] (D&C 88:138-39.)

Peter's impulsive rejection of the ordinance, followed by his equally impulsive response to his Master's solemn rebuke—"If I wash thee not, thou hast no part with me" (John 13:8)—obscured a far more terrible drama when the Son of Man, like any menial slave, knelt before Judas Iscariot and washed and dried his feet. What thoughts besieged the young apostle as he looked down upon the quiet Galilean? What emotions swept through him when his eyes met the eyes of his knowing Lord? What could Jesus have done more calculated to move the alienated disciple with compassion and swerve him from his dark intent than the simple act of kneeling before him in humblest of services? But it was to no avail. The Judean apostle had surrendered his will to another master. His course was fixed. He was committed to betrayal.

The Sacrament: A New Ordinance

John alone recorded the sermon on the bread of life (John 6:26-58) wherein Jesus alluded to the sacrament by saying, among other things, "He that eateth my flesh, and drinketh my blood, dwelleth in me, and I in him." (John 6:56.) It is, therefore, most strange that John failed to mention the institution of the sacrament at the Last Supper.[10] This vital information is found in the other three Gospels and in Paul's letter to the Corinthians. (1 Cor. 11:23-26.)[11]

Jesus introduced the sacrament as a natural, foreordained extension of the Passover meal being eaten at the time. The blood of the paschal lamb—which had temporarily saved the firstborn of ancient Israel from physical death—was a sign of the blood of the Lamb of God, the Firstborn, which permanently delivered all mankind both from physical and (on conditions of repentance) spiritual death. By instituting the ordinance of the sacrament, Jesus used the bread and wine of the Passover. In doing so, the Passover meal, with its limited symbolism, was absorbed into the sacrament of the Lord's supper, with its universal symbolism. The lesser was swallowed up in the greater. Thus, the Passover was fulfilled in the sacrament, even as the Law of Moses was fulfilled in Christ.

The Savior broke and blessed unleavened bread and, giving it to the Twelve, said: "Take, eat; this is in remembrance of my body which I give a ransom for you." (JST, Matt. 26:22.) Mark adds: "For as oft as ye do this ye will remember this hour that I was with you." (JST, Mark 14:21.)

After expressing thanks, Jesus then passed a cup of wine, saying: "Drink ye all of it. For this is in remembrance of my blood of the new testament [the gospel covenant], which is shed for as many as shall believe on my name, for the remission of their sins." (JST, Matt. 26:23-24.)[12] Again Mark adds: "As oft as ye do this ordinance, ye will remember me in this hour that I was with you and drank with you of this cup, even the last time in my ministry." (JST, Mark 14:24.) Such was the common cup Jesus shared with his chosen witnesses, the cup that symbolized another cup he would drink alone—and to its dregs. (See D&C 19:18.)

Yet there would be still another cup, one overflowing with joy, that Jesus would share with the righteous in a glorious reaffirmation of his triumph over death and hell: "I will not drink henceforth of this fruit of the vine, until that day when I shall come and drink it new with you in my Father's kingdom." (JST, Matt. 26:26.) "That day" refers to the millennial day; the setting is the millennial earth; and the partakers will be the first Twelve (less one) and all of the mighty prophets, seers, and revelators, together "with all those whom [the] Father hath given . . . out of the world" since time began. (D&C 27:5-14.) Thus, we partake of the sacramental emblems not only in remembrance of what Jesus has done, but also in testimony of what he will yet do: return as earth's only rightful King and Lawgiver. (D&C 45:59.)[13]

The Traitor

The four Gospels contain a number of passages leading up to the Last Supper in which Jesus alluded to his death.[14] John, stressing Jesus' seership and foreknowledge, stated that Jesus "knew from the beginning who . . . should betray him." (John 6:64, 71; 13:11.)[15] However, although Jesus had explicitly foretold his death on at least three prior occasions to his uncomprehending disciples (Matt. 16:21-22; 17:22-23; 20:17-19), it was not until the Last Supper that he revealed the presence of a traitor among the Twelve (John 13:21).

The Synoptics tell of Judas Iscariot agreeing to inform the chief priests (Sadducees, who controlled the temple) of the most opportune time to arrest Jesus. (Luke 22:3-6.)[16] They also state that each of the apostles—not knowing the traitor's identity, and assuming that Jesus was speaking of some occasion in the distant future—wondered if he himself would be the guilty party: "Lord, is it I?" (Matt. 26:22.)[17] Only Matthew records that when Judas asked "Master, is it I?" Jesus answered, "Thou hast said"—meaning "Yes." (Matt. 26:25.) However, the identity of the traitor remained unknown to the other apostles. Nothing more is said in the Synoptics of the traitor. Nor, strangely, is there any reference to Judas ever leaving the group. And yet, it is obvious that he did so at some time that night, since he was with the arresting soldiers hours later.

According to John, it was following the washing of the apostles' feet that Jesus spoke of a traitor among the Twelve. This prompted Simon Peter to quietly ask John (always unnamed in his Gospel) to ask the Lord the traitor's identity. Jesus signified that it was Judas Iscariot by giving a him a sop (a morsel) from the common dish. John—and presumably Peter—then knew that the betrayer was their Judean brother. Evidently, this byplay went unnoticed by the other apostles. (John 13:21-30.)

Jesus then told Judas, "That thou doest, do quickly." Although heard by all, the Lord's words were understood by none save Judas himself: "Now no man at the table knew for what intent he spake this unto him." (John 13:27-28.) Consequently no one—including Peter and John, who then knew that Judas was the traitor—attached any sinister meaning to Judas's immediate departure. Had they suspected that his perfidy was but hours away, it is doubtful that they would have allowed Judas to leave; but the imminent betrayal and death of Jesus was simply inconceivable to his followers.

The receiving of the sop from the hand of Jesus became a dark sacrament between Satan and Judas. It signified the passage of the treacherous apostle's allegiance from the Son of God to the enemy of all righteousness. Having succumbed to the devil's suggestion that he betray the Master (John 13:2), Judas spurned the Spirit of the Lord and "Satan entered into him" (John 13:27).[18] He became a man possessed by the devil himself! Thus, in reality, the ultimate betrayer of Jesus was the one who despised him above all men—Lucifer, a son of the morning, the brother who became Perdition. (D&C 76:25-26.)

Still, satanic possession does not absolve Judas Iscariot. He epitomized the proverbial warning: "Pride goeth before destruction." (Prov. 16:18.) According to Joseph Smith, Judas would not accept chastisement from Jesus: "Judas was rebuked and immediately betrayed his Lord into the hands of His enemies, because Satan entered into him."[19] Doubtless his defection occurred over a period of time, as little by little he allowed himself to be overcome by that spirit of him who was "a murderer from the beginning." (John 8:44.) This unseen master made Judas the instrument of his evil will and, having used him, discarded the pathetic wretch to his own ignominious destruction. Of the Twelve the Father had given Jesus, "none of them is lost, but the son of perdition."[20] (John 17:6, 9, 12; compare John 18:9.)

The Last Discourse

As we now have it, John's version of the Last Supper is somewhat enigmatic, being characterized by metaphor, abstractions, and a degree of redundancy.[21] It is a scriptural symphony, the movements of which weave back and forth around the great central theme of the Savior's imminent death and resurrection. For purposes of clarity and emphasis, the discourse will be treated in terms of its major concepts.

Jesus was now alone with the faithful eleven apostles. The moment had come for his final words of instruction, admonition, and promise. Some of the things he would say would become clear only after his resurrection. Other things would be made known when these disciples were blessed with the enlightenment of the Holy Ghost. In the meantime, Jesus continued to patiently guide them through their apostolic apprenticeships.

But whatever their initial limitations, we must not forget that the Father had given his Son the Twelve (John 17:6), whom Jesus thereafter chose and ordained (John 15:16). Indeed, Joseph Smith taught that they had been ordained to their holy callings "in the Grand Council of heaven before this world was."[22] This provides added meaning to the Lord's statement to them: "Ye also shall bear witness, because ye have been with me from the beginning." (John 15:27.)

"We Cannot Tell What He Saith"

Blinded by their misconceptions of the nature and mission of the Messiah, the apostles were perplexed by a number of the Lord's comments. Note their apparent lack of understanding in the following instances.[23]

Responding to Jesus' announcement that he would soon go away and that the apostles could not then come with him, Simon Peter asked: "Lord, whither goest thou?" Again told that he could not come with Jesus at that time but would do so later, Peter persisted: "Lord, why cannot I follow thee now? I will lay down my life for thy sake." Peter's boast—so characteristic of those empty commitments we all make but do not expect to be obliged to honor—did not go unchallenged: "Wilt thou lay down thy life for my sake? Verily, verily, I say unto thee, The cock shall not crow, till thou hast denied me thrice." (John 13:33, 36-38; Luke 22:31-34.)[24]

When Jesus told the Twelve that they knew where he was going and "the way" he was taking to get there, Thomas asked: "Lord, we know not whither thou goest; and how can we know the way?" (John 14:5.) Jesus then explained that he himself was the "way" by which men came unto the Father.

Jesus words—"If ye had known me, ye should have known my Father also: and from henceforth ye know him, and have seen him"— prompted Philip to ask: "Lord, shew us the Father, and it sufficeth us." (John 14:7-8.) Jesus then explained that he was the living revelation of the Father. To see and hear him was, in effect, to see and hear the Father.

Having promised the apostles that he would thereafter be seen by them but not by those of the world, Jesus was asked by Judas (Lebbaeus Thaddaeus): "Lord, how is it that thou wilt manifest thyself unto us, and not unto the world?" (John 14:22.) Jesus replied that both he and his Father would appear to, and enter into communion with, those who proved faithful to his teachings. Thereafter, Jesus made another cryptic reference to his approaching death: "A little while, and ye shall not see me: and again, a little while, and ye shall see me, because I go to the Father." (John 16:16.) The apostles were baffled by his words: "What is this that he saith, A little while? we cannot tell what he saith." (John 16:18.) In other words, "We don't know what he is talking about!" Elaborating on his words, the Savior likened his death and resurrection to a mother's delivery pains, which are swallowed up in the joy of her newborn child.

Jesus acknowledged that he had spoken "in proverbs," or figuratively, but he promised to speak plainly thereafter. (John 16:25.) In evidence of this change, he told the disciples that he came into the world from the Father and would leave the world and return to the Father. They responded, "Lo, now speakest thou plainly, and speakest no proverb. Now we are sure that thou knowest all things, . . . by this we believe that thou camest forth from God." But Jesus knew that their belief was flawed: "Do ye now believe? Behold, the hour cometh, yea, is now come, that ye shall be scattered, every man to his own, and shall leave me alone." (John 16:28-32; compare Matt. 26:31.)

The question of the apostles' belief in Jesus was raised several times at the Last Supper. It seems that their Master was trying to prepare the apostles for the devastating events of the next eighteen hours. Consequently, he predicted his betrayal so that "when it is come to pass, ye may believe that I am he." (John 13:19.) He foretold his ascension to the Father so that "when it is come to pass, ye might believe." (John 14:29.) He prophesied their own martyrdoms so that "ye may remember that I told you of them." (John 16:4.)

Acknowledging their belief in God, Jesus asked the apostles to "believe also in me." (John 14:1.) His remark, "If ye had known me, ye should have known my Father also" (John 14:7), prompted the request to show them the Father. Jesus then asked how he could have been with them so long a time without their knowing that he *was* the Father. Inasmuch as the Father—through the Holy Spirit—dwelt in Jesus, the two were effectively one and the same. (John 14:8-10.) However, if the apostles could not yet grasp that profound spiritual truth, Jesus asked them to "believe me for the very works' sake" (John 14:11)—meaning, have faith in me because of the things I have done.[25] He knew that when they were resurrected, these earnest men would comprehend the meaning of oneness: "Ye shall know that I am in my Father, and ye in me, and I in you." (John 14:20.) Possessing this precious knowledge for themselves, his special witnesses would then enjoy eternal life. (John 17:3.) But that greatest of all gifts lay far in the future. For now, Jesus was grateful for their belief in him, however unstable, as one with a mission and a message from God. (John 16:27, 31; 17:8.)

The Savior had lived with, and endured, the pattern of misconceptions—on the part of friends and enemies alike—revealed in the Gospels concerning himself. Insofar as being able to share the deep things of his Father even with his dearest companions, he was alone. "And yet," said he, "I am not alone, because the Father is with me." (John 16:32.) John stresses the great gulf that separated Christ and his true disciples from that unregenerated, human order called the world: "Love not the world, neither the things that are in the world. If any man love the world, the love of the Father is not in him. For all that is in the world, the lust of the flesh, and the lust of the eyes, and the pride of life, is not of the Father, but is of the world." (1 Jn. 2:15-16; John 8:23.)[26] Yet the Father loved humanity enough to sacrifice the life of his Beloved Son "for the life of the world." (John 6:51; 3:16-17.) However, the world as such would not be saved because the world as such would not accept that divine offering. It rejected Christ "because [he] testif[ied] of it, that the works thereof are evil." (John 7:7.) His works of righteousness were in opposition to the evil works of the world.

Being the "light of the world," Christ exposed the depths of its moral and spiritual darkness. (John 8:12; 12:46.) In doing so, he made the choice between good and evil real, compelling, and inescapable: "If I had not come and spoken unto them, they had not had sin: but now they have no cloke for their sin. . . . If I had not done among them the works which none other man did, they had not had sin: but now have they both seen and hated both me and my Father . . . without a cause." (John 15:22-25; Ps. 35:19.) While men may not be faulted for failing to realize that God walked among them (see Acts 3:17), their guilt in mocking virtue and crucifying innocence is unquestionable. The world of Jesus was a microcosm of the universal world in all times and places that rejects God's works in favor of its own.

Jesus proved that it was possible to conquer the world and its accompanying sin because he had conquered them: "I have overcome the world," he said. (John 16:33.) His victory assured a like victory for those who love him. (1 Jn. 5:4-5.) Stripped of its excuses for sin, all mankind is subject to the Lord's righteous judgment against those who remain in sin. (John 12:31; 15:22-25).[27]

The Savior's remarks to the Twelve concerning the world should be understood with the foregoing in mind. The apostles had been given to Jesus by the Father and had been chosen because they were "not of the world, even as [Jesus was] not of the world." (John 17:14, 16.) Consequently, like their Master, they would be hated, persecuted, and killed. (John 15:18-20; 16:1-4.) "In the world ye shall have tribulation," he told them. (John 16:33.) The Lord's intercessory prayer, which follows these words, is so called because it was offered in behalf of his apostles and those "which shall believe on me through their word" (John 17:20): "I pray not for the world, but for them which thou hast given me" (John 17:9). Jesus knew that his servants would need his prayers as long as they lived, for following his ascension, the enemy he had vanquished would concentrate his fury upon his apostles—and they were vulnerable: "The prince of darkness, who is of the world, cometh, but hath no power over me, but he hath power over you." (JST, John 14:30.) However, the apostles would not be left powerless against that evil spirit; they would be armed with the Holy Ghost—the divine opposition to the prince of darkness.

The Two Comforters

There are two Comforters. The first is the Holy Ghost; the second is Jesus Christ. Both are spoken of in this discourse. Both are called "the Spirit of truth." (John 14:17; 15:26; 16:13; D&C 50:17-21.) Both were promised to the Twelve.

The first Comforter reveals, testifies, justifies, sanctifies, and otherwise manifests his spiritual powers and influence in behalf of the second comforter. It is through the Holy Ghost that the Lord dwells in and with the righteous, as, for example, when Paul wrote: "Christ liveth in me." (Gal. 2:20.) Thus, the gift of the Holy Ghost is the gift of the first Comforter, the Spirit of truth.

Unlike the influence of the first Comforter, which can be simultaneously enjoyed by every worthy Saint, the second Comforter can only be experienced in a given place, at a given time, by a given person or group. According to the Prophet Joseph Smith, it is "another Comforter"[28] spoken of in John 14:16-18, 21, and 23, and may be received after one's calling and election has been made sure: "Now what is this other Comforter? It is no more nor less than the Lord Jesus Christ Himself; and this is the sum and substance of the whole matter; that when any man obtains this last Comforter, he will have the personage of Jesus Christ to attend him, or appear unto him from time to time, and even He will manifest the Father unto him, and they will take up their abode with him, and the visions of the heavens will be opened unto him, and the Lord will teach him face to face."[29] Those so blessed enjoy the Lord's confidence to the extent that he shares his mysteries and hidden purposes with them. In that sense, the second comforter abides with them even when Christ is not personally present. (D&C 76:5-10, 116-118.)

John the Baptist was "filled with the Holy Ghost, even from his mother's womb." (Luke 1:15; D&C 84:27.) Such must have been true of Jesus as well. However, this did not preclude the Holy Ghost descending upon Jesus "in bodily shape" following his baptism in water.[30] (JST, Luke 3:29.) Indeed, this unique manifestation of the Holy Spirit was the foreordained sign by which the Baptist was to identify the true Messiah, the Son of God: "He that sent me to baptize with water, the same said unto me, Upon whom thou shalt see the Spirit descending, and remaining on him, the same is he which baptizeth with the Holy Ghost. And I saw, and bare record that this is the Son of God." (John 1:33-34.)

Just as the Holy Ghost identified the true Son of God, so does it identify the true sons and daughters of God. Those who have been "born of water and of the Spirit" (John 3:5)—and they alone—are spiritually begotten or born again as "the children of Christ, his sons, and his daughters" (Mosiah 5:7). Having "received the Spirit of adoption" (Rom. 8:15), they are the eternal children of God, both in spirit and in resurrected flesh. They are sanctified beings. They—and they alone—are "joint-heirs with Christ" (Rom. 8:17) in the riches of the Father's celestial kingdom.

Thus, the same Holy Spirit that empowers the Saints and the Church today was with the Savior throughout his ministry until the hour of his agony in Gethsemane when he trod the winepress of the wrath of God alone. (D&C 76:107; 133:50.)[31] The mortal perfection of Christ stems in part from his long association with the Holy Ghost. Said the Prophet Joseph Smith: "None ever were perfect but Jesus; and why was he perfect? Because He was the Son of God, and had the fullness of the Spirit, and greater power than any man."[32] All that Jesus said, and all that Jesus did, was said and done by virtue of the power of the Spirit within him.

Such was not the case with his apostles or any other disciples.[33] While the Twelve were doubtlessly baptized in water (see JST, John 4:1-4) and exercised a degree of priesthood power (Luke 10:17-20), the Holy Ghost did not descend upon them and remain with them as a constant companion until after Jesus' ascension (John 7:39; Luke 24:49; Acts 1:4-5, 8).[34] After the Last Supper, Jesus told them: "If I go not away, the Comforter will not come unto you." (John 16:7.) Three nights later, the resurrected Savior appeared to the Twelve and "breathed on them, and saith unto them, Receive ye the Holy Ghost." (John 20:22.)

Their long-held traditions,[35] combined with the absence of this vital gift, serve to explain not only the inability of the apostles to comprehend all that Jesus taught, but also their doubts, their dissensions, their flight when Jesus was arrested, Simon Peter's subsequent denials, and their rejection of the testimonies of the women who had seen the risen Lord.

Although it had been but a few months since Peter had testified that Jesus was the Messiah (Matt. 16:15-17), yet at the Last Supper Jesus instructed him, "When thou art converted, strengthen thy brethren" (Luke 22:32). Plainly, a divine revelation, much less an intellectual conversion, is not the same as being spiritually born of God or experiencing that profound change of nature of which King Benjamin and Alma spoke. (Mosiah 3:19; Alma 5:14.) Not having been, as yet, baptized by the Holy Ghost, Peter and his fellow apostles had been "born of water" but not "of the Spirit." (John 3:5.)[36] That spiritual immersion would occur seven weeks later on Pentecost. (Acts 2:1-4.)

No one can give what he himself does not possess. Therefore, when the chief apostle—who had denied Jesus three times, and was later commanded three times, "Feed my sheep" (John 21:17)—was spiritually converted, he was prepared to fulfill his Master's commandment: "Strengthen thy brethren." And strengthen them he did! In the first recorded apostolic sermon ever delivered, the Simon Peter who had been too frightened to acknowledge publicly his discipleship in the predawn hours of history's most terrible night boldly testified: "God hath made that same Jesus, whom ye have crucified, both Lord and Christ." (Acts 2:36.) Filled with the Spirit, Peter possessed great moral courage—the courage that enables men and women to stand in defense of the truth at the peril of their lives. Such courage is born of the strength that comes from knowing. That strength brought martyrdom to several, perhaps all but one, of the faithful Twelve.[37]

Jesus declared himself the "true vine" from which comes all spiritual life and power. (John 15:1-8.) The apostles were to be extensions of their Lord and would be "pruned" by the things they suffered so that they might bring forth an even greater harvest. So it is with us all. It is, therefore, paradoxical that those bitter, humbling experiences that seem to indicate that the Lord has forsaken us may be the very experiences that prove that he has not. To be "pruned" by God is an evidence of his faith in us; we are spiritually alive. To be severed

417

from the "true vine" is to be spiritually dead, for Jesus made it clear that without his Spirit, we can do nothing of lasting meaning.

The gift and powers of the Holy Ghost, the third member of the Godhead, are sent from the Father by the Son. (John 15:26.) To possess this gift is to partake of the very glory of the Father and the Son. (John 17:22.) It is to walk with Christ. In doing so, we come to know him. (See D&C 19:23.) For just as we come unto the Father through the Son, so do we come unto the Son through the Holy Ghost.

Jesus told his apostles: "I have yet many things to say unto you, but ye cannot bear them now." (John 16:12.) Those mysteries would be revealed thereafter by the Holy Spirit: "He shall teach you all things, and bring all things to your remembrance, whatsoever I have said unto you." (John 14:26; see also John 2:22; 12:16; D&C 76:12.) No longer would they be only servants, obeying without comprehending. Because of their obedience, and through the powers of the Spirit, the Twelve were to be elevated to the status of chosen friends and confidants of the Redeemer (John 15:15); he would share all that he had obtained from his Father with them. Receiving grace for grace, they would be glorified in the Son as he was glorified in the Father, thereby entering into the perfect union of the Father and the Son. (John 17:22-23; D&C 93:20.) This exalting process was not to be theirs alone; it was to be offered to all mankind "without money and without price." (2 Ne. 26:24-25.)

Through the apostles and their associates, the Comforter would bear a binding witness of the Son of Man, thereby convicting the world of its guilt in rejecting his sacrifice. It would testify of Jesus' holiness as shown by his ascension to the Father. It would expose the darkness of Satan and his works before all mankind. (John 16:8-11.) And, in spite of all that they were to endure, the Comforter would bless the Lord's faithful witnesses with that promised peace and joy which is forever unknown and unknowable to this alien world. (John 14:27; 15:11; 16:20-22.)

Whereas Jesus' ministry was limited to the house of Israel, his servants were to carry the gospel message to all peoples via the Holy Ghost, the Lord's minister to the Gentiles. (3 Ne. 15:23.) Perhaps this is why Jesus told the Twelve: "It is expedient for you that I go away: for if I go not away, the Comforter will not come unto you." (John 16:7.)

Apparently the ministry of Christ had to end before the ministry of the Twelve could begin. Following the Lord's ascension, the Spirit descended upon the Twelve, enveloping them in "cloven tongues" of fire: "They were all filled with the Holy Ghost." (Acts 2:3-4.) So endowed, the Lord's special witnesses were prepared to be what he had called them to be: a light unto the world and the saviors of men. (Matt. 5:14; D&C 86:11.)

A New Commandment

No sooner had Judas Iscariot left on his malevolent mission than Jesus announced: "Now is the Son of man glorified, and God is glorified in him." (John 13:31.) Significantly, this reference to his death is immediately followed by: "A new commandment I give unto you, That ye love one another; as I have loved you, that ye also love one another." (John 13:34; 15:12, 17.) The Son of Man was a pure prism through which the Father's love had been reflected upon the Twelve. His juxtaposition of the principles of sacrifice and love was not accidental. The truest, purest expression of love is sacrifice. In willingly laying down his life, the Son testified to all the world of his love for his Father. (John 14:31.) By that same act, Jesus demonstrated the supernal affection he felt toward those he called friends. (John 15:13.)

Seemingly, no one could manifest a greater love for others than to surrender his own mortal existence in their behalf. But the Savior did more. He not only laid down his mortal life, but he also surrendered his very soul for friend and enemy alike. The one perfectly obedient, perfectly sinless man voluntarily subjected himself to the fullness of the wrath of God. He did this so that the Father might be glorified through the salvation of his children. Little wonder that the Father loved his beloved and chosen Son from all eternity! (John 17:24; Moses 4:2.)

The Savior was the first, and thus far the only, one to drink the bitter cup of divine justice to its dregs. He descended into the very depths of hell so that others might attain the heights of heaven. (See D&C 19:15-19; 88:6.) The prophet Abinadi said: "God himself shall come down among the children of men, and shall redeem his people." (Mosiah 3:7; Alma 7:11-12.) "God is love." (1 John 4:8.) Therefore, "love" sweat blood in Gethsemane. "Love" was crucified on Golgotha. "Love" atoned for the sins of mankind. "Love" broke the bands of temporal and spiritual death. "Love" overcame the world, the flesh, and the devil. "Love" ascended into the heaven of heavens. This love—the pure love of Christ—was the "new commandment" that Jesus gave the Twelve at the Last Supper. It would motivate them, the greatest of men, to become the servants of the least of men. It would require the sacrifice of their lives even as, in but a matter of hours, it would take the life of their Lord and Master.

To love one another as Jesus loved them was to rise above those imperfect expressions of love characteristic of mankind. Fallen man possesses fallen attributes. Although these attributes originate in God, they cannot be wholly perfected in the untabernacled spirit; the physical body must participate in the final process. Yet, paradoxically, these attributes become vitiated to the extent that the spirit is temporarily weakened by its union with corrupt, mortal flesh. Therefore, human love—compounded as it is with our needs, desires, passions, and fears (as well as with our nobler, altruistic qualities)—is, regardless of how or to whom it is expressed, unavoidably tainted with a greater or lesser degree of selfishness, pride, lust, inconstancy, and change. Lacking ultimate integrity, it is relatively unsanctified. Being, at best, a reflection of the pure love of Christ, human love is to divine love as the moon is to the sun. Only as we permit the Spirit of God to magnify our capacity for acquiring and internalizing divine attributes do we overcome the negative aspects of our fallen nature and grow toward perfect love. Hence, the new commandment.

And it *was* a new commandment. The command to love God and one's neighbor was not new; Israel had been so instructed by Moses himself. (Deut. 6:5; Lev. 19:18.) In his ministry, Jesus simply reconfirmed these foundation principles upon which all else was predicated (Mark 12:28-34.) But before departing, he gave his apostles the "new commandment" because they needed to know love as he knew it: edifying, holy, changeless, all-encompassing, and filled with intelligence. Indeed, a critical factor that sets divine love apart from its earthly counterparts is that it is permeated with light and truth—intelligence—the glory of God.

The Savior's supreme desire for his apostles, reiterated at the close of the intercessory prayer that concluded his farewell discourse, was that they might rise to the summits of love's glory and "be loved of [the] Father" (John 14:21): "The love wherewith thou hast loved me may be in them, and I in them" (John 17:26). Since divine love cannot be manifest beyond one's capacity to receive it, to eventually experience the fullness of the Father's celestial love required that the apostles eventually keep every commandment: "If ye keep my commandments, ye shall abide in my love; even as I have kept my Father's commandments, and abide in his love." (John 15:10.) Knowing the love of the Son, the apostles were, in time, to know the Father's love as well. The fruits of that love are summed up in one word—exaltation.

Where the Lord is concerned, love and obedience are inseparable. Jesus stressed this point again and again: "If you love me, keep my commandments. . . . He that hath my commandments, and keepeth them, he it is that loveth me. . . . If a man love me, he will keep my words. . . . He that loveth me not keepeth not my sayings." (John 14:15, 21, 23-24.) Clearly, one's love for the Lord is directly proportionate to one's obedience to his commandments. To love him is to obey him. To obey him is to know him. To know him is to be one with him and to possess eternal life. (John 17:3.) Such is the formula for exaltation.

However, a formula is one thing, the ability to follow it another. Jesus knew that if his disciples were to love as he loved, they would need to be filled with the Spirit as he was filled with the Spirit: they needed the justifying, sanctifying influence of the Holy Ghost.[38] The new commandment was, therefore, accompanied by the promise of the means to obey it: the Comforter. The Comforter is the bestower of all spiritual gifts, the greatest of which is charity, the pure love of Christ. (1 Cor. 13; Moro. 8:26.) Mormon admonished: "Pray unto the Father with all the energy of heart, that ye may be filled with this love, which he hath bestowed upon all who are true followers of his Son, Jesus Christ; that ye may become the sons of God." (Moro. 7:48.) To be filled with perfect love is to possess God: "If we love one another, God dwelleth in us, and his love is perfected in us." (1 Jn. 4:12.)

It has become popular to preach that God loves everyone unconditionally. This idea suggests much about God's character but little about our own. Further, it tends to promote a dangerous complacency. For while God may love his children unconditionally, he does not bless them unconditionally. (D&C 130:20-21.) Love is one thing; being able to express it, or receive it, another. Where love's rewards are concerned, there is no such thing as literal equality: "Behold, the Lord esteemeth all flesh in one; he that is righteous is favored of God." (1 Ne. 17:35.) The future degrees of glory reflect the broad continuum over which divine love is appropriately expressed by the three members of the Godhead.[39] Therefore, the fruits of God's love are as diverse as the men and women partaking of them. In the last analysis, it is obedience, motivated by divine love, that assures us the blessings of heaven.

As with other statements, the apostles did not at first comprehend the Savior's sealing promise: "In my Father's house [kingdom] are many mansions [glories]. . . . I go to prepare a place for you . . . that where I am, there ye may be also." (John 14:2-3. See also 17:24.) With these words, the calling and election of the first quorum of the Twelve was virtually made sure and confirmed by the more sure word of prophecy of Christ himself. (D&C 131:5.) Years later Peter testified: "We have therefore a more sure *knowledge* of the word of prophecy, to which word of prophecy ye do well that ye take heed, as unto a light which shineth in a dark place, until the day-dawn, and the day-star arise in your hearts." (JST, 2 Pet. 1:19; emphasis added.)

Joseph Smith made it clear that our testimony of Jesus Christ is but a means to an end—Christ's testimony of us: "Though they might hear the voice of God and know that Jesus was the Son of God [as did Peter, James, and John], this would be no evidence that their election and calling was made sure, that they had part with Christ, and were joint heirs with Him. They then would want that more sure word of prophecy, that they were sealed in the heavens and had the promise of eternal life in the kingdom of God."[40] "It is impossible for a man to be saved in ignorance" (D&C 131:6), meaning, we cannot be saved in ignorance of the knowledge that we are saved. In the end, this is the most vital knowledge we can possess.

The Aftermath

The Redeemer's intercessory prayer in behalf of his disciples (John 17) brought to an end the solemn events in the upper room. In the washing of feet, in introducing the sacrament, in giving the new commandment, in promising the Comforters, and in all else that transpired that evening, Jesus had sought to prepare the Twelve—and perhaps himself—for the tragic and triumphant events that lay ahead. Never before or since have the words of Alma been more true: "By small and simple things are great things brought to pass." (Alma 37:6.) A series of incidents of no apparent importance was about to transpire: a man from an obscure Galilean village would kneel alone in agonized prayer and would then be betrayed, arrested, condemned, and crucified while the world at large went on about its business. Yet all eternity was poised in anticipation of his victorious ordeal.

Jesus and his eleven friends left the upper room, walked down the now dark and empty streets of Jerusalem, passed through the golden gate facing the Mount of Olives, and descended to the garden of Gethsemane. The first incident was about to begin.

NOTES

1. It is generally assumed that the apostles regarded Jesus as being the literal offspring of God. Simon Peter's testimony, "Thou art the Christ, the Son of the Living God" (Matt. 16:16), is cited in support of this view. However, the phrase "Son of the living God" does not appear in the parallel accounts in Mark and Luke. (Joseph Smith added this phrase to these two Gospels in his own translation.) Messiah (Christ) and Son of God were considered virtual synonyms by many Jews. (Matt. 26:63.) But more to the point is the fact that among the Jews of that day, such titles were somewhat ambiguous, having no precise denotation. We are prone to impose our own *ex post facto* definitions on them. The Holy Scriptures referred to certain men or supposed angels as "sons of God." (Gen. 6:2, 4; Job 1:6; 38:7.) These "sons" were immortal or spiritual beings of some kind, but their actual relationship to God is never explained. Daniel described the fourth man in the fiery furnace as "like the Son of God." (Dan. 3:25.) Jesus stated that Psalm 82:6 ("Ye are gods; and all of you are children of the most High") applied to all "unto whom the word of God came" and asked why he was guilty of blasphemy for saying, "I am the Son of God." (John 10:34-36.) In identifying his own sonship with that of all men, Jesus obscured his divine paternity, thereby making his

claim to sonship acceptable to the Jewish mind. Following his resurrection, his sonship took on a new and profoundly significant meaning for his disciples. The ambiguous "son of God" of Jewish thought and the precise "Son of God" of the apostolic church were two very different things.

2. Israel's ancient creed was: "Hear, O Israel: The Lord our God is one Lord." (Deut. 6:4.) Jesus quoted this creed with apparent approval. (Mark 12:29.)

3. Certain Jews were prepared to stone Jesus for blasphemy. They said, "Thou, being a man, makest thyself God." (John 10:33.) However, Jesus was never quoted as saying that he *was* God. Indeed, he drew a clear distinction between himself and God, his Father. (John 14:28; 20:17; Matt. 27:46.) He did declare himself to be the Son of God (John 10:36), but left it to his hearers to interpret what he meant by that claim.

4. It was characteristic of pious Jews to refer to God as *'abi* father).

5. Although his disciples were amazed by Jesus' miracles (Matt. 8:27), these works did not establish his divinity. Said Brigham Young: "Did he convince, and prove to twelve men that he was the Christ, by the miracles he performed? He did not. He did not convince them by one or all of the acts, which were called miracles, that he performed upon the earth." (*Journal of Discourses* 3:205). As Paul stated, the thing that set Jesus apart from all other men as the unique Son of God was his resurrection from the dead. (Rom. 1:3-4.)

6. According to 3 Nephi 8:5, the destructions in America that accompanied Jesus' death began on the fourth day of the thirty-fourth year following his birth. (See 3 Ne. 2:7-8.) The supper Mary and Martha prepared for him the night preceding his Messianic entry into Jerusalem may have been in honor of his birthday. (John 12:2.)

7. The synoptic tradition is that Jesus ate the Passover meal (the seder) at the same time as the Jews did. (Mark 14:12-16.) However, the Gospel of John maintains that the Jews observed the Passover the evening of the day of Jesus' death and burial. Despite all efforts, this apparent contradiction has yet to be satisfactorily resolved. Note the following points in John: The Last Supper occurred "before the feast of the passover." (John 13:1.) Some of the apostles assumed that the purpose of Judas Iscariot's sudden departure after supper may have been to purchase things "against the feast." (John 13:29.) The high priest and his associates refused to enter Pilate's hall of judgment (the Praetorium) so that they might remain ceremonially undefiled and "eat the passover." (John 18:28.) Finally, Jesus was tried and crucified on the day of "preparation"—the day on which the paschal lamb was slain and the Passover meal prepared for consumption that evening. (John 19:14, 31, 42.)

It seems, therefore, that if the last supper was a Passover meal (as the Synoptics declare), Jesus celebrated it one day ahead of its observance by the Jewish people.

8. See Moses 5:5-7; Alma 34:10; 3 Ne. 9:19; and Heb. 10:10-18. According to Joseph Smith, the pre-Mosaic practice of animal sacrifice will be reinstituted in connection with the restitution of all things "when the Temple of the Lord shall be built, and the sons of Levi be purified." *(Teachings of the Prophet Joseph Smith,* p. 173.)

9. The washing of feet was observed by the Presidency of the Church and the Twelve in the Nauvoo Temple as well as on subsequent occasions.

10. Whether John deliberately omitted reference to the sacrament—perhaps because of its sacred nature—or whether his reference was somehow deleted from all extant manuscripts (which is unlikely) is unknown.

11. If, as many scholars believe, Paul's letters antedate the four Gospels, his is the oldest account of the institution of the sacrament and one possible source of the accounts found in the Synoptics.

12. Note that the Joseph Smith Translation, unlike the King James, makes it clear that the bread and wine were *in remembrance* of the Savior's flesh and blood, and not, in fact, his flesh and blood.

13. *Journal of Discourses* 9:315-16.

14. See John 3:14; 5:25; 7:33-34; 8:21-22, 28; 10:11, 15, 18; 12:7, 23-28, 32-36. Allusions by Jesus to his death in the Synoptics are Matt. 9:15; 12:40; 21:37-39; 26:12; Luke 9:22; 20:13-15. However, if the texts faithfully convey Jesus' actual teachings, we can only conclude that his disciples either failed to grasp their import or chose to ignore or relegate them to some far distant time. Mark 9:32 and Luke 9:45 and 18:34 state that Jesus' predictions of his approaching betrayal and death were incomprehensible to his apostles. This is evident in the exchange between Jesus and Peter on the matter. (Matt. 16:21-23; Mark 8:31-33.) The apostles entertained the common notion that the Messiah would be a mighty, but mortal, spiritual and temporal leader whom God would raise up to deliver the Jews from their oppressors and reestablish the Davidic kingdom. (Acts 1:6.) Thus, in their minds, the destiny of the Messiah was not a cross but a crown, not death but dominion. He would rule forever. (John 12:34.) The very practical ambition of the apostles concerning the Messianic kingdom is shown in their arguments as to who among them should be the greatest or the most prominent (Luke 9:46), and by the request of James and John for chief positions in the kingdom—a request that angered the other apostles (Mark 10:35-41). Luke wrote that the apostles, believing that Jesus was about to set up an earthly government, even quarreled at the Last Supper over their future positions therein. (Luke

22:24.) The limited understanding of the disciples as to Jesus' true mission is indicated by John. (John 2:22; 12:16; 20:9.) It is also evident in several post-resurrection passages. (Luke 24:13-27, 45; Mark 16:14.)

15. John indicates that Jesus' seeric powers and foreknowledge enabled him to anticipate and control every situation. See John 1:42, 48-51; 2:24-25; 4:16-19; 6:6, 64; 13:1, 21.

16. Contrary to the arguments of some writers, Judas Iscariot's motivation for betraying Jesus was malevolent, not benevolent. Apparently chastised by Jesus for something he had said or done, the defensive young apostle refused to confess his error and sought revenge. The Prophet Joseph Smith revealed: "Judas was rebuked and immediately betrayed his Lord into the hands of His enemies, because Satan entered into him." *(Teachings of the Prophet Joseph Smith,* p. 67.) It was a day or two before the Last Supper that Judas committed himself to the betrayal. (Matt. 26:14-16.)

17. This is a further evidence that the apostles were unmindful of any imminent danger to their Master or themselves.

18. Judas Iscariot is a classic example of the parable of the empty house wherein a soul once cleansed of all evil becomes, as a result of subsequent blasphemy, the habitation of devils. (JST, Matt. 12:38-39.) Said Joseph Smith: "There is a superior intelligence bestowed upon such as obey the Gospel with full purpose of heart, which, if sinned against, the apostate is left naked and destitute of the Spirit of God, and he is, in truth, nigh unto cursing, and his end is to be burned. . . . And they, Judas like, seek the destruction of those who were their greatest benefactors. What nearer friend on earth, or in heaven, had Judas than the Savior? And his first object was to destroy Him." *(Teachings of the Prophet Joseph Smith,* p. 67.)

19. Ibid.

20. According to Matthew, the distraught Judas sought to undo his crime by returning the thirty pieces of silver. He then committed suicide by hanging. (Matt. 27:3-5.) Luke, probably reflecting John's less charitable view of Judas, describes his death as resulting from an accidental fall on property he had purchased with the bribery money. (Acts 1:16-20.) JST, Matt. 27:6 combines the two accounts. Satan is called perdition. (D&C 76:26.) Therefore, all who yield to his enticings and die in their sins are sons (or daughters) of perdition and will have to suffer in hell for a given length of time. (Moses 7:37-39.) The risen Christ compared Nephite apostates to Judas: "For they are led away captive by him [Satan] even as was the son of perdition; for they will sell me for silver." (3 Ne. 27:32.) Those Gentiles who deny Christ "shall become like unto the son of perdition, for whom there was no mercy." (3 Ne.

29:7.) "No mercy" means they must bear the full weight of divine justice (the wrath of God or hell) before being saved. They are *temporary* sons or daughters of perdition as opposed to those who, failing to ever repent, are termed the "filthy still" (D&C 88:35, 102) and are consigned to the fullness of the second death (D&C 29:27-30, 41). Likening Nephite and Gentile sinners to Judas suggests that there is hope for him as well. Consequently, whether or not Judas committed the unpardonable sin and is, in fact, a son of perdition in the direst sense of the term is debatable. Although an apostle, he had received neither the baptism nor the gift of the Holy Ghost. Like Peter, he was not yet converted. (Luke 22:32.) Then too, if, as Matthew suggests, he attempted to repent—something a totally lost son of perdition would not do (D&C 29:44)—he may yet obtain some measure of salvation. This issue has had proponents among Church leaders on both sides of the question.

21. Many biblical critics regard John's account of the Last Supper as a product of later reconstruction or redaction on the part of unknown editors. While it is not unlikely that some editing has occurred (see John 21:24b), modern revelation confirms and supports the essential character and doctrinal content of this scripture.

22. *Teachings of the Prophet Joseph Smith,* p. 365.

23. It is characteristic of John's Gospel to employ what has been called a foil technique in which the literal questions or statements of men serve as bases for the Lord's spiritual pronouncements. The exchange between Jesus and Nicodemus (John 3:1-6) is a good example of this technique. The responses of the apostles in John 13–16 may, therefore, be somewhat contrived since they serve to justify lengthy commentary by Jesus.

24. Matthew and Mark recorded that all of the apostles joined Peter in promising loyalty to the death. (Matt. 26:35; Mark 14:31.)

25. John emphasized that the Lord's miracles, his works, were sufficient for men to believe in him—at least as a man of God. (John 3:2; 10:38; 15:24.)

26. The term *world* is used in a double sense, sometimes referring to the earth, but more often to human society. Both senses are present in John 1:10.

27. The fifth Lecture on Faith states that in spite of the fact that Christ "suffered greater sufferings, and was exposed to more powerful contradictions than any man can be, . . . He kept the law of God, and remained without sin, showing thereby that it is in the power of man to keep the law and remain also without sin." Therefore, willful sinners "may be justly condemned by the law, and have no excuse for their sins."

28. The phrase "another Comforter" is also applied to the Holy Ghost or Holy Spirit of promise in D&C 88:3-4, where it is defined as the promise of

eternal life or celestial glory. (See 2 Cor. 1:22; 5:5; Eph. 1:13-14.) Elder Marion G. Romney equated this Comforter with the more sure word of prophecy. (*Conference Report,* April 1977, p. 62.)

29. *Teachings of the Prophet Joseph Smith,* pp. 150-51. Commenting on John 14:23, Doctrine and Covenants 130:3 states: "The appearing of the Father and the Son, in that verse, is a personal appearance; and the idea that the Father and the Son dwell in a man's heart is an old sectarian notion, and is false."

30. The presence of a dove at Jesus' baptism signified the presence of the Holy Ghost. "The Holy Ghost cannot be transformed into a dove, but the sign of a dove was given to John to signify the truth of the deed." (*Teachings of the Prophet Joseph Smith,* p. 276.) That the Holy Ghost descended upon Jesus "in bodily shape" suggests that Jesus was literally enveloped in the very person of the third member of the Godhead rather than merely in the spiritual influence he controls. The Doctrine and Covenants states that one reason the Holy Ghost "is a personage of Spirit," as opposed to one with flesh and bones, is so that he might "dwell in us. A man may receive the Holy Ghost, and it may descend upon him and not tarry with him." (D&C 130:22-23.) In Jesus' case, the Holy Ghost descended upon him and remained with him. (John 1:33.)

31. *Journal of Discourses* 3:206.

32. *Teachings of the Prophet Joseph Smith,* pp. 187-88. See also John 3:34; D&C 93:15-17.

33. However, John the Baptist was filled with the Holy Ghost from his mother's womb. (Luke 1:15; D&C 84:27.)

34. *Teachings of the Prophet Joseph Smith,* p. 149. Simon Peter's testimony that Jesus was the Messiah (Matt. 16:15-16) was based upon the *witness,* not the *gift* of the Holy Ghost.

35. Brigham Young noted: "Though he [Jesus] was diligent in teaching his disciples, their traditions were such that, after he had been with them a long time, there were many points that they did not fully understand." (*Journal of Discourses* 7:7.)

36. The first modern Quorum of the Twelve was organized in February 1835. However, two years later members of that body also were in need of a more profound conversion: "If they harden not their hearts, and stiffen not their necks against me, they shall be converted, and I will heal them." (D&C 112:13.)

37. John requested that his life be lengthened so that he might continue to serve the Lord in this world. He became a translated being. (John 21:21-23; D&C 7.)

38. It was subsequent to the Nephite Twelve being "filled with the Holy Ghost and with fire" (3 Ne. 19:13) that Jesus told them, "Therefore, what manner of men ought ye to be? Verily I say unto you, even as I am" (3 Ne. 27:27).

39. The three members of the Godhead may be thought of as bestowing three different measures of God's manifest love. The telestial order partakes of that love via the Holy Spirit, the terrestrial via the Son. Only heirs of the celestial kingdom receive a fullness of the Father's love as it is made manifest in terms of thrones, kingdoms, principalities, powers, glories, and so forth. (D&C 76:71, 77, 86, 92-94.)

40. *Teachings of the Prophet Joseph Smith,* p. 298. Compare pp. 299, 301, 303-6. A number of righteous men have received the more sure word of prophecy pertaining to their own salvation. See D&C 132:49; 2 Ne. 33:6; Moro. 10:34; Moses 7:59.

28

TREADING THE WINEPRESS ALONE
(Matthew 26:36-46; Mark 14:32-42; Luke 22:39-46)

ROBERT L. MILLET

Having finished the Last Supper, the Passover meal having now been subsumed into an even greater occasion, the little band of apostles, with Jesus at their head, left the Upper Room. The disciples, no doubt, had been deeply touched by our Lord's moving and much-needed Intercessory Prayer. (John 17.) Mark records: "When they had sung an hymn, they went out into the mount of Olives." (Mark 14:26.) East of the temple mount, outside the walls of the holy city, on the slopes of the Mount of Olives was a garden spot, a place where "Jesus oftimes resorted . . . with his disciples." (John 18:2.) Gethsemane, the "garden of the oil press" (or winepress), was indeed one of the three "gardens of God." With the Garden of Eden and the Garden of the Empty Tomb, the Garden of Gethsemane would be forever enshrined in the hearts and minds of Christians as one of those profoundly sacred spots on earth where the works of God—Creation, Fall, and Atonement—took place.[1]

A lifetime of purity and preparation and performance was now a part of the past; the private battles of the soul, the unwritten struggles over Satan and his minions, had been waged and won. Now, for the Lord of Life, the time of preparation was over: the hour of ordeal, the major reason for which the great Jehovah had come to earth, was now at hand. This fateful occasion, transcendent in scope and incomprehensible to mortal minds, was the hinge upon which the door into

---

Robert L. Millet is assistant professor of ancient scripture and New Testament area coordinator at Brigham Young University.

430

all eternity turned. Surely the heavens were hushed and the spirits of men and women from ages past and for ages to come paused and prayed during this precious segment of time. In a way perhaps much more profound than on that joyous Christmas eve some thirty-three years earlier, "The hopes and fears of all the years are met in thee tonight." (*Hymns*, 1985, no. 208.)

The Awful Ordeal

"They came to a place which was named Gethsemane, which was a garden; and the disciples began to be sore amazed, and to be very heavy, and to complain in their hearts, wondering if this be the Messiah. And Jesus, knowing their hearts, said to his disciples, Sit ye here, while I shall pray." (JST, Mark 14:36-37.) As Elder Bruce R. McConkie wrote: "Though they all knew, as Jesus himself attested in the private sermons and prayer just delivered [the Intercessory Prayer], that he was the Son of God, yet he did not fit the popular pattern for the Jewish Messiah, and the disciples, of course, had not yet received the gift of the Holy Ghost."[2] The hours of anguish and alienation had begun. That for which the Lamb of God had been foreordained and that of which the prophets had spoken for millennia was under way. "When the unimaginable burden began to weigh upon Christ," Elder Neal A. Maxwell has observed, "it confirmed His long-held and intellectually clear understanding as to what He must now do."[3]

There is no weight heavier than the burden of sin, and the Sinless One (and those closest to him) began to sense and feel the bitterness of this singular occasion, a time when the weight of the world was about to be placed upon the shoulders of Him who had made the world. To approximate an understanding of Gethsemane, it seems appropriate to consider things in perspective. Jesus was morally perfect. He had never taken a backward step or a moral detour. He was "in all points tempted like as we are, yet without sin." (Heb. 4:15; compare 1 Pet. 2:22.) According to the Prophet Joseph Smith, Jesus was "the Son of God, and had the fullness of the Spirit, and greater power than any man."[4] He had never known the feelings of guilt and remorse, the pain of alienation from God that characterizes the whole of mankind. Note the following statements from Jesus, utterances that evidence the closeness and intimacy between God the Father and God the Son:

"My Father worketh hitherto, and I work." (John 5:17.)

"The Son can do nothing of himself, but what he seeth the Father do; for what things soever he doeth, these also doeth the Son likewise." (John 5:19.)

"I seek not mine own will, but the will of the Father which hath sent me." (John 5:30.)

"I am come in my Father's name." (John 5:43.)

"My doctrine is not mine, but his that sent me." (John 7:16.)

"I and my Father are one." (John 10:30.)

"The Father hath not left me alone; for I do always those things that please him." (John 8:29.)

There was a tragic aura surrounding this night of nights, then, when he who had always pleased the Father and had thus never been alone (so far as being separated from his Father) was subjected to the forces and effects of sin that he had never known, forces that must have been poignantly and excruciatingly intense to that pure and clean soul of the Son of Man. The God of the Fathers, the Holy One of Israel, the Lord God Omnipotent, as he was known among the ancients, knew all things. In the language of Jacob, son of Lehi, "O how great the holiness of our God! For he knoweth all things, and there is not anything save he knows it." (2 Ne. 9:20.) And yet there was something he had never known personally: sin or its effects. Christ knew all things as a Spirit Being; "nevertheless," Alma taught, "the Son of God suffereth *according to the flesh* that he might take upon him the sins of his people, that he might blot out their transgressions according to the power of his deliverance." (Alma 7:13, emphasis added.) In the words of Elder Maxwell, a modern apostle, "The suffering Jesus began to be 'sore amazed' (Mark 14:33), or, in the Greek, 'awestruck' and 'astonished.' Imagine, Jehovah, the Creator of this and other worlds, 'astonished'! Jesus knew cognitively what he must do, but not experientially. He had never personally known the exquisite and exacting process of an atonement before. Thus, when the agony came in its fulness, it was so much, much worse than even he with his unique intellect had ever imagined!"[5]

"He went forward a little, and fell on the ground, and prayed that, if it were possible, the hour might pass from him. And he said, Abba, Father, all things are possible unto thee; take away this cup from me: nevertheless not what I will, but what thou wilt." (Mark 14:35-36.) Being withdrawn from his apostolic associates "about a stone's cast" (Luke 22:41), the Master pleaded in prayer with God. The Son of God called out in tender tones, "Abba," an intimate and familiar form of *father*, perhaps something like what we know as *"Daddy."* Was there not another way, he asked? It did not appear so. Could the plan of salvation have been operative without Jesus' selfless submission to the torturous experiences of the hour? It would seem not. We have no scriptural or prophetic indication that some substitute Savior waited in the wings, some person who could fill in should Jesus of Nazareth not complete the task at hand. We sing with conviction: "There was no other good enough to pay the price of sin. He only could unlock the gate of heaven and let us in." (*Hymns*, 1985, no. 194.) Indeed, no one else qualified for such an assignment. Earlier the Savior had spoken in soliloquy. "Now is my soul troubled," he had said, "and what shall I say? Father, save me from this hour: but for this cause came I unto this hour. Father, glorify thy name." The Father then spoke: "I have both glorified it, and will glorify it again." (John 12:27-28.)

Isaiah had prophesied of this event some seven hundred years earlier: "Surely he hath borne our griefs, and carried our sorrows. . . . He was wounded for our transgressions, he was bruised for our iniquities. . . . He was oppressed, and he was afflicted. . . . Yet it pleased the Lord [the Father] to bruise him; he hath put him to grief." (Isa. 53:4-5, 7, 10.) The bitter cup of justice (see Mosiah 3:26) had been passed by the Father to the Son, all as part of the foreordained plan of the Father, and the Son had begun to imbibe the dreadful draught.

Luke added two important details to the story. He wrote: "There appeared an angel unto him from heaven, strengthening him. And being in an agony, he prayed more earnestly; and he sweat as it were great drops of blood falling down to the ground." (JST, Luke 22:43-44.) An angel, sent from the courts of glory, came to strengthen the God of Creation in his hour of greatest need. What an assignment! What an honor! "If we might indulge in speculation," Elder Bruce R. McConkie wrote, "we would suggest that the angel who came into this second Eden was the same person who dwelt in the first Eden. At least Adam, who is Michael, the archangel—the head of the whole heavenly hierarchy of angelic ministrants—seems the logical one to give aid and comfort to his Lord on such a solemn occasion. Adam fell, and Christ redeemed men from the fall; theirs was a joint enterprise, both parts of which were essential for the salvation of the Father's children."[6]

Luke added the additional detail concerning the intensity of our Lord's suffering—so great that drops of blood came to the surface of his body and fell to the ground. This was in fulfillment of the prophecy delivered by the angel to King Benjamin: "He shall suffer temptations, and pain of body, hunger, thirst, and fatigue, even more than man can suffer, except it be unto death; for behold, blood cometh from every pore, so great shall be his anguish for the wickedness and the abominations of his people." (Mosiah 3:7.)

In a modern revelation, the Savior pleaded with his people to repent, recalling the painful episode in Gethsemane: "I command you to repent—repent, lest I smite you by the rod of my mouth, and by my wrath, and by my anger, and your sufferings be sore—how sore you know not, how exquisite you know not, yea, how hard to bear you know not. For behold, I, God, have suffered these things for all, that they might not suffer if they would repent; but if they would not repent they must suffer even as I; which suffering caused myself, even God, the greatest of all, to tremble because of pain, and to bleed at every pore, and to suffer both body and spirit—and would that I might not drink the bitter cup, and shrink—nevertheless, glory be to the Father, and I partook and finished my preparations unto the children of men." (D&C 19:15-18.)

The immediate consequence of sin is withdrawal of the Spirit of the Father. (See Alma 34:35.) It may be that such a withdrawal from an individual is what leads to feelings of guilt and pain and emptiness. Jesus Christ, in taking upon him the effects of the sins of all mankind, was thus exposed to the awful (and to Jesus, unusual) withdrawal of that Spirit which had been his constant companion from birth. In speaking of the atoning mission of Jesus Christ (and the ordeals related thereto), President Brigham Young explained:

> The Father withdrew His Spirit from His Son, at the time he was to be crucified. Jesus had been with his Father, talked with Him, dwelt in His bosom, and knew all about heaven, about making the earth, about the transgression of man, and

what would redeem the people, and that he was the character to redeem the sons of earth, and the earth itself from all sin that had come upon it. The light, knowledge, power, and glory with which he was clothed were far above, or exceeded that of all others who had been upon the earth after the fall, consequently at the very moment, at the hour when the crisis came for him to offer up his life, the Father withdrew Himself, withdrew His Spirit. . . . That is what made him sweat blood. If he had had the power of God upon him, he would not have sweat blood.[7]

Concerning the suffering of Christ in Gethsemane, Elder James E. Talmage wrote:

Christ's agony in the garden is unfathomable by the finite mind, both as to intensity and cause. The thought that He suffered through fear of death is untenable. Death to Him was preliminary to resurrection and triumphal return to the Father from whom He had come, and to a state of glory even beyond what He had before possessed; and, moreover, it was within His power to lay down His life voluntarily. He struggled and groaned under a burden such as no other being who has lived on earth might even conceive as possible. It was not physical pain, nor mental anguish alone, that caused Him to suffer such torture as to produce an extrusion of blood from every pore; but a spiritual agony of soul such as only God was capable of experiencing. No other man, however great his powers of physical or mental endurance, could have suffered so. . . . In some manner, actual and terribly real though to man incomprehensible, the Savior took upon Himself the burden of the sins of mankind from Adam to the end of the world.[8]

Just as ancient Israel had sent the scapegoat into the wilderness (Lev. 16:5-10), even so the Lamb of God, suffering outside Jerusalem's walls and outside the pale of God's healing and redemptive Spirit, met and faced the obstacles and assaults of Lucifer and his hosts. Delivered over to "the buffetings of Satan," Christ "met and overcame all the horrors that Satan, 'the prince of this world,' could inflict. The frightful struggle incident to the temptations immediately following the Lord's baptism was surpassed and overshadowed by this supreme contest with the powers of evil."[9]

The night of atonement was a night of irony. He who was sinless became, as it were, the great Sinner. In Paul's words, God the Father had "made him to be sin for us, who knew no sin." (2 Cor. 5:21.) To the Galatian Saints, Paul also taught that "Christ hath redeemed us from the curse of the law, being made a curse for us." (Gal. 3:13.) He who deserved least of all to suffer now suffered most—more than mortal mind can fathom. He who had brought life—the more abundant life (John 10:10)—was subjected to the powers of death and darkness. As the Prophet Joseph Smith taught the brethren of the School of the Prophets, Jesus Christ is called the *Son* of God because he "descended in suffering below that which man can suffer; or, in other words, suffered greater sufferings, and was exposed to more powerful contradictions than any man can be."[10]

Through most of our Lord's infinite ordeal—which may have lasted for three or four hours[11]—the chief apostles slept. It is almost impossible to imagine that these good and noble and obedient servants of the Lord, called to be special witnesses of his name in all the world, could not control the demands of the body for a brief moment—indeed, a moment that mattered. Elder McConkie suggested the following explanation for this most unusual scene: "Finite minds can no more comprehend how and in what manner Jesus performed his redeeming labors than they can comprehend how matter came into being, or how Gods began to be. Perhaps the very reason Peter, James, and John slept was to enable a divine providence to withhold from their ears, and seal up from their eyes, those things which only Gods can comprehend."[12]

Below All Things

Alma spoke with poetic and prophetic power when he described the coming of the Messiah and the suffering necessary to accomplish the Atonement: "He shall be born of Mary, at Jerusalem which is the land of our forefathers, she being a virgin, a precious and chosen vessel, who shall be overshadowed and conceive by the power of the Holy Ghost, and bring forth a son, yea, even the Son of God. And he shall go forth, suffering pains and afflictions and temptations of every kind; and this that the word might be fulfilled which saith he will take upon him the pains and the sicknesses of his people. And he will take upon him death, that he may loose the bands of death which bind his people; and he will take upon him their infirmities, that his bowels may be filled with mercy, according to the flesh, that he may know according to the flesh how to succor his people according to their infirmities." (Alma 7:10-12.) In commenting upon these verses, Elder Neal A. Maxwell observed:

> Can we, even in the depths of disease, tell Him anything at all about suffering? In ways we cannot comprehend, our sicknesses and infirmities were borne by Him even before they were borne by us. The very weight of our combined sins caused Him to descend below all. We have never been, nor will we be, in depths such as He has known. Thus His atonement made perfect His empathy and His mercy and His capacity to succor us, for which we can be everlastingly grateful as He tutors us in our trials. There was no ram in the thicket at Calvary to spare Him, this Friend of Abraham and Isaac. . . .
>
> And when we feel so alone, can we presume to teach Him who trod "the wine-press alone" anything at all about feeling forsaken? . . .
>
> Should we seek to counsel Him in courage? Should we rush forth eagerly to show Him our press clippings and mortal medals—our scratches and bruises—as He bears His five special wounds? . . .
>
> Indeed, we cannot teach Him anything! But we can listen to Him. We can love Him; we can honor Him; we can worship Him. We can keep His commandments, and we can feast upon His scriptures.[13]

And so it was that our Savior descended below all things. (See Eph. 4:8-10; D&C 88:6.) The Redeemer has indeed "trodden the wine-press alone, even the wine-press of the fierceness of the wrath of Almighty God." (D&C 76:107; 88:106; Isa. 63:3.) And the voice of him who shall come again to reward the righteous and heap vengeance upon the ungodly shall yet be heard: "I have trodden the wine-press alone, and have brought judgment upon all people; and none were with me; and I have trampled them in fury, and I did tread upon them in mine anger, and their blood have I sprinkled upon my garments, and stained all my raiment." (D&C 133:50-51.) In the meantime, the miracle, the miracle and blessings of the Atonement—timeless in their scope—continue to be extended to all who come to the Lord with righteous intent.

"I am Christ," the Lord declared in a modern revelation, "and in mine own name, by the virtue of the blood which I have spilt, have I pleaded before the Father for them." (D&C 38:4.) The nature of that pleading, that intercession, was elucidated some two months later in another revelation: "Listen to him who is the advocate with the Father, who is pleading your cause before him—saying: Father, behold the sufferings and death of him who did no sin, in whom thou wast well pleased; behold the blood of thy Son which was shed, the blood of him whom thou gavest that thyself might be glorified; wherefore, Father, spare these my brethren that believe on my name, that they may come unto me and have everlasting life." (D&C 45:3-5.)

NOTES

1. See Bruce R. McConkie, *Conference Report,* April 1985, p. 11.
2. Bruce R. McConkie, *The Mortal Messiah,* 4 vols. (Salt Lake City: Deseret Book, 1979-81), 4:123.
3. Neal A. Maxwell, *Conference Report,* April 1985, p. 92.
4. *Teachings of the Prophet Joseph Smith,* p. 188; compare JST, John 3:34.
5. Neal A. Maxwell, *Conference Report,* April 1985, p. 92.
6. *The Mortal Messiah* 4:125. See also *Conference Report,* April 1985, p. 10.
7. *Journal of Discourses* 3:206.
8. James E. Talmage, *Jesus the Christ* (Salt Lake City: 1977), p. 613.
9. Ibid. President John Taylor wrote: "Groaning beneath this concentrated load, this intense, incomprehensible pressure, this terrible exaction of Divine justice, from which feeble humanity shrank, and through the agony thus experienced sweating great drops of blood, He was led to exclaim, 'Father, if it be possible, let this cup pass from me.' He had wrestled with all the superincumbent load in the wilderness, He had struggled against the powers of darkness that had been let loose upon him there; placed below all

things, His mind surcharged with agony and pain, lonely and apparently help-less and forsaken, in his agony the blood oozed from His pores." (*The Media-tion and Atonement of Our Lord and Savior Jesus the Christ* [Salt Lake City; Deseret News Co., 1882], p. 150.)

10. *Lectures on Faith* (Salt Lake City: Deseret Book, 1985), 5:2.

11. See Bruce R. McConkie, *Conference Report,* April 1985, p. 10.

12. *The Mortal Messiah* 4:124.

13. Neal A. Maxwell, *Even As I Am* (Salt Lake City: Deseret Book, 1982), pp. 116-19.

29

THE ARREST, TRIAL, AND CRUCIFIXION—
A LESSON IN LOYALTY
(Luke 22:47–23:56)

ANDREW C. SKINNER

Though the Lord endured incomprehensible suffering in Gethsemane, his pain and humiliation were far from finished as he completed his prayer, arose, and walked a stone's throw distance to awaken the fatigued apostles from the sleep to which they finally had succumbed. (Luke 22:41, 45-46.) The Gospels record with varying degrees of completeness the scene of the Master's arrest while he was speaking to his disciples. (Matt. 26:45-57; Mark 14:41-53; Luke 22:45-54; John 18:1-12.) However, concerning one detail there is exact and poignant agreement: Judas, one of the Twelve, was leading an incited and armed crowd! So began the series of exhausting events of an already long evening, events that culminated in the Crucifixion, events that provide us with a profound lesson in loyalty.

Betrayal and Arrest

That the wording is exactly the same in the Synoptic Gospels regarding Judas's position as a member of the Twelve while at the same time he was the Lord's betrayer perhaps reflects the shock and intensity with which that moment was felt by those disciples present. Surely it must have added to the Savior's grief as Judas singled him out. Do we not learn that in all dispensations of time loyalty to one's brethren always was and always will be essential? (See, for example, Prov. 6:16, 19; John 17:11; D&C 38:27.)

Andrew C. Skinner is an instructor in the department of History at Metro State College in Denver, Colorado.

Both Matthew and Mark, whose Gospels contain fuller accounts of the betrayal than Luke's, indicate that Jesus was hailed with a kiss. Luke, however, explains that as Judas drew near to kiss the Savior, the latter chided him, asking if such a symbolic act was in harmony with such treachery. We come to appreciate the significance of this question when we recall that Paul exhorted the Thessalonian saints to greet all the brethren with a holy kiss or salutation. (1 Thes. 5:26.) In latter-day revelation we are told that the Lord's people and Enoch's city will be reunited in a holy place "and [they] will kiss each other." (Moses 7:63.) It is not unlikely that as Judas employed this singular method of greeting, the Savior remembered the prophetic words of Proverbs 27:6: "Faithful are the wounds of a friend; but the kisses of an enemy are deceitful."

After the betrayal and the seizure of Jesus by the mob, all four Gospels report the scuffle involving the servant of the high priest. Only John declared specifically that it was Simon Peter who drew his sword and cut off the servant's ear. Likewise only John reported that his name was Malchus. (John 18:10.) The Lord immediately rebuked Peter, and, as Luke, the physician, said, the servant was made whole by this, the Lord's last miracle of healing. Even in the time of his greatest extremity or danger, the Savior's compassion and concern for mankind were evident. This is seen not only in the incident concerning the healing of Malchus but also in the Savior's reply to Peter, as reported by Matthew: "Put up again thy sword. . . . Thinkest thou that I cannot now pray to my Father, and he shall presently give me more than twelve legions of angels? But how then shall the scriptures be fulfilled, that thus it must be?" (Matt. 26:52-54.) In Roman Palestine, a legion was the chief subdivision of the army, containing about six thousand soldiers. Certainly Jesus had great power at his disposal (seventy-two thousand angels against mere mortals). But his purpose was not to destroy those around him. Rather, he wanted to carry out the supreme saving mission of the Father (John 18:11) and thus fulfill the scriptures. He was loyal to the Father at all costs.

Peter's Denial

As Jesus was being led away to Caiaphas, the high priest, "all the disciples forsook him, and fled." (Matt. 26:56; Mark 14:50.) Though we might be tempted to view this circumstance in a harsh light, perhaps even regard it as another example of supreme disloyalty and thus become highly critical of the Savior's followers, other discussions may help to temper our attitudes.

Elder James E. Talmage observed that any resistance to the arrest of Jesus was useless. He also noted that the apostles were actually in jeopardy themselves.[1] Furthermore, we have the testimony of John, who indicated that Jesus was very protective of his apostles, perhaps even encouraging their flight or dispersal from the garden, and not wanting any harm to come to them: "Then asked he them again, Whom seek ye? And they said, Jesus of Nazareth. Jesus answered, I have told you that I am he: if therefore ye seek me, let these go their way: that the saying might be fulfilled, which he spake, Of them which thou gavest me have I lost none." (John 18:7-9.)

Finally we turn to President Spencer W. Kimball's remarks concerning the apostle Peter, who, as all four Gospels tell us, followed Jesus at a distance while he was being taken first to Annas and then to Caiaphas. (See John 18:13.) There can be no doubt that Peter denied knowing the Savior, for, again, all four texts report this, though the events are arranged in slightly different order. (Matt. 26:69-75; Mark 14:66-72; Luke 22:54-62; John 18:15-18, 25-27.) As to Peter's motives for the denial, President Kimball stated: "Much of the criticism of Simon Peter is centered in his denial of his acquaintance with the Master. This has been labeled 'cowardice.' Are we sure of his motive in that recorded denial? He had already given up his occupation and placed all worldly goods on the altar for the cause."[2] Certainly this assessment coincides with the general New Testament picture of a chief apostle who was far from cowardly, as demonstrated by his readiness to draw the sword against a mob armed with swords and clubs.

Jesus and the Sanhedrin

At daylight, when the chief priests and scribes came together to hear Jesus in their council meeting (Luke 22:66), the Savior had already been awake for an entire day and night, having experienced the bloody agony in Gethsemane; having been forced to cross the Kidron Valley and march up the steep western slope to the residences of

Annas (father-in-law to Caiaphas) and then Caiaphas the High Priest; and having been forced to endure blows to the face and being blindfolded, mocked, and spit upon. Such an ordeal would have caused exhaustive collapse in most mortals.

At this point Jesus was examined by a group of Jewish leaders, with the high priest taking the lead as interrogator. (John 18:19-22.) Whether this body of leaders constituted the Great Sanhedrin of 72, the lesser Sanhedrin of 23, or some smaller informal group is a question for debate among scholars.[3] It was expressly forbidden for the Sanhedrin to meet in the house of the high priest, for that body had as its place of convocation the "Hall of Hewn Stones" from which the "law went out to all Israel."[4] As Elder Talmage observed, the size of the body is uncertain and of small importance.[5] One thing is certain, however: based upon Mishnaic writings and legal procedures—codified after the time of Jesus—the proceedings were illegal on several points of Jewish law. The ultimate irony seems to be that though every element of Mishnaic or rabbinic legal tradition was theoretically designed to ensure that the innocent not be made scapegoats or railroaded into conviction (that is, no one-day trials resulting in capital punishment, no self-incrimination or confession without two corroborating witnesses, no conviction unless self-knowledge of wrongdoing was positively proven[6]), all the safeguards were ignored in the case of Jesus of Nazareth. Perhaps the most sinister aspect of the whole business is recorded by Matthew: "Now the chief priests, and elders, and all the council, sought false witness against Jesus, to put him to death." (Matt. 26:59.)

Throughout this pretense of a proper trial, Jesus stood before his accusers calm, not reviling though he was reviled against. Finally, the leaders of the Jews, having convinced themselves that he was guilty, delivered him to Pilate. This little note is most significant, for rabbinic law explicitly stated that a unanimous verdict of guilt rendered on the same day of a trial was the same as an acquittal and gave freedom to the defendant.[7] Furthermore, the charge for which Jesus was to be put to death was blasphemy. According to the Mishna, a "blasphemer is not liable to the death penalty, unless he has pronounced the Ineffable Name [YAHWEH]."[8] Blaspheming or cursing God without pronouncing the "Ineffable Name" was punishable by flogging only.

Arraignment Before Pilate and Herod

Bound and condemned, Jesus was taken from the residence of Caiaphas to the hall of judgment to stand before the Roman governor, Pontius Pilate. This move, on top of all that Jesus had already endured, can only but have compounded the exhaustion—physically, emotionally, and spiritually—that he was feeling at that point. We do not know for certain the location of the Praetorium or judgment hall, but tradition holds it to be the Antonia Fortress. Rebuilt and strengthened by Herod, who named it in honor of his friend Mark Antony, the Antonia was situated at the northwest corner of the temple precinct for purposes of temple defense and surveillance. John 19:13 notes that the place of the judgment seat was called the "pavement," in Hebrew (Aramaic) *Gabbatha.* A portion of an ancient pavement found below the present-day surface of the ground may represent the site in question.

In bringing Jesus to Pilate, the leaders responsible for the previous trial at the palace of Caiaphas would not enter the judgment hall lest they be made ritually unclean owing to Passover requirements as well as Jewish regulations. (John 18:28; compare Acts 10:28.) Consequently, Pilate went out to meet them. It is ironic that Jesus, who had the power to make these Jewish leaders clean every whit (not just ritually clean), was the object of their vile persecutions and buffetings.

At this point the Jews began to accuse Jesus not just of blasphemy but also of sedition against Rome. This then prompted Pilate to ask Jesus if he was indeed the King of the Jews. (Luke 23:2-3.) Sometime during the course of this arraignment, a very interesting exchange occurred, as recorded by John. (See John 18:33-38.) In answer to Pilate's query, Jesus told the governor that he was a king, but that his kingdom was not of this world. However, he said, "Every one that is of the truth heareth my voice." Then Pilate asked his very famous question, "What is truth?" As Latter-day Saints, we possess the divinely inspired answer to that question, given to us from the very God who once stood before Pilate: "Truth is knowledge of things as they are, and as they were, and as they are to come." (D&C 93:24.) No plainer declaration could be made.

Interposed between the account of Jesus' early morning trial and this first arraignment before Pilate is Matthew's unique (among the Gospels) report on the suicide of Judas, the Lord's betrayer. (Matt. 27:3-10.) Owing to the brief mention of Judas's demise in Acts, it is a little surprising that nothing is mentioned in Luke about this episode. Judas Iscariot is one of eight men with that given name mentioned in the New Testament. His surname, Iscariot, probably means "man (Hebrew *'îsh*) of Kerioth." John (14:22) is careful to distinguish between Iscariot and another apostle named Judas, owing perhaps to the odium attached to the reputation of the former. Elder Talmage eloquently summarized the events leading to the death of Judas; how he became remorseful, consumed by the enormity of his crime; how he tried to undo the damage by returning the thirty pieces of silver (the price of a slave); and finally how "under the goading impulse of his master, the devil" he himself had become the slave, and he went and committed suicide.[9]

Pilate's interrogation of Jesus was interrupted when he learned that the prisoner was a Galilean and belonged in Herod's jurisdiction. He therefore sent the accused man to Herod Antipas, who was in Jerusalem at the time, evidently for the feast of Passover. Luke 23:6-12 reports that meeting and indicates that Herod was glad to see the Savior because he had hopes of witnessing a miracle performed by him.

Herod Antipas, son of Herod the Great, was at this time tetrarch of Galilee. We know he had been referred to by the Savior as "that fox" (Luke 13:31-32), and we know that he was the one who ordered the murder of John the Baptist. In fact, at some point he apparently had thought that Jesus was John the Baptist reincarnated.[10]

The meeting between Herod and Jesus was evidently short, since Jesus did not speak. No doubt upset by such silence, Herod had the Savior mocked, arrayed in a gorgeous robe that some modern authorities believe was white, the usual color of dress among Jewish nobility,[11] and sent back to Pilate. Luke concludes his report of the meeting with a very interesting note that tells us something of the political climate in Jesus' day: "The same day Pilate and Herod were made friends together: for before they were at enmity between themselves." (Luke 23:12.)

Since Herod refused to exercise jurisdiction, Pilate was now forced to act. Recognizing the Savior's innocence, he attempted to release him by giving the assembled crowd the choice to set free either Jesus or Barabbas. Matthew and Mark contain the fullest accounts of this episode (Matt. 27:16-26; Mark 15:7-15), though all of the Gospels recount the crowd's decision. It is noteworthy that each of the Gospel authors offers us a different perspective regarding the life of the prisoner who was released in place of the Savior. Matthew calls him a "notable prisoner." (Matt. 27:16.) From Mark and Luke we learn that he was an insurrectionist as well as a murderer, and John calls him a robber. (Mark 15:7; Luke 23:19, 25; John 18:40.) At any rate, Pilate, no doubt afraid to go against the insistent Jewish rulers who had by now stirred up and poisoned the crowd against Jesus (Mark 15:11), finally gave in after having appealed to the crowd several times that he found no fault in Jesus. All four Gospels record the cry of the mob, which demanded (at the instigation of the Jewish leaders) that Jesus should be crucified. Therefore Pilate scourged Jesus and delivered him up to be crucified.[12] (Matt. 27:24-26; Mark 15:12-15; Luke 23:23-25; John 18:40—19:1.)

Pilate was not a very appealing figure, though he did attempt to have Jesus released and later allowed the release of Jesus' body for burial. He ruled for ten years (A.D. 26-36) as procurator in Judea. He was first mentioned to Gospel readers in Luke 3:1; of the four Gospel writers, Luke probably was more interested in the man than the others. We begin to get a glimpse of his personality and the disdain he felt for the Jews when we are told that he mingled the blood of Galileans with their sacrifices. (Luke 13:1.) We understand more fully Pilate's character when we study the story of our Lord's Passion. Above all, he appears to have been a man who ultimately acted to preserve his own interests. Though he had acquitted the Savior of wrongdoing and wanted to release him as justice demanded, he gave in to the Jewish rulers and the rabble, fearing that any other decision would further increase his unpopularity.

Josephus and Philo indicate that Pilate was not the wisest of rulers, having offended various segments of the populace long before the mock trial of Jesus took place. Probably near the beginning of his rule Pilate had sent a detachment of troops into Jerusalem at night carrying ensigns of the Roman empire, consisting of images of the emperor and small eagles, which had always been left outside the city. This set off mass demonstrations, and Pilate ordered the offending symbols removed only after attempting to first intimidate his subjects.[13] Later in his administration the procurator built an aqueduct to bring water from Bethlehem to Jerusalem, and paid for the project with funds from the temple treasury. Though he must have had some cooperation from certain Jewish authorities in Jerusalem, this incident nevertheless caused another demonstration which resulted in bloodshed as Pilate suppressed the rioters.[14]

All of this tells us that Pilate reigned over an uneasy internal situation in Palestine at the time of the Savior's arraignment. We do not know with certainty the fate of Pilate. One story, propagated by the Church historian Eusebius, claims that Pilate fell into such misfortune that he committed suicide. Because Pilate's wife attested to Jesus' innocence as the result of an unusual dream (Matt. 27:19), she was later honored as a saint by the Greek Orthodox Church.[15]

The Crucifixion and Burial

The four accounts of the Crucifixion taken together give us a fairly detailed account of what happened. (Matt. 27:26-66; Mark 15:15-47; Luke 23: 26-56; John 19:16-42.) All four Gospel writers tell us that Jesus was led away to be crucified, though Luke contains the fullest account of the events immediately after the Savior left the presence of Pilate. Since victims carried either the traverse portion (crossbar) of their crosses or the whole thing, we do not know for certain what Jesus was required to do, although we suppose the latter. John 19:17 states simply that the Savior went forth "bearing his cross." At this point it appears that the cumulative effects of the past twenty-four hours took their toll; and Jesus, in his weakened condition, needed to be given assistance in carrying the cross. The Synoptic Gospels record that the man (a passerby, Mark says) who was pressed into service was Simon of Cyrene (a town of Libya).

Here Luke gives us valuable information not presented elsewhere. A great multitude of people (no doubt including both disciples and curiosity seekers) followed behind the Savior, with women bewailing and lamenting his fate. Jesus, ever the master teacher, turned and uttered a warning prophecy that was fulfilled some thirty-five years later when Jerusalem and the temple were devastated by the Romans. (Luke 23:27-31.) The Joseph Smith Translation of Luke 23:32 tells us this warning was meant to include the desolation of the gentiles as well as the scattering of Israel.

When the party reached the place called "the Skull" (*Golgotha* in Aramaic, *Calvaria* in Latin), the actual crucifixion took place. All the Gospels report that the Savior hung between two criminals. From John we learn that four soldiers comprised the crucifixion detail (John 19:23), and that they divided the garments of Jesus between themselves. In this action the Gospel writers saw the fulfillment of the psalmist's prophetic statement: "They part my garments among them, and cast lots upon my vesture." (Ps. 22:18.)

All of the Gospels tell of the superscription placed on the cross above Jesus' head. However, only Luke and John explain that it was written in Hebrew, Greek, and Latin, and only John informs us that it was authored by Pilate himself. This gives us an important clue as to the languages current among the inhabitants of Palestine in the time of Jesus. There are significant questions as to whether Hebrew in the Gospels really means Hebrew or Aramaic. By the first century, both used the same script and shared some words, but they were two distinct languages. For our purposes, it is significant to note that this trilingual inscription implies that Jerusalem was a real crossroads and that the place of crucifixion was located in a spot where people of varying linguistic backgrounds would have passed by.

As to which languages Jesus used, one can only speculate. However, he was certainly exposed to both classical (biblical) and Mishnaic (Talmudic) Hebrew (see Luke 2:46, 4:16); Aramaic, the *lingua franca* of the entire ancient Near East; Greek, the language of the Septuagint; and Latin, the official language of the Empire. It is possible that he used Aramaic for everyday speech and Hebrew for religious performances and biblical quotations.

The act of fixing a victim to a cross for the purposes of capital punishment was well known among many peoples of the ancient world. Alexander the Great employed it. According to Josephus, Cyrus the Great threatened with crucifixion anyone who interfered with the Jews returning to Israel from Babylon.[16] Apparently Darius the Persian also threatened to crucify those who did not obey his decrees. (Ezra 6:11.) Among the Romans, it was a punishment inflicted on those who were guilty of the most heinous crimes, though the ordinary Roman citizen was usually exempted from it.

Crucifixion was carried out either by tying the victim's hands and feet to the cross or by using nails while the victim was laid on the ground and then raising the cross upright. Frederic Farrar provides a detailed description of the effects of crucifixion on the human body:

> Death by crucifixion seems to include all that pain and death can have of [the] horrible and ghastly—dizziness, cramp, thirst, starvation, sleeplessness, traumatic fever, tetanus, publicity of shame, long continuance of torment, horror of anticipation, mortification of untended wounds—all intensified just up to the point at which they can be endured at all, but all stopping just short of the point which would give to the sufferer the relief of unconsciousness. The unnatural position made every movement painful; the lacerated veins and crushed tendons throbbed with incessant anguish; the wounds, inflamed by exposure, gradually gangrened; the arteries—especially of the head and stomach—became swollen and oppressed with surcharged blood; and while each variety of misery went on gradually increasing, there was added to them the intolerable pang of a burning and raging thirst; and all these physical complications caused an internal excitement and anxiety, which made the prospect of death itself . . . bear the aspect of a delicious and exquisite release.[17]

Such was the lot of our Lord as he hung and suffered on the cross.

It has been said that nothing reveals a person's true self as much as when he faces personal catastrophe. As incidents on the cross indicate, Jesus truly is the supreme exemplar. His actions indicate that even at this moment of tremendous suffering, his concern was for the welfare of others. Luke 23:34 recounts how he asked our Father in heaven to forgive those who crucified him. The Joseph Smith Translation of Luke 23:35 makes it clear that Jesus had reference to the soldiers who were carrying out orders. John's account tells us something about the compassion of the Master: As Jesus' mother stood by the cross, he directed his beloved disciple to care for and protect her—"and from that hour that disciple took her unto his own home." (John 19:27.)

Mark 15:25 tells us the Crucifixion began at the third hour (9 A.M.). All of the writers report that from the sixth hour (noon) to the ninth hour (3 P.M.), great darkness covered the land. Luke 23:45 adds that at that time "the veil of the temple was rent in the midst." This was followed by one of the most dramatic moments recorded in all of religious history. In a cry more anguish-laden than any mortal will ever be able to understand, the Savior of mankind called out, "Eloi, Eloi, lama sabachthani? which is, being interpreted, My God, my God, why hast thou forsaken me?" (Mark 15:34.)

I have sometimes marveled at how certain theologians could detachedly discuss this one passage—whether it was Hebrew or Aramaic, whether it represented the actual words of Jesus, who first recorded it, and so forth—and miss its profound implications. How close the Father and the Son must have been throughout the Son's earthly ministry! How sustaining the influence of the Father must have been to the Son! How utterly devastating the withdrawal of that influence must have been to one so accustomed to it! Now the Savior was alone. The agonies of Gethsemane had returned.[18]

As to why the Father withdrew himself, the words of Elder Talmage are instructive: "In that bitterest hour the dying Christ was alone, alone in most terrible reality. That the supreme sacrifice of the Son might be consummated in all its fulness, the Father seems to have withdrawn the support of His immediate Presence, leaving to the Savior of men the glory of complete victory over the forces of sin and death."[19]

The rest of the narrative following the death of the Savior is fairly well known. It is important to note that while all the Gospels discuss the role of Joseph of Arimathaea, only John mentions that Nicodemus brought spices to the burial. (John 19:38-42.) Both men were leaders of the Jews who recognized the special nature of the Savior's life and teachings. In the end they remained loyal to him and performed a special act of love and service.

Conclusion

The image of Jesus, bloody, bruised and humiliated, stumbling along while attempting to bear the weight of the cross, in many ways seems to symbolize and capsulize the profound lessons we need to learn from the Savior's life. Under the most adverse circumstances he moved along that course which would take him to the completion of his mission. He was loyal to the Father.

Perhaps that is why one of the greatest, if not the greatest, discourses ever given on the Atonement uses the symbolic imagery of enduring "the crosses of the world." (2 Ne. 9:18.) Faithfully bearing up under such loads prepares us for the kingdom of God. We cannot enjoy the association of the Savior without offering sacrifice in the similitude of the Savior, suffering tribulation in his name. (D&C 138:12-13.) We must be loyal to him as he was loyal to the Father. However, we can be sure that our Lord will be with us in our trials, lifting the burden of our crosses. After all, who understands better those kinds of needs than one whose cross was carried by someone else for a while?

NOTES

1. James E. Talmage, *Jesus the Christ* (Salt Lake City: Deseret Book, 1961), p. 617.

2. Spencer W. Kimball, "Peter, My Brother," *Brigham Young University Speeches of the Year* (Provo: Brigham Young University Publications, 1971), pp. 1-2.

3. See, for example, S. G. F. Brandon, *The Trial of Jesus of Nazareth* (New York: Stein and Day, 1968) or Kaim Cohn, *The Trial and Death of Jesus* (New York: Harper and Row, 1971).

4. Mishna Sanhedrin 11.2.

5. Talmage, *Jesus the Christ,* p. 623.

6. See ibid., pp. 645-48, where twelve violations of the law are discussed.

7. Mishna Sanhedrin 4.1.

8. Mishna Sanhedrin 7.5.

9. Talmage, *Jesus the Christ,* p. 642. See the Joseph Smith Translation of Matthew 27:6 for the manner in which Judas met his death.

10. Ibid., p. 636.

11. Ibid.

12. The name of the insurrectionist, Barabbas, literally "son of the father," is but another element of irony in the Savior's days of passion.

13. Josephus, *Antiquities* xviii. 3, 1; *War* ii. 9, 2-3.

14. Josephus, *Antiquities* xviii. 3, 2; *War* ii. 9, 4.

15. Madeleine Miller and J. Lane Miller, eds. *Harper's Bible Dictionary* (New York: Harper and Row, 1973), p. 753.

16. Josephus, *Antiquities* xi. 1, 3; 4, 6.

17. Frederic W. Farrar, *The Life of Christ* (Portland: Fountain Publishers, 1964), p. 641.

18. See Bruce R. McConkie, *Conference Report,* April 1985, p. 10.

19. Talmage, *Jesus the Christ,* p. 661.

30

THE WITNESSES OF THE RESURRECTION
(Matthew 28, Mark 16, Luke 24, John 20)

MONTE S. NYMAN

The testaments of Matthew, Mark, Luke, and John give many witnesses of the resurrection of Jesus Christ. Despite these witnesses, however, the world still doubts or rejects, in one way or another, this vital message of the New Testament. A review of these witnesses can bolster our faith today and help bring a personal witness to us in compliance with Moroni's declaration, "Ye receive no witness until after the trial of your faith." (Ether 12:6.)

The Witnesses in Jerusalem

A most unusual witness of the resurrection comes from the enemies of the Savior and of the truth. The chief priests and Pharisees came to Pilate and asked him to command that "the sepulchre be made sure until the third day, lest his disciples come by night, and steal him away, and say unto the people, He is risen from the dead: so the last error shall be worse than the first." Pilate complied with their wish; the sepulchre was sealed with a large stone, and a watch, or guard, was set upon it. (Matt. 27:62-66.) As analyzed by President Joseph F. Smith, such actions only verified the reality of the resurrection, for thereafter the leaders of the Jews could not claim that the Savior's disciples had stolen the body.[1] Nonetheless they attempted such a claim. When some of that watch reported to the chief priests

---

Monte S. Nyman is professor of ancient scripture, associate dean of Religious Education, and director of Book of Mormon research in the Religious Studies Center at Brigham Young University.

what had happened, the soldiers were given a large sum of money to say that indeed the disciples had stolen the Savior's body while the guards had slept, which negligence was a capital offense. They were told that the chief priests would intercede with the governor for them if the incident were brought before him. (Matt. 28:11-15.) Despite the chief priests' and others' attempts at deception, the guards stand as a witness to the world that it was a supernatural power that brought Jesus from the grave.

Jesus had taught his disciples that he had the power to take up his body again after he had laid it down. (John 10:17-18.) Although we have no account of his actual resurrection, we do have accounts of other supernatural powers that attended his resurrection. First there was a great earthquake, a means whereby God often speaks to man (see D&C 43:25), and then an angel appeared and rolled back the stone. These actions brought fear upon the guards, and they "became as dead men" (Matt. 28:2-4), which suggests they fainted or were subdued to total silence.

A companion witness to the removal of the stone is that of the women who visited the tomb. Although the account in Matthew 28:1-5 suggests that the two Marys who visited the sepulchre at dawn of the first day of the week were witnesses to the angel's rolling back the stone, Mark 16:1-5 records that as the women approached the sepulchre, they discussed how they might get the stone rolled away, and upon their arrival they saw that the stone had already been rolled away. They also saw the young man—an angel—sitting inside the entrance. Both Luke and John support Mark's account.

Upon seeing the angel, the women were told that Jesus had risen, and they were invited to "see the place where the Lord lay." They were then told to go quickly and tell the disciples that Christ had risen and was going to Galilee, where they would see him. They hurried to obey these instructions. (Matt. 28:5-8.) The account in Luke records that the women entered the sepulchre and were perplexed because they did not find the body. Then two men in shining garments appeared and informed them of Christ's prophesied resurrection. (Luke 24:1-7.) The Joseph Smith Translation of Luke states that these men were angels and were outside the sepulchre upon the arrival of the women. The Joseph Smith Translation of John 20:1 adds that the two angels were sitting on the stone. Apparently, both Matthew and Mark were concerned only with the angelic message and overlooked recording that there were two angels present. Regardless of the number, the angels were a spiritual witness to support the physical evidence of the stone having been removed. The Lord's law of witnesses was met (Deut. 19:15), and the women had two witnesses—including both physical and spiritual affirmation that Jesus had risen.

Upon hearing the report of the women, Peter and John the Beloved ran to the sepulchre and saw the linen clothes but no body of Jesus. Not fully comprehending Jesus' prophecy that he would rise again, they returned to their own homes. (John 20:2-10.)

After the disciples left, Mary Magdalene remained outside the sepulchre weeping. She looked into the sepulchre, and again she saw the two angels, who asked why she wept. After responding that her Lord had been taken away, she turned and saw Jesus but did not recognize him. There was another exchange of questions concerning why she wept and where the body was laid, and then Jesus called her by name. Recognizing him, she called him *Rabboni* or "Master" and apparently stepped toward him; she was cautioned against holding or touching him, because he had "not yet ascended to [his] Father." He then instructed her to go to the disciples and tell them that he was ascending to his Father. Mary reported to the disciples, telling them that she had seen the Lord, and relaying his message to them. (John 20:11-18.)[2] Mark records that the disciples "believed not." (Mark 16:9-11.)

Mary Magdalene was thus given the privilege of being the first mortal to see the resurrected Lord. Why such a privilege was granted to her is not known.

The next appearance of Jesus is not recorded but merely referred to by Luke. In describing a report of two disciples to the eleven apostles, Luke wrote that the Lord had appeared to Simon. (Luke 24:33-34.) Although none of the other Gospels mention this appearance to Peter, Paul did tell the Corinthian saints that following the resurrection on the third day, as foretold in the scriptures, the Savior "was seen of Cephas, then of the Twelve." (1 Cor. 15:3-5.) This appearance to Peter was undoubtedly because of Peter's position as president of the Church. (Matt. 16:19.)

Matthew records that there was also an appearance to the other women who had gone to the sepulchre early that morning. As they were rushing to tell the disciples that Jesus' body was not in the tomb, Jesus met them and addressed them. Matthew names only the other Mary, while Mark identifies the women as Salome and Mary the mother of James. (Mark 16:1.) Luke names Joanna as being with Mary the mother of James and other women. (Luke 24:10.) While the exact number is not known, there were apparently several women. That this is a separate appearance from Mary Magdalene's is evident from the fact that they "held [Jesus] by the feet, and worshipped him." Mary had been told not to touch him, but these women were allowed to do so. He then instructed them to tell the brethren to go to Galilee, where they would see him. (Matt. 28:9-10.) Since some time had lapsed, Jesus having in the meantime ascended to his Father, it is assumed that this appearance to the women also occurred after Jesus appeared to Simon Peter. However, no account tells us the exact sequence of events.

The next recorded appearance of Jesus in Jerusalem was to two disciples on the road to Emmaus. While there is uncertainty about the exact geographical location of the village of Emmaus, it was in the Jerusalem area. (Luke 24:13.) Why Jesus chose to appear to these two brethren (one of whom is identified as Cleopas) is again not stated. Perhaps it was a reward for their faith, or perhaps it was to give a witness to the common people in addition to the leadership of the Church. Regardless, Jesus appeared and asked concerning the seriousness of their conversation. He then opened the scriptures and expounded, "beginning at Moses and all the prophets" (Luke 24:27), on how all of the events associated with the resurrection had been foretold. When they arrived at their destination, Jesus accepted their invitation to tarry with them, and as he partook of food with them, "he took bread, and blessed it, and brake, and gave to them." (Luke 24:30.) At this point their eyes were opened, and they recognized Jesus, who promptly vanished from their sight. The witness was now complete; they praised the Lord, saying: "Did not our heart burn within us, while he talked with us by the way, and while he opened to us the scriptures?" (Luke 24:32.) These two disciples also had two witnesses: the testimony of the Holy Ghost—a spiritual confirmation—and the recognition of Jesus as a physical being who indeed had once been dead.

Legend suggests that Luke, the author of the account, was one of the two men.

That evening Jesus appeared in Jerusalem to ten of the apostles and others who were assembled. Luke records that eleven apostles were present (Luke 24:34), but from the account in John 20:24, it is apparent that Thomas was not present. The two Emmaus disciples had hastened to Jerusalem to inform the apostles of their great spiritual experience, and found the apostles discussing the appearance of Jesus to Peter.

As the two disciples made their report, "Jesus himself stood in the midst of them, and saith unto them, Peace be unto you." The apostles, despite the previous reports, "were terrified and affrighted, and supposed that they had seen a spirit." But Jesus calmed them and showed them his hands and feet, which apparently had the marks of the crucifying nails upon them: "Handle me, and see; for a spirit hath not flesh and bones, as ye see me have." He then requested food—a further witness of his physical resurrected body—and ate the fish and honeycomb they brought him. After he ate, he opened the scriptures, this time including the Psalms, and helped them to understand how these scriptures had testified of him. He also charged them to be witnesses of the things they had seen, to labor as special witnesses of his resurrection and divinity. He admonished them, however, to remain in Jerusalem until the promised endowment of power from on high came from the Father. Jesus then led them to Bethany, where they witnessed his ascension into heaven. Now special witnesses of the Son of God, they "returned to Jerusalem with great joy" and proclaimed their witness in the temple. (Luke 24:33-53.)

John's account of the Savior's appearance records that the apostles were given the Holy Ghost and the power to remit or forgive sins. (John 20:22-23.) The phrase used, that he "breathed on them" to give the Holy Ghost, can be understood through the teachings of the Book of Mormon, where we learn that the Holy Ghost was given to the apostles through the laying on of hands. (See 3 Ne. 18:36-37; Moro. 2:1-2.)

The final recorded appearance of Jesus in his resurrected body in Jerusalem occurred eight days later. Thomas, a member of the Twelve who had not been present at the previous appearance, was with the other apostles on this occasion.[3] Jesus appeared and said to him, "Reach hither thy finger, and behold my hands; and reach hither thy hand, and thrust it into my side: and be not faithless, but believing." To Thomas's response, "My Lord and my God," Jesus commented that Thomas was blessed because he had seen and believed; however, "blessed are they that have not seen, and yet have believed." (John 20:26-29.)

The Witness in Galilee

In Jesus' appearances in Jerusalem, he repeatedly instructed his apostles to assemble in Galilee, where he would appear to them. This promise he kept both collectively and individually.

The first appearance in Galilee was to seven of the apostles at the Sea of Tiberias (Galilee). This was actually the third recorded appearance to a majority of the Twelve. Seven of the apostles, led by Peter, had gone fishing. They fished all night but caught nothing. Unrecognized by the apostles, Jesus stood on the shore and inquired as to their success. When they reported that they had caught no fish, he instructed them to throw their net on the right side of the boat. They did so, and the result was a catch of a "multitude of fishes." Suddenly John the Beloved recognized Jesus and told Peter, "It is the Lord." Jesus invited them to eat with him. Then he taught them more concerning their mission. (John 21.)

The appearance on the coast of Tiberias was not the promised appearance in Galilee to the apostles, possibly because they were not all present or perhaps because of the impatience shown by Peter and the others. According to Matthew, the place of the apostles' meeting had been designated by Jesus, "a mountain . . . appointed them." (Matt. 28:16.) Little is known of the appearance on the mount other than that the apostles were instructed to go forth and preach the gospel to all nations. (Matt. 28:17-20; Mark 16:14-18.) This is further evidence that the appearance was after the Pentecost, where the Spirit was collectively poured out on the Saints.

Other Witnesses

For other appearances, we are indebted to Paul's epistles to the saints in Corinth. In addition to reporting the appearance to Peter (Luke 24:33-34), Paul referred to an appearance of Jesus to "above five hundred brethren at once." (1 Cor. 15:6.) We have no record of where this event took place. This appearance to such a large group might be compared with the Savior's appearance to twenty-five hundred Nephites in America, a group that included men, women, and children. (3 Ne. 17:25.) Both of these experiences were undoubtedly a reward to the faithful followers who had endured the trial of their faith.

Paul also told the saints at Corinth that Jesus had appeared to James. He did not identify which James, although it is reasonable to assume that it was the one who was a member of the presidency of the church. (D&C 7:7; Matt. 17:1-2.) However, the James who was prominent in Paul's day, who would have been more familiar to the saints of Corinth, was James the brother of Jesus. What the Savior told James is not known. And, finally, Paul told the Corinthians that the Lord had appeared to him (this was, of course, many years later).

In addition to these appearances, there have been many appearances to apostles and prophets in the latter days. (D&C 76:23; 110:1-10.)

The New Testament answers the Old Testament question of Job, "If a man die, shall he live again?" (Job 14:14.) Not only were there multiple witnesses of the resurrection of Jesus, but Matthew also recorded that "the graves were opened; and many bodies of the saints which slept arose, and came out of the graves after his resurrection, and went into the holy city, and appeared unto many." (Matt. 27:52-53.) To those who will accept it, a second witness is found in the Book of Mormon, which reports that many others were brought forth from the grave in another hemisphere following Christ's resurrection. (3 Ne. 23:9-11.)

The Lord has provided the witnesses, the world is on trial, and the judgment will be rendered after a trial of our faith. Those who accept the witnesses will know "that Jesus is the Christ, the Son of God; and that believing [they] might have life through his name." (John 20:31.) This is the purpose of John's testimony, and it should be the objective for every seeker after truth.

NOTES

1. Joseph F. Smith, *Gospel Doctrine* (Salt Lake City: Deseret Book, 1977), pp. 463-64.

2. Many theories have been advanced as to why Mary was told not to touch Jesus. These must remain as theories, because we have no substantial answer. Although the present Joseph Smith Translation of John 20:17 changes the word *touch* to *hold,* it is not certain whether Joseph Smith intended the word *hold* to mean *embrace* or *detain.*

3. John records that the doors were shut, an indication that Jesus did not come into the room in the usual manner. As an immortal resurrected being, he was not bound by the normal physical laws but could enter closed rooms without there being an opening. This is substantiated by Moroni's appearance to Joseph Smith. (JS–H 1:43.)

31

THE RESURRECTED LORD AND HIS APOSTLES
(John 21)

THOMAS W. MACKAY

The Setting

Of the postresurrection appearances of the Savior recorded in the New Testament, John 21 is striking in a quiet but penetrating way. After having recounted, in the preceding chapter, the resurrection and some of the experiences of Mary and the apostles with the Lord, John relates a simple experience on the Sea of Galilee (called the Sea of Tiberias in John 21:1, as well as in John 6:1). Because the directive "feed my sheep" is often quoted, we should examine it in context.

Despite having seen the resurrected Savior and despite having received personal assurance of his divinity, the disciples are portrayed as still foundering, still lacking direction and motivation. From our perspective, on the basis of both Luke's account in Acts and John's statement (John 7:39; see also John 14:16, 26; 15:26; 16:13) that the Holy Ghost had not yet been given, we may conclude that the disciples had been touched by the Holy Ghost but had not yet received that cleansing, revitalizing force we term the birth of the Spirit. Although they had been promised they would receive the Holy Ghost, the gift itself was not made manifest until Pentecost (Acts 2), more than a month and a half after the resurrection. It was during the forty-day ministry that the events of John 21 took place.

Seven disciples were in Galilee: Simon Peter, Thomas (or Didymos), Nathanael, the two sons of Zebedee (John the Beloved and his

---

Thomas W. Mackay is professor of Greek and Latin at Brigham Young University.

brother James), and two other disciples. (John 21:2.) Manifesting his natural leadership, Peter stated that he was going fishing; the others concurred. Implicit in Peter's words was a growing impatience about waiting to learn what they should do. His response to the situation was to return to his former work by going fishing. In the structure of John's Gospel, this setting is reminiscent of Peter's call recorded in John 1:35-42. Peter's brother, Andrew, had been one of the adherents of John the Baptist, from whom he learned the identity of the Redeemer, the Messiah or anointed Savior (Greek *Christos* means "the anointed one"). It is in Matthew 4:18-20 that we learn more about Peter and Andrew as fishermen by trade; and so, echoing Jeremiah 16:16, Jesus invited them to join him, saying, "I will make you fishers of men."

Then, with characteristic irony, John notes that though they fished throughout the night, they caught nothing. As dawn came, Jesus stood at the shore, unrecognized by the disciples even when he spoke. At his instructions, the disciples cast their nets to the right side; the net was so full of fish—John states that there were 153 (John 21:11)—that they could not pull it into the boat, and the net nearly broke. Immediately John realized who it was on the shore. Peter's impetuous response, after clothing himself, was to hurl himself into the sea to hasten to the Lord. The event may have been so recorded by John to counterbalance Matthew's account of Peter walking on the water, which Matthew alone appends to the story of Jesus approaching the disciples by walking across the water. (John 6:15-21; Matthew 14:22-23; Mark 6:45-52.) Certainly the very setting of this postresurrection appearance of the Lord brings vividly to mind other instances in John where Jesus was around the boats, the sea, and fishermen. And the disciples knew well his identity without inquiring.

Bread, Fish, and Wine

But even more important, as the disciples came ashore, they saw a fire as well as fish and bread. When Jesus had them eat of the bread and fish, it was a symbolic reminder of the great multitude that he fed during his mortal ministry. In John's account of the setting for the "Bread of Life" sermon in John 6, the multitude wanted to make Jesus king, but his subsequent discourse turned many away. (John 6:66.) For he was the true manna that had come down from heaven, the bread of life, and his doctrine was hard. Since many deserted, he asked the disciples whether they, too, would leave. In John's way of writing, the miracle of the feeding of the multitude recorded in John 6 was a situation in which the Lord was being tested in a true-life circumstance parallel to Satan's testing his fortitude and self-discipline during Jesus' solitary fasting in the desert. (Matthew 4:1-11.) As the divinely appointed Messiah, Jesus had the power to create life (John 1:3-4, a passage that echoes Genesis), to sustain it (as with wine, fish, bread), and to renew it (John 11—the resurrection of Lazarus). The symbols of sustaining life were the bread and the fish (or, elsewhere, the wine), and the Jews knew that the Messiah would be able to produce them. Satan's efforts in the temptations were directed at getting Jesus to doubt or question his Messianic powers and to use them either for personal satisfaction or to gain the adulation of the crowds. Whether confronting Satan directly or whether confronting the pressure of a large multitude ready to worship and to adore, Jesus chose the course his Father directed him to choose: I do only that which the Father has shown me. (John 5:19; 8:28.)

Bread, fish, and wine are the characteristic symbols found throughout John that unify the stories and the teachings. The presence of bread and fish beside the Lord when he bid the disciples come ashore ties this scene back to earlier events in John, and they all point to the great Messianic banquet when he will come in his glory and eat with Abraham, Isaac, Jacob, holy prophets, and all who are worthy. (See Matt. 8:11, where "sit down" properly means to recline at a meal with someone; see also D&C 27:5-14.) Just as he had broken bread with the two disciples in Emmaus, here, on the shore of the Sea of Galilee, the resurrected Lord shared a sacramental meal with his disciples. The very word *sacrament* comes from the Latin *sacramentum*, meaning an oath of allegiance such as was made by a Roman soldier to his general. In a sense, in the sacrament we partake of the emblems of our oath of allegiance to the Lord. It is thus natural and appropriate that loyalty and fidelity to the cause of the Messiah should be bound up with eating the sustaining forces of life he produced; it is entirely in harmony with the rest of John's Gospel that he should imply such here.

"Lovest Thou Me?"

Only a short while before, Peter had categorically denied his affiliation with the Lord on three occasions. (John 18:17, 25-27.) President David O. McKay suggested that the threefold questioning of Peter in John 21:15-19 was the Lord's way of letting Peter make good his error, of having him purge his soul with a reaffirmation of loyalty and of energetic, devoted action.[1] Just as Peter had denied the Lord three times, three times the Lord invited Peter to assert his love and commitment.

Some writers have confused readers about the nature of John's words for *love* in chapter 21 of his Gospel. Let us, therefore, rather patiently and carefully examine the passage in question. After they had eaten (that is, after the sacramental meal reestablishing the open expression of the disciples' devotion to the Savior), the Lord said to Simon Peter, "Simon, son of Jonah, do you love me more than these?" Peter replied, "Oh, yes, my Lord; you know that I love you." (John 21:15; translation by the author.) In Jesus' words "than these," we understand "than you love these [fish]," a gentle chastisement of Peter. For he (and we) ought to love the Lord's work more than the things of this world. Without directly raising the question, the Lord caused Peter to reflect: Why should I be more concerned about material goods than about preaching the gospel? Even lacking specific instructions, Peter should try to help others. His responsibility as one of the apostles gave new direction to life, or at least it should have done so. After Pentecost it did.

But Peter was afflicted with one of the most common diseases of mankind: discouragement. Even while anticipating the success of the Lord's kingdom, he had experienced the death of his Master, whom he had denied knowing three times. Perhaps the anguish of his actions and of his dashed expectations weighed upon him. In such circumstances people often revert to old habitual pursuits. That is what Peter did. He went fishing, taking with him other apostles. So when the Lord inquired whether Peter loved him more than worldly pursuits or tangible goods, the question acted as a purging influence, bringing Peter to acknowledge the strength and depth of his testimony, which had been temporarily obscured. The resurrected Lord masterfully taught Peter by having him recognize and state the true priorities of his life. He then exhorted Peter to put these priorities into practice.

While it is true that there are several words for *love* in Greek, John 21:15-17 is probably not the best passage to differentiate the meanings. But because many have treated this exchange as though it were intended to urge Peter to a higher form of love, we should examine more closely John's account of Jesus' words here. Since the Greek language is extremely rich in vocabulary and grammar, it exhibits many synonyms. In the New Testament, at least four different word groups (verbs, nouns, or adjectives based on the same stem) may be translated by a meaning in the range of the English *love: phileo, agapao, stergo, aspazomai.* Furthermore, another word group based on *eros,* commonly used in classical literature to describe a purely sensuous or passionate love, does not appear in the New Testament (though it appears twice in the Septuagint or Greek Old Testament used by the early Christian Church).

In Greek, the noun *eros* is used both for *love* and for the boy Cupid (from the Latin noun *cupido* or "desire"), who, according to the myths of classical antiquity, stirs up longing and desire in the hearts of people by shooting them with his arrows. We would expect that the notion of *eros* would receive a strong condemnation in the scriptures, particularly in cataloguing evils and vices that are prevalent in the world and that members of the church should avoid. But the entire word group is lacking from the New Testament, and only occasionally does it appear in later Christian writings. John does not use it; to suggest the word in the context of John 21 is offensive, contrary to the entire episode.

The word *aspazomai* (often translated "greet" or "salute") includes warm and affectionate greetings, often with a kiss. The welcome may include a friend, relative, or peer, or it may extend to acclaiming a king; in Matthew 5:47 it clearly means to cherish, love, and be fond of someone. While the verb and its related noun are common enough in the synoptic Gospels, and while John uses the verb in his epistles, he does not include it in his Gospel. If he had intended to convey a development of love, he likely would have used this word to mean general, natural human love, warmth, and respect for one another.

Another word with a more specific sense was *stergo*. It was originally used by poets for the word *love*, with the nuance of love between parents and children; but by the time of the New Testament, prose writers also used it. Most commonly, the meaning was the love a parent felt for a child; Euripides pathetically used it thus in his play *Medea*. While *love* as a verb does not occur in the New Testament, other early Christian writers in the late first and second centuries used it. But one form of the stem does appear in the writings of Paul in a very pejorative or negative sense. In Romans 1:31 (in a list of vices) and in 2 Timothy 3:3 (talking of the last days), Paul uses an adjective with a negative prefix (like *un*loving): *astorgos*. This is not surprising, for Paul had an extensive familiarity with Greek literature and quoted from some Greek poets. John knew Greek very well, though he probably did not enjoy Paul's familiarity with classical literature. Nevertheless, inasmuch as John wrote the Gospel in Greek (and that, too, quite probably for the church at the Greek city of Ephesus after he wrote Revelation, according to early Christian sources), he could well have drawn upon Paul and other Christian or non-Christian Greek works for this sense of the word. He did not. Never, even speaking of God's love for his own Son, does he use the positive sense of the verb. Instead, he writes *phileo* or *agapao,* without making a distinction between the two words.

Generally, *phileo* has a broad meaning of love and affection, from kindness to a passionate kiss, from respect to deep love. John used the verb *phileo* to describe God's love for his Son (John 5:20) and the disciples (John 16:27), and Christ's love for Lazarus (John 11:3, 36). Jesus uses the noun *friends (philoi)* in an elevated manner (John 15:15); the disciples are his friends *(philoi)* if they keep his commandments (John 15:14). Negatively, *phileo* is used to describe a person loving his own life (John 12:25), just as John in 1 John 2:15 uses *agapao* to describe loving or lusting after the things of this world. (At James 4:4 "friendship of the world" is *philia*.)

In Greek, *agapao* and its related words (for example, *agapazo* in Homer) carry a range of meaning: to treat with affection, to caress, to be fond of, to love, to be contented with or pleased at, to show affection, to value or esteem. In John we find *agapao* to describe God loving the world (John 3:16; 1 Jn. 4:9-10), God loving his Son, and his Son loving the disciples (John 15:9), the love of his disciples for one another (John 13:34-35; 15:12, 17), and the obedience stemming from love (John 14:23-24; 15:10). But in Christian usage the noun came to mean a love-feast or meal shared in connection with church services (much as we might say sacrament meeting). The adjective *beloved (agapetos)* is used of Christ in the synoptics (Matt. 3:17; 17:5) and of members of the church in the writings of Paul and the general epistles, including John.

In John 21 Jesus twice asks, "Do you love me?" *(agapas me)* and Peter responds, "I love you" *(philo se)*. Jesus asks the same question the third time, now using the other verb, *phileis me,* to which Peter responds with *philo se,* the same as the first two times. His protestation of love would be ludicrous if he had replied with a word that had a distinctly lesser meaning than the word used by the Lord. Likewise, if the words were not synonymous, why would John have Jesus alter his words?

Thus we conclude that *agapao* and *phileo* occur interchangeably in this context of John's Gospel. Although some popular Christian ministers and Latter-day Saint speakers have endeavored to see in John 21 levels of love and some sort of qualitative personal growth, there is nothing in John's words to warrant such a conclusion. Literary, stylistic, and vocabulary considerations require interpreting the phrases as deliberate repetition of the same point by using synonyms.

Peter's Death Foretold

As we read in Eusebius's account of early Christian history, Peter did indeed die in Rome, crucified upside down.[2] That he had developed the determination of character to emulate the Savior and remain true to the testimony he had uttered three times on the shore to his resurrected Lord illustrates that at least for John, the sealing of the Atonement by the Resurrection was the focal point of the life of Christ. To gain and to bear testimony of that event was far more significant than the utterance by Peter near Caesarea. (Matt. 16:16.) Hence, John's account minimizes the very things that some people at Rome were extolling: Peter and his confession of faith.

This same attitude toward Peter may be seen in John's references to "the beloved disciple" and to the walking on the sea (John 6:16-21) without mentioning Peter walking on the water, an event recorded only in Matthew 14:28-33. In John 21 the postresurrection appearance of the Lord furnishes an analogous situation, but John notes only that Peter attempted to approach Jesus—by swimming. Similarly, at the beginning of John 20, both Peter and John hastened to the tomb, though John, perhaps with an inward smile, notes that "the other disciple" ran ahead faster than Peter. Yet, after looking inside, he did not have the audacity to enter the tomb. Peter, on the other hand, rushed right in. (John 20:4-7.)

Whereas Matthew gives us the magnificent testimony of Peter at Caesarea shortly after Jesus fed the multitude, John's report of the event is somewhat more subdued: "Lord, to whom will we go? Thou hast the words of eternal life. And we have come to trust [or, in Greek, have faith, believe] and know that thou art God's holy one." (John 6:68-69; translation by the author.) Like most of us, Peter's actions warranted occasional reproach and encouragement, but he was at base a good, dedicated, and energetic person. He willingly surrendered his life to and for his Lord.

John's Mortal Life Extended But Transformed

Of all the events recounted in John 21, the translation or transformed physical condition of John is most enigmatic for the world. That it stands in stark contrast to Peter's future is only one aspect, for John was the *beloved* disciple. Curiously, although this scripture states that John would not die until the Savior returned (John 21:23), Eusebius records that John met death.[3] The compression of John's narrative has deliberately obscured the circumstances of the Lord's promise to John presupposed by John 21:21-23. Early commentators are perplexed by the passage; Latter-day Saints fare better because we have other sources on the subject, section 7 of the Doctrine and Covenants and chapter 28 of 3 Nephi.

In the Doctrine and Covenants we have a brief transcript of a writing of John from a leather scroll that Joseph Smith saw in a vision. Since the language of that text is close to the Gospel of John but more expansive and in a more personal tone, we may have in section 7, as well as in section 93, some of John's earlier or more complete Gospel that we are told will be brought forth in our dispensation (D&C 93:18), depending on our faith. Certainly the first-person narrative of section 7 contrasts sharply with the third-person account in John ("the disciple whom Jesus loved" [*phileo* at John 20:2 and *agapao* at John 21:20]). But section 7 requires that the reader know John 21 or at least the point made in John 21:20-23. Yet section 7 clarifies why John would remain untouched by death, while the other disciples would come to the Lord: John was to preach the gospel and to prophesy among the nations in order to prepare the way for the return of the Lord. From John 21:22-23 we learn that John was to remain until Jesus should come, but, as noted above, John does not elaborate the point in his Gospel that has been transmitted to us.

In 3 Nephi 28 we find a reference to John's condition, for three of the Nephite Twelve sought the same promise and privilege that Jesus had granted to John. From Mormon's statements we conclude that John and the three Nephite disciples entered a condition analogous to that experienced by Enoch and his city: they are no longer subjected to mortal conditions and restrictions known to us; they can disguise themselves; they have supernatural mobility; they can exercise tremendous priesthood powers; Satan no longer has power over them to tempt them; and they will undergo another change to their eternal condition when the Lord comes. Mormon himself, curious as to how they could be above death, asked and learned that when they were changed, pain, sorrow, and death could not affect them. (3 Nephi 28:37-38.) Therefore, 3 Nephi 28 is really our best description of what happened also to John.

Given the long interval between that occasion and the present, we may well wonder whether any of the Nephite disciples or John might have regretted that choice. Still, the world has been blessed through their ministry even without knowing its source or nature. Their actions have been a manifestation of a deep and abiding love for their fellowmen and for the gospel. Like Peter, we will go to our Master; others will remain until his coming.

In John 21 we have a precious record of the Lord's postresurrection appearance to some disciples on the Sea of Galilee. The sacramental meal of fish and bread provided by the Lord only reinforced his lesson: his kingdom requires full dedication. If John reported that Jesus, in helping Peter to understand this message, used two different words for *love,* he did so only for stylistic variation and not to differentiate meanings or qualities of love. John's own devotion to the cause led him to request the privilege of continuing to manifest this love to others by remaining in a mortal, though transformed, condition. Whether our lives are of long or short duration, we too should be motivated to minister to the Lord's sheep.

NOTES

1. David O. McKay, "Christ, the Light of Humanity," *Improvement Era* 71 (June 1968): 5.
2. Eusebius *HE* II.xxv. 5.

SCRIPTURE INDEX

THE OLD TESTAMENT

GENESIS

6:2	423
6:4	423
6:9	243
12:6	211
17:1	243
17:11, JST	147
33:18	211
35:4	211
37:14	211
49:9	263

EXODUS

3:14	118
6:3	342
12:1-11	406
13:1-2	147
19:18	180
20:17	206
21:12	243
23:14-17	209
29:42	241
30:19	407
30:30-31	162
40:15	162
40:31	407

LEVITICUS

2:13	239
12:1-8	147
16:5-10	435
19:18	316, 420
23:4-8	209
23:15-21	209
23:33-44	209

NUMBERS

15:37-41	202
18:19	239

21:8-9	196
25:1-8	26

DEUTERONOMY

5:21	206
6:4	202, 424
6:4-6	153
6:4-7	32, 203
6:4-9	202
6:5	316, 420
11:13-21	202
11:29	211
12:5	206
18:15	292, 326
18:15-19	324
18:18	208
18:18-19	292
19:15	256, 455
22:20-21	143
24:1-4	366
27:11-13	211
34:1-8	307

JOSHUA

3:17	178
24:32	211

JUDGES

5:10	389
10:4	389
16:17	56

1 SAMUEL

26:9	386

2 SAMUEL

5:2	56
7:12-16	374
13:29	389
18:9	389

1 KINGS

8:48	210

2 KINGS

2:6-8	178
2:9-12	307
2:14	178
5:10-14	178
17:24	204
17:24-41	204

2 CHRONICLES

24:20-22	390

EZRA

4	205
4:1-4	28
4:2	204
4:10	204
6:11	449

NEHEMIAH

2:19-20	205
4	205
13:28	204

JOB

1:1	243
1:6	423
14:14	459
38:7	423

PSALMS

22:18	448
23	118
24:3-6	239
35:19	414
45:6	342
45:6-7	341

45:7 | 342
78:2 | 56
82:6 | 405
107:4-7 | 238
107:9 | 238
110:1 | 385
113-118 | 153
118:22 | 380
118:26 | 402
120-126 | 153
135-136 | 153
137:5-6 | 12

PROVERBS

6:16 | 440
16:18 | 410
27:6 | 441

ISAIAH

4:3 | 56
6:9-10 | 56, 269
7:14 | 56
8:23-9:1 | 56
12:3 | 332
14:6 | 185
14:12-14 | 184
14:15 | 184
29:13 | 298
40:2-3 | 81
40:3 | 56, 77, 81
40:7-8 | 81
42:1-4 | 56
44:3 | 331
49:6 | 328

50:7 | 322
52:11 | 407
52:13-53:12 | 82
53:4 | 56
53:4-5 | 433
53:7 | 433
53:10 | 433
53:12 | 60
55:1 | 331
55:1-2 | 352
55:10-11 | 129
58 | 187
59:5 | 314
60:1-3 | 328
60:12 | 186
61:1-2 | 203, 237
62:11 | 56
63:3 | 437
64:8 | 315

JEREMIAH

1:5 | 328
2:2 | 399
7 | 391
7:4 | 392
7:6 | 392, 401
7:9 | 392
7:10 | 392
7:11 | 392
12:7 | 402
16:16 | 462
18:2-3 | 56
22:5 | 402
26 | 391

26:9 | 392
31:15 | 56
31:31-33 | 7
31:31-34 | 406
32:6-15 | 56

EZEKIEL

8:16 | 210
10:18-19 | 402
11:22-23 | 402
17:2 | 264
17:2-10 | 277
24:3-8 | 277
24:19 | 277

DANIEL

3:25 | 423
6:10 | 203
11:31 | 396
12:11 | 396

HOSEA

2 | 399
11:1 | 56

MICAH

5:1 | 56

ZECHARIAH

9:9 | 56, 374
11:12-13 | 56

MALACHI

3:1 | 81

THE NEW TESTAMENT

MATTHEW

1:1-17 | 51, 141
1:18 | 48, 142
1:18-21 | 142
1:19 | 142-43
1:20 | 143, 157
1:21 | 6, 147
1:22-23 | 56
1:24 | 157
2:1, JST | 48
2:1 | 148
2:1-12 | 52
2:5 | 56
2:5b-6 | 56
2:7 | 148
2:7-16 | 52

2:8 | 150
2:12 | 150
2:13 | 157
2:15b | 56
2:16 | 148
2:17 | 56
2:17-18 | 56
2:19 | 157
2:23 | 153
2:23b | 56
2:33 | 157
3:1-2 | 175
3:1-17 | 166
3:2, JST | 149
3:3 | 56, 175, 176
3:4 | 172

3:4-6, JST | 150
3:8 | 176
3:13 | 177
3:13, JST | 151
3:14 | 178
3:16 | 178-79
3:17 | 179, 467
3:21-22, JST | 153
3:24-25, JST | 156
3:38, JST | 176-77
3:43, JST | 178
4:1, JST | 181
4:1-11 | 463
4:3 | 181
4:4 | 182
4:5, JST | 183

4:6	183-84	6:33	363	10:11-15	232
4:7	185, 319	6:34	246	10:14, JST	232
4:8	185	7:1	237, 246	10:16	233
4:9, JST	185	7:1, JST	231	10:16-40, JST	341
4:10	186	7:6	267	10:17	31
4:11	186	7:6-7, JST	54	10:17-18	233
4:11, JST	170	7:7-8	247	10:19	233
4:14-16	56	7:11	247	10:22	233
4:18, JST	55	7:11, JST	231	10:23	233
4:18-20	462	7:12	247	10:30	233
4:22	228	7:13	247	10:32-39	363
5:1, JST	231	7:14, JST	54	10:34-36	233
5:1-4, JST	51	7:21	247	10:37	363
5:3-6	238	7:21-23	403	10:37-38	233
5:7-10	238	7:24-27	274	11:1-11	295
5:13	239, 262	7:24-30	225	11:3-5	214
5:14	240, 419	7:28-29	250	11:15	309
5:14-16	274	7:37, JST	155	12:1-8	229
5:17	55, 241	8:1-4	217, 224	12:10-13	217, 224
5:18	407	8:5-13	218, 224	12:17-21	56
5:20-21, JST	53	8:11	463	12:22	224, 251
5:21	55	8:11-12	218	12:23, JST	253
5:21-22	36	8:14-15	218, 223	12:24	261
5:21-26	242	8:16-17	217, 224	12:26	252
5:21-48	241	8:17	56	12:26-28, JST	255
5:27	55	8:19-20	208	12:27	252
5:27-28	36	8:23-27	219, 224	12:28	253
5:27-32	243	8:26	220	12:29	253
5:31	55	8:27	424	12:30	253
5:31-32	365	8:28-29	252	12:31-33	255
5:31-34	36	8:28-32	220	12:34	257
5:33	55	8:28-34	224	12:34-45	259
5:33-37	243	9:1-8	224	12:35	257
5:35-36, JST	365	9:2-6	221	12:36-37	257
5:38	55	9:14-15	274	12:36-37	257
5:38-39	36	9:15	425	12:37-39, JST	259
5:38-47	243	9:15-16	53	12:38	258
5:40	34	9:16	274	12:38-39, JST	426
5:43	55	9:16-22, JST	53	12:39	258
5:43-44	320	9:17	274	12:39-40	258
5:47	465	9:18	222	12:40	425
5:48	243-44	9:18-19	224	12:41-42	259
5:50, JST	51	9:20-22	219, 224	12:45	260
6:5	210	9:23-25	222	12:46-47	260
6:10	52, 277	9:23-26	224	12:48-49	260
6:12	364	9:27-31	224	12:50	260
6:18	245	9:32-34	220, 224	13:1-52	52
6:14-15	364	9:35-36, JST	51	13:3-8	271
6:18	245	10	232, 305, 306	13:3-23	274
6:24	245	10:1	222	13:11-13	267
6:25-27, JST	231	10:2-4	230	13:13	269
6:25-34	231, 245	10:6	232	13:14-15	56
6:27	245	10:7	232	13:19-23	271
6:29-30, JST	51	10:7-8	222	13:24	398

13:24-30	271, 275	16:21	322, 348	20:1	398
13:31	398	16:21-22	409	20:1-16	276
13:31-32	273, 275	16:21-23	425	20:1-34	369
13:32	263	16:22-23	347	20:1-34, JST	369
13:33	272, 275, 398	16:24-25	348	20:4	370
13:35	56	16:25-29, JST	51	20:7	370
13:36-43	272, 275	16:26	346	20:12	370
13:44	263, 275	17:1	308	20:16	308, 370
13:44-46	272	17:1-2	459	20:17-19	322, 336, 409
13:45	398	17:1-9	306	20:23	370
13:45-46	275	17:2	305	20:25-28	4
13:47	398	17:5	467	20:26-28	371
13:47-50	273, 275	17:10	308	20:29-34	225
13:49-50	278	17:12-13	170	20:30	371
13:55	324	17:13-14, JST	309	20:30-34	217
13:55-56	260	17:14-21	220, 225	21:1-11	52, 295, 321,
14:1-10	35	17:22-23	409		389
14:1-12	171	17:24-27	219, 225	21:4-5	56
14:3	170	18:1	361	21:5, JST	374
14:12-13	289	18:1-5, JST	361	21:9	374
14:13	289	18:1-6	361	21:12-13	377
14:14	289	18:2-3	362	21:13, JST	389
14:15-21	219	18:2-5	51	21:13	392
14:16	289	18:6-14, JST	362	21:15	377
14:16-21	182, 225	18:7-14	362	21:18-22	225
14:19	290	18:8	362	21:23-22:14	269
14:21	295	18:9	362	21:23-32	168
14:22-23	225, 462	18:9, JST	362	21:26	377
14:24-33	219	18:10-11, JST	51	21:27	378
14:29-31	290	18:12-14	275, 363	21:28-32	276, 378
14:32	290	18:12-14, JST	41	21:31-34, JST	378
14:33	291	18:15-17	364	21:33-34	276, 379
14:34-36	225, 291	18:15-17, JST	51	21:33-34, JST	168
15:1-9	35	18:16	256	21:34, JST	379
15:11	275	18:17	51	21:37-38	379
15:12-14	300	18:18	230	21:37-39	425
15:14	274	18:21	364	21:40-41	379
15:15	300	18:21-35	51, 364	21:42	380
15:15-20	275	18:23	398	21:42-44	277
15:21-28	225	18:23-35	275, 364	21:46	380
15:22-28	218	19:1-12	365	21:51-53, JST	380
15:30-38	219	19:3	365	21:54-56, JST	380
15:32-38	225	19:7-9	36	22:1-14	277, 380
16:1-2	300	19:8	365	22:2	398
16:4	258, 300	19:9	366	22:2-3	386
16:6	301	19:13-15	361	22:10	381
16:7-8	301	19:16	361, 367	22:13-14	381
16:11-12	301	19:16-22	368	22:14, JST	382
16:13	308	19:16-30	367	22:16-17	383
16:13-19, JST	51	19:21	352	22:18-21	383
16:15-16	303, 428	19:24	368	22:24	384
16:15-17	417	19:26, JST	367	22:32	384
16:16	423, 467	19:27	368	22:36	385
16:19	304, 455	19:30	370	22:37-40	385

22:42	385	24:36-51	395	27:46	424
22:44-45	385	24:40-41	398	27:52-53	459
22:46	386	24:42-44	398	27:62-66	406, 453
23:3	393	24:42-51	277	27:63	406
23:4	386	24:45-51	398	28:1-5	454
23:12	387	24:46	393	28:1-10	295
23:13	387	24:55, JST	394	28:2-4	454
23:14	387	25:1	398, 404	28:5-8	454
23:15	387	25:1-13	265, 277	28:9-10	456
23:16-22	387	25:13	399	28:11-15	454
23:21, JST	54	25:14-30	277	28:16	458
23:23	298	25:19	400	28:16-18	322
23:23-24	387	25:21	199	28:17	405
23:24	265	25:31	52	28:17-20	458
23:29	388	25:31-34	401		
23:35	388	25:31-46	277	**MARK**	
23:37-38	389	25:34	393	1:1	75-77
23:37-39	253	25:34-36	401	1:1-13	76
23:38-39	391	25:35-46	400	1:4	77
23:38-41, JST	57	25:37-40	401	1:7-8	76
23:39	395	26:12	425	1:8	77
24	403	26:14-16	426	1:10	77
24, JST	394	26:20-35	295	1:11	77
24:1-2	391	26:22	409	1:12	77
24:1-5	395	26:22, JST	408	1:13	77
24:4-8	396	26:23-24, JST	408	1:14	77
24:4-31	395	26:25	409	1:15	277
24:6	396	26:26, JST	408	1:21-28	223
24:6-7	395	26:28	7	1:23-27	220
24:8	395	26:31	412	1:25	78
24:9	233	26:35	427	1:28	78
24:9-13	395	26:36-56	295	1:29-31	218, 223
24:9-14	396	26:45-47	440	1:30	85
24:12	395	26:52-54	441	1:32-34	217, 224
24:13	393	26:53	184	1:34	78
24:13	393	26:56	56, 441	1:40-45	217, 224
24:14	396	26:57-27:31	295	1:44	78
24:14-15	395	26:59	443	1:45	78
24:15	397, 403	26:63	423	2:1-12	221, 224
24:15-21	395	26:69-75	442	2:11-12	78
24:15-22	396	27:2	66	2:18-20	274
24:22	395, 397	27:3-5	230, 426	2:21	274
24:23-24	395	27:3-10	445	2:22	274
24:25-28	395	27:5	234	3:1-5	78, 217, 224
24:25-31	397	27:6, JST	426, 451	3:12	78
24:27	397	27:9-10	56	3:14	230
24:28	397	27:16	446	3:15	230
24:29	395	27:16-26	446	3:16-19	230
24:30-33	395	27:16-26	446	3:19, JST	252
24:32-33	277	27:19	447	3:21-25, JST	255
24:32-35	397	27:24-26	446	3:22	261
24:34	398	27:26-66	447	3:26	252
24:34-35	395	27:32-66	295	3:28-29	255
24:36	398	27:37	52	4:3-8	271

4:3-25	274	8:15	301	13:5	68
4:10-20	78	8:17	301	13:5-23	69
4:11-12	268	8:17-21	78	13:6	68
4:14-20	271	8:21	301	13:7	68
4:26	275	8:22-26	81, 217, 225	13:8	68
4:26-29	272	8:26	78	13:9	68-69
4:30-32	273, 275	8:29	76	13:9-12	77
4:34	78	8:29-30	51	13:12	69
4:35-41	219, 224	8:30	78-79	13:13	69
4:37-39	84	8:31-33	82, 425	13:13	70
4:41	78	8:34-38	87	13:13	85
5:1-20	220, 224	8:38	79	13:14	68
5:7-10	78	9:1	65	13:14-16	375
5:19	78	9:1-4	308	13:21-22	69
5:21-22	224	9:2-9	306	13:23	68, 70
5:22-24	222	9:2-13	79	13:28-29	277
5:25-26	99	9:3	305	24:34-37	277
5:25-34	219, 224	9:9	79	13:35	67
5:35-43	222, 224	9:14-29	220, 225	14:12-16	424
5:43	78	9:30-35, JST	361	14:17-31	295
6:14-29	171	9:31-50	87	14:21, JST	408
6:17	170	9:32	78, 425	14:24	7
6:21, JST	170	9:33-37	361	14:24, JST	408
6:30-31	289	9:40-50, JST	362	14:26	430
6:31	289	9:43-50	362	14:31	427
6:33	289	9:46, JST	363	14:32-52	295
6:33-34	219, 225	9:49-50	239	14:33	432
6:33-44	84	10:1-10, JST	365	14:35-36	433
6:34	289, 303	10:1-12	365	14:36-37, JST	431
6:37	289	10:2-4	365	14:41-53	440
6:44	295	10:10	366	14:49	56
6:45-52	225, 462	10:11-12	366	14:50	441
6:47-51	219	10:17-31	367	14:53-15:20	295
6:48	67, 290	10:26, JST	367-68	14:66-72	442
6:51	78, 84, 290	10:28-31	369	15:1	66
6:51-52	291	10:30, JST	370	15:5	450
6:53-55	291	10:33	78	15:7	446
6:53-56	225	10:33-45	87	15:7-15	446
7:1-13	35	10:35-41	425	15:11	446
7:2-6, JST	298	10:46-52	79, 217, 225	15:12-15	446
7:7, JST	298	11:1	85	15:15-47	447
7:8-11, JST	299	11:1-11	389	15:16	66
7:9	35	11:12-14	225, 376	15:21	65
7:12-13, JST	299	11:13, JST	375	15:21-47	295
7:13	35	11:20-24	376	15:28	60
7:14-21, JST	300	11:20-26	225	15:34	450
7:22-23	302	11:25	210	15:39	76
7:24	302	12:1-12	276	16:1	456
7:25-30	218	12:28-34	420	16:1-11	295
7:31-37	225	12:29	424	16:8	85
7:32-37	217	12:32-34	385	16:9-11	405, 455
7:36	78	12:42	66	16:9-20	87
8:1-9	84, 219, 225	13:1-2, JST	340	16:14	405, 426
8:12	301	13:2-37	67	16:14-18	458

16:17-18	222	4:29	204	8:49-56	222, 224
16:20	234	4:31-37	223	9:6	234
		4:33-36	220	9:10	289
LUKE		4:38-39	218, 223	9:11	295
1:1-4	95	4:40-41	217, 224	9:11-17	219, 225
1:3	90	5:1-11	229	9:13	289
1:5-7	162	5:4-9	219	9:14	295
1:5-25	141	5:4-11	223	9:16-17	289
1:7-17	162	5:12-14	217	9:20-21, JST	51
1:13	349	5:12-15	224	9:22	425
1:15	163, 415, 428	5:17-26	221, 224	9:28-36	306
1:31	147	5:23-24	244	9:29	305
1:36-57	163	5:33-35	274	9:37-42	220
1:41	177, 304	5:36	274	9:37-43	225
1:48	236	5:37-38	274	9:45	425
1:56-61	163	5:39	274	9:46	361, 425
1:67	304	6:6-10	217, 224	9:46-48	361
1:67-79	163	6:12-13	229	9:46-48, JST	361
2:1-20	144	6:13-16	306	9:62	189, 192
2:7, JST	144	6:14-16	230	10:1	312
2:8	145	6:30	360	10:1-20	306
2:12, JST	146	6:38	265	10:4-9	312-13
2:14	146	6:39	274	10:9	313
2:19	146	6:41-42	274	10:10-16	313
2:20, JST	146	6:44	262	10:16	313
2:25-26	148	7:1	251	10:17	313
2:28-31	148	7:1-10	224	10:17-20	416
2:35, JST	148	7:2-10	218	10:19, JST	313
2:36-38, JST	148	7:3-5	218	10:20	314
2:42-50	190	7:11-16	222	10:20, JST	314
2:46	448	7:11-17	224	10:21	316
2:46-47, JST	155	7:24	169	10:22, JST	315
2:48-49, JST	155	7:24-25	173	10:25	316, 367
2:51, JST	155	7:24-30	168	10:25-37	275, 367
2:52	155	7:24-35	168	10:26	316
3:1	66, 446	7:28	160, 173	10:27	316
3:1-25, JST	166	7:29	166	10:28	316
3:9	166	7:33	165	10:29	316
3:9-13	166	7:36-50	274	10:30-35	317
3:15	165	7:39	416	10:33, JST	318
3:23-38	141	7:48-50	221	10:36	317
3:29, JST	416	8:1	251	10:37	317
4:1	304	8:1, JST	251	11:1	349
4:12	319	8:2	260	11:5-9	349
4:13	186	8:2	260	11:5-13	275
4:16	203, 448	8:5-8	271	11:13	349
4:16-20	238	8:5-18	274	11:14-15	225
4:16-21	32	8:11-15	271	11:14-26	220
4:16-24	201	8:16-39	220	11:24-26	275
4:16-30	203	8:22-25	219, 224	11:27-28	350
4:17	211	8:26-39	224	11:34-36	348
4:18-19	204	8:41-42	222, 224	12:1	353
4:20	203	8:43	99	12:2-3	353
4:28-30	184, 216, 223	8:43-48	219, 224	12:13-15	351

12:13-21	275	19:11-27	277	24:32	456
12:20-21	351	19:29-40	389	24:33-34	455,459
12:28-31	352	19:29-44	295	24:33-53	457
12:32-34	352	19:40	375	24:34	457
12:36-40	275	19:41-44	375	24:40	105
12:41-48	276	20:9	406	24:44	60
12:43-44	347	20:9-18	276	24:45	426
13:1	446	20:13-15	425	24:49	416
13:1-5	297	20:24	34	28:37, JST	368
13:6-9	276	21	94		
13:11-17	219, 225	21:24	104	**JOHN**	
13:18-29	275	21:29-31	277	1:1	128-30
13:20-21	275	22:3-6	409	1:1-18	127
13:23-30	276	22:14-34	295	1:2	131
13:31	60	22:20	7	1:3-4	463
13:31-32	445	22:24	426	1:3-9	131
13:32	265	22:31-34	411	1:3-17	136
13:34-36, JST	340	22:32	417, 427	1:4-5	119
14:1-6	217, 225	22:37	60	1:6-9	137
14:7-11	277	22:39-53	295	1:9	133
14:7-14	276	22:41	433, 440	1:10	133
14:15-24	276	22:43-44	103	1:10-13	131
14:16-24	277	22:43-44, JST	433	1:11	133, 321
14:25-30	276	22:45-46	440	1:11-12	117
14:26-27	347	22:45-54	440	1:12	133
14:28-30	347	22:50-51	217, 226	1:13	134
14:31-33	276	22:54-23:25	295	1:14	101, 112, 129
14:33	347	22:54-62	442		134-35
15:3-7	275	22:66	442	1:16	136
15:4-10	266	23:2-3	444	1:17	136
15:8-10	276	23:6-12	445	1:18	137-38
15:11-32	265, 276, 355	23:12	445	1:18-40	166
16:1-3	276	23:19	446	1:19	174
16:15	357	23:23-25	446	1:19, JST	137,303
16:16, JST	358	23:25	446	1:20-25, JST	167
16:19-21, JST	54	23:25-56	295	1:21-28	309
16:19-31	276-77, 357	23:26-56	447	1:26-33, JST	168
16:20-22, JST	301	23:27-31	448	1:27	173
16:20-23, JST	357	23:32	448	1:28, JST	173
16:20-36, JST	357	23:34	104, 449	1:29	165
16:31	361	23:35, JST	449	1:29-34	168
17:7-10	276	23:45	450	1:30, JST	227
17:11-19	217, 225	23:56-24:12	295	1:33	428
18:1	349	24:1-7	454	1:33-34	416
18:1-8	276	24:6-12	405	1:35-42	462
18:2-8	349	24:10	456	1:36	227, 285
18:9-14	276	24:11	406	1:39	228
18:11	210	24:13	456	1:41	7, 228, 405
18:18-30	367	24:13-27	426	1:42	228, 426
18:27, JST	353, 367	24:22-25	405	1:42, JST	228
18:34	425	24:27	456	1:43	228
18:35-43	217, 225	24:30	456	1:45-51	229

1:48-51   426
1:49   24
2:1-11   113, 188, 219
    223
2:4   189
2:4, JST   189
2:9-10   188
2:11   189
2:12   189
2:13-17   376
2:16   183
2:17   26
2:18   191, 377
2:19   191
2:19-22   274
2:22   418, 426
2:23   121
2:24   426
2:24-25   426
3:1-2   192, 405
3:1-6   427
3:2   24, 427
3:3   192
3:5   175, 416-17
3:9   122
3:10   122
3:11   122
3:13   195
3:14   196, 425
3:16   196, 466
3:16-17   413
3:16-21   342
3:19   117, 123, 197
3:19-20   336
3:22-36   165
3:25-36   166
3:26   198
3:28-30   198
3:30-31   173
3:34   428
3:34, JST   438
4:1   206
4:1-4, JST   416
4:3-4   206
4:4-42   36, 208
4:9   206
4:10-11   208
4:12   207-8
4:16-19   426
4:19-24   282
4:19-25   208
4:20   207

4:21   207
4:23   207
4:25   207
4:25-26   201
4:28-29   125
4:39-42   208
4:43-54   226
4:46-54   223
5:1-15   217
5:2-16   224
5:6-9   281
5:13   415
5:17   282, 322, 432
5:18   322
5:19   432, 463
5:20   466
5:22   283
5:22-23   135
5:25   425
5:25-29   283
5:26-27   135
5:30   432
5:31   285
5:32, JST   285
5:32-35   168, 285
5:32-36   168
5:36   285
5:37-38   117, 285
5:39   285
5:39-40   117
5:43   432
5:45   116, 286
5:46-47   116
6   116
6:1   461
6:1-15   115
6:5-6   289
6:5-14   219, 225
6:6   426
6:10   295
6:12-59   291
6:13   115
6:14   292
6:15   292
6:15-21   225, 462
6:16-21   219, 468
6:24   324
6:26, JST   292
6:26-58   407
6:27   292
6:28-35   182
6:30   292

6:31   292
6:32-33   292
6:34   292
6:35   265, 293
6:41   116, 293
6:44   117
6:47-51   182
6:48   293
6:48-51   293
6:49   116
6:50   293
6:51   293, 413
6:52   116, 293
6:53-54   293-94
6:56   408
6:56-57   182
6:58   293
6:60   293
6:60-61   294
6:63   182, 294
6:64   409, 426
6:65   117
6:66   116, 293, 462
6:66-67   294
6:68-69   295, 468
6:71   409
7:1   322
7:1-8   322
7:1-9   323
7:7   414
7:15   323
7:16   432
7:19-26   323
7:20   323
7:27   323
7:30   204, 323
7:31   323
7:32   323
7:33-34   425
7:37-39, JST   331
7:39   256, 304, 461
7:40-43   324, 405
7:44-46   323
8:12   414
8:12-15   328
8:13   285
8:18-20   328
8:21   336
8:21-22   425
8:23   413
8:23-25   336
8:28   336, 425, 463

8:29	135, 432	11	463	14:1	413
8:31-34	338	11:1	334	14:2-3	422
8:36	338	11:1-45	332	14:5	412
8:37-41	336	11:3	466	14:6	175
8:39-59	117	11:3-7	334	14:7	413
8:43-45	324, 336	11:4	332	14:7-8	412
8:44	328, 410	11:17	334	14:8-10	413
8:47	336	11:17-46	222, 225	14:9	130
8:51-53	338	11:21-22	335	14:10-11	130
8:52-59	328	11:23-27	339	14:11	413
8:58	338	11:27	335	14:15	421
8:58-59	323	11:36	466	14:16	461
8:59	204, 216, 223	11:45	335	14:16-18	415
9	118	11:47-53	323	14:17	415
9:1-3	333	11:48	36	14:20	413
9:1-7	217, 225	11:49-52	340	14:21	415, 421
9:1-38	332	11:53	335	14:22	412, 445
9:2	296	11:54	323	14:23	415, 428
9:3	332	11:57	323	14:23-24	421, 467
9:4-5	120	12:2	424	14:26	41, 418, 461
9:6-7	333	12:7	425	14:27	418
9:8-12	333	12:12-19	295, 389	14:28	424
9:26-34	334	12:16	418, 426	14:29	413
9:30-33	215	12:23-28	425	14:30, JST	414
9:33	214	12:25	466	14:31	419
9:34	297	12:26	175	15:1-8	417
9:35-38	121	12:27-28	433	15:3	419
9:35-41	325	12:31	414	15:5	248
9:41	121, 123	12:32-36	425	15:8-11	418
10	118	12:34	425	15:9	467
10:1-6	276	12:35	132	15:10	421, 467
10:2-5	330	12:37	269	15:11	418
10:10	345, 436	12:39-40	269	15:12	419, 467
10:11	425	12:42	405	15:14	466
10:14	175, 330-31	12:46	414	15:15	418, 466
10:15	425	13	295	15:16	411
10:17-18	454	13-16	427	15:17	419, 467
10:18	425	13:1	424, 426	15:18-20	414
10:19-25	405	13:2	410	15:22-25	414
10:23-25	325	13:8	407	15:26	415, 418, 461
10:24-25	332	13:10, JST	407	15:27	411
10:25	214	13:11	409	15:42	427
10:26-29	330	13:19	413	16:1-4	414
10:27	175	13:21	409, 426	16:4	413
10:30	135, 432	13:21-30	410	16:7	416, 418
10:30-33	323, 325	13:27	410	16:12	418
10:33	118, 424	13:27-28	410	16:13	461
10:34-36	423	13:29	424	16:16	412
10:36	215, 424	13:31	419	16:18	412
10:38	427	13:33	411	16:20-22	418
10:39	204, 323	13:34	419	16:25	412
10:40-11:16	323	13:34-35	467	16:27	413, 466
10:41	166	13:36-38	411	16:28-32	412

16:31	413	20:11-18	455	11:19-26	91
16:32	413	20:17	424	11:27-30	85, 93
16:33	112, 414	20:17, JST	460	12:2	234
17	422, 430	20:22	416	12:12-13;13	74, 82
17:3	413, 421	20:22-23	457	12:12-17	63
17:5	1, 327	20:24	457	12:20	20
17:6	410-11	20:24-29	361, 405	12:25	85
17:8	413	20:26-29	458	12:25-13:13	63
17:9	410, 414	20:30-31	126, 215	13:14-15	211
17:11	440	20:31	75, 459	13:15	203
17:12	410	21	458	16:10-13	91
17:14	414	21:1	461	16:33	414
17:16	414	21:1-14	226	19:5-15	91
17:19	240	21:2	462	21:1-18	91
17:20	414	21:6-14	220	21:8	92
17:20-21	136	21:11	462	21:10	93
17:22	418	21:15	464	21:16	93
17:22-23	418	21:15-17	465	21:18	94
17:24	135, 419, 422	21:15-19	464	23:6-10	36
17:26	421	21:17	417	24:23	92
18:1-12	295, 440	21:20	469	26:16	96
18:3-6	226	21:20-23	469	27:1	92
18:7-9	442	21:21-23	428, 468	27:2	91
18:9	410	21:23	468	28:16	91
18:10	217, 441	21:24b	427		
18:11	441	21:25	47, 72, 126,	**ROMANS**	
18:13	442		128	1:31	466
18:15-18	442	**ACTS**		6:6	241
18:17	464	1:1	92	8:15	416
18:19-22	443	1:1-2	90	8:17	416
18:25-27	442, 464	1:2	92	10:17	57
18:28	424, 444	1:4-5	416		
18:33-38	444	1:6	425	**1 CORINTHIANS**	
18:40	446	1:8	416	1:10	42
18:40-19:1	446	1:13	230	2:9-16, JST	315
19:13	444	1:15-19	230	10:9	319
19:13-25	333	1:16-20	426	11:23-25	97, 100
19:14	424	1:22-23	96	11:23-26	408
19:16-42	295, 447	1:25-26	96	11:25	7
19:17	447	2	304, 461	12:13	303
19:23	448	2:1-4	242, 417	13	421
19:25	148	2:3-4	419	15	97
19:27	449	2:22	214	15:3-4	47
19:31	424	2:22-36, JST	341	15:3-5	455
19:38-42	450	2:36	417	15:3-7	97
19:42	424	3:17	414	15:6	65, 94, 459
20:1, JST	454	3:19	104		
20:1-18	295	3:19-21	286	**2 CORINTHIANS**	
20:2	469	4:12	303	1:22	426
20:2-10	455	6:1-6	92	5:5	428
20:4-17	468	7:58	93	5:21	436
20:9	426	8:5-40	93	7:10	344
20:9-15	405	10:28	444	13:1	284

GALATIANS

2:20	415
3:13	436
3:19-20, JST	55
3:24	240, 366

EPHESIANS

1:13-14	428
4:8-10	437

PHILIPPIANS

2:6	1
2:7-8	2
2:8	3
2:9-11	4
2:12	286
4:13	344

COLOSSIANS

1:9-11	344
1:15	327
3:9-10	193
4:10	90
4:14	89

1 THESSALONIANS

5:26	441

2 THESSALONIANS

2:1-4	68

2 TIMOTHY

3:3	466

3:7, JST	315
4:11	89

HEBREWS

1:2	327
1:3	1
1:8-12	342
1:9	327
2:17-18	3, 181
4:14	177
4:15	3, 181, 431
5:5-6	342
6:4-6	344
6:20	306
8:6-13	406
8:8-13	7
9:12	339
9:25-28	339
10:10-18	425
10:14	339
12:9	327

JAMES

1:5	283
1:8	245
1:27	402
2:19	361

1 PETER

2:2	194
2:22	431
5:13	62

2 PETER

1:16-18	305
1:16-19	310
1:19, JST	422
1:21	304

1 JOHN

1:1	128
1:3	128
2:15-16	413
4:8	419
4:9-10	466
4:12	421
4:12, JST	303
5:4-5	414

REVELATIONS

2:11	293
5:2, JST	176
5:3-4	176
5:5-7	177
5:9	177
6:35	293
6:48-51	293
6:53-54	293
6:58	293
7:14	382
11:15	186
13:18	114
19:7-9	399
19:8-9	382
19:10	45, 303
19:16	4

BOOK OF MORMON

1 NEPHI

1:19	7, 341-42
1:20	41
3:29-31	361
7:16-20	361
8:20	188
10:4-5	341
10:9	177
10:10	178
10:17	304
11:16-25	142
13	60
13:28	46
13:34-41	325
13:39-40	8
14:10	253

15:13	326
15:28-29	360
16:37-39	361
17:35	422
17:45-55	361
18:8-21	361
19:23	182

2 NEPHI

1:10	341
1:13	360
2:6-8	342
2:7	326
2:8	339
2:9-10	337
2:10	326, 341

2:18	182, 252, 314
2:25	345
2:27-29	344
3:5	327
5:1-7	361
5:28-32	41
6:13-14	342
9:7-9	337
9:7-10	5
9:10-15	337
9:18	451
9:20	432
9:38	335
9:41-42	198
9:46	343
12:6	344

16:9-10	269	**ALMA**		13:6-7	146
25:1	9	5:13	195	14:5	149
25:4	9	5:14	195, 417		
25:16	327	5:25	195	**3 NEPHI**	
25:18	327	5:26	195	2:7-8	424
25:19	147, 327, 342	7:10	142, 147	8:5	424
25:20	303	7:10-12	437	9:16	321
26:24-25	418	7:11-12	419	9:18-20	242
26:26	210	7:13	432	9:19	425
30:2	382	11:36	5	11:32	285
31:5-7	178	11:37	5	11:39-40	281
31:5-17	338	11:37-40	403	12:2	237
31:7	180	12:9-11	47	12:6	238
31:8	180	12:9-13	327	12:29-30	244
31:9	181	12:14	258	13:25	231
31:18	331	19:6	344	13:34	231
31:19-32:3	344	21:4	210	15:5	55, 260, 298
32:5	331	25:16	241	15:9	328
33:1	304	26:20	360	15:23	418
33:6	429	26:29	210	17:17	40
		29:4-5	344	17:25	459
JACOB		30:50-53	343	18:16	328
4:14	53	31:12	210	18:24	186, 240, 328
7:11	55, 303	32:26-43	361	18:32	210
		32:28-35	342	18:36-37	457
JAROM		34:10	6, 344, 425	19:13	429
1:11	342	34:32	255	20:27	256
		34:35	434	23:9-11	459
OMNI		37:6	423	27:16	244
1:26	249	38:9	339	27:27	429
		40:11-14	359	27:32	426
MOSIAH		40:12	359	28	468
2:38	359	41:3-7	344	28:37-38	469
3:3	145	41:14	246	29:5-7	335
3:5-8	146	41:14-15	238	29:7	427
3:7	419, 434	42:9-15	337		
3:8	147	42:11	337	**ETHER**	
3:13-17	366	42:14	337	3:2	344
3:17	303	42:15-25	326	12:6	453
3:19	362, 417	42:17-21	343		
3:26	433	45:19	307	**MORONI**	
4:27	371	48:11	243	2:1-2	457
5:7	194, 362, 416	50:37	243	6:8	364
12:31-37	366			7:1	210
13:28-35	366			7:12	328
13:29-32	297	**HELAMAN**		7:16-19	337
13:30-31	240	3:9	210	7:48	421
13:33	342	5:9	303	8:8	362
15:1	341	5:12	360	8:26	421
26:29-30	364	8:13	342	10:22	354
27:24-27	343	8:13-20	303	10:26	335
27:25	194, 344	8:14-15	196	10:34	429
27:25-26	362	8:17-18	342		

THE DOCTRINE AND COVENANTS

1	393	42:22	365	82:2-4	268
1:8-9	232	42:84-92	51	82:4	335
1:31	335	43	393, 402	84:19-22	242
1:33	133	43:25	545	84:23-27	297
4:6	198	43:34	326	84:25	242
5:2	326	45	393, 402	84:26-28	173
6:37	403	45:3-4	339	84:27	163, 415, 428
7	428, 468-69	45:3-5	438	84:28-29	163
7:7	459	45:16-25	394	84:33-39	319
10:5	343	45:26-59	394	84:43-47	342
10:55	403	45:40-59	397	84:43-48	331
11:13	344	45:52	394	84:46	337
12:8	198	45:56	400	84:51-52	328
13:1	326	45:59	409	84:109-10	370
15:1	325	50:17-21	415	84:117	397
16:1	326	50:34-35	344	86:1-7	278
18:10	346	53:3	177	86:11	419
18:23	303, 339	55:1	177	88:3-4	427
18:33	326	56:4	343	88:6	419, 437
19:15-18	434	56:14-15	343	88:12-13	342
19:15-19	419	58:2	403	88:21-24	360
19:18	408	58:43	338	88:22	366
19:23	418	60:4	342	88:35	427
19:27	57	61:27	220	88:38	360
19:30	339	63:7-11	259	88:40	348
20:11	8	63:20-21	308	88:67-68	348
20:13-15	259	63:54	400	88:81-88	341
20:26-27	304	63:64	348-49	88:84-85	397
20:27	198	64:9-10	364	88:92	400
20:73-74	178	65:3	400	88:102	427
22	54	67:10	198	88:106	437
24:15	232	67:13	245	88:119	191
27:5-14	409, 463	68:3-4	38	88:138-139	407
27:6	164	68:6	341	88:141	75
29	393, 402	75:21	232	93:6-18	174
29:1	326	76:5-10	415	93:8	130
29:12	232	76:12	418	93:12-13	136
29:27-30	427	76:15-20	284	93:12-20	156
29:28-32	328	76:23	459	93:15-17	179, 428
29:36-37	328	76:24	327	93:18	469
29:39-40	343	76:25	314	93:20	418
29:41	337, 427	76:25-26	410	93:21	327
29:44	427	76:26	426	93:24	444
29:47	181	76:40-42	38	93:25	184, 328
33:17-18	400	76:71	429	93:29-33	327
35:15-16	278	76:77	429	93:36	342
38:1-3	327	76:86	429	93:36-39	133
38:4	438	76:92-94	429	93:38	362
38:27	440	76:107	416, 437	98:11	187
41:1	376	76:115-16	40	98:39-48	364
42:14	348	76:116-18	415	98:41-48	364

101:43-65	278	128:18	388	133:50	416
103:9-10	240	130:18-19	342, 355	133:50-51	438
107:20	177	130:20-21	422	133:55	173
107:23	227	130:22	179	136:32-33	198
107:43	243	130:22-23	428	136:36-39	341
107:99	370	131:5	310, 422	138	359
109:67	326	131:6	422	138:12-13	451
110:1-10	459	132:15-19	384	138:22	360
112:13	428	132:49	429	138:30	360
116	393, 402	132:49-50	243	138:31	360
121:45	239	133	393, 402	138:32	360
124:2-3	341	133:10	400	138:35	360
124:7-10	341	133:19	400	138:37	360

THE PEARL OF GREAT PRICE

MOSES

1:39	4, 156, 346
4:1-4	314
4:2	419
4:14	328
5:5-7	425
5:6-9	213
5:14-15	213
5:18	182
6:48	337
6:52	147, 303
6:57	195, 362
6:59-61	193
6:64-65	180
7:30	180
7:35	196
7:37-39	426
7:50	147
7:59	429
7:63	441
8:24	147

ABRAHAM

1:16	342
3:19	327
3:22	1
3:22-23	327-28
3:24	1
3:24-26	328

JOSEPH SMITH–MATTHEW

1:1	395, 402
1:1-21a	394
1:2-6	395
1:4	402
1:7-11	395
1:10	396
1:12	397
1:12-18	395
1:19	395
1:20-21a	395
1:21b-22	395

1:21b-55	394
1:23	395
1:24-27	395
1:27	397
1:28-29	395
1:30	395, 396
1:31-32	395
1:32	397
1:33	395
1:34	398
1:34-35	395
1:36-39	395
1:40-54	395
1:55	395

JOSEPH SMITH–HISTORY

1:43	460
1:68-74	171

ARTICLES OF FAITH

2	366

SUBJECT INDEX

Aaronic Priesthood: restored by John the
   Baptist, 171; lesser law of, 297
Abomination of desolation, 67-71, 396
Abraham, 147; seed of, 336; in parable of
   Lazarus and rich man, 360; trials of, 363
Accountability, 388
Acts, book of, 90-95
Adultery: and sign seeking, 258, 300, 301; and
   divorce, 365-67
Alexander the Great, 13
Allegory, 263
Àm ha-áretz, nonaffiliated Jews, 29
Andrew, 227-28
Angel: glad tidings of, 145-46; Gabriel, 161,
   163-64; strengthens Christ in
   Gethsemane, 433-34; at empty tomb,
   454-55
Anna, 148
Annunciation, 142-43
Anointed One, Messiah as, 6-7
Antipater, 17, 18
Apostles: power imparted to, 222, 230; calling
   of, 227-30; training period of, 229, 251;
   sermon directed to, 231; mission of,
   232-34; Jesus warns, of persecution, 233,
   341 n. 3, 414; fate of, 234, 417; Jesus
   washes feet of, 407; final instructions to,
   411; confusion of, over Jesus' destiny,
   411-12, 425-26 n. 14; Jesus prays for, 414;
   receive more sure word of prophecy, 422;
   appearances to, of resurrected Christ, 457,
   458, 461-62; receive Holy Ghost, 457
Assyrians, Israel conquered by, 11
Atonement: humility involved in, 3; lessons
   taught by, 3-4; made repentance possible,
   5-6; role of, in salvation, 337-38;
   requirements of, 339; as supreme act of
   love, 419-20; agony of, 432, 434-35
Authority of Jesus, 377-78. See also Keys

Babes, secrets revealed to, 315
Babylonians, Israel conquered by, 11
Baptism: of Jesus, 175, 177-81; explained to
   Nicodemus, 193
Bar Kokhba revolt, 21-22
Barabbas, 446, 452 n. 12
Beatitudes, 237-40
Benson, Ezra Taft, 369
Bethany, 373, 375
Bethesda, pool of, 281
Blasphemy: against Holy Ghost, 254-57; Jesus
   accused of, 282, 325, 424 n. 3
Blind man, healing of, 120-21, 324-25,
   332-34
Blindness, spiritual, 324-25
Born again, process of being, 193-95
Bread: temptation of, 182; symbolism of, 463
Bread of Life sermon, 115-16, 291-94, 407-8
Brown, Raymond, 57, 143
Bultmann, Rudolph, 71-72

Caesar, render unto, his own, 382-83
Caiaphas, 340, 441-42
Caius, Roman emperor, 20
Capernaum, Jesus visits, 189-90
Child, becoming as, 361-62
Christ, definition of, 7. See also Jesus Christ
Christians: fleeing of, to Pella, 67-68, 397, 403
   n. 8; persecution of, 69-70
"Christmas Story," 144-46
Church of Jesus Christ: Matthew's emphasis
   on, 50-52; hard doctrines of, 294-95;
   forgiveness in, 355
Circumcision, 147
Clark, J. Reuben, Jr., 105, 371
Clement of Alexandria, 63-64
Comforters, two, 415-19
Compassion: in spite of weariness, 302; based
   on real needs, 353; for "least of these," 401

Contrite spirit, definition of, 242-43
Corban, principle of, 35 n. 27, 299
Creation, John's account of, 112-13
Crosses, bearing our own, 451
Crucifixion of Jesus, 447-50

Daniel, 203, 396
David: prosperity of Israel under, 10; Jesus as heir of, 374; Messiah to be son of, 385-86
Davies, W. D., 42, 43
Dead Sea Scrolls, 25, 26
Death: physical and spiritual, 5, 337; Jesus' power over, 221-22, 334-36; salvation from, 337-38
Deliverer, definition of, 6
Despair, 354
Devils: Jesus' power over, 220-21, 251; cast out by others, 252-53; possession by, after initial cleansing, 259-60
Diaspora, 14
Divine Sonship of Jesus, 279, 282-83
Divorce, 365-67
Dove, sign of, 179, 428 n. 30

Edersheim, Alfred, 149, 151, 153-54
Elias, 167-68, 308-9
Elijah, 305, 307
Elisabeth, 162-63
Emmaus, 456
Endowments, 309-10
Epiphanes, Antiochus, 15, 392, 396
Eschatology, 402 n. 4
Essenes, 16, 25-26
Eternal life, requirements for, 361-71
Eusebius, 41, 59-60 n. 28; 403 n. 8
Evil spirits. *See* Devils
Eyewitnesses, Luke's emphasis on, 96
Ezra, 12

Faith, 361
Farrar, Frederic, 144, 191, 449
Fasting, 181, 187 n. 11
Fear, overcoming, 245-48
Feeding of five thousand, 288-90; misinterpretations of, 292
Feet, washing of, 407, 425 n. 9
Fig tree, cursing of, 375-76
Fire, symbolism of, 239-40
Foreordination, 44, 164
Forgiveness, 355, 364-65, 449
Form criticism, 71-73, 96-97

Gabriel, 161, 163-64
Galilee, resurrected Christ in, 461-70
Genealogies of Jesus, 141
Geography in Gospel of Mark, 74-75
Gerizim, Mount, 205-6, 211-12 n. 16
Gethsemane, garden of, 430-31; Christ's suffering in, 431-38
Gift of Holy Ghost, 304, 416, 419, 457
Glory: premortal, of Jesus, 1-2; Jesus' return to, 4-5; of Jesus described by John, 135; equated with intelligence, 342 n. 16
God the Father: distinctness of, from Christ, 130-31; becoming children of, 133-34, 416; relationship of, with Son, 135, 137-38, 413; at Jesus' baptism, 179; as Man of Holiness, 195; love of, evidenced by gift of Son, 196-97; is known only by revelation, 213; submitting to will of, 247; love for, is first great commandment, 384-85; withdrawal of, during Atonement, 434-35, 450
Golgotha, 448
Good Samaritan, parable of, 315-19
Gospel, oral testimonies of, 38-39
Gospels, four: as testimonies of Christ, 7, 75; keys to studying, 8-9; barriers to writing of, 39-40; necessity for, 41-43; writers of, 44-45; addressed to varying audiences, 45, 111; purpose served by, 47; comparison of, 48-50; critical approaches to, 71-73. *See also* John, Gospel of; Luke, Gospel of; Mark, Gospel of; Matthew, Gospel of
Gossip, John, 192, 197
Grace: role of, in salvation, 5; Jesus being full of, 135-36; for grace, receiving, 136-37, 155-56
Greek influence in Jesus' day, 13-15, 34 n. 7

Haggai, 12
Hannukah, 16
Happiness, 345-46
Hasmonean family, 15-17
Healing power of Jesus, 216-17, 332-34; exercised on Sabbath, 281, 322-23
Heart, defilement from, 299-300
Hell, 358-59
Hellenism, 13-15, 34 n. 9
Hengel, Martin, 64, 67, 80
Herod Antipas, 19, 34 n. 15, 170-71, 445
Herod the Great, 18-19, 149-52, 164
Herodians, 382

Holy Ghost: relying on, in scripture study, 9; descent of, at Jesus' baptism, 179, 415-16, 428 n. 30; sin against, 254-57; revelation comes through, 303; power vs. gift of, 303-4; blessings possible through, 349; as first Comforter, 415; given to apostles, 457

Humility: of Jesus, 2-3, 180; of John the Baptist, 198; necessity for, 198-99

Hunger, spiritual, 238, 293

Husbandmen, wicked, parable of, 379-80

Hyperbole, 263

Hypocrites, Jesus' denunciation of, 298, 376, 386-88

Hyrcanus, John, 16-17

Innocents, slaughter of, 150-51

Intelligence, 342 n. 16

Intercessory prayer, 414, 430

Irenaeus, 44, 63, 89

Israel: under King David, 10; division of, 10-11; exile and return of, 11-12; apostles' mission to, 232; covenant of, likened to marriage, 399. See also Jews

Jacob's well, 124, 207

James, 305-8, 459

Jannaeus, Alexander, 17

Jehovah, 405

Jeremiah, 392

Jerusalem, 340 n. 1; fall of, to Rome, 21, 67-71, 389 n. 4; danger to Jesus in, 322, 323; triumphal entry into, 374-75; Jesus weeps over, 375, 388-89

Jesus, definition of, 6, 147

Jesus Christ: premortal glory of, 1-2; mission of, 2; humble mortality of, 2-3, 180; terms describing, 5-7; biography of, impossibility of writing, 39-40; condemns early Judaism, 52-54, 297-300; as fulfillment of prophecy, 55-57, 76-77, 112-18; as Bread of Life, 115-16, 291-94, 462-63; as living water, 124, 331-32; as *logos,* or the Word, 128-31; relationship of, with Father, 135, 137-38, 413; genealogies of, 141; birth of, 144-46; naming of, 146-47; early training of, 153-54; teaches in temple as youth, 154-55; baptism of, 175, 177-81; gift of, demonstrates God's love, 196-97; preaching of, in synagogue, 203-4; rejection of, in his own town, 204, 208; divinity of, shown by miracles, 214-15;

powers of, shown by miracles, 216-22; fulfilled law of Moses, 241; new law of, 242-45; condemns scribes and Pharisees, 252-53, 257-60; brothers and sisters of, 260; divine Sonship of, 279, 282-83; power of, to effect resurrection, 283; compassion of, 302; transfiguration of, 305; Judean ministry of, 321; conflicting views of, 323-25; messianic roles of, 325-27; triumphal entry of, 374-75; as second comforter, 415; suffering of, in Gethsemane, 431-38; betrayal and arrest of, 440-41; trial of, before Sanhedrin, 442-43; trials of, before Pilate, 444-46; is taken before Herod, 445; crucifixion of, 447-50; resurrection of, 453-59. See also Atonement; Messiah, Miracles of Jesus; Parables; Savior

Jews: exile of, 11-12; Greek influence on, 13-15; sects of, in Jesus' day, 22-29; institutions of, 30-33; early training of, 153-54; attitude of, toward Samaritans, 204-6; leaders of, reject Christ, 335-36. See also Israel

John, Gospel of: directed to Saints, 45, 111-12; authorship of, 109-10; dating of, 110-11; Old Testament allusions in, 112-18; style of, 118-19; light and dark imagery in, 119-25, 132-33; conclusions about, 125-26; prologue of, 127-39

John the Baptist: birth of, 141-42; preserved from decreed slaughter, 151, 164-65; biographical summary of, 160-61; Aaronic lineage of, 162; naming of, 163; foreordained mission of, 164; preaching of, 165-66; Pharisee's "opinion" of, 167-68; two disciples of, sent to Jesus, 168-69; death of, 170-71; "interview" with, 172-74; as fulfillment of prophecy, 175; Aaronic baptism by, 176-77; baptizes Jesus, 177-79; humility of, 198; testified of Jesus to disciples, 227; at Mount of Transfiguration, 308; as Elias, 308-9; authority of, 377, 379

John the Beloved, 305-8, 468-70. See also John, Gospel of

Jonah: book of, 34 n. 4; sign of, 258-59

Joseph, stepfather of Jesus, 142-44, 157 n. 6

Joseph Smith Translation of Bible, 53-54

Josephus, Flavius, 152, 446, 448

Judah, kingdom of, 11

Judah the Maccabee, 15-16

Judaism: Jesus' denunciation of, 52-54, 297; Mark's portrait of, 66; traditions of, 280,

296-97; monotheistic views of, 405. *See also* Jews

Judas Iscariot, 407, 409-10, 426 n. 16, 426-27 n. 20; betrays Christ with kiss, 440-41; death of, 445

Judean ministry of Christ, 321

Judgment: righteous, 246; of living and dead, 283; according to deeds, 401

Justice: mercy cannot rob, 326; God of, 336; demands of, satisfied by Jesus, 419

Keys: promised to Peter, 304; given to Peter, James, and John, 305-6; restored in latter days, 306

Kimball, Spencer W., 137, 192, 442

Kingdom, divided, fallacy of, 252

Kingdom of God: Matthew's emphasis on, 50-52; establishment of, declared, 253; as subject of parables, 266; keys of, 305-6; to be first priority, 362-63

Kiss, betrayal of Christ with, 441

Laborers in vineyard, parable of, 369-70

Languages, 448

Last days, 393

Last Supper, 406

Latin terms in Mark, 66-67

Law of Moses: Jesus' reverence for, 52; sacrifices of, pointed to Christ, 240-41; fulfillment of, in Christ, 241; compared to new law, 242-43; Aaronic order of, 297; end of, with Christ's death, 406

Lawyer, questions of, 315-16

Lazarus: raising of, 334-36; Jesus visits, in Bethany, 373

Leaven of Pharisees and Sadducees, 301

Lee, Harold B., 369

Lehi, 177, 178

Leprosy, curing of, 216-17

Light: and darkness, imagery of, 112, 119-25, 132-33; of world, Christ as, 328-29

Literary devices, 262-64

Logos, or the Word, 129-31

Love: new commandment of, 419; manifested in Atonement, 419-20; human, vs. divine, 420; connection of, with obedience, 421; three measures of, bestowed by Godhead, 429 n. 39; Christ asks Peter concerning, 464; Greek terms for, 465-67

Luke: obscurity of, 88-89; Paul's profile of, 89-90; as author of Acts, 90; glimpses of, in writings, 90-91, 102; education of, 101. *See also* Luke, Gospel of

Luke, Gospel of: directed to Greeks, 45; authorship heading of, 88; sources for, 92-95, 96; verifying role of, 95, 101; historical accuracy of, 97-98; distinctive contributions of, 100; alterations in text of, 103-6; "Christmas Story" in, 144-46

Maccabean revolt, 15-16, 396

Maccabees, apocryphal books of, 34 n. 12

Magi, 148-50, 157-58 n. 14

Manna, true, 116, 292-93

Mark: as Peter's interpreter, 61, 62; identity of, 74-75, 82; travels of, 85 n. 39. *See also* Mark, Gospel of

Mark, Gospel of: directed to Gentiles, 45; alterations in, 46; as possible source for Matthew and Luke, 49, 60 n. 30, 65 n. 13, 83; dating of, 63-71; geography in, 74-75; opening of, 75-76, 81; tone of, 76-79, 81-82; theological/historical focus of, 79-80; conclusions about, 82; ending of, 86-87 n. 52

Marriage: in resurrection, 384, 390 n. 14; symbolism of, 399

Mary, mother of Jesus, 142-43, 146-48, 155, 449

Mary Magdalene, 454, 455

Mattathias, 15

Matthew, 47-48. *See also* Matthew, Gospel of

Matthew, Gospel of: directed to Jews, 45; prominent themes in, 50-57; citations of prophecy in, 56

Maxwell, Neal A., 247, 432, 437

McConkie, Bruce R.: on writing Jesus' "biography," 39-40; on Moses' editorial labors, 44; on Gospel audiences, 45; on fulfilling law of Moses; 55; on sons of God, 134; on advent of Savior, 140; on Mary, 142; on Jesus' birthplace, 145; on new star, 149; on Magi, 149; on Jesus' baptism, 179, 180; on temptation of Jesus, 182; on Melchizedek Priesthood, 187 n. 3; on being born again, 193, 194; on power of faith, 220; on calling of apostles, 229-30; on mission of apostles, 232; on miracles as threat to scribes, 251; on parables, 264, 268; on Mount of Transfiguration, 308, 309-10; on Jesus' final months, 322; on light of world, 329; on living water, 331-32; on divorce, 365-66; on rich young man, 368; on angel in Gethsemane, 433-34

McKay, David O., 186

Melchizedek Priesthood: rejected by Israel, 297; keys of 305-6

Mercy, 238, 326

Messiah: definition of, 6-7; secrecy of Jesus' role as, 77-79; was to provide abundance, 114-15; coming of, heralded by star, 149; miracles testify of, 215, 217, 251; rejection of Jesus as, 323-24; role of, 325-27; mention of, in Book of Mormon, 341 n. 7-8; to be son of David, 385-86

Metaphor, 263, 291, 295 n. 7

Miracles of Jesus: water changed to wine, 113-15, 188-89; feeding of five thousand, 115, 288-90; walking on sea, 115, 290-91; healing of man blind from birth, 120-21, 332-34; literal reality of, 213-14; divinity shown by, 214-15, 251, 332; purposes for, 215-16; healing sick and leprous, 216-17; healing of centurion's servant, 218; demonstrating power over nature, 219-20; overcoming devils, 220-21, 251; raising of people from dead, 221-22; conclusions concerning, 223; catalog of, 223-26; healing of cripple on Sabbath, 281; raising of Lazarus, 334-36

Missionary work: of Twelve, 232-34; of Seventy, 312-13

Money changers: reason for, 34 n. 11; Jesus drives out, from temple, 190-91, 376-77

More sure word of prophecy, 422, 429 n. 40

Mormon, 44-45

Moses, 44, 58 n. 12; acceptance of, implies acceptance of Christ, 116-17, 286; brazen serpent lifted by, 196; held Melchizedek Priesthood, 197; on Mount of Transfiguration, 305, 307; translation of, 307; as prototype of Christ, 326. See also Law of Moses

Mount of Transfiguration, 305-8

Mountain: Jesus taken to, 185; relative sanctity of, 310

Nathanael, 228-29

Nature: Jesus' power over, 219-20; breaking laws of, 343 n. 30

Nazarene, Christ to be, 153, 158 n. 25

Nehemiah, 12

Neighbor, definition of, 316-17, 319-20 n. 11

Nephi, 41, 180

Nero, 69, 84 n. 21

Nicodemus, 121-23, 192-93, 450

Obedience: of Jesus, 180; connection of, with love, 421

Old Testament: quotations from, in Matthew, 56; allusions to, in John, 112-18; allusions to, in Sermon on Mount, 236, 237-39

Olivet Discourse, 393

Oral law of Pharisees, 22-23, 297. See also Traditions of the elders

Oral testimonies of gospel, 38-39, 72

Papias, 39, 61-62

Parables: disciples puzzled by, 262; definition of, 263-64; purpose for, 264-65; of Savior, compared to rabbinic, 265-67; power of, to conceal, 267-68; power of, to reveal, 268-69; interpreting, 270, 402 n. 3; first recorded, 270-73; catalog of, 274-77; of good Samaritan, 315-19; about prayer, 349; of foolish rich man, 351; of prodigal son, 355-56; of rich man and Lazarus, 357-61; of unforgiving servant, 364; of laborers in vineyard, 369-70; of two sons, 378; of wicked husbandmen, 379-80; of royal marriage feast, 380-82; of ten virgins, 398-400; of talents, 400

Parents, failure to honor, 299

Parthians, 18

Passover, 406, 408, 424-25 n. 7

Paul, 89-92, 459

Pentateuch, 203

Pentecost, 461

Perdition, sons of, 426-27 n. 20

Perfection, commandment of, clarified, 243-45

Persecution: of early Christians, 69-70; Jesus warns apostles of, 233, 341 n. 3, 414; mentioned in Beatitudes, 239

Peter: Mark as interpreter for, 61, 62; mother-in-law of, Jesus heals, 218-19; meets Jesus, 228; attempts to walk on water, 290-91; testifies of Christ, 303; keys promised to, 304; on Mount of Transfiguration, 305-8; receives endowment, 309-10; Jesus prophesies denial of, 411; cuts off servant's ear, 441; denies Christ, 442; appearance to, of resurrected Christ, 455; Christ asks, "Lovest thou me?" 464-67; death of, 467

Pharisees: description of, 22-24; and John the Baptist, 167-68; miracles disclaimed by, 251-52; signs sought by, 300-301; denunciation of, by Jesus, 301, 386-88; spiritual blindness of, 324-25; alliance of, with Herodians, 382; demanded guard for Christ's tomb, 453

Philip, 228

Pilate, Pontius, 20, 35 n. 20, 444-47, 453

Pompey, 17

Power of Jesus: shown by miracles, 216; over sickness, 216-17; extended to all people, 218-19; over nature, 219-20; over devils, 220-21; over sins, 221; over death, 221-22; imparted to apostles, 222, 230

Prayer: offered in synagogue, 202-3; Jesus' teachings on, 348-49; of Jesus for apostles, 414

Premortal life: Jesus' glory in, 1-2, 327; ordination in, 44, 328; knowledge of Christ in, 329-30

Priesthood government, order of, 290

Prodigal son, 355-56

Prologue of John, 127-39

Prophecy: fulfilled by Jesus, 55-57, 76-77, 112-18; fulfilled by John the Baptist, 175; more sure word of, 422, 429 n. 40

Prophets, blood of, 388

Publicans, 29

Reality, 353

Redaction criticism, 73, 99

Redeemer, definition of, 6, 326

Repentance: depends on Atonement, 6; preached by John the Baptist, 175-76; possibility for, 254-56, 338, 354-55

Resurrection: through grace of Savior, 5; Luke's account of, 102; of just and unjust, 283-84; marriage in, 384, 390 n. 14; lack of understanding regarding, 405-6; witnesses of, of Jesus, 453-59; of many Saints, 459; nature of body after, 460 n. 3

Revelation: modern, clarifies ancient, 8-9; continuing, denial of, 23, 35 n. 26; necessity of, in knowing God, 213; is true source of testimony, 303; continuing, need for, 367

Reynolds, George, 42

Rich man and Lazarus, parable of, 357-61

Rich young man, 367-68

Romans: rising power of, 17; Jewish revolts against, 20-22, 69; fall of Jerusalem to, 21, 67-71, 389 n. 4

Sabbath: perversion of laws of, 280; Jesus heals man on, 281, 321-22

Sacrament, 294, 408-9, 463

Sacrifice: Mosaic, pointed to Christ, 240-41; of broken heart and contrite spirit, 242; power of, 248-49; to save souls, 346-48, 356; rewards for, 369; is truest expression of love, 419

Sadducees, 24-25, 300-301, 384

Salt, symbolism of, 239-40

Salvation: from two deaths, 5-6, 337-38; is available to all, 255; through testimony of Christ, 303

Samaritan, good, parable of, 315-19

Samaritan woman at Jacob's well, 123-25, 206-8

Samaritans, 11, 16, 27-28, 204-6

Samuel the Lamanite, 149

Sanhedrin: description of, 30-31; Jesus' trial before, 442-43

Satan: Jesus tempted by, 181-86; miracles attributed to, 252; spirit of, 257; desires a body, 260; fall of, from heaven, 313-14, 328; priesthood power over, 314-15; power of, over Judas, 410. *See also* Devils

Savior: definition of, 5; Jesus' role as, 5-6, 326

Scribes: description of, 29, 261 n. 1; attempts of, to confound Jesus, 259-60, 385; Jesus' denunciation of, 386-88

Scriptures: effects of studying, 8; keys to understanding, 8-9; alterations in, 45-46; quotations from, in Matthew, 56; literary devices in, 262-64; misusing, to deny gospel, 286

Second Coming, 397-98

Sepulchres, whited, 387-88

Sermon on the Mount: directed to apostles, 231; setting for, 236; audience of, 237; Beatitudes in, 237-40

Serpent: brazen, 196; Satan as, 314-15

Seventy: mission of, 312-13; power of, over Satan, 314-15

Shechem, 211 n. 16

Shema, 202-3

Shepherd, good, Jesus as, 118, 330

Shepherds, 145-46, 330-31

Simile, 273

Sign, seeking for, 191, 258-59, 300-301

Signs of the times, 395-98

Simeon, 147-48

Simon of Cyrene, 447

Sin: Jesus' power over, 221; unpardonable, 254-57; weight of, 431, 435

Sjodahl, Janne, 42

Smith, B. T. D., 265-66

Smith, Joseph, 41; on foreordination, 44; on John the Baptist, 171-72; on being born again, 193-94; on sacrifice, 249; on salvation and sin, 255-56, 257-58; on sign seekers, 258; on parables, 270, 271-73; on resurrection of just and unjust, 284; on priesthood keys, 305; on Elijah, 307;

on hell, 359; on second comforter, 415; on more sure word of prophecy, 422

Smith, Joseph F., 359-60, 453

Solomon, 10

"Son of God," ambiguity in term of, 423-24 n. 1

Sons of perdition, 426-27 n. 20

Sophists, 13-14

Sorrow, godly, 343-44 n. 33

Souls, worth of, 346-47

Sower, parable of, 271

Spirit world, 358-60

Spiritual rebirth, 193-95

Star, new, 149

Synagogue: description of, 31-32, 201-2; services in, 202-3, 211 n. 13; Jesus preaches in, 203-4; antiquity of, 209-10 n. 4; segregation of sexes in, 210 n. 8

Synoptic Problem, 48-49, 65, 98

Taheb, or restorer, 207-8

Talents, parable of, 400

Talmage, James E.: on genealogies of Christ, 141; on Mary, 155; on Jesus' first Passover, 190; on Son of Man, 195; on humility of John the Baptist, 198; on charge to apostles, 233-34; on power over serpents, 314; on rendering unto Caesar his own, 383; on whited sepulchres, 388; on Gethsemane, 435

Taylor, John, 363, 438-39 n. 9

Temple: rebuilding of, under Zerubbabel, 12; desecration of, by Epiphanes, 15; cleansing of, by Maccabees, 15-16; remodeled by Herod, 19; burning of, 21; description of, 32-33; youthful Jesus teaching in, 154-55; pinnacle of, Jesus placed upon, 183; Jesus drives money changers from, 190-91, 376-77; differentiated from synagogue, 201-2, 209 n. 3; Jesus prophesies destruction of, 391-92; veil of, rent, 450

Temptations of Jesus, 181-86

Ten Tribes, lost, 11

Ten virgins, parable of, 398-400

Testament, definition of, 7

Testimony: of Christ, scriptures bear, 7; oral, 38-39; Peter's, 303; of Savior, necessity of, 303

Theophilus, 90

Thomas, 457-58

Three Nephites, 469

Time and perspective, 41

Titus, 67-71, 389 n. 4, 396

Traditions of the elders, 22-23, 280, 296-97, 341 n. 5. *See also* Judaism

Transfiguration: of Jesus, 305; Mount of, 305-8; of earth, 307-8

Translated beings, 468-69

Treasures in heaven, 350-52

Triumphal entry of Jesus, 374-75

Truth, Pilate asks about, 444

Unpardonable sin, 254-57

Values, 345-46, 350

Virgins, ten, parable of, 398-400

Washing: ceremonial, 296-97, 298-99; of feet, 407, 425 n. 9

Water, living, 124, 331-32

Wealth, worldly, 350-53, 367-68

Wedding feast, parable of, 380-82

Wheat and tares, parable of, 271-72

Wilderness, 76-77, 181

Wine, water changed to, 113-14, 188-89

Wise men, 148-50

Witnesses: law of, 256, 284-86; of Resurrection, 453-59

Word, the, Jesus as, 128-31

Words, men condemned by, 257

World: values of, 345-46, 350; hatred of, for Jesus, 413-14

Wrede, Wilhelm, 77-79

Young, Brigham, 59 n. 23, 424 n. 5, 428 n. 35, 434-35

Zacharias, 151, 158 n. 21, 161-65

Zealots, 21, 26-27

Zechariah, 12, 374

Zerubbabel, 12